Professional
Microsoft® SharePoint® 2007 Workflow Programming

Professional
Microsoft® SharePoint® 2007 Workflow Programming

Professional Microsoft® SharePoint® 2007 Workflow Programming

Dr. Shahram Khosravi

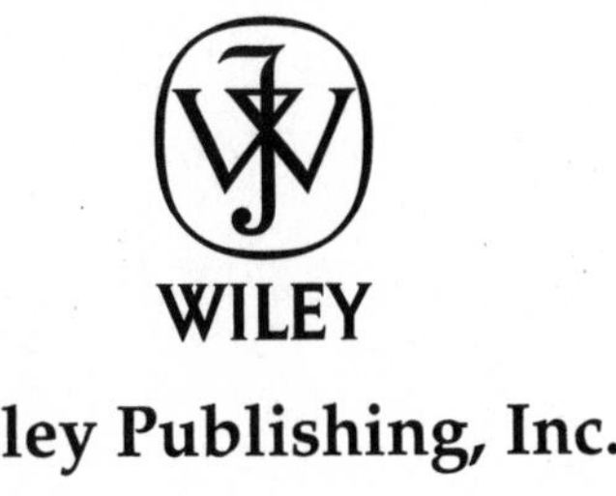

Wiley Publishing, Inc.

Professional Microsoft® SharePoint® 2007 Workflow Programming

Published by
Wiley Publishing, Inc.
10475 Crosspoint Boulevard
Indianapolis, IN 46256
www.wiley.com

Published simultaneously in Canada

ISBN: 978-0-470-40251-1

Manufactured in the United States of America

10 9 8 7 6 5 4 3 2 1

Library of Congress Cataloging-in-Publication Data is available from the publisher.

For general information on our other products and services please contact our Customer Care Department within the United States at (800) 762-2974, outside the United States at (317) 572-3993 or fax (317) 572-4002.

Wiley also publishes its books in a variety of electronic formats. Some content that appears in print may not be available in electronic books.

To my wife, Xiaodong Gong

About the Author

Shahram Khosravi, Ph.D., is a lead technical consultant, architect, author, and instructor specializing in Microsoft Windows SharePoint Services (WSS) 3.0, Microsoft Office SharePoint Server (MOSS) 2007, SharePoint 2007 workflow programming, Windows Workflow Foundation (WF), ASP.NET, Windows Communication Foundation (WCF), ASP.NET AJAX, IIS7 and ASP.NET Integrated Programming, ADO.NET, web services, .NET, and XML technologies such as XSD, XSLT, XPath, SOAP, and WSDL. He also has years of experience in object-oriented analysis, design, and programming; architectural and design patterns; service-oriented analysis, design, and programming; 3D computer graphics programming; user interface design; and usability.

He is the sole author of the following six books: *Expert WSS 3.0 and MOSS 2007 Programming, Professional Microsoft SharePoint 2007 Workflow Programming, Professional ASP.NET 2.0 and .NET 3.0 Programming (ASP.NET Internals plus ASP.NET AJAX, IIS 7, Windows Workflow Foundation, and Workflow Communication Foundation), ASP.NET AJAX Programmer's Reference with ASP.NET 2.0 or ASP.NET 3.5, Professional IIS7 and ASP.NET Integrated Programming,* and *Professional ASP.NET Server Control and Component Development*. He has authored numerous articles about the ASP.NET, ADO.NET, .NET, and XML technologies for the industry's leading journals, including *Dr. Dobb's Journal, asp.netPRO magazine,* and *Microsoft MSDN Online.*

About the Technical Editors

Matt Ranlett, a SharePoint Server MVP, has been a member of the Atlanta .NET developer community for many years. He is a founding member of the Atlanta Dot Net Regular Guys (`www.devcow.com`) and the SharePoint Guys (`www.sharepointguys.com`). He has also formed and led several area user groups. He and his wife, Kim, are raising a child and three dogs.

Brendon Schwartz is a principal consultant in Atlanta, GA, specializing in SharePoint 2007. A Microsoft MVP for Microsoft Office SharePoint Server, he is a co-author of *Professional SharePoint 2007 Development* (Wrox Press, 2007) and has contributed to other Wrox titles. He is a seasoned conference speaker and has authored several magazine articles.

Credits

Executive Editor
Chris Webb

Development Editor
William Bridges

Technical Editors
Matt Ranlett
Brendon Schwartz

Production Editor
William A. Barton
Daniel Scribner

Copy Editor
Luann Rouff

Editorial Manager
Mary Beth Wakefield

Production Manager
Tim Tate

Vice President and Executive Group Publisher
Richard Swadley

Vice President and Executive Publisher
Joseph B. Wikert

Project Coordinator, Cover
Lynsey Stafford

Proofreaders
Corina Copp
Scott Klemp
Word One

Indexer
Robert Swanson

Acknowledgments

My greatest thanks go to my beautiful wife, Xiaodong Gong, who never wavered in her support. I could not have written this book without her. Xiaodong, thanks very much for always being there for me and for your continuous love, understanding, support, and patience.

Huge thanks go to Chris Webb, the book's senior acquisitions editor, for giving me this unique opportunity to work on this exciting project and for all his guidance. Special thanks go to Jim Minatel, the senior acquisitions editor on the book, for all his support. Huge thanks go to William Bridges, the development editor on the book, for all his valuable input and comments. William, it's been a great pleasure working with you on this exciting project. I'd also like to thank Matt Ranlett and Brendon Schwartz, the book's technical editors, for all their valuable input. Thanks also go to Bill Barton, the book's production editor. Additional thanks go to Luann Rouff, the copy editor.

Contents

Introduction

Welcome to *Professional Microsoft SharePoint 2007 Workflow Programming*. SharePoint 2007 provides both workflow and activity developers with rich workflow programming facilities, which enable them to implement and deploy their own custom SharePoint workflows and activities.

This book presents numerous detailed step-by-step recipes for developing and deploying SharePoint workflows and activities, and numerous real-world examples in which these recipes are used. This book uses an approach based on analysis of detailed code and in-depth technical discussions to help you gain the skills, knowledge, and experience you need to develop and deploy your own custom SharePoint workflows and activities.

Whom This Book Is For

This book is aimed at the SharePoint developer who already has a basic knowledge of Windows Workflow Foundation (WF) and SharePoint 2007 workflow and activity programming, and is looking for more advanced coverage of SharePoint 2007 workflow and activity programming.

What This Book Covers

The book is divided into 10 chapters:

- **Chapter 1, "Workflow Programming Principles,"** first discusses the main similarities and differences between workflow programming and traditional procedural programming languages such as C#. It then dives into the implementation of two main types of activities: leaf activities and composite activities. The section on leaf activities covers activity initialization, uninitialization, and execution. The section on composite activities covers the two main types of composite activities: flow control constructs and composite activities that inherit from the flow control constructs but do not change the flow control logic implemented in the flow control constructs from which they inherit.

  The chapter covers two main types of flow control constructs: non-iterative, such as SequenceActivity and ParallelActivity, and iterative, such as WhileActivity. The chapter also shows you how to implement custom WF conditions and use them in your own workflows.

- **Chapter 2, "Developing Custom Workflows,"** presents a detailed step-by-step recipe for implementing and deploying custom SharePoint workflows, and an example where this recipe is used. This chapter also covers the OnWorkflowActivated and LogToHistoryListActivity activities in detail, where the activity binding and the SPActivationEventArgs, SPWorkflowActivationProperties, SPWorkflow, and SPWorkflowTask classes are also discussed in detail. Next, the chapter covers workflow association and initiation input forms in detail in the context of examples that also demonstrate the SPWorkflowAssociation class. Finally, the chapter describes how to implement workflow templates in CAML, and discusses the SPWorkflowTemplate class.

- **Chapter 3, "Programming SharePoint External Data Exchange Services,"** begins by showing you how SharePoint takes advantage of the extensibility features of Windows Workflow Foundation (WF) to extend this framework to add support for SharePoint-specific functionality, including registering four important SharePoint-specific external data exchange services with the workflow run time. These four external data exchange services, respectively, implement the ITaskService, ISharePointService, IWorkflowModificationService, and IListItemService external data exchange service interfaces. The chapter provides detailed coverage of these four external data exchange service interfaces and their associated event data classes — that is, SPTaskServiceEventArgs, SPItemEventArgs, SPListItemServiceEventArgs, and SPModificationEventArgs, and the related ExternalDataEventArgs and SPWorkflowTaskProperties classes. Also included are examples showing how to use the CallExternalMethodActivity and HandleExternalEventActivity activities to invoke the methods of these SharePoint-specific external data exchange services and to wait for these services to fire desired events. Finally, the chapter provides in-depth coverage of correlation parameters and the important role they play in workflow programming.

- **Chapter 4, "CallExternalMethodActivity-Based SharePoint Activities,"** provides complete coverage of the CallExternalMethodActivity activity and those standard SharePoint activities that inherit from this activity, including CreateTask, CreateTaskWithContentType, UpdateTask, DeleteTask, CompleteTask, SendEmail, and EnableWorkflowModification. Numerous examples show you how to use these standard SharePoint activities to implement your custom SharePoint workflows. In the process, you'll also learn about the WorkflowParameterBinding and ActivityBind classes and how to implement site content types, which are used with the CreateTaskWithContentType activity. Finally, the chapter explains how to implement your own custom CallExternalMethodActivity-based SharePoint activities to invoke those methods of the SharePoint external data exchange services that are not covered by the standard CallExternalMethodActivity-based SharePoint activities.

- **Chapter 5, "HandleExternalEventHandler-Based SharePoint Activities,"** covers those standard SharePoint activities that inherit from the HandleExternalEventActivity activity, including OnTaskChanged, OnTaskCreated, OnTaskDeleted, OnWorkflowItemChanged, OnWorkflowItemDeleted, and OnWorkflowModified. The chapter uses examples to show you how to use these standard SharePoint activities to implement your own custom SharePoint workflows. The chapter also discusses the standard ListenActivity, EventDrivenActivity, DelayActivity, EventHandlingScopeActivity, and EventHandlersActivity activities and shows you how to use them in your own custom workflows.

- **Chapter 6, "Workflow Security and Management, and Fault Handling,"** first discusses the SPWorkflowManager class and its public members. It then provides a section on workflow security, where you learn a great deal about the WorkflowRole, WorkflowRoleCollection, and SPWorkflowWorkflowRoleCreator workflow security classes, the SPBasePermissions enumeration, and SharePoint securable objects. Included is an example to show you how to take advantage of workflow security in your own custom workflows. Finally, the chapter covers fault handling in detail, and describes the FaultHandlersActivity and FaultHandlerActivity activities and how to use them in your own workflows to handle faults.

- **Chapter 7, "Workflow Modification and Task Editing,"** begins with coverage of workflow modifications, and provides a two-step recipe for implementing a workflow modification. In the first step you learn how to use the EventHandlingScopeActivity, EnableWorkflowModification, EventHandlersActivity, EventDrivenActivity, and OnWorkflowModified activities to make required changes in the workflow itself to enable it to support a workflow modification. In the second step you learn how to implement and deploy a workflow modification input form.

The chapter then deals with workflow task editing, where you learn how to implement a custom workflow edit task input form and how to deploy it as part of the deployment of a site content type. Finally, the chapter shows you how to implement a workflow that uses a workflow edit task input form.

- **Chapter 8, "Developing Custom Office SharePoint Designer 2007 Actions and Conditions,"** first provides you with a detailed recipe for developing, deploying, and testing a custom Office SharePoint Designer 2007 action and an example that uses this recipe. The chapter then presents a recipe for developing and deploying custom Office SharePoint Designer 2007 conditions and uses this recipe to implement and deploy a custom condition.
- **Chapter 9, "Workflow Actions and Conditions XML Markup Language,"** provides comprehensive coverage of the workflow actions and conditions XML markup language. Using numerous examples, the chapter helps you gain the skills you need to use this markup language to describe your own custom actions and conditions to Office SharePoint Designer 2007. In the process, you'll get to implement numerous custom SharePoint activities and expose them as Office SharePoint Designer 2007 actions.
- **Chapter 10, "Deploying Workflows and Actions Through SharePoint Solution Package,"** first provides detailed coverage of the data description file (DDF) and the role it plays in creating a SharePoint solution package. It then discusses the manifest file and its role. Next, the chapter shows you how to implement data description and manifest files to deploy your custom workflows and actions through SharePoint solution packages.

1

Workflow Programming Principles

Business process modeling has many of the same characteristics as the traditional procedural programming model such as C#. However, it also exhibits characteristics that are fundamentally different from the traditional procedural programming model. This mismatch between the two models has always been the main stumbling block in workflow programming. This chapter first covers those characteristics that business process modeling has in common with the traditional procedural programming model such as C#. Then it dives into their main differences. Finally, the chapter discusses different types of custom activities that you can develop and shows you how to implement each type of custom activity.

Workflow Programming Language

A traditional procedural program such as a C# program consists of program statements, which are executed in a certain prescribed order. A business process or workflow also consists of activities that are executed in a certain prescribed order. For example, consider a vacation request processing workflow, which consists of the following activities:

1. **Employee activity:** An employee makes a vacation request.
2. **Section manager activity:** The employee's section manager approves or denies the request.
3. **Personnel activity:** The personnel staff approves or denies the vacation request. For example, the personnel staff may deny the request if the employee does not have any more vacation days left.

These activities must be executed in the correct order. You wouldn't want the personnel staff to approve the vacation request before the section manager approves it.

Therefore, you can think of a business process or workflow as a logical program, just like a traditional procedural program such as a C# program, and its constituent activities as logical program statements, just like such traditional procedural program statements such as C# program statements.

The order in which the program statements are executed in a traditional procedural program such as a C# program is determined at design time — that is, when the developer is writing the program. The same concept applies to both a business process and a logical program. That is, the order in which the activities or logical program statements of a business process or a logical program are executed is determined at design time when the workflow developer is designing the workflow.

In a traditional procedural program such as a C# program, we normally think in terms of the concept of program control. When the program control reaches a program statement, the statement executes. We can also envision a logical program control that passes from one activity to another just like a traditional procedural program control. When the logical program control reaches an activity or logical program statement in a business process or workflow or logical program, the logical program statement executes.

There are two types of program statements in a traditional procedural programming model such as C#: *flow controls* and *non-flow controls*. A flow control program statement is a composite program statement, which executes its constituent program statements in a certain order. For example, the C# { } flow control program statement executes its constituent program statements in sequential linear order. The { } flow control program statement is also the fundamental flow control program statement, which is used to define other C# flow controls. For example, the C# "for" flow control program statement contains a single { } flow control program statement and executes this { } flow control program statement repeatedly for a specified number of times. The C# "while" flow control program statement also contains a single { } flow control program statement and executes this { } flow control program statement repeatedly as long as a specified condition is met. The C# "if" flow control program statement also contains a single { } flow control program statement and executes this { } flow control program statement once only if a specified condition is met.

Business processes or workflows exhibit the same characteristics. For example, it is quite common in a business process or workflow for the same set of activities to execute repeatedly for a specified number of times. A good example of this scenario is the approval process whereby the approval activity must be repeated several times, once for each approver. It is also quite common in a business process or workflow for a set of activities to execute only if a certain business condition is met. A good example of this scenario is the vacation request process whereby the personnel department approves or disapproves a vacation request only if the employee's section manager has already approved the request.

Therefore, you can envision the following: a logical { } flow control program statement that executes its constituent activities or logical program statements in sequential linear order; a logical "for" flow control program statement that contains a single logical { } flow control program statement and executes it repeatedly for a specified number of times; a logical "while" flow control program statement that contains a single logical { } flow control program statement and executes it repeatedly as long as a specified condition is met; and a logical "if" flow control program statement that contains a single logical { } flow control program statement and executes it once only if a specified condition is met.

As you can see, you can envision a logical workflow programming language that exhibits many of the same characteristics of a traditional procedural programming language such as C#. This logical workflow programming language is known as Windows Workflow Foundation (WF). The WF logical workflow programming language exposes many of the same types of traditional procedural flow control constructs such as "for," "while," "if," "{ }," and so on.

So far, I've discussed the characteristics that WF workflow programming has in common with traditional programming such as C#. Next, I'll discuss the characteristics that make workflow programming fundamentally different from a traditional programming such as C#.

When the program control in a single-threaded C# program reaches a program statement, the program statement executes continuously in synchronous fashion until it completes its execution. This concept is so obvious and rudimentary in traditional programming models that we never think about it.

When the logical program control in a logical program (business process or workflow) reaches a logical program statement (activity), the logical program statement may or may not execute continuously in synchronous fashion. For example, consider the section manager activity in the aforementioned vacation request workflow. After an employee makes a vacation request — that is, after the employee activity or logical program statement completes its execution — the execution of the section manager activity or logical program statement begins. However, the section manager may be stuck in meetings for several days and may not be able to respond to the vacation request immediately. In the meantime, the section manager logical program statement cannot continue its execution because it is waiting for the section manager to approve or deny the vacation request.

This is a common characteristic of business activities or logical program statements. They execute for a very short while and then suspend their execution, waiting for an indefinite period of time for an external entity to deposit the required data before they resume their execution.

This introduces a huge challenge. What should a business activity or logical program statement do when it suspends its execution and waits for an indefinite period of time for an external entity to deposit the required data? Should it hold on to the thread on which it is running?

Holding on to the thread for an indefinite period of time is not a viable solution for two main reasons:

- Threads are expensive resources and should not be wasted.
- Threads and the processes owning the threads would not stay around for an indefinite period of time. For one thing, Windows processes do crash.

Therefore, the activity must let go of the thread when it suspends its execution and waits for an indefinite period of time for an external entity to deposit the data.

Another resource-related issue is the fact that activities consume memory. It would not make sense to let an activity remain in memory while waiting indefinitely for external input. This would waste a lot of server resources, especially when too many inactive activities are sitting in memory waiting for external inputs. A better solution is to serialize these inactive activities into a durable storage.

When the required data is finally deposited in the appropriate location, the activity or logical program statement can then be brought back to memory to retrieve the required data and resume its execution where it left off. However, there is no guarantee that the activity or logical program statement will resume its execution on the same Windows process, let alone the same thread, because by the time the external entity deposits the data — which could be days or weeks later — the process on which the activity or logical program statement was running when it suspended its execution is long gone! There is no guarantee even that the activity or logical program statement will resume its execution on the same machine!

Clearly, the execution model of an activity or logical program statement is fundamentally different from that of a C# program statement. A C# program statement does not suspend its execution and resume it later on a different thread, process, or machine. A C# program statement cannot be resumed. That is why when a C# program crashes, you have to rerun the program. When a C# program is rerun, it does not resume its execution from the last program statement that was executing. That's because a C# program relies on the thread on which it is running to maintain its execution context. This execution context is gone when the thread is gone.

A business activity or logical program statement must be resumable. As such, a business process or workflow or logical program must not rely on the thread on which it is running to maintain its execution context. Instead, it must explicitly allocate memory for its execution context on the heap so it can serialize its execution context into a durable storage such as a database when it suspends its execution and waits indefinitely for an external entity to deposit data. This enables the logical program to deserialize its execution context from the durable storage and resume its execution where it left off when the external data finally arrives.

Now you can see the type of challenges you face when you're implementing a workflow or logical program. If you were to handle all these challenges on your own, you would end up writing a tremendous amount of infrastructural code that has nothing to do with the specifics of your application requirements. This is where Windows Workflow Foundation (WF) comes into play. WF provides you with a comprehensive workflow programming framework that enables you to implement workflows or logical programs with minimal time and effort.

Custom Activities

A traditional procedural program such as a C# program is a hierarchy, or tree, of program statements. For example, consider the following C# program:

```
public class Program
{
  public static void Main (string[] args)
  {
    bool bcontinue = bool.Parse(Console.ReadLine());
    while (bcontinue)
    {
      if (args[0] == "String1")
        Console.WriteLine("String one was entered");
      else
        Console.WriteLine("String one was not entered");

      bcontinue = bool.Parse(Console.ReadLine());
    }
  }
}
```

Figure 1-1 presents the program statement hierarchy, or tree, for this C# program.

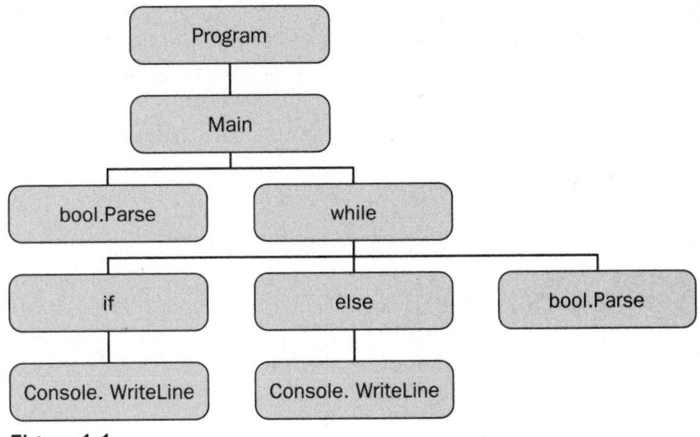

Figure 1-1

Note that the C# program itself is the root program statement in this program statement hierarchy. Also note that this program statement hierarchy, like any other hierarchy, consists of two types of nodes. The first type includes those program statements such as "while," "if," and "else" that contain other program statements. These program statements are known as *composite program statements*. The second type includes the leaf program statements — that is, those program statements such as "bool.Parse" and "Console.WriteLine" that do not contain other program statements.

A business process or workflow as a logical program also consists of a hierarchy of logical program statements or activities, where the business process or workflow itself is the root of the tree. An activity hierarchy, just like a C# program statement hierarchy, consists of two types of nodes. The first type includes those activities such as a "while" activity that contain other activities. These activities are known as *composite activities*. The second type includes leaf activities — that is, those activities that do not contain other activities.

Therefore, you have two options when it comes to developing a custom activity: leaf activities and composite activities, as discussed in the following sections.

Developing Custom Leaf Activities

As mentioned earlier, a leaf activity is an activity that does not contain other activities. When it comes to developing a custom leaf activity, the first order of business is to decide from which base activity to inherit your custom leaf activity. Take these steps to make this determination:

1. List all the features that your custom leaf activity must support.
2. Search through the existing standard and custom activities for an activity that supports more of these features than other activities. Inherit your leaf activity from this activity to take advantage of the features that this activity already supports, consequently saving yourself a lot of unnecessary coding effort.

One of the base classes from which you can inherit your leaf activity is the standard Activity base class, which is discussed thoroughly in this section. Every activity in Windows Workflow Foundation inherits from the Activity base class directly or indirectly. Listing 1-1 presents some of the methods, properties, and events of this base class.

Listing 1-1: The Activity base class

```
public class Activity : DependencyObject
{
  // Events
  public event EventHandler<ActivityExecutionStatusChangedEventArgs>
                    Canceling;
  public event EventHandler<ActivityExecutionStatusChangedEventArgs>
                    Closed;
  public event EventHandler<ActivityExecutionStatusChangedEventArgs>
                    Compensating;
  public event EventHandler<ActivityExecutionStatusChangedEventArgs>
                    Executing;
  public event EventHandler<ActivityExecutionStatusChangedEventArgs>
                    Faulting;

  // Methods
  protected internal virtual ActivityExecutionStatus
               Cancel(ActivityExecutionContext executionContext);
  protected internal virtual ActivityExecutionStatus
              Execute(ActivityExecutionContext executionContext);
  protected internal virtual ActivityExecutionStatus
      HandleFault(ActivityExecutionContext executionContext, Exception exception);
  protected internal virtual void Initialize(IServiceProvider provider);
  protected internal virtual void Uninitialize(IServiceProvider provider);

  // Properties
  public string Description { get; set; }
  public bool Enabled { get; set; }
  public ActivityExecutionResult ExecutionResult { get; }
  public ActivityExecutionStatus ExecutionStatus { get; }
  public bool IsDynamicActivity { get; }
  public string Name { get; set; }
  public CompositeActivity Parent { get; }
}
```

I discuss the members of the Activity base class in the following sections. You need to have a thorough understanding of these members if you're going to inherit from this base class to implement your custom activity, because your custom activity must override the appropriate methods of this base class.

Activity Initialization

The Initialize method of an activity is the first method of the activity to execute. An activity overrides this method to initialize itself. Note that when this method is invoked, an activity has not yet started its execution because the Execute method of the activity has not yet been invoked. When the Initialize method of an activity returns, the activity is in a state known as *Initialized*, which is different from another state known as *Executing*, the state an activity enters when its Execute method is scheduled for execution.

It is very important to understand when the Initialize and Execute methods of the activities making up a workflow are invoked. The Initialize methods are invoked when the CreateWorkflow method is invoked on the workflow run time. This method loads the workflow into memory and synchronously invokes the Initialize methods of the activities making up the workflow. Because this is done synchronously, you can rest assured that when the CreateWorkflow method returns, the Initialize methods of all activities have returned and all activities are in Initialized state.

This shows one of the main differences between the Execute and Initialize methods of the activities making up a workflow. The Initialize methods are all invoked in one shot before the workflow instance begins its execution. The Execute method of an activity is invoked only when the logical program control reaches the activity, which could be days, months, or years after the workflow instance has begun its execution. In other words, in principle, there is an indefinite time lag between when the Initialize method of an activity is invoked and when its Execute method is invoked.

The Initialize method of an activity is a good place to perform initialization that must be done once in the lifetime of an activity, which could be days, months, or even years. It is also a good place to perform one-time initialization that must be performed to avoid possible problems caused by the indefinite time lag between the executions of the Initialize and Execute methods. Following is an example of such a scenario.

As discussed earlier, an activity may need to suspend its execution for an indefinite period of time waiting for external input. The execution logic of the activity, which is contained inside the Execute method of the activity, must create what is known as a *workflow queue*, whereby an external entity deposits the data that the activity needs to resume its execution. Creating the workflow queue inside the Execute method could cause problems because of the indefinite time lag between when the workflow instance starts and when the Execute method of the activity is invoked. This is because the external entity may attempt to deposit the data long before the Execute method of the activity is invoked. To tackle this problem, the Initialize method of the activity should create the required workflow queues to enable the external entities to deposit the required data even before the activity actually starts it execution.

An activity normally needs to use one or more local services to initialize itself. These local services are registered with the workflow "run time" and are made available to an activity through an IServiceProvider object that is passed into the Initialize method of the activity when this method is invoked. The next chapter discusses the local services that SharePoint registers with the workflow run time. The Initialize method of your custom activity can access these SharePoint local services through the IServiceProvider object passed into it as its argument.

The workflow run time automatically registers some basic standard services that every activity needs. One of these standard services is a service named WorkflowQueuingService. As the name suggests, the WorkflowQueuingService service provides workflow queuing services such as creating, deleting, and accessing workflow queues.

Your implementation of the Initialize method can use the IServiceProvider object passed into it as its argument to access the WorkflowQueingService service and use this service to create the workflow queues whereby external entities must deposit the data that the execution logic of your activity needs.

Listing 1-2 presents an example of the implementation of the Initialize method of an activity whereby the activity creates a workflow queue.

Listing 1-2: A typical implementation of the Initialize method

```
Using System;
using System.Workflow.ComponentModel;
using System.Workflow.Runtime;

namespace Chapter1
{
  public class CustomActivity : Activity
  {
    protected override void Initialize(IServiceProvider provider)
    {
      WorkflowQueuingService workflowQueuingService =
        provider.GetService(typeof(WorkflowQueuingService))
                                        as WorkflowQueuingService;
      if (!workflowQueuingService.Exists(this.Name))
        workflowQueuingService.CreateWorkflowQueue(this.Name, true);
    }
  }
}
```

Follow these steps to create a workflow queue:

1. Invoke the GetService method on the IServiceProvider object, passing in the Type object that represents the type of workflow queuing service to access the WorkflowQueuingService service:

```
WorkflowQueuingService workflowQueuingService =
        provider.GetService(typeof(WorkflowQueuingService))
                                        as WorkflowQueuingService;
```

2. Invoke the Exists method on the WorkflowQueuingService service, passing in the workflow queue name to ensure that the service does not already contain a workflow queue with the same name. If your custom activity needs to create only a single workflow queue, use the name of your activity as the workflow queue name. The name of your activity is set by the workflow designer that uses your activity. You can access this name through the Name property of your activity:

```
if (!workflowQueuingService.Exists(this.Name))
```

3. If the workflow queuing service does not already contain a workflow queue with the same name, then invoke the CreateWorkflowQueue method on the WorkflowQueuingService service, passing in the workflow queue name to create the workflow queue:

```
workflowQueuingService.CreateWorkflowQueue(this.Name, true);
```

You will see throughout this book that you don't need to create workflow queues when programming SharePoint activities, because SharePoint workflow programming abstracts you away from workflow queues. That said, you still need to have a solid understanding of workflow queues to understand SharePoint workflow programming, which is thoroughly covered throughout this book.

Keep in mind that the Initialize method of an activity is invoked only once in the lifetime of the activity. This is important considering the fact that the lifetime of an activity could span multiple threads, processes, or machine boundaries and could last an indefinitely long period of time.

Also keep in mind that initializing an activity as a logic program statement in a workflow as a logical program is different from initializing the Common Language Runtime (CLR) object that transiently represents the activity in memory. Object initialization is a CLR concept, whereas activity initialization is a WF concept. The same activity or logical program statement may be represented by numerous CLR objects during its lifetime, whereby each CLR object is initialized when it springs into life. While numerous CLR initializations could be associated with the same activity or logical program statement, only one WF initialization is associated with the activity.

This has an important consequence. You must not contain one-time initialization logic of your activity in the constructor of your activity class, because the contructor of your activity class is invoked every time a new CLR object springs into life — that is, every time your activity resumes its execution after an external entity deposits data. If you include the one-time initialization logic of your activity inside the constructor of your activity class, your activity will be initialized multiple times during its lifetime. That being the case, you must contain all your activity's one-time initialization logic inside the Initialize method.

At this point, you may be wondering how an external entity accesses a workflow queue. As mentioned, you can think of a workflow as a logical program, somewhat like a C# program, and its constituent activities as logical program statements, somewhat like C# program statements. Just as you can have multiple instances of the same C# program running in memory, you can also have multiple instances of the same logical program running. Every running instance of a logical program in WF is represented by an instance of a class named WorkflowInstance.

The WorkflowInstance class exposes a method named EnqueueItem, which an external entity can use to deposit data into a workflow queue with the specified name:

```
public sealed class WorkflowInstance
{
  public void EnqueueItem(IComparable queueName, object item,
                          IPendingWork pendingWork, object workItem);
}
```

The external entity simply passes the workflow queue name as the first argument of the EnqueueItem method, and the data that needs to be deposited as the second argument of this method.

Note that workflow queue names are treated as IComparable objects in WF. This means that you can use any IComparable object as the workflow queue name. However, a string generally does the job.

As you can see, the external entity needs to know the name of the workflow queue in which it needs to deposit the data. It also needs access to the WorkflowInstance object on which it needs to invoke the EnqueueItem method. You do not have to worry about this in SharePoint because SharePoint provides you with a convenient layer on top of WorkflowInstance that enables you to deposit data into the appropriate workflow queue much more conveniently. This will all be clear later in the book.

Activity Uninitialization

If your custom activity overrides the Initialize method of the Activity base class, it must also override the UnInitialize method to uninitialize itself. The UnIntialize method undoes what the Initialize method does. For example, if the Initialize method creates and adds a new workflow queue to the workflow queuing service, the UnInitialize method must remove the same workflow queue from the workflow queuing service.

Listing 1-3 shows a typical implementation of the Uninitialize method of a custom activity.

Listing 1-3: A typical implementation of the Uninitialize method

```
Using System;
using System.Workflow.ComponentModel;
using System.Workflow.Runtime;

namespace Chapter1
{
  public class CustomActivity : Activity
  {
    . . .

    protected override void Uninitialize(IServiceProvider provider)
    {
      WorkflowQueuingService workflowQueuingService =
        provider.GetService(typeof(WorkflowQueuingService))
                                          as WorkflowQueuingService;
      if (workflowQueuingService.Exists(this.Name))

        workflowQueuingService.DeleteWorkflowQueue(this.Name);
    }
  }
}
```

The Uninitialize method takes these steps to remove the workflow queue:

1. It accesses the WorkflowQueuingService service:

```
WorkflowQueuingService workflowQueuingService =
        provider.GetService(typeof(WorkflowQueuingService))
                                                as WorkflowQueuingService;
```

2. It checks whether the WorkflowQueuingService service contains the workflow queue with the specified name. If so, it invokes the DeleteWorkflowQueue method on the WorkflowQueuingService service to remove the workflow queue:

```
if (workflowQueuingService.Exists(this.Name))
  workflowQueuingService.DeleteWorkflowQueue(this.Name);
```

Keep in mind that the Uninitialize method of an activity, just like its Initialize method, is invoked only once during the lifetime of an activity, which could last an indefinitely long time and span multiple thread, process, or machine boundaries.

The Uninitialize method, which is a WF concept, is very different from the Dispose method, which is a CLR concept. You mustn't include one-time uninitialization logic of your activity in the Dispose method because the Dispose method is invoked every time the CLR object that represents your activity is about to be disposed of — that is, every time your activity suspends its execution and is serialized into the durable storage. You must include one-time uninitialization logic of your activity in the Uninitialize method because WF guarantees that this method is invoked only once during the lifetime of your activity.

Activity Execution

As the name suggests, the Execute method is where the execution logic of your activity should go. Every activity inherits this method from the Activity base class:

```
protected void ActivityExecutionStatus Execute(
                                   ActivityExecutionContext executionContext)
```

When the logical program control reaches an activity or logical program statement, the Execute method of the activity is automatically scheduled for execution. It is very important to realize that the Execute method is not invoked immediately. Instead, it is scheduled for execution. When an execution method such as Execute is scheduled for execution, a work item is added to the WF scheduler's work queue. This work item is basically a delegate that wraps the method. The WF scheduler uses a strict FIFO (First in-First out) algorithm to run scheduled work items.

When the WF scheduler invokes a work item and consequently the method that it encapsulates, it passes an instance of a class named ActivityExecutionContext into the method. The ActivityExecutionContext class plays several important roles in Windows Workflow Foundation:

- It represents the execution context within which the method must run. Recall from earlier that the execution context of an activity is allocated on the heap because an activity cannot rely on the thread on which it is running to maintain its execution context. When a method of an activity is invoked, an object that represents its execution context is explicitly passed into it as an argument. This is very different from method invocation in traditional programming models such as C#, where the execution context is implicit and is maintained in the thread's stack.
- The ActivityExecutionContext class implements the IServiceProvider interface, which is the standard interface that every .NET service provider implements. Your activity's implementation of the Execute method can use the ActivityExecutionContext object passed into it as its argument to access the services that its execution logic needs. As you'll see in the next chapter, SharePoint registers several services with the workflow run time. The Execute method of your custom activity can use the ActivityExecutionContext object to access these services.
- The ActivityExecutionContext enables you to create subordinate activity execution contexts. This is discussed later in this chapter.

The Execute method of activities that expect data from external entities must check whether the workflow queues they created during their initialization phase (inside the Initialize method) contain the data they need. If not, then they should return ActivityExecutionStatus.Executing and let go of the thread on which they're running. Listing 1-4 presents an example of an Execute method.

Listing 1-4: An example implementation of the Execute method

```
Using System;
using System.Workflow.ComponentModel;
using System.Workflow.Runtime;

namespace Chapter1
{
  public class CustomActivity : Activity
  {
    protected override ActivityExecutionStatus Execute(
                        ActivityExecutionContext executionContext)
    {
      WorkflowQueuingService workflowQueuingService =
        executionContext.GetService<WorkflowQueuingService>();
      WorkflowQueue workflowQueue =
             workflowQueuingService.GetWorkflowQueue(
                                                   this.Name);
      if (workflowQueue.Count > 0)
      {
        object data = workflowQueue.Dequeue();
        // Consume the data here
        return ActivityExecutionStatus.Closed;
      }

      workflowQueue.QueueItemAvailable +=
              new EventHandler<QueueEventArgs>(
                      WorkflowQueue_QueueItemAvailable);
      return ActivityExecutionStatus.Executing;
    }
  }
}
```

As shown in the preceding code, the Execute method takes these steps:

1. The ActivityExecutionContext class exposes a generic GetService method in addition to the standard GetService method that returns a strongly typed service. Execute invokes this generic method to access the WorkflowQueuingService service:

```
WorkflowQueuingService workflowQueuingService =
                              executionContext.GetService<WorkflowQueuingService>();
```

2. Execute invokes the GetWorkflowQueue method on the WorkflowQueuingService service, passing in the workflow queue name, to access the WorkflowQueue object that represents the workflow queue that the activity created in its initialization phase inside its Initialize method:

```
WorkflowQueue workflowQueue =
                        workflowQueuingService.GetWorkflowQueue(this.Name);
```

3. Execute then checks whether the external entity has deposited the data in the workflow queue. If so, it invokes the Dequeue method on the WorkflowQueue object to dequeue the data, consumes the data, and returns ActivityExecutionStatus.Closed to inform the workflow run time that it has completed its execution.

If not, it first registers a method named WorkflowQueue_QueueItemAvailable as event handler for the QueueItemAvailable event of the WorkflowQueue object and then returns ActivityExecutionStatus.Executing to inform the workflow run time that it hasn't completed its execution because it needs to wait indefinitely for the external entity to deposit the data into the workflow queue.

When the external entity finally deposits the data in the workflow queue, the WorkflowQueue_QueueItemAvailable event handler is scheduled for execution. This means that a work item (a delegate that wraps this event handler) is added to the WF scheduler's work queue. When the WF scheduler finally invokes the event handler, it passes an instance of the ActivityExecutionContext object into the method as its first argument. Listing 1-5 presents the implementation of the WorkflowQueue_QueueItemAvailable event handler.

Listing 1-5: The WorkflowQueue_QueueItem event handler

```
using System.Workflow.ComponentModel;
using System.Workflow.Runtime;
using System;

namespace Chapter1
{
  public class CustomActivity : Activity
  {
    void WorkflowQueue_QueueItemAvailable(object sender,
                                          QueueEventArgs e)
    {
      ActivityExecutionContext activityExecutionContext =
                               sender as ActivityExecutionContext;
      WorkflowQueuingService workflowQueuingService =
                activityExecutionContext.GetService<WorkflowQueuingService>();
      WorkflowQueue workflowQueue =
               workflowQueuingService.GetWorkflowQueue(
                                             e.QueueName);
      object data = workflowQueue.Dequeue();
      // Consume the data
      activityExecutionContext.CloseActivity();
    }
  }
}
```

This method takes the following steps:

1. As just mentioned, the WF scheduler passes an ActivityExecutionContext object as the first argument of this method when it invokes the method. Therefore, this method first casts its first argument to the ActivityExecutionContext type:

```
ActivityExecutionContext activityExecutionContext =
                                      sender as ActivityExecutionContext;
```

2. The method then invokes the GetService generic method on this ActivityExecutionContext object to access the WorkflowQueuingService service:

```
WorkflowQueuingService workflowQueuingService =
              activityExecutionContext.GetService<WorkflowQueuingService>();
```

3. It then invokes the GetWorkflowQueue method to access the WorkflowQueue object that represents the workflow queue that the activity created in its initialization phase. Note that the method passes the QueueName property of its second argument into the GetWorkflowQueue method. This is not important in our case because this activity creates a single workflow queue in its initialization phase. However, in cases where the activity creates more than one workflow queue in its initialization phase, you should use the QueueName property to ensure that you're accessing the right workflow queue.

```
WorkflowQueue workflowQueue =
                            workflowQueuingService.GetWorkflowQueue(e.QueueName);
```

4. The method then invokes the Dequeue method on the WorkflowQueue object to access the deposited data, and consumes it:

```
object data = workflowQueue.Dequeue();
```

5. The WorkflowQueue_QueueItemAvailable method is part of the execution logic of our activity because it was the Execute method of our activity that registered this method as an event handler for the QueueItemAvailable event of the workflow queue. Once the event handler is registered, our activity can resume its execution where it left off when the external entity finally deposits the data into the workflow queue. The workflow run time expects every execution method to notify it when the execution status of the activity changes. Such notification can occur in two different forms.

   If the method returns a value of the ActivityExecutionStatus type, then it must return the appropriate ActivityExecutionStatus enumeration value. Otherwise, it must invoke the appropriate method on the ActivityExecutionContext to inform the workflow run time of the execution status change. Execution methods such as Execute, Cancel, and HandleFault return a value of the ActivityExecutionStatus type. Execution methods such as event handlers do not. In this case, the WorkflowQueue_QueueItemAvailable method invokes the CloseActivity method on the ActivityExecutionContext to inform the workflow run time that the execution logic of the current activity is now completed:

```
activityExecutionContext.CloseActivity();
```

The following example presents the complete code for the custom activity that we've been developing in last few sections:

```
using System.Workflow.ComponentModel;
using System.Workflow.Runtime;
using System;

namespace Chapter1
{
  public class CustomActivity : Activity
  {
    protected override void Initialize(IServiceProvider provider)
    {
      WorkflowQueuingService workflowQueuingService =
        provider.GetService(typeof(WorkflowQueuingService))
                                                as WorkflowQueuingService;
```

```
      if (!workflowQueuingService.Exists(this.Name))
        workflowQueuingService.CreateWorkflowQueue(this.Name, true);
    }

    protected override void Uninitialize(System.IServiceProvider provider)
    {
      WorkflowQueuingService workflowQueuingService =
        provider.GetService(typeof(WorkflowQueuingService))
                                                as WorkflowQueuingService;
      if (workflowQueuingService.Exists(this.Name))
        workflowQueuingService.DeleteWorkflowQueue(this.Name);
    }

    protected override ActivityExecutionStatus Execute(
                                    ActivityExecutionContext executionContext)
    {
      WorkflowQueuingService workflowQueuingService =
        executionContext.GetService<WorkflowQueuingService>();
      WorkflowQueue workflowQueue =
                            workflowQueuingService.GetWorkflowQueue(this.Name);
      if (workflowQueue.Count > 0)
      {
        object data = workflowQueue.Dequeue();
        // Consume the data here
        return ActivityExecutionStatus.Closed;
      }

      workflowQueue.QueueItemAvailable +=
                new EventHandler<QueueEventArgs>(WorkflowQueue_QueueItemAvailable);
      return ActivityExecutionStatus.Executing;
    }

    void WorkflowQueue_QueueItemAvailable(object sender, QueueEventArgs e)
    {
      ActivityExecutionContext activityExecutionContext =
                                        sender as ActivityExecutionContext;
      WorkflowQueuingService workflowQueuingService =
          activityExecutionContext.GetService<WorkflowQueuingService>();
      WorkflowQueue workflowQueue =
                            workflowQueuingService.GetWorkflowQueue(e.QueueName);
      object data = workflowQueue.Dequeue();
      // Consume the data
      activityExecutionContext.CloseActivity();
    }
  }
}
```

As mentioned earlier, you will not directly use lower-level objects such as workflow queues and WorkflowQueuingService to implement custom activities in SharePoint. However, you do need a solid understanding of these lower-level objects and the fundamental role they play in WF in order to be a successful activity developer. Such an understanding is the key to understanding standard SharePoint workflow activities and workflow programming discussed throughout this book.

Developing Custom Composite Activities

A composite activity or logical program statement, just like a C# composite program statement such as "{ }," "for,""while," and so on, is a logical program statement that contains other logical program statements or activities. In general, there are two types of composite activities. The first type includes flow control constructs such as "{ }," "for," and "while." The second type includes those composite activities that inherit from the flow control constructs but do not change the flow control logic implemented in the flow control constructs from which they inherit. The main purpose behind implementing this second type of composite activity is to assemble a custom activity from other composite or leaf activities. This enables you to reuse the functionality implemented in other composite or leaf activities when you're building your own custom activity.

Both types of composite activity directly or indirectly inherit from a base activity named CompositeActivity, which in turn inherits from the Activity base class and exposes the members shown in Listing 1-6.

Listing 1-6: The CompositeActivity activity

```
public class CompositeActivity : Activity
{
  // Methods
  protected internal override void Initialize(
                                   IServiceProvider provider);
  protected internal override void Uninitialize(
                                   IServiceProvider provider);

  // Properties
  public ActivityCollection Activities { get; }
  protected internal bool CanModifyActivities { get; set; }
  public ReadOnlyCollection<Activity> EnabledActivities { get; }
}
```

Note that the CompositeActivity activity does not override the Execute method. It is the responsibility of the flow control constructs that inherit from the CompositeActivity activity to override this method to include the logic that determines in which order the child activities of the composite activity should be executed. You'll see examples of this later in this chapter.

CompositeActivity does override the Initialize method where it invokes the Initialize method of all its containing child activities. CompositeActivity also overrides the Uninitialize method where it invokes the Uninitialize methods of all its containing child activities.

Note that the CompositeActivity activity exposes a collection property named Activities, which is of the ActivityCollection type. This is where the CompositeActivity activity maintains its child activities. The CompositeActivity activity also exposes a read-only collection property named EnabledActivities, which is of the ReadOnlyCollection<Activity> type. This collection contains references to all enabled activities of the composite activity. An enabled activity is an activity whose Enabled property is set to true.

Disabling an activity or logical program statement is like commenting out a C# program statement. A disabled activity does not participate in the execution of the composite activity. It is like dead code.

As Listing 1-6 shows, the CompositeActivity activity exposes a Boolean property named CanModifyActivities. As the name suggests, you must set this property to true before you can add child activities to the Activities collection property of the composite activity or before you can modify any child activity in the Activities collection property. Note that this property is marked as protected. This means that only the subclasses of the CompositeActivity class can set this property, and consequently only the subclasses of the CompositeActivity class can add child activities to its Activities collection property or modify child activities in this collection.

To put it differently, only a composite activity itself is allowed to add child activities to its own Activities collection property or to modify its own child activities. No outsider is allowed to add child activities to it or modify any of its child activities. This puts a composite activity in complete control of its child activities. This is very similar to C# composite program statements. For example, it would not make sense for the code outside of a C# { } composite program statement to add new program statements to this composite program statement or to modify any of its child program statements. You'll see numerous examples of custom composite activities throughout this book.

Developing Custom Flow Control Activities

As discussed earlier, workflows as logical programs, just like C# programs, need control flow program statements such as "if," "while,""for," "{ }," and so on. Just as you cannot write a useful C# program without using these control flow program statements, you cannot implement useful workflows without using logical "if," "while,""for," "{ }," and other control flow program statements.

One big difference between WF as a logical workflow programming language and a standard procedural programming language such as C# is that the set of control flow program statements in WF is extensible. This means that you can implement your own custom control flow program statements and use them in your workflows just like standard control flow contructs that ship with WF. This section provides several examples to help you gain the skills you need to implement your own custom flow control activities.

A traditional procedural programming language such as C# comes with two types of flow control constructs: *iterative* and *non-iterative*. Thus, "for" and "while" are examples of iterative flow control constructs whereby the flow control program statement repeatedly executes its child program statement, which is a { } program statement. Conversely, "if," "else if," "{ }," and "else" are examples of non-iterative flow control constructs whereby the flow control program statement executes its child program statements once in the prescribed order.

Developing Non-Iterative Flow Control Constructs

This section explains how to implement non-iterative flow control constructs that execute their child program statements once in the prescribed order.

SequenceActivity

Here, I'll walk you through the implementation of the logical { } control flow construct, which does exactly what the C# { } flow control construct does. That is, it executes its constituent child activities in sequential linear fashion. This implementation provides you with a simplified duplicate of the standard WF SequenceActivity activity, as shown in Listing 1-7.

Listing 1-7: The SequenceActivity activity

```
using System.Workflow.ComponentModel;
using System.Workflow.Runtime;
using System;

namespace Chapter1
{
  public class SequenceActivity : CompositeActivity
  {
    protected override ActivityExecutionStatus Execute(
                      ActivityExecutionContext executionContext)
    {
      if (this.EnabledActivities.Count == 0)
        return ActivityExecutionStatus.Closed;

      Activity activity = this.EnabledActivities[0];
      activity.Closed += Activity_Closed;
      executionContext.ExecuteActivity(activity);
      return ActivityExecutionStatus.Executing;
    }

    void Activity_Closed(object sender,
                      ActivityExecutionStatusChangedEventArgs e)
    {
      e.Activity.Closed -= this.Activity_Closed;
      ActivityExecutionContext executionContext =
                              sender as ActivityExecutionContext;
      int index = this.EnabledActivities.IndexOf(e.Activity);
      index++;
      if (index == this.EnabledActivities.Count)
        executionContext.CloseActivity();
      else
      {
        Activity activity = this.EnabledActivities[index];
        activity.Closed += this.Activity_Closed;
        executionContext.ExecuteActivity(activity);
      }
    }
  }
}
```

The SequenceActivity activity, just like any other control flow activity, inherits from the CompositeActivity base class and overrides its Execute method. The SequenceActivity's implementation of the Execute method first checks whether the EnabledActivities collection is empty. Recall that this collection contains the child activities of the composite activity. If the collection is empty, then the

SequenceActivity activity returns ActivityExecutionStatus.Closed to inform the workflow run time that it has completed its execution. A SequenceActivity activity without any child activities is the WF equivalence of an empty C# { } statement block.

If the EnabledActivities collection is not empty — that is, if the SequenceActivity activity or logical { } flow control contains logical program statements or activities — then the Execute method takes the following steps to execute the first child activity or logical program statement (keep in mind that the SequenceActivity activity executes its child activities one activity at a time):

1. It accesses the first child activity or logical program statement:

```
Activity activity = this.EnabledActivities[0];
```

2. It registers an event handler named Activity_Closed for the Closed event of the first child activity:

```
activity.Closed += Activity_Closed;
```

3. It invokes the ExecuteActivity method on the ActivityExecutionContext object that represents the execution context within which the Execute method is executing to schedule the first child activity for execution:

```
executionContext.ExecuteActivity(activity);
```

   Note that the SequenceActivity activity does not directly invoke the Execute method of its child activity. Instead, it invokes the ExecuteActivity method to schedule the Execute method of its child activity for execution. As discussed earlier, scheduling a method for execution basically adds a work item to the WF scheduler. This work item is basically nothing but a delegate that encapsulates the Execute method of the first child activity. In order to ensure that no one can directly call the Execute method of an activity, this method is marked as protected internal.

4. Finally, the method returns ActivityExecutionStatus.Executing to inform the workflow run time that it hasn't completed its execution yet:

```
return ActivityExecutionStatus.Executing;
```

As just discussed, the Execute method of the SequenceActivity activity schedules the Execute method of its first child activity with the WF scheduler for execution. At some point, the WF scheduler finally invokes the Execute method of the first child activity. The execution logic of the first child activity may require the activity to suspend its execution indefinitely until the required data is deposited into the appropriate workflow queue, at which point the activity resumes its execution. This process may be repeated any number of times until the first child activity finally completes its execution, at which point the activity raises its Closed event and consequently the Activity_Closed event handler that the SequenceActivity activity has registered for this event is scheduled with the WF scheduler for execution.

When the WF scheduler finally invokes the Activity_Closed event handler, it passes an ActivityExecutionContext object as its first argument. This object basically represents the execution context within which this event handler must execute.

As Listing 1-7 shows, this event handler takes the following steps:

1. It unregisters the event handler:

```
e.Activity.Closed -= this.Activity_Closed;
```

2. It casts the first argument to the ActivityExecutionContext type:

```
ActivityExecutionContext executionContext =
                                        sender as ActivityExecutionContext;
```

3. It determines the index of the child activity that raised the Closed event and increments the index:

```
int index = this.EnabledActivities.IndexOf(e.Activity);
index++;
```

4. If the child activity that raised the Closed event is the last child activity of the SequenceActivity activity, it invokes the CloseActivity method on the ActivityExecutionContext object to inform the workflow run time that the SequenceActivity activity has now completed its execution:

```
if (index == this.EnabledActivities.Count)
  executionContext.CloseActivity();
```

The SequenceActivity activity, like any other composite activity, notifies the workflow run time that it has completed its execution only after each and every single child activity is in either Initialized or Closed state. In general, a composite activity mustn't report that it has completed its execution if one or more of its child activities are still executing. Imagine how weird it would be if a C# { } statement block were to complete its execution while one or more program statements inside the block were still executing! If a composite activity attempts to report the completion of its execution while one or more of its child activities is not in either Closed or Initialized state, the workflow run time raises an exception. In other words, the workflow run time does not allow a composite activity to transition to the Closed state until all its child activities are either in Closed or Initialized state.

You may be wondering how it would be possible for one or more child activities of a composite activity to remain in the Initialized state. This is very similar to the C# { } statement block that contains "if" and "else if" flow control program statements. Obviously, only the program statements contained in one of these flow control program statements are executed. Similarly, a logical { } flow control program statement may contain logical "if" and "else if" flow control program statements such that only the child activities of one of these flow control program statements are bound to execute — that is, only the Execute methods of the child activities of one these two flow control program statements are bound to be executed. The child activities of the flow control program statements that are not executed will remain in the Initialized state. Keep in mind that the Initialize methods of all activities, including those that are never executed, are invoked when the workflow is loaded into memory. As such, all activities are initially in the Initialized state.

5. If the child activity that raised the Closed event is not the last logical program statement in the logical { } flow control program statement, the Activity_Closed method takes the same steps

discussed earlier to schedule the execution of the Execute method of the next activity with the WF scheduler:

```
else
{
  Activity activity = this.EnabledActivities[index];
  activity.Closed += this.Activity_Closed;
  executionContext.ExecuteActivity(activity);
}
```

ParallelActivity

As mentioned earlier, one of the great things about WF as a workflow programming language versus a standard procedural programming language such as C# is that the set of logical flow control constructs that WF supports are extensible. Another important characteristic of WF as a workflow programming language versus a standard procedural programming language is that WF supports logical flow control constructs that have no counterpart in standard procedural programming languages. One of these logical flow control constructs is the ParallelActivity flow control construct. This flow control construct executes its containing logical program statements or child activities in parallel. The only way to run different sets of C# program statements in parallel is to run each set on a separate .NET thread. You cannot run these sets in parallel on the same thread. WF program statements, conversely, can be executed in parallel on the same .NET thread. You can think of each WF execution branch as running on a separate logical thread, where all these logical threads are running on the same .NET thread.

Listing 1-8 presents the implementation of the ParallelActivity flow control construct, which is a simplified version of the implementation of the standard ParallelActivity flow control construct.

Listing 1-8: The ParallelActivity flow control construct

```
using System.Workflow.ComponentModel;
using System.Workflow.Runtime;
using System;

namespace Chapter1
{
  public class ParallelActivity : CompositeActivity
  {
    protected override ActivityExecutionStatus Execute(
                      ActivityExecutionContext executionContext)
    {
      if (this.EnabledActivities.Count == 0)
        return ActivityExecutionStatus.Closed;

      foreach (Activity activity in this.EnabledActivities)
      {
        activity.Closed += Activity_Closed;
        executionContext.ExecuteActivity(activity);
      }

      return ActivityExecutionStatus.Executing;
```

(continued)

Listing 1-8 *(continued)*

```
        }

        void Activity_Closed(object sender,
                             ActivityExecutionStatusChangedEventArgs e)
        {
          e.Activity.Closed -= this.Activity_Closed;

          foreach (Activity activity in this.EnabledActivities)
          {
            if (activity.ExecutionStatus !=
                             ActivityExecutionStatus.Initialized ||
                activity.ExecutionStatus != ActivityExecutionStatus.Closed)
              return;
          }

          ActivityExecutionContext executionContext =
                                     sender as ActivityExecutionContext;
          executionContext.CloseActivity();
        }
      }
    }
```

The ParallelActivity flow control activity, like any other flow control activity, inherits from the CompositeActivity base class. This is because every flow control activity is a composite activity. As shown in Listing 1-8, the Execute method of ParallelActivity takes these steps:

1. It returns ActivityExecutionStatus.Closed to inform the workflow run time it has completed its execution if ParallelActivity contains no child activities. As mentioned earlier, the execution methods of an activity must inform the workflow run time every time its execution status changes. There are two types of execution methods. The first type contains the Execute, Cancel, and HandleFault methods, which return a value of the ActivityExecutionStatus enumeration type. These methods must notify the workflow run time of their execution status changes by returning the appropriate ActivityExecutionStatus enumeration value. The second type contains event handlers that are registered for events such as the QueueItemAvailable event of a workflow queue or the Closed event of a child activity. Because these event handlers return void, they must use the ClosedActivity method of the ActivityExecutionContext when the respective activity needs to transition to the Closed state. Keep in mind that the workflow run time does not consider a workflow completed until every single activity is in either Initialized or Closed state:

    ```
    if (this.EnabledActivities.Count == 0)
      return ActivityExecutionStatus.Closed;
    ```

2. It iterates through the child activities of ParallelActivity, registers the Activity_Closed method as event handler for the Closed event of each enumerated child activity, and invokes the ExecuteActivity method on the ActivityExecutionContext object for each enumerated child activity to schedule the child activity's Execute method with the WF scheduler for execution:

```
foreach (Activity activity in this.EnabledActivities)
{
  activity.Closed += Activity_Closed;
  executionContext.ExecuteActivity(activity);
}
```

3. Finally, it returns ActivityExecutionStatus.Executing to inform the workflow run time that ParallelActivity has not completed its execution yet because it is waiting for its child activities to complete their execution. As mentioned earlier, a composite activity is not allowed to report the completion of its execution unless every single one of its child activities is in either Initialized or Closed state:

```
return ActivityExecutionStatus.Executing;
```

ParallelActivity scheduled all its child activities with the WF scheduler for execution in one shot. This means that the WF scheduler now contains one work item for each child activity of ParallelActivity. Each work item is basically a delegate that encapsulates a reference to the Execute method of the respective child activity. Because the WF scheduler uses the FIFO algorithm to dispatch work items, the child activities are executed in the order in which they were scheduled, which is basically the order in which they were added to ParallelActivity.

The Execute method of each child activity may need to suspend the execution of the child activity waiting indefinitely for external entities to deposit data into the appropriate workflow queues before the child activity can resume its execution. When a child activity finally completes its execution, it raises its Closed event, which in turn triggers the scheduling of the Activity_Closed event handler for execution. This means that each child activity will end up adding a work item to the WF scheduler, where each work item is a delegate that references the Activity_Closed event handler. In other words, the same Activity_Closed event handler is invoked once for each child activity in the ParallelActivity activity. When the WF scheduler invokes the Activity_Closed event handler, it passes an ActivityExecutionContext object into it as its first argument. This object represents the execution context of the event handler.

Let's walk through the implementation of this event handler (refer to Listing 1-8). The event handler first removes itself from the list of event handlers registered for the Closed event of the child activity that triggered the invocation of the event handler:

```
e.Activity.Closed -= this.Activity_Closed;
```

Next, the event handler iterates through the child activities to check whether all child activities are in either Initialized or Closed state. If even one child activity is not in one of these two states, the event handler returns without reporting any change in the execution status of ParallelActivity. This means that as far as the workflow run time is concerned, ParallelActivity is still in the Executing state because the last time the workflow run time heard of a change in the execution status of ParallelActivity was when the Execute method returned the ActivityExecutionStatus.Executing enumeration value:

```
foreach (Activity activity in this.EnabledActivities)
{
  if (activity.ExecutionStatus != ActivityExecutionStatus.Initialized ||
      activity.ExecutionStatus != ActivityExecutionStatus.Closed)
    return;
}
```

If every single child activity is in either Initialized or Closed state, the event handler calls the CloseActivity method on the ActivityExecutionContext object to inform the workflow run time that ParallelActivity has now completed its execution and is ready to transition from the Executing to the Closed state:

```
ActivityExecutionContext executionContext = sender as ActivityExecutionContext;
executionContext.CloseActivity();
```

Developing Iterative Flow Control Constructs

In this section, I'll show you how to implement custom iterative flow control constructs that repeatedly execute their constituent logical program statement, which is normally a SequenceActivity activity. First you'll learn some basic concepts and techniques that apply to iterative flow control constructs.

Consider the following C# "for" iterative flow control construct:

```
for (int i=0; i<10; i++)
{
  int j = 0;
  Console.WriteLine(j);
  j++;
}
```

The Console.WriteLine in each iteration will write out 0 regardless of the fact that the previous iteration incremented j by one. In other words, the j local variable is reset at the beginning of each iteration. This means that what one iteration does to the local variable j is invisible to other iterations. This is because each iteration allocates memory for its local variables on the stack, which is disposed of after the iteration completes.

In general, each iteration of a C# iterative flow control construct such as "for" and "while" has its own execution context, which is disposed of at the end of the iteration. This ensures that what happens in one iteration does not affect other iterations.

Each iteration of a business or logical iterative flow control construct such as "for," just like a C# iterative flow control construct, must have its own execution context, which is normally disposed of at the end of the iteration. Because each iteration uses a different execution context, no residual effects are carried from one iteration to another.

As discussed earlier, every time the WF scheduler invokes an execution method, such as the Execute method of an activity or an event handler registered for the Closed event of an activity, it passes an ActivityExecutionContext object as the first parameter of the execution method. This object represents the execution context of the execution method.

This execution context contains the states of the CLR objects that represent the enabled activities of the current workflow instance, the state of the WF scheduler's work queue that contains the scheduled work items, and so on. In other words, the execution context captures the essential data stored in the thread's stack in a normal C# program. Because the execution context of a C# program is stored in the stack of the thread on which it is running, the program cannot be suspended on one thread in one process on one machine and resumed where it left off on a different thread in a different process on a different machine. In WF, conversely, the execution context is explicitly allocated on the heap and serialized to the underlying durable storage together with the workflow instance.

As you'll see in next chapter, when you initiate a workflow on a SharePoint list item, SharePoint automatically invokes the CreateWorkflow method on the workflow run time. This method, among other things, creates the global execution context for the workflow instance. If you do not create child execution contexts (I'll show you shortly how to do this), all execution methods of all activities making up the current workflow will be executed within the global execution context.

WF allows composite activities to create child execution contexts within which the child activities of the composite activity can execute. The ActivityExecutionContext exposes a property named ExecutionContextManager, which is of the ActivityExecutionContextManager type. This type exposes the methods and properties that you can use to create, access, and remove child execution contexts. The following code listing presents these members:

```
public sealed class ActivityExecutionContextManager
{
  public void CompleteExecutionContext(ActivityExecutionContext childContext);
  public void CompleteExecutionContext(ActivityExecutionContext childContext,
                                       bool forcePersist);
  public ActivityExecutionContext CreateExecutionContext(Activity activity);
  public ActivityExecutionContext GetExecutionContext(Activity activity);
  public ActivityExecutionContext GetPersistedExecutionContext(Guid contextGuid);

  public ReadOnlyCollection<ActivityExecutionContext> ExecutionContexts { get; }
  public IEnumerable<Guid> PersistedExecutionContexts { get; }
}
```

The next section uses an example to show you how to use the methods and properties of the ActivityExecutionContextManager type.

Listing 1-9 presents the implementation of the WhileActivity activity, which is the WF counterpart of the C# "while" flow control construct.

Listing 1-9: The WhileActivity activity

```
using System.Workflow.ComponentModel;
using System.Workflow.Runtime;
using System;

namespace Chapter1
{
  public class WhileActivity : CompositeActivity
  {
    public static readonly DependencyProperty ConditionProperty =
          DependencyProperty.Register("Condition",
                                       typeof(ActivityCondition),
                                       typeof(WhileActivity));
    public ActivityCondition Condition
    {
      get {
        return (ActivityCondition)base.GetValue(ConditionProperty);
      }
      set { base.SetValue(ConditionProperty, value); }
```

(continued)

Listing 1-9 *(continued)*

```
    }

    protected override ActivityExecutionStatus Execute(
                        ActivityExecutionContext executionContext)
    {
      if (this.EnabledActivities.Count == 0)
        return ActivityExecutionStatus.Closed;

      if (Condition != null &&
          Condition.Evaluate(this, executionContext))
      {
        ActivityExecutionContext childExecutionContext =
          executionContext.ExecutionContextManager.CreateExecutionContext(
                                                     this.EnabledActivities[0]);
        childExecutionContext.Activity.Closed += Activity_Closed;
        childExecutionContext.ExecuteActivity(
                                 childExecutionContext.Activity);
        return ActivityExecutionStatus.Executing;
      }

      return ActivityExecutionStatus.Closed;
    }

    void Activity_Closed(object sender,
                         ActivityExecutionStatusChangedEventArgs e)
    {
      e.Activity.Closed -= this.Activity_Closed;
      ActivityExecutionContext executionContext =
                               sender as ActivityExecutionContext;
      ActivityExecutionContext childExecutionContext =
          executionContext.ExecutionContextManager.GetExecutionContext(
                                   e.Activity);
      executionContext.ExecutionContextManager.CompleteExecutionContext(
                                   childExecutionContext);

      if (Condition != null &&
          Condition.Evaluate(this, executionContext))
      {
        childExecutionContext =
            executionContext.ExecutionContextManager.CreateExecutionContext(
                                 this.EnabledActivities[0]);
        childExecutionContext.Activity.Closed += Activity_Closed;
        childExecutionContext.ExecuteActivity(
                                 childExecutionContext.Activity);
        return;
      }

      executionContext.CloseActivity();
    }
  }
}
```

The WhileActivity activity exposes a property named Condition, which is of the ActivityCondition type, as defined in Listing 1-10. As you can see, this type is an abstract type that exposes a single method named Evaluate, which takes the following two parameters and returns a Boolean value specifying whether the condition is met:

- **activity:** Pass the C# `this` keyword as the value of this parameter.
- **provider:** Pass the ActivityExecutionContext object passed into your execution method as the value of this parameter.

The subclasses of the ActivityCondition type must override the Evaluate method where they must use the preceding two parameters and execute the required custom code to determine whether the condition is met. A subclass's implementation of the Evaluate method can use the IServiceProvider object passed into it as its second argument to access whatever local services it needs. As you'll see in the next chapter, SharePoint registers numerous SharePoint-specific local services that the Evaluate method can access through the IServiceProvider object.

Listing 1-10: The ActivityCondition type

```
public abstract class ActivityCondition : DependencyObject
{
  public abstract bool Evaluate(Activity activity, IServiceProvider provider);
}
```

Next, I'll walk you through the implementation of the WhileActivity activity, starting with the implementation of its Execute method. The Execute method first checks whether the WhileActivity activity contains a child activity. If not, then it returns ActivityExecutionStatus.Closed to inform the workflow run time that it has completed its execution and is ready to transition to its Closed state.

If the WhileActivity activity contains a child activity, and if the condition evaluates to true, then the Execute method takes these steps:

1. It accesses the ActivityExecutionContextManager object referenced through the ExecutionContextManager property of the ActivityExecutionContext object and invokes the CreateExecutionContext method on this ActivityExecutionContextManager object, passing in a reference to the child activity of the WhileActivity activity, to create a child execution context:

   ```
   ActivityExecutionContext childExecutionContext =
     executionContext.ExecutionContextManager.CreateExecutionContext(
                                              this.EnabledActivities[0]);
   ```

   Under the hood, the CreateExecutionContext method takes these steps:

   - It deep copies the child activity of the WhileActivity activity and all its descendant activities. In other words, it deep copies the activity branch rooted at the child activity. The WhileActivity activity, just like the C# "while", contains a single child activity. This requirement is enforced through a component known as an *activity validator*. WF ships with an activity validator that ensures that the WhileActivity activity does not contain more than one child activity. However, the topic of Activity validation is beyond the scope of this book.

- It invokes the Initialize method on all activities in the new activity branch copy. This basically does what a C# "while" loop does for each iteration. Recall that a C# "while" loop resets all the local variables at the beginning of each iteration. In other words, no residual effects are carried over from the previous iteration. The only difference is that C# resets the same local variables, whereas WF creates a new copy of the child activity and its descendants and calls the Initialize method on the new copy of the child activity and its descendants.

- It returns an ActivityExecutionContext object that represents the child execution context.

2. It accesses the new copy of the child activity of the WhileActivity activity and registers the Activity_Closed event handler for the Closed event of this child activity copy:

```
childExecutionContext.Activity.Closed += Activity_Closed;
```

The child execution context exposes a property named Activity of the Activity type, which returns a reference to the new copy of the child activity of the WhileActivity activity.

3. It invokes the ExecuteActivity method on the child execution context, passing in the reference to the new copy of the child activity of the WhileActivity activity to schedule the Execute method of the new copy of this child activity for execution:

```
childExecutionContext.ExecuteActivity(childExecutionContext.Activity);
```

Note that the Execute method of the WhileActivity activity uses the ExecuteActivity method of the child execution context as opposed to the global execution context (keep in mind that the global activity execution context is referenced through the ActivityExecutionContext object passed into the Execute method of the WhileActivity activity) to schedule the Execute method of the new copy of the child activity of the WhileActivity activity for execution. This ensures that the new copy of the child activity is executed within the context of the child execution context as opposed to the global execution context. This is similar to the C# while loop, where the content of the while loop is executed in a local context as opposed to the global context:

```
return ActivityExecutionStatus.Executing;
```

At some point, the WF scheduler dispatches the work item that encapsulates the Execute method of the new copy of the child activity of the WhileActivity activity and consequently invokes the Execute method of the new copy of the child activity, passing in an activity execution context that represents the new child execution context. This means that the Execute method of the new copy of the child activity will be executed within the context of the new child execution context. This Execute method in turn may have to suspend the execution of the new copy of the child activity waiting indefinitely for an external input before it resumes its execution.

When the new copy of the child activity finally completes its execution and raises the Closed event, the Activity_Closed event handler of the WhileActivity activity is scheduled for execution. At some point, the WF scheduler finally invokes the Activity_Closed event handler, passing an ActivityExecutionContext object that represents the global execution context because all execution methods of the WhileActivity activity execute within the context of the global execution context. It is only the execution methods of the new copy of the child activity of the WhileActivity activity that are executed in the context of the new child execution context.

Now let's walk through the implementation of the Activity_Closed event handler. This event handler first removes itself from the list of event handlers registered for the Closed event of the new copy of the child activity of the WhileActivity activity:

```
e.Activity.Closed -= this.Activity_Closed;
```

Next, it casts its first argument to the ActivityExecutionContext type. Keep in mind that this ActivityExecutionContext object represents the global activity execution context:

```
ActivityExecutionContext executionContext =
                              sender as ActivityExecutionContext;
```

It then accesses the ActivityExecutionContextManager object that manages the child execution context that the WhileActivity activity creates and invokes the GetExecutionContext method on this object, passing in the reference to the new copy of the child activity of the WhileActivity activity, to return a reference to the ActivityExecutionContext object that represents the child execution context:

```
ActivityExecutionContext childExecutionContext =
    executionContext.ExecutionContextManager.GetExecutionContext(e.Activity);
```

Next, it calls the CompleteExecutionContext method on the same ActivityExecutionContextManager object, passing in the ActivityExecutionContext object that represents the child execution context, to complete and to consequently discard the child execution context:

```
executionContext.ExecutionContextManager.CompleteExecutionContext(
                                                  childExecutionContext);
```

Finally, it checks whether the condition is met again. If so, it repeats the same steps discussed earlier to deep copy the child activity of the WhileActivity activity and all its descendant activities once again, create a new child execution context, and schedule the Execute method of the new copy of the child activity for execution.

Developing Custom Conditions

As you saw, the WhileActivity activity exposes a property named Condition, which is of the ActivityCondition type. You must assign an ActivityCondition object to this property before executing the WhileActivity activity. The WhileActivity activity invokes the Evaluate method on this ActivityCondition object at the beginning of every iteration to determine whether to execute the iteration or complete its execution. Recall that the ActivityCondition is an abstract class. Every activity condition must inherit from this abstract base class or one of its subclasses.

In this section we'll develop a custom condition named CustomCondition that inherits from the ActivityCondition class and overrides its Evaluate method, as shown in Listing 1-11. My main goal in this example is to show you that the full power of the SharePoint object model is at your disposal when you're developing a custom activity or condition.

Listing 1-11: The CustomCondition activity condition

```
using System;
using System.Workflow.ComponentModel;
using Microsoft.SharePoint.WorkflowActions;
using Microsoft.SharePoint;

namespace Chapter1
{
 public class CustomCondition: ActivityCondition
 {
    public static readonly DependencyProperty ListNameProperty =
            DependencyProperty.Register("ListName", typeof(string),
                                        typeof(CustomCondition));
    public string ListName
    {
      get { return (string)base.GetValue(ListNameProperty); }
      set { base.SetValue(ListNameProperty, value); }
    }

    public static readonly DependencyProperty ItemIdProperty =
            DependencyProperty.Register("ItemId", typeof(int),
                                        typeof(CustomCondition));
    public int ItemId
    {
      get { return (int)base.GetValue(ItemIdProperty); }
      set { base.SetValue(ItemIdProperty, value); }
    }

    public static readonly DependencyProperty FieldNameProperty =
           DependencyProperty.Register("FieldName", typeof(string),
                                       typeof(CustomCondition));
    public string FieldName
    {
      get { return (string)base.GetValue(FieldNameProperty); }
      set { base.SetValue(FieldNameProperty, value); }
    }

    public static readonly DependencyProperty KeywordsProperty =
           DependencyProperty.Register("Keywords", typeof(string),
                                       typeof(CustomCondition));
    public string Keywords
    {
      get { return (string)base.GetValue(KeywordsProperty); }
      set { base.SetValue(KeywordsProperty, value); }
    }

    public static readonly DependencyProperty SiteUrlProperty =
           DependencyProperty.Register("SiteUrl", typeof(string),
                                       typeof(CustomCondition));
    public string SiteUrl
    {
      get { return (string)base.GetValue(SiteUrlProperty); }
```

```
      set { base.SetValue(SiteUrlProperty, value); }
    }

    public override bool Evaluate(Activity activity,
                                  IServiceProvider provider)
    {
      bool success = false;
      using (SPSite siteCollection = new SPSite(this.SiteUrl))
      {
        using( SPWeb web = siteCollection.OpenWeb())
        {
          SPList list = web.Lists[ListName];
          SPListItem item = list.GetItemById(ItemId);
          string str = item[FieldName].ToString();
          success = ((str != null) && str.Contains(Keywords));
        }
      }
      return success;
    }
  }
}
```

This custom condition basically determines whether a specified field of a specified list item of a specified SharePoint list in the top-level site of a specified site collection contains the specified keywords. As such, the condition exposes five properties that must be set for this condition to operate properly. As shown in the example, your condition can expose as many properties as necessary. Next, let's look at the implementation of the Evaluate method. This method first instantiates an SPSite object so it can programmatically access the site collection with the specified URL:

```
SPSite siteCollection = new SPSite(this.SiteUrl);
```

Next, it accesses the SPWeb object that represents the top-level site in this site collection:

```
SPWeb web = siteCollection.OpenWeb();
```

It then uses the list name as an index into the Lists collection property of this SPWeb object to return a reference to the SPList object that represents the list:

```
SPList list = web.Lists[ListName];
```

Next, it invokes the GetItemById method on this SPList object, passing in the ID of the list item, to return a reference to the SPListItem object that represents the list item:

```
SPListItem item = list.GetItemById(ItemId);
```

Then, it uses the field name as an index into this SPListItem object to return the value of the field:

```
string str = item[FieldName].ToString();
```

Finally, it returns a Boolean value that specifies whether this field value contains the specified keywords:

```
return ((str != null) && str.Contains(Keywords));
```

Listing 1-11 follows the best practice of instantiating SPSite and SPWeb objects in the context of using statements to ensure that the Dispose methods of these objects are automatically invoked when they go out of scope.

Next, we'll design a workflow that uses the custom activities and condition that we've developed in this chapter, as shown in Listing 1-12.

Listing 1-12: A workflow that uses the custom activities and condition developed in this chapter

```
using System;
using System.ComponentModel;
using System.ComponentModel.Design;
using System.Collections;
using System.Drawing;
using System.Linq;
using System.Workflow.ComponentModel.Compiler;
using System.Workflow.ComponentModel.Serialization;
using System.Workflow.ComponentModel;
using System.Workflow.ComponentModel.Design;
using System.Workflow.Runtime;
using System.Workflow.Activities;
using System.Workflow.Activities.Rules;
using Microsoft.SharePoint;
using Microsoft.SharePoint.Workflow;
using Microsoft.SharePoint.WorkflowActions;
using Microsoft.Office.Workflow.Utility;

namespace Chapter1
{
  public sealed class Workflow1 : SequentialWorkflowActivity
  {
    private LogToHistoryListActivity logToHistoryListActivity2;
    private LogToHistoryListActivity logToHistoryListActivity3;
    private OnWorkflowActivated onWorkflowActivated1;
    private WhileActivity whileActivity1;
    private LogToHistoryListActivity logToHistoryListActivity1;
    private LogToHistoryListActivity logToHistoryListActivity4;
    private SequenceActivity sequenceActivity1;
    private SequenceActivity sequenceActivity2;

    public Workflow1()
    {
      InitializeComponent();
    }

    private void InitializeComponent()
    {
      this.CanModifyActivities = true;
      Chapter1.CustomCondition customcondition1 =
                                    new Chapter1.CustomCondition();
```

```
System.Workflow.Runtime.CorrelationToken correlationtoken1 =
                                    new CorrelationToken();
System.Workflow.ComponentModel.ActivityBind activitybind1 =
                                         new ActivityBind();
this.logToHistoryListActivity3 = new LogToHistoryListActivity();
this.sequenceActivity1 = new SequenceActivity();
this.sequenceActivity2 = new SequenceActivity();
this.logToHistoryListActivity2 = new LogToHistoryListActivity();
this.whileActivity1 = new Chapter1.WhileActivity();
this.logToHistoryListActivity1 = new LogToHistoryListActivity();
this.onWorkflowActivated1 = new OnWorkflowActivated();
this.logToHistoryListActivity4 = new LogToHistoryListActivity();

//
// logToHistoryListActivity3
//
this.logToHistoryListActivity3.Duration =
                 TimeSpan.Parse("-10675199.02:48:05.4775808");
this.logToHistoryListActivity3.EventId =
              SPWorkflowHistoryEventType.WorkflowComment;
this.logToHistoryListActivity3.HistoryDescription =
                                  "Condition succeeded";
this.logToHistoryListActivity3.HistoryOutcome =
                                  "Condition succeeded";
this.logToHistoryListActivity3.Name =
                             "logToHistoryListActivity3";
this.logToHistoryListActivity3.OtherData = "";
this.logToHistoryListActivity3.UserId = -1;
this.logToHistoryListActivity3.MethodInvoking +=
   new EventHandler(logToHistoryListActivity3_MethodInvoking);
//
// logToHistoryListActivity4
//
this.logToHistoryListActivity4.Duration =
        System.TimeSpan.Parse("-10675199.02:48:05.4775808");
this.logToHistoryListActivity4.EventId =
                 SPWorkflowHistoryEventType.WorkflowComment;
this.logToHistoryListActivity4.HistoryDescription =
                                   "Iteration completed!";
this.logToHistoryListActivity4.HistoryOutcome =
                                   "Iteration completed!";
this.logToHistoryListActivity4.Name =
                               "logToHistoryListActivity4";
this.logToHistoryListActivity4.OtherData = "";
this.logToHistoryListActivity4.UserId = -1;

//
// sequenceActivity1
//
this.sequenceActivity1.Activities.Add(
                                this.logToHistoryListActivity3);
this.sequenceActivity1.Activities.Add(
                                this.logToHistoryListActivity4);
```

(continued)

Listing 1-12 *(continued)*

```
        this.sequenceActivity1.Name = "sequenceActivity1";
        //
        // logToHistoryListActivity2
        //
        this.logToHistoryListActivity2.Duration =
                      TimeSpan.Parse("-10675199.02:48:05.4775808");
        this.logToHistoryListActivity2.EventId =
                      SPWorkflowHistoryEventType.WorkflowComment;
        this.logToHistoryListActivity2.HistoryDescription = "Completed";
        this.logToHistoryListActivity2.HistoryOutcome = "Completed";
        this.logToHistoryListActivity2.Name =
                                        "logToHistoryListActivity2";
        this.logToHistoryListActivity2.OtherData = "";
        this.logToHistoryListActivity2.UserId = -1;
        //
        // whileActivity1
        //
        this.whileActivity1.Activities.Add(this.sequenceActivity1);
        customcondition1.FieldName = "Title";
        customcondition1.ItemId = 1;
        customcondition1.Keywords = "Document";
        customcondition1.ListName = "Documents";
        customcondition1.SiteUrl = "EnterSiteURLHere";
        this.whileActivity1.Condition = customcondition1;
        this.whileActivity1.Name = "whileActivity1";
        //
        // logToHistoryListActivity1
        //
        this.logToHistoryListActivity1.Duration =
                 System.TimeSpan.Parse("-10675199.02:48:05.4775808");
        this.logToHistoryListActivity1.EventId =
                    SPWorkflowHistoryEventType.WorkflowComment;
        this.logToHistoryListActivity1.HistoryDescription = "Started";
        this.logToHistoryListActivity1.HistoryOutcome = "Started";
        this.logToHistoryListActivity1.Name =
                                    "logToHistoryListActivity1";
        this.logToHistoryListActivity1.OtherData = "";
        this.logToHistoryListActivity1.UserId = -1;
        //
        // onWorkflowActivated1
        //
        correlationtoken1.Name = "worflowToken";
        correlationtoken1.OwnerActivityName = "Workflow1";
        this.onWorkflowActivated1.CorrelationToken = correlationtoken1;
        this.onWorkflowActivated1.EventName = "OnWorkflowActivated";
        this.onWorkflowActivated1.Name = "onWorkflowActivated1";
        activitybind1.Name = "Workflow1";
        activitybind1.Path = "workflowProperties";
        this.onWorkflowActivated1.SetBinding(
                    OnWorkflowActivated.WorkflowPropertiesProperty,
                                ((ActivityBind)(activitybind1)));
        //
```

```
            // Workflow1
            //
            this.Activities.Add(this.onWorkflowActivated1);
            this.Activities.Add(this.logToHistoryListActivity1);
            this.Activities.Add(this.whileActivity1);
            this.Activities.Add(this.logToHistoryListActivity2);
            this.Name = "Workflow1";
            this.CanModifyActivities = false;
        }

        void logToHistoryListActivity3_MethodInvoking(object sender,
                                                     EventArgs e)
        {
            System.Threading.Thread.Sleep(5000);
        }

        public Guid workflowId = default(System.Guid);
        public SPWorkflowActivationProperties workflowProperties =
                              new SPWorkflowActivationProperties();
    }
}
```

This workflow is a class named Workflow1, which inherits from the SequentialWorkflowActivity activity, which is the base class for all sequential workflows. The workflow itself is nothing but a custom activity, which is composed of other activities. In other words, the workflow itself is a custom composite activity. Composite activities are the most common custom activities that you, as an activity developer, will be developing, because it enables you to compose your custom activity from existing activities, which promotes reusability (as opposed to starting from scratch and implementing the features that existing activities already support). For example, our custom SequenceActivity activity already contains the logic for executing a set of activities sequentially in linear fashion. By having our custom activity use this activity, we save ourselves the effort of reimplementing this logic all over again.

Now back to the implementation of Workflow1. As you can see, the InitializeComponent method is where the workflow instantiates and initializes its containing activities. This workflow is a sequence of the following activities:

- An OnWorkflowActivated activity named onWorkflowActivated1. This activity suspends its execution and consequently the execution of the workflow and waits for the current workflow instance to be activated. This activity must be the first activity in every SharePoint workflow. I discuss this activity in more detail in the next chapter.
- A LogToHistoryListActivity activity named logToHistoryListActivity1, which logs a workflow history event to the workflow history list stating that the workflow has started. I also discuss the LogToHistoryListActivity activity in the next chapter.
- An instance of our custom WhileActivity activity.
- A LogToHistoryListActivity activity named logToHistoryListActivity2, which logs a workflow history event to the workflow history list stating that the workflow has completed.

Note that the workflow instantiates an instance of our CustomCondition condition, initializes its properties, and assigns it to the Condition property of the WhileActivity activity:

```
customcondition1.FieldName = "Title";
customcondition1.ItemId = 1;
customcondition1.Keywords = "Document";
customcondition1.ListName = "Documents";
customcondition1.SiteUrl = "EnterSiteUrlHere";
this.whileActivity1.Condition = customcondition1;
```

Also note that the WhileActivity activity contains an instance of our SequenceActivity custom activity, which in turn contains two LogToHistoryListActivity activities.

The next chapter discusses in detail how to deploy your workflow for SharePoint. First you will learn how to create a workflow with Visual Studio 2008. Start by launching Visual Studio 2008. Select File ⇨ New Project to launch the New Project dialog shown in Figure 1-2.

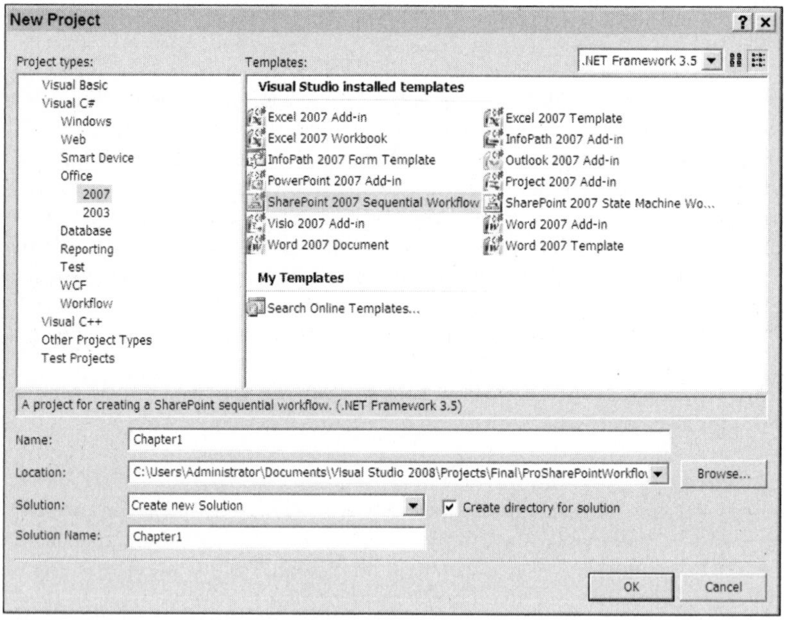

Figure 1-2

Enter Chapter1 as the name of the project and click OK. Visual Studio will automatically take you to the dialog shown in Figure 1-3.

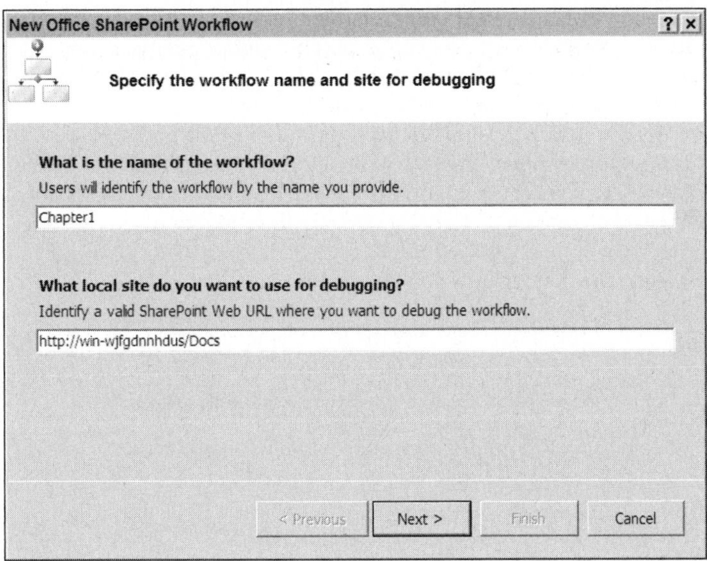

Figure 1-3

Enter Chapter1 as the name of the workflow template and choose a local site for debugging. Click Next to navigate to the dialog shown in Figure 1-4.

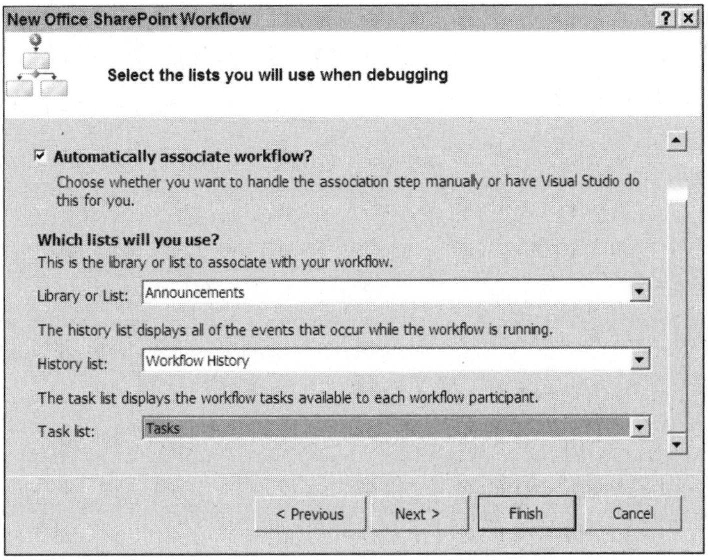

Figure 1-4

Leave the "Automatically associate workflow?" toggle checked because we want to have Visual Studio automatically create the workflow association for us. The next chapter discusses workflow associations in detail. As you can see, this dialog contains three drop-down list boxes. Select a list from the top drop-down list box to have Visual Studio associate the workflow with this SharePoint list. Select a list from the middle drop-down list box to have Visual Studio use this list as the history list for our workflow when it is creating the workflow association. Select a list from the bottom drop-down list box to have Visual Studio use this list as the task list for our workflow when it's creating the workflow association. Our workflow does not create any tasks. SharePoint tasks are thoroughly discussed later in this book.

Click Next to navigate to the dialog shown in Figure 1-5.

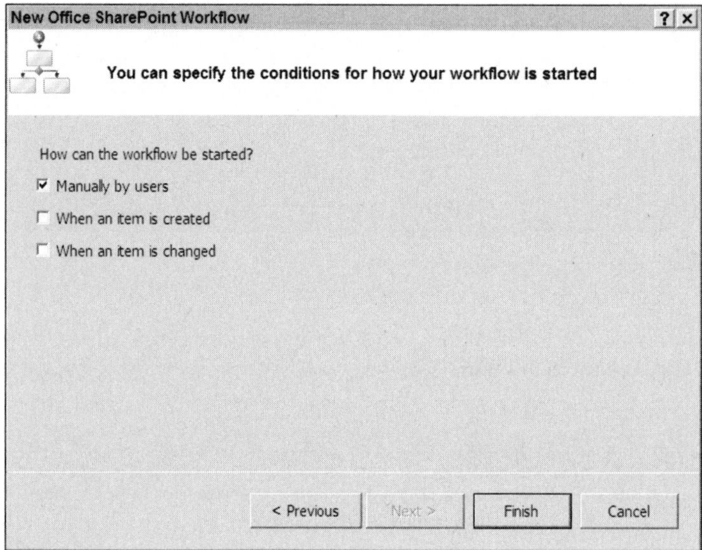

Figure 1-5

This dialog enables you to choose how the workflow should be initiated. You have three options:

- **Manually by users:** In this case the user initiates a workflow manually on a list item in the list with which the workflow is associated.
- **When an item is created:** In this case an instance of the workflow is automatically initiated every time an item is added to the list with which the workflow is associated.
- **When an item is changed:** In this case an instance of the workflow is automatically initiated every time an item is updated in the list with which the workflow is associated.

Check the "Manually by users" option and uncheck the other two options. Click Finish to create the project. As Figure 1-6 shows, Visual Studio creates the following files:

- **feature.xml:** This file defines the feature that references the element manifest file containing the definition of the workflow template. I discuss workflow templates in the next chapter.
- **workflow.xml:** This file is the element manifest file containing the definition of the workflow template.

- **key.snk:** This is the key file that is used to sign the assembly. As you can see, Visual Studio always compiles the workflow code-behind class into a strong-named assembly. Every time you build this project, Visual Studio automatically compiles the workflow into a strong-named assembly and installs this assembly in the global assembly cache (GAC). As you'll see later in this book, SharePoint expects the workflow code-behind class to be compiled into a strong-named assembly and installed in the GAC.
- **Workflow1.cs:** This file contains the first portion of the workflow code-behind class. Keep in mind that the workflow code-behind class in this file is defined as a partial class.
- **Workflow1.designer.cs:** This file contains the second portion of the workflow code-behind class.

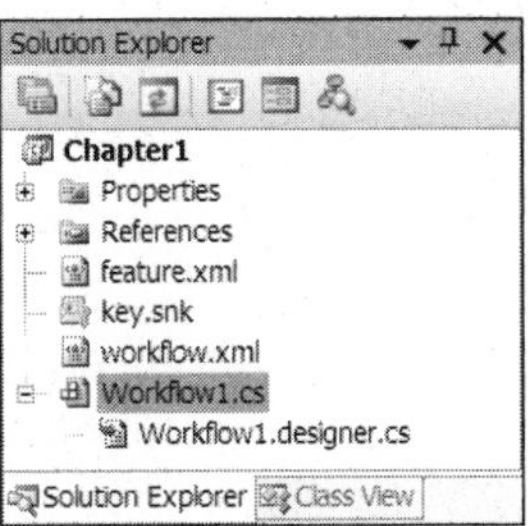

Figure 1-6

Now go ahead and delete the Workflow1.designer.cs file and replace the contents of the Workflow1.cs file with Listing 1-12, earlier in this chapter. Add the following files to the project:

- **CustomConditions.cs:** Add Listing 1-11 to this file.
- **SequenceActivity.cs:** Add Listing 1-7 to this file.
- **WhileActivity.cs:** Add Listing 1-9 to this file.

The Solution Explorer should now look like Figure 1-7.

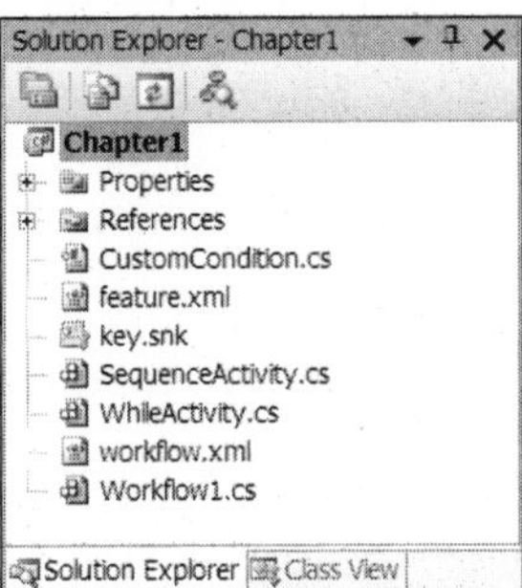

Figure 1-7

Press F5 to build the project. Visual Studio will automatically take the following steps:

1. It compiles all .cs files into a single strong-named assembly.
2. It deploys this assembly to the global assembly cache.
3. It creates a feature-specific subfolder named Chapter1 in the following folder in the file system of the front-end Web server:

```
C:\Program Files\Common Files\microsoft shared\Web Server Extensions\12\
TEMPLATE\FEATURES
```

4. It deploys the feature.xml feature file and the workflow.xml element manifest file into the Chapter1 feature-specific folder.
5. It uses the STSADM command-line utility to install the feature.
6. It uses the STSADM command-line utility to activate the feature in the site that you specified earlier (refer to Figure 1-3).
7. It creates a workflow association for the workflow with the history and task lists that you specified in the middle and bottom drop-down list boxes in Figure 1-4.
8. It adds this workflow association to the list that you specified in the top drop-down list box in Figure 1-4.
9. It navigates to the page displaying the list you specified in the top drop-down list box in Figure 1-4. This page is shown in Figure 1-8.

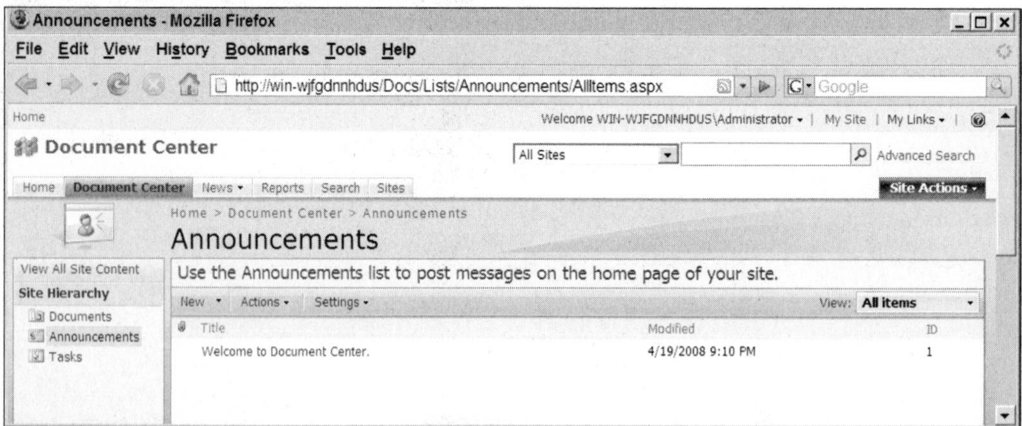

Figure 1-8

Select the Workflows options from the ECB menu of a list item in the list as shown in Figure 1-9.

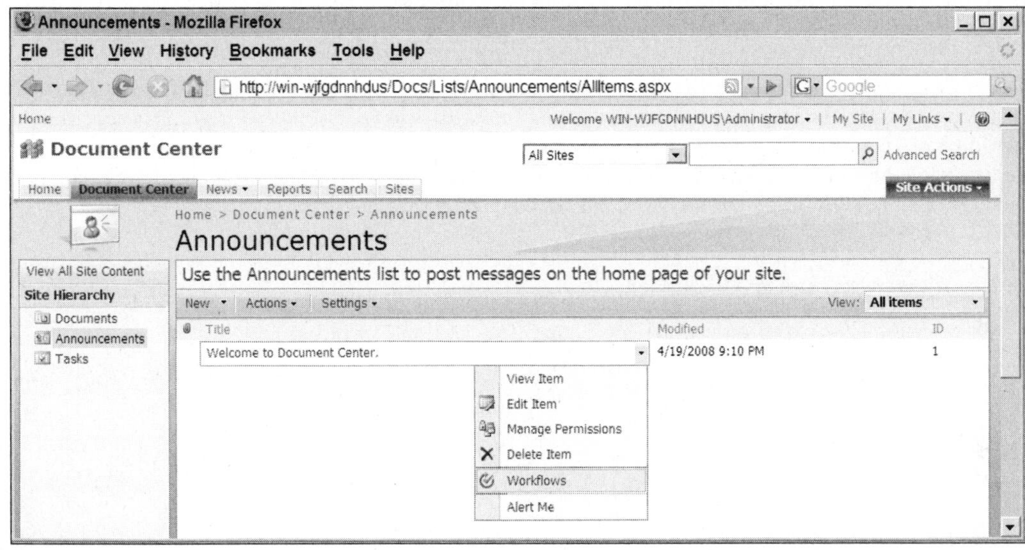

Figure 1-9

This will take you to the Workflow.aspx page shown in Figure 1-10. This page shows the workflow association added to the list. This page contains a link titled Chapter1, which is the name of the workflow association that Visual Studio created and added to the list. This is the same name that you specified earlier (refer to Figure 1-3).

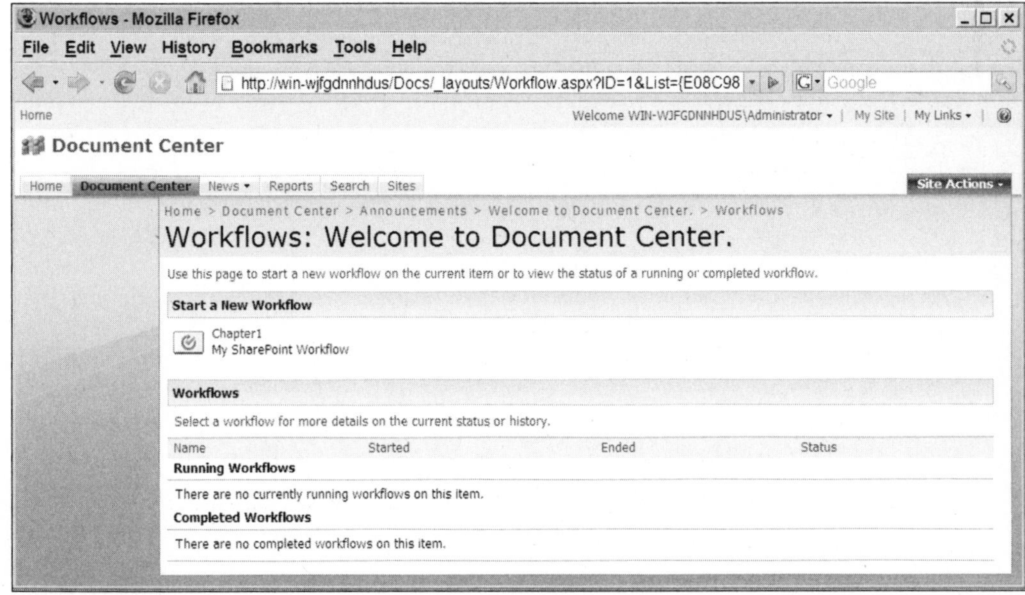

Figure 1-10

Before you click the Chapter1 link shown in Figure 1-10, open another browser window or a new tab in the existing browser window and navigate to the page that shows the SharePoint list whose name is specified in the ListName property of our custom condition, which is Documents in this case. Now go ahead and click the Chapter1 link to initiate an instance of the workflow.

Now return to the new browser window or new tab and change the value of the field whose name is specified in the FieldName property of our custom condition in the list item whose ID is specified in the ItemId property of our custom condition. Now, if you revisit the list item on which you initiated the workflow instance, you should see a column named Chapter1 with the value of Completed (see Figure 1-11), signaling that the workflow instance has completed.

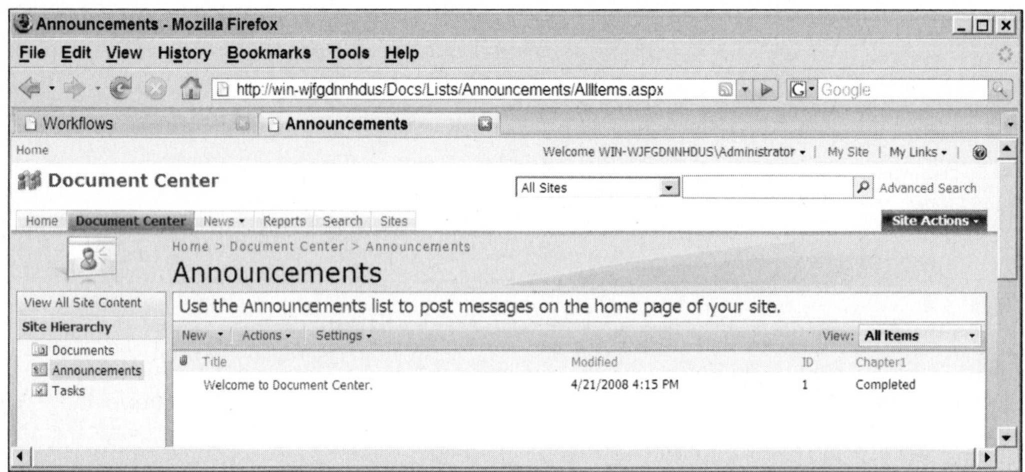

Figure 1-11

Click the Completed link to navigate to the WrkStat.aspx page shown in Figure 1-12. Here, the two LogToHistoryListActivity child activities of our custom SequenceActivity activity are executed multiple times.

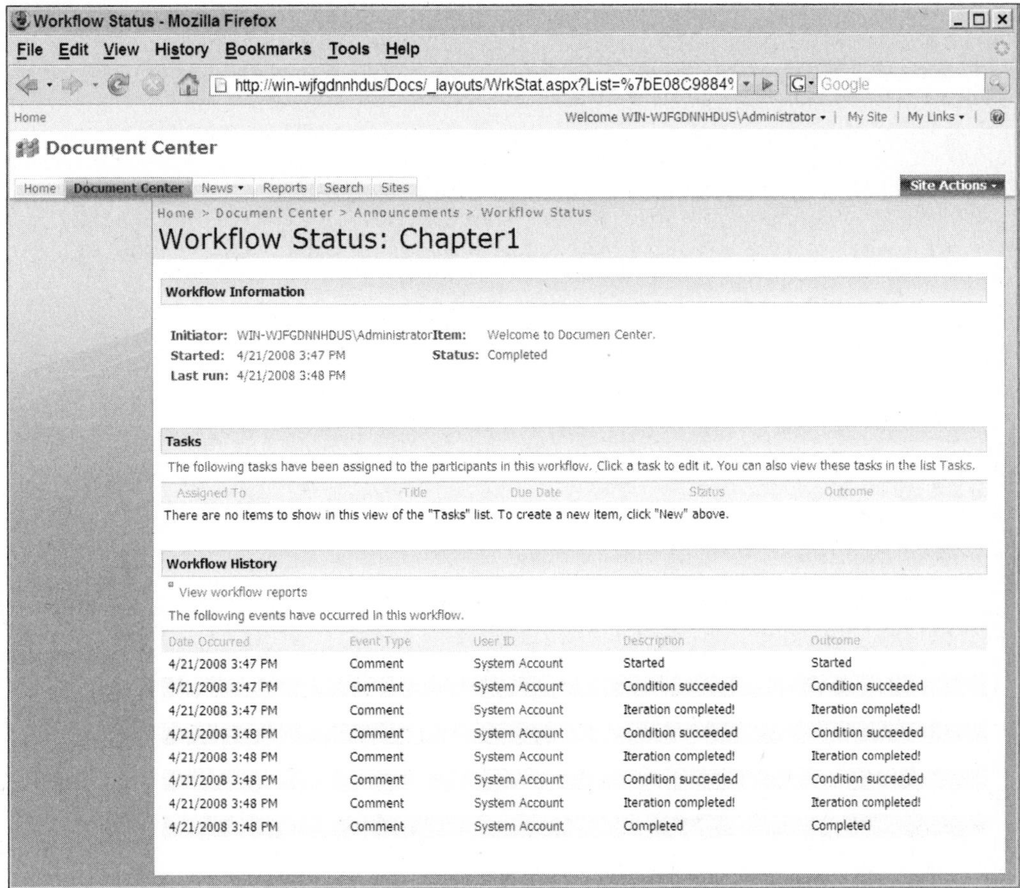

Figure 1-12

Summary

This chapter first provided an overview of the similarities and fundamental differences between WF as a logical workflow programming language and a procedural programming language such as C#. It then discussed the different types of custom activities that you can implement and showed you how to implement each type.

2

Developing Custom Workflows

The previous chapter provided you with an overview of activity development. It also briefly showed you how to implement a workflow that uses your custom activities. This chapter provides the details of SharePoint workflow programming.

SharePoint Workflow Terminology

Before diving into the nuts and bolts of implementing SharePoint workflows, you need to understand the terminology that SharePoint uses to describe the various components involved in SharePoint workflow development. Some of these terms are WF terms and some others are SharePoint-specific terms. The first term is the *workflow* itself, which is a WF term. A workflow is a class that normally inherits from a SequentialWorkflowActivity or StateMachineWorkflowActivity and contains a tree, or hierarchy, of activities. The workflow itself is the root activity of this activity hierarchy.

The next term is *workflow input form,* which is a SharePoint-specific term. As the name suggests, a workflow input form is a form that collects workflow inputs. In general, there are four types of workflow input forms:

- **Association Form:** An association workflow input form is used to collect the workflow association data when a workflow association is being created from a workflow template. I discuss workflow associations and workflow templates shortly.
- **Initiation Form:** An initiation workflow input form is used to collect the workflow initiation data when a workflow instance is being created from a workflow association. I discuss workflow instances shortly.
- **Task Edit Form:** A task edit workflow input form is used to edit workflow tasks.
- **Modification Form:** A modification workflow input form is used to modify workflow instances.

The next term you need to understand is *workflow template,* which is a SharePoint-specific term. A workflow template is a SharePoint construct that represents a workflow and its associated workflow input forms. A workflow template is defined in a CAML-based file, which is referenced from a SharePoint feature file. The SharePoint object model comes with a class named SPWorkflowTemplate whose instances represent workflow templates.

The next term is a SharePoint-specific term named *workflow association.* A workflow association is a SharePoint construct that represents a workflow template, a workflow history list, and a workflow task list. A workflow association associates a workflow template with a SharePoint list, a list content type, or a site content type. The SharePoint object model comes with a class named SPWorkflowAssociation whose instances represent workflow associations.

The next term is *workflow instance.* A workflow instance represents an initiated or activated workflow. A workflow instance is created from a workflow association on a SharePoint list item or document. This means that you must first create the workflow association on the SharePoint list, list content type, or site content type before you can create a workflow instance on a SharePoint list item or document library that belongs to the SharePoint list or document library or is of the specified content type. The SharePoint object model comes with a class named SPWorkflow whose instances represent workflow instances.

SharePoint Solution Package

The examples and recipes presented in this and subsequent chapters do not use SharePoint solution packages for deployment. Instead, they use a manual approach to make the steps involved in the deployment of SharePoint workflows explicit so you can gain a better understanding of these steps. For example, as you'll see later, this manual approach requires you to directly create the required folders in the file system of the front-end Web server and copy the required files into these folders.

This manual approach is taken for educational purposes. You should not use it to deploy your SharePoint workflows to a production machine. Instead, you should use SharePoint solution packages. A SharePoint solution package automatically creates the specified folders and copies the specified files to these folders.

Implementing a SharePoint solution package requires you to know what files you need to deploy and to which folders on the file system of each front-end Web server in the server farm to deploy these files. The manual approach explicitly specifies what these files are and where they should be deployed. I'll postpone the discussion of SharePoint solution packages to Chapter 10, where you'll learn how to use SharePoint solution packages to deploy your workflows.

Recipe for Developing a Custom SharePoint Workflow

Now that you have a better understanding of the terminology that SharePoint uses to describe various components involved in SharePoint workflow development, you're ready to get down to the details of SharePoint workflow programming. Take the following steps to implement, test, and run a SharePoint workflow:

1. Implement the workflow itself, which is a class that inherits from SequentialWorkflowActivity or StateMachineWorkflowActivity.
2. Implement the necessary workflow input forms:
   - **Association Form:** SharePoint automatically displays this form to users when they are creating a workflow association on a SharePoint list, list content type, or site content type. This form basically collects the default settings required to initialize the workflow instances that are created from this workflow association. As such, this form is only necessary for workflows whose instances must be initialized with the appropriate default settings to operate properly.
   - **Initiation Form:** SharePoint automatically displays this form to users when they are creating a workflow instance from a workflow association on a SharePoint list item or document. This form normally displays the same user interface as the association form. This user interface is initially populated with the association data so users can see the default settings for the workflow instance being initiated. As such, this form enables users to optionally modify the default settings and customize them for the workflow instance being activated. Again, this form is only necessary for workflows whose instances must be initialized with the appropriate settings to operate properly.
   - **Edit Task Form:** SharePoint automatically displays this form to users when they attempt to update a SharePoint task for this workflow. A workflow can optionally create SharePoint tasks and assign them to external entities, which could be people or programs, and can then optionally suspend its execution and wait for these people or programs to update these tasks before it resumes its execution where it left off. I discuss SharePoint tasks and edit task forms later in the book.
   - **Modification Form:** SharePoint automatically displays this form to users when they click the specified link to modify a workflow instance. I discuss workflow modification and modification forms later in the book.
3. Compile the workflow itself and the code-behind files for the workflow input forms into a strong-named assembly and install this assembly in the global assembly cache (GAC).
4. Implement the workflow template: As discussed earlier, the workflow template represents the workflow and its respective workflow input forms. A workflow template is defined in a CAML-based file, which is referenced from the feature file that is used to deploy the workflow template. As such, you need to understand the CAML constructs that you need to use to define the workflow template. I cover these constructs later in this chapter. The workflow template CAML document references the strong-named assembly that contains the workflow.
5. Implement a site-collection-scoped SharePoint feature that references the workflow template.

6. Deploy the SharePoint feature and the workflow template that it references to a feature-specific subfolder under the standard TEMPLATE\FEATURE folder on the file system of the front-end Web server:

```
Local_Drive:\Program Files\Common Files\microsoft shared\Web Server
Extensions\12\TEMPLATE\FEATURE
```

7. Deploy the workflow input forms to a feature-specific subfolder under the standard LAYOUTS folder on the file system of the front-end web server. In this book we'll implement workflow input forms as custom application pages:

```
Local_Drive:\Program Files\Common Files\microsoft shared\Web Server
Extensions\12\TEMPLATE\LAYOUTS
```

8. Install the SharePoint feature with SharePoint.
9. Activate the SharePoint feature in a site collection.
10. Create a workflow association from the workflow template on a SharePoint list, list content type, or site content type.
11. Activate a workflow instance from the workflow association on a SharePoint list item or document.

We'll follow this 11-step recipe in the following sections to implement, deploy, and run a SharePoint workflow.

Implementing a SharePoint Workflow

According to the 11-step recipe, the first order of business is to implement the workflow itself, which is a class that normally inherits from SequentialWorkflowActivity or StateMachineWorkflowActivity. As an example, we'll implement a simple workflow that logs a few workflow history events into the workflow history list.

A workflow history list is a SharePoint list where a workflow logs its workflow history events. As you'll see later, when you're creating a workflow association on a SharePoint list, list content type, or a site content type, SharePoint automatically displays a page where you can select a SharePoint list as the history list for your workflow. This is where your workflow can log its history events as it is executing. This provides visibility into the execution of your workflow, enabling you to see what your workflow is doing at every step of the way.

SharePoint comes with an activity named LogToHistoryListActivity that your workflow can use to log its history events to the workflow history list. I discuss this activity later in this chapter. The first activity of every SharePoint workflow must be an activity named OnWorkflowActivated. Our workflow will consist of two activities, OnWorkflowActivated and LogToHistoryListActivity. The next section provides in-depth coverage of the OnWorkflowActivated activity.

OnWorkflowActivated

There are different ways to request SharePoint to activate a workflow:

- Users use the SharePoint user interface to request SharePoint to activate a workflow on a SharePoint list item or document.
- Workflow developers use an activity to request SharePoint to activate a workflow.
- Applications running on the local server use the SharePoint object model to request SharePoint to activate a workflow.
- Code running inside SharePoint uses the SharePoint object model to request SharePoint to activate a workflow.
- External applications use SharePoint Web services to request SharePoint to activate a workflow.

When SharePoint receives a workflow activation request, the following sequence of actions occur:

1. The CreateWorkflow method is invoked on the workflow run time to create the workflow instance. This method invokes the Initialize methods of all constituent activities of the workflow synchronously. In other words, you can rest assured that the Initialize methods of all constituent activities have already completed when the CreateWorkflow method returns. The Initialize methods of those activities whose execution logic requires inputs from external entities normally create the workflow queues where external entities can deposit the inputs. Because the Initialize method of an activity is invoked before its Execute method, external entities are allowed to deposit the required inputs into the workflow queues long before the activities begin their executions.

   SharePoint comes with an activity named OnWorkflowActivated whose Initialize method creates a workflow queue. Every SharePoint activity must include an instance of the OnWorkflowActivated activity as its first child. In other words, this instance must come before any other activities of the workflow. You'll see the reason for this shortly.

2. The OnWorkflowActivated event of a local service known as SharePoint service is fired. I discuss this service in more detail in the next chapter. When the SharePoint service raises this event, it instantiates an instance of an event data class named SPActivationEventArgs (see Listing 2-1). As you'll see in the next chapter, this SPActivationEventArgs instance is finally deposited into the workflow queue that the Initialize method of the OnWorkflowActivated created. As Listing 2-1 shows, the SPActivationEventArgs instance exposes the following two important public fields:

   - **workflowId:** Returns a GUID that uniquely identifies the activated workflow instance
   - **properties:** Returns a reference to an SPWorkflowActivationProperties object that exposes the complete information about the activated workflow instance and its environment

3. The Start method is invoked on the workflow instance to start its execution. As mentioned earlier, the first activity of every SharePoint workflow must be an OnWorkflowActivated activity. Therefore, this activity is the first activity to execute. The Execute method of this activity takes the following steps in order:

   - It retrieves the SPActivationEventArgs instance from the workflow queue.

- It calls the OnInvoked method of the OnWorkflowActivated activity, passing in the SPActivationEventArgs instance as its argument. As Listing 2-2 shows, the OnInvoked method assigns the value of the workflowId field of the SPActivationEventArgs instance to the WorkflowId property of the OnWorkflowActivated activity and assigns the value of the properties field of the SPActivationEventArgs instance to the WorkflowProperties property of the OnWorkflowActivated activity. As discussed earlier, the value of the properties field is a reference to an SPWorkflowActivationProperties object that contains complete information about the workflow instance and its environment.
- It fires its Invoked event and consequently invokes all event handlers registered for the Invoked event, passing in the SPActivationEventArgs instance as their arguments. You can register an event handler for the Invoked method of the OnWorkflowActivated activity to run custom code. Your event handler must have the following signature:

```
void OnWorkflowActivated1_Invoked(object sender, ExternalDataEventArgs e) { . . . }
```

4. Every SharePoint workflow should expose two public fields named workflowId and workflowProperties, which are of type GUID and SPWorkflowActivationProperties, respectively. The values of these two workflow fields should be bound to the WorkflowId and WorkflowProperties properties of the OnWorkflowActivated activity. Therefore, when the OnInvoked method of the WorkflowActivated activity sets the values of the WorkflowId and WorkflowProperties properties of the OnWorkflowActivated activity, these values are automatically assigned to the workflowId and workflowProperties public fields of the workflow through a process known as *activity binding*.

   These two workflow fields basically expose the values of the WorkflowId and WorkflowProperties of the OnWorkflowActivated activity to other activities of the workflow. For example, a LogToHistoryListActivity activity can access the value of the WorkflowProperties property of the OnWorkflowActivated activity through the workflow field that exposes this value to log some of the information content of the referenced SPWorkflowActivationProperties object to the workflow history list.

Listing 2-1: The SPActivationEventArgs event data class

```
public class SPActivationEventArgs : ExternalDataEventArgs
{
  public SPWorkflowActivationProperties properties;
  public Guid workflowId;
}
```

Listing 2-2: The OnWorkflowActivated activity

```
public sealed class OnWorkflowActivated : HandleExternalEventActivity
{
  public static DependencyProperty WorkflowIdProperty;
  public static DependencyProperty WorkflowPropertiesProperty;

  public OnWorkflowActivated()
  {
    this.InterfaceType = typeof(ISharePointService);
    this.EventName = "OnWorkflowActivated";
  }
```

```
    protected override void OnInvoked(EventArgs e)
    {
      this.WorkflowId = ((SPActivationEventArgs)e).workflowId;
      this.WorkflowProperties = ((SPActivationEventArgs)e).properties;
    }

    public override Type InterfaceType
    {
      get { return typeof(ISharePointService); }
    }

    public Guid WorkflowId
    {
      get
      {
        Guid workflowInstanceId = (Guid)base.GetValue(WorkflowIdProperty);
        if (Guid.Empty == workflowInstanceId)
          workflowInstanceId = WorkflowEnvironment.WorkflowInstanceId;
        return workflowInstanceId;
      }
      set { base.SetValue(WorkflowIdProperty, value); }
    }

    public SPWorkflowActivationProperties WorkflowProperties { get; set; }
  }
```

Listing 2-3 presents the public API of SPWorkflowActivationProperties. Recall that the workflowProperties public field of the workflow references an SPWorkflowActivationProperties object.

Listing 2-3: The SPWorkflowActivationProperties class

```
  public class SPWorkflowActivationProperties : SPAutoSerializingObject, ISerializable
  {
    public SPWorkflowActivationProperties();
    protected SPWorkflowActivationProperties(SerializationInfo info,
                                             StreamingContext context);
    public override void GetObjectData(SerializationInfo info,
                                       StreamingContext context);

    public string AssociationData { get; }
    public SPList HistoryList { get; }
    public Guid HistoryListId { get; }
    public string HistoryListUrl { get; }
    public string InitiationData { get; }
    public SPListItem Item { get; }
    public int ItemId { get; }
    public string ItemUrl { get; }
    public SPList List { get; }
```

(continued)

Listing 2-3 *(continued)*

```
        public Guid ListId { get; }
        public string ListUrl { get; }
        public string Originator { get; }
        public string OriginatorEmail { get; }
        public SPUser OriginatorUser { get; }
        public SPSite Site { get; }
        public Guid SiteId { get; }
        public string SiteUrl { get; }
        public SPList TaskList {  get; }
        public Guid TaskListId { get; }
        public string TaskListUrl { get; }
        public string TemplateName { get; }
        public SPWeb Web { get; }
        public Guid WebId { get; }
        public string WebUrl { get; }
        public SPWorkflow Workflow { get; }
        public Guid WorkflowId { get; }
    }
```

Here are the descriptions of the public properties of SPWorkflowActivationProperties against which you can program from within your workflow:

- **AssociationData:** Gets a string that contains the association data passed to the workflow instance
- **HistoryList:** Gets a reference to the SPList object that represents the workflow history list
- **HistoryListId:** Gets a GUID that uniquely identifies the workflow history list
- **HistoryListUrl:** Gets a string that contains the URL of the workflow history list
- **InitiationData:** Gets a string that contains the initiation data passed to the workflow instance
- **Item:** Gets a reference to the SPListItem object that represents the SharePoint list item or document on which the workflow instance is running
- **ItemId:** Gets an integer that uniquely identifies the SharePoint list item or document on which the workflow instance is running
- **ItemUrl:** Gets a string that contains the URL of the SharePoint list item or document on which the workflow instance is running
- **List:** Gets a reference to the SPList object that represents the SharePoint list or document library containing the SharePoint list item or document on which the workflow instance is running
- **ListId:** Gets a GUID that uniquely identifies the SharePoint list or document library containing the SharePoint list item or document on which the workflow instance is running
- **ListUrl:** Gets a string that contains the URL of the SharePoint list or document library containing the SharePoint list item or document on which the workflow instance is running

- **Originator:** Gets a string that contains the user name of the user who initiated the workflow instance
- **OriginatorEmail:** Gets a string that contains the e-mail address of the user who initiated the workflow instance
- **OriginatorUser:** Gets a reference to the SPUser object that represents the user who initiated the workflow instance
- **Site:** Gets a reference to the SPSite object that represents the SharePoint site collection where the workflow instance is running
- **SiteId:** Gets a GUID that uniquely identifies the SharePoint site collection where the workflow instance is running
- **SiteUrl:** Gets a string that contains the URL of the SharePoint site collection where the workflow instance is running
- **TaskList:** Gets a reference to the SPList object that represents the workflow task list. The workflow task list is the SharePoint list containing the workflow tasks that this workflow instance creates and assigns to external entities, which could be people or programs.
- **TaskListId:** Gets a GUID that uniquely identifies the workflow task list
- **TaskListUrl:** Gets a string that contains the URL of the workflow task list
- **TemplateName:** Gets a string that specifies the name of the workflow association from which the workflow instance was created
- **Web:** Gets a reference to the SPWeb object that represents the SharePoint site where the workflow instance is running
- **WebId:** Gets a GUID that uniquely identifies the SharePoint site where the workflow instance is running
- **WebUrl:** Gets a string that contains the URL of the SharePoint site where the workflow instance is running
- **Workflow:** Gets a reference to the SPWorkflow object that represents the workflow instance
- **WorkflowId:** Gets a GUID that uniquely identifies the workflow instance

As you can see, the SPWorkflowActivationProperties object contains complete information about the workflow instance and its environment.

The SPWorkflowActivationProperties object exposes a property named Workflow that references the SPWorkflow object representing the workflow instance. Listing 2-4 presents the public API of the SPWorkflow class against which you can program from within your SharePoint workflow.

Listing 2-4: The SPWorkflow class

```
public sealed class SPWorkflow : IComparable<SPWorkflow>
{
  public SPWorkflow(SPListItem item, Guid workflowInstanceId);
  public SPWorkflow(SPWeb web, Guid workflowInstanceId);
  public int CompareTo(SPWorkflow wf);
  public void CreateHistoryDurationEvent(int eventId, object groupId,
                                         SPMember user, TimeSpan duration,
                                         string outcome, string description,
                                         string otherData);
  public void CreateHistoryEvent(int eventId, object groupId,
                                 SPMember user, string outcome,
                                 string description, string otherData);
  public static void CreateHistoryEvent(SPWeb web, Guid workflowId,
                                        int eventId, SPMember user,
                                        TimeSpan duration, string outcome,
                                        string description, string otherData);

  public Guid AssociationId { get; }
  public int Author { get; }
  public SPUser AuthorUser { get; }
  public DateTime Created { get; }
  public bool HasNewEvents { get; }
  public SPList HistoryList { get; }
  public Guid HistoryListId { get; }
  public Guid InstanceId { get; }
  public SPWorkflowState InternalState { get; }
  public bool IsCompleted { get; }
  public bool IsLocked { get; }
  public Guid ItemGuid { get; }
  public int ItemId { get; }
  public Guid ListId { get; }
  public SPWorkflowModificationCollection Modifications { get; }
  public DateTime Modified { get; }
  public SPWorkflowAssociation ParentAssociation { get; }
  public SPListItem ParentItem { get; }
  public SPList ParentList { get; }
  public SPWeb ParentWeb { get; }
  public Guid SiteId { get; }
  public SPWorkflowFilter TaskFilter { get; set; }
  public SPList TaskList { get; }
  public Guid TaskListId { get; }
  public SPWorkflowTaskCollection Tasks { get; }
  public bool VisibleParentItem { get; }
  public Guid WebId { get; }
  public string Xml { get; }
}
```

Here are the descriptions of the public properties of SPWorkflow:

- **Author:** Gets an integer that specifies the user ID of the user who initiated the workflow instance from the workflow association
- **AuthorUser:** Gets a reference to the SPUser object that represents the user who initiated the workflow instance from the workflow association
- **HistoryList:** Gets a reference to the SPList object that represents the workflow history list
- **HistoryListId:** Gets a GUID that uniquely identifies the workflow history list
- **InstanceId:** Gets a GUID that uniquely identifies the workflow instance
- **InternalState:** Gets a SPWorkflowState enumeration value that represents the current internal state of the workflow instance. Here is the definition of the SPWorkflowState enumeration:

```
[Flags]
public enum SPWorkflowState
{
  All = 0xfff,
  Cancelled = 8,
  Completed = 4,
  Expired = 0x20,
  Expiring = 0x10,
  Faulting = 0x40,
  HasNewEvents = 0x400,
  Locked = 1,
  None = 0,
  NotStarted = 0x800,
  Orphaned = 0x200,
  Running = 2,
  Suspended = 0x100,
  Terminated = 0x80
}
```

  As you can see, SPWorkflowState is marked with the FlagsAttribute metadata attribute to specify that this enumeration supports bitwise operations among its members.

- **IsCompleted:** Gets a Boolean value that specifies whether the workflow instance has completed its execution
- **ItemGuid:** Gets a GUID that uniquely identifies the SharePoint list item or document on which the workflow instance was initiated
- **ParentItem:** Gets a reference to the SPListItem object representing the SharePoint list item or document on which this workflow instance was initiated from the respective workflow association
- **ItemId:** Gets an integer that uniquely identifies the SharePoint list item or document on which the workflow instance was initiated from the workflow association
- **ListId:** Gets a GUID that uniquely identifies the SharePoint list or document library containing the SharePoint list item or document on which the workflow instance was initiated from the workflow association

- **ParentList:** Gets a reference to the SPList object representing the SharePoint list or document library that contains the SharePoint list item or document on which this workflow instance was initiated from the respective workflow association
- **Modifications:** Gets a reference to an SPWorkflowModificationCollection that contains references to the SPWorkflowModification objects that represent the workflow modifications currently in scope for the workflow instance. As described later, when a workflow modification is in scope, SharePoint displays a link to the workflow modification form in the workflow status page. Here is the definition of SPWorkflowModification:

```
public sealed class SPWorkflowModification
{
  public string ContextData { get; }
  public Guid Id { get; }
}
```

As you can see, each workflow modification is associated with two parameters: a string that contains the context data for the workflow modification and a GUID that uniquely identifies the workflow modification.

- **Modified:** Gets a DateTime object that specifies the last modification to the workflow instance. As shown later, users use a link displayed in the workflow status page to navigate to the respective workflow modification form to modify the workflow instance.
- **Created:** Gets a DateTime object that specifies when the workflow instance was initiated from the workflow association
- **ParentAssociation:** Gets a reference to an SPWorkflowAssociation object that represents the workflow association from which the workflow instance was initiated
- **AssociationId:** Gets a GUID that uniquely identifies the workflow association from which the workflow instance was created
- **ParentWeb:** Gets a reference to the SPWeb object representing the SharePoint site containing the SharePoint list or document library that contains the SharePoint list item or document on which this workflow instance was initiated from the respective workflow association
- **WebId:** Gets a GUID that uniquely identifies the SharePoint site containing the SharePoint list or document library that contains the SharePoint list item or document on which the workflow instance was initiated from the respective workflow association
- **SiteId:** Gets a GUID that uniquely identifies the SharePoint site collection containing the SharePoint site for the SharePoint list or document library that contains the SharePoint list item or document on which this workflow instance was initiated from the respective workflow association
- **Tasks:** Gets a reference to the SPWorkflowTaskCollection containing references to the SPWorkflowTask objects that represent the workflow tasks that the workflow instance creates

- **TaskFilter:** Gets or sets an SPWorkflowFilter object which specifies the filter criteria for filtering the workflow task collection specified in the Tasks property. Here is the definition of SPWorkflowFilter:

```
public sealed class SPWorkflowFilter
{
  public SPWorkflowFilter();
  public SPWorkflowFilter(SPWorkflowAssignedToFilter filterAssignedTo);
  public SPWorkflowFilter(SPWorkflowState inclusiveFilterStates,
                          SPWorkflowState exclusiveFilterStates);
  public SPWorkflowFilter(SPWorkflowState inclusiveFilterStates,
                          SPWorkflowState exclusiveFilterStates,
                          SPWorkflowAssignedToFilter filterAssignedTo);

  public SPWorkflowAssignedToFilter AssignedTo { get; set; }
  public SPWorkflowState ExclusiveFilterStates { get; set; }
  public SPWorkflowState InclusiveFilterStates { get; set; }
}
```

  As you can see, SPWorkflowFilter exposes a public read-write property of type SPWorkflowAssignedToFilter that specifies a filter criterion based on to whom the workflow task is assigned:

```
public enum SPWorkflowAssignedToFilter
{
  None,
  CurrentUserAndGroups
}
```

  SPWorkflowFilter also exposes two properties of type SPWorkflowState named ExclusiveFilterStates and InclusiveFilterStates that respectively specify a filter criteria based on including or excluding workflow instances with specified states.

- **TaskList:** Gets a reference to the SPList object that represents the workflow task list
- **TaskListId:** Gets a GUID that uniquely identifies the workflow task list

Here are the descriptions of the methods of SPWorkflow:

- **CreateHistoryDurationEvent:** This method logs the specified workflow history duration event to the workflow history list of the workflow instance. This method takes the following parameters:
  - **eventId:** An integer that identifies the workflow history event type
  - **groupId:** An object that identifies the group to which the workflow history duration event belongs
  - **user:** An SPMember object identifying the user under which to log the workflow history duration event
  - **duration:** A TimeSpan object that specifies the duration of the workflow history duration event
  - **outcome:** A string that contains a short description of the workflow history duration event (limited to 255 characters). SharePoint displays this string on the workflow status page.

- **description:** A string that contains a longer description of the workflow history duration event. SharePoint displays this string on the workflow status page.
- **otherData:** A string that contains any other extra information about the workflow history duration event. SharePoint does not display this string to end users.

- **CreateHistoryEvent:** This method logs the specified workflow history event to the workflow history list of the workflow instance. This method has two overloads.

  The first overload takes the following parameters:

  - **eventId:** An integer that identifies the event type
  - **groupId:** An object that identifies the group to which the workflow history event belongs
  - **user:** An SPMember object identifying the user under which to log the workflow history event
  - **outcome:** A string that contains a short description of the workflow history event (limited to 255 characters). SharePoint displays this string on the workflow status page.
  - **description:** A string that contains a longer description of the workflow history event. SharePoint displays this string on the workflow status page.
  - **otherData:** A string that contains any other extra information about the workflow history event. SharePoint does not display this string to end users.

  The second overload takes the following parameters:

  - **web:** An SPWeb object that represents the SharePoint site containing the SharePoint list or document library that contains the SharePoint list item or document on which the workflow instance was initiated from the respective workflow association
  - **workflowId:** A GUID that uniquely identifies the workflow instance
  - **eventId:** An integer that identifies the workflow history event type
  - **user:** An SPMember object identifying the user under which to log the workflow history event
  - **duration:** A TimeSpan object that specifies the duration of the workflow history event
  - **outcome:** A string that contains a short description of the workflow history event (limited to 255 characters). SharePoint displays this string on the workflow status page.
  - **description:** A string that contains a longer description of the workflow history event. SharePoint displays this string on the workflow status page.
  - **otherData:** A string that contains any other extra information about the workflow history event. SharePoint does not display this string to end users.

SPWorkflowTask represents a workflow task. As the following code listing shows, SPWorkflowTask inherits from SPListItem. As such, SPWorkflowTask exposes all the public properties and methods that SPListItem exposes.

```
public sealed class SPWorkflowTask : SPListItem
{
  public static bool AlterTask(SPListItem task, Hashtable htData,
                               bool fSynchronous);
```

```
    public static Hashtable GetExtendedPropertiesAsHashtable(SPListItem task);
    public static string GetWorkflowData(SPListItem task);

    public Guid WorkflowId { get; }
    public string Xml { get; }
}
```

SPWorkflowTask exposes two properties of its own, WorkflowId and XML. These properties get the GUID that uniquely identifies the workflow instance, and a string that contains the workflow task definition in XML format. SPWorkflowTask also exposes three static methods of its own:

- **AlterTask:** This static method takes the following parameters and updates the specified fields of the specified workflow task:
    - **task:** an SPListItem object that represents the workflow task to update
    - **htData:** A Hashtable collection that contains the names and new values of the workflow task fields to update
    - **fSynchronous:** A Boolean value that specifies whether the update should be done synchronously
- **GetExtendedPropertiesAsHashtable:** This static method returns a Hashtable collection that contains the extended properties of the specified workflow task. The method takes an SPListItem object as its argument, representing the workflow task.
- **GetWorkflowData:** This static method returns a string that contains the workflow data associated with a specified workflow task.

Using OnWorkflowActivated

This section explains how you can use and configure the OnWorkflowActivated activity in Visual Studio 2008. Add a new workflow to your Visual Studio project and drag and drop the OnWorkflowActivated activity onto the designer surface. Next, select this activity. You should see the properties shown in Figure 2-1.

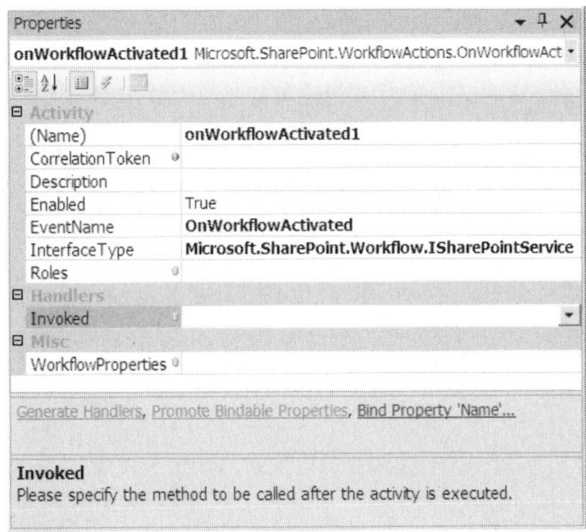

Figure 2-1

The Name, InterfaceType, and EventName properties of the OnWorkflowActivated activity are already set. Next, we'll set the CorrelationToken property. I provide in-depth coverage of correlation tokens in the next chapter. Enter a name for the correlation token and select the workflow as the owner activity, as shown in Figure 2-2.

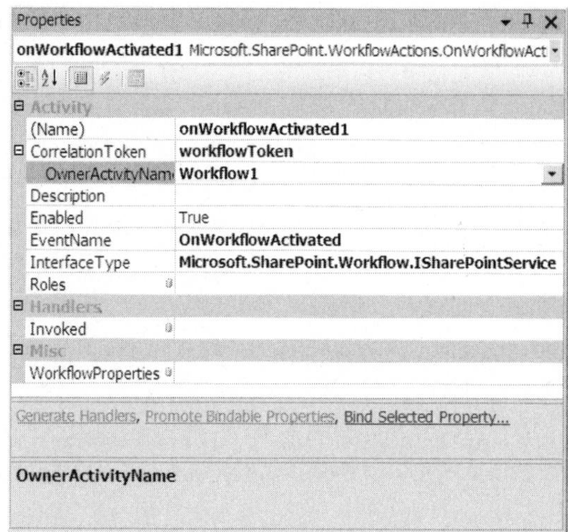

Figure 2-2

This instructs Visual Studio to generate and add the code shown in Listing 2-5 to your workflow class. This code instantiates an instance of a class named CorrelationToken and assigns it to the CorrelationToken property of the OnWorkflowActivated activity.

Listing 2-5: An excerpt showing the CorrelationToken object

```
CorrelationToken correlationtoken1 = new CorrelationToken();
this.onWorkflowActivated1 = new OnWorkflowActivated();
correlationtoken1.Name = "workflowToken";
correlationtoken1.OwnerActivityName = "Workflow1";
this.onWorkflowActivated1.CorrelationToken = correlationtoken1;
```

You should now bind the WorkflowProperties property of the OnWorkflowActivated activity to a local workflow field to make the value of this property available to other activities in the workflow. To do so, click the text box next to the WorkflowProperties property to view the button shown in Figure 2-3.

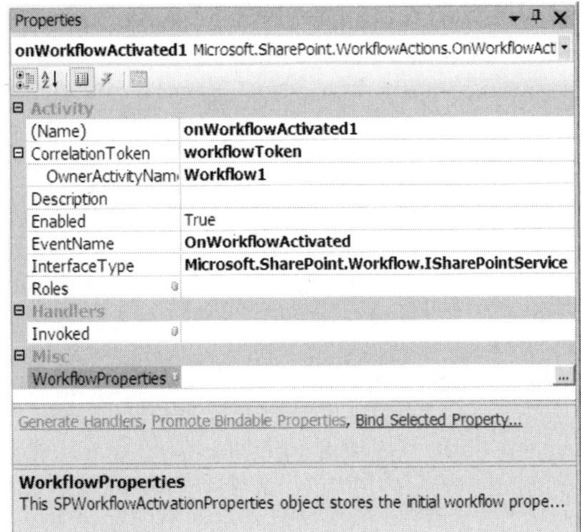

Figure 2-3

Click this button to launch the dialog shown in Figure 2-4. Switch to the "Bind to a new member" tab, select the Create Field toggle, enter "WorkflowProperties" in the "New Member Name" text box as the field name, and click OK.

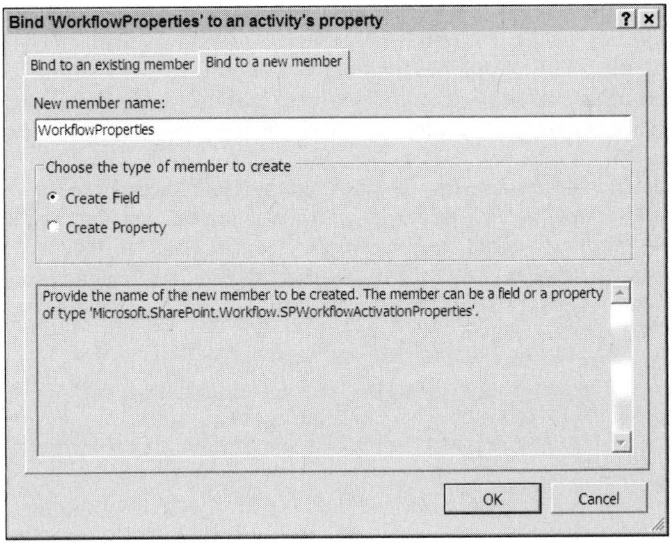

Figure 2-4

When you click the OK button, Visual Studio automatically generates and adds the following code to your workflow:

```
public SPWorkflowActivationProperties WorkflowProperties =
                                            new SPWorkflowActivationProperties();

ActivityBind activitybind1 = new ActivityBind();
activitybind1.Name = "Workflow1";
activitybind1.Path = "WorkflowProperties";
this.onWorkflowActivated1.SetBinding(OnWorkflowActivated
                    .WorkflowPropertiesProperty, activitybind1);
```

This code adds a new public field named WorkflowProperties to the workflow. Then it instantiates an ActivityBind object, sets its Path property to the name of the new field (that is, WorkflowProperties), and sets it Name property to the name of the class that owns this field (that is, the name of the workflow). Finally, it invokes the SetBinding method on the OnWorkflowActivated activity to bind this ActivityBind object to the WorkflowPropertiesProperty of the OnWorkflowActivated activity. This means that every time the value of the field — whose name is provided by the Path property of the ActivityBind object — of the object whose name is provided by the Name property of the ActivityBind object changes, that is, every time the value of the WorkflowProperties field of the Workflow1 workflow changes, WF automatically assigns the new value to the WorkflowPropertiesProperty of the OnWorkflowActivated activity.

In our case, this means that the same SPWorkflowActivationProperties object that the following line of code instantiates is assigned to the WorkflowPropertiesProperty of the OnWorkflowActivated activity. The OnWorkflowActivated activity populates the SPWorkflowActivationProperties object that its WorkflowPropertiesProperty references with the complete information about the workflow instance and its environment. This means that this complete information is now available to all other activities in the workflow through the WorkflowProperties field of the workflow. Other activities can now bind this field or subproperties of the SPWorkflowActivationProperties that this field references to their own bindable properties so these properties automatically pick up these values without any coding.

This is the power of activity binding. However, this only works if the field to which the ActivityBind object is bound is of the DependencyProperty type, because the first argument of the SetBinding method must be a DependencyProperty object. For example, in the case of the OnWorkflowActivated activity, the WorkflowPropertiesProperty field of this activity is of the DependencyProperty type, as shown in the following excerpt, which contains the internal implementation of the WorkflowPropertiesProperty field of the OnWorkflowActivated activity:

```
public static DependencyProperty WorkflowPropertiesProperty =
    DependencyProperty.Register("WorkflowProperties",
              typeof(SPWorkflowActivationProperties), typeof(OnWorkflowActivated));
```

The WorkflowProperties property of the OnWorkflowActivated activity uses the WorkflowPropertiesProperty DependencyProperty field as its backing store, as shown in the following excerpt, which contains the internal implementation of the workflowProperties property of the OnWorkflowActivated activity:

```
public SPWorkflowActivationProperties WorkflowProperties
{
  get
  {
    return (SPWorkflowActivationProperties)
                                    base.GetValue(WorkflowPropertiesProperty);
```

```
    }
    set
    {
      base.SetValue(WorkflowPropertiesProperty, value);
    }
  }
```

A property such as WorkflowProperties of the OnWorkflowActivated activity that uses a DependencyProperty field as its backing store is known as a *bindable property*. You must make the properties of your custom activities bindable if you want to enable other activities or the containing workflow to bind their properties and fields to the properties of your custom activities. This enables data transfer from the bindable properties of your custom activities to the properties of other activities or the fields of the containing workflow through activity binding without any coding.

Take these two steps to make a property of your custom activity bindable:

1. Define a field of the DependencyProperty type. The name of this field should be the name of the property that will use this field as its backing store followed by the word "Property." Use the Register static method on the DependencyProperty class to initialize and register the field:

```
public static DependencyProperty PropertyNameProperty =
    DependencyProperty.Register("PropertyName",
              TypeObjectThatRepresentsTheTypeOfProperty,
              TypeObjectThatRepresentsTheTypeOfYourCustomActivity);
```

   As you can see, the Register static method takes the following parameters:

   - A string that contains the name of the property that will use this field as its backing store
   - A Type object that represents the type of this property
   - A Type object that represents the type of your custom activity

2. Define a property that uses the field from Step 1 as its backing store. The getter and setter of this property must use the GetValue and SetValue methods to get and set that value of this property. Note that the first argument of these two methods uses the field from Step 1:

```
public TypeOfProperty WorkflowProperties
{
  get
  {
    return (TypeOfProperty)base.GetValue(PropertyNameProperty);
  }
  set
  {
    base.SetValue(PropertyNameProperty, value);
  }
}
```

As Figure 2-3 shows, the OnWorkflowActivated activity exposes an event named Invoked. You can optionally register an event handler for this event. This activity raises this event after the underlying SharePoint service fires the OnWorkflowActivated event. To add an event handler to any activity in

Visual Studio, right-click the activity and select the Generate Handlers menu option. This will automatically add an event handler with an empty body:

```
private void onWorkflowActivated1_Invoked(object sender, ExternalDataEventArgs e)
{
}
```

LogToHistoryListActivity

Listing 2-6 presents the public API of the LogToHistoryListActivity activity.

Listing 2-6: The LogToHistoryListActivity activity

```
public class LogToHistoryListActivity : Activity
{
  public static DependencyProperty DurationProperty;
  public static DependencyProperty EventIdProperty;
  public static DependencyProperty HistoryDescriptionProperty;
  public static DependencyProperty HistoryOutcomeProperty;
  public static DependencyProperty MethodInvokingEvent;
  public static DependencyProperty OtherDataProperty;
  public static DependencyProperty UserIdProperty;

  public event EventHandler MethodInvoking { add; remove; }

  protected override ActivityExecutionStatus Execute(
                                ActivityExecutionContext context)
  {
    ISharePointService service =
              (ISharePointService)context.GetService(
                                typeof(ISharePointService));
    base.RaiseEvent(MethodInvokingEvent, this, EventArgs.Empty);
    this.OnMethodInvoking(EventArgs.Empty);
    service.LogToHistoryList(base.WorkflowInstanceId,
                          this.EventId, this.UserId,
                          this.Duration, this.HistoryOutcome,
                          this.HistoryDescription, this.OtherData);
    return ActivityExecutionStatus.Closed;
  }

  protected virtual void OnMethodInvoking(EventArgs e) { }

  public TimeSpan Duration { get; set; }
  public SPWorkflowHistoryEventType EventId { get; set; }
  public string HistoryDescription { get; set; }
  public string HistoryOutcome { get; set; }
  public string OtherData { get; set; }
  public int UserId { get; set; }
}
```

LogToHistoryListActivity exposes the following properties:

- **EventId:** Gets or sets a SPWorkflowHistoryEventType enumeration value that represents the type of the workflow history event to log. The following listing presents the possible values of the SPWorkflowHistoryEventType enumeration:

```
public enum SPWorkflowHistoryEventType
{
  None,
  WorkflowStarted,
  WorkflowCompleted,
  WorkflowCancelled,
  WorkflowDeleted,
  TaskCreated,
  TaskCompleted,
  TaskModified,
  TaskRolledBack,
  TaskDeleted,
  WorkflowError,
  WorkflowComment
}
```

- **UserId:** Gets or sets an integer specifying the user ID under which the workflow history event is logged
- **Duration:** Gets or sets a TimeSpan object specifying the duration of the workflow history event
- **HistoryDescription:** Gets or sets a string that describes the workflow history event
- **HistoryOutcome:** Gets or sets a string that specifies the outcome of the workflow history event
- **OtherData:** Gets or sets a string that specifies any other data associated with the workflow history event. SharePoint does not display this information to end users.

Next, I'll walk you through the internal implementation of the Execute method of the LogToHistoryListActivity shown in Listing 2-6. One of my main goals in this book is to teach you the skills that you need in order to implement your own custom activities. One great way to learn about activity development is to study the internal implementation of the activities that ship with SharePoint. As such, I cover the internal implementation of several important SharePoint activities throughout this book. The internal implementation of each activity teaches you some of the skills you need to implement your own custom activities. The internal implementation of the LogToHistoryListActivity activity shows you how to take advantage of the SharePoint-specific local services in your own custom activities. As shown in the next chapter, SharePoint automatically registers these local services with the workflow run time when it starts the run time. The next chapter also provides comprehensive coverage of these SharePoint-specific local services.

Returning now to the internal implementation of the Execute method of the LogToHistoryListActivity activity shown in Listing 2-6, this method, like the Execute method of any other WF activity, contains the execution logic of the activity. The method first invokes the GetService method on the ActivityExecution Context object, passing in the Type object that represents the type of the ISharePointService interface, to return a reference to the SharePoint service that SharePoint has registered with the workflow run time. Chapter 3 discusses the ISharePointService interface and the SharePoint service that implements this interface. For now, it suffices to say that the SharePoint service enables a workflow activity such as

LogToHistoryListActivity to make calls into SharePoint to perform operations such as logging workflow history events to a workflow history list:

```
ISharePointService service =
          (ISharePointService)context.GetService(typeof(ISharePointService));
```

Next, the Execute method raises the MethodInvoking event of the LogToHistoryListActivity activity; consequently, it invokes all event handlers registered for this event. You can register an event handler for this event to execute custom code. You'll see an example of this later in this section.

```
base.RaiseEvent(MethodInvokingEvent, this, EventArgs.Empty);
```

Now the Execute method invokes the OnMethodInvoking method. As Listing 2-6 shows, the OnMethodInvoking method of the LogToHistoryListActivity activity doesn't do anything. However, you can implement a custom activity that inherits from the LogToHistoryListActivity activity and overrides the OnMethodInvoking method to run custom code. In other words, the OnMethodInvoking method is an extensibility point of the LogToHistoryListActivity activity.

```
this.OnMethodInvoking(EventArgs.Empty);
```

Next, the Execute method invokes the LogToHistoryList method on the SharePoint service to log the specified workflow history event to the workflow history list. Note that the Execute method passes the values of its properties directly into the LogToHistoryList method of the SharePoint service. As such, you must set the values of these properties before you use this activity:

```
service.LogToHistoryList(base.WorkflowInstanceId, this.EventId, this.UserId,
                         this.Duration, this.HistoryOutcome,
                         this.HistoryDescription, this.OtherData);
```

Finally, the Execute method returns the ActivityExecutionStatus enumeration value of Closed to signal the workflow run time that it has completed its execution. The LogToHistoryListActivity activity completes its execution in one shot because it does not need to wait for any inputs from external entities:

```
return ActivityExecutionStatus.Closed;
```

Note that all properties of the LogToHistoryListActivity activity are defined as bindable properties. As such, you can use activity binding to set the values of these properties. This enables you to bind these properties to the public fields of the containing workflow so they can automatically pick up their values from these fields through a process known as *activity binding*. As such, every workflow that uses the LogToHistoryListActivity should expose the following public fields and bind them to the respective properties of LogToHistoryListActivity:

```
    public string historyDescription = default(string);
    public string historyOutcome = default(string);
    public string otherData = default(string);
    public int userId = default(int);
    public TimeSpan duration = default(TimeSpan);
```

Using LogToHistoryListActivity

Visual Studio enables you to drag the LogToHistoryListActivity activity from the toolbox and drop it onto the designer surface when you're designing a workflow or developing a custom composite activity.

When you drop the LogToHistoryListActivity activity onto the designer surface of a workflow or a custom composite activity and select the activity, you should see its properties in the Properties pane, as shown in Figure 2-5.

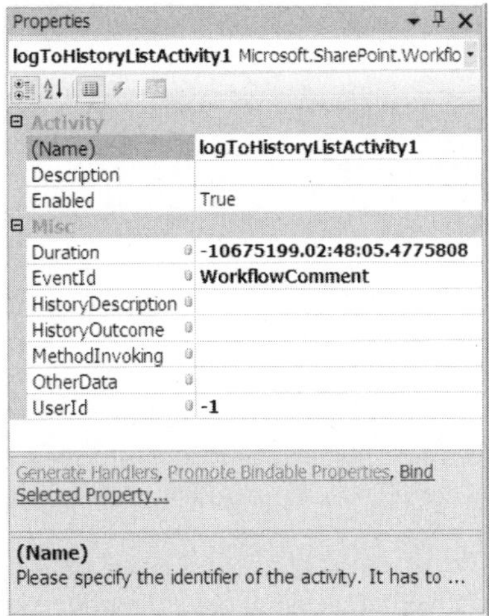

Figure 2-5

Click the HistoryDescription property to make the button shown in Figure 2-6 visible.

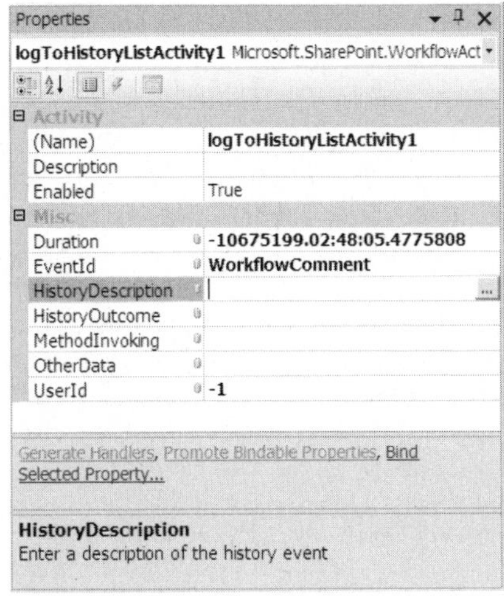

Figure 2-6

Click this button to launch the dialog shown in Figure 2-7. Switch to the "Bind to a new member" tab and check the Create Field radio button. Enter HistoryDescription as the name for the new member.

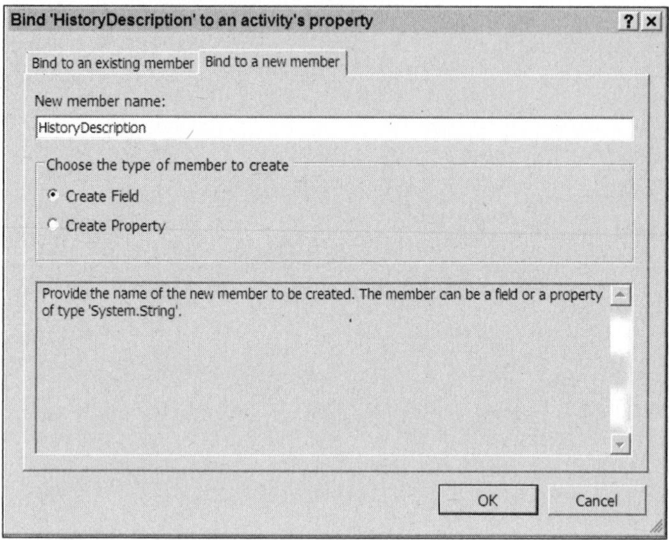

Figure 2-7

When you click the OK button on this dialog, Visual Studio will automatically generate the following code and add it to your workflow if you're designing a workflow, or to your custom composite activity if you're developing a custom composite activity:

```
public string HistoryDescription = default(System.String);
ActivityBind activitybind1 = new ActivityBind();
activitybind1.Name = "Workflow1";
activitybind1.Path = "HistoryDescription";
this.logToHistoryListActivity1.SetBinding(
            LogToHistoryListActivity.HistoryDescriptionProperty, activitybind1);
```

This code adds a new public field named HistoryDescription of the string type to the workflow or composite activity. Then it instantiates an ActivityBind object, sets its Path property to the name of the new field, and its Name property to the name of the workflow or composite activity, because the field belongs to the workflow or composite activity. Finally, it calls the SetBinding method on the LogToHistoryListActivity activity to bind this ActivityBind object to the HistoryDescriptionProperty DependencyProperty of the LogToHistoryListActivity. This means that every time the value of the HistoryDescription field of the workflow or composite activity is set, this value is automatically assigned to the HistoryDescriptionProperty field of the LogToHistoryListActivity activity. Here is the definition of the HistoryDescriptionProperty field of the LogToHistoryListActivity activity:

```
public static DependencyProperty HistoryDescriptionProperty =
        DependencyProperty.Register("HistoryDescription", typeof(string),
                                    typeof(LogToHistoryListActivity));
```

As you may have already guessed, the HistoryDescription property of the LogToHistoryListActivity activity uses this HistoryDescriptionProperty DependencyProperty field as its backing store:

```
public string HistoryDescription
{
  get { return (string) base.GetValue(HistoryDescriptionProperty); }
  set { base.SetValue(HistoryDescriptionProperty, value); }
}
```

Because the LogToHistoryListActivity activity has defined its HistoryDescription property as a bindable property, we can set its value through activity binding.

So far, we've looked at the code that Visual Studio generates and adds to your workflow or custom composite activity when you select the Create Field radio button in the dialog box shown in Figure 2-7. Next, we'll study the code that Visual Studio generates and adds to your workflow or custom composite activity when you select the Create Property radio button in this dialog, as shown here:

```
public static DependencyProperty HistoryDescriptionProperty =
           DependencyProperty.Register("HistoryDescription", typeof(System.String),
                                         typeof(Chapter2.CompositeActivity));
public String HistoryDescription
{
  get
  {
    return ((string)(base.GetValue(
                         Chapter2CompositeActivity.HistoryDescriptionProperty)));
  }
  set
  {
    base.SetValue(Chapter2CompositeActivity.HistoryDescriptionProperty, value);
  }
}

ActivityBind activitybind1 = new ActivityBind();
activitybind1.Name = "CompositeActivity";
activitybind1.Path = "HistoryDescription";
this.logToHistoryListActivity1.SetBinding(
            LogToHistoryListActivity.HistoryDescriptionProperty, activitybind1);
```

In this case, Visual Studio adds a new DependencyProperty field named HistoryDescriptionProperty and a new bindable property that uses this DependencyProperty field as its backing store. In other words, selecting the Create Property radio button, rather than the Create Field radio button, creates a bindable property for your workflow or custom composite activity so its value can be set through activity binding.

Note that the preceding code also creates an ActivityBind object, sets its Path property to the name of the new bindable property — that is, HistoryDescription — and sets its Name property to the name of the class that owns this bindable property — that is, the name of your workflow or custom composite activity. The code listing then invokes the SetBinding method on the LogToHistoryListActivity activity to bind this ActivityBind object to the HistoryDescriptionProperty DependencyProperty as usual.

Therefore, when you're deciding whether to select the Create Field or Create Property radio button, the deciding factor should be whether you want to allow others to set the property or field that you're creating through activity binding. For instance, if the LogToHistoryListActivity activity that you're adding to your custom composite activity is only used internally in your custom composite control to log history events to the workflow history list, then there is no need to expose the HistoryDescription field of your custom composite control, which is bound to the LogToHistoryListActivity activity's HistoryDescription bindable property, as a bindable property.

As Figure 2-6 shows, the LogToHistoryListActivity activity exposes an event named MethodInvoking. Next, we'll add an event handler for this event. When you right-click an activity such as LogToHistoryListActivity activity that supports bindable events, a menu pops up that contains an option named Generate Handlers, as shown in Figure 2-8.

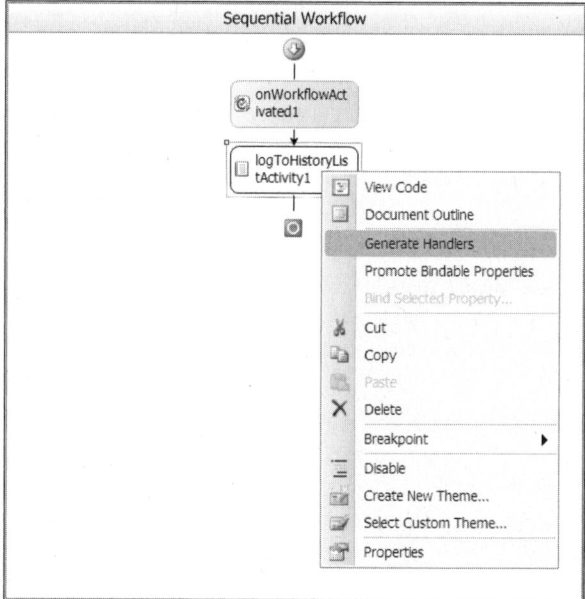

Figure 2-8

If you select this menu option, Visual Studio automatically generates and adds the code shown in boldface to your workflow or custom composite activity:

```
private void logToHistoryListActivity1_MethodInvoking(object sender, EventArgs e)
{
}

private void InitializeComponent()
{
  . . .
  this.logToHistoryListActivity1.MethodInvoking +=
            new System.EventHandler(this.logToHistoryListActivity1_MethodInvoking);
  . . .
}
```

As you can see, this code defines an event handler named logToHistoryListActivity1_MethodInvoking and registers it for the MethodInvoking event of the LogToHistoryListActivity activity. Next, add the following lines to the event handler:

```
private void logToHistoryListActivity1_MethodInvoking(object sender,
                                                      EventArgs e)
{
  this.HistoryDescription = . . .;
  this.HistoryOutcome = . . .;
  this.Duration = . . .;
  this.UserId = . . .;
  this.OtherData = . . .;
}
```

This event handler basically sets the values of the HistoryDescription, HistoryOutcome, Duration, OtherData, and UserId workflow or composite fields or properties. Because these fields or properties are bound to the HistoryDescription, HistoryOutcome, Duration, OtherData, and UserId properties of the LogToHistoryListActivity activity, the values of these fields or properties are automatically assigned through activity binding. Because this event handler is registered for the MethodInvoking event and because the LogToHistoryListActivity activity raises this event before it logs the workflow history event into the workflow history list, the values of these properties are set before the workflow history event is logged. Keep in mind that the LogToHistoryListActivity activity basically logs the values of these properties into the workflow history list.

Note that Visual Studio shows the Generate Handlers option and consequently generates and adds code like the preceding only if the activity exposes bindable events. A bindable event, just like a bindable property, uses a DependencyProperty field as its backing store. The MethodInvoking event of the LogToHistoryListActivity activity is a bindable event, as you can see from the following code listing, which presents the internal definition of this event:

```
public static DependencyProperty MethodInvokingEvent =
                DependencyProperty.Register("MethodInvoking", typeof(EventHandler),
                                            typeof(LogToHistoryListActivity));

public event EventHandler MethodInvoking
{
  add { base.AddHandler(MethodInvokingEvent, value); }
  remove { base.RemoveHandler(MethodInvokingEvent, value); }
}
```

Follow these steps to add a bindable event to your own custom composite activity:

1. Add a DependencyProperty event field like so:

```
public static DependencyProperty MethodInvokingEvent =
                DependencyProperty.Register("MethodInvoking", typeof(EventHandler),
                                            typeof(LogToHistoryListActivity));
```

2. Add an event property whose add method invokes the AddHandler method, passing in the DependencyProperty event field from Step 1 and the event handler being added and whose remove method invokes the RemoveHandler method, passing in the DependencyProperty event field from Step 1 and the event handler being removed, like so:

```
public event EventHandler MethodInvoking
{
  add { base.AddHandler(MethodInvokingEvent, value); }
  remove { base.RemoveHandler(MethodInvokingEvent, value); }
}
```

In summary, based on the discussions in this and the previous section, you should follow this recipe to add an activity to your workflow or custom composite activity when you're designing your workflow or custom composite activity in Visual Studio:

1. Drag the activity from the toolbox and drop it onto the designer surface of your workflow or custom composite activity.
2. Click the activity to view its properties in the Properties pane.
3. Take these steps to set each property:
   - ❑ Click the property to make the button shown in Figure 2-6 visible.
   - ❑ Click the button to launch the dialog shown earlier in Figure 2-7.
   - ❑ Switch to the "Bind to a new member" tab if you need to add a new member to your workflow or custom composite activity. For example, if you've already added an instance of the LogToHistoryListActivity activity to your workflow or custom composite activity and now you're adding another instance, you don't need to add a new member because you can reuse the members that you defined for the first instance. That said, if you need to use different members for different instances of the same type of activity, you should switch to the "Bind to a new member" tab to add a new member.
   - ❑ Select the Create Field radio button to create a nonbindable member if you do not want other activities to bind their properties to this member.
   - ❑ Select the Create Property radio button to create a bindable member if you do want other activities to bind their properties to this member.
4. Right-click the activity and select Generate Handlers from the pop-up menu to generate empty event handlers for the events of the activity. Note that selecting this menu option automatically adds event handlers for all events of the activity.
5. Add the required code to the body of these event handlers.

Putting It All Together

The previous two sections provided you with in-depth coverage of two SharePoint activities named OnWorkflowActivated and LogToHistoryListActivity. In this section, we'll implement a workflow that uses these two activities. Following the same pattern as Visual Studio, this workflow is implemented in two separate files using partial classes. Listing 2-7 presents the content of theWorkflow1.cs file, which contains the event handlers for the activities that make up the workflow.

Listing 2-7: The content of the Workflow1.cs file

```
using System;
using System.Workflow.Activities;
using Microsoft.SharePoint.Workflow;
using System.Xml;
using System.Xml.Serialization;
using System.IO;

namespace Chapter2
{
  public sealed partial class Workflow1 : SequentialWorkflowActivity
  {
    public Workflow1()
    {
      InitializeComponent();
    }

    public Guid workflowId = default(System.Guid);
    public SPWorkflowActivationProperties workflowProperties;
    public string HistoryDescription = default(string);
    public string HistoryOutcome = default(string);
    public string OtherData = default(string);
    public int UserId = default(int);
    public TimeSpan Duration  = default(TimeSpan);

    private void onWorkflowActivated1_Invoked(object sender,
                                              ExternalDataEventArgs e)
    {
      this.workflowId = workflowProperties.WorkflowId;
    }

    private void logToHistoryListActivity1_MethodInvoking(
                                    object sender, EventArgs e)
    {
      this.HistoryDescription = "WorkflowProperties";
      this.HistoryOutcome =
        "AssociationId: " +
        workflowProperties.Workflow.AssociationId.ToString() +
        "&&Author: " + workflowProperties.Workflow.Author.ToString() +
        "&&Created: " +
        workflowProperties.Workflow.Created.ToShortDateString() +
        "&&InstanceId: " +
        workflowProperties.Workflow.InstanceId.ToString() +
        "&&InternalState: " +
        workflowProperties.Workflow.InternalState.ToString();
    }
  }
}
```

Note that the constructor of the workflow invokes a method named InitializeComponent. This method is defined in the Workflow1.designer.cs file. As the name suggests, this method is responsible for instantiating and initializing the activities that make up the workflow, as shown in Listing 2-8. Note that the workflow exposes a public field of type SPWorkflowActivationProperties named workflowProperties as discussed earlier.

Listing 2-8: The content of the Workflow1.designer.cs file

```
using System;
using System.ComponentModel;
using System.ComponentModel.Design;
using System.Workflow.Runtime;
using System.Workflow.Activities;
using System.Workflow.ComponentModel;
using Microsoft.SharePoint.WorkflowActions;
using Microsoft.SharePoint.Workflow;

namespace Chapter2
{
  public sealed partial class Workflow1
  {
    private LogToHistoryListActivity logToHistoryListActivity1;
    private OnWorkflowActivated onWorkflowActivated1;

    private void InitializeComponent()
    {
      this.CanModifyActivities = true;

      // logToHistoryListActivity1
      this.logToHistoryListActivity1 = new LogToHistoryListActivity();
      this.logToHistoryListActivity1.Description =
                  "Logs the information content of " +
                  "SPWorkflowActivationProperties1";
      this.logToHistoryListActivity1.EventId =
                      SPWorkflowHistoryEventType.WorkflowComment;
      this.logToHistoryListActivity1.Name =
                                    "logToHistoryListActivity1";
      ActivityBind activitybind1 = new ActivityBind();
      activitybind1.Name = "Workflow1";
      activitybind1.Path = "Duration ";
      this.logToHistoryListActivity1.SetBinding(
          LogToHistoryListActivity.DurationProperty, activitybind1);
      ActivityBind activitybind2 = new ActivityBind();
      activitybind2.Name = "Workflow1";
      activitybind2.Path = "HistoryDescription";
      this.logToHistoryListActivity1.SetBinding(
           LogToHistoryListActivity.HistoryDescriptionProperty,
           activitybind2);
      ActivityBind activitybind3 = new ActivityBind();
      activitybind3.Name = "Workflow1";
      activitybind3.Path = "HistoryOutcome";
```

```
            this.logToHistoryListActivity1.SetBinding(
                    LogToHistoryListActivity.HistoryOutcomeProperty,
                    activitybind3);
            ActivityBind activitybind4 = new ActivityBind();
            activitybind4.Name = "Workflow1";
            activitybind4.Path = "OtherData";
            this.logToHistoryListActivity1.SetBinding(
                    LogToHistoryListActivity.OtherDataProperty,
                    activitybind4);
            ActivityBind activitybind5 = new ActivityBind();
            activitybind5.Name = "Workflow1";
            activitybind5.Path = "UserId";
            this.logToHistoryListActivity1.SetBinding(
                    LogToHistoryListActivity.UserIdProperty, activitybind5);
            this.logToHistoryListActivity1.MethodInvoking +=
                  new System.EventHandler(
                      this.logToHistoryListActivity1_MethodInvoking);

            // onWorkflowActivated1
            this.onWorkflowActivated1 = new OnWorkflowActivated();
            CorrelationToken correlationtoken1 = new CorrelationToken();
            correlationtoken1.Name = "workflowToken";
            correlationtoken1.OwnerActivityName = "Workflow1";
            this.onWorkflowActivated1.CorrelationToken = correlationtoken1;
            this.onWorkflowActivated1.Description =
                        "Responds to the OnWorkflowActivation event!";
            this.onWorkflowActivated1.EventName = "OnWorkflowActivated";
            this.onWorkflowActivated1.Name = "onWorkflowActivated1";
            ActivityBind activitybind6 = new ActivityBind();
            activitybind6.Name = "Workflow1";
            activitybind6.Path = "workflowProperties";
            this.onWorkflowActivated1.SetBinding(
                        OnWorkflowActivated.WorkflowPropertiesProperty,
                        activitybind6);
            ActivityBind activitybind7 = new ActivityBind();
            activitybind7.Name = "Workflow1";
            activitybind7.Path = "workflowId";
            this.onWorkflowActivated1.SetBinding(
                              OnWorkflowActivated.WorkflowIdProperty,
                              activitybind7);
            this.onWorkflowActivated1.Invoked +=
              new System.EventHandler<ExternalDataEventArgs>(
                                  this.onWorkflowActivated1_Invoked);

            // Workflow1
            this.Activities.Add(this.onWorkflowActivated1);
            this.Activities.Add(this.logToHistoryListActivity1);
            this.Name = "Workflow1";
            this.CanModifyActivities = false;
        }
    }
}
```

Implementing Workflow Input Forms

Recall that there are four types of workflow input forms: association, initiation, edit task, and modification. This section walks you through the details of the implementation of the association and initiation workflow input forms, starting with the association form. Chapter 7 covers the edit task and modification forms.

Implementing an Association Workflow Input Form

The association form is a form that collects what is known as *association data* from users when they are associating a workflow template with a SharePoint list, site content type, or list content type. The association data basically provides default parameterization for a workflow. Every workflow association is represented by an instance of a class named SPWorkflowAssociation. Because you're going to use this class in the implementation of your association form, I cover this class first before diving into the details of the implementation of our association form.

A SharePoint workflow association associates a workflow template with a SharePoint list, site content type, or list content type. You can use different workflow associations to associate the same workflow template with the same SharePoint list, site content type, or list content type multiple times. This enables you to run the same workflow with different parameterizations. Listing 2-9 presents the public API of SPWorkAssociation, against which you can program.

Listing 2-9: The SPWorkflowAssociation class

```
public sealed class SPWorkflowAssociation : SPAutoSerializingObject,
                                            IComparer
{
  public static SPWorkflowAssociation CreateListAssociation(
                                      SPWorkflowTemplate baseTemplate,
                                      string name, SPList taskList,
                                      SPList historyList);

  public static SPWorkflowAssociation CreateListContentTypeAssociation(
                                      SPWorkflowTemplate baseTemplate,
                  string name, SPList taskList, SPList historyList);

  public static SPWorkflowAssociation CreateSiteContentTypeAssociation(
                                      SPWorkflowTemplate baseTemplate,
              string name, string strTaskList, string strHistoryList);

  public void SetHistoryList(SPList list);
  public void SetTaskList(SPList list);

  public bool AllowAsyncManualStart { get; set; }
  public bool AllowManual { get; set; }
  public string AssociationData { get; set; }
  public int Author { get; }
  public bool AutoStartChange { get; set; }
  public bool AutoStartCreate { get; set; }
```

```
    public Guid BaseId { get; }
    public SPWorkflowTemplate BaseTemplate { get; }
    public DateTime Created { get; }
    public string Description { get; set; }
    public Guid HistoryListId { get; }
    public string HistoryListTitle { get; set; }
    public Guid Id { get; }
    public string InstantiationUrl { get; }
    public bool IsDeclarative { get; }
    public string ModificationUrl { get; }
    public DateTime Modified { get; }
    public string Name { get; set; }
    public Guid ParentAssociationId { get; }
    public SPContentType ParentContentType { get; }
    public SPList ParentList { get; }
    public SPSite ParentSite { get; }
    public SPWeb ParentWeb { get; }
    public int RunningInstances { get; }
    public Guid SiteId { get; }
    public string SoapXml { get; }
    public bool StatusColumn { get; }
    public string StatusUrl { get; }
    public SPContentTypeId TaskListContentTypeId { get; }
    public Guid TaskListId { get; }
    public string TaskListTitle { get; set; }
    public Guid WebId { get; }
}
```

Following are descriptions of the properties of SPWorkflowAssociation:

- **BaseTemplate:** Gets a reference to the SPWorkflowTemplate object that represents the workflow template from which this workflow association is created
- **Created:** Gets a DateTime object that specifies when this workflow association was created
- **Description:** Gets and sets a string that contains a short description about the workflow association. SharePoint displays this description to end users.
- **HistoryListId:** Gets a GUID that uniquely identifies the history list for this workflow association
- **HistoryListTitle:** Gets or sets a string that specifies the title of the history list for this workflow association
- **Id:** Gets a GUID that uniquely identifies this workflow association
- **InstantiationUrl:** Gets a string that specifies the URL of the workflow initiation form for this workflow association
- **ModificationUrl:** Gets a string that specifies the URL of the workflow modification form for this workflow association
- **Name:** Gets or sets a string that contains the name of the workflow association
- **ParentContentType:** Gets a reference to an SPContentType object that represents the content type to which the workflow association is assigned if the workflow association is indeed assigned to a content type

- **ParentList:** Gets a reference to the SPList object that represents the parent SharePoint list. The parent SharePoint list is either the list to which the workflow association is assigned or the list to one of whose list content types the workflow association is assigned.
- **TaskListContentTypeId:** Gets an SPContentTypeId object that represents the content type ID of the content type assigned to the workflow task list
- **TaskListId:** Gets a GUID that uniquely identifies the workflow task list for this workflow association
- **TaskListTitle:** Gets or sets an string that specifies the title of the workflow task list for this workflow association
- **ParentSite:** Gets a reference to an SPSite object representing the SharePoint site collection that contains the SharePoint list, list content type, or site content type to which the workflow association is assigned
- **SiteId:** Gets a GUID that uniquely identifies the SharePoint site collection containing the SharePoint list, list content type, or site content type to which this workflow association is assigned
- **ParentWeb:** Gets a reference to an SPWeb object that represents the SharePoint site containing the SharePoint list, list content type, or site content type to which the workflow association is assigned
- **WebId:** Gets a GUID that uniquely identifies the SharePoint site containing the SharePoint list, list content type, or site content type to which this workflow association is assigned
- **RunningInstances:** Gets an integer that specifies the number of running workflow instances initiated from this workflow association
- **SoapXml:** Gets a string containing the XML document that defines the workflow template from which the workflow association was created
- **StatusColumn:** Gets or sets a Boolean value that specifies whether to display a status column for workflow instances initiated from this workflow association in the SharePoint user interface. This status column is displayed on a SharePoint list that contains the SharePoint list item on which the workflow instance is running.
- **StatusUrl:** Gets a string that specifies the URL of a custom workflow status page for the workflow instances initiated from this workflow association
- **AllowAsyncManualStart:** Gets or sets a Boolean value that specifies whether to allow SharePoint to initiate a workflow instance from this workflow association asynchronously, even if the workflow instance was manually initiated
- **AllowManual:** Gets and sets a Boolean value that specifies whether workflow instances can be manually initiated from this workflow association
- **AssociationData:** Gets or sets a string that contains the association data for this workflow association
- **Author:** Gets an integer that specifies the user ID of the author of the workflow association
- **AutoStartChange:** Gets or sets a Boolean value that specifies whether to initiate a new workflow instance from this workflow association every time:

    - A SharePoint list item belonging to the SharePoint list to which the workflow association is assigned changes
    - A SharePoint list item of the list content type to which the workflow association is assigned changes
    - A SharePoint list item of the site content type to which the workflow association is assigned changes

- **AutoStartCreate:** Gets or sets a Boolean value that specifies whether to initiate a new workflow instance from this workflow association every time:
    - A new SharePoint list item is added to the SharePoint list to which the workflow association is assigned
    - A new SharePoint list item of the list content type to which the workflow association is assigned is added
    - A new SharePoint list item of the site content type to which the workflow association is assigned is added

Here are descriptions of the methods of SPWorkflowAssociation:

- **CreateListAssociation:** This static method takes an SPWorkflowTemplate object, a string, an SPList object, and another SPList object as its arguments and creates a workflow association from the workflow template represented by the SPWorkflowTemplate object with the name specified in the string argument, with the task list represented by the first SPList object, and with the history list represented by the second SPList object.

    This method returns an SPWorkflowAssociation object that represents the newly created workflow association, which can then be assigned to a SharePoint list. As such, the workflow association that this method creates is used to associate the specified workflow template with the SharePoint list to which the workflow association is added.

- **CreateListContentTypeAssociation:** This static method takes an SPWorkflowTemplate object, a string, an SPList object, and another SPList object as its arguments and creates a workflow association from the workflow template represented by the SPWorkflowTemplate object with the name specified in the string argument, with the task list represented by the first SPList object, and with the history list represented by the second SPList object.

    This method returns an SPWorkflowAssociation object that represents the newly created workflow association, which can then be added to a SharePoint list content type. As such, the workflow association that this method creates associates the specified workflow template with the SharePoint list content type to which the workflow association is added.

- **CreateSiteContentTypeAssociation:** This static method takes an SPWorkflowTemplate object, a string, an SPList object, and another SPList object as its arguments and creates a workflow association from the workflow template represented by the SPWorkflowTemplate object with the name specified in the string argument, with the task list represented by the first SPList object, and with the history list represented by the second SPList object.

    This method returns an SPWorkflowAssociation object that represents the newly created workflow association, which can then be added to a SharePoint site content type. As such, the workflow association that this method creates associates the specified workflow template with the SharePoint site content type to which the workflow association is added.

- **SetHistoryList:** This method takes an SPList object as its only argument and specifies the SharePoint list represented by this object as the history list for the workflow association. A history list is where workflow instances initiated from the workflow association log their history events.
- **SetTaskList:** This method takes an SPList object as its only argument and specifies the SharePoint list represented by this object as the task list for the workflow associations. A task list is the SharePoint list containing the workflow tasks that workflow instances initiated from the workflow association create.

Note that the call into the CreateListAssociation, CreateListContentTypeAssociation, or CreateSiteContentTypeAssociation only creates the workflow association and returns an SPWorkflowAssociation object that represents this workflow association. It does not assign the workflow association to the SharePoint list, list content type, or site content type. The actual assignment must be done through an explicit call into the AddWorkflowAssociation method of the SPList object that represents the SharePoint list, SPContentType object that represents the list content type, or SPContentType object that represents the site content type. In a typical scenario, you'll first invoke the CreateListAssociation, CreateListContentTypeAssociation, or CreateSiteContentTypeAssociation static method on the SPWorkflowAssociation to create a new workflow association and to return the SPWorkflowAssociation object that represents this workflow association. You'll then configure this SPWorkflowAssociation object by setting its properties before you call the AddWorkflowAssociation method to do the actual assignment. You'll see an example of this typical scenario later in this section.

Now that you have a good understanding of the public API of the SPWorkflowAssociation class, let's get down to the implementation of the association form for our workflow, as shown in Listing 2-10.

Listing 2-10: The association form

```
<%@ Page Language="C#" MasterPageFile="~/_layouts/application.master" EnableSession
State="true" ValidateRequest="False" Inherits="Chapter2.AssociationForm1" %>

<%@ Assembly Name="Chapter2, Version=1.0.0.0, Culture=neutral, PublicKeyToken=f589c
fc210e77624" %>

<%@ Register TagPrefix="SharePoint" Namespace="Microsoft.SharePoint.WebControls"
Assembly="Microsoft.SharePoint, Version=12.0.0.0, Culture=neutral, PublicKeyToken=7
1e9bce111e9429c" %>

<%@ Register TagPrefix="Utilities" Namespace="Microsoft.SharePoint.Utilities"
Assembly="Microsoft.SharePoint, Version=12.0.0.0, Culture=neutral, PublicKeyToken=7
1e9bce111e9429c" %>

<%@ Register TagPrefix="wssuc" TagName="InputFormSection" Src="/_controltemplates/
InputFormSection.ascx" %>

<%@ Register TagPrefix="wssuc" TagName="InputFormControl" Src="/_controltemplates/
InputFormControl.ascx" %>

<%@ Register TagPrefix="wssuc" TagName="ButtonSection" Src="/_controltemplates/
ButtonSection.ascx" %>

<asp:Content ID="Main" ContentPlaceHolderID="PlaceHolderMain" runat="server">
```

```
<SharePoint:FormDigest ID="FormDigest1" runat="server" />
<asp:Table CellSpacing="0" CellPadding="0" BorderWidth="0">
  <wssuc:InputFormSection Title="Default username"
  Description="Specify the default name for this workflow association."
  runat="server">
    <template_inputformcontrols>
      <wssuc:InputFormControl runat="server" LabelText="Name:">
        <Template_Control>
          <SharePoint:InputFormTextBox Title="Name" width="300"
          runat="server"/>
        </Template_Control>
      </wssuc:InputFormControl>
    </template_inputformcontrols>
  </wssuc:InputFormSection>

  <wssuc:InputFormSection Title="Default retirement status"
  Description="Specify the default retirement setting for this workflow
  association." runat="server">
    <template_inputformcontrols>
      <wssuc:InputFormControl Runat="server" LabelText="Retired:">
        <Template_Control>
          <SharePoint:InputFormCheckbox ID="retiredcbx"
          runat="server" />
        </Template_Control>
      </wssuc:InputFormControl>
    </template_inputformcontrols>
  </wssuc:InputFormSection>

  <wssuc:ButtonSection runat="server" ShowStandardCancelButton="false">
    <template_buttons>
      <asp:PlaceHolder runat="server">
        <asp:Button runat="server" OnClick="OKCallback" Text="OK" />
        <asp:Button runat="server" OnClick="CancelCallback"
        Text="Cancel" />
      </asp:PlaceHolder>
    </template_buttons>
  </wssuc:ButtonSection>
</asp:Table>

<input type="hidden" name="WorkflowDefinition"
value='<% SPHttpUtility.NoEncode(SPHttpUtility.HtmlEncode(
       Request.Form["WorkflowDefinition"]),Response.Output); %>'/>

<input type="hidden" name="WorkflowName"
value='<% SPHttpUtility.NoEncode(SPHttpUtility.HtmlEncode(
       Request.Form["WorkflowName"]),Response.Output); %>'/>

<input type="hidden" name="AddToStatusMenu"
value='<% SPHttpUtility.NoEncode(SPHttpUtility.HtmlEncode(
       Request.Form["AddToStatusMenu"]),Response.Output); %>'/>

<input type="hidden" name="AllowManual"
value='<% SPHttpUtility.NoEncode(SPHttpUtility.HtmlEncode(
```

(continued)

Listing 2-10 *(continued)*

```
            Request.Form["AllowManual"]),Response.Output); %>'/>

    <input type="hidden" name="RoleSelect"
    value='<% SPHttpUtility.NoEncode(SPHttpUtility.HtmlEncode(
            Request.Form["RoleSelect"]),Response.Output); %>'/>

    <input type="hidden" name="GuidAssoc"
    value='<% SPHttpUtility.NoEncode(SPHttpUtility.HtmlEncode(
            Request.Form["GuidAssoc"]),Response.Output); %>'/>

    <input type="hidden" name="SetDefault"
    value='<% SPHttpUtility.NoEncode(SPHttpUtility.HtmlEncode(
            Request.Form["SetDefault"]),Response.Output); %>'/>

    <input type="hidden" name="HistoryList"
    value='<% SPHttpUtility.NoEncode(SPHttpUtility.HtmlEncode(
            Request.Form["HistoryList"]),Response.Output); %>'/>

    <input type="hidden" name="TaskList"
    value='<% SPHttpUtility.NoEncode(SPHttpUtility.HtmlEncode(
            Request.Form["TaskList"]),Response.Output); %>'/>

    <input type="hidden" name="UpdateLists"
    value='<% SPHttpUtility.NoEncode(SPHttpUtility.HtmlEncode(
            Request.Form["UpdateLists"]),Response.Output); %>'/>

    <input type="hidden" name="AutoStartCreate"
    value='<% SPHttpUtility.NoEncode(SPHttpUtility.HtmlEncode(
            Request.Form["AutoStartCreate"]),Response.Output); %>'/>

    <input type="hidden" name="AutoStartChange"
    value='<% SPHttpUtility.NoEncode(SPHttpUtility.HtmlEncode(
            Request.Form["AutoStartChange"]),Response.Output); %>'/>
    </asp:Content>

  <asp:Content ID="Content1" ContentPlaceHolderID="PlaceHolderPageTitle"
  runat="server">
    <%= PlaceHolderPageTitleContent %>
  </asp:Content>

  <asp:Content ID="Content2" ContentPlaceHolderID="PlaceHolderPageTitleInTitleArea"
  runat="server">
    <%= PlaceHolderPageTitleInTitleAreaContent %>
  </asp:Content>
```

The association form for our workflow is a custom application page, which like any other application page is a content page that uses the application.master master page. This master page is located in the

LAYOUTS folder on the file system of the front-end web server. This folder is mapped to an IIS virtual directory named _layouts inside the Web application. As such, you can reference the application.master page using the following web application-relative URL:

```
~/_layouts/application.master
```

This master page contains numerous optional content placeholders whose contents you can override in your application pages. In the case of our association form, we've chosen to override the contents of the PlaceHolderMain, PlaceHolderPageTitle, and PlaceHolderPageTitleInTitleArea content placeholders.

Note that our association form inherits from a code-behind class named Chapter2.AssociationForm1, which is discussed later in this section. We must compile our code-behind class into a strong-named assembly and install the assembly in the global assembly cache. As such, we also need to add an @ Assembly directive to our association form so it knows where the code-behind class comes from:

```
<%@ Assembly Name="Chapter2, Version=1.0.0.0,
Culture=neutral, PublicKeyToken=f589cfc210e77624" %>
```

Another option is to add the assembly information to the Inherits attribute of the @Page directive itself.

Because our association form uses a few server controls from the Microsoft.SharePoint.WebControls namespace, which resides in the Microsoft.SharePoint.dll assembly, we need to add a reference to this assembly and specify a tag prefix for the namespace:

```
<%@ Register TagPrefix="SharePoint" Namespace="Microsoft.SharePoint.WebControls"
Assembly="Microsoft.SharePoint, Version=12.0.0.0, Culture=neutral,
PublicKeyToken=71e9bce111e9429c" %>
```

Our association form also uses three user controls that reside in the InputFormSection.ascx, InputFormControl.ascx, and ButtonSection.ascx files. These files, like all .ascx files, reside in the CONTROLTEMPLATES folder on the file system of the front-end web server. This folder is mapped into an IIS virtual directory named _controltemplates inside the web application. As such, you can assign the following web application-relative URLs to the Src attributes of the associated @Register directives:

```
/_controltemplates/InputFormSection.ascx
/_controltemplates/InputFormControl.ascx
/_controltemplates/ButtonSection.ascx
```

As shown in Listing 2-10, our association form consists of a text field in which users enter their name, a checkbox in which they specify whether they are retired, an OK button to submit the form, and a Cancel button to cancel the form.

Note that our association form defines several hidden fields and uses the Form property of the Request object to specify their values. To help you understand the role of these hidden fields, let's go over a typical scenario in which our association form, like any other association form, is used to collect the association data when the user is associating our workflow with a SharePoint list, list content type, or site content type.

The user first navigates to the desired SharePoint list, list content type, or site content type, as shown in Figure 2-9.

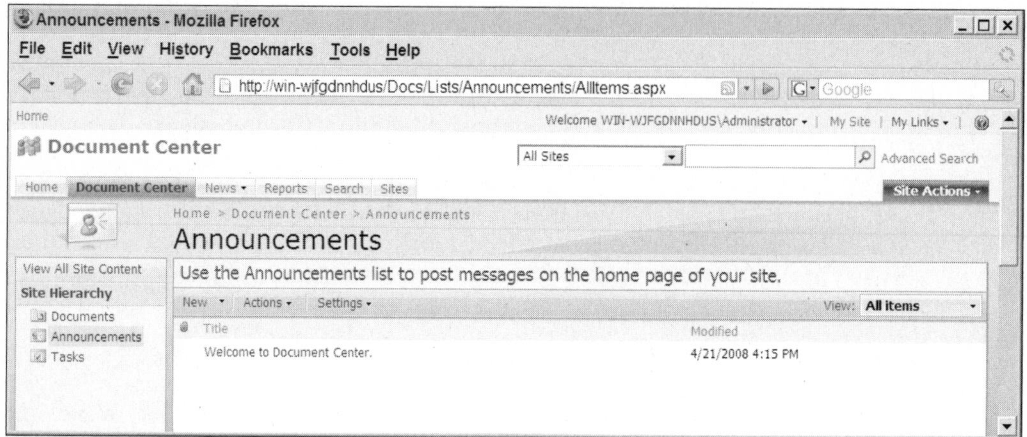

Figure 2-9

Using the Settings drop-down menu, the user then selects the option to navigate to the page shown in Figure 2-10.

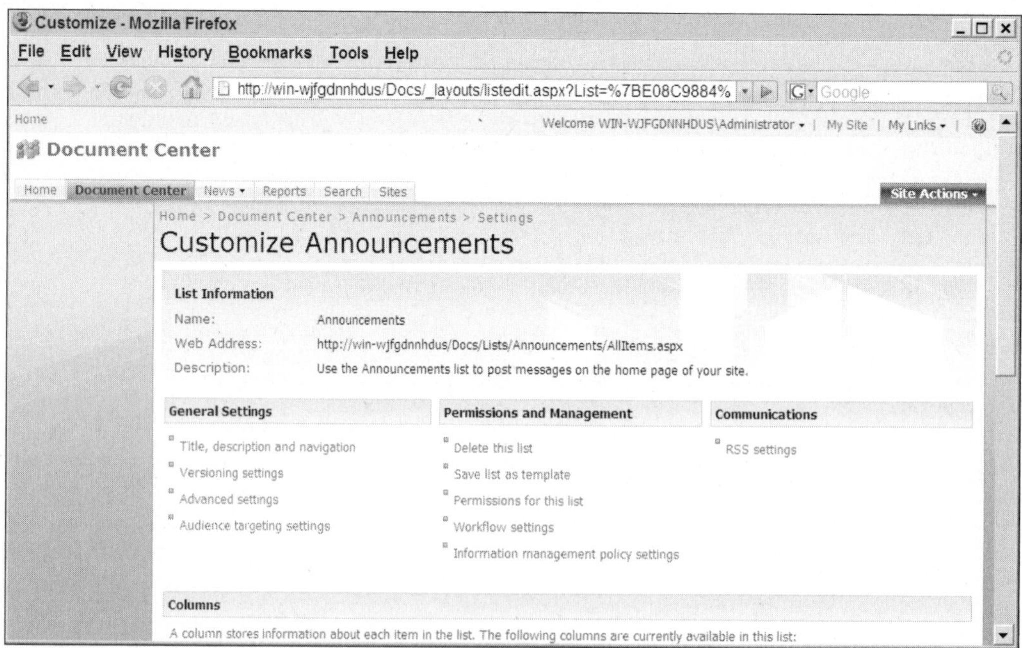

Figure 2-10

The user then selects the Workflow Settings option from the page shown in Figure 2-10 to navigate to the WrkSetng.aspx page shown in Figure 2-11.

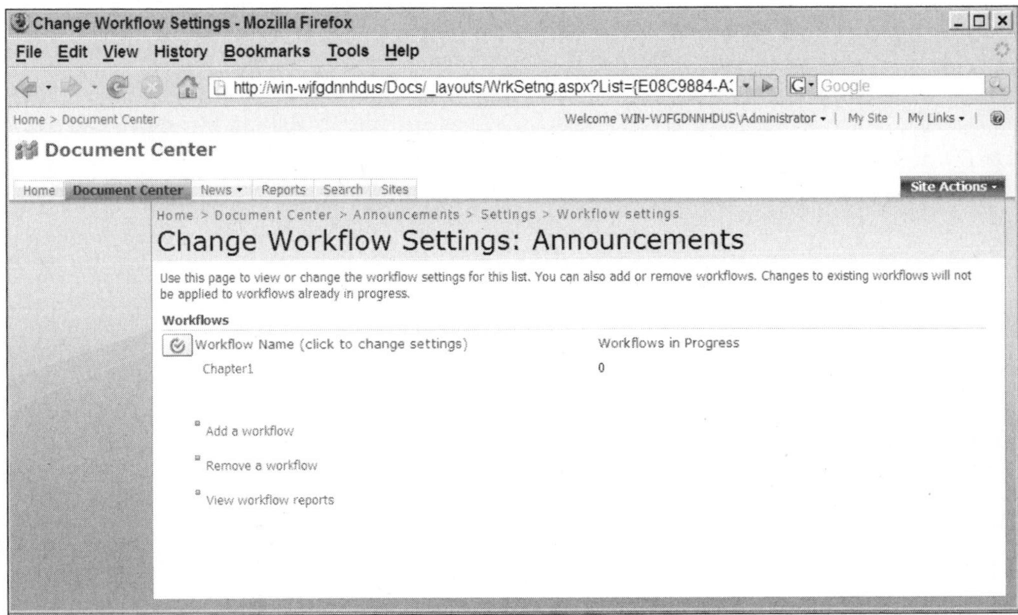

Figure 2-11

This page contains a number of links:

- **Chapter1:** This link takes users to the page shown in Figure 2-12 where they can update the workflow association named "Chapter1." There is one link for each workflow association on the page shown in Figure 2-11. The page shown in Figure 2-11 contains only one link because the current SharePoint list contains one workflow association.
- **Add a workflow:** This link takes users to the page shown in Figure 2-13 where they can create a new workflow association for the SharePoint list.
- **Remove a workflow:** This link takes users to the page where they can remove one or more workflow associations from the SharePoint list or document library.

- **View workflow reports:** This link takes users to the page where they can view the workflow instances currently running on the SharePoint list or document library or the workflow instances that ran on the SharePoint list or document library in the past.

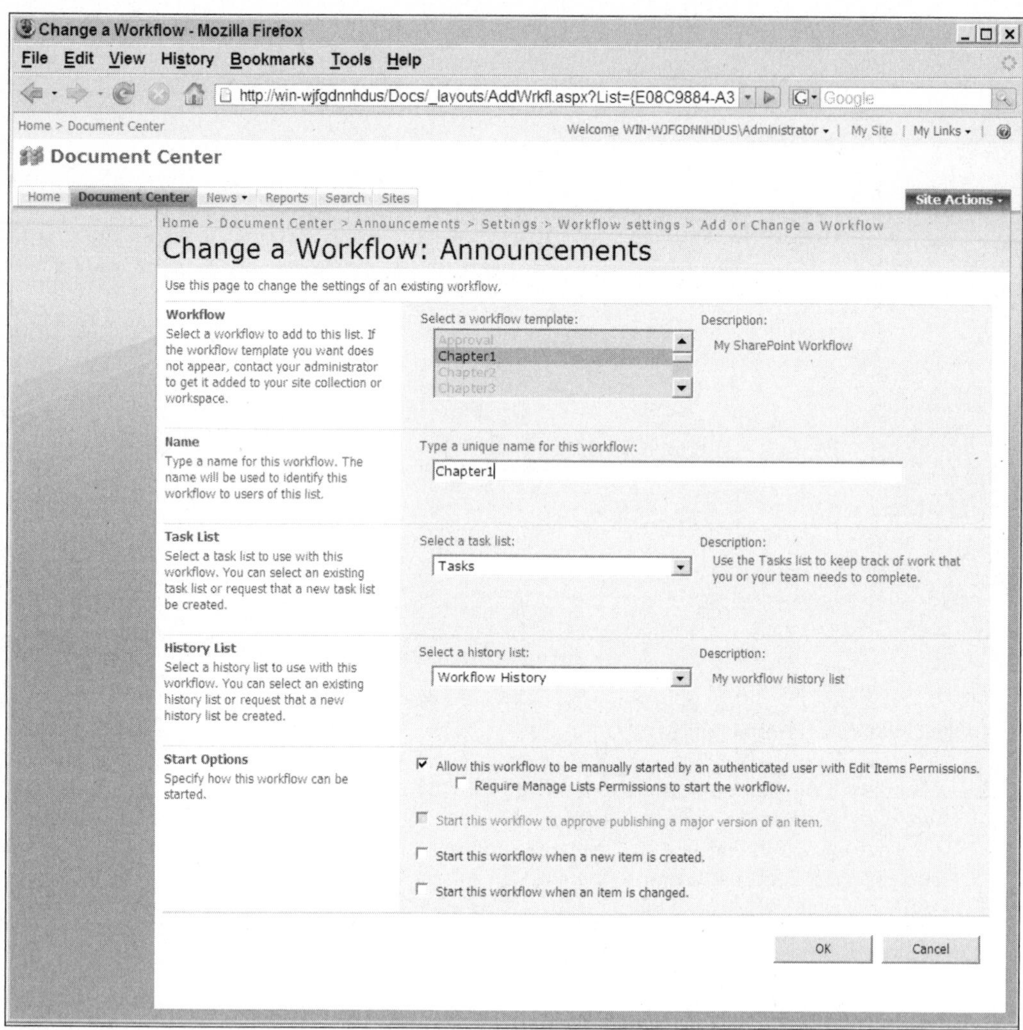

Figure 2-12

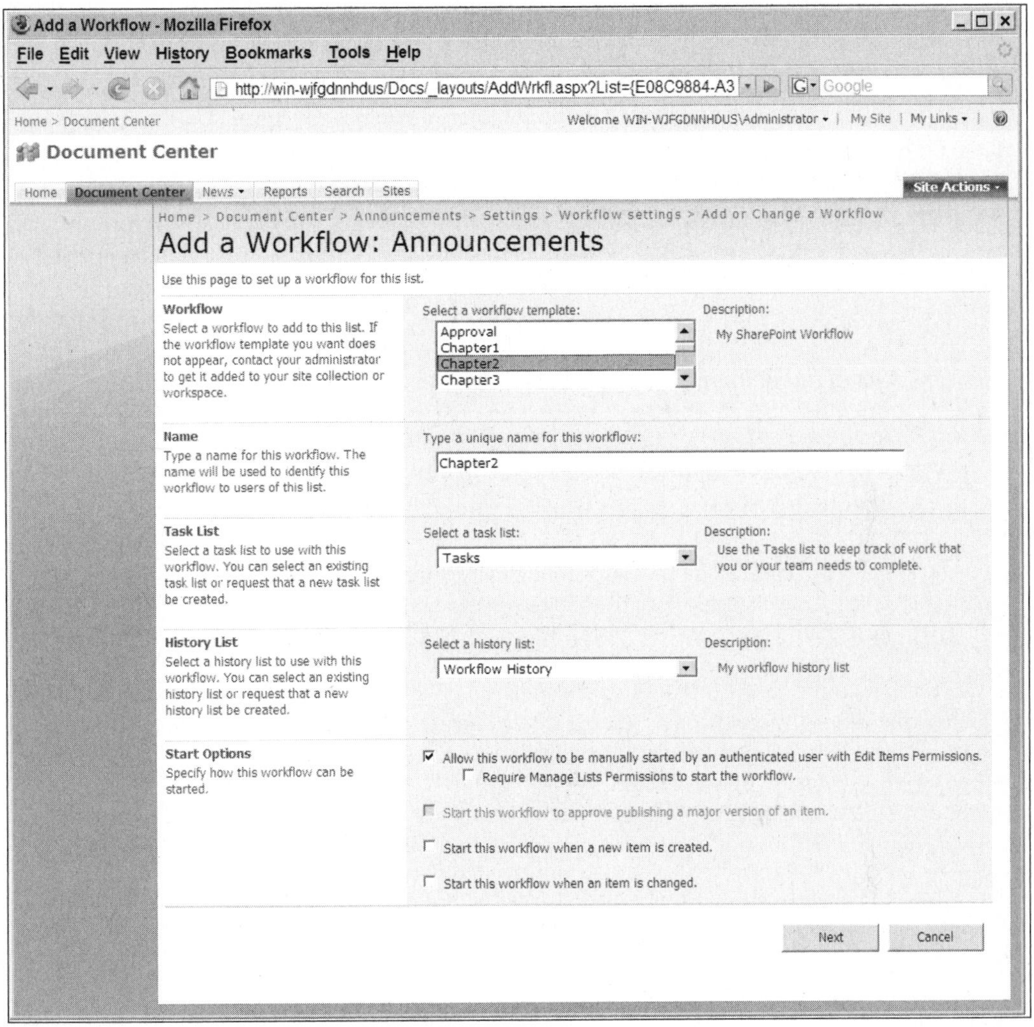

Figure 2-13

Because we're creating a new workflow association, we select the "Add a workflow" link to navigate to the page shown in Figure 2-13. This page enables the user to create a new workflow association on the SharePoint list or document library. Users take the following steps to create the workflow association:

1. Select a workflow template from the list of available workflow templates. Every SharePoint workflow association is created from a workflow template. When you install a feature that contains one or more workflow templates, SharePoint automatically adds them to the list of available workflow templates. In our case, the user will select our workflow template named Chapter2.
2. Specify a name for the workflow association. SharePoint workflow associations are named entities. We've chosen the name Chapter2 for our workflow association. Keep in mind that users

can create as many workflow associations as they wish from the same workflow template. The relationship between a template and its workflow associations is one to many.

3. Select a task list for the workflow association. A task list is a SharePoint list that contains the SharePoint tasks that a workflow instance creates during its execution. Users can choose an existing SharePoint list from the list or have SharePoint create a new task list. I discuss SharePoint tasks in the next chapter.

4. Select a history list for the workflow association. A history list is where a workflow instance logs its history events. Users can choose an existing SharePoint list from the list or have SharePoint create a new history list.

5. Choose one or more of the following workflow instance initiation options:

    - **Manual initiation:** This option enables users to manually initiate a workflow instance from the workflow association. To do so, the user must navigate to the SharePoint list or document library, drop down the EditControlBlock menu of a list item or document, and select the Workflows option to navigate to the page that enables the user to select a workflow association from which to initiate a workflow instance on the list item or document.

    - **Auto initiation:** This option automatically initiates a workflow instance from the workflow association every time a new list item or document is added to the SharePoint list or document library and/or every time an existing list item or document is updated.

The user then clicks the Next button. What happens next depends on whether the workflow template from which the workflow association is being created has an association form. If not, SharePoint, under the hood, uses the settings that the user has specified for the workflow association to create the workflow association from the specified workflow template and adds the association to the list of available workflow associations on the SharePoint list, list content type, or site content type.

Now let's look at what happens when the workflow template from which the workflow association is being created has an association form. The best way to understand what happens next is to take a look at the source for the page shown in Figure 2-11. You can use the View Source option of Internet Explorer to view this source.

This source contains the following important HTML elements:

- A <select> element whose name HTML attribute is set to "WorkflowDefinition":

```
<label for="WorkflowDefinition">Select a workflow template:</label><BR>
<SELECT style="width:20em" ID="WorkflowDefinition" Name="WorkflowDefinition"
Size=4 onchange="OnChangeSelect();">
  <OPTION value="c6964bff-bf8d-41ac-ad5e-b61ec111731c">Approval</OPTION>
  <OPTION value="46c389a4-6e12-476c-aa17-289b0c79fb8f">Collect Feedback</OPTION>
  <OPTION value="2f213931-3b93-4f81-b021-3022434a3114">Collect Signatures</OPTION>
  <OPTION value="dd19a800-37c1-43c0-816d-f8eb5f4a4145">Disposition Approval
  </OPTION>
  <OPTION value="b5f1576e-9f64-49f3-8b6c-89cf01b1291f">My Workflow Template
  </OPTION>
</SELECT>
```

This <select> element displays the list of available workflow templates to choose from. Note that the value HTML attribute of each <option> child element contains the GUID that uniquely identifies the associated workflow template. As such, the selected value of this <select> element contains the GUID that uniquely identifies the workflow template from which the workflow association is being created.

- An <input> element of type text whose name HTML attribute is set to "WorkflowName":

```
Type a unique name for this workflow:
<input size=65 class="ms-input" Type=Text
Title="Type a unique name for this workflow" Name="WorkflowName" ID="WorkflowName"
maxLength="255">
```

This is where the user enters a unique name for the workflow association being created.

- A hidden field whose name HTML attribute is set to "GuidAssoc":

```
<input type="hidden" Name="GuidAssoc" ID="GuidAssoc"/>
```

SharePoint sets the value of this hidden field when the page shown in either Figure 2-12 or 2-13 is shown to users. This value depends on whether the user is updating an existing workflow association (Figure 2-12) or creating a new workflow association (Figure 2-13). Recall that the user clicks the link that displays the name of an existing workflow association (e.g., the Chapter1 link shown in Figure 2-11) to navigate to the page shown in Figure 2-12 to update the workflow association. In this case, SharePoint automatically sets the value of the "GuidAssoc" hidden field to the string representation of the GUID that uniquely identifies the workflow association being updated when it first displays the page shown in Figure 2-12.

- If the user clicks the Add New Workflow link shown in Figure 2-11 to navigate to the page shown in Figure 2-13 to create a new workflow association, SharePoint automatically sets the value of the "GuidAssoc" hidden field to an empty string "". The presence of an empty string as the value of this hidden field is an indication that the page is accessed to create a new workflow association.
- A <select> element whose name HTML attribute is set to "HistoryList":

```
Select a history list:
<SELECT ID="HistoryList" Name="HistoryList" style="width:20em" Size=1
align=absmiddle onchange="OnChangeSelectHistoryList();">
  <OPTION value="368d098a-4a59-428f-a13a-55363f6f76df">Workflow History</OPTION>
  <OPTION ID="OptCreateNewHistoryList" value="" />
</SELECT>
```

- This <select> element displays the list of available history lists to choose from. The value attribute of each <option> element contains the string representation of the GUID that uniquely identifies the associated history list. As such, the selected value of this <select> element specifies the GUID that uniquely identifies the selected history list. The <select> element also contains an <option> element with the ID attribute value of optCreateNewHistoryList. The user selects this option to have SharePoint or the association form create a new history list for the workflow association.

- A <select> element whose name HTML attribute is set to "TaskList":

```
Select a task list:
<SELECT ID="TaskList" Name="TaskList" style="width:20em" Size=1 align=absmiddle
  onchange="OnChangeSelectTaskList();">
  <OPTION value="026e68bf-306d-4d2f-aa73-54a0798ca815">Tasks</OPTION>
  <OPTION ID="OptCreateNewTaskList" value="" />
</SELECT>
```

- This <select> element displays the list of available task lists to choose from. Each <option> element of this <select> element displays an available task list. Note that the value attribute of each <option> element contains the string representation of the GUID that uniquely identifies the associated task list. As such, the selected value of this <select> element specifies the GUID that uniquely identifies the selected task list. The <select> element also contains an <option> element with the ID attribute value of OptCreateNewTaskList. The user selects this option to have SharePoint or the association form create a new task list for the workflow association.
- A checkbox whose name HTML attribute is set to "AutoStartCreate":

```
<INPUT id=onetidIOAutoStartCreate type="checkbox" name="AutoStartCreate" value="ON"
title="Start this workflow when a new item is created."> <span id="spanAutoSta
rtCreate">Start this workflow when a new item is created.</span>
```

- The user enables this checkbox to specify that a workflow instance must be automatically initiated from the workflow association whenever a new SharePoint list item or document is added to the SharePoint list or document on which the new workflow association is being created.
- A checkbox whose name HTML attribute is set to "AutoStartChange":

```
<INPUT id=onetidIOAutoStartChange type="checkbox" name="AutoStartChange" value="ON"
title="Start this workflow when an item is changed."> <span id="spanAutoStartC
hange">Start this workflow when an item is changed.</span>
```

- The user enables this checkbox to specify that a workflow instance must be automatically initiated from the workflow association whenever a SharePoint list item or document of the SharePoint list or document on which the new workflow association is being created is updated.

Listing 2-11 presents the JavaScript function that handles the click event of the Next button.

Listing 2-11: The JavaScript function that handles the click event of the Next button

```
function OnClickNext()
{
 if (_spFormOnSubmit())
 {
    var elSelect = document.getElementById("WorkflowDefinition");
    var actionUrl = document.getElementById("Act_" + elSelect.value).value;
    actionUrl += "?List={BBB0C541-DEFF-45E6-82B1-6579C65F9473}";
    form.action = actionUrl;
    form.submit();
 }
}
```

This JavaScript function first invokes another JavaScript function named _spFormOnSubmit, shown in Listing 2-12.

Listing 2-12: The _spFormOnSubmit JavaScript function

```
function _spFormOnSubmit()
{
  if (form["TaskList"].value.length == 0)
  {
    var strTaskPattern = "{0} Tasks";
    strTaskListNew = strTaskPattern.replace("{0}",
                                  form["WorkflowName"].value);
    var elCreateNewTaskList =
                     document.getElementById("OptCreateNewTaskList");
    elCreateNewTaskList.value = 'z' + strTaskListNew;
  }

  if (form["HistoryList"].value.length == 0)
  {
    var strHistoryPattern = "{0} History";
    strHistoryListNew = strHistoryPattern.replace("{0}",
                                  form["WorkflowName"].value);
    var elCreateNewHistoryList =
                     document.getElementById(
                           "OptCreateNewHistoryList");
    elCreateNewHistoryList.value = 'z' + strHistoryListNew;
  }

  form["__VIEWSTATE"].value = "";
  form["WorkflowDefinition"].disabled = false;
  return true;
}
```

The _spFormOnSubmit JavaScript function first checks whether the user has requested SharePoint or the association form to create a new task list for the workflow association being created. If so, it creates a string that consists of two substrings, which are separated by a space. The first substring contains the name of the workflow association. Recall that the user enters the workflow association name in a text field whose name HTML attribute is set to "WorkflowName". The second substring is "Tasks":

```
var strTaskPattern = "{0} Tasks";
strTaskListNew = strTaskPattern.replace("{0}", form["WorkflowName"].value);
```

_spFormOnSubmit then prepends the letter "z" to this string and assigns the string to the value attribute of the <option> child element whose ID attribute is set to "OptCreateNewTaskList." This is the <option> child element that the user selects to request SharePoint or the association form to create a new task list for the workflow association:

```
var elCreateNewTaskList = document.getElementById("OptCreateNewTaskList");
elCreateNewTaskList.value = 'z' + strTaskListNew;
```

Therefore, if the selected value of the <select> element that displays the list of available task lists — the one whose name attribute is set to "TaskList" — follows the pattern just described, this indicates that the user has requested SharePoint or the association form to create a new task list for the workflow association.

Next, _spFormOnSubmit does the same thing for the <select> element that displays the list of available history lists. That is, it first checks whether the user has requested SharePoint or the association form to create a new history list for the workflow association being created. If so, it creates a string that consists of two substrings, separated by a space. The first substring contains the name of the workflow association. The second substring is "History":

```
var strHistoryPattern = "{0} History";
strHistoryListNew = strHistoryPattern.replace("{0}", form["WorkflowName"].value);
```

_spFormOnSubmit then prepends the letter "z" to this string and assigns the string to the value attribute of the <option> child element whose ID attribute is set to "OptCreateNewHistoryList". This is the <option> child element that the user selects to request SharePoint or the association form to create a new history list for the workflow association:

```
var elCreateNewHistoryList = document.getElementById("OptCreateNewHistoryList");
elCreateNewHistoryList.value = 'z' + strHistoryListNew;
```

Therefore, if the selected value of the <select> element that displays the list of available history lists — the one whose name attribute is set to "HistoryList" — follows the pattern just described, this indicates that the user has requested SharePoint or the association form to create a new history list for the workflow association.

Now back to Listing 2-11 — that is, the JavaScript function that handles the click event of the Next button. After invoking _spFormOnSubmit, this JavaScript function accesses the <select> element that displays the list of available workflow templates:

```
var elSelect = document.getElementById("WorkflowDefinition");
```

It then prepends the string "Act_" to the value property of this <select> element. The resultant string contains the value of the ID attribute of the hidden field that contains the action URL. As you'll see shortly, this URL is the URL of the association form if the workflow template is configured with an association form:

```
var actionUrl = document.getElementById("Act_" + elSelect.value).value;
```

Next, it appends a query string to this URL. This query string includes a single query string parameter named List whose value is set to the GUID that uniquely identifies the SharePoint list or document library on which the workflow association is being created:

```
actionUrl += "?List={BBB0C541-DEFF-45E6-82B1-6579C65F9473}";
```

Note that if the workflow association were being created on a site content type, the query string appended to the URL of the association form would include a single query string parameter named ctype whose value would contain the content type ID of the site content type. For example, if the workflow association was being created on the Document site content type, the query string would include a single query string parameter named ctype whose value would be 0x0101, which is the content type ID of the Document site content type:

```
actionUrl += "?ctype=0x0101";
```

If the workflow association were being created on a list content type, the query string appended to the URL of the association form would include two query string parameters named List and ctype whose values would contain the GUID that uniquely identifies the SharePoint list or document library owning the content type and the content type ID of the list content type, respectively:

```
actionUrl += "?ctype=0x01010091DDD7097E6EA14FBA7E933A3AA48054&List=bbb0c541-deff-
45e6-82b1-6579c65f9473";
```

Next, the JavaScript function assigns the preceding URL, plus query string, to the action attribute of the form:

```
form.action = actionUrl;
```

Finally, it invokes the submit function on the form to post the page back to the specified action URL:

```
form.submit();
```

Here are typical examples of hidden fields whose ID attribute values start with the string "Act_":

```
<input Type=Hidden ID="Act_c6964bff-bf8d-41ac-ad5e-b61ec111731c"
Value="http://win-wjfgdnnhdus/Docs/_layouts/CstWrkflIP.aspx" />

<input Type=Hidden ID="Act_46c389a4-6e12-476c-aa17-289b0c79fb8f"
Value="http://win-wjfgdnnhdus/Docs/_layouts/CstWrkflIP.aspx" />

<input Type=Hidden ID="Act_2f213931-3b93-4f81-b021-3022434a3114"
Value="http://win-wjfgdnnhdus/Docs/_layouts/AssocWrkfl.aspx" />

<input Type=Hidden ID="Act_dd19a800-37c1-43c0-816d-f8eb5f4a4145"
Value="http://win-wjfgdnnhdus/Docs/_layouts/AssocWrkfl.aspx" />

<input Type=Hidden ID="Act_b5f1576e-9f64-49f3-8b6c-89cf01b1291f"
Value="http://win-wjfgdnnhdus/Docs_layouts/SharePointWorkflow2/
AssociationForm1.aspx" />
```

The preceding listing contains an entry for our association form:

```
<input Type=Hidden ID="Act_b5f1576e-9f64-49f3-8b6c-89cf01b1291f"
Value="http://win-wjfgdnnhdus/Docs_layouts/SharePointWorkflow2/
AssociationForm1.aspx" />
```

This is because our workflow template is configured with an association form. In other words, if the user selects a workflow template that is configured with an association form, the JavaScript function that handles the click event for the Next button posts the page back to the association form, passing in one of the following pieces of information:

- A GUID that uniquely identifies a SharePoint list if the workflow association is associated with a SharePoint list
- A content type ID and a GUID that uniquely identifies the SharePoint list owning the content type if the workflow association is associated with a list content type
- A content type ID if the workflow association is associated with a site content type

This means that when the association form is first displayed to users it has access to all input form elements of the previous page — that is, the page shown in Figure 2-12 or 2-13 plus a GUID that uniquely identifies a SharePoint list, a GUID and a content type ID that uniquely identifies a list content type, or a content type ID that uniquely identifies a site content type. Thanks to this cross-page postback mechanism, our association form can retrieve all selections that the user has made or the inputs the user has entered into the page shown in Figure 2-12 or 2-13, which is as follows:

- The workflow template the user selected from the list of available workflow templates
- The name the user entered for the workflow association
- The task list the user selected for the workflow association
- The history list the user selected for the workflow association
- The workflow instance initiation choice the user made

ASP.NET loads all this data into the Form property of the Request object. Your custom association form must use the Form property to access this data when it is first displayed to the user. This data is lost forever when your custom association form is posted back to the server. Therefore, it is very important that you capture this data when your custom association form is first displayed. To do so, your custom association form needs to define hidden fields and populate them with this data, as the following excerpt from Listing 2-10 shows:

```
<input type="hidden" name="WorkflowDefinition"
value='<% SPHttpUtility.NoEncode(SPHttpUtility.HtmlEncode(
                    Request.Form["WorkflowDefinition"]),Response.Output); %>'/>

<input type="hidden" name="WorkflowName"
value='<% SPHttpUtility.NoEncode(SPHttpUtility.HtmlEncode(
                         Request.Form["WorkflowName"]),Response.Output); %>'/>

<input type="hidden" name="AddToStatusMenu"
value='<% SPHttpUtility.NoEncode(SPHttpUtility.HtmlEncode(
                      Request.Form["AddToStatusMenu"]),Response.Output); %>'/>

<input type="hidden" name="AllowManual"
value='<% SPHttpUtility.NoEncode(SPHttpUtility.HtmlEncode(
                          Request.Form["AllowManual"]),Response.Output); %>'/>

<input type="hidden" name="RoleSelect"
value='<% SPHttpUtility.NoEncode(SPHttpUtility.HtmlEncode(
                           Request.Form["RoleSelect"]),Response.Output); %>'/>

<input type="hidden" name="GuidAssoc"
```

```
value='<% SPHttpUtility.NoEncode(SPHttpUtility.HtmlEncode(
                              Request.Form["GuidAssoc"]),Response.Output); %>'/>

<input type="hidden" name="SetDefault"
value='<% SPHttpUtility.NoEncode(SPHttpUtility.HtmlEncode(
                             Request.Form["SetDefault"]),Response.Output); %>'/>

<input type="hidden" name="HistoryList"
value='<% SPHttpUtility.NoEncode(SPHttpUtility.HtmlEncode(
                            Request.Form["HistoryList"]),Response.Output); %>'/>

<input type="hidden" name="TaskList"
value='<% SPHttpUtility.NoEncode(SPHttpUtility.HtmlEncode(
                               Request.Form["TaskList"]),Response.Output); %>'/>

<input type="hidden" name="UpdateLists"
value='<% SPHttpUtility.NoEncode(SPHttpUtility.HtmlEncode(
                            Request.Form["UpdateLists"]),Response.Output); %>'/>

<input type="hidden" name="AutoStartCreate"
value='<% SPHttpUtility.NoEncode(SPHttpUtility.HtmlEncode(
                        Request.Form["AutoStartCreate"]),Response.Output); %>'/>

<input type="hidden" name="AutoStartChange"
value='<% SPHttpUtility.NoEncode(SPHttpUtility.HtmlEncode(
                        Request.Form["AutoStartChange"]),Response.Output); %>'/>
```

This excerpt shows the following:

- The hidden field named "WorkflowDefinition" stores the value Request.Form ["WorkflowDefinition"], which returns the selected value of the <select> element named "WorkflowDefinition" that displays the list of available workflow templates. In other words, this hidden field contains the GUID that uniquely identifies the workflow template selected by the user. This is the workflow template from which the workflow association will be created.
- The hidden field named "WorkflowName" stores the value Request.Form["WorkflowName"], which returns the value that the user entered into the text field named "WorkflowName" as the name of the workflow association.
- The hidden field named "GuidAssoc" stores the value Request.Form["GuidAssoc"], which returns the value of a hidden field named "GuidAssoc". Recall that this hidden field contains the GUID that uniquely identifies the workflow association being updated. This hidden field contains an empty string if a new workflow association is being created.
- The hidden field named "HistoryList" stores the value Request.Form["HistoryList"], which returns the selected value of the <select> element named "HistoryList" that displays the list of available history lists. In other words, this hidden field contains the GUID that uniquely identifies the history list selected by the user.
- The hidden field named "TaskList" stores the value Request.Form["TaskList"], which returns the selected value of the <select> element named "TaskList" that displays the list of available task lists. In other words, this hidden field contains the GUID that uniquely identifies the task list selected by the user.

Figure 2-14 shows our association form in action.

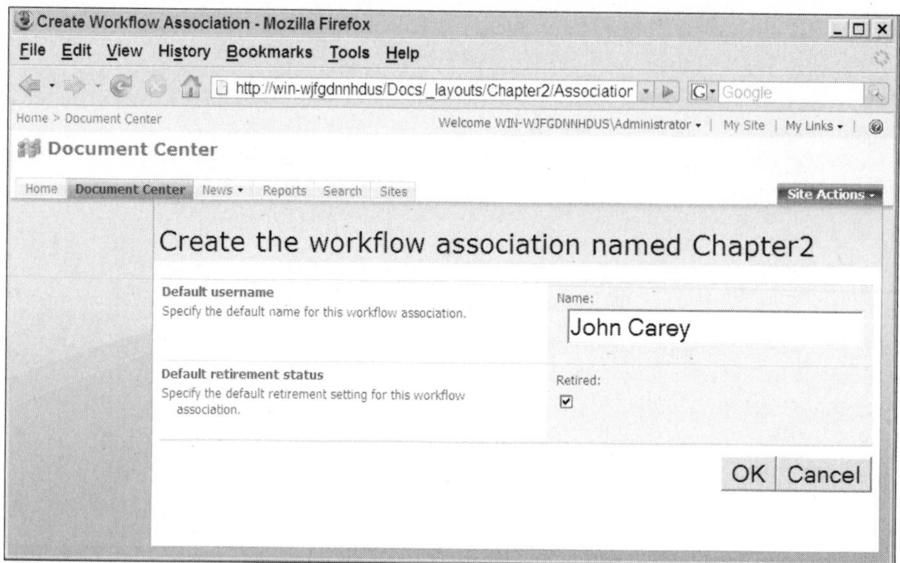

Figure 2-14

Listing 2-13 presents the code-behind for the association form.

Listing 2-13: Code-behind for the association form

```
using System;
using System.IO;
using System.Text;
using System.Web;
using System.Web.UI;
using System.Web.UI.WebControls;
using System.Web.UI.HtmlControls;
using System.Xml;
using System.Xml.Serialization;
using Microsoft.SharePoint;
using Microsoft.SharePoint.Utilities;
using Microsoft.SharePoint.WebControls;
using Microsoft.SharePoint.Workflow;

namespace Chapter2
{
  public class AssociationForm1 : LayoutsPageBase
  {
    private SPList taskList;
    private SPList historyList;

    private string workflowAssociationName;
```

```
private SPWorkflowAssociation workflowAssociation;
private Guid workflowAssociationId;

protected InputFormTextBox nametbx;
protected InputFormCheckBox retiredcbx;
protected string PlaceHolderPageTitleContent;
protected string PlaceHolderPageTitleInTitleAreaContent;

private bool isUpdatingWorkflowAssociation;
private WorkflowAssociationTarget workflowAssociationTarget;
private Guid workflowAssociationTargetListId;
private SPList workflowAssociationTargetList;
private SPContentTypeId workflowAssociationTargetContentTypeId;
private SPContentType workflowAssociationTargetContentType;

private void DetermineTaskAndHistoryLists()
{
  if (Request.Params["TaskList"][0] == 'z' &&
      Request.Params["TaskList"].EndsWith(" Tasks"))
  {
    string newTaskListName =
                 Request.Params["TaskList"].Substring(1);
    Guid newTaskListId = Web.Lists.Add(newTaskListName,
                                       "Workflow Tasks",
                                       SPListTemplateType.Tasks);
    taskList = Web.Lists[newTaskListId];
  }

  else
  {
    if (workflowAssociationTarget ==
                 WorkflowAssociationTarget.SiteContentType)
      taskList = Web.Lists[Request.Params["TaskList"]];

    else
      taskList = Web.Lists[new Guid(Request.Params["TaskList"])];
  }

  if (Request.Params["HistoryList"][0] == 'z' &&
      Request.Params["HistoryList"].EndsWith(" History"))
  {
    string newHistoryListName =
                 Request.Params["HistoryList"].Substring(1);
    Guid newHistoryListId = Web.Lists.Add(newHistoryListName,
                                          "Workflow History",
                          SPListTemplateType.WorkflowHistory);
    historyList = Web.Lists[newHistoryListId];
  }

  else
  {
    if (workflowAssociationTarget ==
              WorkflowAssociationTarget.SiteContentType)
```

(continued)

Listing 2-13 *(continued)*

```
        historyList = Web.Lists[Request.Params["HistoryList"]];

      else
        historyList =
            Web.Lists[new Guid(Request.Params["HistoryList"])];
    }
  }

  private void UpdateWorkflowAssociation()
  {
    workflowAssociation.Name = workflowAssociationName;
    workflowAssociation.AutoStartCreate =
                    (Request.Params["AutoStartCreate"] == "ON");
    workflowAssociation.AutoStartChange =
                    (Request.Params["AutoStartChange"] == "ON");
    workflowAssociation.AllowManual =
                       (Request.Params["AllowManual"] == "ON");

    Person person = new Person();
    person.Name = this.nametbx.Text;
    person.Retired = this.retiredcbx.Checked;

    using (StringWriter sw = new StringWriter())
    {
      XmlSerializer serializer = new XmlSerializer(typeof(Person));
      serializer.Serialize(sw, person);
      workflowAssociation.AssociationData = sw.ToString();
    }

    if (workflowAssociation.TaskListTitle != taskList.Title)
      workflowAssociation.SetTaskList(taskList);

    if (workflowAssociation.HistoryListTitle != historyList.Title)
      workflowAssociation.SetHistoryList(historyList);
  }

  public void CancelCallback(object sender, EventArgs e)
  {
    string url = String.Empty;
    switch (workflowAssociationTarget)
    {
      case WorkflowAssociationTarget.SiteContentType:
        url = "WrkSetng.aspx?ctype=" +
            this.workflowAssociationTargetContentTypeId.ToString();
        break;
      case WorkflowAssociationTarget.List:
        url = "WrkSetng.aspx?List=" +
                this.workflowAssociationTargetListId.ToString();
        break;
      case WorkflowAssociationTarget.ListContentType:
```

```
            url = "WrkSetng.aspx?List=" +
                    this.workflowAssociationTargetListId.ToString() +
                                             "&ctype=" +
                this.workflowAssociationTargetContentTypeId.ToString();
            break;
        }
        SPUtility.Redirect(url, SPRedirectFlags.RelativeToLayoutsPage,
                           HttpContext.Current);
    }

    public void OKCallback(object sender, EventArgs e)
    {
        DetermineTaskAndHistoryLists();
        bool updateChildContentTypesAndLists =
                           (Request.Params["UpdateLists"] == "TRUE");
        Guid workflowTemplateId =
                      new Guid(Request.Params["WorkflowDefinition"]);
        SPWorkflowTemplate workflowTemplate =
                      this.Web.WorkflowTemplates[workflowTemplateId];

        string url = "";
        switch (workflowAssociationTarget)
        {
          case WorkflowAssociationTarget.SiteContentType:
            if (isUpdatingWorkflowAssociation)
            {
              workflowAssociation =
              workflowAssociationTargetContentType.WorkflowAssociations[
                                                   workflowAssociationId];
              UpdateWorkflowAssociation();
              workflowAssociationTargetContentType.UpdateWorkflowAssociation(
                                                   workflowAssociation);
              if (updateChildContentTypesAndLists)
    workflowAssociationTargetContentType.UpdateWorkflowAssociationsOnChildren(true,
true, true);
            }

            else
            {
              workflowAssociation =
                SPWorkflowAssociation.CreateSiteContentTypeAssociation(
                             workflowTemplate, workflowAssociationName,
                             taskList.Title, historyList.Title);
              UpdateWorkflowAssociation();
              workflowAssociationTargetContentType.AddWorkflowAssociation(
                                                workflowAssociation);
              if (updateChildContentTypesAndLists)
        workflowAssociationTargetContentType.UpdateWorkflowAssociationsOnChildren
(true, true, true);
            }

            url = "WrkSetng.aspx?ctype=" +
                  workflowAssociationTargetContentTypeId.ToString();
```

(continued)

Listing 2-13 *(continued)*

```
        break;
      case WorkflowAssociationTarget.List:
        if (isUpdatingWorkflowAssociation)
        {
          UpdateWorkflowAssociation();
          workflowAssociationTargetList.UpdateWorkflowAssociation(
                                                  workflowAssociation);
        }

        else
        {
          workflowAssociation =
            SPWorkflowAssociation.CreateListAssociation(workflowTemplate,
                                              workflowAssociationName,
                                              taskList, historyList);
          UpdateWorkflowAssociation();
          workflowAssociationTargetList.AddWorkflowAssociation(
                                                  workflowAssociation);
        }
        url = "WrkSetng.aspx?List=" +
                     workflowAssociationTargetListId.ToString();
        break;
      case WorkflowAssociationTarget.ListContentType:
        if (isUpdatingWorkflowAssociation)
        {
          workflowAssociation =
          workflowAssociationTargetContentType.WorkflowAssociations[
                                                  workflowAssociationId];
          UpdateWorkflowAssociation();
          workflowAssociationTargetContentType.UpdateWorkflowAssociation(
                                                  workflowAssociation);
        }

        else
        {
          workflowAssociation =
            SPWorkflowAssociation.CreateListContentTypeAssociation(
                         workflowTemplate, workflowAssociationName,
                             taskList, historyList);
          UpdateWorkflowAssociation();
        workflowAssociationTargetContentType.AddWorkflowAssociation(
                                                workflowAssociation);
        }

        url = "WrkSetng.aspx?List=" +
                     workflowAssociationTargetListId.ToString() +
                                              "&ctype=" +
                workflowAssociationTargetContentTypeId.ToString();
```

```
        break;
    }

    SPUtility.Redirect(url, SPRedirectFlags.RelativeToLayoutsPage,
                       HttpContext.Current);
  }

  protected override void OnLoad(EventArgs e)
  {
    workflowAssociationName = Request.Params["WorkflowName"];

    if (!string.IsNullOrEmpty(Request.Params["GuidAssoc"]))
    {
      isUpdatingWorkflowAssociation = true;
      workflowAssociationId = new Guid(Request.Params["GuidAssoc"]);
    }

    if (!string.IsNullOrEmpty(Request.Params["List"]))
    {
      workflowAssociationTargetListId =
                          new Guid(Request.Params["List"]);
      workflowAssociationTargetList =
                  Web.Lists[workflowAssociationTargetListId];
      if (!string.IsNullOrEmpty(Request.Params["ctype"]))
      {
        workflowAssociationTarget =
                  WorkflowAssociationTarget.ListContentType;
        workflowAssociationTargetContentType =
                workflowAssociationTargetList.ContentTypes[
                  new SPContentTypeId(Request.Params["ctype"])];
        if (isUpdatingWorkflowAssociation)
          workflowAssociation =
             workflowAssociationTargetContentType.WorkflowAssociations[
                                             workflowAssociationId];
      }

      else
      {
        workflowAssociationTarget = WorkflowAssociationTarget.List;
        if (isUpdatingWorkflowAssociation)
          workflowAssociation =
             workflowAssociationTargetList.WorkflowAssociations[
                                             workflowAssociationId];
      }
    }

    else
    {
      workflowAssociationTarget =
                  WorkflowAssociationTarget.SiteContentType;
```

(continued)

Listing 2-13 *(continued)*

```
          workflowAssociationTargetContentTypeId =
                      new SPContentTypeId(Request.Params["ctype"]);
          workflowAssociationTargetContentType =
    this.Web.AvailableContentTypes[workflowAssociationTargetContentTypeId];
          if (isUpdatingWorkflowAssociation)
            workflowAssociation =
             workflowAssociationTargetContentType.WorkflowAssociations[
                                                  workflowAssociationId];
        }

        if (isUpdatingWorkflowAssociation)
        {
          PlaceHolderPageTitleContent =
                           "Update an existing workflow association";
          PlaceHolderPageTitleInTitleAreaContent =
                  "Update the existing workflow association called " +
                  workflowAssociationName;

          Person person = null;

          using (StringReader sr =
                 new StringReader(workflowAssociation.AssociationData))
          {
            XmlSerializer serializer = new XmlSerializer(typeof(Person));
            person = (Person)serializer.Deserialize(sr);
          }

          this.nametbx.Text = person.Name;
          this.retiredcbx.Checked = person.Retired;
        }

        else
        {
          PlaceHolderPageTitleContent =
                              "Create a new workflow association";
          PlaceHolderPageTitleInTitleAreaContent =
                      "Create a new workflow association called " +
                              workflowAssociationName;
        }
      }
    }
  }
```

The code-behind class for our association form, like the code-behind class for any other application page, inherits from LayoutsPageBase. This code-behind class overrides the OnLoad method where it performs these tasks. It first retrieves the value of the hidden field named "WorkflowName" and stores it in a private field named workflowAssociationName. Recall that this hidden field contains the name of the workflow association being created or updated:

```
workflowAssociationName = Request.Params["WorkflowName"];
```

Next, it checks whether the hidden field named "GuidAssoc" contains a value. If so, this value is the string representation of the GUID that uniquely identifies the workflow association being updated. In other words, the presence of this value indicates that the user is using the association form to update a workflow association, as opposed to creating a new workflow association. As such, a local field named isUpdatingWorkflowAssociation is set to true to indicate that the association form is being used to update a workflow association:

```
if (!string.IsNullOrEmpty(Request.Params["GuidAssoc"]))
{
  isUpdatingWorkflowAssociation = true;
  workflowAssociationId = new Guid(Request.Params["GuidAssoc"]);
}
```

Next, OnLoad determines whether the URL contains a query string parameter named "List." Recall that the page that posts back to the association form passes this query string parameter along without the query string parameter named "ctype" when the workflow association either is assigned to (in the case of updating an existing workflow association) or is to be assigned to (in the case of creating a new workflow association) a list. As such, this page sets the value of the query string parameter "List" to the GUID that uniquely identifies the SharePoint list with which the workflow association is associated or is to be associated.

Conversely, the page that posts back to the association form passes the query string parameter "List" along with the query string parameter "ctype" when the workflow association either is assigned to (in the case of updating an existing workflow association) or is to be assigned to (in the case of creating a new workflow association) a list content type as opposed to a list. As such, this page sets the value of the query string parameter "List" to the GUID that uniquely identifies the SharePoint list containing the list content type and sets the value of the query string parameter "ctype" to the content type ID that uniquely identifies the SharePoint list content type with which the workflow association is associated or is to be associated.

Therefore, when OnLoad determines that the URL contains a query string parameter "List", it takes the following steps:

1. It stores the GUID that uniquely identifies the SharePoint list in a field named workflowAssociationTargetListId:

    ```
    workflowAssociationTargetListId = new Guid(Request.Params["List"]);
    ```

2. It uses this GUID as an index into the Lists collection property of the SPWeb object representing the current SharePoint site to return a reference to an SPList object that represents the SharePoint list, and stores this reference in a field named workflowAssociationTargetList:

    ```
    workflowAssociationTargetList = Web.Lists[workflowAssociationTargetListId];
    ```

3. It checks whether the URL contains the query string parameter "ctype." If so, this indicates that the workflow association is assigned to or is to be assigned to a list content type as discussed earlier. As such, the code takes the following steps:

   - It assigns the ListContentType enumeration value to a field named workflowAssociationTarget to indicate that the target of this workflow association is a list content type:

```
workflowAssociationTarget = WorkflowAssociationTarget.ListContentType;
```

   - It uses the content type ID as an index into the ContentTypes collection property of the SharePoint list, which contains all the list content types for this list, to return a reference to the SPContentType object that represents this list content type, and stores this reference in a field named workflowAssociationTargetContentType:

```
workflowAssociationTargetContentType =
                  workflowAssociationTargetList.ContentTypes[
                                    new SPContentTypeId(Request.Params["ctype"])];
```

   - It uses the GUID that uniquely identifies the workflow association as an index into the WorkflowAssociations collection property of this SPContentType object to return a reference to the SPWorkflowAssociation object that represents the workflow association being updated. The WorkflowAssociation collection property contains all the workflow associations assigned to the content type:

```
if (isUpdatingWorkflowAssociation)
  workflowAssociation =
      workflowAssociationTargetContentType.WorkflowAssociations[
                                                        workflowAssociationId];
```

If the URL does not contain the query string parameter "ctype," then this indicates that the workflow association is assigned to or is to be assigned to a SharePoint list, as discussed earlier. Therefore, OnLoad takes the following steps:

- It stores the List enumeration value in the workflowAssociationTarget field to indicate that the target of the workflow association is a list:

```
workflowAssociationTarget = WorkflowAssociationTarget.List;
```

- It uses the GUID that uniquely identifies the workflow association as an index into the WorkflowAssociations collection property to return a reference to the SPWorkflowAssociation object that represents the workflow association being updated. The WorkflowAssociations collection property contains all workflow associations assigned to the list:

```
if (isUpdatingWorkflowAssociation)
  workflowAssociation =
         workflowAssociationTargetList.WorkflowAssociations[workflowAssociationId];
```

If the URL does not contain the query string parameter "List," then this indicates that the workflow association is not associated with or is not to be associated with a SharePoint list. Therefore, the workflow association is assigned to or is to be assigned to a SharePoint site content type. As such, OnLoad takes the following steps:

1. It assigns the SiteContentType enumeration value to the workflowAssociationTarget field to indicate that the target of the workflow association is a SharePoint site content type:

```
workflowAssociationTarget = WorkflowAssociationTarget.SiteContentType;
```

2. It uses the content type ID as an index into the AvailableContentTypes collection property of the SPWeb object that represents the current site to return a reference to the SPContentType object representing the site content type. The AvailableContentTypes collection contains all the site content types in the site and all its descendant sites:

```
workflowAssociationTargetContentTypeId =
                                      new SPContentTypeId(Request.Params["ctype"]);
workflowAssociationTargetContentType =
            this.Web.AvailableContentTypes[workflowAssociationTargetContentTypeId];
```

3. It uses the GUID that uniquely identifies the workflow association as an index into the WorkflowAssociations collection property of this SPContentType to return a reference to the SPWorkflowAssociation object representing the workflow association being updated. The WorkflowAssociations collection contains all the workflow associations assigned to the site content type:

```
if (isUpdatingWorkflowAssociation)
  workflowAssociation =
             workflowAssociationTargetContentType.WorkflowAssociations[
                                                       workflowAssociationId];
```

If the association form is being used to update an existing workflow association, OnLoad takes the following steps:

1. It specifies the proper labels:

```
PlaceHolderPageTitleContent = "Update an existing workflow association";
PlaceHolderPageTitleInTitleAreaContent =
                           "Update the existing workflow association called " +
                                         workflowAssociationName;
```

2. It deserializes a Person object from the association data:

```
Person person = null;
using (StringReader sr =
                  new StringReader(workflowAssociation.AssociationData))
{
  XmlSerializer serializer = new XmlSerializer(typeof(Person));
  person = (Person)serializer.Deserialize(sr);
}
```

3. It uses the Person object to populate the association form:

```
this.nametbx.Text = person.Name;
this.retiredcbx.Checked = person.Retired;
```

The following code presents the definitions of Person and WorkflowAssociationTarget:

```
namespace Chapter2
{
 public class Person
 {
    private string name;
    public string Name
    {
      get { return this.name; }
      set { this.name = value; }
    }

    private bool retired;
    public bool Retired
    {
      get { return this.retired; }
      set { this.retired = value; }
    }
 }

 public enum WorkflowAssociationTarget
  {
    SiteContentType,
    List,
    ListContentType
  }
}
```

If the association form is being used to create a new workflow association, OnLoad uses the following proper labels:

```
PlaceHolderPageTitleContent = "Create a new workflow association";
PlaceHolderPageTitleInTitleAreaContent = "Create a new workflow association called " +
                       workflowAssociationName;
```

So far, I've covered the implementation of the OnLoad method, which is automatically invoked when the page is loaded into memory. After users complete the association form, they click the OK button and post the page back to the server, where the OKCallback method is invoked. As shown earlier in Listing 2-13, this method first invokes another method named DetermineTaskAndHistoryLists to determine whether the user has requested a new task list and/or history list to be created for the workflow association. If so, it creates the lists. If the user has selected an existing task list and/or history list from the list of available SharePoint task and history lists, it simply accesses them and assigns them to the appropriate fields:

```
DetermineTaskAndHistoryLists();
```

Next, OKCallback determines whether the hidden field named "UpdateLists" contains the value "TRUE". Recall that the page that posts back to the association form specifies this value for this hidden field to indicate that the user has requested updates to be propagated to all child content types and lists of a given site content type. This obviously applies only when the workflow association is assigned to or is to be assigned to a site content type. When a workflow association is assigned to a site content type or when an existing workflow association of a site content type is updated, the user can choose to propagate this update to all content types that inherit from the site content type and all lists that contain the site content type or content types that inherit from the site content type:

```
bool updateChildContentTypesAndLists = (Request.Params["UpdateLists"] == "TRUE");
```

Next, OKCallback uses the GUID that uniquely identifies the workflow template associated with the workflow association as an index into the WorkflowTemplates collection property of the SPWeb object representing the current SharePoint site to return a reference to the SPWorkflowTemplate object that represents the workflow template. The WorkflowTemplates collection contains all the workflow templates of the SharePoint site:

```
Guid workflowTemplateId = new Guid(Request.Params["WorkflowDefinition"]);
SPWorkflowTemplate workflowTemplate =
                              this.Web.WorkflowTemplates[workflowTemplateId];
```

Next, OKCallback takes the following steps if the workflow association is assigned to or is to be assigned to a SharePoint list:

1. If the association form is being used to update the workflow association, then it invokes the UpdateWorkflowAssociation method to update the properties of the workflow association and then invokes the UpdateWorkflowAssociation method on the SharePoint list to which the workflow association is assigned to commit the changes:

```
if (isUpdatingWorkflowAssociation)
{
  UpdateWorkflowAssociation();
  workflowAssociationTargetList.UpdateWorkflowAssociation(
                                                   workflowAssociation);
}
```

2. If the association form is being used to create the workflow association, then it takes these steps:

   - It invokes the CreateListAssociation static method on the SPWorkflowAssociation class, passing in the workflow template, workflow association name, task list, and history list to create the workflow association. Note that the creation does not assign the workflow association to the respective SharePoint list:

```
workflowAssociation =
    SPWorkflowAssociation.CreateListAssociation(workflowTemplate,
                                                workflowAssociationName,
                                                taskList,
                                                historyList);
```

   - It invokes UpdateWorkflowAssociation to update the properties of the workflow association:

```
UpdateWorkflowAssociation();
```

- It invokes the AddWorkflowAssociation method on the SPList object that represents the SharePoint list to assign the workflow association to the list:

```
workflowAssociationTargetList.AddWorkflowAssociation(
                                                     workflowAssociation);
```

3. It specifies the redirect URL, which the URL of the SharePoint WrkSetng.aspx standard page appended with the query string containing the GUID of the SharePoint list to which the workflow association is assigned:

```
url = "WrkSetng.aspx?List=" + workflowAssociationTargetListId.ToString();
```

OKCallback takes the following steps if the workflow association is assigned to or is to be assigned to a SharePoint site content type:

1. If the association form is being used to update the workflow association, it performs the following tasks:

    - It uses the GUID that uniquely identifies the workflow association as an index into the WorkflowAssociations collection property of the SPContentType object representing the site content type to return a reference to the SPWorkflowAssociation object that represents the workflow association being updated:

```
workflowAssociation =
              workflowAssociationTargetContentType.WorkflowAssociations[
                                                       workflowAssociationId];
```

    - It invokes UpdateWorkflowAssociation to update the properties of the workflow association:

```
UpdateWorkflowAssociation();
```

    - It invokes the UpdateWorkflowAssociation method on the SPContentType object that represents the site content type to commit the changes:

```
workflowAssociationTargetContentType.UpdateWorkflowAssociation(
                                                     workflowAssociation);
```

    - If the user has requested the update to be propagated to all content types that inherit from this site content type and all list content types originated from this site content type, it invokes the UpdateWorkflowAssociationsOnChildren method on the SPContentType object that represents the site content type to propagate the update:

```
if (updateChildContentTypesAndLists)
  workflowAssociationTargetContentType.UpdateWorkflowAssociationsOnChildren(
                                                          true, true, true);
```

2. If the association form is being used to create the workflow association, it performs the following tasks:

    - ❑ It invokes the CreateSiteContentTypeAssociation static method on the SPWorkflowAssociation class, passing in the workflow template, workflow association name, task list title, and history list title to create the workflow association. Keep in mind that the call into CreateSiteContentTypeAssociation does not assign the workflow association to the site content type. It simply creates the workflow association:

```
workflowAssociation = SPWorkflowAssociation.CreateSiteContentTypeAssociation(
                          workflowTemplate, workflowAssociationName,
                          taskList.Title, historyList.Title);
```

    - ❑ It invokes UpdateWorkflowAssociation to update the properties of the SPWorkflowAssociation object that represents the workflow association:

```
UpdateWorkflowAssociation();
```

    - ❑ It invokes the AddWorkflowAssociation method on the SPContentType object that represents the site content type to assign the workflow association to the site content type:

```
workflowAssociationTargetContentType.AddWorkflowAssociation(workflowAssociation);
```

    - ❑ If the user has requested that the same workflow association be assigned to all content types that inherit from the site content type and all list content types originated from the site content type, it invokes the UpdateWorkflowAssociationsOnChildren method on the SPContentType object that represents the site content type to assign the workflow association to all its children:

```
if (updateChildContentTypesAndLists)
  workflowAssociationTargetContentType.UpdateWorkflowAssociationsOnChildren(
                                                          true, true, true);
```

3. It specifies the redirect URL, which the URL for the SharePoint WrkSetng.aspx standard page appended with a query string containing the content type ID of the site content type:

```
url = "WrkSetng.aspx?ctype=" +
               workflowAssociationTargetContentTypeId.ToString();
```

OKCallback performs the following tasks if the workflow association is assigned to or is to be assigned to a list content type:

1. If the association form is being used to update the workflow association, then OKCallback takes these steps:

    - ❑ It uses the GUID that uniquely identifies the workflow association as an index into the WorkflowAssociations collection property of the SPContentType object that represents the list content type, to return a reference to the SPWorkflowAssociation object that represents the workflow association. The WorkflowAssociations collection contains all workflow associations assigned to the site content type:

```
workflowAssociation =
  workflowAssociationTargetContentType.WorkflowAssociations[
                                              workflowAssociationId];
```

- It invokes UpdateWorkflowAssociation to update the properties of the SPWorkflowAssociation object:

```
UpdateWorkflowAssociation();
```

- It invokes UpdateWorkflowAssociation on the SPContentType object representing the list content type to commit the changes:

```
workflowAssociationTargetContentType.UpdateWorkflowAssociation(
                                              workflowAssociation);
```

2. If the association form is being used to create the workflow association, then OKCallback takes the following steps:

- It invokes the CreateListContentTypeAssociation static method on the SPWorkflowAssociation class, passing the workflow template, workflow association name, task list, and history list to create the workflow association and return an SPWorkflowAssociation object that represents the workflow association:

```
workflowAssociation =
    SPWorkflowAssociation.CreateListContentTypeAssociation(
                    workflowTemplate, workflowAssociationName,
                    taskList, historyList);
```

- It calls UpdateWorkflowAssociation to update this SPWorkflowAssociation object:

```
UpdateWorkflowAssociation();
```

- It calls AddWorkflowAssociation on the SPContentType object that represents the list content type to assign the workflow association to the site content type:

```
workflowAssociationTargetContentType.AddWorkflowAssociation(
                                              workflowAssociation);
```

- It specifies the URL to which the user will be redirected afterward, which is the URL of the SharePoint WrkSetng.aspx standard page. Note that OKCallback passes the content type ID of the list content type and the GUID of the list that contains the content type as the values of the List and ctype query string parameters:

```
url = "WrkSetng.aspx?List=" +
              workflowAssociationTargetListId.ToString() +
                                    "&ctype=" +
              workflowAssociationTargetContentTypeId.ToString();
```

Finally, OKCallback redirects the browser to the specified redirect URL:

```
SPUtility.Redirect(url, SPRedirectFlags.RelativeToLayoutsPage,
                   HttpContext.Current);
```

Implementing an Initiation Workflow Input Form

When a user attempts to initiate a new workflow instance from a workflow association whose respective workflow template is configured with an initiation form, the user is automatically redirected to the initiation form. You must populate the user interface of your initiation form with the association data when the form is first displayed. The user has the option to either leave the association data as is so that the same association data is used as the initiation data for the workflow instance being initiated, or the user can edit the data. In other words, the association data provides the default settings that apply to all workflow instances initiated from the workflow association, whereas initiation data provides the settings that only apply to a specific workflow instance. Any changes that the user makes in the initiation form only affect the workflow instance being initiated. They have no impact on other workflow instances currently running or the workflow instance that will run in the future. Put differently, the user uses the initiation form to customize the default settings specified in the association data.

The initiation form normally displays the same user interface as the instantiation form. Listing 2-14 presents the implementation of our initiation form.

Listing 2-14: The initiation form

```
<%@ Page Language="C#" MasterPageFile="~/_layouts/application.master" EnableSession
State="true" ValidateRequest="False" Inherits="ProWSSMOSSProg.InitiationForm1" %>

<%@ Assembly Name="ProWSSMOSSProg, Version=1.0.0.0, Culture=neutral, PublicKeyToken
=f589cfc210e77624" %>

<%@ Register TagPrefix="SharePoint" Namespace="Microsoft.SharePoint.WebControls"
Assembly="Microsoft.SharePoint, Version=12.0.0.0, Culture=neutral, PublicKeyToken=7
1e9bce111e9429c" %>

<%@ Register TagPrefix="Utilities" Namespace="Microsoft.SharePoint.Utilities"
Assembly="Microsoft.SharePoint, Version=12.0.0.0, Culture=neutral, PublicKeyToken=7
1e9bce111e9429c" %>

<%@ Register TagPrefix="wssuc" TagName="InputFormSection" Src="/_controltemplates/
InputFormSection.ascx" %>

<%@ Register TagPrefix="wssuc" TagName="InputFormControl" Src="/_controltemplates/
InputFormControl.ascx" %>

<%@ Register TagPrefix="wssuc" TagName="ButtonSection" Src="/_controltemplates/
ButtonSection.ascx" %>

<asp:Content ID="Main" ContentPlaceHolderID="PlaceHolderMain" runat="server">
  <asp:Table CellSpacing="0" CellPadding="0" BorderWidth="0">
```

(continued)

Listing 2-14 *(continued)*

```
        <wssuc:InputFormSection Title="Name"
        Description="Specify the name for this workflow instance."
        runat="server">
          <template_inputformcontrols>
            <wssuc:InputFormControl runat="server" LabelText="Name:">
              <Template_Control>
                <SharePoint:InputFormTextBox Title="Name" width="300"
                runat="server"/>
              </Template_Control>
            </wssuc:InputFormControl>
          </template_inputformcontrols>
        </wssuc:InputFormSection>

        <wssuc:InputFormSection Title="Retirement status"
        Description="Specify the retirement setting for this workflow
        instance." runat="server">
          <template_inputformcontrols>
            <wssuc:InputFormControl Runat="server" LabelText="Retired:">
              <Template_Control>
                <SharePoint:InputFormCheckbox ID="retiredcbx"
                runat="server" />
              </Template_Control>
            </wssuc:InputFormControl>
          </template_inputformcontrols>
        </wssuc:InputFormSection>

        <wssuc:ButtonSection runat="server"
        ShowStandardCancelButton="false">
          <template_buttons>
            <asp:PlaceHolder runat="server">
              <asp:Button runat="server" OnClick="OKCallback" Text="OK" />
              <asp:Button runat="server" OnClick="CancelCallback"
              Text="Cancel" />
            </asp:PlaceHolder>
          </template_buttons>
        </wssuc:ButtonSection>
      </asp:Table>

      <SharePoint:FormDigest ID="FormDigest1" runat="server" />
    </asp:Content>

    <asp:Content ID="Content1" ContentPlaceHolderID="PlaceHolderPageTitle"
    runat="server">
      <%= PlaceHolderPageTitleContent %>
    </asp:Content>

    <asp:Content ID="Content2" ContentPlaceHolderID="PlaceHolderPageTitleInTitleArea"
    runat="server">
      <%= PlaceHolderPageTitleInTitleAreaContent %>
    </asp:Content>
```

If you compare this with Listing 2-10 (our association form), you'll notice that this code listing is missing all the hidden fields that we used in the association form. Recall that the page that performs the cross-page postback to the association form posts its form data to this form. As discussed, the association form needs those hidden fields to store this form data. Because no one is making a cross-page postback to the initiation form, these hidden fields are no longer needed.

Listing 2-15 presents the code-behind class of our initiation form.

Listing 2-15: Code-behind class of the initiation form

```
using System;
using System.IO;
using System.Text;
using System.Web;
using System.Web.UI;
using System.Web.UI.WebControls;
using System.Web.UI.HtmlControls;
using System.Xml;
using System.Xml.Serialization;
using Microsoft.SharePoint;
using Microsoft.SharePoint.Utilities;
using Microsoft.SharePoint.WebControls;
using Microsoft.SharePoint.Workflow;

namespace Chapter2
{
  public class InitiationForm1 : LayoutsPageBase
  {
    protected InputFormTextBox nametbx;
    protected InputFormCheckBox retiredcbx;
    protected string PlaceHolderPageTitleContent;
    protected string PlaceHolderPageTitleInTitleAreaContent;

    protected SPList targetList;
    SPListItem targetListItem;
    protected SPWorkflowAssociation workflowAssociation;

    protected override void OnLoad(EventArgs e)
    {
      targetList = Web.Lists[new Guid(Request.Params["List"])];
      Guid workflowAssociationId =
                          new Guid(Request.Params["TemplateID"]);
      workflowAssociation =
            targetList.WorkflowAssociations[workflowAssociationId];
      targetListItem =
             targetList.GetItemById(int.Parse(Request.Params["ID"]));
      if (workflowAssociation == null)
      {
        SPContentTypeId targetContentTypeID =
                   (SPContentTypeId)targetListItem["ContentTypeId"];
        SPContentType targetContentType =
                        targetList.ContentTypes[targetContentTypeID];
```

(continued)

Listing 2-15 *(continued)*

```
        workflowAssociation =
          targetContentType.WorkflowAssociations[workflowAssociationId];
      }

      PlaceHolderPageTitleContent = "Initiate a workflow instance";
      PlaceHolderPageTitleInTitleAreaContent =
                        "Initiate a workflow instance on " +
                     (string)targetListItem["Title"] + " list item";

      Person person = null;

      using (StringReader sr =
              new StringReader(workflowAssociation.AssociationData))
      {
        XmlSerializer serializer = new XmlSerializer(typeof(Person));
        person = (Person)serializer.Deserialize(sr);
      }

      this.nametbx.Text = person.Name;
      this.retiredcbx.Checked = person.Retired;
    }

    public void CancelCallback(object sender, EventArgs e)
    {
      SPUtility.Redirect(targetList.DefaultViewUrl,
                         SPRedirectFlags.Default,
                         HttpContext.Current);
    }

    public void OKCallback(object sender, EventArgs e)
    {
      try
      {
        Person person = new Person();
        person.Name = this.nametbx.Text;
        person.Retired = this.retiredcbx.Checked;
        string initiationData;

        using (StringWriter sw = new StringWriter())
        {
          XmlSerializer serializer = new XmlSerializer(typeof(Person));
          serializer.Serialize(sw, person);
          initiationData = sw.ToString();
        }

        Web.Site.WorkflowManager.StartWorkflow(targetListItem,
                                               workflowAssociation,
```

```
                                            initiationData);
        }

        catch (SPException exception)
        {
          SPUtility.Redirect("Error.aspx",
                          SPRedirectFlags.RelativeToLayoutsPage,
                          HttpContext.Current,
                          "ErrorText=" +
            SPHttpUtility.UrlKeyValueEncode(exception.Message));
        }

        SPUtility.Redirect(targetList.DefaultViewUrl,
                           SPRedirectFlags.Default,
                           HttpContext.Current);
      }
    }
  }
```

As Listing 2-15 shows, the InitiationForm1 code-behind initiation form, like any other application page, inherits from LayoutsPageBase. InitiationForm1 overrides the OnLoad method, where it performs the following steps. First, it accesses the GUID that uniquely identifies the SharePoint list containing the SharePoint list item on which the workflow instance is being initiated. This GUID is passed to the initiation form as the value of a query string parameter named List. OnLoad uses this GUID as an index into the Lists collection property of the SPWeb object that represents the current SharePoint site, to return a reference to the SPList object representing the SharePoint list. The Lists collection is where the SharePoint site stores the SPList objects that represent its SharePoint lists:

```
targetList = Web.Lists[new Guid(Request.Params["List"])];
```

Next, OnLoad accesses the GUID that uniquely identifies the workflow association from which the workflow instance is being initiated. This GUID is passed to the initiation form as the value of a query string parameter named TemplateID:

```
Guid workflowAssociationId = new Guid(Request.Params["TemplateID"]);
```

OnLoad uses this GUID as an index into the WorkflowAssociations collection property of the SPList object that represents the SharePoint list to return a reference to the SPWorkflowAssociation object representing the workflow association from which the workflow instance is being initiated:

```
workflowAssociation = targetList.WorkflowAssociations[workflowAssociationId];
```

OnLoad then accesses the integer that identifies the SPList item on which the workflow instance is being initiated. This integer is passed to the initiation form as the value of a query string parameter named ID. OnLoad then invokes the GetItemById method on the SPList object to return a reference to the SPListItem object that represents the SharePoint list item on which the workflow instance is being initiated:

```
targetListItem = targetList.GetItemById(int.Parse(Request.Params["ID"]));
```

If the WorkflowAssociations collection property of the SPList object does not contain a workflow association with the specified GUID, then this indicates that the workflow association from which the workflow instance is being initiated is not assigned to the SharePoint list. Instead, it is assigned to a content type. As such, OnLoad takes the following steps to access the workflow association:

1. It uses the string "ContentTypeId" as an index into the SPListItem object representing the SharePoint list item on which the workflow instance is being initiated, to return a reference to the SPContentTypeId object that represents the content type ID of the content type:

```
SPContentTypeId targetContentTypeID =
                                    (SPContentTypeId)targetListItem["ContentTypeId"];
```

2. It uses this SPContentTypeId object as an index, into the ContentTypes collection property of the SPList object that represents the SharePoint list, to return a reference to the SPContentType object representing the content type:

```
SPContentType targetContentType = targetList.ContentTypes[targetContentTypeID];
```

3. It uses the GUID that uniquely identifies the workflow association as an index into the WorkflowAssociations collection property of this SPContentType object, to return a reference to the SPWorkflowAssociation object representing the workflow association from which the workflow instance is being initiated. The WorkflowAssociation collection contains the SPWorkflowAssociation objects that represent all workflow associations assigned to the content type:

```
workflowAssociation =
                    targetContentType.WorkflowAssociations[workflowAssociationId];
```

Next, OnLoad deserializes a Person object from the association data and uses it to populate the initiation form. This enables the user to view and optionally customize this data for the workflow instance being initiated:

```
Person person = null;

using (StringReader sr =
                  new StringReader(workflowAssociation.AssociationData))
{
  XmlSerializer serializer = new XmlSerializer(typeof(Person));
  person = (Person)serializer.Deserialize(sr);
}

this.nametbx.Text = person.Name;
this.retiredcbx.Checked = person.Retired;
```

The user optionally edits the data shown in the initiation form and clicks OK to post the form back to the server, where the OKCallback method is invoked. As Listing 2-15 shows, this method first instantiates a Person object and populates it with the data the user has entered into the initiation form:

```
Person person = new Person();
person.Name = this.nametbx.Text;
person.Retired = this.retiredcbx.Checked;
```

Next, OKCallback serializes this Person object into a string, which contains the initiation data:

```
using (StringWriter sw = new StringWriter())
{
  XmlSerializer serializer = new XmlSerializer(typeof(Person));
  serializer.Serialize(sw, person);
  initiationData = sw.ToString();
}
```

The SPSite object that represents the current site collection exposes a property of named WorkflowManager, which references an object of type SPWorkflowManager. This object enables you to manage workflow instances from your managed code. I provide in-depth coverage of this method later in the chapter. This object exposes a method named StartWorkflow that you can use to initiate a workflow instance on a given SharePoint list item from a given workflow association with the specified initiation data:

```
Web.Site.WorkflowManager.StartWorkflow(targetListItem, workflowAssociation,
                                       initiationData);
```

Implementing a Workflow Template

As shown in the previous section, every workflow instance is initiated from a workflow association, which in turn is created from a workflow template. As the name implies, the workflow template defines the template from which new workflow associations, and consequently new workflow instances, are created. A workflow template represents a workflow and its associated workflow input forms.

A workflow template is defined in a CAML-based file, which is referenced from a SharePoint feature. As such, it is deployed alongside its associated feature to the application-specific folder under the FEATURES folder on the file system of the front-end web server.

Listing 2-16 shows an excerpt from the wss.xsd file, which is located in the following directory on the file system of the front-end web server:

```
Local_Drive:\Program Files\Common Files\microsoft shared\Web Server
Extensions\12\TEMPLATE\XML
```

Listing 2-16: CAML schema for defining a workflow template

```
<xs:element name="Elements" type="ElementDefinitionCollection" />

<xs:complexType name="ElementDefinitionCollection">
  <xs:sequence>
    <xs:choice minOccurs="0" maxOccurs="unbounded">
      <xs:element name="ContentType" type="ContentTypeDefinition" />
      <xs:element name="ContentTypeBinding"
      type="ContentTypeBindingDefinition" />
      <xs:element name="DocumentConverter"
      type="DocumentConverterDefinition" />
      <xs:element name="FeatureSiteTemplateAssociation"
```

(continued)

Listing 2-16 *(continued)*

```
        type="FeatureSiteTemplateAssociationDefinition" />
        <xs:element name="Field" type="SharedFieldDefinition" />
        <xs:element name="CustomAction" type="CustomActionDefinition" />
        <xs:element name="CustomActionGroup"
        type="CustomActionGroupDefinition" />
        <xs:element name="HideCustomAction"
        type="HideCustomActionDefinition" />
        <xs:element name="Module" type="ModuleDefinition" />
        <xs:element name="ListInstance" type="ListInstanceDefinition" />
        <xs:element name="ListTemplate" type="ListTemplateDefinition" />
        <xs:element name="Control" type="DelegateControlDefinition" />
        <xs:element name="Receivers"
        type="ReceiverDefinitionCollection" />
        <xs:element name="Workflow" type="WorkflowDefinition" />
        <xs:element name="UserMigrator" type="UserMigratorDefinition" />
      </xs:choice>
    </xs:sequence>
    <xs:attribute name="Id" type="UniqueIdentifier" />
  </xs:complexType>

  <xs:complexType name="WorkflowDefinition" mixed="true">
    <xs:all>
      <xs:element name="AssociationData" type="xs:anyType" minOccurs="0"
      maxOccurs="1" />
      <xs:element name="MetaData" type="xs:anyType" minOccurs="0"
      maxOccurs="1" />
      <xs:element name="Categories" type="xs:anyType" minOccurs="0"
      maxOccurs="1" />
    </xs:all>
    <xs:attribute name="Title" type="xs:string" />
    <xs:attribute name="Name" type="xs:string" />
    <xs:attribute name="CodeBesideAssembly" type="AssemblyStrongName" />
    <xs:attribute name="CodeBesideClass" type="AssemblyClass" />
    <xs:attribute name="Description" type="xs:string" />
    <xs:attribute name="Id" type="UniqueIdentifier" />
    <xs:attribute name="EngineClass" type="AssemblyClass" />
    <xs:attribute name="EngineAssembly" type="AssemblyStrongName" />
    <xs:attribute name="AssociationUrl" type="RelativeUrl" />
    <xs:attribute name="InstantiationUrl" type="RelativeUrl" />
    <xs:attribute name="ModificationUrl" type="RelativeUrl" />
    <xs:attribute name="StatusUrl" type="RelativeUrl" />
    <xs:attribute name="TaskListContentTypeId" type="ContentTypeId" />
  </xs:complexType>
```

The CAML schema excerpt shown in Listing 2-16 defines an XML element named <Elements>, which is of schema type ElementDefinitionCollection. This element must be the document element of the CAML file that defines a workflow template. According to its schema type, the <Elements> element can contain an element named <Workflow>. The <Workflow> element is the XML element that you must use to define a workflow template. As shown in Listing 2-16, the <Workflow> element is of schema type WorkflowDefinition. According to this schema type, the <Workflow> element can contain the following child elements:

- A single instance of an XML element named <AssociationData>, which is of schema type xs: anyType. This means that this element can contain any valid XML data. SharePoint automatically assigns this XML data to the AssociationData property of the SPWorkflowAssociation object that represents a workflow association associated with this workflow template. The association form with which this workflow template is configured can then load this XML data into an IXPathNavigable object such as an XmlDocument or XPathDocument and consume it.

  For example, in the case of our previous example, we may want to pass the following XML data, which contains information about the company:

```
<Company>
  <Name>OurCompany</Name>
  <Address>
    <Street>456 SomeStreet</Street>
    <City>SomeCity</City>
    <State>SomeState</State>
  </Address>
</Company>
```

- The association form can then use a code snippet such as the following to parse and consume this data:

```
StringReader sr = new StringReader(workflowAssociation.AssociationData);
XmlDocument xdoc = new XmlDocument();
xdoc.Load(sr);
sr.Close();
```

  - A single instance of an XML element named <MetaData>, which is of schema type xs: anyType. This means that this element, just like the <AssociationData> element, can contain any valid XML data. Use the <MetaData> element to provide metadata information about the workflow template. SharePoint provides the following standard XML elements that you can use within the <MetaData> element to specify metadata information about the workflow template:

- **<InitiationType>:** Use this XML element to specify how workflow instances can be initiated from the workflow associations created from this workflow template. The possible values for the <InitiationType> element are Manual, OnNewItem, OnItemUpdate, and OnMajorCheckIn. Use Manual to enable users to manually initiate workflow instances from the SharePoint user interface. Use OnNewItem, OnItemUpdate, and OnMajorCheckIn to specify that a workflow instance must be automatically initiated from each workflow association created from this workflow template on a given SharePoint list, list content type, or site content type every time a list item is added or updated, or every time a major version of a list item is checked in. Note that the added, updated, or checked-in list item must be of the content type on which the workflow association is created. As the following example shows, you can use two or more of these values together provided that you separate them with ";#":

```
<MetaData>
  <InitiationType>Manual;#OnNewItem;#OnItemUpdate;#OnMajorCheckIn</InitiationType>
</MetaData>
```

  If you don't specify the <InitiationType> element, SharePoint uses the default value, shown in the preceding example, which contains all the four values.

- **<Modification_GUID_Name>:** Use this XML element to specify the name of a workflow modification with the specified GUID. SharePoint displays this name as a link to end users on the workflow status page. Users click this link to navigate to the specified modification form to modify the workflow instance. Note that you must include the GUID that uniquely identifies the modification form as part of the name of this XML element because SharePoint uses this GUID to identify the modification form and consequently to determine the URL of the form, which is needed for the link that SharePoint displays to the user.

```
<Modification_e6eb12e9-83ca-4272-ba72-53aec4c3639c_Name>Modify this workflow
instance</Modification_e6eb12e9-83ca-4272-ba72-53aec4c3639c_Name>
```

- **<StatusPageUrl>:** Use this XML element to specify the URL for a custom workflow status page. Keep in mind that all URLs specified in the CAML file that defines a workflow template must be either absolute or Web application-relative:

```
<StatusPageUrl>_layouts/MyDir/MyWrkStat.aspx</StatusPageUrl>
```

If you do not specify the <StatusPageUrl> element, SharePoint uses _layouts/WrkStat.aspx page.

- **<ExtendedStatusColumnValues>:** Use this XML element to specify custom status column values. This element contains one or more <StatusColumnValue> child elements, where each child element specifies a custom status column value. These values form an ordered list whereby each value is uniquely identified by its 0-based index in the list. The first 15 indexes are reserved, so the index of your first custom status column value will be 15. For example, the following defines two custom status column values:

```
<ExtendedStatusColumnValues>
  <StatusColumnValue>Completed</StatusColumnValue>
  <StatusColumnValue>Canceled</StatusColumnValue>
</ExtendedStatusColumnValues>
```

You can use the index of a custom status column value to access the custom status column value from within your code. Using this index, as opposed to the actual name of the custom status column value specified in the above, enables you to change the names without affecting your code. It also enables you to localize the names of the custom status column values.

- A single instance of an XML element named <Categories>, which is of schema type xs:anyType. This XML element is reserved and should not be used.

At this point, you have seen all the child elements that the <Workflow> element can contain. According to the schema type WorkflowDefinition shown in Listing 2-16, the <Workflow> element exposes the following attributes:

- **Title:** Specifies the title of the workflow template
- **Name:** Specifies the name of the workflow template. SharePoint displays this name in the list of available workflow templates on the SharePoint page that allows users to create a new workflow association
- **CodeBesideClass:** Specifies the fully qualified name of the code-beside class for the workflow, including its complete namespace containment hierarchy

- **CodeBesideAssembly:** Specifies complete information about the assembly that contains the code-beside class for the workflow, including assembly name, version, culture, and public key token
- **Description:** Provides a short description about the workflow template. SharePoint displays this description on the SharePoint page that allows users to create a new workflow association when the user selects the name of the workflow template from the list of available workflow templates.
- **Id:** Specifies the GUID that uniquely identifies the workflow template
- **EngineClass:** This attribute is reserved and should not be used.
- **EngineAssembly:** This attribute is reserved and should not be used.
- **AssociationUrl:** Specifies the absolute or web-application-relative virtual path to the association form for this workflow template
- **InstantiationUrl:** Specifies the absolute or web-application-relative virtual path to the initiation form for this workflow template
- **ModificationUrl:** Specifies the absolute or web-application-relative virtual path to the modification form for this workflow template
- **StatusUrl:** This attribute is obsolete and should not be used.
- **TaskListContentTypeId:** Specifies the content type ID of the content type assigned to the task list. This will be clear in Chapter 7 when we cover edit task forms.

Listing 2-17 presents the CAML document that defines the workflow template for the workflow example we've been using in this chapter.

Listing 2-17: CAML document that defines the workflow template

```
<?xml version="1.0" encoding="utf-8" ?>
<Elements xmlns="http://schemas.microsoft.com/sharepoint/">
  <Workflow
  Name="My Workflow Template"
  Description="This is My Workflow Template!"
  Id="94477ddb-45f3-4eb2-8cde-19348a43ef71"
  CodeBesideClass="Chapter2.Workflow1"
  CodeBesideAssembly="Chapter2, Version=1.0.0.0, Culture=neutral,
                      PublicKeyToken=5782d297fbd1147f"
  AssociationUrl="_layouts/SharePointWorkflow2/AssociationForm1.aspx"
  InstantiationUrl="_layouts/SharePointWorkflow2/InitiationForm1.aspx">
    <Categories/>
    <MetaData>
      <StatusPageUrl>_layouts/WrkStat.aspx</StatusPageUrl>
    </MetaData>
  </Workflow>
</Elements>
```

The SharePoint object model comes with a class named SPWorkflowTemplate whose instances represent SharePoint workflow templates. You can use the public API of this class to program against the SharePoint workflow templates. Listing 2-18 presents this public API.

Listing 2-18: The SPWorkflowTemplate class

```
public sealed class SPWorkflowTemplate : SPAutoSerializingObject,
                                          IComparer, ICloneable
{
  public StringCollection GetStatusChoices(SPWeb web);
  public static bool IsCategoryApplicable(string strAllCategs,
                                           string[] rgReqCateg);

  public bool AllowAsyncManualStart { get; set; }
  public bool AllowManual { get; set; }
  public string AssociationData { get; set; }
  public string AssociationUrl { get; }
  public int AutoCleanupDays { get; set; }
  public bool AutoStartChange { get; set; }
  public bool AutoStartCreate { get; set; }
  public Guid BaseId { get; }
  public bool CompressInstanceData { get; set; }
  public string Description { get; set; }
  public Guid Id { get; }
  public string InstantiationUrl { get; }
  public bool IsDeclarative { get; }
  public object this[string property] { get; set; }
  public string ModificationUrl { get; }
  public string Name { get; }
  public SPBasePermissions PermissionsManual { get; set; }
  public bool StatusColumn { get; set; }
  public string StatusUrl { get; }
  public SPContentTypeId TaskListContentTypeId { get; }
  public string Xml { get; }
  public Hashtable UpgradedPersistedProperties { get; }
}
```

Here are the descriptions of the properties of SPWorkflowTemplate against which you can program from within your managed code:

- **AllowAsyncManualStart:** Gets or sets a Boolean value that specifies whether to allow SharePoint to initiate workflow instances from workflow associations created from this workflow template asynchronously, even if the workflow instance was manually initiated
- **AllowManual:** Gets or sets a Boolean value that specifies whether workflow instances can be manually initiated from workflow associations created from this workflow template
- **AssociationData:** Gets or sets a string that contains the association data for workflow associations
- **AssociationUrl:** Gets a string that contains the absolute or web-application-relative virtual path to the workflow association form for this workflow template. This property basically returns the value of the AssociationUrl attribute of the <Workflow> element in the underlying CAML file that defines the workflow template.

- **AutoStartChange:** Gets or sets a Boolean value that specifies whether workflow instances can be automatically initiated from the workflow associations created from this workflow template every time the following occurs:
    - A SharePoint list item of the same content type on which the workflow association was created changes
    - A SharePoint list item contained in a SharePoint list on which the workflow association was created changes
- **AutoStartCreate:** Gets or sets a Boolean value that specifies whether workflow instances can be automatically initiated from the workflow associations created from this workflow template every time the following occurs:
    - A SharePoint list item of the same content type on which the workflow association was created is added
    - A SharePoint list item is added to a SharePoint list on which the workflow association was created
- **BaseId:** Gets a GUID that uniquely identifies the workflow template
- **Description:** Gets and sets a string that contains a short description for the workflow template. SharePoint displays this description to end users when they select the workflow template from the list of available workflow templates when they are creating workflow associations from the workflow template.
- **Id:** Gets a GUID that uniquely identifies the workflow template
- **InstantiationUrl:** Gets a string that contains the absolute or web-application-relative virtual path to the workflow initiation form for this workflow template. This property basically returns the value of the InstantiationUrl attribute of the <Workflow> element in the underlying CAML file that defines the workflow template.
- **IsDeclarative:** Gets a Boolean value that specifies whether the workflow template is declarative — that is, whether its associated workflow is defined declaratively in an XAML file. This property returns false if the associated workflow is contained in an assembly.
- **ModificationUrl:** Gets a string that contains the absolute or web-application-relative virtual path to the workflow modification form for this workflow template. This property basically returns the value of the ModificationUrl attribute of the <Workflow> element in the underlying CAML file that defines the workflow template.
- **Name:** Gets a string that contains the name of the workflow template. SharePoint displays this name to end users in the list of available workflow templates to choose from on the SharePoint page where they create a new workflow association.
- **StatusColumn:** Gets or sets a Boolean value that specifies whether to display a status column for workflow instances created from this workflow template in the SharePoint user interface. The default is true.
- **StatusUrl:** Gets a string that specifies the URL of a custom workflow status page for the workflow instances created from this workflow template. This property basically returns the value of the <StatusPageUrl> element.

- **TaskListContentTypeId:** Gets an SPContentTypeId object that represents the content type ID of the content type assigned to the workflow task list.
- **Xml:** Gets a string that contains the XML definition of the workflow template.

Implementing a Workflow Feature

You need to implement a site-collection-scoped SharePoint point feature that references the CAML-based file that defines the workflow template. Listing 2-19 presents the feature that references the CAML-based workflow template definition file shown in Listing 2-18.

Listing 2-19: Feature that references the workflow template definition file

```
<?xml version="1.0" encoding="utf-8" ?>

<Feature
Id="d9c446cc-37db-4164-8294-76ad66faf4e7"
Title="Chapter2 feature"
Description="My SharePoint Workflow Feature"
Version="12.0.0.0"
Scope="Site"
ReceiverAssembly="Microsoft.Office.Workflow.Feature, Version=12.0.0.0,
                  Culture=neutral, PublicKeyToken=71e9bce111e9429c"
ReceiverClass="Microsoft.Office.Workflow.Feature.WorkflowFeatureReceiver"
xmlns="http://schemas.microsoft.com/sharepoint/">
  <ElementManifests>
    <ElementManifest Location="workflow.xml" />
  </ElementManifests>
  <Properties>
    <Property Key="GloballyAvailable" Value="true" />
    <!-- Value for RegisterForms key indicates the path to the forms relative to
feature file location -->
    <!-- if you don't have forms, use *.xsn -->
    <Property Key="RegisterForms" Value="*.xsn" />
  </Properties>
</Feature>
```

Note that the Scope attribute of the <Feature> element is set to "Site" to specify that this feature must be activated at the site collection level to make it available to all sites in the site collection.

Deploying Workflow Template Files and Feature

Following our 11-step recipe, the next order of business is to deploy the feature.xml file that contains our feature and the workflow.xml file that defines our workflow template to an application-specific folder under the FEATURES folder on the file system of the front-end web server. If you are using Visual Studio 2008, Visual Studio automatically does this for you every time you run your application. If you're not using Visual Studio 2008, you need to manually copy these two files to the application-specific folder just mentioned.

Deploying Workflow Input Forms

Still following our 11-step recipe, we now need to deploy our association and initiation forms to an application-specific folder under that LAYOUTS folder on the file system of the front-end web server. Recall that our association and initiation forms are custom application pages, and every custom application page must be deployed to the LAYOUTS folder, which is mapped to the _layouts virtual directory of the web application. This enables others to use the web-application-relative virtual path of _layout/application_specific_folder/custom_application_page.aspx to access the custom application page.

Installing a Workflow Feature

The next order of business is to install the SharePoint feature that references our workflow template definition file. If you're using Visual Studio 2008, then Visual Studio automatically does this for you every time you run your application. Otherwise, you need to use the STSADM command-line utility as follows:

```
stsadm.exe -o InstallFeature -filename
   application_specific_folder\feature.xml -force
```

Activating a Workflow Feature

Next, you need to activate the SharePoint feature that references your workflow template definition file in a SharePoint site collection. Visual Studio 2008 automatically does this for you every time you run your application if you are working in the Visual Studio 2008 environment. Otherwise, you can use the STSADM command-line utility or the SharePoint user interface to activate the feature.

At this point, your workflow template is available to all sites within the site collection in which you activated the SharePoint feature. Now authorized users can navigate to a SharePoint list, list content type, or site content type to create workflow associations from your workflow template. Note that users can create multiple workflow associations from the same workflow template on the same SharePoint list, list content type, or site content type. They can optionally configure each workflow association differently as follows:

- Have each workflow association use a different task list
- Have each workflow association use a different history list
- Specify different workflow instance initiation options for different workflow associations. For example, one workflow association can be configured so that users can manually initiate workflow instances from it. Another workflow association can be configured so that workflow instances are automatically initiated every time the following occurs:
    - A new SharePoint list item is added to the SharePoint list on which the workflow association is created
    - A new SharePoint list item of the content type on which the workflow association is created is added
- Have each workflow association use different association data if your workflow template is configured with an association form

Summary

This chapter presented the following 11-step recipe for developing and deploying a custom SharePoint workflow and its respective association and initiation forms. It also included an example showing how to use this recipe in your SharePoint applications:

1. Implement the workflow itself, which is a class that inherits from SequentialWorkflowActivity or StateMachineWorkflowActivity.
2. Implement the necessary workflow input forms: Association, Initiation, Edit Task, and/or Modification forms.
3. Compile the workflow itself and the code-behind files for the workflow input forms into a strong-named assembly and install this assembly in the global assembly cache.
4. Implement the workflow template.
5. Implement a site-collection-scoped SharePoint feature that references the workflow template.
6. Using a SharePoint Solution file, deploy the SharePoint feature and the workflow template that it references to a feature-specific subfolder under the standard TEMPLATE\FEATURE folder on the file system of the front-end web server:

```
Local_Drive:\Program Files\Common Files\microsoft shared\Web Server
Extensions\12\TEMPLATE\FEATURE
```

7. Deploy the workflow input forms to a feature-specific subfolder under the standard LAYOUTS folder on the file system of the front-end web server:

```
Local_Drive:\Program Files\Common Files\microsoft shared\Web Server
Extensions\12\TEMPLATE\LAYOUTS
```

8. Install the SharePoint feature with SharePoint.
9. Activate the SharePoint feature in a site collection.
10. Create a workflow association from the workflow template on a SharePoint list, list content type, or site content type.
11. Activate a workflow instance from the workflow association on a SharePoint list item or document.

3

Programming SharePoint External Data Exchange Services

SharePoint workflow programming is built on top of Windows Workflow Foundation (WF). One of the great things about WF is its extensibility model, which enables it to work in different hosting scenarios. This chapter begins by taking you under the hood of the SharePoint workflow programming infrastructure to help you see how SharePoint takes full advantage of the WF extensibility model. Then I'll dive into the details of the SharePoint-specific external data exchange services that SharePoint registers with the workflow run time when it starts the run time. These services play a central role in SharePoint workflow programming. Finally, you'll learn how to implement custom composite activities that take advantage of these services.

Extending WF

One of the most important aspects of the WF extensibility model is that WF can be hosted in any .NET application. Hosting WF involves several important steps. First, the host must instantiate the workflow run time, which is represented by a WF class called WorkflowRuntime. Second, the host must create the required local services and register them with the workflow run time. A local service facilitates two-way communications between the host and activities that make up a workflow. A local service is a .NET class that implements one or more interfaces known as *local service interfaces*. Each interface defines one or more events and methods. Workflow activities invoke the methods of a local service in order to have the local service perform the specified tasks on their behalf. The nature of these tasks depends on the specifics of your workflow activities. Workflow activities also subscribe to the events of a local service so they are notified when the local service fires these events. Events facilitate the flow of communications from the local service to workflow activities.

WF comes with two types of workflow activities, HandleExternalEventActivity and CallExternalMethodActivity, which only work with local services that meet certain requirements. These local services are known as *external data exchange services*. A workflow uses one or more instances of CallExternalMethodActivity to invoke one or more methods of one or more external data exchange services. Each CallExternalMethodActivity instance is configured to invoke a specific method of a specific external data exchange service. A workflow uses one or more instances of HandleExternalEventActivity to handle one or more events of one or more external data exchange services. Each HandleExternalEventActivity instance is configured to handle a specific event of a specific external data exchange service.

An external data exchange service interface is a local service interface that meets specific requirements that enables it to work with HandleExternalEventActivity and CallExternalMethodActivity. These requirements are as follows:

- An external data exchange service interface is annotated with the ExternalDataExchangeAttribute metadata attribute.
- The event data classes associated with the events of an external data exchange service interface directly or indirectly inherit from the ExternalDataEventArgs event data class.

Listing 3-1 presents the internal implementation of the ExternalDataEventArgs event data class.

Listing 3-1: The ExternalDataEventArgs class

```
[Serializable]
public class ExternalDataEventArgs : EventArgs
{
  private IPendingWork workHandler;
  private object workItem;
  private string identity;
  private Guid instanceId;
  private bool waitForIdle;

  public ExternalDataEventArgs(Guid instanceId)
    : this(instanceId, null, null, false) { }

  public ExternalDataEventArgs(Guid instanceId, IPendingWork workHandler,
                               object workItem)
    : this(instanceId, workHandler, workItem, false) { }

  public ExternalDataEventArgs(Guid instanceId, IPendingWork workHandler,
                               object workItem, bool waitForIdle)
  {
    this.instanceId = instanceId;
    this.workHandler = workHandler;
    this.workItem = workItem;
    this.waitForIdle = waitForIdle;
  }

  public string Identity
```

```
    {
      get { return this.identity; }
      set { this.identity = value; }
    }

    public Guid InstanceId
    {
      get { return this.instanceId; }
      set { this.instanceId = value; }
    }

    public bool WaitForIdle
    {
      get { return this.waitForIdle; }
      set { this.waitForIdle = value; }
    }

    public IPendingWork WorkHandler
    {
      get { return this.workHandler; }
      set { this.workHandler = value; }
    }

    public object WorkItem
    {
      get { return this.workItem; }
      set { this.workItem = value; }
    }
  }
```

As shown in the preceding example, ExternalDataEventArgs exposes the following public properties:

- **Identity:** Gets or sets a string that contains the identity (username) under which the external data exchange service runs the event handlers registered for the associated event and consequently the username under which the external data exchange service communicates with the HandleExternalEventActivity instance that is configured to handle the event. HandleExternalEventActivity first determines the roles that this identity is in and then determines whether this identity is in any of the roles that are allowed to communicate with HandleExternalEventActivity. HandleExternalEventActivity exposes a property of type WorkflowRoleCollection named Roles, which can be populated with a list of the roles that are allowed to communicate with HandleExternalEventActivity. Note that none of the constructors of ExternalDataEventArgs take the identity as its argument. This information is passed through setting the Identity property of ExternalDataEventArgs, which is a read-write property.
- **InstanceId:** Gets or sets a GUID that uniquely identifies the current workflow instance. When an external data exchange service raises an event, it passes the workflow instance ID as part of the ExternalDataEventArgs-derived object that it passes to the HandleExternalEventActivity instance configured to handle the event. The workflow run time uses the workflow instance ID to identify the workflow instance that contains the HandleExternalEventActivity instance configured to handle this event, and consequently the workflow instance ID enables the workflow run time to route the ExternalDataEventArgs-derived object to the correct workflow instance. Keep in mind that the same workflow run-time instance could handle numerous workflow instances.

- **WaitForIdle:** Gets or sets a Boolean that specifies whether to wait for the work flow instance to become idle before passing the ExternalDataEventArgs-derived object to the workflow instance. Internally, any external data such as an ExternalDataEventArgs-derived object is passed into a workflow instance through a call into the EnqueueItem method of the workflow instance. This method comes with two overloads:

```
public sealed class WorkflowInstance
{
  public void EnqueueItem(IComparable queueName, object item,
                          IPendingWork pendingWork, object workItem);
  public void EnqueueItemOnIdle(IComparable queueName, object item,
                                IPendingWork pendingWork, object workItem);
}
```

As the name suggests, the second overload waits for the workflow instance to become idle before it enqueues the data in the specified workflow queue.

- **WorkHandler:** Gets or sets the IPendingWork object that handles pending work items
- **WorkItem:** Gets or sets the pending work item

Also note that ExternalDataEventArgs exposes three public constructors:

- **ExternalDataEventArgs (Guid instanceId, IPendingWork workHandler, object workItem, bool waitForIdle):** This constructor takes four parameters — a GUID that uniquely identifies the workflow instance, an IPendingWork object that handles pending work items, a pending work item, and a Boolean that specifies whether to wait for the workflow instance to become idle. This constructor is used when an external data exchange service must pass data to the running workflow instance in transactional fashion. Discussion of IPendingWork and pending work items is deferred to a subsequent section in this chapter where you'll see an example of a transactional data exchange.
- **ExternalDataEventArgs (Guid instanceId, IPendingWork workHandler, object workItem):** This constructor takes three parameters — a GUID that uniquely identifies the workflow instance, an IPendingWork object that handles pending work items, and a pending work item. Note that this constructor simply delegates to the first constructor, passing in false for the fourth parameter. This constructor is used when an external data exchange service must pass data to the running workflow instance in transactional fashion but does not need to wait for the workflow instance to become idle.
- **ExternalDataEventArgs (Guid instanceId):** This constructor takes a GUID that uniquely identifies the associated workflow instance. This contructor simply delegates to the first constructor, passing in null, null, and false for the second, third, and fourth parameters, respectively. This constructor is used when an external data exchange service does not need to pass data to the running workflow instance in transactional fashion.

An external data exchange service interface may also be annotated with one or more instances of a CorrelationParameterAttribute metadata attribute to define one or more of what are known as *correlation parameters*. As mentioned earlier, a workflow uses a CallExternalMethodActivity instance to invoke a specific method of a specific external data exchange service. CallExternalMethodActivity normally passes the correlation parameter values into the associated method as its arguments when it invokes the method. Recall that a workflow uses a HandleExternalEventActivity instance to handle a specified event of a specified external data exchange service. The event data class associated with an external data exchange service event derives from ExternalDataEventArgs. This event data class normally exposes properties that contain the correlation parameter values. When the external data exchange service fires its event, it instantiates an instance of this ExternalDataEventArgs-derived event data class and populates its correlation parameter-related properties with the correlation parameter values before it finally passes this instance to HandleExternalEventActivity.

In summary, CallExternalMethodActivity passes the correlation parameter values to the external data exchange service when it is invoking its associated method. The external data exchange service, conversely, passes the correlation parameter values to HandleExternalEventActivity when it is firing its event. As you'll see later, these correlation parameter values are used to determine which messages exchanged between a running workflow instance and the external data exchange service map to which destination. This will all be clear by the end of this chapter.

So far, you've learned that hosting WF requires two fundamental steps. First, the host must instantiate the workflow run time. Second, the host must create the required local services, such as external data exchange services, and register them with the workflow run time. There is also a third requirement: The host must start the workflow run time.

The SharePoint object model comes with an internal class named SPWinOeHostServices that takes care of these three requirements and hosts the workflow run time. The constructor of this class is where all the action is, as shown in Listing 3-2. As you can see, this constructor takes an SPSite object that represents the current SharePoint site collection, an SPWeb object that represents the current SharePoint site, and an SPWorkflowManager object as its argument. As the name suggests, SPWorkflowManager manages workflow instances. Chapter 6 provides in-depth coverage of SPWorkflowManager.

Listing 3-2: The SPWinOeHostServices class

```
internal class SPWinOeHostServices : SPWorkflowHostServiceBase, IDisposable
{
  public SPWinOeHostServices(SPSite site, SPWeb web, SPWorkflowManager manager,
                             SPWorkflowEngine engine)
    : base("SPWinOeHostServices", site, web, manager, engine)
  {
    this.m_engine = engine;
    this.m_manager = manager;
    WorkflowRuntimeSection settings = new WorkflowRuntimeSection();
    settings.ValidateOnCreate = true;
    this.m_WinOeHostServices = new WorkflowRuntime(settings);
    SPWinOePersistenceService pservice =
                              new SPWinOePersistenceService();
    this.m_WinOeHostServices.AddService(pservice);
    pservice.Host = this;
    . . .
    this.m_WinOeHostServices.StartRuntime();
    this.m_WinOeHostServices.AddService(new SPWinOESubscriptionService(this));
    ExternalDataExchangeService service = new ExternalDataExchangeService();
    this.m_WinOeHostServices.AddService(service);
```

(continued)

Listing 3-2 *(continued)*

```
            service.AddService(new SPWinOETaskService(this));
            service.AddService(new SPWinOEWSSService(this));
            manager.OnStop += new SPWorkflowManager.StopHandler(this.Stop);
        }
    }
```

This constructor first instantiates a WorkflowRuntimeSection and sets its ValidationOnCreate property to true. When this property is true, the workflow validation logic executes every single time the CreateWorkflow method is invoked on the WorkflowRuntime and raises a WorkflowValidationFailedException exception if the validation fails:

```
WorkflowRuntimeSection settings = new WorkflowRuntimeSection();
settings.ValidateOnCreate = true;
```

The constructor then instantiates the WorkflowRuntime and stores it in a private field for future references:

```
this.m_WinOeHostServices = new WorkflowRuntime(settings);
```

Next, the constructor instantiates a SPWinOePersistenceService persistence service and registers it with the WorkflowRuntime:

```
SPWinOePersistenceService pservice = new SPWinOePersistenceService();
this.m_WinOeHostServices.AddService(pservice);
pservice.Host = this;
```

SharePoint uses this SPWinOePersistenceService persistence service to store workflow instances in the content database. This persistence service, like any other WF persistence service, inherits from the WorkflowPersistenceService base class. As you can see, SharePoint uses its own persistence service because the WF standard SqlWorkflowPersistenceService persistence service stores workflow instances in the WF standard SQL Server database. SharePoint, conversely, needs to store workflow instances in the content database. Persistence service is yet another example of the WF extensibility model, which enables the application hosting WF (SharePoint in our case) to use its own persistence service to persist workflow instances in the desired storage.

The constructor then starts the WorkflowRuntime instance:

```
this.m_WinOeHostServices.StartRuntime();
```

Next, it instantiates an ExternalDataExchangeService and registers it with the WorkflowRuntime instance. This ExternalDataExchangeService instance is used to register external data exchange services with the run time:

```
ExternalDataExchangeService service = new ExternalDataExchangeService();
this.m_WinOeHostServices.AddService(service);
```

It then instantiates the SPWinOETaskService and SPWinOEWSSService external data exchange services and registers them with the WorkflowRuntime instance:

```
service.AddService(new SPWinOETaskService(this));
service.AddService(new SPWinOEWSSService(this));
```

As the preceding discussion shows, an external data exchange service must be registered with the workflow run time via an ExternalDataExchangeService object. They should not be registered directly with the workflow run time. The reason for this is discussed later in this chapter. For now, understand that all external data exchange services are registered through the same ExternalDataExchangeService instance.

SPWinOETaskService is an external data exchange service that implements a single external data exchange service interface named ITaskService. SPWinOEWSSService, conversely, is an external data exchange service that implements three external data exchange service interfaces: ISharePointService, IListItemService, and IWorkflowModificationService. These four external data exchange service interfaces together facilitate a rich two-way communication between workflow activities and SharePoint hosting the workflow run time. The following sections provide in-depth coverage of these four external data exchange service interfaces.

The methods of your custom activities can access these SharePoint external data exchange services through the service provider, which is passed into the method as its argument as follows:

- When the WF scheduler invokes the execution methods of your custom activity, such as the Execute, Cancel, and HandleFault methods and event handlers registered for the Closed events of child activities, it passes an ActivityExecutionContext object into these methods as their argument. These methods can use the GetService generic method of this object to access these SharePoint external data exchange services.
- When the workflow run time invokes the Initialize and Uninitialize methods of your custom activity, it passes an IServiceProvider object into these methods as their argument. These methods can use the GetService method on this object to access these SharePoint external data exchange services.

ITaskService

As the name implies, the ITaskService external data exchange service interface defines the API that every task service must implement, as shown in Listing 3-3. A task service is an external data exchange service that manages workflow tasks for workflow instances. A workflow instance uses this service to create, update, delete, rollback, and complete SharePoint workflow tasks and to respond to the events raised when SharePoint workflow tasks are updated, created, or deleted.

Listing 3-3: The ITaskService interface

```
[ExternalDataExchange,
CorrelationParameter("taskId")]
public interface ITaskService
{
  [CorrelationAlias("taskId", "e.taskId")]
  event EventHandler<SPTaskServiceEventArgs> OnTaskChanged;

  [CorrelationAlias("taskId", "e.taskId")]
  event EventHandler<SPTaskServiceEventArgs> OnTaskCreated;

  [CorrelationAlias("taskId", "e.taskId")]
  event EventHandler<SPTaskServiceEventArgs> OnTaskDeleted;

  void CompleteTask(Guid taskId, string taskOutcome);

  [CorrelationInitializer]
  int CreateTask(Guid taskId, SPWorkflowTaskProperties properties,
              HybridDictionary specialPermissions);

  [CorrelationInitializer]
  int CreateTaskWithContentType(Guid taskId, SPWorkflowTaskProperties properties,
                             string taskContentTypeId,
                             HybridDictionary specialPermissions);

  void DeleteTask(Guid taskId);
  void RollbackTask(Guid taskId, string reason);
  void UpdateTask(Guid taskId, SPWorkflowTaskProperties properties);
}
```

Note that ITaskService, like any other external data exchange service interface, is annotated with the ExternalDataExchangeAttribute metadata attribute. Also note that ITaskService is marked with an instance of the CorrelationParameterAttribute metadata attribute, which defines a correlation parameter named taskId. As you'll see later in this chapter, correlation parameter values (in this case the task ID) are used to direct the incoming messages from an external data exchange service to the appropriate location within a workflow instance. An external data exchange service sends a message in the form of an ExternalDataEventArgs-derived object (which is of type SPTaskServiceEventArgs in the case of ITaskService) when it raises an event. This object, among other properties, exposes properties that contain correlation parameter values.

ITaskService exposes three events, which are annotated with the CorrelationAliasAttribute metadata attribute to create an alias for the taskId correlation parameter. In all three cases the correlation parameter is aliased to the taskId public field of the SPTaskServiceEventArgs object that the ITaskService object passes to the HandleExternalEventActivity instances configured to handle the respective event.

Note that the CreateTask and CreateTaskWithContentType methods are marked with the CorrelationInitializerAttribute metadata attribute to specify that these two methods initialize the taskId correlation parameter. Don't worry if you don't quite understand what a correlation parameter is and what role it plays. This will all be crystal-clear by the end of this chapter.

Here are the descriptions of the members of the ITaskService interface:

- **OnTaskChanged:** A task service raises this event when a SharePoint task is updated. A SharePoint task can be updated through the SharePoint user interface, object model, workflow activities, or web services.
- **OnTaskCreated:** A task service raises this event when a SharePoint task is created. A SharePoint task can be created through the SharePoint user interface, object model, workflow activities, or web services.
- **OnTaskDeleted:** A task service raises this event when a SharePoint task is deleted. A SharePoint task can be deleted through the SharePoint user interface, object model, workflow activities, or web services.
- **CreateTask:** This method creates a SharePoint task with a specified task ID (GUID), task properties (SPWorkflowTaskProperties), and permissions (HybridDictionary).
- **CreateTaskWithContentType:** This method creates a SharePoint task with a specified content type ID (string), task ID (GUID), task properties (SPWorkflowTaskProperties), and permissions (HybridDictionary). Recall that every workflow association is configured with a task list. A task list, just like any other SharePoint list, can support several content types. CreateTaskWithContentType enables a workflow to create a task with a specified content type. The respective task list of the workflow association from which the respective workflow instance is initiated must support the content type.
- **UpdateTask:** This method updates a SharePoint task with a specified task ID (GUID). The method takes a SPWorkflowTaskProperties that contains the names and new values of the properties of the SharePoint task.
- **RollbackTask:** This method rolls back a SharePoint task with a specified task ID (GUID) for a specified reason (string). Keep in mind that a SharePoint task is nothing but a list item in the task list associated with the workflow association from which the workflow instance is initiated. The SPListItem class exposes a collection property named Versions that keeps track of versioning. RollbackTask basically rolls back to the previous version of the task or list item.
- **DeleteTask:** This method deletes a SharePoint task with a specified task ID (GUID).
- **CompleteTask:** This method completes a SharePoint task with a specified task ID (GUID). The method takes a string parameter that contains the task outcome.

When the external data exchange task service — recall that this service is an instance of a class named SPWinOETaskService, which implements ITaskService — raises its OnTaskChanged, OnTaskCreated, or OnTaskDeleted event and consequently invokes the registered event handlers, it passes an SPTaskServiceEventArgs object into these event handlers. Listing 3-4 presents the public API of the SPTaskServiceEventArgs class.

Listing 3-4: The SPTaskServiceEventArgs class

```
public class SPTaskServiceEventArgs : ExternalDataEventArgs
{
  public SPWorkflowTaskProperties afterProperties;
  public SPWorkflowTaskProperties beforeProperties;
  public string executor;
  public Guid taskId;
}
```

Notice that SPTaskServiceEventArgs exposes the following four public fields, which are available to the event handlers for the OnTaskChanged, OnTaskDeleted, and OnTaskCreated events:

- **afterProperties:** An SPWorkflowTaskProperties dictionary that contains the names and values of the properties of the task after the event has occurred
- **beforeProperties:** An SPWorkflowTaskProperties dictionary that contains the names and values of the properties of the task before the event has occurred
- **executor:** A string that contains the identity or username under which the current code is executing
- **taskId:** A GUID that uniquely identifies the task

SPTaskServiceEventArgs, like the event data class associated with the events of any other external data exchange service, inherits from ExternalDataEventArgs.

In a typical scenario, a workflow first uses one or more CallExternalMethodActivity instances to invoke the CreateTask, CreateTaskWithContentType, DeleteTask, UpdateTask, RollbackTask, and/or CompleteTask methods, and then uses one or more HandleExternalEventActivity instances to handle the OnTaskChanged, OnTaskCreated, and OnTaskDeleted events.

A workflow must take the following steps to use a CallExternalMethodActivity instance to invoke the CreateTask, CreateTaskWithContentType, DeleteTask, UpdateTask, RollbackTask, or CompleteTask method:

- Instantiate a CallExternalMethodActivity instance:

```
CallExternalMethodActivity cemc = new CallExternalMethodActivity();
```

- Set the Name property of the CallExternalMethodActivity instance to a string value, which is unique within the scope of the instance's parent activity. The parent activity could be the workflow itself.

```
cemc.Name = "CallExternalMethodActivity1";
```

- Set the InterfaceType property of the CallExternalMethodActivity instance to the Type object that represents the type of the ITaskService interface:

```
cemc.InterfaceType = typeof(Microsoft.SharePoint.Workflow.ITaskService);
```

- Set the MethodName property of the CallExternalMethodActivity instance to the name of the ITaskService method. For example, set this property to the string "CreateTask" to configure the instance to invoke the CreateTask method:

```
cemc.MethodName = "CreateTask";
```

- Implement a method that takes two parameters and returns void. The first parameter must be of type System.Object, which is normally named "sender," and the second parameter must be of type ExternalDataEventArgs, which is normally named "e." Inside this method, populate the ParameterBindings public property with the WorkflowParameterBinding objects that represent the parameters of the method being invoked. For example, suppose the CallExternalMethodActivity instance is configured to invoke the CreateTask method. As Listing 3-3 shows, this method takes three parameters — taskId, properties, and specialPermissions — which are of type GUID, SPWorkflowTaskProperties, and HybridDictionary, respectively. In this case, the workflow must do the following:

```
private void MethodInvokingHandler(object sender, ExternalDataEventArgs e)
{
  WorkflowParameterBinding taskIdBinding = new WorkflowParameterBinding();
  taskIdBinding.ParameterName = "taskId";
  taskIdBinding.Value = Guid.NewGuid();
  ParameterBindings.Add(taskIdBinding);
  SPWorkflowTaskProperties properties = new SPWorkflowTaskProperties();
  properties.AssignedTo = "";
  properties.Description = "";
  properties.DueDate = DateTime.Now.AddDays(2);
  properties.EmailBody = "";
  properties.ExtendedProperties[""] = . . .;
  properties.HasCustomEmailBody = false;
  properties.OnBehalfEmail = "";
  properties.OnBehalfReason = "";
  properties.PercentComplete = 0.0;
  properties.SendEmailNotification = true;
  properties.StartDate = DateTime.Now.AddDays(1);
  properties.TaskItemId = 5;
  properties.TaskType = 7;
  properties.Title = "";
  WorkflowParameterBinding propertiesBinding = new WorkflowParameterBinding();
  propertiesBinding.ParameterName = "properties";
  propertiesBinding.Value = properties;
  ParameterBindings.Add(propertiesBinding);
  HybridDictionary specialPermissions = new HybridDictionary();
  specialPermissions[""] = . . .;
  specialPermissions[""] = . . .;
  WorkflowParameterBinding specialPermissionsBinding =
                                          new WorkflowParameterBinding();
  specialPermissionsBinding.ParameterName = "specialPermissions";
  specialPermissionsBinding.Value = specialPermissions;
  ParameterBindings.Add(specialPermissionsBinding);
}
```

- Register the preceding method as the event handler for the MethodInvoking event of the CallExternalMethodActivity instance:

```
cemc.MethodInvoking += MethodInvokingHandler;
```

  Note that the CallExternalMethodActivity instance fires this event right before it actually invokes the specified method. This allows the MethodInvokingHandler method to specify the values of the parameters of the method before it is invoked.

- Declare a public field of type CorrelationToken named correlationToken, instantiate a CorrelationToken instance, set the Name and OwnerActivityName properties of the instance, and finally assign the instance to the public field:

```
public CorrelationToken correlationToken;
. . .
correlationToken = new CorrelationToken();
correlationToken.Name = "MyToken";
correlationToken.OwnerActivityName = "MyActivity";
```

- The OwnerActivityName property is set to the name of the parent activity of the HandleExternalEventActivity instance, which could be the workflow itself.
- Assign the preceding public field to the CorrelationToken property of the HandleExternalEventActivity instance:

```
cemc.CorrelationToken = correlationToken;
```

- Use the Add method of the Activities property of the parent activity, which could be the workflow itself, to add the HandleExternalEventActivity instance as its child activity:

```
parentActivity.Activities.Add(cemc);
```

A workflow must take the following steps to use a HandleExternalEventActivity activity to handle the OnTaskChanged, OnTaskCreated, or OnTaskDeleted event:

- Instantiate a HandleExternalEventActivity instance:

```
HandleExternalEventActivity heea = new HandleExternalEventActivity();
```

- Set the Name property of the HandleExternalEventActivity instance to a string value, which is unique within the scope of the instance's parent activity. The parent activity could be the workflow itself:

```
heea.Name = "HandleExternalEventActivity1";
```

- Set the InterfaceType property of the HandleExternalEventActivity instance to the Type object that represents the type of the ITaskService interface:

```
heea.InterfaceType = typeof(Microsoft.SharePoint.Workflow.ITaskService);
```

- Set the EventName property of the HandleExternalEventActivity instance to the name of the ITaskService event. For example, set this property to the string "OnTaskChanged" to configure the instance to handle the OnTaskChanged event:

```
heea.EventName = "OnTaskChanged";
```

- Populate the ParameterBinding public property with the WorkflowParameterBinding objects representing the parameters that the external data exchange task service will pass along to the HandlerExternalEventActivity instance when it finally raises the event. Following the .NET event implementation pattern, the external data exchange task service passes two parameters, "sender" and "e," where the first parameter references the external data exchange task service itself and the second parameter references an SPTaskServiceEventArgs object that contains the event data:

```
WorkflowParameterBinding ebinding = new WorkflowParameterBinding();
ebinding.ParameterName = "e";
heea.ParameterBindings.Add(ebinding);
WorkflowParameterBinding senderbinding = new WorkflowParameterBinding();
senderbinding.ParameterName = "sender";
heea.ParameterBindings.Add(senderbinding);
```

  Note that the workflow does not set the Value properties of these WorkflowParameterBinding objects because the Value properties are dynamically set when the external data exchange task service finally raises the associated event.

- When the event is finally raised, the external data exchange task service instantiates an SPTaskServiceEventArgs object, populates the object with the event data, and passes the object along with a reference to the external data exchange task service itself to the HandleExternalEventActivity instance. This, in turn, assigns the SPTaskServiceEventArgs object to the Value property of the WorkflowParameterBinding whose ParameterName property was set to "e" and assigns the reference to the external data exchange task service to the Value property of the WorkflowParameterBinding whose ParameterName property was set to "sender."
- Implement a method that takes two parameters and returns void. The first parameter must be of type System.Object, which is normally named "sender," and the second parameter must be of type ExternalDataEventArgs, which is normally named "e":

```
private void InvokedHandler(object sender, ExternalDataEventArgs e)
{
  // Access the ParameterBindings public property and consume the event data
}
```

- Register the preceding method as event handler for the Invoked event of the HandleExternalEventActivity instance:

```
heea.Invoked += InvokedHandler;
```

  Note that when the external data exchange task service fires the event, the HandleExternalEventActivity instance in turn fires its own Invoked event and consequently invokes the InvokedHandler method, which in turn accesses the content of the ParameterBindings public property and consumes the event data.

Strictly speaking, you do not have to use the ParameterBindings public property because you can easily type-cast the ExternalDataEventArgs object passed into the InvokedHandler method to SPTaskServiceEventArgs type and directly access the event data.

- Declare a public field of type CorrelationToken named correlationToken and assign the same CorrelationToken object that was assigned to the associated CallExternalMethodActivity instance in the workflow instance:

```
public CorrelationToken correlationToken;
```

Keep in mind that in a typical scenario, a workflow first uses one or more CallExternalMethodActivity instances to invoke the CreateTask, CreateTaskWithContentType, DeleteTask, UpdateTask, RollbackTask, and/or CompleteTask methods, and then uses one or more HandleExternalEventActivity instances to handle the OnTaskChanged, OnTaskCreated, and OnTaskDeleted events. For example, the workflow may use a CallExternalMethodActivity instance to invoke the CreateTask method to create a new SharePoint task and then use a HandleExternalEventActivity instance to handle the OnTaskChanged event, which is raised when the same SharePoint task is updated.

- Assign the preceding public field to the CorrelationToken property of the HandleExternalEventActivity instance:

```
heea.CorrelationToken = correlationToken;
```

- Use the Add method of the Activities property of the parent activity, which could be the workflow itself, to add the HandleExternalEventActivity instance as its child activity:

```
parentActivity.Activities.Add(heea);
```

ISharePointService

SPWinOEWSSService implements three important external data exchange service interfaces named ISharePointService, IWorkflowModificationService, and IListItemService. It is possible to have an external data exchange service that implements several external data exchange service interfaces:

```
internal class SPWinOEWSSService : ISharePointService, IWorkflowModificationService,
                                   IListItemService, IEventProcessor
{
   . . .
}
```

This section covers the ISharePointService interface; the IWorkflowModificationService and IListItemService interfaces are covered in subsequent sections.

The ISharePointService external data exchange service interface (see Listing 3-5) defines the API that the SPWinOEWSSService external data exchange service implements. The external data exchange SharePoint service facilitates the communications between workflow activities and SharePoint facilities such as logging workflow history events into the workflow history list, updating workflow tasks, and sending e-mail.

Listing 3-5: The ISharePointService SharePoint service

```
[ExternalDataExchange,
CorrelationParameter("workflowId")]public interface ISharePointService
{
  [CorrelationAlias("workflowId", "e.workflowId"), CorrelationInitializer]
  event EventHandler<SPActivationEventArgs> OnWorkflowActivated;
  [CorrelationAlias("workflowId", "e.workflowId")]
  event EventHandler<SPItemEventArgs> OnWorkflowItemChanged;
  [CorrelationAlias("workflowId", "e.workflowId")]
  event EventHandler<SPItemEventArgs> OnWorkflowItemDeleted;

  [CorrelationInitializer]
  void InitializeWorkflow(Guid workflowId);
  void LogToHistoryList(Guid workflowId, SPWorkflowHistoryEventType eventId,
                        int userId, TimeSpan duration, string outcome,
                        string description, string otherData);
  void SendEmail(Guid workflowId, bool includeStatus,
                 StringDictionary headers, string body);
  void SetState(Guid workflowId, int index, int state);
  void UpdateAllTasks(Guid workflowId, SPWorkflowTaskProperties properties);
}
```

Notice the following important aspects of the ISharePointService external data exchange SharePoint service interface:

- It is annotated with the ExternalDataExchangeAttribute metadata attribute just like any other WF external data exchange service interface.
- It is annotated with a CorrelationParameterAttribute metadata attribute that defines a correlation parameter named workflowId.
- It exposes the following three events:
  - **OnWorkflowActivated:** The external data exchange SharePoint service raises this event when the current workflow instance is first initiated. A workflow instance can be initiated through the SharePoint user interface, the SharePoint object model, workflow activities, or SharePoint web services.
  - **OnWorkflowItemChanged:** The external data exchange SharePoint service raises this event when the SharePoint list item or document on which the current workflow instance is running is updated. This SharePoint list item or document can be updated through the SharePoint user interface, the SharePoint object model, workflow activities, or SharePoint web services.
  - **OnWorkflowItemDeleted:** The external data exchange SharePoint service raises this event when the SharePoint list item or document on which the current workflow instance is running is deleted. This SharePoint list item or document can be updated through the SharePoint user interface, the SharePoint object model, workflow activities, or SharePoint web services.

Note that all three events are annotated with the CorrelationAliasAttribute metadata attribute, which aliases the workflowId correlation parameter to e.workflowId, where "e" references the SPActivationEventArgs or SPItemEventArgs object that the external data exchange SharePoint service passes along to the HandleExternalEventActivity instance configured to handle the event. The SPActivationEventArgs and SPItemEventArgs event data classes are covered shortly.

- It exposes a method named InitializeWorkflow, which initiates the workflow instance with the specified instance id. This method takes a single parameter of type GUID, which specifies the workflow instance id. Note that this method is annotated with the CorrelationInitializerAttribute metadata attribute to mark the method as the initializer of the workflowId correlation parameter.
- It exposes a method named LogToHistoryList, which logs the specified workflow history event into the history list of the workflow instance with the specified instance id. This method takes the following parameters:
  - **workflowId:** Specifies the workflow instance id for logging the specified workflow history event
  - **SPWorkflowHistoryEventType:** An enumeration value that represents the type of the workflow history event to log. The following listing presents the possible values of the SPWorkflowHistoryEventType enumeration:

```
public enum SPWorkflowHistoryEventType
{
  None,
  WorkflowStarted,
  WorkflowCompleted,
  WorkflowCancelled,
  WorkflowDeleted,
  TaskCreated,
  TaskCompleted,
  TaskModified,
  TaskRolledBack,
  TaskDeleted,
  WorkflowError,
  WorkflowComment
}
```

  - **userId:** Specifies the user id under which to log the workflow history event
  - **duration:** Specifies the duration of the workflow history event
  - **description:** Describes the workflow history event to log
  - **outcome:** Specifies the outcome of the workflow history event
  - **otherData:** Specifies any other data associated with the workflow history event. SharePoint does not display this information to end users.
- **SendEmail:** This method sends an e-mail about the workflow instance with the specified instance id. The following describes the parameters of this method:
  - **workflowId:** Specifies the workflow instance id
  - **includeStatus:** Specifies whether to include the workflow status in the e-mail

- **headers:** A StringDictionary that contains the e-mail header names and values
- **body:** Specifies the body of the e-mail

- **SetState:** This method sets the status of the workflow instance with the specified instance id. This method takes the following parameters:
  - **workflowId:** Specifies the workflow instance id
  - **index:** Specifies the 0-based index of the workflow status column that appears in the SharePoint list or document library that contains the SharePoint list item or document on which the workflow instance is running
  - **state:** Specifies the status of the workflow
- **UpdateAllTasks:** This method updates all workflow tasks of the workflow instance with the specified instance id with the specified task properties. This method takes the following parameters:
  - **workflowId:** Specifies the workflow instance id
  - **properties:** A SPWorkflowTaskProperties collection that contains the task property names and values

Listing 3-6 presents the definition of the SPItemEventArgs event data class associated with the OnWorkflowItemChanged and OnWorkflowItemDeleted events. Note that SPItemEventArgs, like the event data class associated with the events of any other external data exchange service, inherits from ExternalDataEventArgs.

Listing 3-6: The SPItemEventArgs class

```
public class SPItemEventArgs : ExternalDataEventArgs
{
  public Hashtable afterProperties;
  public Hashtable beforeProperties;
  public Guid workflowId;
}
```

As shown in the preceding code, SPItemEventArgs exposes the following public fields:

- **afterProperties:** Gets a reference to the Hashtable that contains the field names and values of the SharePoint list item or document after the list item or document was updated or deleted
- **beforeProperties:** Gets a reference to the Hashtable that contains the field names and values of the SharePoint list item or document before the list item or document was updated or deleted
- **workflowId:** Gets a GUID that uniquely identifies the current workflow instance

As discussed earlier, the external data exchange SharePoint service exposes a method named UpdateAllTasks that enables a workflow to update all tasks in a workflow task list. This method takes a parameter of type SPWorkflowTaskProperties that contains the names and new values of the fields of the tasks being updated. Listing 3-7 presents the public API of this type.

Listing 3-7: The SPWorkflowTaskProperties class

```
public class SPWorkflowTaskProperties : SPAutoSerializingObject, ISerializable
{
  public SPWorkflowTaskProperties();
  public override void GetObjectData(SerializationInfo info,
                                     StreamingContext context);

  public string AssignedTo { get; set; }
  public string Description { get; set; }
  public DateTime DueDate { get; set; }
  public string EmailBody { get; set; }
  public Hashtable ExtendedProperties { get; }
  public bool HasCustomEmailBody { get; set; }
  public string OnBehalfEmail { get; set; }
  public string OnBehalfReason { get; set; }
  public float PercentComplete { get; set; }
  public bool SendEmailNotification { get; set; }
  public DateTime StartDate { get; set; }
  public int TaskItemId { get; set; }
  public int TaskType { get; set; }
  public string Title { get; set; }
  public Hashtable UpgradedPersistedProperties { get; }
}
```

Here are the descriptions of the properties of SPWorkflowTaskProperties:

- **AssignedTo:** Gets or sets a string that contains the user name to which the workflow task is assigned
- **Description:** Gets or sets a string that contains a short description about the assigned workflow task
- **DueDate:** Gets or sets a DateTime object that specifies when the workflow task is due
- **EmailBody:** Gets or sets a string that contains the body text of an e-mail to send
- **ExtendedProperties:** Gets a reference to the Hashtable that contains the names and values of the extended fields of the assigned task
- **HasCustomEmailBody:** Gets or sets a Boolean that specifies whether the task has a custom e-mail body text
- **PercentComplete:** Gets or sets a float value (between 0.0 and 1.0) that specifies what percentage of the task is completed. Set this property to 1.0 to mark the task as completed.
- **SendEmailNotification:** Gets or sets a Boolean that specifies whether to send an e-mail notification
- **StartDate:** Gets or sets a DateTime object that specifies when the task starts
- **TaskItemId:** Gets or sets an integer that uniquely identifies the assigned task
- **TaskType:** Gets or sets an integer that specifies the task type
- **Title:** Gets or sets a string that contains the title of the task

IListItemService

As discussed earlier, SPWinOEWSSService implements three important external data exchange service interfaces: ISharePointService, IWorkflowModificationService, and IListItemService:

```
internal class SPWinOEWSSService : ISharePointService, IWorkflowModificationService,
                                   IListItemService,IEventProcessor
{
  . . .
}
```

I covered the ISharePointService interface in the previous section. This section covers the IListItemService interface. This interface defines the API that the SPWinOEWSSService external data exchange list item service implements to provide list item services to workflow activities, including the following: checking in and out, copying, creating, deleting, and updating a list item; creating and updating a document and registering for list item events, such as adding an attachment to and deleting an attachment from a list item; and updating, checking in and out, deleting, creating, moving, and unchecking a list item, as shown in Listing 3-8.

Listing 3-8: The IListItemService list item service

```
[ExternalDataExchange,
CorrelationParameter("itemId"),
CorrelationParameter("listId"),
CorrelationParameter("id")]
public interface IListItemService
{
  [CorrelationAlias("listId", "e.listId"),
   CorrelationAlias("itemId", "e.itemId"),
   CorrelationAlias("id", "e.id")]
  event EventHandler<SPListItemServiceEventArgs> OnItemAttachmentAdded;

  [CorrelationAlias("itemId", "e.itemId"),
   CorrelationAlias("listId", "e.listId"),
   CorrelationAlias("id", "e.id")]
  event EventHandler<SPListItemServiceEventArgs> OnItemAttachmentDeleted;

  [CorrelationAlias("listId", "e.listId"),
   CorrelationAlias("itemId", "e.itemId"),
   CorrelationAlias("id", "e.id")]
  event EventHandler<SPListItemServiceEventArgs> OnItemChanged;

  [CorrelationAlias("listId", "e.listId"),
   CorrelationAlias("id", "e.id"),
   CorrelationAlias("itemId", "e.itemId")]
  event EventHandler<SPListItemServiceEventArgs> OnItemCheckedIn;

  [CorrelationAlias("listId", "e.listId"),
   CorrelationAlias("id", "e.id"),
```

(continued)

Listing 3-8 *(continued)*

```
 CorrelationAlias("itemId", "e.itemId")]
event EventHandler<SPListItemServiceEventArgs> OnItemCheckedOut;

[CorrelationAlias("itemId", "e.itemId"),
 CorrelationAlias("listId", "e.listId"),
 CorrelationAlias("id", "e.id")]
event EventHandler<SPListItemServiceEventArgs> OnItemCreated;

[CorrelationAlias("id", "e.id"),
 CorrelationAlias("itemId", "e.itemId"),
 CorrelationAlias("listId", "e.listId")]
event EventHandler<SPListItemServiceEventArgs> OnItemDeleted;

[CorrelationAlias("itemId", "e.itemId"),
 CorrelationAlias("listId", "e.listId"),
 CorrelationAlias("id", "e.id")]
event EventHandler<SPListItemServiceEventArgs> OnItemFileMoved;

[CorrelationAlias("id", "e.id"),
 CorrelationAlias("listId", "e.listId"),
 CorrelationAlias("itemId", "e.itemId")]
event EventHandler<SPListItemServiceEventArgs> OnItemUncheckedOut;

[CorrelationInitializer]
void CheckInListItem(Guid id, Guid listId, int itemId, string comment);

[CorrelationInitializer]
void CheckOutListItem(Guid id, Guid listId, int itemId);

[CorrelationInitializer]
void CopyListItem(Guid id, Guid listId, int itemId, Guid toList, bool overwrite);

[CorrelationInitializer]
int CreateDocument(Guid id, Guid listId, int itemId,
                   Hashtable itemProperties, byte[] fileContents);

[CorrelationInitializer]
int CreateListItem(Guid id, Guid listId, int itemId,
                   Hashtable itemProperties);

[CorrelationInitializer]
void DeleteListItem(Guid id, Guid listId, int itemId);

[CorrelationInitializer]
void InitializeForEvent(Guid id, Guid listId, int itemId);

[CorrelationInitializer]
void UndoCheckOutListItem(Guid id, Guid listId, int itemId);
```

```
    [CorrelationInitializer]
    void UpdateDocument(Guid id, Guid listId, int itemId,
                        Hashtable itemProperties, bool
                        overwriteFromTemplate,
                        byte[] fileContents);

    [CorrelationInitializer]
    void UpdateListItem(Guid id, Guid listId, int itemId,
                        Hashtable itemProperties);
}
```

IListItemService, like any other external data exchange service interface, is annotated with the ExternalDataExchangeAttribute metadata attribute to make it work with the HandleExternalEventActivity and CallExternalMethodActivity activities, as discussed later. IListItemService is also marked with three instances of the CorrelationParameterAttribute metadata attribute, which define three correlation parameters named itemId, listId, and id. These parameters, respectively, represent an integer that specifies a list item, a GUID that specifies a list, and a GUID reserved for internal use.

IListItemService contains the following events, where all these events are annotated with three instances of the CorrelationAliasAttribute metadata attribute. These instances, respectively, alias the itemId, listId, and id correlation parameters to e.itemId, e.listId, and e.id. Note that "e" represents the SPListItemServiceEventArgs object (see Listing 3-8) that contains the event parameters for these events:

- **OnItemAttachmentAdded:** The external data exchange list item service — which is an instance of the SPWinOEWSSService class that implements the IListItemService interface as discussed earlier — fires this event when an attachment is added to a SharePoint list item.
- **OnItemAttachmentDeleted:** The external data exchange list item service fires this event when an attachment is removed from a SharePoint list item.
- **OnItemChanged:** The external data exchange list item service fires this event when a SharePoint list item is updated.
- **OnItemCheckedIn:** The external data exchange list item service fires this event when a SharePoint list item is checked in.
- **OnItemCheckedOut:** The external data exchange list item service fires this event when a SharePoint list item is checked out.
- **OnItemCreated:** The external data exchange list item service fires this event when a SharePoint list item is created.
- **OnItemDeleted:** The external data exchange list item service fires this event when a SharePoint list item is deleted.
- **OnItemFileMoved:** The external data exchange list item service fires this event when a SharePoint list item is moved from the SharePoint list in which it resides into another SharePoint list.
- **OnItemUncheckedOut:** The external data exchange list item service fires this event when the checkout of a SharePoint list item is undone.

All the events of IListItemService have the same associated event data class named SPListItemServiceEventArgs, as shown in Listing 3-9. This event data class, like the event data class of any other external data exchange service, inherits from ExternalDataEventArgs.

Listing 3-9: The SPListItemServiceEventArgs event data class

```
public class SPListItemServiceEventArgs : ExternalDataEventArgs
{
  public Hashtable afterProperties;
  public Hashtable beforeProperties;
  public string executor;
  public Guid id;
  public int itemId;
  public Guid listId;
}
```

SPListItemServiceEventArgs exposes the following public fields:

- **afterProperties:** Specifies a Hashtable that contains the names and values of the associated SharePoint list item or document after the event was raised
- **beforeProperties:** Specifies a Hashtable that contains the names and values of the associated SharePoint list item or document before the event was raised
- **executor:** Specifies a string that contains the executor user id
- **id:** Specifies a GUID reserved for internal use
- **itemId:** Specifies an integer that uniquely identifies the associated SharePoint list item or document
- **listId:** Specifies a GUID that uniquely identifies the SharePoint list in which the associated SharePoint list item resides

The IListItemService list item service contains the following methods, where all methods are annotated with the CorrelationInitializerAttribute metadata attribute to mark them all as initializers of the correlation parameters itemId, listId, and id:

- **CheckInListItem:** This method takes the following parameters and checks in the specified SharePoint list item contained in the specified SharePoint list:
  - **id:** Specifies a GUID reserved for internal use
  - **listId:** Specifies a GUID that uniquely identifies the SharePoint list containing the SharePoint list item to check in
  - **itemId:** Specifies an integer that uniquely identifies the SharePoint list item to check in
  - **comment:** Specifies any comment to accompany the SharePoint list item check-in
- **CheckOutListItem:** This method takes the following parameters and checks out the specified list item contained in the specified SharePoint list:
  - **id:** Specifies a GUID reserved for internal use

- **listId:** Specifies a GUID that uniquely identifies the SharePoint list containing the SharePoint item to check out
- **itemId:** Specifies an integer that uniquely identifies the SharePoint list item to check out

- **CopyListItem:** This method takes the following parameters and copies the specified SharePoint list item contained in the specified SharePoint list:
    - **id:** Specifies a GUID reserved for internal use
    - **listId:** Specifies a GUID that uniquely identifies the SharePoint list containing the SharePoint list item to copy
    - **itemId:** Specifies an integer that uniquely identifies the SharePoint list item to copy
    - **toList:** Specifies a GUID that uniquely identifies the SharePoint list to which to copy the specified SharePoint list item
    - **overwrite:** Specifies whether to overwrite the list item that already exists in the target SharePoint list
- **CreateDocument:** This method takes the following parameters and creates a new document with the specified properties and content in a specified document library:
    - **id:** Specifies a GUID reserved for internal use
    - **listId:** Specifies a GUID that uniquely identifies the SharePoint document library in which to create the specified SharePoint document
    - **itemId:** Specifies an integer that uniquely identifies the SharePoint document to create
    - **itemProperties:** Specifies a Hashtable that contains the names and values of the properties of the document to create
    - **fileContents:** Specifies a byte array containing the content of the document to create
- **CreateListItem:** This method takes the following parameters and creates a new SharePoint list item with the specified properties in the specified SharePoint list:
    - **id:** Specifies a GUID reserved for internal use
    - **listId:** Specifies a GUID that uniquely identifies the SharePoint list in which to create the specified SharePoint list item
    - **itemId:** Specifies an integer that uniquely identifies the SharePoint list item to create
    - **itemProperties:** Specifies a Hashtable containing the names and values of the properties of the list item to create
- **DeleteListItem:** This method takes the following parameters and deletes the specified SharePoint list item from the specified SharePoint list:
    - **id:** Specifies a GUID reserved for internal use
    - **listId:** Specifies a GUID that uniquely identifies the SharePoint list containing the SharePoint list item to delete
    - **itemId:** Specifies an integer that uniquely identifies the SharePoint list item to delete

- **InitializeForEvent:** This method takes the following parameters and initializes the specified SharePoint list item residing in the specified SharePoint list for the specified event:
    - **id:** Specifies a GUID that uniquely identifies the event
    - **listId:** Specifies a GUID that uniquely identifies the SharePoint list containing the SharePoint item list to initialize for the event
    - **itemId:** Specifies an integer that uniquely identifies the SharePoint list item to initialize for the event
- **UndoCheckOutListItem:** This method takes the following parameters and undoes the checkout of the specified SharePoint list item in the specified SharePoint list:
    - **id:** Specifies a GUID reserved for internal use
    - **listId:** Specifies a GUID that uniquely identifies the SharePoint list in which the SharePoint list item whose checkout to undo resides
    - **itemId:** Specifies an integer that uniquely identifies the SharePoint list item whose checkout should be undone.
- **UpdateDocument:** This method takes the following parameters and updates the specified document in the specified document library:
    - **id:** Specifies a GUID reserved for internal use
    - **listId:** Specifies a GUID that uniquely identifies the SharePoint document library in which the SharePoint document to update resides
    - **itemId:** Specifies an integer that uniquely identifies the SharePoint document to update
    - **itemProperties:** Specifies a Hashtable containing the names and updated values of the document's properties
    - **fileContents:** Specifies a byte array that contains the updated content of the document
- **UpdateListItem:** This method takes the following parameters and updates the specified SharePoint list item in the specified SharePoint list:
    - **id:** Specifies a GUID reserved for internal use
    - **listId:** Specifies a GUID that uniquely identifies the SharePoint list in which the SharePoint list item to update resides
    - **itemId:** Specifies an integer that uniquely identifies the SharePoint list item to update
    - **itemProperties:** Specifies a Hashtable containing the names and updated values of the properties of the SharePoint list item to update

Using CallExternalMethodActivity and HandleExternalEventActivity Activities

In this section, we'll implement a custom composite activity named CreateListItemAndWaitForChange. This composite activity creates a SharePoint list item and then suspends its execution waiting for the list item to change before it resumes and completes its execution.

Launch Visual Studio 2008. Select File ⇨ New Project to launch the New Project dialog. Under Visual C# ⇨ Office Project types, select 2007, select SharePoint 2007 Sequential Workflow template, and click OK.

Select Add ⇨ New Item to launch the Add New Item dialog and then select Activity to add a new activity named CreateListItemAndWaitForChange. This custom composite activity inherits from the SequenceActivity activity to execute its child activities sequentially. Figure 3-1 shows this custom composite activity on the designer surface of Visual Studio. Currently, it contains no child activities.

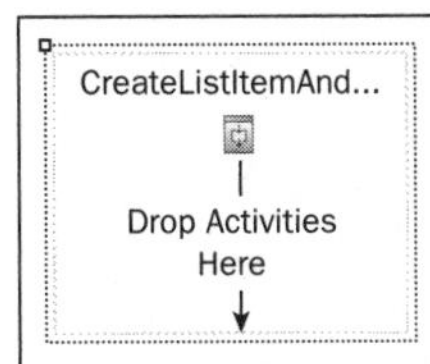

Figure 3-1

Drag a LogToHistoryListActivity activity from the toolbox and drop it inside the CreateListItemAndWaitForChange composite activity on the designer surface. We will use this activity to log a history event to the workflow history list, signaling that the execution of our custom activity has started when the logical program control finally reaches our custom activity and our custom activity starts its execution. You should follow this as a best practice in your own custom composite activities.

Click the LogToHistoryListActivity activity to view its properties in the Properties pane. Follow the steps discussed in the previous chapter:

- Add four public fields named Duration, HistoryDescription, HistoryOutcome, and OtherData, and a public property named UserId to our CreateListItemAndWaitForChange composite activity.
- Bind these fields to the Duration, HistoryDescription, HistoryOutcome, and OtherData bindable properties of the LogToHistoryListActivity activity, and the UserId public property to the UserId bindable property of this activity.

Note that we've made UserId a bindable public property, rather than a field, to enable the clients of our custom composite activity to set the value of this property through activity binding.

This will add the code shown in boldface to the CreateListItemAndWaitForChange activity:

```
public String HistoryDescription = default(System.String);
public TimeSpan Duration = default(System.TimeSpan);
public String HistoryOutcome = default(System.String);
public String OtherData = default(System.String);

[DesignerSerializationVisibilityAttribute(DesignerSerializationVisibility.Visible)]
[BrowsableAttribute(true)]
[CategoryAttribute("Misc")]
[DefaultValue(-1)]
[Description("Please specify the user ID.")]
public Int32 UserId
{
  get
  {
    return ((int)(base.GetValue(
              SharePointWorkflow1.CreateListItemAndWaitForChange.UserIdProperty)));
  }
  set
  {
    base.SetValue(
         SharePointWorkflow1.CreateListItemAndWaitForChange.UserIdProperty, value);
  }
}

private void InitializeComponent()
{
  . . .
  ActivityBind activitybind1 = new ActivityBind();
  ActivityBind activitybind2 = new ActivityBind();
  ActivityBind activitybind3 = new ActivityBind();
  ActivityBind activitybind4 = new ActivityBind();
  ActivityBind activitybind5 = new ActivityBind();

  activitybind1.Path = "Duration";
  activitybind1.Name = "CreateListItemAndWaitForChange";
  activitybind2.Path = "HistoryDescription";
  activitybind2.Name = "CreateListItemAndWaitForChange";
  activitybind3.Path = "HistoryOutcome";
  activitybind3.Name = "CreateListItemAndWaitForChange";
  activitybind4.Path = "OtherData";
  activitybind4.Name = "CreateListItemAndWaitForChange";
  activitybind5.Path = "UserId";
  activitybind5.Name = "CreateListItemAndWaitForChange";

  this.logToHistoryListActivity1.SetBinding(
             LogToHistoryListActivity.HistoryDescriptionProperty, activitybind2);
  this.logToHistoryListActivity1.SetBinding(
                         LogToHistoryListActivity.DurationProperty, activitybind1);
  this.logToHistoryListActivity1.SetBinding(
                  LogToHistoryListActivity.HistoryOutcomeProperty, activitybind3);
```

```
    this.logToHistoryListActivity1.SetBinding(
                        LogToHistoryListActivity.OtherDataProperty, activitybind4);
    this.logToHistoryListActivity1.SetBinding(
                           LogToHistoryListActivity.UserIdProperty, activitybind5);
    . . .
  }
```

Note that the UserId bindable property is annotated with the following design-time metadata attributes:

```
[DesignerSerializationVisibilityAttribute(DesignerSerializationVisibility.Visible)]
[BrowsableAttribute(true)]
[CategoryAttribute("Misc")]
[DefaultValue(-1)]
[Description("Please specify the user ID.")]
```

The BrowsableAttribute(true) design time metadata attribute instructs the designer to display this property and its value in the Properties pane. The CategoryAttribute("Misc") design-time metadata attribute instructs the designer to place this property under the Misc category in the Properties pane. The DefaultValue(−1) design-time metadata attribute instructs the designer to use −1 as the default value of this property. The [Description("Please specify the user ID.")] design-time metadata attribute instructs the designer to display the "Please specify the user ID" text when the property is selected in the Properties pane.

Be sure to annotate the bindable properties of your custom activities to enable users to experience your custom activities as they do standard WF and SharePoint activities.

Right-click the LogToHistoryListActivity activity and select Generate Handlers to generate an event handler for the MethodInvoking event of the LogToHistoryListActivity activity. Add the following code to this event handler:

```
private void logToHistoryListActivity1_MethodInvoking(object sender, EventArgs e)
{
  this.HistoryDescription = "Information";
  this.HistoryOutcome = "Activity named " + this.Name + " started!";
}
```

Because the LogToHistoryListActivity activity fires its MethodInvoking event right before it logs the history event to the workflow history list, this event handler is the best place to specify the values of those fields of our custom composite activity that are bound to the properties of the LogToHistoryListActivity activity. Keep in mind that the LogToHistoryListActivity activity basically logs the information content of its properties to the workflow history list.

Next, drag a CallExternalMethodActivity activity from the toolbox and drop it inside the CreateListItemAndWaitForChange activity on the designer surface, as shown in Figure 3-2.

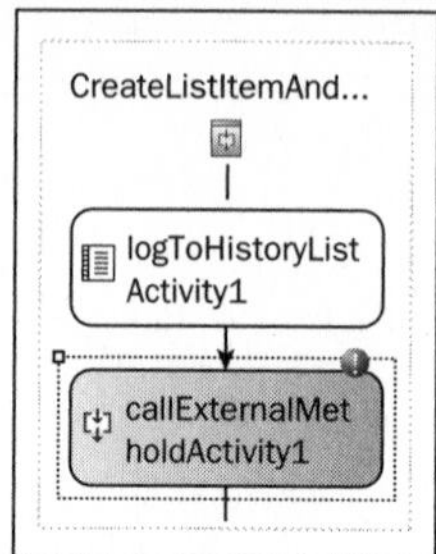

Figure 3-2

Click this activity to view its properties in the Properties pane, as shown in Figure 3-3.

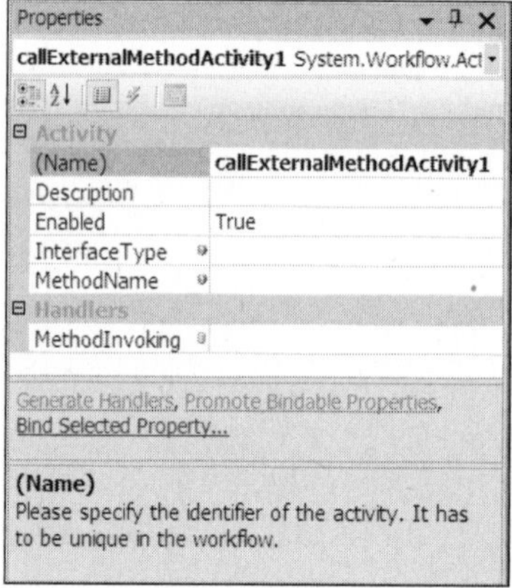

Figure 3-3

Click the InterfaceType property to make the button shown in Figure 3-4 visible.

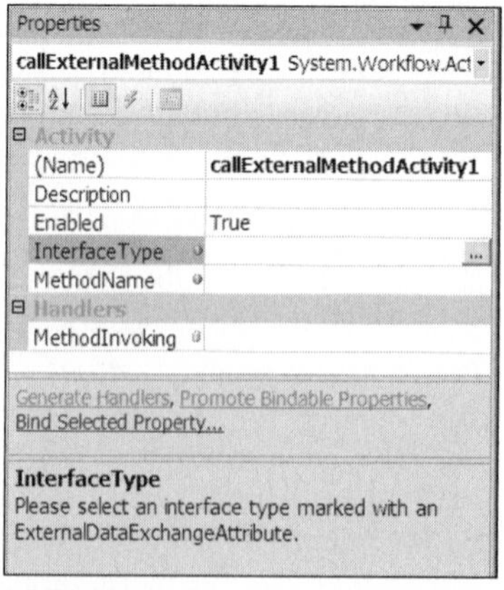

Figure 3-4

Click this button to launch the dialog shown in Figure 3-5. Click the Microsoft.SharePoint node on the left pane to view the list of SharePoint-specific local service interfaces that we've been discussing in this chapter.

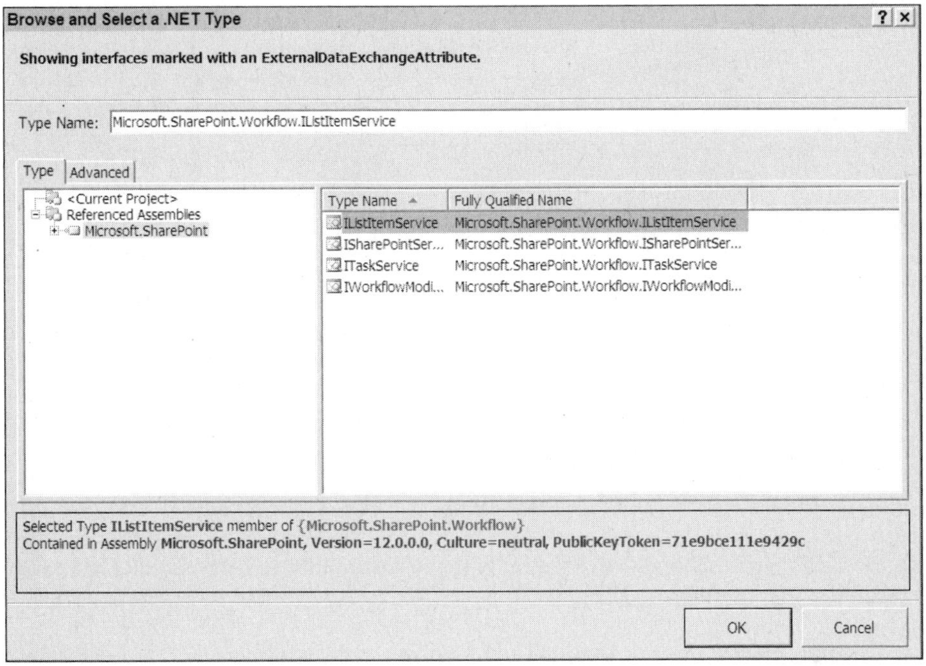

Figure 3-5

Select the IListItemService local service interface from this list and click OK. This will generate and add the following line of code to our custom composite activity. This line of code basically sets the value of the InterfaceType property of the CallExternalMethodActivity activity. This tells this activity that the method we want to invoke belongs to the SharePoint list item service:

```
this.callExternalMethodActivity1.InterfaceType =
                        typeof(Microsoft.SharePoint.Workflow.IListItemService);
```

Now, if you go back to the Properties pane, click the MethodName property, and check the drop-down list, you'll see that Visual Studio lists all the methods of the IListItemService interface in this drop-down list, as shown in Figure 3-6.

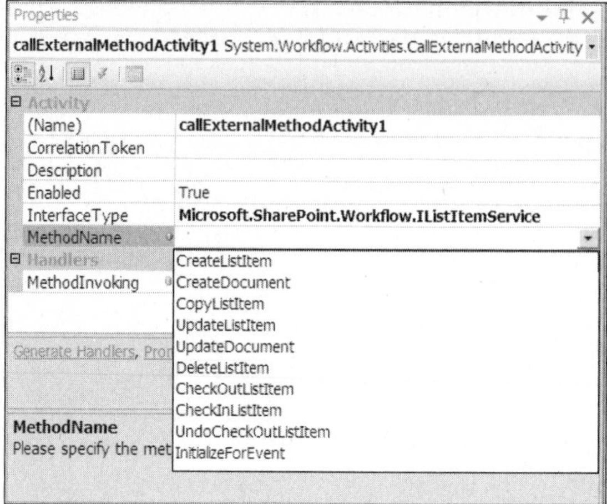

Figure 3-6

Select CreateListItem from this list. This will add the following line of code to our CreateListItemAndWaitForChange composite activity:

```
this.callExternalMethodActivity1.MethodName = "CreateListItem";
```

This tells the CallExternalMethodActivity activity that we want to invoke the CreateListItem method of the SharePoint list item service.

If you return to the Properties pane, you'll see that it displays the parameters of the CreateListItem method, as shown in Figure 3-7.

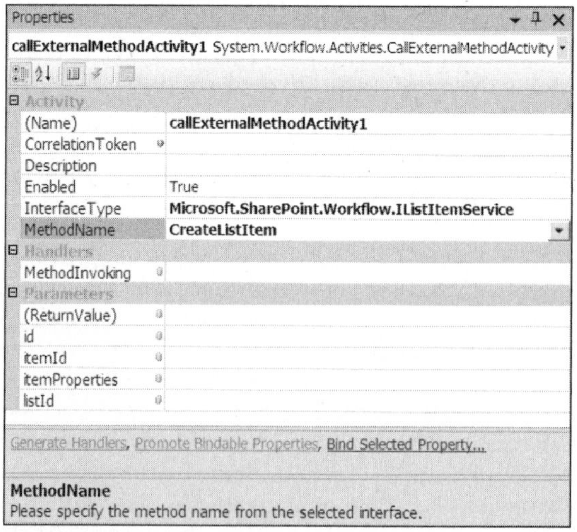

Figure 3-7

As expected, the CreateListItem method exposes four input parameters: id, itemId, itemProperties, and listId, and a return parameter. Use the steps discussed in the previous chapter to do the following:

- Add four bindable properties named Id, ItemId, ItemProperties, and ListId to our custom composite activity. Here is the definition of the ListId bindable property as an example:

```
public static DependencyProperty ListIdProperty =
              DependencyProperty.Register("ListId", typeof(System.Guid),
                                          typeof(CreateListItemAndWaitForChange));
[DesignerSerializationVisibilityAttribute(DesignerSerializationVisibility.Visible)]
[BrowsableAttribute(true)]
[CategoryAttribute("Parameters")]
[Description("Please specify the list ID.")]
public Guid ListId
{
  get
  {
    return (System.Guid)base.GetValue(
                              CreateListItemAndWaitForChange.ListIdProperty));
  }
  set
  {
    base.SetValue(CreateListItemAndWaitForChange.ListIdProperty, value);
  }
}
```

  We're making Id, ListId, ItemId, and ItemProperties properties bindable because we want to enable the clients of our custom composite activity to set the values of these properties through activity binding. Note that the Id, ListId, and ItemId properties are annotated with the appropriate design-time metadata attributes discussed earlier.

- Bind these four properties to the id, listId, itemId, and itemProperties parameters of the CreateListItem method. As an example, consider the code that binds the ListId property of our custom composite activity to the listId parameter of the CreateListItem method:

```
ActivityBind activitybind4 = new ActivityBind();
activitybind4.Name = "CreateListItemAndWaitForChange";
activitybind4.Path = "ListId";
WorkflowParameterBinding workflowparameterbinding4 =
                                        new WorkflowParameterBinding();
workflowparameterbinding4.ParameterName = "listId";
workflowparameterbinding4.SetBinding(
                          WorkflowParameterBinding.ValueProperty, activitybind4);
  this.callExternalMethodActivity1.ParameterBindings.Add(workflowparameterbinding4);
```

  This code fragment first instantiates an ActivityBind object and sets its Path property to the ListId bindable property and its Name property to the name of our custom composite activity because this activity owns the ListId property. It then instantiates a WorkflowParameterBinding object and sets its ParameterName property to the name of the parameter of the CreateListItem method to which the ListId property is to be bound, which is the listId parameter in this case. Next, this example invokes the SetBinding method on the WorklowParameterBinding object to bind the previous ActivityBind object to the ValueProperty of the WorkflowBinding object. This means that when the value of the ListId property of our custom composite activity is set or changed, this value is automatically assigned to the listId parameter of the CreateListItem method through activity binding. Finally, the WorkflowParameterBinding object is added to the ParameterBindings collection property of the CallExternalMethodActivity activity.

- ❑ Add a new field named ReturnValue to our custom composite activity:

```
public Int32 ReturnValue = default(System.Int32);
```

We're defining ReturnValue as a nonbindable field because the value of this field is used internally by our custom activity.

- ❑ Bind the ReturnValue field to the return value of the CreateListItem method:

```
ActivityBind activitybind1 = new ActivityBind();
activitybind1.Name = "CreateListItemAndWaitForChange";
activitybind1.Path = "ReturnValue";
WorkflowParameterBinding workflowparameterbinding1 =
                                           new WorkflowParameterBinding();
workflowparameterbinding1.ParameterName = "(ReturnValue)";
workflowparameterbinding1.SetBinding(
                            WorkflowParameterBinding.ValueProperty, activitybind1);
this.callExternalMethodActivity1.ParameterBindings.Add(workflowparameterbinding1);
```

This code fragment first creates an ActivityBind object and sets its Path property to ReturnValue, which is the name of the field that maps to the return value of the method, and set its Name property to the name of the class that owns this field, which is our custom composite activity. The example then creates a WorkflowParameterBinding object and sets its ParameterName property to the name of the parameter to which we would like to bind the ReturnValue field of our custom composite activity. In this case this parameter is the return value of the CreateListItem method.

Next, this code fragment invokes the SetBinding method on the WorkflowParameterBinding object to bind our ReturnValue field to the ValueProperty DependencyProperty of the WorkflowParameterBinding object. The ValueProperty basically maps to the parameter whose name is provided by the ParameterName property, which is the return value of the CreateListItem method in this case.

Finally, this WorkflowParameterBinding object is added to the ParameterBindings collection property of the CallExternalMethodActivity activity. This collection property basically contains all the WorkflowParameterBinding objects associated with the parameters of the method that the CallExternalMethodActivity activity is configured to invoke, which is the CreateListItem method in our case.

Next, we need to set the CorrelationToken property of the CallExternalMethodActivity activity. Back in the Properties pane, shown in Figure 3-8, enter a name for the correlation token and specify our custom composite activity as the owner activity.

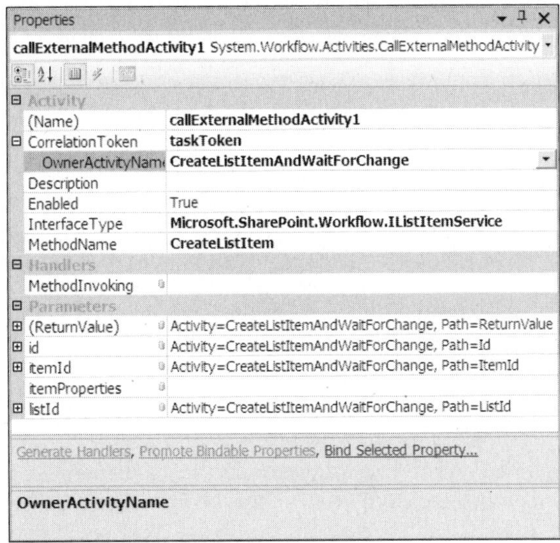

Figure 3-8

This will automatically generate and add the following code to our custom composite activity:

```
CorrelationToken correlationtoken1 = new CorrelationToken();
correlationtoken1.Name = "taskToken";
correlationtoken1.OwnerActivityName = "CreateListItemAndWaitForChange";
this.callExternalMethodActivity1.CorrelationToken = correlationtoken1;
```

This code fragment defines and instantiates a CorrelationToken object and sets its Name property to the name that we entered before, and sets its OwnerActivityName property to the name of our custom composite activity because we specified our custom composite activity as the owner activity. Finally, this CorrelationToken object is assigned to the CorrelationToken property of the CallExternalMethodActivity activity.

Next, right-click the CallExternalMethodActivity activity and select Generate Handlers to add the following handler:

```
private void callExternalMethodActivity1_MethodInvoking(object sender, EventArgs e)
{
  ItemProperties.Add("Title", "MyTitle");
}
```

Drag a HandleExternalEventActivity activity from the toolbox and drop it onto the designer surface as shown in Figure 3-9.

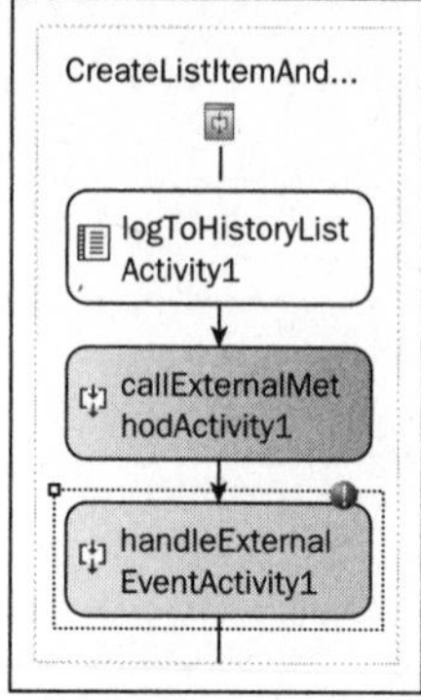

Figure 3-9

Next, we'll configure this HandleExternalEventActivity activity to suspend its execution and consequently the execution of our custom composite activity to wait for the SharePoint list item service to fire the OnItemUpdated event. The SharePoint list item service will fire this event after the list item (which the CallExternalMethodActivity activity created) is updated. Select the HandleExternalEventActivity activity to view its properties in the Properties pane, as shown in Figure 3-10.

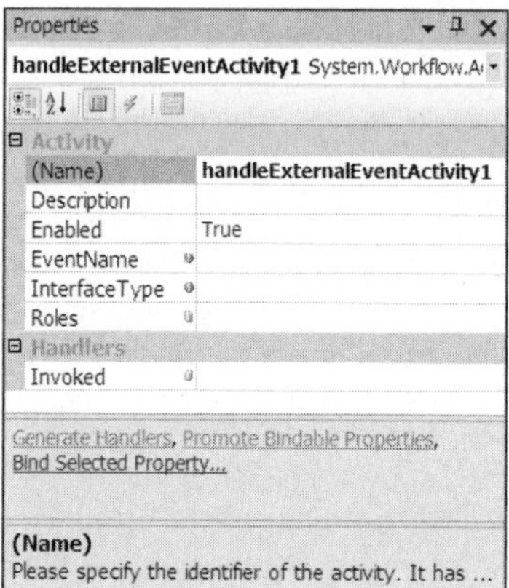

Figure 3-10

Follow the steps discussed earlier to set the value of the InterfaceType property to the Type object that represents the type of the IListItemService interface:

```
this.handleExternalEventActivity1.InterfaceType = typeof(IListItemService);
```

Note that the EventName drop-down list displays all the events that the IListItemService interface exposes, as shown in Figure 3-11.

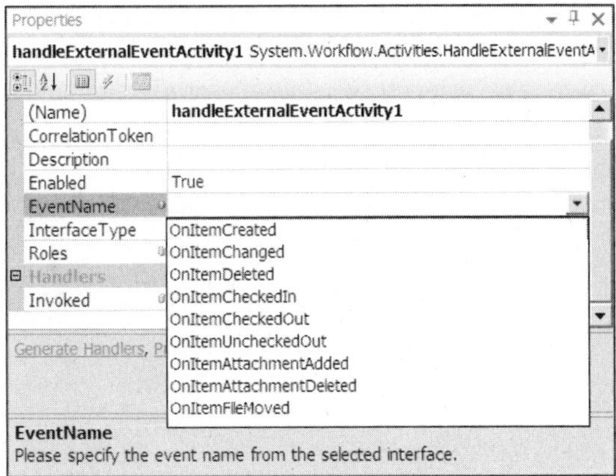

Figure 3-11

Select the OnItemChanged event from this list. This will automatically generate and add the following line of code to our custom composite activity:

```
this.handleExternalEventActivity1.EventName = "OnItemChanged";
```

Next, we'll set the CorrelationToken property of the HandleExternalEventActivity activity. Enter the same name that you entered for the CorrelationToken property of the CallExternalMethodActivity activity for the CorrelationToken property of the HandleExternalEventActivity activity (see Figure 3-12). This instructs Visual Studio to assign the same CorrelationToken object to the CorrelationToken property of the HandleExternalEventActivity that it assigned to the CorrelationToken property of the CallExternalMethodActivity. If you enter a different name for the correlation token property of the HandleExternalEventActivity activity, Visual Studio will generate a new CorrelationToken object and assign this new object to the CorrelationToken property of the HandleExternalEventActivity activity.

The net effect of assigning the same CorrelationToken object, which is assigned to the CorrelationToken property of the CallExternalMethodActivity activity, to the CorrelationToken property of the HandleExternalEventActivity activity is as follows: The HandleExternalEventActivity activity will only respond to the OnItemUpdated event that the SharePoint list item service fires when the list item, which the CallExternalMethodActivity activity created, is updated. It will not respond to the OnItemUpdated event that the SharePoint list item service fires when other list items are updated.

```
CorrelationToken correlationtoken1 = new CorrelationToken();
correlationtoken1.Name = "taskToken";
correlationtoken1.OwnerActivityName = "CreateListItemAndWaitForChange";
this.callExternalMethodActivity1.CorrelationToken = correlationtoken1;
this.handleExternalEventActivity1.CorrelationToken = correlationtoken1;
```

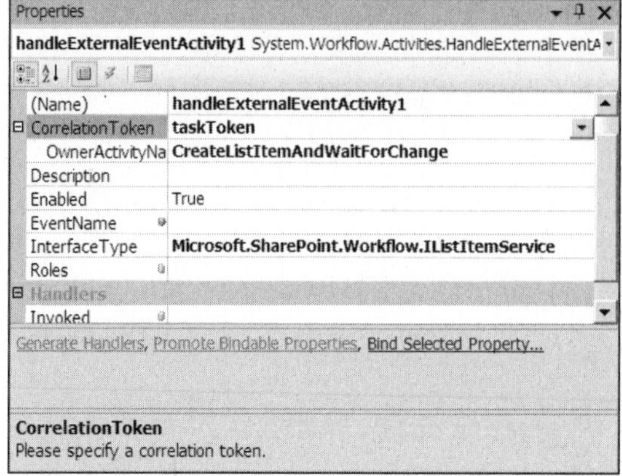

Figure 3-12

Next, drag a LogToHistoryListActivity activity from the toolbox and drop it onto the designer surface as shown in Figure 3-13.

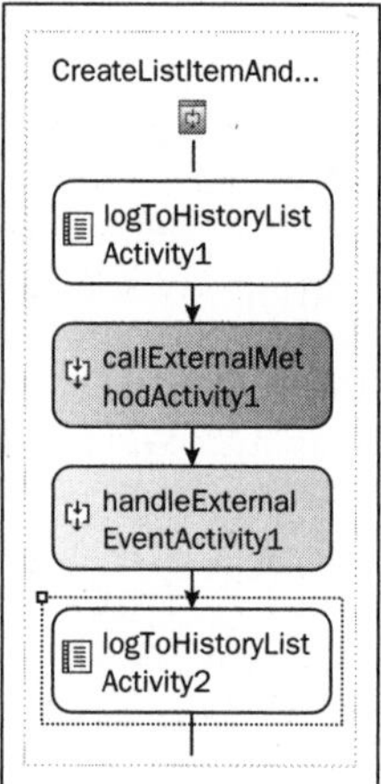

Figure 3-13

We'll use this activity to log a history event to the workflow history list to signal that our activity has completed its execution. To set the properties of this LogToHistoryListActivity activity, click the button in front of the HistoryDescription property to launch the dialog shown in Figure 3-14.

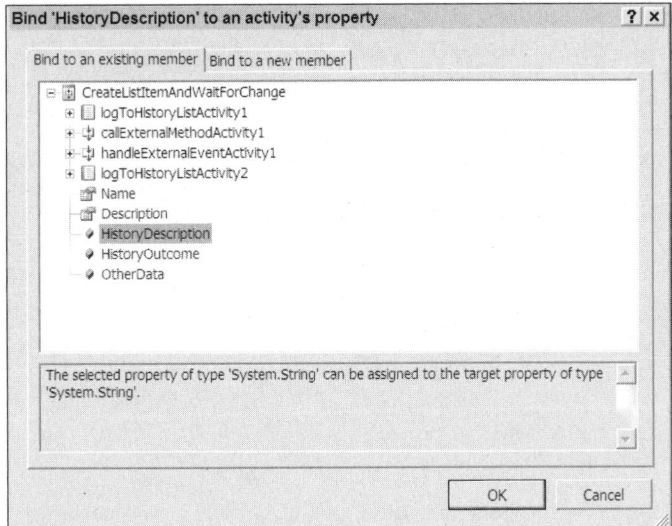

Figure 3-14

In this case we don't really need to create new fields in our composite activity. Instead, we'll reuse the existing fields. For instance, as Figure 3-14 shows, we bind the existing HistoryDescription field to the HistoryDescription property of the LogToHistoryListActivity activity. Do the same for the rest of the properties of this activity. This will generate the following code. Note that the same fields of the composite activity are bound to the respective bindable properties of this LogToHistoryList activity:

```
private void InitializeComponent()
{
  . . .
ActivityBind activitybind6 = new ActivityBind();
ActivityBind activitybind7 = new ActivityBind();
ActivityBind activitybind8 = new ActivityBind();
ActivityBind activitybind9 = new ActivityBind();
ActivityBind activitybind10 = new ActivityBind();

Activitybind6.Path = "Duration";
Activitybind6.Name = "CreateListItemAndWaitForChange";
Activitybind7.Path = "HistoryDescription";
Activitybind7.Name = "CreateListItemAndWaitForChange";
Activitybind8.Path = "HistoryOutcome";
Activitybind8.Name = "CreateListItemAndWaitForChange";
Activitybind9.Path = "OtherData";
Activitybind9.Name = "CreateListItemAndWaitForChange";
Activitybind10.Path = "UserId";
Activitybind10.Name = "CreateListItemAndWaitForChange";

this.logToHistoryListActivity2.SetBinding(LogToHistoryListActivity
    .HistoryDescriptionProperty, activitybind7);
```

(continued)

(continued)

```
    this.logToHistoryListActivity1.SetBinding(LogToHistoryListActivity
        .DurationProperty, activitybind6);
    this.logToHistoryListActivity1.SetBinding(LogToHistoryListActivity
    .HistoryOutcomeProperty, activitybind8);
    this.logToHistoryListActivity1.SetBinding(LogToHistoryListActivity
                                              .OtherDataProperty, activitybind9);
    this.logToHistoryListActivity1.SetBinding(LogToHistoryListActivity.UserIdProperty,
                                              activitybind10);

      . . .
    }
```

The following listing presents the content of the CreateListItemAndWaitForChange.cs file:

```
using System;
using System.ComponentModel;
using System.ComponentModel.Design;
using System.Collections;
using System.Workflow.ComponentModel;
using System.Workflow.ComponentModel.Design;
using System.Workflow.ComponentModel.Compiler;
using System.Workflow.ComponentModel.Serialization;
using System.Workflow.Runtime;
using System.Workflow.Activities;
using System.Workflow.Activities.Rules;

namespace SharePointWorkflow1
{
  public partial class CreateListItemAndWaitForChange : SequenceActivity
  {
    public CreateListItemAndWaitForChange()
    {
      InitializeComponent();
    }

    public String HistoryDescription = default(System.String);
    public String HistoryOutcome = default(System.String);
    public String OtherData = default(System.String);
    public TimeSpan Duration = default(System.TimeSpan);
    public Hashtable ItemProperties = new Hashtable();

    private void logToHistoryListActivity1_MethodInvoking(object sender,
                                                          EventArgs e)
    {
      this.HistoryDescription = "Information";
      this.HistoryOutcome = "Activity named " + this.Name + " started!";
    }

    public static DependencyProperty IdProperty =
              DependencyProperty.Register("Id", typeof(System.Guid),
                       typeof(SharePointWorkflow1.CreateListItemAndWaitForChange));
```

```
[DesignerSerializationVisibilityAttribute(
                                DesignerSerializationVisibility.Visible)]
[BrowsableAttribute(true)]
[CategoryAttribute("Parameters")]
public Guid Id
{
  get
  {
    return ((System.Guid)(base.GetValue(
             SharePointWorkflow1.CreateListItemAndWaitForChange.IdProperty)));
  }
  set
  {
    base.SetValue(
         SharePointWorkflow1.CreateListItemAndWaitForChange.IdProperty, value);
  }
}

public static DependencyProperty ItemIdProperty =
           DependencyProperty.Register("ItemId", typeof(System.Int32),
                   typeof(SharePointWorkflow1.CreateListItemAndWaitForChange));

[DesignerSerializationVisibilityAttribute(
                                DesignerSerializationVisibility.Visible)]
[BrowsableAttribute(true)]
[CategoryAttribute("Parameters")]
[Description("Please specify the item ID.")]
public Int32 ItemId
{
  get
  {
    return ((int)(base.GetValue(
        SharePointWorkflow1.CreateListItemAndWaitForChange.ItemIdProperty)));
  }
  set
  {
    base.SetValue(
     SharePointWorkflow1.CreateListItemAndWaitForChange.ItemIdProperty, value);
  }
}

public static DependencyProperty ListIdProperty =
            DependencyProperty.Register("ListId", typeof(System.Guid),
                   typeof(SharePointWorkflow1.CreateListItemAndWaitForChange));

[DesignerSerializationVisibilityAttribute(
                                DesignerSerializationVisibility.Visible)]
[BrowsableAttribute(true)]
[CategoryAttribute("Parameters")]
[Description("Please specify the list ID.")]
public Guid ListId
```

(continued)

(continued)

```
{
  get
  {
    return ((System.Guid)(base.GetValue(
       SharePointWorkflow1.CreateListItemAndWaitForChange.ListIdProperty)));
  }
  set
  {
    base.SetValue(
     SharePointWorkflow1.CreateListItemAndWaitForChange.ListIdProperty, value);
  }
}

public Int32 ReturnValue = default(System.Int32);

private void logToHistoryListActivity2_MethodInvoking(object sender,
                                                      EventArgs e)
{
  this.HistoryDescription = "Information";
  this.HistoryOutcome = "Activity named " + this.Name + " completed!";
}

private void callExternalMethodActivity1_MethodInvoking(object sender,
                                                        EventArgs e)
{
  this.ItemProperties.Add("Title", "MyTitle");
}

public static DependencyProperty UserIdProperty =
               DependencyProperty.Register("UserId", typeof(System.Int32),
                  typeof(SharePointWorkflow1.CreateListItemAndWaitForChange));

[DesignerSerializationVisibilityAttribute(
                                 DesignerSerializationVisibility.Visible)]
[BrowsableAttribute(true)]
[CategoryAttribute("Misc")]
[DefaultValue(-1)]
[Description("Please specify the user ID.")]
public Int32 UserId
{
  get
  {
    return ((int)(base.GetValue(
          SharePointWorkflow1.CreateListItemAndWaitForChange.UserIdProperty)));
  }
  set
```

```
        {
          base.SetValue(
           SharePointWorkflow1.CreateListItemAndWaitForChange.UserIdProperty, value);
        }
      }

      private void handleExternalEventActivity1_Invoked(object sender,
                                                         ExternalDataEventArgs e)
      {

      }
    }
  }
```

The following code listing presents the content of the CreateListItemAndWaitForChange.designer.cs file:

```
using System;
using System.ComponentModel;
using System.ComponentModel.Design;
using System.Collections;
using System.Drawing;
using System.Reflection;
using System.Workflow.ComponentModel;
using System.Workflow.ComponentModel.Design;
using System.Workflow.ComponentModel.Compiler;
using System.Workflow.ComponentModel.Serialization;
using System.Workflow.Runtime;
using System.Workflow.Activities;
using System.Workflow.Activities.Rules;

namespace SharePointWorkflow1
{
  public partial class CreateListItemAndWaitForChange
  {
    #region Designer generated code

    /// <summary>
    /// Required method for Designer support - do not modify
    /// the contents of this method with the code editor.
    /// </summary>
    [System.Diagnostics.DebuggerNonUserCode]
    private void InitializeComponent()
    {
      this.CanModifyActivities = true;
      System.Workflow.ComponentModel.ActivityBind activitybind1 =
                                  new System.Workflow.ComponentModel.ActivityBind();
      System.Workflow.ComponentModel.ActivityBind activitybind2 =
                                  new System.Workflow.ComponentModel.ActivityBind();
      System.Workflow.ComponentModel.ActivityBind activitybind3 =
                                  new System.Workflow.ComponentModel.ActivityBind();
      System.Workflow.ComponentModel.ActivityBind activitybind4 =
                                  new System.Workflow.ComponentModel.ActivityBind();
```

(continued)

(continued)

```
System.Workflow.ComponentModel.ActivityBind activitybind5 =
                            new System.Workflow.ComponentModel.ActivityBind();
System.Workflow.Runtime.CorrelationToken correlationtoken1 =
                            new System.Workflow.Runtime.CorrelationToken();
System.Workflow.ComponentModel.ActivityBind activitybind6 =
                            new System.Workflow.ComponentModel.ActivityBind();
System.Workflow.ComponentModel.WorkflowParameterBinding
  workflowparameterbinding1 =
               new System.Workflow.ComponentModel.WorkflowParameterBinding();
System.Workflow.ComponentModel.ActivityBind activitybind7 =
                          new System.Workflow.ComponentModel.ActivityBind();
System.Workflow.ComponentModel.WorkflowParameterBinding
  workflowparameterbinding2 =
               new System.Workflow.ComponentModel.WorkflowParameterBinding();
System.Workflow.ComponentModel.ActivityBind activitybind8 =
               new System.Workflow.ComponentModel.ActivityBind();
System.Workflow.ComponentModel.WorkflowParameterBinding
  workflowparameterbinding3 =
            new System.Workflow.ComponentModel.WorkflowParameterBinding();
System.Workflow.ComponentModel.ActivityBind activitybind9 =
                         new System.Workflow.ComponentModel.ActivityBind();
System.Workflow.ComponentModel.WorkflowParameterBinding
  workflowparameterbinding4 =
              new System.Workflow.ComponentModel.WorkflowParameterBinding();
System.Workflow.ComponentModel.ActivityBind activitybind10 =
               new System.Workflow.ComponentModel.ActivityBind();
System.Workflow.ComponentModel.WorkflowParameterBinding
  workflowparameterbinding5 =
              new System.Workflow.ComponentModel.WorkflowParameterBinding();
System.Workflow.ComponentModel.ActivityBind activitybind11 =
              new System.Workflow.ComponentModel.ActivityBind();
System.Workflow.ComponentModel.ActivityBind activitybind12 =
              new System.Workflow.ComponentModel.ActivityBind();
System.Workflow.ComponentModel.ActivityBind activitybind13 =
              new System.Workflow.ComponentModel.ActivityBind();
System.Workflow.ComponentModel.ActivityBind activitybind14 =
              new System.Workflow.ComponentModel.ActivityBind();
System.Workflow.ComponentModel.ActivityBind activitybind15 =
              new System.Workflow.ComponentModel.ActivityBind();
this.logToHistoryListActivity2 =
        new Microsoft.SharePoint.WorkflowActions.LogToHistoryListActivity();
this.handleExternalEventActivity1 =
         new System.Workflow.Activities.HandleExternalEventActivity();
this.callExternalMethodActivity1 =
                new System.Workflow.Activities.CallExternalMethodActivity();
this.logToHistoryListActivity1 =
        new Microsoft.SharePoint.WorkflowActions.LogToHistoryListActivity();
//
// logToHistoryListActivity2
//
```

```
            activitybind1.Name = "CreateListItemAndWaitForChange";
            activitybind1.Path = "Duration";
            this.logToHistoryListActivity2.EventId =
                Microsoft.SharePoint.Workflow.SPWorkflowHistoryEventType.WorkflowComment;
            activitybind2.Name = "CreateListItemAndWaitForChange";
            activitybind2.Path = "HistoryDescription";
            activitybind3.Name = "CreateListItemAndWaitForChange";
            activitybind3.Path = "HistoryOutcome";
            this.logToHistoryListActivity2.Name = "logToHistoryListActivity2";
            activitybind4.Name = "CreateListItemAndWaitForChange";
            activitybind4.Path = "OtherData";
            activitybind5.Name = "CreateListItemAndWaitForChange";
            activitybind5.Path = "UserId";
            this.logToHistoryListActivity2.MethodInvoking +=
               new System.EventHandler(this.logToHistoryListActivity2_MethodInvoking);
            this.logToHistoryListActivity2.SetBinding(Microsoft.SharePoint
      .WorkflowActions.LogToHistoryListActivity.HistoryDescriptionProperty,
      ((System.Workflow.ComponentModel.ActivityBind)(activitybind2)));
            this.logToHistoryListActivity2.SetBinding(Microsoft.SharePoint
      .WorkflowActions.LogToHistoryListActivity.HistoryOutcomeProperty,
      ((System.Workflow.ComponentModel.ActivityBind)(activitybind3)));
            this.logToHistoryListActivity2.SetBinding(Microsoft.SharePoint
      .WorkflowActions.LogToHistoryListActivity.OtherDataProperty,
      ((System.Workflow.ComponentModel.ActivityBind)(activitybind4)));
            this.logToHistoryListActivity2.SetBinding(Microsoft.SharePoint
      .WorkflowActions.LogToHistoryListActivity.UserIdProperty,
      ((System.Workflow.ComponentModel.ActivityBind)(activitybind5)));
            this.logToHistoryListActivity2.SetBinding(Microsoft.SharePoint
      .WorkflowActions.LogToHistoryListActivity.DurationProperty,
      ((System.Workflow.ComponentModel.ActivityBind)(activitybind1)));
            //
            // handleExternalEventActivity1
            //
            correlationtoken1.Name = "taskToken";
            correlationtoken1.OwnerActivityName = "CreateListItemAndWaitForChange";
            this.handleExternalEventActivity1.CorrelationToken = correlationtoken1;
            this.handleExternalEventActivity1.EventName = "OnItemChanged";
            this.handleExternalEventActivity1.InterfaceType =
                           typeof(Microsoft.SharePoint.Workflow.IListItemService);
            this.handleExternalEventActivity1.Name = "handleExternalEventActivity1";
            this.handleExternalEventActivity1.Invoked +=
         new System.EventHandler<System.Workflow.Activities.ExternalDataEventArgs>(
                                     this.handleExternalEventActivity1_Invoked);
            //
            // callExternalMethodActivity1
            //
            this.callExternalMethodActivity1.CorrelationToken = correlationtoken1;
            this.callExternalMethodActivity1.InterfaceType =
                         typeof(Microsoft.SharePoint.Workflow.IListItemService);
            this.callExternalMethodActivity1.MethodName = "CreateListItem";
            this.callExternalMethodActivity1.Name = "callExternalMethodActivity1";
```

(continued)

(continued)

```
            activitybind6.Name = "CreateListItemAndWaitForChange";
            activitybind6.Path = "Id";
            workflowparameterbinding1.ParameterName = "id";
            workflowparameterbinding1.SetBinding(
                  System.Workflow.ComponentModel.WorkflowParameterBinding.ValueProperty,
                  ((System.Workflow.ComponentModel.ActivityBind)(activitybind6)));
            activitybind7.Name = "CreateListItemAndWaitForChange";
            activitybind7.Path = "ItemId";
            workflowparameterbinding2.ParameterName = "itemId";
            workflowparameterbinding2.SetBinding(
                  System.Workflow.ComponentModel.WorkflowParameterBinding.ValueProperty,
                  ((System.Workflow.ComponentModel.ActivityBind)(activitybind7)));
            activitybind8.Name = "CreateListItemAndWaitForChange";
            activitybind8.Path = "ListId";
            workflowparameterbinding3.ParameterName = "listId";
            workflowparameterbinding3.SetBinding(
                  System.Workflow.ComponentModel.WorkflowParameterBinding.ValueProperty,
                  ((System.Workflow.ComponentModel.ActivityBind)(activitybind8)));
            activitybind9.Name = "CreateListItemAndWaitForChange";
            activitybind9.Path = "ReturnValue";
            workflowparameterbinding4.ParameterName = "(ReturnValue)";
            workflowparameterbinding4.SetBinding(
                  System.Workflow.ComponentModel.WorkflowParameterBinding.ValueProperty,
                  ((System.Workflow.ComponentModel.ActivityBind)(activitybind9)));
            activitybind10.Name = "CreateListItemAndWaitForChange";
            activitybind10.Path = "ItemProperties";
            workflowparameterbinding5.ParameterName = "itemProperties";
            workflowparameterbinding5.SetBinding(
                  System.Workflow.ComponentModel.WorkflowParameterBinding.ValueProperty,
                 ((System.Workflow.ComponentModel.ActivityBind)(activitybind10)));
            this.callExternalMethodActivity1.ParameterBindings.Add(
                                                     workflowparameterbinding1);
            this.callExternalMethodActivity1.ParameterBindings.Add(
                                                     workflowparameterbinding2);
            this.callExternalMethodActivity1.ParameterBindings.Add(
                                                     workflowparameterbinding3);
            this.callExternalMethodActivity1.ParameterBindings.Add(
                                                     workflowparameterbinding4);
            this.callExternalMethodActivity1.ParameterBindings.Add(
                                                     workflowparameterbinding5);
            this.callExternalMethodActivity1.MethodInvoking +=
              new System.EventHandler(this.callExternalMethodActivity1_MethodInvoking);
            //
            // logToHistoryListActivity1
            //
            activitybind11.Name = "CreateListItemAndWaitForChange";
            activitybind11.Path = "Duration";
            this.logToHistoryListActivity1.EventId =
               Microsoft.SharePoint.Workflow.SPWorkflowHistoryEventType.WorkflowComment;
            activitybind12.Name = "CreateListItemAndWaitForChange";
            activitybind12.Path = "HistoryDescription";
```

```
            activitybind13.Name = "CreateListItemAndWaitForChange";
            activitybind13.Path = "HistoryOutcome";
            this.logToHistoryListActivity1.Name = "logToHistoryListActivity1";
            activitybind14.Name = "CreateListItemAndWaitForChange";
            activitybind14.Path = "OtherData";
            activitybind15.Name = "CreateListItemAndWaitForChange";
            activitybind15.Path = "UserId";
            this.logToHistoryListActivity1.MethodInvoking +=
              new System.EventHandler(this.logToHistoryListActivity1_MethodInvoking);
            this.logToHistoryListActivity1.SetBinding(Microsoft.SharePoint
.WorkflowActions.LogToHistoryListActivity.HistoryDescriptionProperty,
((System.Workflow.ComponentModel.ActivityBind)(activitybind12)));
            this.logToHistoryListActivity1.SetBinding(Microsoft.SharePoint
.WorkflowActions.LogToHistoryListActivity.HistoryOutcomeProperty,
((System.Workflow.ComponentModel.ActivityBind)(activitybind13)));
            this.logToHistoryListActivity1.SetBinding(Microsoft.SharePoint
.WorkflowActions.LogToHistoryListActivity.OtherDataProperty,
((System.Workflow.ComponentModel.ActivityBind)(activitybind14)));
            this.logToHistoryListActivity1.SetBinding(Microsoft.SharePoint
.WorkflowActions.LogToHistoryListActivity.UserIdProperty,
((System.Workflow.ComponentModel.ActivityBind)(activitybind15)));
            this.logToHistoryListActivity1.SetBinding(Microsoft.SharePoint
.WorkflowActions.LogToHistoryListActivity.DurationProperty,
((System.Workflow.ComponentModel.ActivityBind)(activitybind11)));
            //
            // CreateListItemAndWaitForChange
            //
            this.Activities.Add(this.logToHistoryListActivity1);
            this.Activities.Add(this.callExternalMethodActivity1);
            this.Activities.Add(this.handleExternalEventActivity1);
            this.Activities.Add(this.logToHistoryListActivity2);
            this.Name = "CreateListItemAndWaitForChange";
            this.CanModifyActivities = false;

        }

        #endregion

        private Microsoft.SharePoint.WorkflowActions.LogToHistoryListActivity
                                        logToHistoryListActivity2;
        private HandleExternalEventActivity handleExternalEventActivity1;
        private CallExternalMethodActivity callExternalMethodActivity1;
        private Microsoft.SharePoint.WorkflowActions.LogToHistoryListActivity
                                        logToHistoryListActivity1;
    }
}
```

Now we will use the CreateListItemAndWaitForChange activity in a workflow and deploy this workflow to SharePoint. When you added the current project, it automatically added a workflow to the project. Go ahead and build the project so our custom composite activity shows up on the toolbox, as shown in Figure 3-15.

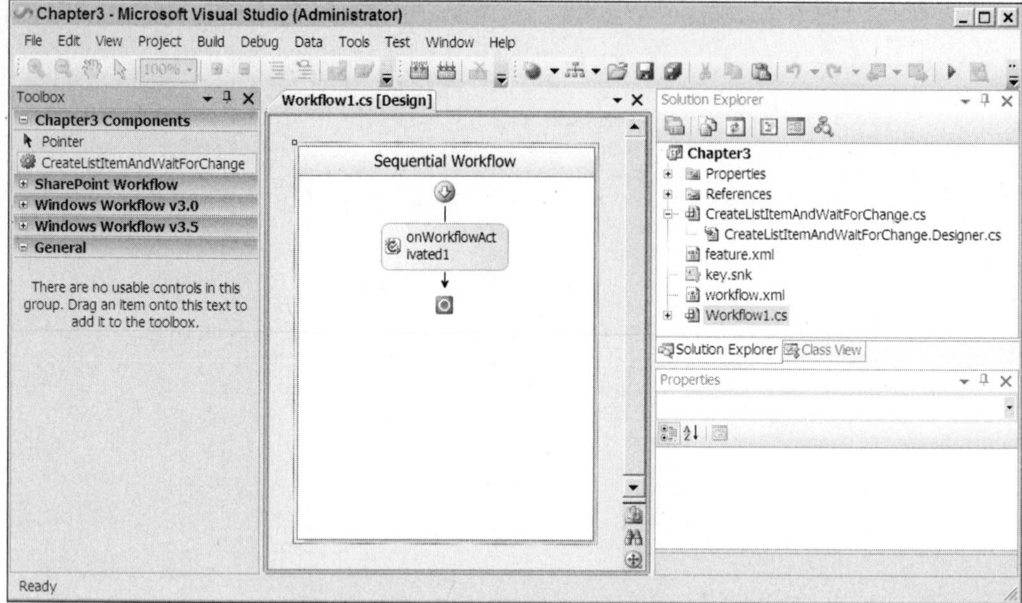

Figure 3-15

Drag and drop the CreateListItemAndWaitForChange custom composite activity below the OnWorkflowActivated activity, as shown in Figure 3-16.

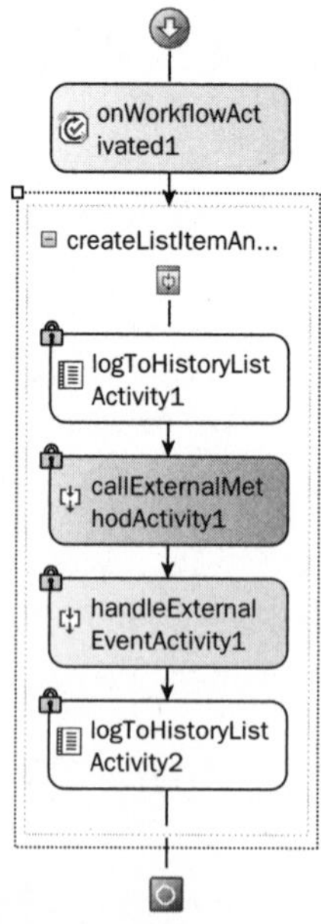

Figure 3-16

You should see the UserId, Id, ItemId, and ItemProperties bindable properties of the CreateListItemAndWaitForChange activity in the Properties pane, as shown in Figure 3-17.

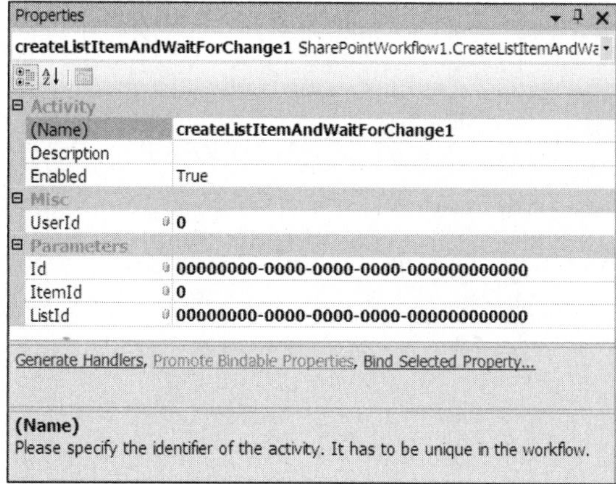

Figure 3-17

Click the UserId text box to make the button shown in Figure 3-18 visible.

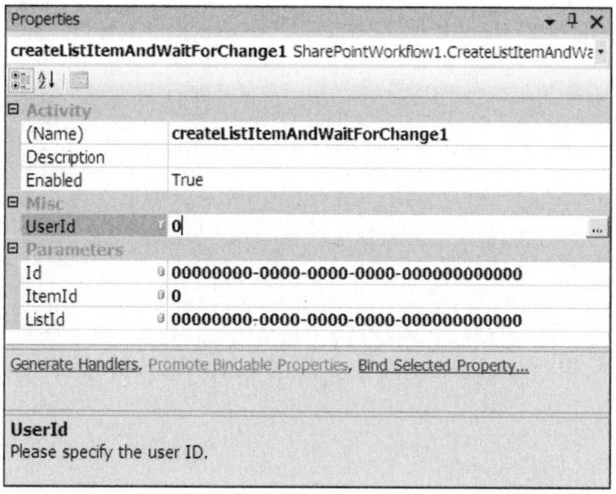

Figure 3-18

Note that the Properties pane displays the "Please specify the user ID" text that the DescriptionAttribute design-time attribute specifies. Click the button shown in Figure 3-18 to launch the dialog shown in Figure 3-19.

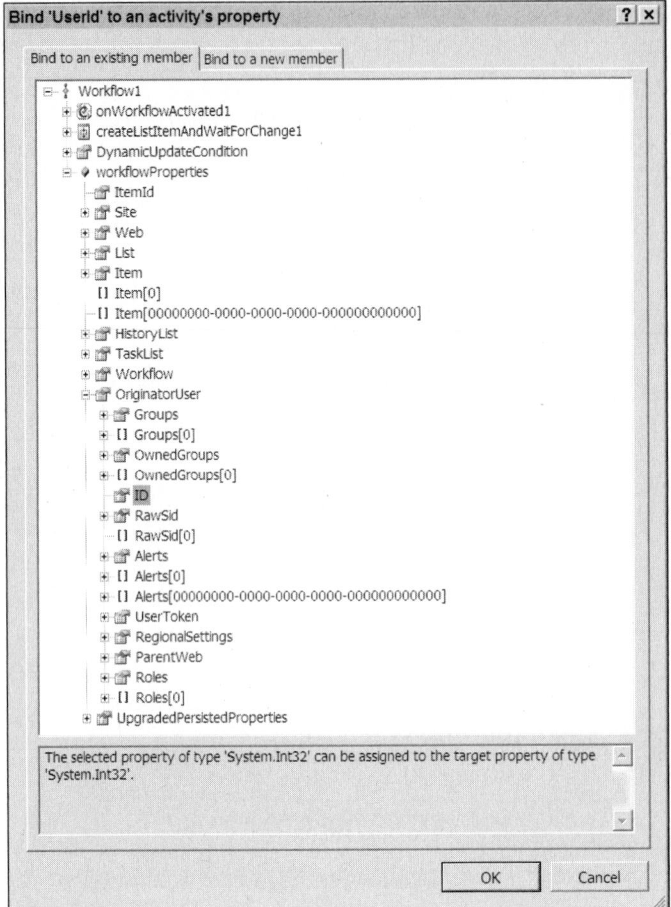

Figure 3-19

Select the ID property under OriginatorUser, which is under workflowProperties, to bind this property to the UserId property of the CreateListItemAndWaitForChange composite activity. This means that the UserId property will now automatically pick up the value of the ID property of the OriginatorUser property of the workflowProperties field of the workflow.

Next, we need to specify the values of the `Id`, ItemId, and ListId properties of the CreateListItemAndWaitForChange composite property. Because the `Id` property maps to the `id` parameter of the underlying CreateListItem method and because this parameter is reserved, it doesn't matter what value we assign to this property as long as we assign a value to it. We will use the same value for the `Id` and ListId properties. First, specify the value of the ListId property. This property basically specifies the GUID of the SharePoint list in which the CreateListItem method will create the new list item. We can use any SharePoint list we wish. In our example, we'll use the same SharePoint list in which the workflow will be running.

Click the ListId property in the Properties pane to make the button visible and click this button to launch the dialog shown in Figure 3-20.

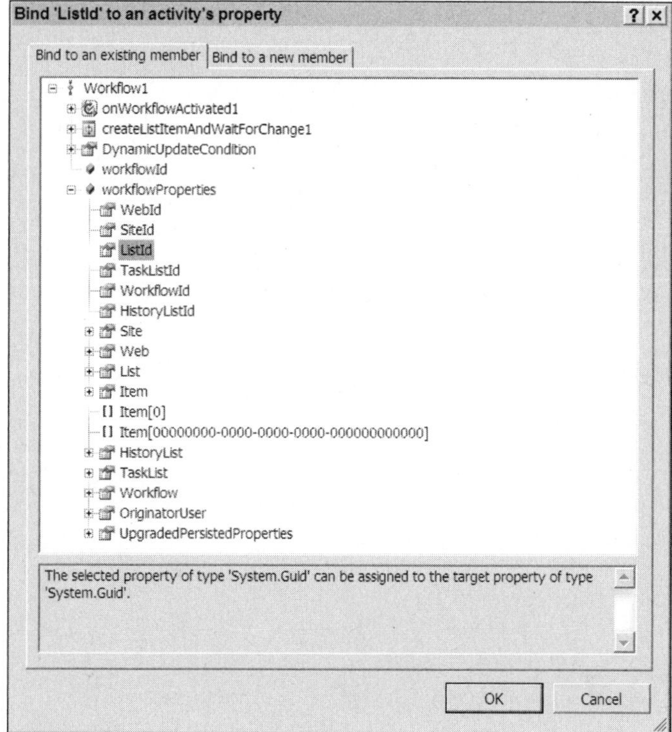

Figure 3-20

Select the ListId property of the workflowProperties field of the workflow. This property contains the ID of the SharePoint list in which the workflow is running. Click OK to bind this ListId property to the ListId property of the CreateListItemAndWaitForChange composite activity. This means that the ListId property of this activity will automatically pick up the value of the ListId property of the workflowProperties field.

Follow the same steps to bind the ListId property of the workflowProperties field to the Id property of the CreateListItemAndWaitForChange composite activity.

Set the ItemId property of the CreateListItemAndWaitForChange composite activity to an integer value. This value must be a value greater than the ID of existing list items in the SharePoint list. You can easily see the ID of the existing list items by turning on the ID column of the list through the SharePoint user interface. As you can see, we're hard-coding the value of the ID in this example to keep our discussions focused.

The following code listing presents the content of the workflow1.cs file:

```
using System;
using System.ComponentModel;
using System.ComponentModel.Design;
using System.Collections;
using System.Drawing;
using System.Linq;
using System.Workflow.ComponentModel.Compiler;
using System.Workflow.ComponentModel.Serialization;
using System.Workflow.ComponentModel;
using System.Workflow.ComponentModel.Design;
using System.Workflow.Runtime;
using System.Workflow.Activities;
using System.Workflow.Activities.Rules;
using Microsoft.SharePoint;
using Microsoft.SharePoint.Workflow;
using Microsoft.SharePoint.WorkflowActions;
using Microsoft.Office.Workflow.Utility;

namespace SharePointWorkflow1
{
  public sealed partial class Workflow1 : SequentialWorkflowActivity
  {
    public Workflow1()
    {
      InitializeComponent();
    }

    public Guid workflowId = default(System.Guid);
    public SPWorkflowActivationProperties workflowProperties =
                                        new SPWorkflowActivationProperties();
    public String HistoryDescription = default(System.String);
    public String HistoryOutcome = default(System.String);
    public String OtherData = default(System.String);

    private void logToHistoryListActivity1_MethodInvoking(object sender,
                                                          EventArgs e)
    {
      LogToHistoryListActivity log = sender as LogToHistoryListActivity;
      FaultHandlerActivity handler = log.Parent as FaultHandlerActivity;
      Exception fault = handler.Fault;
      this.HistoryDescription = fault.Message;
      this.HistoryOutcome = fault.StackTrace;
    }

    private void onWorkflowActivated1_Invoked(object sender,
                                        ExternalDataEventArgs e)
    {
    }
  }
}
```

The following code listing presents the content of the workflow1.designer.cs file:

```
using System;
using System.ComponentModel;
using System.ComponentModel.Design;
using System.Collections;
using System.Drawing;
using System.Reflection;
using System.Workflow.ComponentModel.Compiler;
using System.Workflow.ComponentModel.Serialization;
using System.Workflow.ComponentModel;
using System.Workflow.ComponentModel.Design;
using System.Workflow.Runtime;
using System.Workflow.Activities;
using System.Workflow.Activities.Rules;

namespace SharePointWorkflow1
{
  public sealed partial class Workflow1
  {
    #region Designer generated code

    /// <summary>
    /// Required method for Designer support - do not modify
    /// the contents of this method with the code editor.
    /// </summary>
    [System.Diagnostics.DebuggerNonUserCode]
    private void InitializeComponent()
    {
      this.CanModifyActivities = true;
      System.Workflow.ComponentModel.ActivityBind activitybind1 =
                              new System.Workflow.ComponentModel.ActivityBind();
      System.Workflow.ComponentModel.ActivityBind activitybind2 =
                              new System.Workflow.ComponentModel.ActivityBind();
      System.Workflow.ComponentModel.ActivityBind activitybind3 =
                              new System.Workflow.ComponentModel.ActivityBind();
      System.Workflow.ComponentModel.ActivityBind activitybind4 =
                              new System.Workflow.ComponentModel.ActivityBind();
      System.Workflow.ComponentModel.ActivityBind activitybind5 =
                              new System.Workflow.ComponentModel.ActivityBind();
      System.Workflow.ComponentModel.ActivityBind activitybind6 =
                              new System.Workflow.ComponentModel.ActivityBind();
      System.Workflow.ComponentModel.ActivityBind activitybind7 =
                              new System.Workflow.ComponentModel.ActivityBind();
      System.Workflow.ComponentModel.ActivityBind activitybind9 =
                              new System.Workflow.ComponentModel.ActivityBind();
      System.Workflow.Runtime.CorrelationToken correlationtoken1 =
                              new System.Workflow.Runtime.CorrelationToken();
      System.Workflow.ComponentModel.ActivityBind activitybind8 =
                              new System.Workflow.ComponentModel.ActivityBind();
      this.logToHistoryListActivity1 =
              new Microsoft.SharePoint.WorkflowActions.LogToHistoryListActivity();
```

(continued)

(continued)

```
        this.faultHandlerActivity1 =
                        new System.Workflow.ComponentModel.FaultHandlerActivity();
        this.faultHandlersActivity1 =
                        new System.Workflow.ComponentModel.FaultHandlersActivity();
        this.createListItemAndWaitForChange =
                        new SharePointWorkflow1.CreateListItemAndWaitForChange();
        this.onWorkflowActivated1 =
                        new Microsoft.SharePoint.WorkflowActions
                        OnWorkflowActivated();
        //
        // logToHistoryListActivity1
        //
        this.logToHistoryListActivity1.Duration =
                    System.TimeSpan.Parse("-10675199.02:48:05.4775808");
        this.logToHistoryListActivity1.EventId =
          Microsoft.SharePoint.Workflow.SPWorkflowHistoryEventType.WorkflowComment;
        activitybind1.Name = "Workflow1";
        activitybind1.Path = "HistoryDescription";
        activitybind2.Name = "Workflow1";
        activitybind2.Path = "HistoryOutcome";
        this.logToHistoryListActivity1.Name = "logToHistoryListActivity1";
        activitybind3.Name = "Workflow1";
        activitybind3.Path = "OtherData";
        activitybind4.Name = "Workflow1";
        activitybind4.Path = "workflowProperties.OriginatorUser.ID";
        this.logToHistoryListActivity1.MethodInvoking +=
           new System.EventHandler(this.logToHistoryListActivity1_MethodInvoking);
        this.logToHistoryListActivity1.SetBinding(Microsoft.SharePoint
.WorkflowActions.LogToHistoryListActivity.HistoryDescriptionProperty,
((System.Workflow.ComponentModel.ActivityBind)(activitybind1)));
        this.logToHistoryListActivity1.SetBinding(Microsoft.SharePoint
.WorkflowActions.LogToHistoryListActivity.HistoryOutcomeProperty,
((System.Workflow.ComponentModel.ActivityBind)(activitybind2)));
        this.logToHistoryListActivity1.SetBinding(Microsoft.SharePoint
.WorkflowActions.LogToHistoryListActivity.OtherDataProperty,
((System.Workflow.ComponentModel.ActivityBind)(activitybind3)));
        this.logToHistoryListActivity1.SetBinding(Microsoft.SharePoint
.WorkflowActions.LogToHistoryListActivity.UserIdProperty,
((System.Workflow.ComponentModel.ActivityBind)(activitybind4)));
        //
        // faultHandlerActivity1
        //
        this.faultHandlerActivity1.Activities.Add(this.logToHistoryListActivity1);
        this.faultHandlerActivity1.FaultType = typeof(System.Exception);
        this.faultHandlerActivity1.Name = "faultHandlerActivity1";
        //
        // faultHandlersActivity1
        //
        this.faultHandlersActivity1.Activities.Add(this.faultHandlerActivity1);
        this.faultHandlersActivity1.Name = "faultHandlersActivity1";
        //
        // createListItemAndWaitForChange
        //
```

```
            activitybind5.Name = "Workflow1";
            activitybind5.Path = "workflowProperties.ListId";
            this.createListItemAndWaitForChange.ItemId = 8;
            activitybind6.Name = "Workflow1";
            activitybind6.Path = "workflowProperties.ListId";
            this.createListItemAndWaitForChange.Name = "createListItemAndWaitForChange";
            activitybind7.Name = "Workflow1";
            activitybind7.Path = "workflowProperties.OriginatorUser.ID";
            this.createListItemAndWaitForChange.SetBinding(SharePointWorkflow1
.CreateListItemAndWaitForChange.UserIdProperty,
((System.Workflow.ComponentModel.ActivityBind)(activitybind7)));
            this.createListItemAndWaitForChange.SetBinding(SharePointWorkflow1
.CreateListItemAndWaitForChange.IdProperty,
((System.Workflow.ComponentModel.ActivityBind)(activitybind5)));
            this.createListItemAndWaitForChange.SetBinding(SharePointWorkflow1
.CreateListItemAndWaitForChange.ListIdProperty,
((System.Workflow.ComponentModel.ActivityBind)(activitybind6)));
            activitybind9.Name = "Workflow1";
            activitybind9.Path = "workflowId";
            //
            // onWorkflowActivated1
            //
            correlationtoken1.Name = "workflowToken";
            correlationtoken1.OwnerActivityName = "Workflow1";
            this.onWorkflowActivated1.CorrelationToken = correlationtoken1;
            this.onWorkflowActivated1.EventName = "OnWorkflowActivated";
            this.onWorkflowActivated1.Name = "onWorkflowActivated1";
            activitybind8.Name = "Workflow1";
            activitybind8.Path = "workflowProperties";
            this.onWorkflowActivated1.Invoked +=
                new System.EventHandler<System.Workflow.Activities.ExternalDataEventArgs>(
                                              this.onWorkflowActivated1_Invoked);
            this.onWorkflowActivated1.SetBinding(Microsoft.SharePoint.WorkflowActions
.OnWorkflowActivated.WorkflowIdProperty,
((System.Workflow.ComponentModel.ActivityBind)(activitybind9)));
            this.onWorkflowActivated1.SetBinding(Microsoft.SharePoint.WorkflowActions
.OnWorkflowActivated.WorkflowPropertiesProperty,
((System.Workflow.ComponentModel.ActivityBind)(activitybind8)));
            //
            // Workflow1
            //
            this.Activities.Add(this.onWorkflowActivated1);
            this.Activities.Add(this.createListItemAndWaitForChange);
            this.Activities.Add(this.faultHandlersActivity1);
            this.Name = "Workflow1";
            this.CanModifyActivities = false;

        }

        #endregion

        private CreateListItemAndWaitForChange createListItemAndWaitForChange;
        private Microsoft.SharePoint.WorkflowActions.LogToHistoryListActivity
                          logToHistoryListActivity1;
```

(continued)

(continued)

```
        private FaultHandlerActivity faultHandlerActivity1;
        private FaultHandlersActivity faultHandlersActivity1;
        private Microsoft.SharePoint.WorkflowActions.OnWorkflowActivated
                                  onWorkflowActivated1;
    }
}
```

Build and run the project. This will automatically take the following steps:

1. Deploy the feature and its containing workflow template to SharePoint. This is the feature and workflow template that Visual Studio 2008 automatically created for your project.
2. Activate the feature in the specified site collection. This is the site collection you specified when you created the project in Visual Studio 2008.
3. Create a workflow association on the specified list. This is the SharePoint list you specified when you created the project in Visual Studio 2008.
4. Navigate to the specified list, as shown in Figure 3-21.

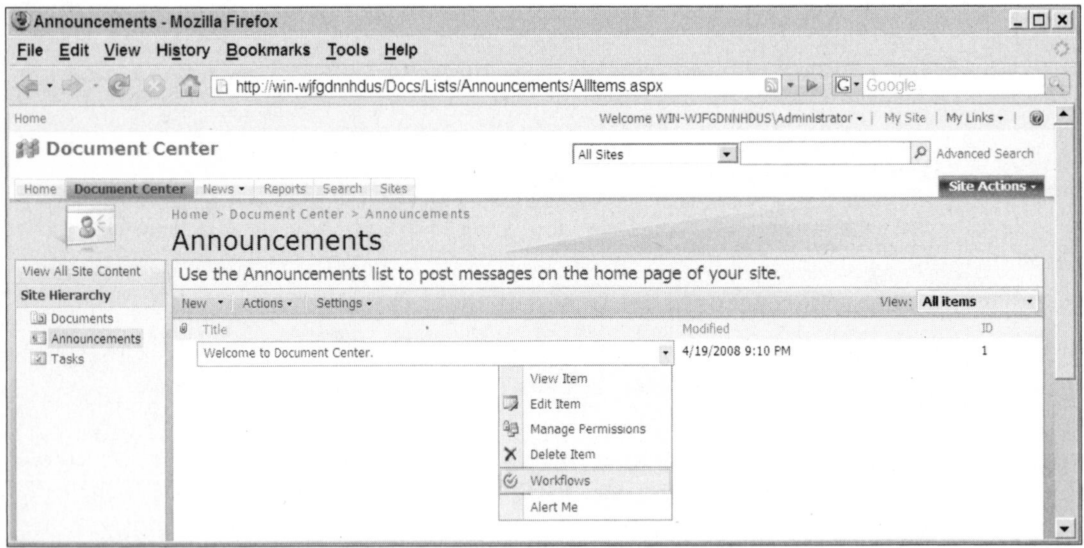

Figure 3-21

Select the Workflows menu item shown in Figure 3-21 to navigate to the Workflow.aspx page, which shows the list of available workflow associations on this SharePoint list, as shown in Figure 3-22.

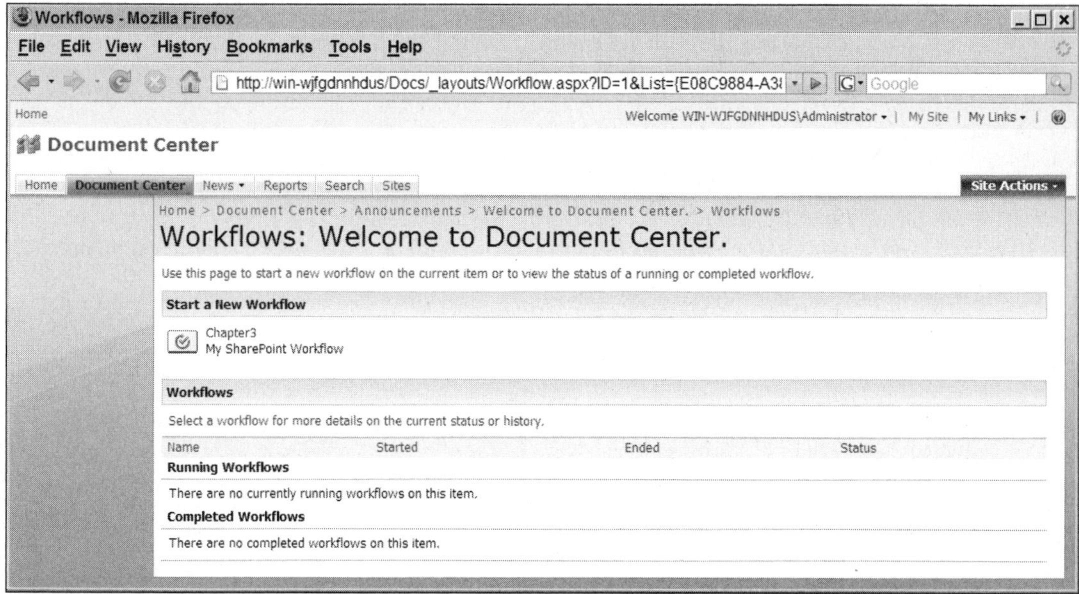
Figure 3-22

Click the workflow association to initiate an instance of the workflow. This should take you back to the list as shown in Figure 3-23.

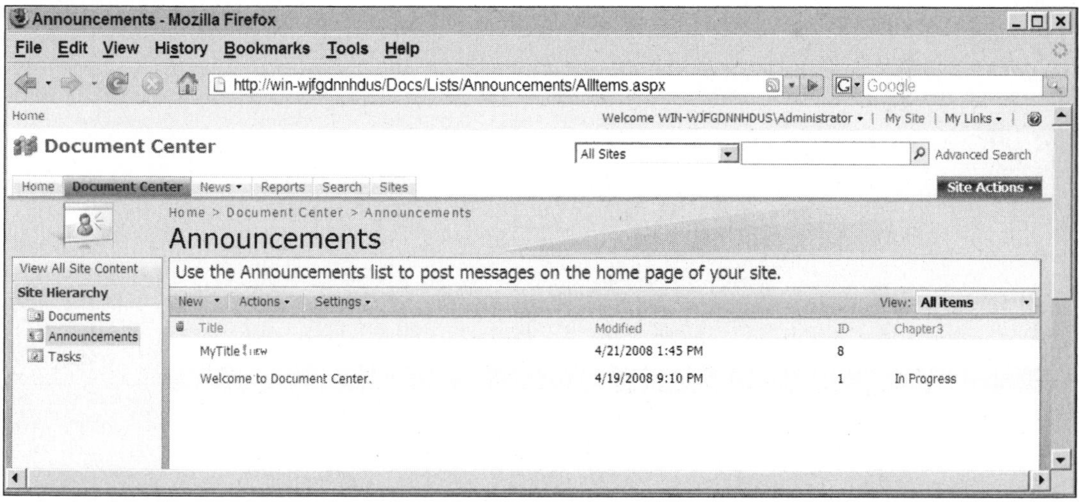
Figure 3-23

If you compare Figures 3-21 and 3-23, you'll see that the list now contains a new list item titled MyTitle. This is the list item that the CallExternalMethodActivity activity of our CreateListItemAndWaitForChange composite activity has created through a call into the CreateListItem method of the IListItemService SharePoint local service.

As Figure 3-23 shows, the list now contains a new column with the same header as the name of the workflow association. Note that the list item on which we initiated the workflow instance has the value of In Progress for this column. This means that the workflow instance has not completed its execution yet. This is expected because the HandleExternalEventActivity activity of our CreateListItemAndWaitForChange composite activity is waiting for the IListItemService local server to raise the OnItemChanged event. This local service raises this event when the list item titled MyTitle is updated. As long as this list item is not updated, the HandlerExternalEventActivity activity will not complete its execution. At this point the workflow instance is idle. This could go on forever. Such indefinite waiting periods are characteristic of activities and workflows. In the meantime, the workflow instance is serialized into the content database.

Now click the In Progress link to navigate to the WrkStat.aspx page shown in Figure 3-24.

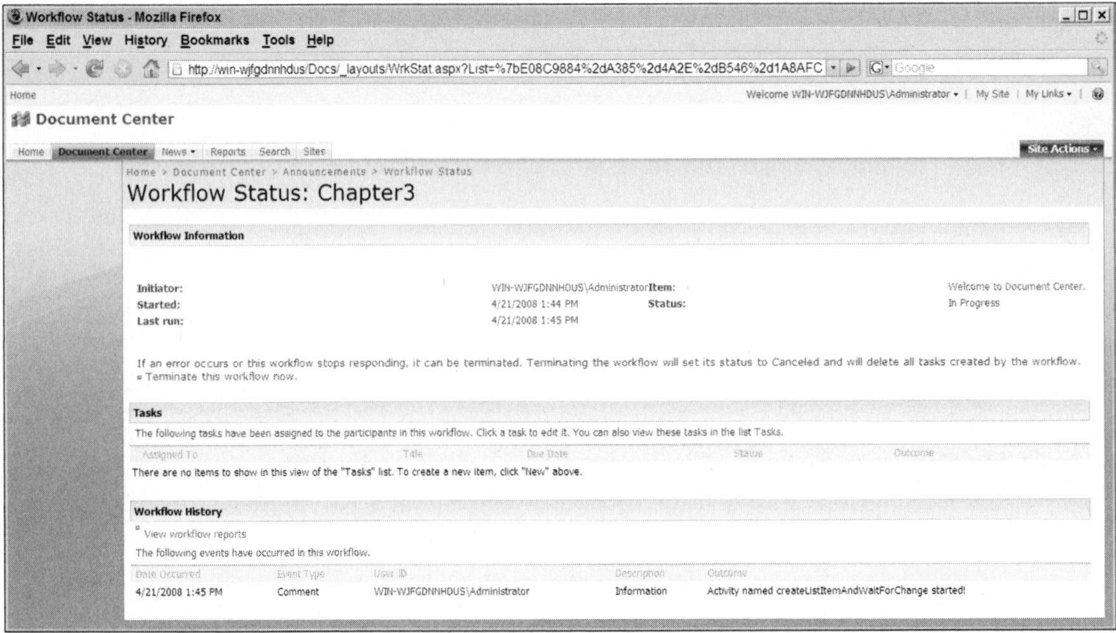

Figure 3-24

Now the Workflow History contains an entry. This is the workflow history event that the first LogToHistoryListActivity activity of our CreateListItemAndWaitForChange adds to the workflow history list. Note that the User ID column is set to the ID of the workflow originator. Thanks to activity binding, the UserId property of our CreateListItemAndWaitForChange composite activity has picked up the value of the UserId property of the OriginatorUser property as discussed earlier.

Now go back to the page shown in Figure 3-21 and update the list item titled MyTitle. You should see the result shown in Figure 3-25.

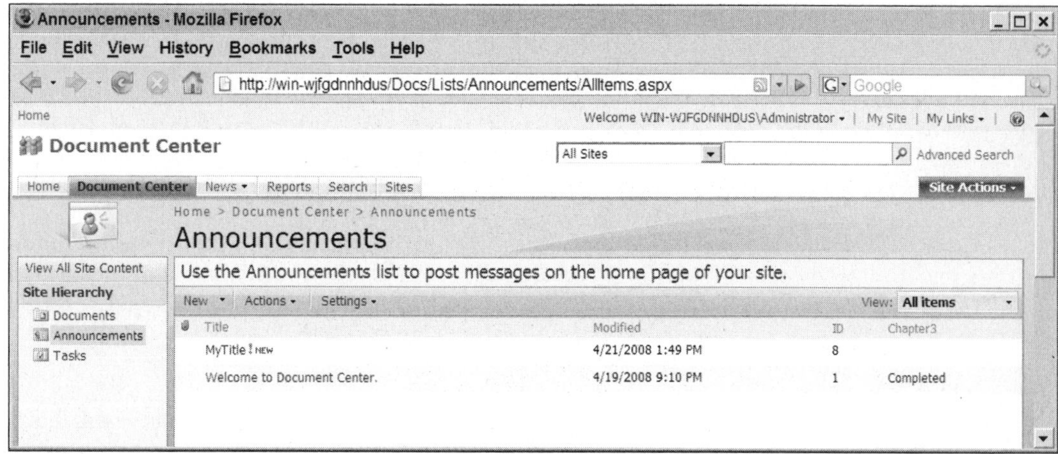

Figure 3-25

The list item on which we initiated the workflow instance now has the value Completed for the column with the same name as the workflow association. This means that the workflow instance has completed. This is because when you updated the list item, the IListItemService raised the OnItemChanged event. This triggered the HandleExternalEventActivity activity of our CreateListItemAndWaitForChange composite activity to resume its execution.

Now click the Completed link to navigate to the WrkStat.aspx page shown in Figure 3-26.

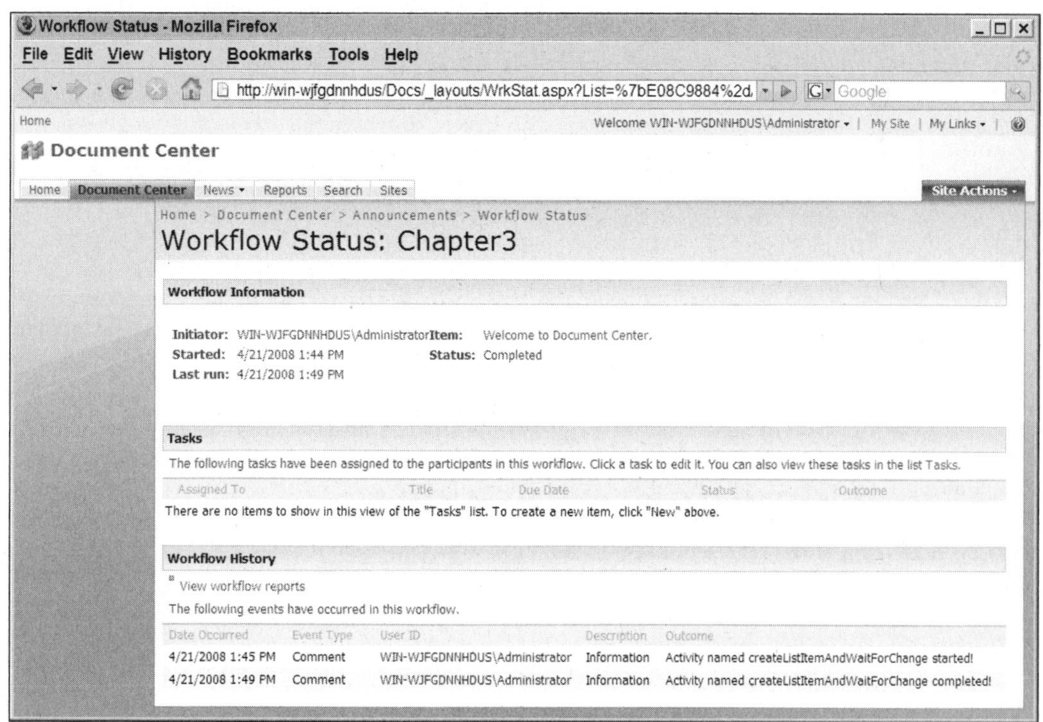

Figure 3-26

The Workflow History now contains a second entry. This is the workflow history event that the second LogToHistoryListActivity activity of our CreateListItemAndWaitForChange composite activity logs.

This example provides important insight into the role of the correlation token. Don't worry if you don't quite grasp how this works right now, because this will all be made clear in the section "Correlation Parameters." I recommend that you read through this part even if you don't quite understand the concept. I also recommend that you revisit this part after you read and understand the aforementioned section.

As you saw, we used the same correlation token name for the CallExternalMethodActivity activity that invokes the CreateListItem method and the HandleExternalEventActivity activity that responds to the OnItemChanged event. This prompted Visual Studio to create and assign the same CorrelationToken object to the CorrelationToken properties of the CallExternalMethodActivity and HandleExternalEventActivity activities.

As discussed earlier, the Execute method of the CallExternalMethodActivity activity populates this CorrelationToken object with the names and values of the correlation parameters if the method that this activity invokes is a correlation parameter initializer. In our case, the CallExternalMethodActivity activity invokes the CreateListItem method, which is indeed a correlation parameter initializer. This means that the Execute method of the CallExternalMethodActivity activity populates the CorrelationToken object with the names and values of the Id, ListId, and ItemId correlation parameters.

The integer identifier (ItemId) of the list item that the CreateListItem method creates is a correlation parameter whose name and value are stored in the CorrelationToken object. You must search the SharePoint list for the list item with the highest item ID, increment this ID by one, and assign the result as the value of the ItemId correlation parameter. This is because the list item that the CreateListItem method creates will have this as its integer identifier (ItemId). The CreateListItem method accepts any integer number as the ItemId correlation parameter as long as it is greater than the current highest integer identifier in the SharePoint list. However, regardless of what value you enter for the ItemId correlation parameter (as long as it is higher than the current highest integer identifier in the SharePoint list), the CreateListItem method always creates a list item whose item ID is the current highest integer identifier plus one.

The Execute method of the CallExternalMethodActivity activity, conversely, uses the item ID that you assigned to the ItemId property as the correlation parameter value. This means that the CorrelationToken object is populated with this item ID, not the actual item ID of the list item that the CreateListItem created. Therefore, if you assign an integer that is not exactly the current highest integer identifier plus one, the HandleExternalEventActivity activity will not respond to the OnItemChanged event that is raised when you update the item, because this activity only responds to the OnItemChanged event that is raised when an item with the same exact item ID that you assigned to the ItemId property is updated.

IWorkflowModificationService

As discussed earlier, SPWinOEWSSService implements three important external data exchange service interfaces named ISharePointService, IWorkflowModificationService, and IListItemService:

```
internal class SPWinOEWSSService : ISharePointService, IWorkflowModificationService,
                                   IListItemService, IEventProcessor
{
  . . .
}
```

I covered the ISharePointService and IListItemService interfaces in the previous sections. This section covers the IWorkflowModificationService interface. IWorkflowModificationService defines the API for the SPWinOEWSSService external data exchange workflow modification services, as shown in Listing 3-10. An external data exchange workflow modification service is a service that allows an activity to enable a specified workflow modification and to respond when a specified workflow instance is modified.

Listing 3-10: The IWorkflowModificationService workflow modification service

```
[ExternalDataExchange,
CorrelationParameter("modificationId"),
SharePointPermission(SecurityAction.InheritanceDemand,
                     ObjectModel = true),
SharePointPermission(SecurityAction.LinkDemand, ObjectModel = true)]
public interface IWorkflowModificationService
{
  [CorrelationAlias("modificationId", "e.modificationId")]
  event EventHandler<SPModificationEventArgs> OnWorkflowModified;

  [CorrelationInitializer]
  void EnableWorkflowModification(Guid modificationId, string contextData);
}
```

IWorkflowModificationService, like any other external data exchange service interface, is annotated with the ExternalDataExchangeAttribute metadata attribute so the HandleExternalEventActivity and CallExternalMethodActivity activities can work with it. IWorkflowModificationService is also marked with a CorrelationParameterAttribute metadata attribute that defines a correlation parameter named modificationId.

IWorkflowModificationService exposes a single event of type EventHandler<SPModificationEventArgs> named OnWorkflowModified. As the name implies, the external data exchange workflow modification service raises this event when a workflow is modified. Note that this event is annotated with a CorrelationAliasAttribute metadata attribute that aliases the modificationId correlation parameter to the modificationId property of the associated SPModificationEventArgs event data object.

IWorkflowModificationService exposes a single method named EnableWorkflowModification that enables a specified workflow modification. This method takes the following two arguments:

- **modificationId:** Specifies a GUID that uniquely identifies the workflow modification to enable
- **contextData:** Specifies a string that contains context data to pass to the workflow modification being enabled

SharePoint comes with an activity named EnableWorkflowModification that inherits from CallExternalMethodActivity and invokes the EnableWorkflowModification method of the workflow modification service to enable a specified workflow modification. The EnableWorkflowModification activity must be added to an EventHandlingScope activity. When the EventHandlingScopeActivity activity is in scope, SharePoint automatically displays a link to end users, enabling them to modify the workflow instance. When the EventHandlingScopeActivity goes out of scope, SharePoint automatically removes the link.

SPModificationEventArgs, like the event data class associated with the events of any other external data exchange service, inherits from ExternalDataEventArgs, as shown in Listing 3-11.

Listing 3-11: The SPModificationEventArgs class

```
public class SPModificationEventArgs : ExternalDataEventArgs
{
  public string data;
  public Guid modificationId;
  public string user;
}
```

SPModificationEventArgs contains the following three fields:

- **data:** Gets and sets a string that contains the context data for the workflow modification
- **modificationId:** Gets or set a GUID that uniquely identifies the workflow modification
- **user:** Gets or sets a string that contains the user name of the user who modified the workflow

Correlation Parameters

As shown in the previous sections, SharePoint exposes the following important external data exchange service interfaces:

- **ITaskService:** This external data exchange service interface defines the API that every task service must implement. Recall that a task service is one that facilitates two-way communications between a workflow and SharePoint workflow task management facilities. SharePoint comes with an implementation of the ITaskService API named SPWinOETaskService.

  A workflow uses the task service to create, delete, update, and complete tasks and to respond to the events raised when a task is created, deleted, updated, and completed. In a typical scenario, a workflow first uses the task service to create and assign a new task to an external entity, which could be a person or a program. The workflow then uses the task service to respond to the events raised when the external entity finally updates, deletes, and/or completes the task.
- **IListItemService:** This external data exchange service interface defines the API that every list item service must implement. Recall that a list item service is one that facilitates two-way communications between a workflow and SharePoint list item management facilities. SharePoint comes with an implementation of IListItemService API named SPWinOEWSSService.

A workflow uses the list item service to check in and out, copy, create, delete, and update SharePoint list items and documents and to respond to the events raised when a SharePoint list item or document is checked in and out, copied, created, deleted, updated, moved, and unchecked, or an attachment is added or removed from a SharePoint list item or document.

- **ISharePointService:** This external data exchange service interface defines the API that every SharePoint service must implement. SharePoint comes with an implementation of ISharePointService API named SPWinOEWSSService.

  A workflow uses the SharePoint service to initiate a workflow instance, log workflow history events to the history list of a workflow instance, send e-mails about a workflow instance, change the status of a workflow instance, and update all tasks of a workflow instance, and to respond to the events raised when a workflow instance is activated and the SharePoint list item or document on which a workflow instance is running is updated or deleted.

- **IWorkflowModificationService:** This external data exchange service interface defines the API that every workflow modification service must implement. SharePoint comes with an implementation of IWorkflowModificationService API named SPWinOEWSSService.

  A workflow uses the workflow modification service to enable a specified workflow modification and to respond to the event raised when a workflow instance is modified.

Clearly, external data exchange services play a significant role in SharePoint workflow programming. They facilitate two-way communications between SharePoint, which hosts the workflow run time, and the activities that make up a workflow. The methods of an external data exchange service enable the flow of communications from activities to SharePoint (the host). The events of an external data exchange service, conversely, enable the flow of communications from SharePoint (the host) to activities.

In a typical scenario, a workflow first uses one or more CallExternalMethodActivity instances to invoke one or more methods of one or more external data exchange services, and then uses one or more HandleExternalEventActivity instances to suspend its execution and wait for these external data exchange services to raise the specified events. For example, a workflow may first use a CallExternalMethodActivity instance to invoke the CreateTask method of the external data exchange task service to create and assign a new SharePoint task to an external entity, which could be a person or a program, and then use a HandleExternalEventActivity instance to suspend its execution and wait for the external data exchange task service to raise the OnTaskChanged event when the external entity finally updates the SharePoint task.

As discussed earlier, the CallExternalMethodActivity and HandleExternalEventActivity activities only work with local services known as external data exchange services. An external data exchange service is a local service interface that meets the following two important requirements:

- It is annotated with the ExternalDataExchangeAttribute metadata attribute.
- The event data classes associated with its events directly or indirectly inherit from ExternalDataEventArgs class. For example, the event data class associated with the OnTaskChanged, OnTaskDeleted, and OnTaskCreated events of ITaskService is a class named SPTaskServiceEventArgs, which inherits from ExternalDataEventArgs.

An external data exchange service is registered with the workflow run time through the following two-step process:

1. An instance of a WF class named ExternalDataExchangeService must be instantiated and registered with the workflow run time like so:

```
WorkflowRuntime runtime;
. . .
ExternalDataExchangeService externalDataExchangeService =
                                              new ExternalDataExchangeService();
runtime.AddService(service);
```

   Note that this is exactly what the constructor of SPWinOeHostServices does in Listing 3-2.

2. An instance of the external data exchange service must be instantiated and registered with the ExternalDataExchangeService instance like so:

```
WorkflowRuntime runtime;
. . .
ExternalDataExchangeService externalDataExchangeService =
                                              new ExternalDataExchangeService();
runtime.AddService(service);
MyLocalService localService = new MyLocalService();
externalDataExchangeService.AddService(localService);
```

   This is exactly what the constructor of SPWinOeHostServices does in Listing 3-2 to register the SPWinOETaskService and SPWinOEWSSService external data exchange services:

```
ExternalDataExchangeService service = new ExternalDataExchangeService();
this.m_WinOeHostServices.AddService(service);
service.AddService(new SPWinOETaskService(this));
service.AddService(new SPWinOEWSSService(this));
```

Under the hood, the AddService method of ExternalDataExchangeService uses .NET reflection to determine whether the external data exchange service being registered contains any events. If so, it instantiates an instance of an internal class named WorkflowMessageEventHandler for each event and registers the EventHandler method of this instance as event handler for the associated event.

When the external data exchange service finally raises an event, it instantiates an instance of the event data class associated with the event and populates the instance with the event data. Recall that this event data class inherits from ExternalDataEventArgs. The external data exchange service then invokes the EventHandler method of the associated WorkflowMessageEventHandler instance, passing in the ExternalDataEventArgs-derived instance that contains the event data.

The EventHandler method of the WorkflowMessageEventHandler instance in turn takes these steps:

1. It instantiates an instance of an internal class named MethodMessage and populates the instance with the following data:

   - ❑ A reference to the Type object that represents the type of the external data exchange service that raised the event
   - ❑ A string that contains the name of the event

- An array that contains a reference to the ExternalDataEventArgs-derived object, among other items. Recall that the external data exchange service passes this object into the EventHandler method when it invokes the method.
- A string that contains the user name

2. It uses the EnqueueItem method of the current workflow instance to deposit this MethodMessage instance in the workflow queue that HandleExternalEventActivity has already created for the associated event (keep in mind that each HandleExternalEventActivity is configured to handle a specified event).

As the second step shows, the EventHandler method of the WorkflowMessageEventHandler instance expects the HandleExternalEventActivity instance, which is configured to handle the event, to create a workflow queue where the EventHandler method can deposit the MethodMessage object. Next, I'll discuss how HandleExternalEventActivity manages to create the required workflow queue.

As mentioned earlier, a workflow uses a HandleExternalEventActivity instance to suspend its execution and wait for the specified external data exchange service to fire the specified event before it continues its execution. HandleExternalEventActivity contains a property named InterfaceType that must be set to the Type object that represents the type of the external data exchange service containing the event, and a property named EventName that must be set to the string containing the name of the event that HandleExternalEventActivity is to handle.

HandleExternalEventActivity, like many other WF activities, directly inherits from the Activity base class and overrides its Initialize, Execute, Cancel, and HandleFault methods. The Initialize method of HandleExternalEventActivity, like the Initialize method of any other WF activity, is invoked before any other methods of the activity. Every activity whose execution logic requires input from external entities should create the required workflow queues — where external entities can deposit the input — inside its Initialize method. This is exactly what the Initialize method of HandleExternalEventActivity does — that is, it creates the workflow queue where the EventHandler method of the associated WorkflowMessageEventHandler instance can deposit the MethodMessage object, which contains the following data:

- A reference to the Type object that represents the type of the external data exchange service the raised the event
- A string that contains the name of the event
- An array that contains a reference to the ExternalDataEventArgs-derived object that contains the event data
- A string that contains the user name

When the Execute method of HandleExternalEventActivity is finally invoked, the method first checks whether the workflow queue that the Initialize method created contains an item. This happens if the external data exchange service raises its event before the HandleExternalEventActivity instance is executed — that is, before its Execute method is invoked. If the workflow queue is still empty, the Execute method subscribes to the QueueItemAvailable event of the workflow queue. At this point, the HandleExternalEventActivity instance suspends its execution and waits for the external data exchange service to fire the event.

When the external data exchange service finally fires the event and the EventHandler method of the associated WorkflowMessageEventHandler finally uses the EnqueueItem method of the current workflow instance to deposit the associated MethodMessage object into the workflow queue, the QueueItemAvailable event of the workflow queue is fired. This in turn triggers the invocation of the OnEvent method of HandleExternalEventActivity, which in turn retrieves the deposited MethodMessage object from the workflow queue. Recall that this MethodMessage object contains two important pieces of information: a reference to the ExternalDataEventArgs-derived object that contains the event data and a string containing the username.

HandleExternalEventActivity first uses the user name to authorize the user. This authorization process ensures that only authorized users can use an external data exchange service to communicate with the workflow instance. This basically secures access to the workflow instance. HandleExternalEventActivity then retrieves the ExternalDataEventArgs-derived object from the deposited MethodMessage object and takes the following two steps:

1. It invokes its OnInvoked method, passing in the ExternalDataEventArgs-derived object. The OnInvoked method of HandleExternalEventActivity does not do anything, but you can implement a custom activity that inherits from HandleExternalEventActivity and overrides the OnInvoked method to run custom code. This custom code must first type-cast the ExternalDataEventArgs-derived object passed into the OnInvoked method to the appropriate ExternalDataEventArgs-derived type so it can access the type-specific properties of the object. As you'll see later, this is exactly what SharePoint does. SharePoint comes with seven activities, named OnTaskCreated, OnTaskChanged, OnTaskDeleted, OnWorkflowActivated, OnWorkflowItemChanged, OnWorkflowItemDeleted, and OnWorkflowModified. that inherit from HandleExternalEventActivity and override the OnInvoked method.
2. It raises the Invoked event and consequently invokes all event handlers registered for this event, passing the ExternalDataEventArgs-derived object. Therefore, you can register an event handler for the Invoked event of HandleExternalEventActivity to run custom code. Again, your custom code must first type-cast this ExternalDataEventArgs-derived object to the appropriate ExternalDataEventArgs-derived type so it can access the type-specific properties of this object.

In summary, the external data exchange service raises the specified event and passes the ExternalDataEventArgs-derived object along to the WorkflowMessageEventHandler, which in turn deposits this object into the workflow queue. HandleExternalEventActivity then retrieves this object from the workflow queue, passes it into its OnInvoked method, fires its Invoked event, and consequently calls all registered event handlers, passing in the same ExternalDataEventArgs-derived object. As such, there are two ways to consume this ExternalDataEventArgs-derived object. One way is to implement a class that derives from HandleExternalEventActivity and overrides its OnInvoked method, as discussed earlier. Another way is to register an event handler for the Invoked event of HandleExternalEventActivity.

As shown here, this whole scenario works only if somehow HandleExternalEventActivity communicates the name of the workflow queue to WorkflowMessageEventHandler, so that WorkflowMessageEventHandler deposits the MethodMessage into the right workflow queue. Keep in mind that every workflow queue is uniquely identified by its name.

Instead of having HandleExternalEventActivity pass the name of the workflow queue to WorkflowMessageEventHandler, WF has both HandleExternalEventActivity and WorkflowMessageEventHandler dynamically generate the same workflow queue name. WF enforces that they both create the same workflow queue name by having both of them dynamically generate a string, which is the concatenation of the following substrings:

- A substring containing the name of the type of the external data exchange service that raises the event
- A substring containing the name of the event

Because both HandleExternalEventActivity and WorkflowMessageEventHandler are configured to work with the same type of external data exchange service and the same event, they both know the name of the type of the external data exchange service and the name of the event. As such, they both end up using the same workflow queue.

As an example, let's see how this works in the case of the OnTaskChanged event of ITaskService. HandleExternalEventActivity creates a workflow queue named "OnTaskChanged\nMicrosoft.SharePoint.Workflow.ITaskService." Note that this name is simply the concatenation of the event name (OnTaskChanged) and the name of the type of the external data exchange service interface (Microsoft.SharePoint.Workflow.ITaskService). HandleExternalEventActivity then registers an event handler for the QueueItemAvailable event of this workflow queue. HandleExternalEventActivity suspends its execution and waits for the external data exchange task service to raise the OnTaskChanged event.

When the external data exchange task service finally raises the OnTaskChanged event, it triggers the invocation of the EventHandler method of the associated WorkflowMessageEventHandler, passing in the SPTaskServiceEventArgs object that contains the event data. The EventHandler method first dynamically generates the same workflow queue name "OnTaskChanged\nMicrosoft.SharePoint.Workflow.ITaskService" because it knows both the name of the event and the name of the type of the external data exchange service interface. The method then instantiates a MethodMessage instance, populates the instance with the SPTaskServiceEventArgs object, among other data, and uses the EnqueueItem method of the current workflow instance to deposit this MethodMessage instance in the workflow queue named "OnTaskChanged\nMicrosoft.SharePoint.Workflow.ITaskService," which is the same workflow queue that the associated HandleExternalEventHandler created.

Depositing this MethodMessage instance into this workflow queue automatically triggers execution of the OnEvent method of HandleExternalEventActivity. This method first retrieves the MethodMessage instance from this workflow queue and then extracts the SPTaskServiceEventArgs object from the instance. The method finally invokes the OnInvoked method, passing in the SPTaskServiceEventArgs object, and then calls all event handlers registered for the Invoked event, passing in the same SPTaskServiceEventArgs object.

Now let's see what happens if the current workflow contains two instances of HandleExternalEventHandler configured for the same OnTaskChanged event of the external data exchange task service. This means that these two HandleExternalEventHandler instances create two workflow queues with the same name because they are both configured to work with the same type of external data exchange service (Microsoft.SharePoint.Workflow.ITaskService) and the same event (OnTaskChanged). This raises the following question: In which workflow queue should the EventHandler method of the associated WorkflowMessageEventHandler deposit the associated MethodMessage object? We've got two HandleExternalEventHandler instances waiting for the same event to occur. That is why WF does not allow two activities to create two workflow queues with the same name in the same workflow instance. Workflow queue names must be unique in the scope of the same workflow instance.

Does this mean that a given workflow cannot contain more than one HandleExternalEventHandler instance configured for the same event of the same external data exchange service? No, because that would exclude very important workflow scenarios. Here is an example. Suppose you have a workflow that uses two instances of CallExternalMethodActivity to invoke the CreateTask method of the external data exchange task service twice to create two SharePoint tasks. Now imagine that the workflow execution logic following these two CallExternalMethodActivity instances consists of two execution branches running in parallel — one branch uses a HandleExternalEventHandler instance to wait for the external data exchange task service to raise the OnTaskChanged event when the first SharePoint task is updated, and the second branch uses another HandleExternalEventHandler instance to wait for the external data exchange task service to raise the OnTaskChanged event when the second SharePoint task is updated.

As this example shows, you can easily run into situations where more than one HandleExternalEventHandler instance may be configured to wait on the same event of the same external data exchange service. Obviously, our previous workflow queue-naming convention, which is a concatenation of the event name and the name of the type of the external data exchange service, will not work in these scenarios. Enter correlation parameters.

To help you understand what a correlation parameter is and what role it plays, let's take a closer look at the example we just discussed. As mentioned, the workflow uses two instances of CallExternalMethodActivity to invoke the CreateTask method of the external data exchange service twice to create two SharePoint tasks. Each SharePoint task is uniquely identified by a GUID known as *task id*. As the following excerpt from Listing 3-3 shows, the external data exchange ITaskService service interface is marked with a metadata attribute named CorrelationParameterAttribute, which defines taskId as a correlation parameter:

```
[ExternalDataExchange,
CorrelationParameter("taskId"),
. . .]
public interface ITaskService
{
   . . .
}
```

This signals both HandleExternalEventHandler and WorkflowMessageEventHandler to append the task id to the dynamically generated string that they use as the workflow queue name. In other words, both HandleExternalEventHandler and WorkflowMessageEventHandler dynamically generate a string, which is a concatenation of the following substrings:

- A substring that contains the name of the type of the external data exchange service that raises the event
- A substring that contains the name of the event
- A substring that contains the task id

Because the two HandleExternalEventHandler instances create workflow queues with two distinct names, the EventHandler method of WorkflowMessageEventHandler gets to deposit the associated MethodMessage object into the right workflow queue.

As Listing 3-3 shows, the external data exchange ITaskService service interface is annotated with a single instance of the CorrelationParameterAttribute metadata attribute, because this service interface supports a single correlation parameter. As the following excerpt from Listing 3-10 shows, the external data exchange IWorkflowModificationService service interface is also annotated with a single instance of the CorrelationParameterAttribute metadata attribute, which defines a correlation parameter named modificationId:

```
[ExternalDataExchange,
CorrelationParameter("modificationId")]
public interface IWorkflowModificationService
{
  [CorrelationAlias("modificationId", "e.modificationId")]
  event EventHandler<SPModificationEventArgs> OnWorkflowModified;

  [CorrelationInitializer]
  void EnableWorkflowModification(Guid modificationId, string contextData);
}
```

This means that you can have a workflow that uses two instances of CallExternalMethodActivity to invoke the EnableWorkflowModification method of the external data exchange workflow modification service twice to enable two workflow modifications with different modification ids, and then uses two instances of HandleExternalEventActivity to wait on the same OnWorkflowModified event of the same external data exchange workflow modification service. This is possible because each HandleExternalEventActivity instance and its associated WorkflowMessageEventHandler are configured to use the modification id as part of the workflow queue name.

The external data exchange ISharePointService service interface is yet another example of an external data exchange service interface that is annotated with a single instance of the CorrelationParameterAttribute metadata attribute to define a single correlation parameter named workflowId, as shown in the following excerpt from Listing 3-5:

```
[ExternalDataExchange,
CorrelationParameter("workflowId")]
public interface ISharePointService
{
  . . .
}
```

So far we have looked at examples of external data exchange services that are annotated with a single instance of the CorrelationParameterAttribute metadata attribute to define a single correlation parameter. As the following excerpt from Listing 3-8 demonstrates, the external data exchange IListItemService service interface is annotated with three instances of the CorrelationParameterAttribute metadata attribute to define three correlation parameters named id, listId, and itemId:

```
[ExternalDataExchange,
CorrelationParameter("itemId"),
CorrelationParameter("listId"),
CorrelationParameter("id")]
public interface IListItemService
{
  . . .
}
```

In this case, HandleExternalEventActivity and WorkflowMessageEventHandler dynamically generate a string, which is a concatenation of the following substrings, and use that as the workflow queue name:

- A substring that contains the name of the type of the external data exchange service interface — that is, Microsoft.SharePoint.Workflow.IListItemService
- A substring that contains the name of the event of the external data exchange service interface, e.g., OnItemCreated
- A substring that contains the values of the id, listId, and itemId correlation parameters

This means that you could have a workflow that uses two instances of CallExternalMethodActivity to invoke the CheckInListItem method of the external data exchange list item service twice to check in two different SharePoint list items belonging to the same or different SharePoint lists, and then uses two instances of HandleExternalEventActivity to wait on the same OnItemCheckedIn event of the external data exchange list item service. Thanks to the fact that the workflow queue name contains the item id of the SharePoint list item, the two HandleExternalEventActivity instances end up creating workflow queues with distinct names, making it possible for the EventHandler method of WorkflowMessageEventHandler to deposit the associated MethodMessage objects into their appropriate workflow queues.

So far you have learned the role of the CorrelationParameterAttribute metadata attribute. Next, I'll discuss the role of the CorrelationInitializerAttribute metadata attribute. Our discussions so far have assumed that HandleExternalEventActivity and WorkflowMessageEventHandler both know the values of the correlation parameters so they both can generate the workflow queue name. This is not a problem for WorkflowMessageEventHandler because the external data exchange service passes the ExternalDataEventArgs-derived object into the EventHandler method of WorkflowMessageEventHandler when it raises the event and invokes this method. This ExternalDataEventArgs-derived object, among other data, contains the values of the correlation parameters.

For example, the event data class associated with the OnTaskChanged event of the external data exchange task service — that is, the SPTaskServiceEventArgs class — exposes a property named taskId, which contains the value of the taskId correlation parameter. Therefore, the WorkflowMessageEventHandler instance, which is configured with the specified event of the specified external data exchange service interface, knows the values of the correlation parameters when it is about to deposit the associated MethodMessage object into the associated workflow queue. As such, this instance can easily generate and determine the name of the workflow queue where it needs to deposit the MethodMessage object.

Where would HandleExternalEventActivity get the values of the correlation parameters? Obviously, it cannot get them from the ExternalDataEventArgs-derived object, because WorkflowMessageEventHandler must deposit this object into the workflow queue to make it available to HandleExternalEventActivity. This requires HandleExternalEventActivity to first create the workflow queue. Creating a workflow queue requires HandleExternalEventActivity to know the values of the correlation parameters so it can create the name of the workflow queue.

As you can see, HandleExternalEventActivity needs to know the values of the correlation parameters long before the associated event is raised and long before the associated ExternalDataEventArgs-derived object is available. Therefore, we need a mechanism to feed HandleExternalEventActivity the required correlation parameter values. Enter CorrelationToken.

HandleExternalEventActivity and CallExternalMethodActivity both expose a property of type CorrelationToken named CorrelationToken. Listing 3-12 presents the public API of the CorrelationToken class.

Listing 3-12: The CorrelationToken class

```
public sealed class CorrelationToken : DependencyObject, IPropertyValueProvider
{
  public CorrelationToken();
  public CorrelationToken(string name);

  public void Initialize(Activity activity,
                 ICollection<CorrelationProperty> propertyValues);

  public void SubscribeForCorrelationTokenInitializedEvent(Activity activity,
             IActivityEventListener<CorrelationTokenEventArgs>
                                                dataChangeListener);

  public void UnsubscribeFromCorrelationTokenInitializedEvent(Activity activity,
             IActivityEventListener<CorrelationTokenEventArgs>dataChangeListener);

  public bool Initialized { get; }
  public string Name { get; set; }
  public string OwnerActivityName { get; set; }
  public ICollection<CorrelationProperty> Properties { get; }
}
```

Every CorrelationToken instance is uniquely identified by its name. You must specify the name of a CorrelationToken instance before you can use the instance. You have two options. One, you can specify the name when you're instantiating the CorrelationToken instance by passing the name as an argument into the constructor of the CorrelationToken class:

```
CorrelationToken token = new CorrelationToken("CorrelationToken1");
```

Alternately, you can first instantiate an unnamed CorrelationToken instance and then set its Name property:

```
CorrelationToken token = new CorrelationToken();
token.Name = "CorrelationToken1";
```

You must also specify the name of the activity that owns the CorrelationToken instance before you can use the instance:

```
token.OwnActivityName = "MyActivity";
```

CorrelationToken exposes a property of type ICollection<CorrelationProperty> named Properties that acts as a container for the CorrelationProperty objects that contain the names and values of the correlation parameters. Listing 3-13 presents the definition of the CorrelationProperty class.

Listing 3-13: The CorrelationProperty class

```
public class CorrelationProperty
{
  private string name;
  private object value;

  public CorrelationProperty(string name, object value)
  {
    this.name = name;
    this.value = value;
  }

  public string Name
  {
    get { return this.name; }
  }

  public object Value
  {
    get { return this.value; }
  }
}
```

As Listing 3-12 shows, CorrelationToken exposes a method named Initialize that takes an ICollection<CorrelationProperty> collection as its argument and performs the following steps:

1. It populates its Properties collection property with the content of this collection. In other words, the Initialize method is responsible for populating the Properties collection property.
2. It raises the correlation token initialized event and consequently invokes all event handlers registered for this event.
3. It sets the value of the Initialized property to true to mark the CorrelationToken instance as initialized.

CorrelationToken also exposes a method named SubscribeForCorrelationTokenInitializeEvent that enables others to register event handlers for the correlation token initialized event:

```
public void SubscribeForCorrelationTokenInitializedEvent(Activity activity,
            IActivityEventListener<CorrelationTokenEventArgs> dataChangeListener);
```

Note that SubscribeForCorrelationTokenInitializedEvent takes an argument of type IActivityEventListener <CorrelationTokenEventArgs>. Listing 3-14 presents the definition of IActivityEventListener<T> generic type.

Listing 3-14: The IActivityEventListener<T> generic type

```
public interface IActivityEventListener<T> where T: EventArgs
{
  void OnEvent(object sender, T e);
}
```

As shown here, the IActivityEventListener<T> generic type exposes a single method named OnEvent that takes two parameters. The first parameter is of type System.Object, which references the object that raised the event. The event raiser in this case is the CorrelationToken instance. The second parameter references an EventArgs-derived class, which is CorrelationTokenEventArgs in this case.

SubscribeForCorrelationTokenInitializedEvent subscribes the OnEvent method of the IActivityEventListener<CorrelationTokenEventArgs> instance to the correlation token initialized event. This means that when this event is raised, the OnEvent method of the IActivityEventListener<CorrelationTokenEventArgs> instance is invoked and a CorrelationTokenEventArgs instance containing the event data is passed into the method. Listing 3-15 presents the definition of the CorrelationTokenEventArgs event data class.

Listing 3-15: The CorrelationTokenEventArgs event data class

```
public sealed class CorrelationTokenEventArgs : EventArgs
{
  private CorrelationToken correlationToken;
  private bool initialized;

  internal CorrelationTokenEventArgs(CorrelationToken correlationToken,
                                     bool initialized)
  {
    this.correlationToken = correlationToken;
    this.initialized = initialized;
  }

  public CorrelationToken CorrelationToken
  {
    get { return this.correlationToken; }
  }

  public bool IsInitializing
  {
    get { return this.initialized; }
  }
}
```

SharePoint comes with an internal class named CorrelationTokenInvalidatorHandler that implements the IActivityEventHandler<CorrelationTokenEventArgs> interface.

Now, let's put everything together to see how CorrelationToken and CorrelationTokenInvalidatorHandler enable HandleExternalEventActivity to access the correlation parameters' values to generate the workflow queue name and consequently to create the workflow queue where WorkflowMessageEventHandler can deposit the MethodMessage object.

The CorrelationToken properties of HandleExternalEventActivity and CallExternalMethodActivity must be set before they can be used. In a typical scenario, you instantiate an instance of CorrelationToken and specify its name and owner activity name. The owner activity is normally the parent activity of HandleExternalEventActivity or CallExternalMethodActivity, which could be the workflow itself. The idea behind the owner activity is to enable multiple HandleExternalEventActivity and CallExternalMethodActivity instances to share the same CorrelationToken instance. You'll learn the benefits of this sharing shortly.

After you instantiate and initialize the CorrelationToken instance, you must assign the instance to the CorrelationToken property of the HandleExternalEventActivity instance. When the Initialize method of the HandleExternalEventActivity instance is invoked, the method checks the value of the Initialized Boolean property of the CorrelationToken object assigned to its CorrelationToken property to determine whether the CorrelationToken object has been initialized. Recall that a CorrelationToken object is initialized when its Initialize method is invoked.

If the CorrelationToken object has been initialized, then the HandleExternalEventActivity instance takes these steps:

1. It retrieves the correlation parameter values from the Properties collection of the CorrelationToken object.
2. It generates the workflow queue name, which includes the correlation parameter values.
3. It creates the workflow queue where WorkflowMessageEventHandler will deposit the MethodMessage object when the external data exchange service raises its event.
4. It registers its OnEvent method as event handler for the QueueItemAvailable event of the workflow queue.
5. It suspends its execution and waits for WorkflowMessageEventHandler to deposit the MethodMessage object into the workflow queue. This happens when the external data exchange service raises the event.

If the CorrelationToken object has not been initialized yet, then the HandleExternalEventActivity instance takes the following steps:

1. It instantiates a CorrelationTokenInvalidatorHandler instance. This instance maintains a reference to the HandleExternalEventActivity instance that instantiates it. The CorrelationTokenInvalidatorHandler instance maintains this reference in a field named eventHandler, which is of type IActivityEventListener<QueueEventArgs>:

```
private IActivityEventListener<QueueEventArgs> eventHandler;
```

   Keep in mind that HandleExernalEventActivity implements the IActivityEventListener<Queue EventArgs> interface. As Listing 3-18 shows, this interface exposes a single method named OnEvent, which takes a parameter of type QueueEventArgs.

2. It invokes the SubscribeForCorrelationTokenInitializedEvent method on the CorrelationToken object, passing in the CorrelationTokenInvalidatorHandler instance as its argument. Recall that the SubscribeForCorrelationTokenInitializedEvent method subscribes the OnEvent method of the instance to the correlation token initialized event of the CorrelationToken object.

When the Initialize method of the CorrelationToken object is finally invoked (you'll see later who invokes this method), this sequence of actions takes place:

1. The Initialize method populates the Properties collection property of the CorrelationToken object with the names and values of the correlation parameters. The caller of the Initialize method passes these names and values into the method when it invokes the method.
2. The Initialize method sets the Initialized property of the CorrelationToken object to true to mark the object as initialized.

3. The Initialize method instantiates an instance of the CorrelationTokenEventArgs event data class. This instance exposes a property of type CorrelationToken that references the CorrelationToken object.

4. The Initialize method invokes the event handlers registered for the correlation token initialized event of the CorrelationToken object, passing in the CorrelationTokenEventArgs instance. Recall that these event handlers are the OnEvent methods of the IActivityEventListener<Correlation TokenEventArgs> objects, such as CorrelationTokenInvalidatorHandler. As such, the OnEvent method of the CorrelationTokenInvalidatorHandler instance is invoked at this point.

5. The OnEvent method of the CorrelationTokenInvalidatorHandler instance accesses the CorrelationToken object through the CorrelationToken property of the CorrelationTokenEventArgs instance.

6. The OnEvent method of the CorrelationTokenInvalidatorHandler instance then retrieves the values of the correlation parameters from the Properties collection property of the CorrelationToken object and uses them to generate the workflow queue name.

7. The OnEvent method of the CorrelationTokenInvalidatorHandler instance then creates the workflow queue name where WorkflowMessageEventHandler will deposit the MethodMessage object when the external data exchange service raises the event.

8. The OnEvent method of the CorrelationTokenInvalidatorHandler instance then accesses the OnEvent method of the HandleExternalEventActivity instance and registers this method as event handler for the QueueItemAvailable event of the workflow queue. Recall that the CorrelationTokenInvalidatorHandler instance maintains a reference to the HandleExternalEventActivity instance in a private field of type IActivityEventListener<Queue EventArgs> named eventHandler. As mentioned earlier, HandleExternalEventActivity implements the IActivityEventListener<QueueEventArgs> interface, which exposes a single method named OnEvent, which takes a parameter of type QueueEventArgs.

9. The OnEvent method of the CorrelationTokenInvalidatorHandler instance then invokes the UnsubscribeFromCorrelationTokenInitializedEvent method on the CorrelationToken object to unsubscribe from the correlation token initialized event.

Now you know where HandleExternalEventActivity gets the values of the correlation parameters: from the Properties collection property of the CorrelationToken object assigned to its CorrelationToken property. As mentioned, it is the Initialize method of the CorrelationToken object that is responsible for populating the Properties collection property with the correlation parameter names and values:

```
public void Initialize(Activity activity,
                       ICollection<CorrelationProperty> propertyValues);
```

The Initialize method takes two parameters. The first parameter references the HandleExternalEventActivity instance. The second parameter references the ICollection<CorrelationProperty> collection that contains the CorrelationProperty objects containing the correlation names and values.

The entire execution logic of HandleExternalEventActivity relies on someone calling the Initialize method of the CorrelationToken object assigned to its CorrelationToken property. There are different ways to trigger the invocation of the Initialize method. One approach is to manually invoke the Initialize method on the CorrelationToken object from within your managed code. For example, the workflow could contain a CodeActivity instance and subscribe a method as an event handler for the ExecuteCode event of this CodeActivity instance. This method can invoke the Initialize method on the CorrelationToken object to initialize the object. This is possible because the Initialize method is marked as public.

Another approach is as follows:

1. Add a CallExternalMethodActivity instance.
2. Set the InterfaceType property of this CallExternalMethodActivity instance to the same Type object assigned to the InterfaceType property of the HandleExternalEventActivity instance.
3. Set the MethodName property of this CallExternalMethodActivity instance to the name of the desired method of the external data exchange service. This method must be annotated with the CorrelationInitializerParameterAttribute metadata attribute.
4. Populate the ParameterBindings collection property of this CallExternalMethodActivity instance with the WorkflowParameterBinding objects that contain the names and values of the parameters of the external data exchange service method. Keep in mind that these parameters, among others, include the correlation parameters, because correlation parameters are passed as arguments into the external data exchange service method. For example, the correlation parameter taskId is passed as an argument into the CreateTask method of the external data exchange task service.
5. Assign the same CorrelationToken object that is assigned to the CorrelationToken property of the HandleExternalEventActivity instance to the CorrelationToken property of this CallExternalMethodActivity instance.

The Execute method of the CallExternalMethodActivity instance internally takes the following steps:

1. It instantiates an ICollection<CorrelationProperty> collection.
2. It extracts the correlation parameter names and values from its ParameterBindings collection property.
3. It instantiates one CorrelationProperty instance for each correlation parameter, populates it with the name and value of the correlation parameter, and adds it to the ICollection<CorrelationProperty> collection.
4. It invokes the Initialize method of the CorrelationToken object assigned to its CorrelationToken property, passing in the ICollection<CorrelationProperty> collection.

The second approach to invoking the Initialize method of the CorrelationToken object requires a CallExternalMethodActivity instance whose MethodName property is set to the name of an external data exchange service method that is annotated with the CorrelationInitializerAttribute metadata attribute.

Next, take a look at a few examples of external data exchange services that make use of CorrelationInitializerAttribute metadata attribute. As the following excerpt from Listing 3-3 shows, the CreateTask and CreateTaskWithContentType methods of ITaskService are annotated with the CorrelationInitializerAttribute metadata attribute:

```
[ExternalDataExchange,
CorrelationParameter("taskId")]
public interface ITaskService
{
  [CorrelationInitializer]
  int CreateTask(Guid taskId, SPWorkflowTaskProperties properties,
                 HybridDictionary specialPermissions);

  [CorrelationInitializer]
  int CreateTaskWithContentType(Guid taskId, SPWorkflowTaskProperties properties,
                                string taskContentTypeId,
                                HybridDictionary specialPermissions);
  . . .
}
```

Note that a method or event can only be annotated with a single instance of the CorrelationInitializerAttribute metadata attribute. This means that the method or event marked with this attribute initializes all correlation parameters. For example, IListItemService is marked with three instances of CorrelationParameter, which define three correlation parameters named id, listId, and itemId. As the following excerpt from Listing 3-8 shows, just about all methods of IListItemService are marked with CorrelationInitializer, which means that all methods of this service initialize all three correlation parameters id, listId, and itemId:

```
[ExternalDataExchange,
CorrelationParameter("itemId"),
CorrelationParameter("listId"),
CorrelationParameter("id")]
public interface IListItemService
{
  . . .

  [CorrelationInitializer]
  void CheckInListItem(Guid id, Guid listId, int itemId, string comment);

  [CorrelationInitializer]
  void CheckOutListItem(Guid id, Guid listId, int itemId);

  [CorrelationInitializer]
  void CopyListItem(Guid id, Guid listId, int itemId, Guid toList, bool overwrite);

  [CorrelationInitializer]
  int CreateDocument(Guid id, Guid listId, int itemId,
                     Hashtable itemProperties, byte[] fileContents);

  [CorrelationInitializer]
  int CreateListItem(Guid id, Guid listId, int itemId, Hashtable itemProperties);

  [CorrelationInitializer]
  void DeleteListItem(Guid id, Guid listId, int itemId);

  [CorrelationInitializer]
  void InitializeForEvent(Guid id, Guid listId, int itemId);

  [CorrelationInitializer]
```

(continued)

(continued)

```
    void UndoCheckOutListItem(Guid id, Guid listId, int itemId);

    [CorrelationInitializer]
    void UpdateDocument(Guid id, Guid listId, int itemId,
                        Hashtable itemProperties, bool overwriteFromTemplate,
                        byte[] fileContents);

    [CorrelationInitializer]
    void UpdateListItem(Guid id, Guid listId, int itemId, Hashtable itemProperties);
  }
```

So far I've covered the CorrelationParameterAttribute and CorrelationInitializerAttribute metadata attributes. Next I'll discuss the CorrelationAliasAttribute metadata attribute. This metadata attribute allows a method or an event of an external data exchange service to create an alias for a correlation parameter. As the following example shows, the OnWorkflowModified event is marked with a CorrelationAliasAttribute metadata attribute, which defines e.modificationId as an alias for the modificationId correlation parameter. "e" in this alias refers to the SPModificationEventArgs object that is passed into the event handlers registered for this event when this event is fired:

```
  [ExternalDataExchange,
  CorrelationParameter("modificationId")]
  public interface IWorkflowModificationService
  {
    [CorrelationAlias("modificationId", "e.modificationId")]
    event EventHandler<SPModificationEventArgs> OnWorkflowModified;

    [CorrelationInitializer]
    void EnableWorkflowModification(Guid modificationId, string contextData);
  }
```

Summary

This chapter provided in-depth coverage of SharePoint external data exchange services and showed you how to implement custom composite activities that make use of these services. Also covered in detail in this chapter were correlation parameters.

CallExternalMethodActivity-Based SharePoint Activities

As shown in a previous chapter, SharePoint provides four external data exchange service interfaces: ITaskService, ISharePointService, IListItemService, and IWorkflowModificationService. A workflow can use CallExternalMethodActivity to invoke the methods of these SharePoint external data exchange services, and HandleExternalEventActivity to wait for these services to fire their events.

The main problem with CallExternalMethodActivity and HandleExternalEventActivity is that they are not strongly typed. As such, they expose generic properties such as InterfaceType, MethodName, and EventName that must be set in a weakly typed manner. SharePoint comes with a standard set of activities that inherit from CallExternalMethodActivity and HandleExternalEventActivity that enable you to invoke the methods of standard SharePoint external data exchange services and to respond to the events of these standard services in strongly typed fashion.

This chapter covers those SharePoint activities that inherit from CallExternalMethodActivity. The next chapter covers those SharePoint activities that inherit from HandleExternalEventActivity.

CallExternalMethodActivity

To help you gain a better understanding of CallExternalMethodActivity-based SharePoint activities, consider the internal implementation of CallExternalMethodActivity shown in Listing 4-1. CallExternalMethodActivity, like many other activities, inherits from the Activity base class and overrides its Execute method.

Listing 4-1: Internal implementation of CallExternalMethodActivity

```
public class CallExternalMethodActivity : Activity, IPropertyValueProvider,
   IDynamicPropertyTypeProvider
{
  public static readonly DependencyProperty CorrelationTokenProperty;
  public static readonly DependencyProperty InterfaceTypeProperty;
  public static readonly DependencyProperty MethodInvokingEvent;
  public static readonly DependencyProperty MethodNameProperty;
  public static readonly DependencyProperty ParameterBindingsProperty;

  public CallExternalMethodActivity()
  {
    base.SetReadOnlyPropertyValue(ParameterBindingsProperty,
             new WorkflowParameterBindingCollection(this));
  }

  public CallExternalMethodActivity(string name): base(name)
  {
    base.SetReadOnlyPropertyValue(ParameterBindingsProperty,
             new WorkflowParameterBindingCollection(this));
  }

  protected sealed override
  ActivityExecutionStatus Execute(
              ActivityExecutionContext executionContext)
  {
    object service = executionContext.GetService(this.InterfaceType);

    base.RaiseEvent(MethodInvokingEvent, this, EventArgs.Empty);
    this.OnMethodInvoking(EventArgs.Empty);
    MethodInfo method = interfaceType.GetMethod(this.MethodName,
              BindingFlags.Public | BindingFlags.Instance);
    ParameterModifier[] parameterModifiers = null;
    object[] messageArgs = InvokeHelper.GetParameters(this.MethodName,
               this.ParameterBindings, out parameterModifiers);
    WorkflowParameterBinding binding = null;
    if (this.ParameterBindings.Contains("(ReturnValue)"))
      binding = this.ParameterBindings["(ReturnValue)"];

    CorrelationService.InvalidateCorrelationToken(this,
                                    this.InterfaceType,
                                  this.MethodName, messageArgs);
    object source = interfaceType.InvokeMember(this.MethodName,
                                  BindingFlags.InvokeMethod,
                         new ExternalDataExchangeBinder(), service,
                       messageArgs, parameterModifiers, null, null);
    if (binding != null)
      binding.Value = InvokeHelper.CloneOutboundValue(source,
                           new BinaryFormatter(), "(ReturnValue)");

    InvokeHelper.SaveOutRefParameters(messageArgs, method,
                               this.ParameterBindings);
```

```
    this.OnMethodInvoked(EventArgs.Empty);
    return ActivityExecutionStatus.Closed;
  }

  protected virtual void OnMethodInvoked(EventArgs e) { }
  protected virtual void OnMethodInvoking(EventArgs e) { }

  public event EventHandler MethodInvoking { add; remove; }
  public virtual CorrelationToken CorrelationToken { get; set; }
  public virtual Type InterfaceType { get; set; }
  public virtual string MethodName { get; set; }
  public WorkflowParameterBindingCollection ParameterBindings { get; }
}
```

As the preceding code shows, CallExternalMethodActivity exposes the following properties and events:

- **InterfaceType:** Gets or sets a reference to the Type object that represents the type of the external data exchange service
- **MethodName:** Gets or sets a string that contains the name of the external data exchange service method to invoke
- **ParameterBindings:** Gets a reference to a WorkflowParameterBindingCollection containing the WorkflowParameterBinding objects that represent the parameters of the external data exchange service method to invoke
- **CorrelationToken:** Gets or sets a reference to a CorrelationToken object that contains the names and values of the correlation parameters
- **MethodInvoking:** CallExternalMethodActivity raises this event before it invokes the external data exchange service method.

Listing 4-2 presents the definition of the WorkflowParameterBinding class.

Listing 4-2: The WorkflowParameterBinding class

```
public sealed class WorkflowParameterBinding : DependencyObject
{
  public static readonly DependencyProperty ParameterNameProperty;
  public static readonly DependencyProperty ValueProperty;

  public WorkflowParameterBinding() { }

  public WorkflowParameterBinding(string parameterName)
  {
    base.SetValue(ParameterNameProperty, parameterName);
  }

  public string ParameterName { get; set; }
  public object Value { get; set; }
}
```

Here, WorkflowParameterBinding exposes the following two properties:

- **ParameterName:** Gets or sets a string containing the name of the parameter that WorkflowParameterBinding represents
- **Value:** Gets or sets the value of the parameter that WorkflowParameterBinding represents

All four InterfaceType, MethodName, ParameterBindings, and CorrelationToken properties of a CallExternalMethodActivity instance must be set before the instance can be used. Here is an example:

```
CallExternalMethodActivity activity = new CallExternalMethodActivity();
activity.InterfaceType = typeof(Microsoft.SharePoint.Workflow);
activity.MethodName = "DeleteTask";
CorrelationToken token = new CorrelationToken();
token.Name = "MyToken";
token.OwnerActivityName = "MyActivity";
activity.CorrelationToken = token;
WorkflowParameterBinding pbinding = new WorkflowParameterBinding();
pbinding.Name = "taskId";
pbinding.Value = taskId;
activity.ParameterBindings.Add(pbinding);
```

As Listing 4-1 shows, all four InterfaceType, MethodName, ParameterBindings, and CorrelationToken properties, plus the MethodInvoking event, are defined as bindable properties. This enables you to use activity binding to specify the values of these properties and event.

Next, I'll walk you through the implementation of the Execute method of CallExternalMethodActivity. This method first accesses the external data exchange service:

```
object service = executionContext.GetService(this.InterfaceType);
```

Then, it raises the MethodInvoking event and consequently invokes all event handlers registered for this event. This enables you to run custom code before CallExternalMethodActivity actually invokes the respective method of the external data exchange service:

```
    base.RaiseEvent(MethodInvokingEvent, this, EventArgs.Empty);
```

Next, it invokes the OnMethodInvoking method. The CallExternalMethodActivity activity's implementation of this method does not do anything. However, you can implement a custom activity that inherits from CallExternalMethodActivity and overrides this method. As a matter of fact, SharePoint comes with several custom activities that inherit from CallExternalMethodActivity and override its OnMethodInvoking method, as discussed later in this chapter.

```
    this.OnMethodInvoking(EventArgs.Empty);
```

The Execute method accesses the MethodInfo object that represents the external data exchange service method with the specified name:

```
    MethodInfo method = interfaceType.GetMethod(this.MethodName,
                                  BindingFlags.Public | BindingFlags.Instance);
```

It then uses a helper method to retrieve an array containing the parameter values of the service method to invoke. Under the hood, this helper method uses .NET reflection and the content of the ParameterBindings collection to retrieve the parameter values. Recall that the ParameterBindings collection contains WorkflowParameterBinding objects containing the names and values of the parameters of the method:

```
ParameterModifier[] parameterModifiers = null;
object[] messageArgs = InvokeHelper.GetParameters(this.MethodName,
                                        this.ParameterBindings, out parameterModifiers);
```

The Execute method calls the InvalidateCorrelationToken method of an internal component named CorrelationService. Under the hood, this method checks whether the service method is annotated with the CorrelationInitializerAttribute metadata attribute. If so, it retrieves the values of the correlation parameters from the messageArgs array and populates the Properties collection property of the CorrelationToken object that the CorrelationToken property of CallExternalMethodActivity references with these correlation parameter values. This causes this CorrelationToken object to raise its correlation token initialized event and consequently invoke all the event handlers registered for this event.

For example, the current workflow instance may contain a HandleExternalEventActivity that has registered its OnEvent method as handler for this event. When the event is raised and this method is invoked, the method simply retrieves the correlation parameter values from the CorrelationToken object and uses them to dynamically generate the name of the required workflow queue. Keep in mind that the CorrelationToken properties of both CallExternalMethodActivity and HandleExternalEventActivity must reference the same CorrelationToken object in order for this to work.

```
CorrelationService.InvalidateCorrelationToken(this, this.InterfaceType,
                                          this.MethodName, messageArgs);
```

Next, the Execute method invokes the service method, passing in the method arguments:

```
object source = interfaceType.InvokeMember(this.MethodName,
                                        BindingFlags.InvokeMethod,
                                        new ExternalDataExchangeBinder(), service,
                                        messageArgs, parameterModifiers, null, null);
```

It then invokes the OnMethodInvoked method. The CallExternalMethodActivity activity's implementation of this method does not do anything, but you can implement a custom activity that inherits from CallExternalMethodActivity and override this method to run custom code. Indeed, SharePoint provides several activities that inherit from CallExternalMethodActivity and override the OnMethodInvoked method, as discussed later in this chapter.

```
this.OnMethodInvoked(EventArgs.Empty);
```

Finally, the Execute method returns ActivityExecutionStatus.Closed to inform the workflow run time that it has completed its execution:

```
return ActivityExecutionStatus.Closed;
```

As you can see, CallExternalMethodActivity invokes its associated service method in synchronous fashion without creating any workflow queues.

Creating SharePoint Tasks

As the following excerpt from Chapter 3 shows, the SharePoint ITaskService external data exchange service interface exposes a method named CreateTask that creates a SharePoint workflow task with the specified task id, task field values, and set of permissions. Note that CreateTask takes a second parameter of type SPWorkflowTaskProperties that contains the task field names and values. Also note that CreateTask is annotated with the CorrelationInitializerAttribute metadata attribute:

```
[ExternalDataExchange,
CorrelationParameter("taskId")]
public interface ITaskService
{
  [CorrelationInitializer]
  int CreateTask(Guid taskId, SPWorkflowTaskProperties properties,
                 HybridDictionary specialPermissions);
  . . .
}
```

SharePoint comes with a workflow activity named CreateTask that a workflow can use to invoke the CreateTask method of ITaskService. Listing 4-3 presents the internal implementation of this activity.

Listing 4-3: The CreateTask activity

```
public sealed class CreateTask : CallExternalMethodActivity
{
  public static DependencyProperty ListItemIdProperty;
  public static DependencyProperty SpecialPermissionsProperty;
  public static DependencyProperty TaskIdProperty;
  public static DependencyProperty TaskPropertiesProperty;

  public CreateTask()
  {
    this.InterfaceType = typeof(ITaskService);
    this.MethodName = "CreateTask";
  }

  protected override void OnMethodInvoked(EventArgs e)
  {
    this.ListItemId =
     (int)base.ParameterBindings["(ReturnValue)"].Value;
  }

  protected override void OnMethodInvoking(EventArgs e)
  {
    base.ParameterBindings["taskId"].Value = this.TaskId;
    base.ParameterBindings["properties"].Value = this.TaskProperties;
    base.ParameterBindings["specialPermissions"].Value =
                         this.SpecialPermissions;
  }

  public override Type InterfaceType
```

```
        {
          get { return typeof(ITaskService); }
        }

        public override string MethodName
        {
          get { return "CreateTask"; }
        }

        public int ListItemId { get; set; }
        public HybridDictionary SpecialPermissions { get; set; }
        public Guid TaskId { get; set; }
        public SPWorkflowTaskProperties TaskProperties { get; set; }
      }
```

The CreateTask activity inherits from CallExternalMethodActivity and extends its functionality as follows:

- It overrides the InterfaceType property of CallExternalMethodActivity to return the Type object that represents the type of ITaskService interface. This enables you to avoid setting the value of this property every time you need to invoke the CreateTask method of ITaskService.
- It overrides the MethodName property of CallExternalMethodActivity to return the string "CreateTask." This enables you to avoid setting this property's value every time you need to invoke the CreateTask method of ITaskService.
- It exposes the three parameters of the underlying CreateTask method (i.e., taskId, properties, and specialPermissions) as three activity-level bindable properties named TaskId, TaskProperties, and SpecialPermissions. This enables you to specify the values of these three parameters through activity binding in purely declarative fashion.
- It exposes the return value of the underlying CreateTask method — that is, the list item id (integer) of the newly created task as an activity-level property named ListItemId.
- It overrides the OnMethodInvoked method of CallExternalMethodActivity where it assigns the return value of the underlying CreateTask method to the ListItemId property. This means that this property can now be bound to a property of another activity inside the current workflow instance, enabling this property of this activity to automatically pick up the ID of the list item.
- It overrides the OnMethodInvoking method of CallExternalMethodActivity where it populates the ParameterBindings property of CallExternalMethodActivity with the values of the TaskId, TaskProperties, and SpecialPermissions properties. This saves you the effort of doing this yourself.

As shown earlier in Listing 4-2, WorkflowParameterBinding derives from DependencyObject. As such, it inherits a method named SetBinding, which is defined as follows:

```
public void SetBinding(DependencyProperty dependencyProperty, ActivityBind bind);
```

This method takes two parameters of type DependencyProperty and ActivityBind. Under the hood, the method uses the ActivityBind object to set the property that the DependencyProperty object represents. This enables you to use an ActivityBind object to specify the value of a parameter of an external data exchange service method.

Listing 4-4 presents the definition of the ActivityBind class. ActivityBind binds an activity's member to another activity's member. This enables the flow of data from one activity to another as the containing workflow instance is executing.

Listing 4-4: The ActivityBind class

```
public sealed class ActivityBind : MarkupExtension
{
  public ActivityBind();
  public ActivityBind(string name);
  public ActivityBind(string name, string path);

  public object GetRuntimeValue(Activity activity);
  public object GetRuntimeValue(Activity activity, Type targetType);
  public override object ProvideValue(IServiceProvider provider);
  public void SetRuntimeValue(Activity activity, object value);

  public string Name { get; set; }
  public string Path { get; set; }
  public IDictionary UserData { get; }
}
```

ActivityBind exposes the following two important properties:

- **Name:** Gets or sets the name of the target activity
- **Path:** Gets or sets the name of the target member. You can use a dotted notation to specify inner members of a specified member as the target member. For example, if you set the value of Path to member1.member2.member3, the target member will be member3, which is a member of member2, which in turn is a member of member1.

For example, suppose you have a custom activity named MyCustomActivity1, which exposes a bindable property of type MyCustomProperty1 named Property1; a custom activity named MyCustomActivity2, which exposes a property of type MyCustomProperty2 named MyProperty1; and a custom type named MyCustomProperty2, which exposes a subproperty of type MyCustomProperty1 named Property1, as shown here:

```
public class MyCustomActivity1 : Activity
{
  public static DependencyProperty Property1Property =
     DependencyProperty.Register("Property1", typeof(MyCustomProperty),
                                 Typeof(MyCustomActivity1));
  public MyCustomProperty1 Property1
  {
    get { return GetValue(Property1Property) as MyCustomProperty1; }
    set { SetValue(Property1Property, value); }
  }

  // More members
}
```

```
public class MyCustomActivity2 : Activity
{
  public MyCustomProperty2 MyProperty1 { get; set; }

  // More members
}

public class MyCustomProperty2
{
  public MyCustomProperty1 Property1 { get; set; }
}
```

The following code snippet shows how to use an ActivityBind object to bind the Property1 subproperty of the MyProperty1 property of an activity of type MyCustomActivity2 to the Property1 property of an activity of type MyCustomActivity1:

```
MyCustomActivity1 sourceActivity;
MyCustomActivity2 targetActivity;
. . .
targetActivity.Name = "MyTargetActivity";
. . .
ActivityBind abind = new ActivityBind();
abind.Name = "MyTargetActivity";
abind.Path = MyProperty1.Property1;
sourceActivity.SetBinding(MyCustomActivity1.Property1Property, abind);
```

Note that the Name property of the ActivityBind object is set to the name of the target activity, and its Path property specifies the target property, which is the Property1 subproperty of the MyProperty1 property of the target activity. This example finally invokes the SetBinding method on the source activity, passing in two parameters, where the first parameter references the Property1Property DependencyObject of MyCustomActivity1, and the second parameter references the ActivityBind object. The SetBinding method uses the ActivityBind object to bind the Property1 subproperty of the MyProperty1 property of the target activity to the Property1 property of the source activity.

The real power of ActivityBind comes into play when you implement your workflow in XAML:

```
<wf:SequenceActivity
xmlns="http://MyCustomActivities"
xmlns:wf="http://schemas.microsoft.com/winfx/2006/xaml/workflow"
xmlns:x="http://schemas.microsoft.com/winfx/2006/xaml">
  <MyCustomActivity1 x:Name="mca1" . . . />
  <MyCustomActivity2 x:Name="mca2"
   Property1="{wf:ActivityBind mca1, Path=MyProperty1.Property1}" . . . />
</wf:SequenceActivity>
```

WF comes with a default workflow loader service named DefaultWorkflowLoaderService that knows how to deserialize an XAML document such as the preceding into a tree of activities rooted at a SequenceActivity. This loader service deserializes the expression

```
{wf:ActivityBind mca1, Path=MyProperty1.Property1}
```

into an ActivityBind object and invokes the SetBinding method on the source activity.

Activity binding reveals the real power of inheriting from CallExternalMethodActivity to implement a dedicated activity such as CreateTask. As Listing 4-3 shows, the CreateTask activity exposes the parameters of the underlying CreateTask method as activity-level bindable properties:

```
public HybridDictionary SpecialPermissions { get; set; }
public Guid TaskId { get; set; }
public SPWorkflowTaskProperties TaskProperties { get; set; }
```

This means that you can use activity binding to specify the values of these properties. For example, imagine a scenario where a workflow includes an activity that exposes three properties of type HybridDictionary, Guid, and SPWorkflowTaskProperties. You can bind the SpecialPermissions, TaskId, and TaskProperties of the CreateTask activity to these three properties to have them pick up their values from these properties. Alternately, the workflow itself may expose three properties of type HybridDictionary, Guid, and SPWorkflowTaskProperties. You can then bind the Special Permissions, TaskId, and TaskProperties of the CreateTask activity to these three properties of the workflow.

Now we'll implement a workflow that uses the CreateTask activity to create a SharePoint task. Take the following steps to implement this workflow: Launch Visual Studio 2008. Select File ⇨ New Project to launch the New Project dialog box.

Select 2007 under Office under Visual C# in the Project types pane and then select SharePoint 2007 Sequential Workflow from the Templates pane (see Figure 4-1). Click OK to add a new SharePoint 2007 Sequential Workflow. Note that the workflow already contains the required OnWorkflowActivated activity as its first child activity.

If you don't want to create a new project, but instead add a new workflow to an existing project, follow these steps: First, add a new Sequential Workflow workflow to your Visual Studio project. Then, drag an OnWorkflowActivated activity from the toolbox and drop it onto the designer surface. Recall that the OnWorkflowActivated activity must always be the first activity in every SharePoint workflow.

Next, enter a name for the CorrelationToken property of the OnWorkflowActivated activity in the Properties pane and specify the workflow as the owner activity. Recall from the previous chapter that this prompts Visual Studio to generate the code that instantiates a CorrelationToken object with the specified Name and OwnerActivityName property values, and assigns this object to the CorrelationToken property of the OnWorkflowActivated activity.

Place your cursor in the WorkflowProperties property of the OnWorkflowActivated activity in the Properties pane and then click the ellipsis button that appears in front of this property to launch the dialog that enables you to bind another property or field to this property. Switch to the "Bind to a new member" tab in this dialog box and check Create Field radio button to add a new field named WorkflowProperties to the workflow. Visual Studio automatically generates the code that instantiates a SPWorkflowActivationProperty object, assigns this object to the WorkflowProperty field of the workflow, and uses an ActivityBind object and the SetBinding method on the OnWorkflowActivated activity to bind the WorkflowProperties field of the workflow to the WorkflowProperties property of the OnWorkflowActivated activity.

Thanks to activity binding, the SPWorkflowActivationProperty object assigned to the WorkflowProperties field of the workflow is automatically assigned to the WorkflowProperties property of the OnWorkflowActivated activity. When the ISharePointService object finally fires its OnWorkflowActivated event and consequently the OnWorkflowActivated activity resumes its execution, this activity populates the SPWorkflowActivationProperties object that its WorkflowProperties references with complete information about the current workflow instance and its environment.

Whether you've created a new project or added a new workflow to an existing project, you should have a workflow that contains an OnWorkflowActivity activity as its child activity.

Now, drag a CreateTask activity from the toolbox and drop it onto the designer surface right below the OnWorkflowActivated activity, as shown in Figure 4-1.

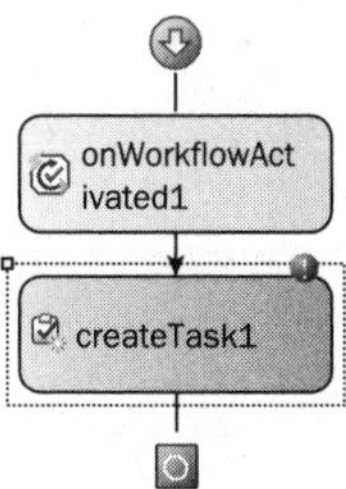

Figure 4-1

As shown in the Properties in Figure 4-2, the InterfaceType and MethodName properties of the CreateTask activity are automatically set to Microsoft.SharePoint.Workflow.ITaskService and CreateTask, respectively. This is because the default constructor of the CreateTask activity explicitly sets the values of these two properties even though the InterfaceType and MethodName properties of this activity return these values as well, as shown in the following excerpt from Listing 4-3:

```
public CreateTask()
{
  this.InterfaceType = typeof(ITaskService);
  this.MethodName = "CreateTask";
}

public override Type InterfaceType
{
  get { return typeof(ITaskService); }
}

public override string MethodName
{
  get { return "CreateTask"; }
}
```

You must follow the same implementation pattern when you're implementing your own custom CallExternalMethodActivity-based activities. That is, the default constructor of your custom activity must explicitly set the values of the InterfaceType and MethodName properties in this constructor in addition to overriding the InterfaceType and MethodName properties. Otherwise, Visual Studio would not show these values in the Properties pane.

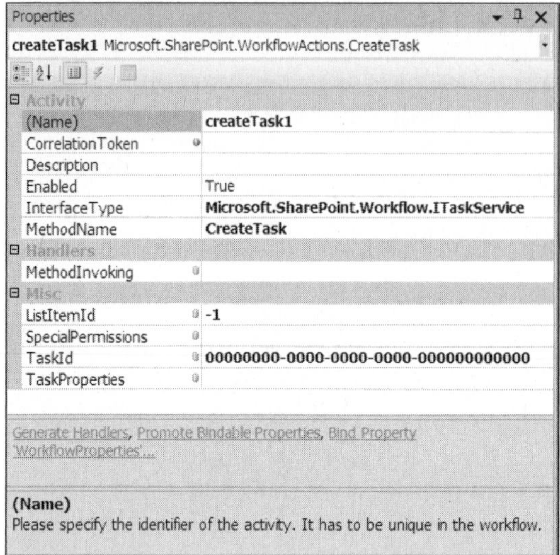

Figure 4-2

Enter a name for the CorrelationToken property of the CreateTask activity in the Properties pane. Make sure you do not use the same name that we assigned to the CorrelationToken property of the OnWorkflowActivated activity. Instead enter a new name such as "taskToken" for the CorrelationToken property in the Properties pane. This will automatically generate and add the following code to our workflow:

```
CorrelationToken correlationtoken1 = new CorrelationToken();
correlationtoken1.Name = "taskToken";
correlationtoken1.OwnerActivityName = null;
this.createTask1.CorrelationToken = correlationtoken1;
```

The preceding code instantiates a new CorrelationToken object, sets its Name property to whatever name you've entered in the Properties pane, and assigns this object to the CorrelationToken property of the CreateTask activity. At this point the OwnerActivityName property of the CorrelationToken property is set to null because you haven't yet specified an owner activity for this correlation token. That's also why the exclamation sign still appears in the top-right corner of the CreateTask activity on the designer surface.

You may be wondering why you shouldn't use the same correlation token name that you used for the correlation token of the OnWorkflowActivated activity. As discussed thoroughly in the previous section, the Execute method of CallExternalMethodActivity, which is the base class from which CreateTask inherits, internally populates the CorrelationToken object assigned to its CorrelationToken property with the correlation parameter values. The correlation parameter in the case of the CreateTask activity is the task ID, which is different from the correlation parameter in the case of the OnWorkflowActivated activity, which is the workflow instance ID.

Next, select the workflow, which is workflow2 in this project, as the owner activity for this correlation token in the Properties pane. This automatically resets the value of the OwnerActivityName property as follows:

```
correlationtoken1.OwnerActivityName = "Workflow2";
```

The Properties pane should now look like Figure 4-3.

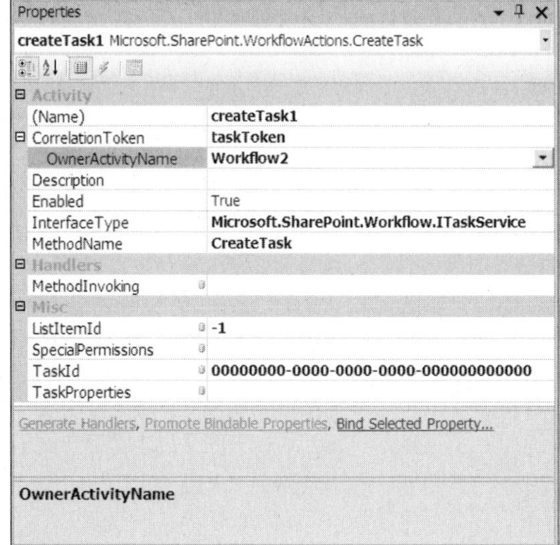

Figure 4-3

Click the text box in front of the TaskId property in the Properties pane to make the ellipsis button shown in Figure 4-4 visible.

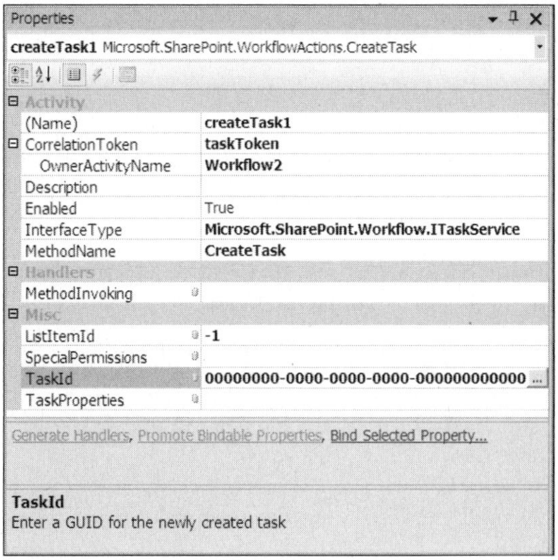

Properties
createTask1 Microsoft.SharePoint.WorkflowActions.CreateTask
Activity
(Name) createTask1
CorrelationToken taskToken
OwnerActivityName Workflow2
Description
Enabled True
InterfaceType Microsoft.SharePoint.Workflow.ITaskService
MethodName CreateTask
Handlers
MethodInvoking
Misc
ListItemId -1
SpecialPermissions
TaskId 00000000-0000-0000-0000-000000000000 ...
TaskProperties
Generate Handlers, Promote Bindable Properties, Bind Selected Property...
TaskId
Enter a GUID for the newly created task

Figure 4-4

Click this button to launch the dialog shown in Figure 4-5. Switch to the "Bind to a new parameter" tab, check the Create Field radio button, enter TaskId for the name of the field, and click OK.

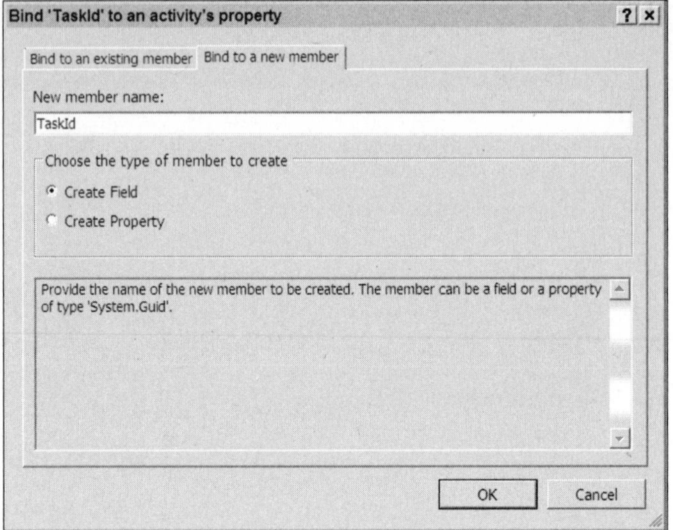

Figure 4-5

This will automatically generate and add the following code to our workflow:

```
public Guid TaskId = default(System.Guid);

private void InitializeComponent()
{
  . . .
  ActivityBind activitybind1 = new ActivityBind();
  activitybind1.Name = "Workflow2";
  activitybind1.Path = "TaskId";
  this.createTask1.SetBinding(CreateTask.TaskIdProperty, activitybind1);
  . . .
}
```

This code declares a new field named TaskId for our workflow. It then instantiates an ActivityBind object, sets its Path property to the name of this new field — that is, "TaskId" — and sets its Name property to the name of our workflow because this field belongs to the workflow. Finally, it invokes the SetBinding method on the CreateTask activity to bind this ActivityBind object to the TaskId property of this activity. This means that when the workflow sets the value of its TaskId field, this value will be automatically assigned to the TaskId property of the CreateTask activity through activity binding. You'll see shortly where the value of the TaskId field is set.

Next, click the text box in front of the TaskProperties property in the Properties pane to make the button shown in Figure 4-6 visible.

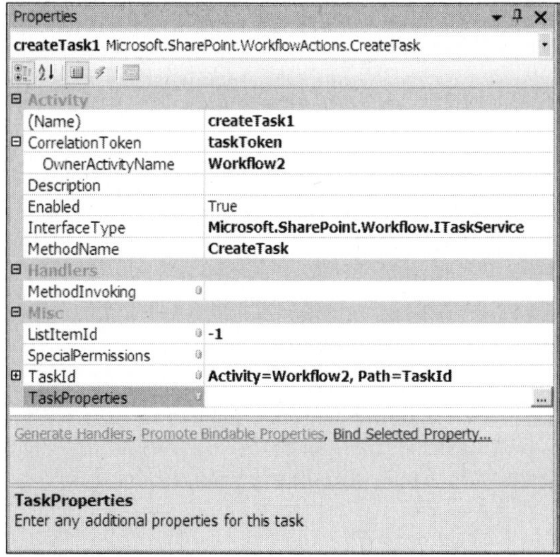

Figure 4-6

Click this button to launch the dialog shown in Figure 4-7. Switch to the "Bind to a new member" tab, check the Create Field radio button, enter TaskProperties for the name of the new field, and click OK.

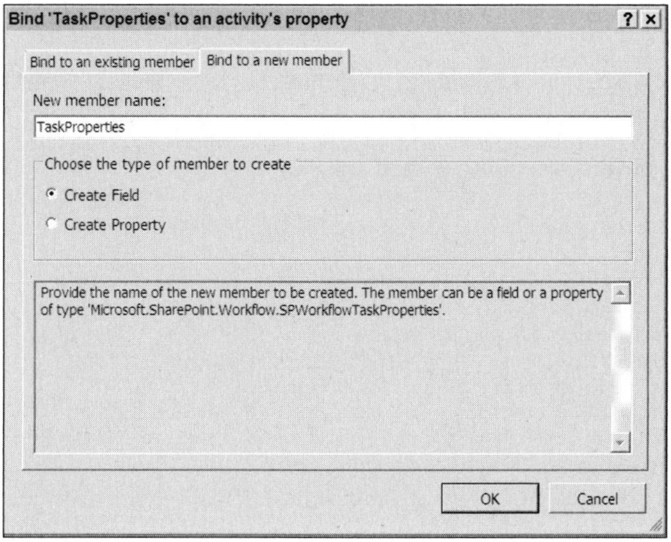

Figure 4-7

This will automatically generate and add the following code to our workflow:

```
public SPWorkflowTaskProperties TaskProperties = new SPWorkflowTaskProperties();

private void InitializeComponent()
{
  . . .
  ActivityBind activitybind2 = new ActivityBind();
  activitybind2.Name = "Workflow2";
  activitybind2.Path = "TaskProperties";
  this.createTask1.SetBinding(CreateTask.TaskPropertiesProperty, activitybind2);
  . . .
}
```

Next, right-click the CreateTask activity in the designer surface and select the Generate Handlers option from the pop-up menu. This will automatically generate an event handler with an empty body for you and register this event handler for the MethodInvoking event of the CreateTask activity:

```
private void InitializeComponent()
{
  . . .
  this.createTask1.MethodInvoking +=
                       new EventHandler(this.createTask1_MethodInvoking);
  . . .
}

private void createTask1_MethodInvoking(object sender, EventArgs e)
{
}
```

This event handler is where you must specify the properties of the SharePoint task that you want the CreateTask activity to create, as shown in Listing 4-5.

Listing 4-5: The MethodInvoking event handler

```
private void createTask1_MethodInvoking(object sender, EventArgs e)
{
  this.TaskId = Guid.NewGuid();
  this.TaskProperties.Title = "My Title";
  this.TaskProperties.PercentComplete = 0;
  this.TaskProperties.DueDate = DateTime.Now.AddMinutes(2);
  this.TaskProperties.StartDate = DateTime.Now;
  this.TaskProperties.AssignedTo = workflowProperties.Originator;
}
```

Click F5 to build and run the project. Visual Studio will automatically perform the following tasks:

1. It deploys the feature and the workflow template that it references to a feature-specific folder under the FEATURES folder on the file system of the front-end Web server. Visual Studio automatically creates this feature and the workflow template files when you create a SharePoint 2007 Sequential Workflow project.

2. It uses the STSADM command-line utility to install and activate the feature in the site collection that you specified when you created the project.
3. It compiles the workflow into a strong-named assembly.
4. It deploys the assembly to the global assembly cache.
5. It creates a workflow association with the name that you specified when you created the project on the same SharePoint list that you specified when you created the project.
6. It navigates to the AllItems.aspx page that displays this SharePoint list, as shown in Figure 4-8.

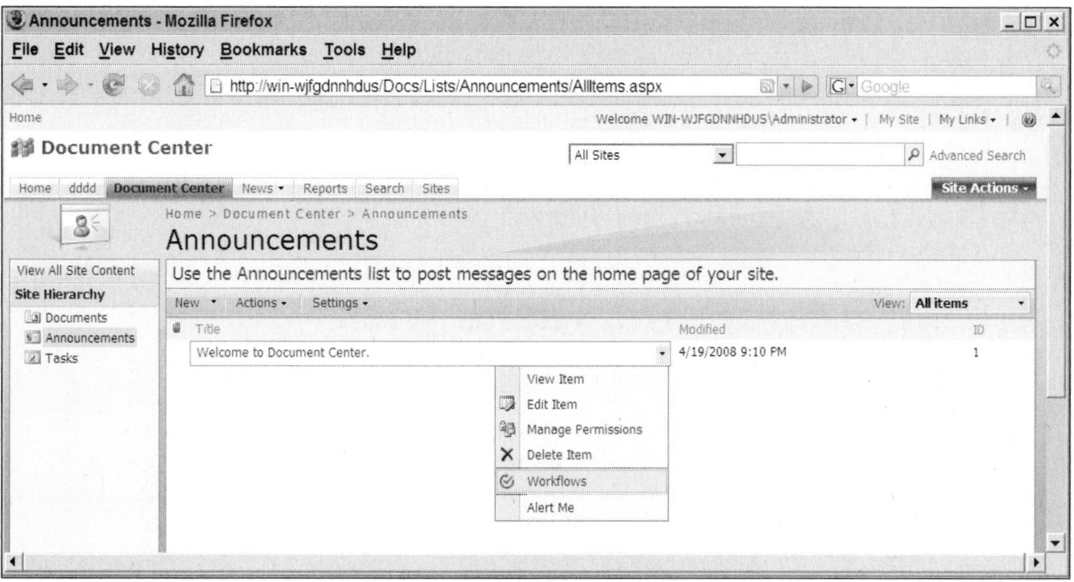

Figure 4-8

Select the Workflows menu option (refer to Figure 4-8) from the Edit Control Block (ECB) menu of a list item from this SharePoint list to navigate to the Workflow.aspx page, which displays the list of available workflow associations. Select the workflow association that Visual Studio just created to initiate a workflow instance. Because this workflow is not waiting for input from an external entity, it should complete its execution. Then click the Tasks node shown in the View All Site Content pane shown in Figure 4-8 to navigate to the AllItems.aspx page that displays the content of the Tasks list, as shown in Figure 4-9.

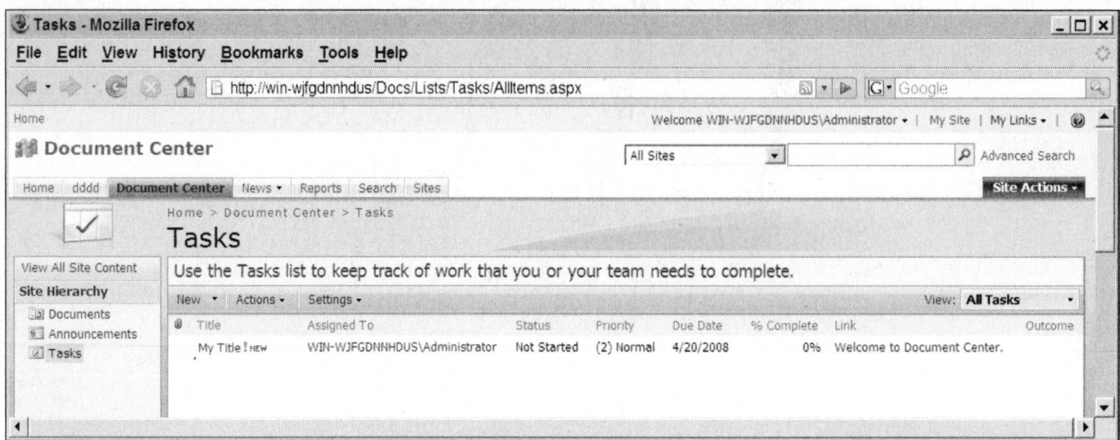

Figure 4-9

As you can see, the Tasks list contains a new task with the same properties that you specified in the MethodInvoking event handler shown in Listing 4-5.

Creating SharePoint Tasks with Content Types

SharePoint comes with an activity named CreateTaskWithContentType that inherits from CallExternalMethodActivity, as shown in Listing 4-6.

Listing 4-6: The CreateTaskWithContentType activity

```
public sealed class CreateTaskWithContentType : CallExternalMethodActivity
{
  public static DependencyProperty ContentTypeIdProperty;
  public static DependencyProperty ListItemIdProperty;
  public static DependencyProperty SpecialPermissionsProperty;
  public static DependencyProperty TaskIdProperty;
  public static DependencyProperty TaskPropertiesProperty;

  public CreateTaskWithContentType()
  {
    this.InterfaceType = typeof(ITaskService);
    this.MethodName = "CreateTaskWithContentType";
  }

  protected override void OnMethodInvoked(EventArgs e)
  {
    this.ListItemId =
     (int)base.ParameterBindings["(ReturnValue)"].Value;
  }

  protected override void OnMethodInvoking(EventArgs e)
```

```
    {
      base.ParameterBindings["taskId"].Value = this.TaskId;
      base.ParameterBindings["properties"].Value = this.TaskProperties;
      base.ParameterBindings["taskContentTypeId"].Value =
                            this.ContentTypeId;
      base.ParameterBindings["specialPermissions"].Value =
                            this.SpecialPermissions;
    }

    public override Type InterfaceType
    {
      get { return typeof(ITaskService); }
    }

    public override string MethodName
    {
      get { return "CreateTaskWithContentType"; }
    }

    public string ContentTypeId { get; set; }
    public int ListItemId { get; set; }
    public HybridDictionary SpecialPermissions { get; set; }
    public Guid TaskId { get; set; }
    public SPWorkflowTaskProperties TaskProperties { get; set; }
  }
```

CreateTaskWithContentType takes the following steps:

- It overrides the InterfaceType property of CallExternalMethodActivity to return the Type object that represents the type of ITaskService.
- It overrides the MethodName property of CallExternalMethodActivity to return the string "CreateTaskWithContentType". This means that the CreateTaskWithContentType activity is specifically designed to invoke the CreateTaskWithContentType method of ITaskService.
- It exposes the taskId, properties, taskContentTypeId, and specialPermissions parameters of the underlying CreateTaskWithContentType method as activity-level bindable properties named TaskId, TaskProperties, ContentTypeId, and SpecialPermissions. Because these properties are defined as bindable properties, the properties of the containing workflow or other activities can be bound to them to automatically pick up the values of these properties through activity binding.
- It exposes the return value of the underlying CreateTaskWithContentType method as an activity-level bindable property named ListItemId. Recall that this method returns the list item id of the newly created task. This means that a property of the containing workflow or one of its activities can be bound to the ListItemId property to automatically pick up this value through activity binding.
- It overrides the OnMethodInvoking method of CallExternalMethodActivity to populate the ParameterBindings property with the values of the TaskId, TaskProperties, ContentTypeId, and SpecialPermissions properties before the underlying CreateTaskWithContentType method is invoked.

- It overrides the OnMethodInvoked method of CallExternalMethodActivity to assign the return value of the underlying CreateTaskWithContentType method to the ListItemId property after the underlying method is invoked.

For example, consider a large company that is organizing a conference for a selected group of employees. Interested employees are required to send a request to their respective manager to get approval before they can participate in this conference. Because the conference lasts for several days, employees must get approval for the days they wish to participate. To keep the example simple, assume that every request is made for consecutive days.

We'll develop a workflow named ConferenceRequestWorkflow. This workflow consists of several SharePoint activities. We'll add these activities one by one as we proceed through the discussions in this chapter and subsequent chapters. For now, here's an overview of this workflow and its constituent activities (this section adds only the first two activities):

1. An employee who needs to make a conference request initiates an instance of this workflow on a list item in the SharePoint list with which this workflow is associated.
2. SharePoint redirects the employee to the initiation form, where the employee enters his or her first and last name and the starting and ending dates.
3. The first activity of this workflow, OnWorkflowActivated, is executed first. This activity suspends its execution and waits for the ISharePointService external data exchange service to raise the OnWorkflowActivated event. When this event is finally raised, the OnWorkflowActivated activity resumes its execution and raises its Invoked event.
4. The event handler that the workflow has registered for this event is then invoked. This event handler populates the workflow fields named EmployeeFirstName, EmployeeLastName, StartingDate, and EndingDate with the initiation data.
5. The OnWorkflowActivated activity then completes its execution.
6. The second activity of this workflow, CreateTaskWithContentType, is executed next. This activity creates a task with the content type of ManagerContentType, populates the respective fields of this task with the values of the EmployeeFirstName, EmployeeLastName, StartingDate, and EndingDate workflow fields, and finally completes its execution. I'll discuss ManagerContentType shortly.
7. The third activity of this workflow, OnTaskChanged, is executed next. This activity suspends its execution and waits for the manager to update the task that the CreateTaskWithContentType activity from Step 6 created.
8. The manager selects the Edit Item option menu from the ECB of the task to navigate to the edit task form, where he or she approves or denies the request, optionally enters a comment, and finally clicks the OK button on this form to update and complete the task.
9. Updating the task triggers the OnTaskChanged activity from Step 7 to resume its execution. This activity then fires its Invoked event and consequently invokes the event handler that the workflow has registered for this event.
10. This event handler retrieves the manager approval and comment from the task and stores them in the workflow fields named ManagerApproval and ManagerComment.
11. The OnTaskChanged activity finally completes its execution.

12. The fourth activity of this workflow, which is another CreateTaskWithContentType activity, is executed next. This activity creates a task with the content type of PersonnelContentType, populates the respective fields of this task with the values of the EmployeeFirstName, EmployeeLastName, StartingDate, EndingDate, ManagerApproval, and ManagerComment workflow fields, and finally completes its execution. I discuss PersonnelContentType shortly. This activity hasn't been added to our workflow because it is very similar to Step 6. As such, I'll leave this as an exercise.

13. The fifth activity of this workflow, an OnTaskChanged activity, is executed next. This activity suspends its execution and waits for the personnel department of the employee to update the task that the CreateTaskWithContentType activity from Step 12 created. I have not added this activity to our workflow because it is very similar to Step 7. Again, it is left as an exercise.

14. Personnel selects the Edit Item option menu from the ECB of the task to navigate to the edit task form, where Personnel approves or denies the employee's request, optionally adds a comment, and clicks the OK button on this form to update and complete the task.

15. Updating the task triggers the OnTaskChanged activity from Step 13 to resume and complete its execution.

ConferenceRequestWorkflow contains two instances of the CreateTaskWithContentType activities that create tasks with the content types of ManagerContentType and PersonnelContentType, respectively. Next, we'll implement and deploy these two content types to SharePoint.

First, we need to define these two content types and store them in an XML file named ConferenceRequestSiteContentTypes.xml. This XML file is an example of what is known as an *element manifest file*. Listing 4-7 presents the content of this XML file.

Listing 4-7: Content of the ConferenceRequestSiteContentTypes.xml file

```
<?xml version="1.0" encoding="utf-8" ?>
<Elements xmlns="http://schemas.microsoft.com/sharepoint/">
  <ContentType
    ID="0x01080100A3440F3CB4E74e5e8B4CF07BAEBAB9B1"
    Name="ConferenceRequestContentType"
    Description="Provision a new ConferenceRequestContentType"
    Version="0"
    Group="Conference Request Content Types" >
    <FieldRefs>
      <FieldRef ID="{C936B73E-5607-462f-9623-5AACD5765CBF}"
      Name="EmployeeFirstName" DisplayName="Employee First Name" />
      <FieldRef ID="{481FD88F-4964-4924-A25B-FF1C3882CD0F}"
      Name="EmployeeLastName"
      DisplayName="Employee Last Name" />
      <FieldRef ID="{7FF39930-F6CD-4728-8000-9AA39B50995F}"
      Name="ConferenceStartDate" DisplayName="Conference Start Date" />
      <FieldRef ID="{D5601EC5-FCE3-4ea8-ABA6-8A1503DB8D22}"
      Name="ConferenceEndDate"
      DisplayName="Conference End Date" />
      <FieldRef ID="{7E26EA7A-A5A6-4dc3-B257-442FB62E84EB}"
      Name="EntitledDays"
```

(continued)

Listing 4-7 *(continued)*

```
          DisplayName="Entitled Days" />
      </FieldRefs>
    </ContentType>

    <ContentType
      ID="0x01080100A3440F3CB4E74e5e8B4CF07BAEBAB9B101"
      Name="ManagerContentType"
      Description="Provision a new ManagerContentType"
      Version="0"
      Group="Conference Request Content Types" >
      <FieldRefs>
        <FieldRef ID="{D90A2BE9-0230-4d0e-8C33-192CF9F54A27}"
        Name="ManagerComment"
        DisplayName="Manager Comment" />
        <FieldRef ID="{29BBEEC4-BE8E-4efb-9646-F4A132222B45}"
        Name="ManagerApproval"
        DisplayName="Manager Approval" />
      </FieldRefs>
    </ContentType>

    <ContentType
      ID="0x01080100A3440F3CB4E74e5e8B4CF07BAEBAB9B10101"
      Name="PersonnelContentType"
      Description="Provision a new PersonnelContentType"
      Version="0"
      Group="Conference Request Content Types" >
      <FieldRefs>
        <FieldRef ID="{4296281E-3EC8-42d6-AD17-7CCB52483E66}"
        Name="PersonnelComment"
        DisplayName="Personnel Comment" />
        <FieldRef ID="{D382F1DA-5FA5-4478-A2F8-C96FCE95293C}"
        Name="PersonnelApproval" DisplayName="Personnel Approval" />
      </FieldRefs>
    </ContentType>
  </Elements>
```

This element manifest file, like any other element manifest file, has a document element named <Elements>. This document element contains three <ContentType> child elements that define the ConferenceRequestContentType, ManagerContentType, and PersonnelContentType site content types, respectively. The value of the ID attribute of a <ContentType> element is known as the content type ID of the site content type that the element defines. As a matter of fact, the SharePoint object model comes with a class named SPContentTypeId whose instances represent the content type IDs of SharePoint content types.

Note that the value of the ID attribute on the <ContentType> element that defines the ConferenceRequestContentType site content type (that is, the content type ID of the ConferenceRequestContentType site content type) consists of the following parts:

- **0x010801:** This hexadecimal number is the content type ID of a standard SharePoint site content type named WorkflowTask. The WorkflowTask site content type, like any other standard SharePoint site content type, is defined in an element manifest file named ctypes.xml, which is located in the following folder on the file system of the front-end web server:

```
Local_Drive:\Program Files\Common Files\microsoft shared\Web Server
Extensions\12\TEMPLATE\FEATURES\ctypes
```

The following excerpt from ctypes.xml presents the definition of the WorkflowTask site content type:

```
<ContentType
ID="0x010801"
Name="$Resources:WorkflowTask"
Group="_Hidden"
Hidden="TRUE"
Description="$Resources:WorkflowTaskCTDesc"
Version="0">
  <FieldRefs>
    <FieldRef ID="{58ddda52-c2a3-4650-9178-3bbc1f6e36da}" Name="Link" />
    <FieldRef ID="{16b6952f-3ce6-45e0-8f4e-42dac6e12441}"
    Name="OffsiteParticipant" />
    <FieldRef ID="{4a799ba5-f449-4796-b43e-aa5186c3c414}"
    Name="OffsiteParticipantReason" />
    <FieldRef ID="{18e1c6fa-ae37-4102-890a-cfb0974ef494}" Name="WorkflowOutcome" />
    <FieldRef ID="{e506d6ca-c2da-4164-b858-306f1c41c9ec}" Name="WorkflowName" />
    <FieldRef ID="{ae069f25-3ac2-4256-b9c3-15dbc15da0e0}" Name="GUID" />
    <FieldRef ID="{8d96aa48-9dff-46cf-8538-84c747ffa877}" Name="TaskType" />
    <FieldRef ID="{17ca3a22-fdfe-46eb-99b5-9646baed3f16}" Name="FormURN" />
    <FieldRef ID="{78eae64a-f5f2-49af-b416-3247b76f46a1}" Name="FormData" />
    <FieldRef ID="{8cbb9252-1035-4156-9c35-f54e9056c65a}" Name="EmailBody" />
    <FieldRef ID="{47f68c3b-8930-406f-bde2-4a8c669ee87c}"
    Name="HasCustomEmailBody" />
    <FieldRef ID="{cb2413f2-7de9-4afc-8587-1ca3f563f624}"
    Name="SendEmailNotification" />
    <FieldRef ID="{4d2444c2-0e97-476c-a2a3-e9e4a9c73009}" Name="PendingModTime" />
    <FieldRef ID="{35363960-d998-4aad-b7e8-058dfe2c669e}" Name="Completed" />
    <FieldRef ID="{1bfee788-69b7-4765-b109-d4d9c31d1ac1}" Name="WorkflowListId" />
    <FieldRef ID="{8e234c69-02b0-42d9-8046-d5f49bf0174f}" Name="WorkflowItemId" />
    <FieldRef ID="{1c5518e2-1e99-49fe-bfc6-1a8de3ba16e2}"
    Name="ExtendedProperties" />
  </FieldRefs>
</ContentType>
```

- The WorkflowTask site content type defines the columns that appear in all workflow task lists. As shown in the excerpt, the ID attribute of the WorkflowTask site content type is set to 0x010801, which is the same value with which the content type ID of the ConferenceRequestContentType begins. This tells SharePoint that the ConferenceRequestContentType site content type inherits from the WorkflowTask site content type. This means that the ConferenceRequestContentType site content type inherits all the columns that the WorkflowTask site content type references.

- **00:** This hexadecimal number is used to separate the content type ID of the base site content type, which is 0x010801 in this case, from the rest of the content type ID of the derived content type, which is discussed in the next bulleted item.

- **A3440F3CB4E74e5e8B4CF07BAEBAB9B1:** This is a GUID that uniquely identifies the ConferenceRequestContentType site content type from all other content types that inherit from the same base site content type, which is the WorkflowTask site content type in this case. Visual Studio comes with a command-line utility named guidgen.exe, shown in Figure 4-10, that you can use to generate and copy and paste GUIDs. Select Start ⇨ All Programs ⇨ Microsoft Visual Studio 2008 ⇨ Visual Studio Tools ⇨ Visual Studio 2008 Command Prompt to launch the Visual Studio command prompt, and then enter guidgen.exe at the command line to launch the guidgen command-line utility.

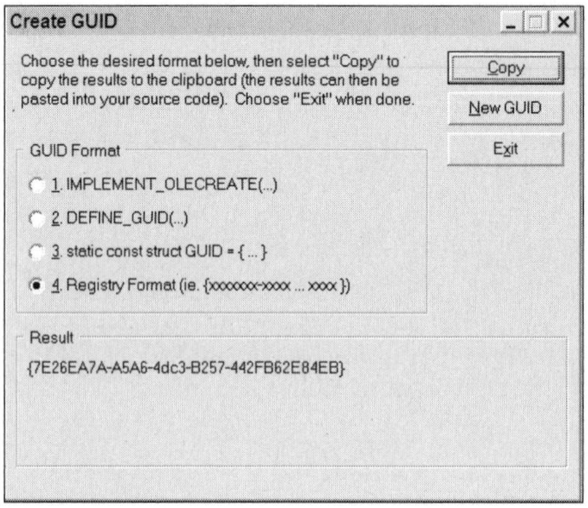

Figure 4-10

As shown in Listing 4-7, the ConferenceRequestContentType site content type references five site columns named EmployeeFirstName, EmployeeLastName, and StartDate, EndDate, and Days (which specifies the number of days the employee is entitled to):

```
<FieldRefs>
  <FieldRef ID="{C936B73E-5607-462f-9623-5AACD5765CBF}"
  Name="EmployeeFirstName" DisplayName="Employee First Name" />
  <FieldRef ID="{C936B73E-5607-462f-9623-5AACD5765CBF}" Name="EmployeeLastName"
  DisplayName="Employee Last Name" />
  <FieldRef ID="{7FF39930-F6CD-4728-8000-9AA39B50995F}"
  Name="StartDate" DisplayName=" Start Date" />
  <FieldRef ID="{D5601EC5-FCE3-4ea8-ABA6-8A1503DB8D22}" Name="EndDate"
  DisplayName=" End Date" />
  <FieldRef ID="{7E26EA7A-A5A6-4dc3-B257-442FB62E84EB}" Name="Days"
  DisplayName="Days" />
</FieldRefs>
```

In other words, the ConferenceRequestContentType site content type extends the columns that it inherits from the WorkflowTask site content type to add support for these five site columns. This means that when you add the ConferenceRequestContentType site content type to a SharePoint list, it will add the columns that it inherits from the WorkflowTask site content type plus the preceding five columns. I provide the definitions of these five site columns later in this section.

As shown in Listing 4-7, the ConferenceRequestContentTypes.xml element manifest file also defines a site content type named ManagerContentType. The ID attribute of the <ContentType> element that defines this site content type, like the ID attribute of any other <ContentType> element, specifies the content type ID of the site content type that the <ContentType> element defines. This content type ID consists of the following sections:

- **0x01080100A3440F3CB4E74e5e8B4CF07BAEBAB9B1:** This is the content type ID of the ConferenceRequestContentType site content type. This means that the ManagerContentType site content type inherits from the ConferenceRequestContentType site content type. As such, it inherits all the site column references that the ConferenceRequestContentType site content type contains. This includes those site column references that the ConferenceRequestContentType site content type inherits from the WorkflowTask site content type plus the five site column references that the ConferenceRequestContentType site content type contains — that is, EmployeeFirstName, EmployeeLastName, StartDate, EndDate, and Days.
- **01:** This hexadecimal number uniquely identifies the ManagerContentType site content type from all other site content types that inherit from the ConferenceRequestContentType site content type.

The ManagerContentType site content type references two new site columns named ManagerComment and ManagerApproval:

```
<FieldRefs>
  <FieldRef ID="{D90A2BE9-0230-4d0e-8C33-192CF9F54A27}" Name="ManagerComment"
  DisplayName="Manager Comment" />
  <FieldRef ID="{29BBEEC4-BE8E-4efb-9646-F4A132222B45}" Name="ManagerApproval"
  DisplayName="Manager Approval" />
</FieldRefs>
```

As Listing 4-7 illustrates, the ConferenceRequestContentTypes.xml element manifest file also defines a site content type named PersonnelContentType. The content type ID of this site content type consists of the following sections:

- **0x01080100A3440F3CB4E74e5e8B4CF07BAEBAB9B101:** This is the content type ID of the ManagerContentType site content type. This means that the PersonnelContentType site content type inherits from the ManagerContentType site content type. As such, it inherits all the site column references that the ManagerContentType site content type contains. This includes those site column references that the ManagerContentType site content type inherits from the ConferenceRequestContentType site content type plus the two site column references that the ManagerContentType site content type contains — that is, ManagerApproval and ManagerComment.
- **01:** This hexadecimal number uniquely identifies the PersonnelContentType site content type from all other site content types that inherit from the ManagerContentType site content type.

As shown in Listing 4-7, the PersonnelContentType site content type references two new site columns named PersonnelComment and PersonnelApproval:

```
<FieldRefs>
  <FieldRef ID="{D90A2BE9-0230-4d0e-8C33-192CF9F54A27}" Name="PersonnelComment"
  DisplayName="Personnel Comment" />
  <FieldRef ID="{29BBEEC4-BE8E-4efb-9646-F4A132222B45}"
  Name="PersonnelApproval" DisplayName="Personnel Approval" />
</FieldRefs>
```

Listing 4-8 presents the content of another element manifest file named ConferenceRequestSiteColumns.xml that defines the site columns that the ConferenceRequestContentType, ManagerContentType, and PersonnelContentType site content types reference.

Listing 4-8: Content of the ConferenceRequestSiteColumns.xml file

```
<?xml version="1.0" encoding="utf-8" ?>
<Elements xmlns="http://schemas.microsoft.com/sharepoint/">
  <Field
    ID="{C936B73E-5607-462f-9623-5AACD5765CBF}"
    Name="EmployeeFirstName"
    SourceID="http://schemas.microsoft.com/sharepoint/v3"
    StaticName="EmployeeFirstName"
    Group="Conference Request Site Columns"
    DisplayName="Employee First Name"
    Type="Text" />

  <Field
    ID="{481FD88F-4964-4924-A25B-FF1C3882CD0F}"
    Name="EmployeeLastName"
    SourceID="http://schemas.microsoft.com/sharepoint/v3"
    StaticName="EmployeeLastName"
    Group="Conference Request Site Columns"
    DisplayName="Employee Last Name"
    Type="Text" />

  <Field
    ID="{7FF39930-F6CD-4728-8000-9AA39B50995F}"
    Name="ConferenceStartDate"
    SourceID="http://schemas.microsoft.com/sharepoint/v3"
    StaticName="ConferenceStartDate"
    Group="Conference Request Site Columns"
    DisplayName="Conference Start Date"
    Type="DateTime" />

  <Field
    ID="{D5601EC5-FCE3-4ea8-ABA6-8A1503DB8D22}"
    Name="ConferenceEndDate"
    SourceID="http://schemas.microsoft.com/sharepoint/v3"
    StaticName="ConferenceEndDate"
    Group="Conference Request Site Columns"
    DisplayName="Conference End Date"
    Type="DateTime" />
```

```
  <Field
    ID="{7E26EA7A-A5A6-4dc3-B257-442FB62E84EB}"
    Name="EntitledDays"
    SourceID="http://schemas.microsoft.com/sharepoint/v3"
    StaticName="EntitledDays"
    Group="Conference Request Site Columns"
    DisplayName="EntitledDays"
    Type="Number" />

  <Field
    ID="{D90A2BE9-0230-4d0e-8C33-192CF9F54A27}"
    Name="ManagerComment"
    SourceID="http://schemas.microsoft.com/sharepoint/v3"
    StaticName="ManagerComment"
    Group="Conference Request Site Columns"
    DisplayName="Manager Comment"
    Type="Note" />

  <Field
    ID="{29BBEEC4-BE8E-4efb-9646-F4A132222B45}"
    Name="ManagerApproval"
    SourceID="http://schemas.microsoft.com/sharepoint/v3"
    StaticName="ManagerApproval"
    Group="Conference Request Site Columns"
    DisplayName="Manager Approval"
    Type="Boolean" />

  <Field
    ID="{4296281E-3EC8-42d6-AD17-7CCB52483E66}"
    Name="PersonnelComment"
    SourceID="http://schemas.microsoft.com/sharepoint/v3"
    StaticName="PersonnelComment"
    Group="Conference Request Site Columns"
    DisplayName="Personnel Comment"
    Type="Note" />

  <Field
    ID="{D382F1DA-5FA5-4478-A2F8-C96FCE95293C}"
    Name="PersonnelApproval"
    SourceID="http://schemas.microsoft.com/sharepoint/v3"
    StaticName="PersonnelApproval"
    Group="Conference Request Site Columns"
    DisplayName="Personnel Approval"
    Type="Boolean" />
</Elements>
```

This element manifest file contains a group of <Field> elements, each of which defines a site column. The ID attribute of each <Field> element must be set to a GUID that uniquely identifies the site column. Use the guidgen.exe utility shown in Figure 4-10 to generate and copy-and-paste the required GUIDs. The Type attribute of each <Field> element specifies the data type of the site column that the element defines.

Note that a site column does not define its own data type. Instead, it uses an existing data type. In addition, the ID attribute of a <Field> element that defines a site column does not follow the same pattern as the ID attribute of a <ContentType> element that defines a site content type. In other words, the ID attribute of a <Field> element that defines a site column does not contain the ID attribute value of another site column. This means that you cannot inherit from a site column to define a new site column. This is very different from content types, whereby you must inherit your site content type from another site content type.

Listings 4-7 and 4-8, respectively, present the contents of the ConferenceRequestContentTypes.xml and ConferenceRequestSiteColumns.xml element manifest files that define the ConferenceRequestContentType, ManagerContentType, and PersonnelContentType site content types and the site columns that these site content types reference. Next, we need to implement a feature that references these element manifest files, as shown in Listing 4-9.

Listing 4-9: Feature that references the element manifest files that define our site columns and site content types

```
<?xml version="1.0" encoding="utf-8" ?>
<Feature
Id="AC1C2E35-20BE-4418-917F-34AB8689F711"
Title="Conference Request Feature"
Description="This is Conference Request Feature!"
Version="1.0.0.0"
Scope="Site"
ReceiverAssembly="Microsoft.Office.Workflow.Feature, Version=12.0.0.0,
                  Culture=neutral, PublicKeyToken=71e9bce111e9429c"
ReceiverClass="Microsoft.Office.Workflow.Feature.WorkflowFeatureReceiver"
xmlns="http://schemas.microsoft.com/sharepoint/">
  <ElementManifests>
    <ElementManifest Location="ConferenceRequestSiteColumns.xml"/>
    <ElementManifest Location="ConferenceRequestSiteContentTypes.xml"/>
  </ElementManifests>
  <Properties>
    <Property Key="GloballyAvailable" Value="true" />
    <!-- Value for RegisterForms key indicates the path to the forms relative to
feature file location -->
    <!-- if you don't have forms, use *.xsn -->
    <Property Key="RegisterForms" Value="*.xsn" />
  </Properties>
</Feature>
```

Next, we need to take the following steps:

1. Create a feature-specific folder named ConferenceRequest under the FEATURES folder in the following folder on the file system of the front-end web server:

```
Local_Drive:\Program Files\Common Files\microsoft shared\Web Server
Extensions\12\TEMPLATE
```

2. Copy the feature.xml feature file whose content is shown in Listing 4-9 into the ConferenceRequest folder.
3. Copy the ConferenceRequestContentTypes.xml and ConferenceRequestSiteColumns.xml element manifest files whose contents are shown in Listings 4-7 and 4-8 into the ConferenceRequest folder.

4. Run the STSADM.exe command-line utility to install the feature:

```
stsadm.exe -o installfeature -name ConferenceRequest
```

   Note that the -name switch expects the name of the feature-specific folder under which the feature.xml file is stored, which is the ConferenceRequest folder in our case.

5. Run the STSADM.exe command-line utility or use the SharePoint user interface to activate the feature in your favorite site.

Activating the feature on a site makes the ConferenceRequestContentType, ManagerContentType, and PersonnelContentType site content types and the site columns that they reference available to all SharePoint lists in that site and its descendant sites. In other words, you can add these site content types to any SharePoint list in that site and its descendant sites. In our case, we would like to add these content types to the task list of the workflow association that associates our ConferenceRequestWorkflow workflow with a SharePoint list.

Next, go ahead and use the SharePoint user interface to add our ManagerContentType site content type to the task list that you're going to use with our workflow. Because the ManagerContentType site content type inherits from the ConferenceRequestContentType site content type, you do not need to add the ConferenceRequestContentType site content type to the task list.

Now that we're done with the implementation and deployment of our site content types, we need to move on to the next order of business, which is the workflow association form. As discussed in previous chapters, the workflow association form is used to collect the workflow association data, which is normally default values for the workflow initialization parameters. In the case of the ConferenceRequestWorkflow workflow, the initialization parameters are the employee first and last names and the starting and ending dates. As such, our workflow association form consists of four input fields to collect the default values of these parameters, and two buttons named OK and Cancel.

Launch Visual Studio 2008. Select File ⇨ New Project to launch the New Project dialog. Select Office ⇨ 2007 under "Project types," and then select SharePoint 2007 Sequential Workflow under Templates, and click OK. Note that this newly created project already contains a workflow. We will add activities to this workflow later in this chapter. For now, we want to focus on the implementation of the workflow association form shown in Listing 4-10.

Listing 4-10: The ConferenceRequestWorkflowAssociationForm workflow association form

```
<%@ Page Language="C#" MasterPageFile="~/_layouts/application.master" EnableSession
State="true" ValidateRequest="False"
Inherits="SharePointWorkflow5.ConferenceRequestWorkflowAssociationForm" %>

<%@ Assembly Name="SharePointWorkflow5, Version=1.0.0.0, Culture=neutral, PublicKey
Token=1c4a9ebab9f0532c" %>

<%@ Register TagPrefix="SharePoint" Namespace="Microsoft.SharePoint.WebControls"
Assembly="Microsoft.SharePoint, Version=12.0.0.0, Culture=neutral, PublicKeyToken=7
1e9bce111e9429c" %>
```

(continued)

Listing 4-10 *(continued)*

```
<%@ Register TagPrefix="Utilities" Namespace="Microsoft.SharePoint.Utilities"
Assembly="Microsoft.SharePoint, Version=12.0.0.0, Culture=neutral, PublicKeyToken=7
1e9bce111e9429c" %>

<%@ Register TagPrefix="wssuc" TagName="InputFormSection" Src="/_controltemplates/
InputFormSection.ascx" %>

<%@ Register TagPrefix="wssuc" TagName="InputFormControl" Src="/_controltemplates/
InputFormControl.ascx" %>

<%@ Register TagPrefix="wssuc" TagName="ButtonSection" Src="/_controltemplates/
ButtonSection.ascx" %>

<asp:Content ID="Main" ContentPlaceHolderID="PlaceHolderMain" runat="server">
  <SharePoint:FormDigest ID="FormDigest1" runat="server" />
  <asp:Table CellSpacing="0" CellPadding="0" BorderWidth="0">
    <wssuc:InputFormSection Title="Default first name"
    Description="Specify the default first name for this workflow association."
    runat="server">
      <template_inputformcontrols>
        <wssuc:InputFormControl runat="server" LabelText="First Name:">
          <Template_Control>
            <SharePoint:InputFormTextBox ID="FirstNameTbx"
            Title="FirstName" width="300" runat="server"/>
          </Template_Control>
        </wssuc:InputFormControl>
      </template_inputformcontrols>
    </wssuc:InputFormSection>

    <wssuc:InputFormSection Title="Default last name"
    Description="Specify the default last name for this workflow association."
    runat="server">
      <template_inputformcontrols>
        <wssuc:InputFormControl runat="server" LabelText="Last Name:">
          <Template_Control>
            <SharePoint:InputFormTextBox ID="LastNameTbx"
            Title="LastName"
            width="300" runat="server"/>
          </Template_Control>
        </wssuc:InputFormControl>
      </template_inputformcontrols>
    </wssuc:InputFormSection>

    <wssuc:InputFormSection Title="Default starting date"
    Description="Specify the default starting date for this workflow association."
    runat="server">
      <template_inputformcontrols>
        <wssuc:InputFormControl runat="server"
        LabelText="Starting Day:">
          <Template_Control>
            <SharePoint:InputFormTextBox ID="StartingDateTbx"
            Title="StartingDate" width="300" runat="server"/>
          </Template_Control>
```

```
        </wssuc:InputFormControl>
      </template_inputformcontrols>
    </wssuc:InputFormSection>

    <wssuc:InputFormSection Title="Default ending date"
    Description="Specify the default ending date for this workflow association."
    runat="server">
      <template_inputformcontrols>
        <wssuc:InputFormControl runat="server" LabelText="ending Day:">
          <Template_Control>
            <SharePoint:InputFormTextBox ID="EndingDateTbx"
            Title="EndingDate" width="300" runat="server"/>
          </Template_Control>
        </wssuc:InputFormControl>
      </template_inputformcontrols>
    </wssuc:InputFormSection>

    <wssuc:ButtonSection runat="server"
    ShowStandardCancelButton="false">
      <template_buttons>
        <asp:PlaceHolder runat="server">
          <asp:Button runat="server" OnClick="OKCallback" Text="OK" />
          <asp:Button runat="server" OnClick="CancelCallback"
          Text="Cancel" />
        </asp:PlaceHolder>
      </template_buttons>
    </wssuc:ButtonSection>
  </asp:Table>

  <input type="hidden" name="WorkflowDefinition"
  value='<% SPHttpUtility.NoEncode(SPHttpUtility.HtmlEncode(
         Request.Form["WorkflowDefinition"]),Response.Output); %>'/>

  <input type="hidden" name="WorkflowName"
  value='<% SPHttpUtility.NoEncode(SPHttpUtility.HtmlEncode(
         Request.Form["WorkflowName"]),Response.Output); %>'/>

  <input type="hidden" name="AddToStatusMenu"
  value='<% SPHttpUtility.NoEncode(SPHttpUtility.HtmlEncode(
         Request.Form["AddToStatusMenu"]),Response.Output); %>'/>

  <input type="hidden" name="AllowManual"
  value='<% SPHttpUtility.NoEncode(SPHttpUtility.HtmlEncode(
         Request.Form["AllowManual"]),Response.Output); %>'/>

  <input type="hidden" name="RoleSelect"
  value='<% SPHttpUtility.NoEncode(SPHttpUtility.HtmlEncode(
         Request.Form["RoleSelect"]),Response.Output); %>'/>

  <input type="hidden" name="GuidAssoc"
  value='<% SPHttpUtility.NoEncode(SPHttpUtility.HtmlEncode(
         Request.Form["GuidAssoc"]),Response.Output); %>'/>
```

(continued)

Listing 4-10 *(continued)*

```
    <input type="hidden" name="SetDefault"
    value='<% SPHttpUtility.NoEncode(SPHttpUtility.HtmlEncode(
           Request.Form["SetDefault"]),Response.Output); %>'/>

    <input type="hidden" name="HistoryList"
    value='<% SPHttpUtility.NoEncode(SPHttpUtility.HtmlEncode(
           Request.Form["HistoryList"]),Response.Output); %>'/>

    <input type="hidden" name="TaskList"
    value='<% SPHttpUtility.NoEncode(SPHttpUtility.HtmlEncode(
           Request.Form["TaskList"]),Response.Output); %>'/>

    <input type="hidden" name="UpdateLists"
    value='<% SPHttpUtility.NoEncode(SPHttpUtility.HtmlEncode(
           Request.Form["UpdateLists"]),Response.Output); %>'/>

    <input type="hidden" name="AutoStartCreate"
    value='<% SPHttpUtility.NoEncode(SPHttpUtility.HtmlEncode(
           Request.Form["AutoStartCreate"]),Response.Output); %>'/>

    <input type="hidden" name="AutoStartChange"
    value='<% SPHttpUtility.NoEncode(SPHttpUtility.HtmlEncode(
           Request.Form["AutoStartChange"]),Response.Output); %>'/>
</asp:Content>

<asp:Content ID="Content1" ContentPlaceHolderID="PlaceHolderPageTitle"
   runat="server">
  <%= PlaceHolderPageTitleContent %>
</asp:Content>

<asp:Content ID="Content2" ContentPlaceHolderID="PlaceHolderPageTitleInTitleArea"
   runat="server">
  <%= PlaceHolderPageTitleInTitleAreaContent %>
</asp:Content>
```

Next, create a subfolder named ConferenceRequest in the following folder on the file system of the front-end web server:

```
Local_Drive:\Program Files\Common Files\microsoft shared\Web Server
Extensions\12\TEMPLATE\LAYOUTS
```

Recall that the LAYOUTS folder is where SharePoint application pages such as ConferenceRequestWorkflowAssociationForm.aspx are deployed. Next, create a file named ConferenceRequestWorkflowAssociationForm.aspx in the ConferenceRequest folder and add the contents of Listing 4-10 to this file.

As shown in Listing 4-10, the Inherits attribute on the @Page directive references a code-behind class named ConferenceRequestWorkflowAssociationForm. Listing 4-11 presents the implementation of this class.

Listing 4-11: The ConferenceRequestWorkflowAssociationForm class

```
using System;
using System.IO;
using System.Text;
using System.Web;
using System.Web.UI;
using System.Web.UI.WebControls;
using System.Web.UI.HtmlControls;
using System.Xml;
using System.Xml.Serialization;
using Microsoft.SharePoint;
using Microsoft.SharePoint.Utilities;
using Microsoft.SharePoint.WebControls;
using Microsoft.SharePoint.Workflow;

namespace SharePointWorkflow5
{
  public class ConferenceRequestWorkflowAssociationForm :
                                                  LayoutsPageBase
  {
    private SPList taskList;
    private SPList historyList;

    private string workflowAssociationName;
    private SPWorkflowAssociation workflowAssociation;
    private Guid workflowAssociationId;

    protected InputFormTextBox FirstNameTbx;
    protected InputFormTextBox LastNameTbx;
    protected InputFormTextBox StartingDateTbx;
    protected InputFormTextBox EndingDateTbx;
    protected string PlaceHolderPageTitleContent;
    protected string PlaceHolderPageTitleInTitleAreaContent;

    private bool isUpdatingWorkflowAssociation;
    private WorkflowAssociationTarget workflowAssociationTarget;
    private Guid workflowAssociationTargetListId;
    private SPList workflowAssociationTargetList;
    private SPContentTypeId workflowAssociationTargetContentTypeId;
    private SPContentType workflowAssociationTargetContentType;

    private void DetermineTaskAndHistoryLists()
    {
      if (Request.Params["TaskList"][0] == 'z' &&
          Request.Params["TaskList"].EndsWith(" Tasks"))
      {
        string newTaskListName =
             Request.Params["TaskList"].Substring(1);
```

(continued)

Listing 4-11 *(continued)*

```
        Guid newTaskListId = Web.Lists.Add(newTaskListName,
"Workflow Tasks",
                                          SPListTemplateType.Tasks);
        taskList = Web.Lists[newTaskListId];
      }

      else
      {
        if (workflowAssociationTarget ==
                WorkflowAssociationTarget.SiteContentType)
          taskList = Web.Lists[Request.Params["TaskList"]];

        else
          taskList = Web.Lists[new Guid(Request.Params["TaskList"])];
      }

      if (Request.Params["HistoryList"][0] == 'z' &&
          Request.Params["HistoryList"].EndsWith(" History"))
      {
        string newHistoryListName =
                Request.Params["HistoryList"].Substring(1);
        Guid newHistoryListId = Web.Lists.Add(newHistoryListName,
"Workflow History",
                                 SPListTemplateType.WorkflowHistory);
        historyList = Web.Lists[newHistoryListId];
      }

      else
      {
        if (workflowAssociationTarget ==
              WorkflowAssociationTarget.SiteContentType)
          historyList = Web.Lists[Request.Params["HistoryList"]];

        else
          historyList =
             Web.Lists[new Guid(Request.Params["HistoryList"])];
      }
    }

    private void UpdateWorkflowAssociation()
    {
      workflowAssociation.Name = workflowAssociationName;
      workflowAssociation.AutoStartCreate =
                    (Request.Params["AutoStartCreate"] == "ON");
      workflowAssociation.AutoStartChange =
                     (Request.Params["AutoStartChange"] == "ON");
      workflowAssociation.AllowManual =
                       (Request.Params["AllowManual"] == "ON");

      ConferenceRequestInfo info = new ConferenceRequestInfo();
      info.EmployeeFirstName = this.FirstNameTbx.Text;
```

```
    info.EmployeeLastName = this.LastNameTbx.Text;
    info.StartingDate = DateTime.Parse(this.StartingDateTbx.Text);
    info.EndingDate = DateTime.Parse(this.EndingDateTbx.Text);

    using (StringWriter sw = new StringWriter())
    {
      XmlSerializer serializer =
              new XmlSerializer(typeof(ConferenceRequestInfo));
      serializer.Serialize(sw, info);
      workflowAssociation.AssociationData = sw.ToString();
    }

    if (workflowAssociation.TaskListTitle != taskList.Title)
      workflowAssociation.SetTaskList(taskList);

    if (workflowAssociation.HistoryListTitle != historyList.Title)
      workflowAssociation.SetHistoryList(historyList);
  }

  protected override void OnLoad(EventArgs e)
  {
    workflowAssociationName = Request.Params["WorkflowName"];

    if (!string.IsNullOrEmpty(Request.Params["GuidAssoc"]))
    {
      isUpdatingWorkflowAssociation = true;
      workflowAssociationId = new Guid(Request.Params["GuidAssoc"]);
    }

    if (!string.IsNullOrEmpty(Request.Params["List"]))
    {
      workflowAssociationTargetListId =
             new Guid(Request.Params["List"]);
      workflowAssociationTargetList =
             Web.Lists[workflowAssociationTargetListId];
      if (!string.IsNullOrEmpty(Request.Params["ctype"]))
      {
        workflowAssociationTarget =
               WorkflowAssociationTarget.ListContentType;
        workflowAssociationTargetContentType =
             workflowAssociationTargetList.ContentTypes[
            new SPContentTypeId(Request.Params["ctype"])];
        if (isUpdatingWorkflowAssociation)
          workflowAssociation =
          workflowAssociationTargetContentType.WorkflowAssociations[
                                         workflowAssociationId];
      }

      else
      {
        workflowAssociationTarget = WorkflowAssociationTarget.List;
        if (isUpdatingWorkflowAssociation)
```

(continued)

Listing 4-11 *(continued)*

```
                workflowAssociation =
                   workflowAssociationTargetList.WorkflowAssociations[
                                                workflowAssociationId];
          }
        }

        else
        {
          workflowAssociationTarget =
                   WorkflowAssociationTarget.SiteContentType;
          workflowAssociationTargetContentTypeId =
                      new SPContentTypeId(Request.Params["ctype"]);
          workflowAssociationTargetContentType =
                           this.Web.AvailableContentTypes[
                      workflowAssociationTargetContentTypeId];
          if (isUpdatingWorkflowAssociation)
            workflowAssociation =
             workflowAssociationTargetContentType.WorkflowAssociations[
                                                workflowAssociationId];
        }

        if (isUpdatingWorkflowAssociation)
        {
          PlaceHolderPageTitleContent =
    "Update an existing workflow association";
          PlaceHolderPageTitleInTitleAreaContent =
    "Update the existing workflow association called " +
                               workflowAssociationName;

          ConferenceRequestInfo info = null;

          using (StringReader sr =
             new StringReader(workflowAssociation.AssociationData))
          {
            XmlSerializer serializer =
                 new XmlSerializer(typeof(ConferenceRequestInfo));
            info = (ConferenceRequestInfo)serializer.Deserialize(sr);
          }

          this.FirstNameTbx.Text = info.EmployeeFirstName;
          this.LastNameTbx.Text = info.EmployeeLastName;
          this.StartingDateTbx.Text = info.StartingDate.ToString();
          this.EndingDateTbx.Text = info.EndingDate.ToString();
        }

        else
        {
          PlaceHolderPageTitleContent = "Create a new workflow association";
```

```
        PlaceHolderPageTitleInTitleAreaContent =
"Create a new workflow association called " +
                              workflowAssociationName;
      }
    }

    public void CancelCallback(object sender, EventArgs e)
    {
      string url = String.Empty;
      switch (workflowAssociationTarget)
      {
        case WorkflowAssociationTarget.SiteContentType:
          url = "WrkSetng.aspx?ctype=" +
                 this.workflowAssociationTargetContentTypeId.ToString();
                 break;
        case WorkflowAssociationTarget.List:
          url = "WrkSetng.aspx?List=" +
                this.workflowAssociationTargetListId.ToString();
          break;
        case WorkflowAssociationTarget.ListContentType:
          url = "WrkSetng.aspx?List=" +
                 this.workflowAssociationTargetListId.ToString() +
"&ctype=" +
          this.workflowAssociationTargetContentTypeId.ToString();
          break;
      }
      SPUtility.Redirect(url, SPRedirectFlags.RelativeToLayoutsPage,
                         HttpContext.Current);
    }

    public void OKCallback(object sender, EventArgs e)
    {
      DetermineTaskAndHistoryLists();
      bool updateChildContentTypesAndLists =
                    (Request.Params["UpdateLists"] == "TRUE");
      Guid workflowTemplateId =
              new Guid(Request.Params["WorkflowDefinition"]);
      SPWorkflowTemplate workflowTemplate =
                 this.Web.WorkflowTemplates[workflowTemplateId];

      string url = "";
      switch (workflowAssociationTarget)
      {
        case WorkflowAssociationTarget.SiteContentType:
          if (isUpdatingWorkflowAssociation)
          {
            workflowAssociation =
          workflowAssociationTargetContentType.WorkflowAssociations[
                                             workflowAssociationId];
            UpdateWorkflowAssociation();
            workflowAssociationTargetContentType.UpdateWorkflowAssociation(
                                             workflowAssociation);
```

(continued)

Listing 4-11 *(continued)*

```
              if (updateChildContentTypesAndLists)
    workflowAssociationTargetContentType.UpdateWorkflowAssociationsOnChildren(true,
    true, true);
            }

            else
            {
              workflowAssociation =
                SPWorkflowAssociation.CreateSiteContentTypeAssociation(
                           workflowTemplate, workflowAssociationName,
                           taskList.Title, historyList.Title);
              UpdateWorkflowAssociation();
              workflowAssociationTargetContentType.AddWorkflowAssociation(
                                            workflowAssociation);
              if (updateChildContentTypesAndLists)
            workflowAssociationTargetContentType.UpdateWorkflowAssociationsOnChildren
    (true, true, true);
            }

            url = "WrkSetng.aspx?ctype=" +
                  workflowAssociationTargetContentTypeId.ToString();
            break;
          case WorkflowAssociationTarget.List:
            if (isUpdatingWorkflowAssociation)
            {
              UpdateWorkflowAssociation();
              workflowAssociationTargetList.UpdateWorkflowAssociation(
                                            workflowAssociation);
            }

            else
            {
              workflowAssociation =
                SPWorkflowAssociation.CreateListAssociation(workflowTemplate,
                                 workflowAssociationName,
                                                   taskList, historyList);
              UpdateWorkflowAssociation();
              workflowAssociationTargetList.AddWorkflowAssociation(
                                            workflowAssociation);
            }
            url = "WrkSetng.aspx?List=" +
                       workflowAssociationTargetListId.ToString();
            break;

          case WorkflowAssociationTarget.ListContentType:
            if (isUpdatingWorkflowAssociation)
```

```
          {
            workflowAssociation =
              workflowAssociationTargetContentType.WorkflowAssociations[
                                            workflowAssociationId];
            UpdateWorkflowAssociation();
            workflowAssociationTargetContentType.UpdateWorkflowAssociation(
                                            workflowAssociation);
          }

          else
          {
            workflowAssociation =
              SPWorkflowAssociation.CreateListContentTypeAssociation(
                          workflowTemplate, workflowAssociationName,
                               taskList, historyList);
            UpdateWorkflowAssociation();
            workflowAssociationTargetContentType.AddWorkflowAssociation(
                                                 workflowAssociation);
          }

          url = "WrkSetng.aspx?List=" +
                       workflowAssociationTargetListId.ToString() +
"&ctype=" +
             workflowAssociationTargetContentTypeId.ToString();
          break;
      }

      SPUtility.Redirect(url, SPRedirectFlags.RelativeToLayoutsPage,
                         HttpContext.Current);
    }
  }
}
```

Note that the ConferenceRequestWorkflowAssociationForm class makes use of another class named ConferenceRequestInfo, shown in Listing 4-12.

Listing 4-12: The ConferenceRequestInfo class

```
using System;

namespace SharePointWorkflow5
{
  public class ConferenceRequestInfo
  {
    private string employeeFirstName;
    public string EmployeeFirstName
    {
      get { return employeeFirstName; }
      set { employeeFirstName = value; }
    }

    private string employeeLastName;
    public string EmployeeLastName
```

(continued)

Listing 4-12 *(continued)*

```
    {
      get { return employeeLastName; }
      set { employeeLastName = value; }
    }

    private DateTime startingDate;
    public DateTime StartingDate
    {
      get { return startingDate; }
      set { startingDate = value; }
    }

    private DateTime endingDate;
    public DateTime EndingDate
    {
      get { return endingDate; }
      set { endingDate = value; }
    }

    private bool managerApproval;
    public bool ManagerApproval
    {
      get { return managerApproval; }
      set { managerApproval = value; }
    }

    private string managerComment = string.Empty;
    public string ManagerComment
    {
      get { return managerComment; }
      set { managerComment = value; }
    }

    private bool personnelApproval;
    public bool PersonnelApproval
    {
      get { return personnelApproval; }
      set { personnelApproval = value; }
    }

    private string personnelComment = string.Empty;
    public string PersonnelComment
    {
      get { return personnelComment; }
      set { personnelComment = value; }
    }
  }

  public enum WorkflowAssociationTarget
```

```
    {
      SiteContentType,
      List,
      ListContentType
    }
  }
```

Next, add two .cs files named ConferenceRequestWorkflowAssociationForm.cs and ConferenceRequestInfo.cs to the workflow project. Then add Listing 4-11 to ConferenceRequestWorkflowAssociationForm.cs and Listing 4-12 to ConferenceRequestInfo.cs. When you compile the workflow project, these two files will be compiled into the same assembly as the workflow assembly and deployed to the global assembly cache.

Figure 4-11 shows the workflow association form in action.

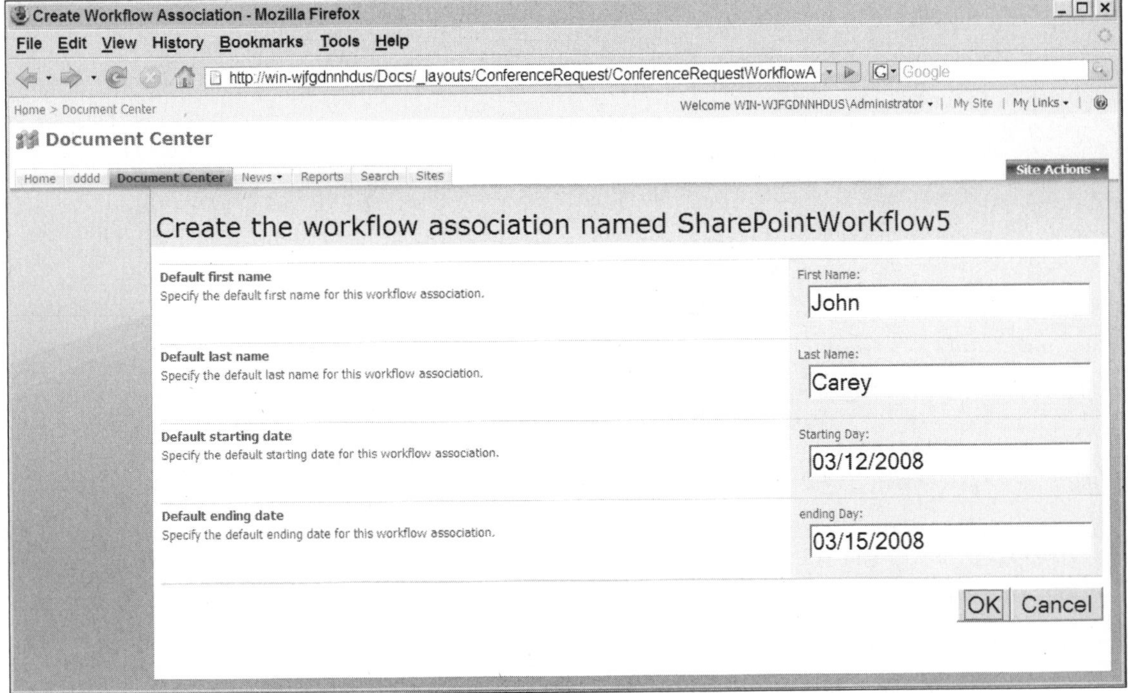

Figure 4-11

The next order of business is to implement the initiation form for our ConferenceRequestWorkflow workflow. When employees initiate a ConferenceRequestWorkflow instance, SharePoint automatically redirects the employees to the ConferenceRequestWorkflowInitiationForm.aspx page to enter their first and last name and starting and ending dates. The workflow initiation form exposes the same GUID as the workflow association form.

Listing 4-13 presents the implementation of the ConferenceRequestWorkflowInitiationForm.aspx page.

Listing 4-13: The ConferenceRequestWorkflowInitiationForm.aspx page

```
<%@ Page Language="C#" MasterPageFile="~/_layouts/application.master"
EnableSessionState="true"
ValidateRequest="False"
Inherits="SharePointWorkflow5.ConferenceRequestWorkflowInitiationForm" %>

<%@ Assembly Name="SharePointWorkflow5, Version=1.0.0.0, Culture=neutral, PublicKey
Token=1c4a9ebab9f0532c" %>

<%@ Register TagPrefix="SharePoint" Namespace="Microsoft.SharePoint.WebControls"
Assembly="Microsoft.SharePoint, Version=12.0.0.0, Culture=neutral, PublicKeyToken=7
1e9bce111e9429c" %>

<%@ Register TagPrefix="Utilities" Namespace="Microsoft.SharePoint.Utilities"
Assembly="Microsoft.SharePoint, Version=12.0.0.0, Culture=neutral, PublicKeyToken=7
1e9bce111e9429c" %>

<%@ Register TagPrefix="wssuc" TagName="InputFormSection" Src="/_controltemplates/
InputFormSection.ascx" %>

<%@ Register TagPrefix="wssuc" TagName="InputFormControl" Src="/_controltemplates/
InputFormControl.ascx" %>

<%@ Register TagPrefix="wssuc" TagName="ButtonSection" Src="/_controltemplates/
ButtonSection.ascx" %>

<asp:Content ID="Main" ContentPlaceHolderID="PlaceHolderMain" runat="server">
  <SharePoint:FormDigest ID="FormDigest1" runat="server" />
  <asp:Table CellSpacing="0" CellPadding="0" BorderWidth="0">
    <wssuc:InputFormSection Title="First name"
    Description="Specify the first name for this workflow instance."
    runat="server">
      <template_inputformcontrols>
        <wssuc:InputFormControl runat="server" LabelText="First Name:">
          <Template_Control>
            <SharePoint:InputFormTextBox ID="FirstNameTbx"
            Title="FirstName" width="300" runat="server"/>
          </Template_Control>
        </wssuc:InputFormControl>
      </template_inputformcontrols>
    </wssuc:InputFormSection>

    <wssuc:InputFormSection Title="Last name"
    Description="Specify the last name for this workflow instance."
    runat="server">
      <template_inputformcontrols>
        <wssuc:InputFormControl runat="server" LabelText="Last Name:">
          <Template_Control>
            <SharePoint:InputFormTextBox ID="LastNameTbx"
            Title="LastName" width="300" runat="server"/>
          </Template_Control>
```

```
        </wssuc:InputFormControl>
      </template_inputformcontrols>
    </wssuc:InputFormSection>

    <wssuc:InputFormSection Title="Starting date"
    Description="Specify the starting date for this workflow instance."
    runat="server">
      <template_inputformcontrols>
        <wssuc:InputFormControl runat="server"
        LabelText="Starting Day:">
          <Template_Control>
            <SharePoint:InputFormTextBox ID="StartingDateTbx"
            Title="StartingDate" width="300" runat="server"/>
          </Template_Control>
        </wssuc:InputFormControl>
      </template_inputformcontrols>
    </wssuc:InputFormSection>

    <wssuc:InputFormSection Title="Ending date"
    Description="Specify the ending date for this workflow instance."
    runat="server">
      <template_inputformcontrols>
        <wssuc:InputFormControl runat="server" LabelText="Ending Day:">
          <Template_Control>
            <SharePoint:InputFormTextBox ID="EndingDateTbx"
            Title="EndingDate" width="300" runat="server"/>
          </Template_Control>
        </wssuc:InputFormControl>
      </template_inputformcontrols>
    </wssuc:InputFormSection>

    <wssuc:ButtonSection runat="server"
    ShowStandardCancelButton="false">
      <template_buttons>
        <asp:PlaceHolder runat="server">
          <asp:Button runat="server" OnClick="OKCallback" Text="OK" />
          <asp:Button runat="server" OnClick="CancelCallback"
          Text="Cancel" />
        </asp:PlaceHolder>
      </template_buttons>
    </wssuc:ButtonSection>
  </asp:Table>
</asp:Content>

<asp:Content ID="Content1" ContentPlaceHolderID="PlaceHolderPageTitle"
runat="server">
  <%= PlaceHolderPageTitleContent %>
</asp:Content>

<asp:Content ID="Content2" ContentPlaceHolderID="PlaceHolderPageTitleInTitleArea"
runat="server">
  <%= PlaceHolderPageTitleInTitleAreaContent %>
</asp:Content>
```

Next, add a new file named ConferenceRequestWorkflowInitiationForm.aspx to the ConferenceRequest folder that you created under the following folder on the file system of the front-end web server:

```
Local_Drive:\Program Files\Common Files\microsoft shared\Web Server
Extensions\12\TEMPLATE\LAYOUTS
```

Then, add Listing 4-13 to this file and save it.

As shown in Listing 4-13, the Inherits attribute on the @Page directive references a code-behind class named ConferenceRequestWorkflowAssociationForm. Listing 4-14 presents the implementation of this class.

Listing 4-14: The ConferenceRequestWorkflowInitiationForm class

```
using System;
using System.IO;
using System.Text;
using System.Web;
using System.Web.UI;
using System.Web.UI.WebControls;
using System.Web.UI.HtmlControls;
using System.Xml;
using System.Xml.Serialization;
using Microsoft.SharePoint;
using Microsoft.SharePoint.Utilities;
using Microsoft.SharePoint.WebControls;
using Microsoft.SharePoint.Workflow;

namespace SharePointWorkflow5
{
  public class ConferenceRequestWorkflowInitiationForm : LayoutsPageBase
  {
    protected InputFormTextBox FirstNameTbx;
    protected InputFormTextBox LastNameTbx;
    protected InputFormTextBox StartingDateTbx;
    protected InputFormTextBox EndingDateTbx;
    protected string PlaceHolderPageTitleContent;
    protected string PlaceHolderPageTitleInTitleAreaContent;

    protected SPList targetList;
    SPListItem targetListItem;
    protected SPWorkflowAssociation workflowAssociation;

    protected override void OnLoad(EventArgs e)
    {
      targetList = Web.Lists[new Guid(Request.Params["List"])];
      Guid workflowAssociationId =
                new Guid(Request.Params["TemplateID"]);
      workflowAssociation =
         targetList.WorkflowAssociations[workflowAssociationId];
      targetListItem =
       targetList.GetItemById(int.Parse(Request.Params["ID"]));
      if (workflowAssociation == null)
```

```
      {
        SPContentTypeId targetContentTypeID =
              (SPContentTypeId)targetListItem["ContentTypeId"];
        SPContentType targetContentType =
                    targetList.ContentTypes[targetContentTypeID];
        workflowAssociation =
         targetContentType.WorkflowAssociations[
                                    workflowAssociationId];
      }

      PlaceHolderPageTitleContent = "Initiate a workflow instance";
      PlaceHolderPageTitleInTitleAreaContent =
"Initiate a workflow instance on " +
                      (string)targetListItem["Title"] +
" list item.";

      if (!this.Page.IsPostBack)
      {
        ConferenceRequestInfo info = null;

        using (StringReader sr =
                    new StringReader(workflowAssociation.AssociationData))
        {
          XmlSerializer serializer =
               new XmlSerializer(typeof(ConferenceRequestInfo));
          info = (ConferenceRequestInfo)serializer.Deserialize(sr);
        }

        this.FirstNameTbx.Text = info.EmployeeFirstName;
        this.LastNameTbx.Text = info.EmployeeLastName;
        this.StartingDateTbx.Text = info.StartingDate.ToString();
        this.EndingDateTbx.Text = info.EndingDate.ToString();
      }
    }

    public void CancelCallback(object sender, EventArgs e)
    {
      SPUtility.Redirect(targetList.DefaultViewUrl,
                         SPRedirectFlags.Default,
                         HttpContext.Current);
    }

    public void OKCallback(object sender, EventArgs e)
    {
      try
      {
        ConferenceRequestInfo info = new ConferenceRequestInfo();
        info.EmployeeFirstName = this.FirstNameTbx.Text;
        info.EmployeeLastName = this.LastNameTbx.Text;
```

(continued)

Listing 4-14 *(continued)*

```
          info.StartingDate = DateTime.Parse(this.StartingDateTbx.Text);
          info.EndingDate = DateTime.Parse(this.EndingDateTbx.Text);
          string initiationData;

          using (StringWriter sw = new StringWriter())
          {
            XmlSerializer serializer =
                   new XmlSerializer(typeof(ConferenceRequestInfo));
            serializer.Serialize(sw, info);
            initiationData = sw.ToString();
          }

          Web.Site.WorkflowManager.StartWorkflow(targetListItem,
                                                    workflowAssociation,
                                                       initiationData);
        }

        catch (SPException exception)
        {
          SPUtility.Redirect("Error.aspx",
                             SPRedirectFlags.RelativeToLayoutsPage,
                              HttpContext.Current,
  "ErrorText=" +
              SPHttpUtility.UrlKeyValueEncode(exception.Message));
        }

        SPUtility.Redirect(targetList.DefaultViewUrl,
                             SPRedirectFlags.Default,
                             HttpContext.Current);
      }
    }
  }
```

Next, add a .cs file named ConferenceRequestWorkflowInitiationForm.cs to the workflow project and add Listing 4-14 to this file. When you compile the workflow project, this file will be compiled into the same assembly as the workflow and deployed to the global assembly cache.

Now that we're done with the implementation of our workflow association and initiation forms, let's get down to the implementation of the workflow itself. As discussed earlier, our ConferenceRequestWorkflow workflow consists of several activities. In this section, we'll add and discuss two of these activities: OnWorkflowActivated and CreateTaskWithContentType. The rest will be added and discussed in subsequent chapters.

Note that the workflow project that we created already includes a workflow that contains an OnWorkflowActivated activity as its first child activity. Go ahead and add the following four fields to the workflow:

```
public string EmployeeFirstName = default(string);
public string EmployeeLastName = default(string);
public DateTime StartingDate = default(DateTime);
public DateTime EndingDate = default(DateTime);
```

Right-click the OnWorkflowActivated activity and select Generate Handlers to generate an empty event handler for the Invoked event of this activity and implement the body of this event handler as follows:

```
private void onWorkflowActivated1_Invoked(object sender, ExternalDataEventArgs e)
{
  ConferenceRequestInfo info = null;

  using (StringReader sr = new StringReader(workflowProperties.InitiationData))
  {
    XmlSerializer serializer = new XmlSerializer(typeof(ConferenceRequestInfo));
    info = (ConferenceRequestInfo)serializer.Deserialize(sr);
  }

  this.EmployeeFirstName = info.EmployeeFirstName;
  this.EmployeeLastName = info.EmployeeLastName;
  this.StartingDate = info.StartingDate;
  this.EndingDate = info.EndingDate;
}
```

As discussed in the previous chapter, the OnWorkflowActivated activity suspends its execution and waits for the ISharePointService external data exchange service to fire its OnWorkflowActivated event. When this service finally fires this event, the OnWorkflowActivated activity resumes its execution and fires its Invoked event. This in turn triggers the invocation of the event handler registered for this event. As the preceding code shows, this event handler first deserializes a ConferenceRequestInfo object from the initiation data:

```
info = (ConferenceRequestInfo)serializer.Deserialize(sr);
```

Then it assigns the properties of this ConferenceRequestInfo object to the respective workflow fields. The result is that this event handler stores the initiation data in these workflow fields to make them available to other activities of the workflow.

Now drag a CreateTaskWithContentType activity from the toolbox and drop it onto the designer surface right below the OnWorkflowActivated activity, as shown in Figure 4-12. Recall that the OnWorkflowActivated activity must always be the first activity in any SharePoint workflow.

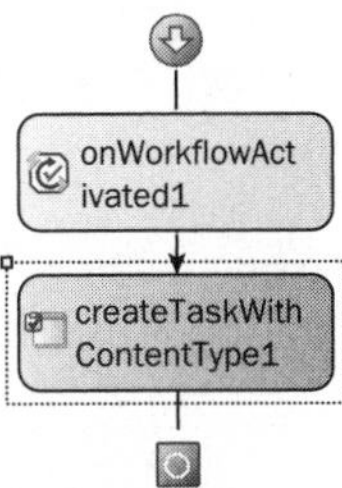

Figure 4-12

Select the CreateTaskWithContentType activity, if it hasn't already been selected, to view its properties in the Properties pane, as shown in Figure 4-13.

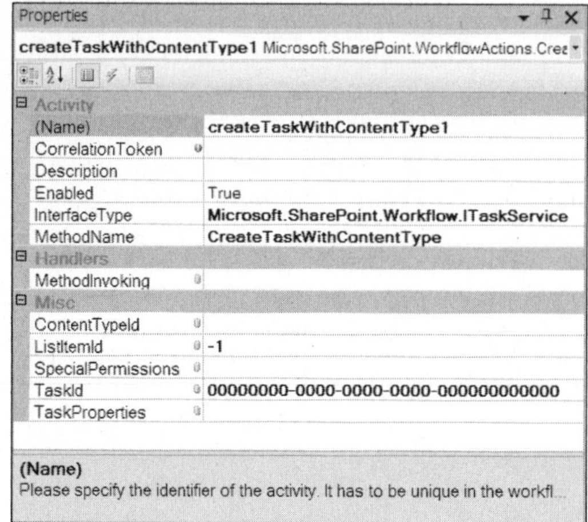

Figure 4-13

Now compare Figures 4-2 and 4-13. Recall that the Properties pane shown in Figure 4-2 displays the properties of the CreateTask activity. As you can see, CreateTaskWithContentType exposes the same properties as CreateTask except for one property named ContentTypeId. You must set the value of this property to the content type ID of the desired content type. In our case, we want the CreateTaskWithContentType activity to add a task with the content type of ManagerContentType to the task list. Therefore, we must set the ContentTypeId property to 0x01080100A3440F3CB4E74e5e8B4CF07B AEBAB9B101, which is the value of the ID attribute of the <ContentType> element that defines the ManagerContentType site content type, as shown in Listing 4-7. Enter this value into the ContentTypeId text box.

Follow the same steps discussed in the previous section to set the rest of the properties of the CreateTaskWithContentType activity:

1. Enter taskToken (or any value other than workflowToken) as the correlation token name.
2. Select the workflow (ConferenceRequestWorkflow by default) as the correlation token owner activity.
3. Add a new workflow field named TaskId and bind it to the TaskId property of the CreateTaskWithContentType activity.
4. Add a new workflow field named TaskProperties and bind it to the TaskProperties property of the CreateTaskWithContentType activity.
5. Right-click the CreateTaskWithContentType activity on the designer surface to add an empty event handler for the MethodInvoking event of the activity and implement the body of this event handler as follows:

```
private void createTaskWithContentType1_MethodInvoking(object sender, EventArgs e)
{
  this.TaskId = Guid.NewGuid();
  this.TaskProperties.Title = "Process the request";
  this.TaskProperties.PercentComplete = 0;
  this.TaskProperties.DueDate = DateTime.Now.AddMinutes(2);
```

```
    this.TaskProperties.StartDate = DateTime.Now;
    this.TaskProperties.ExtendedProperties["EmployeeFirstName"] =
                                                     this.EmployeeFirstName;
    this.TaskProperties.ExtendedProperties["EmployeeLastName"] =
                                                      this.EmployeeLastName;
    this.TaskProperties.ExtendedProperties["StartDate"] = this.StartingDate;
    this.TaskProperties.ExtendedProperties["EndDate"] = this.EndingDate;
  }
```

As discussed earlier, this event handler is invoked before the CreateTaskWithContentType activity creates the task. This method basically specifies the values of the Title, PercentComplete, DueDate, and StartDate properties of the task. The Title value simply instructs the manager to use the edit task form to process the request. Note that this event handler also instructs SharePoint to store the values of the EmployeeFirstName, EmployeeLastName, StartingDate, and EndingDate workflow fields in the respective fields of the task.

Listing 4-15 presents the content of the ConferenceRequestWorkflow.cs file that contains the implementation of our workflow.

Listing 4-15: The implementation of our workflow

```
using System;
using System.ComponentModel;
using System.ComponentModel.Design;
using System.Collections;
using System.Drawing;
using System.Linq;
using System.Workflow.ComponentModel.Compiler;
using System.Workflow.ComponentModel.Serialization;
using System.Workflow.ComponentModel;
using System.Workflow.ComponentModel.Design;
using System.Workflow.Runtime;
using System.Workflow.Activities;
using System.Workflow.Activities.Rules;
using Microsoft.SharePoint;
using Microsoft.SharePoint.Workflow;
using Microsoft.SharePoint.WorkflowActions;
using Microsoft.Office.Workflow.Utility;
using System.Xml;
using System.Xml.Serialization;
using System.IO;

namespace SharePointWorkflow5
{
  public sealed partial class ConferenceRequestWorkflow :
SequentialWorkflowActivity
  {
    public ConferenceRequestWorkflow()
    {
      InitializeComponent();
    }

    public Guid workflowId = default(System.Guid);
```

(continued)

Listing 4-15 *(continued)*

```
        public SPWorkflowActivationProperties workflowProperties =
                    new SPWorkflowActivationProperties();
        public Guid TaskId = default(System.Guid);
        public SPWorkflowTaskProperties TaskProperties =
            new Microsoft.SharePoint.Workflow.SPWorkflowTaskProperties();

        private void createTaskWithContentType1_MethodInvoking(
                                          object sender, EventArgs e)
        {
          this.TaskId = Guid.NewGuid();
          this.TaskProperties.Title = "Enter the request information";
          this.TaskProperties.PercentComplete = 0;
          this.TaskProperties.DueDate = DateTime.Now.AddMinutes(2);
          this.TaskProperties.StartDate = DateTime.Now;
          this.TaskProperties.ExtendedProperties["EmployeeFirstName"] =
                    this.EmployeeFirstName;
          this.TaskProperties.ExtendedProperties["EmployeeLastName"] =
                    this.EmployeeLastName;
          this.TaskProperties.ExtendedProperties["StartDate"] =
                    this.StartingDate;
          this.TaskProperties.ExtendedProperties["EndDate"] =
                    this.EndingDate;

        }

        public string EmployeeFirstName = default(string);
        public string EmployeeLastName = default(string);
        public DateTime StartingDate = default(DateTime);
        public DateTime EndingDate = default(DateTime);

        private void onWorkflowActivated1_Invoked(
                      object sender, ExternalDataEventArgs e)
        {
          ConferenceRequestInfo info = null;

          using (StringReader sr =
              new StringReader(workflowProperties.InitiationData))
          {
            XmlSerializer serializer =
               new XmlSerializer(typeof(ConferenceRequestInfo));
            info = (ConferenceRequestInfo)serializer.Deserialize(sr);
          }

          this.EmployeeFirstName = info.EmployeeFirstName;
          this.EmployeeLastName = info.EmployeeLastName;
          this.StartingDate = info.StartingDate;
          this.EndingDate = info.EndingDate;
        }
      }
    }
```

Listing 4-16 presents the content of the ConferenceRequestWorkflow.designer.cs file.

Listing 4-16: The ConferenceRequestWorkflow.designer.cs file

```
using System;
using System.ComponentModel;
using System.ComponentModel.Design;
using System.Collections;
using System.Drawing;
using System.Reflection;
using System.Workflow.ComponentModel.Compiler;
using System.Workflow.ComponentModel.Serialization;
using System.Workflow.ComponentModel;
using System.Workflow.ComponentModel.Design;
using System.Workflow.Runtime;
using System.Workflow.Activities;
using System.Workflow.Activities.Rules;

namespace SharePointWorkflow5
{
  public sealed partial class ConferenceRequestWorkflow
  {
    #region Designer generated code

    /// <summary>
    /// Required method for Designer support - do not modify
    /// the contents of this method with the code editor.
    /// </summary>
    [System.Diagnostics.DebuggerNonUserCode]
    private void InitializeComponent()
    {
      this.CanModifyActivities = true;
      System.Workflow.Runtime.CorrelationToken correlationtoken1 =
            new System.Workflow.Runtime.CorrelationToken();
      System.Workflow.ComponentModel.ActivityBind activitybind1 =
            new System.Workflow.ComponentModel.ActivityBind();
      System.Workflow.ComponentModel.ActivityBind activitybind2 =
            new System.Workflow.ComponentModel.ActivityBind();
      System.Workflow.ComponentModel.ActivityBind activitybind4 =
            new System.Workflow.ComponentModel.ActivityBind();
      System.Workflow.Runtime.CorrelationToken correlationtoken2 =
            new System.Workflow.Runtime.CorrelationToken();
      System.Workflow.ComponentModel.ActivityBind activitybind3 =
            new System.Workflow.ComponentModel.ActivityBind();
      this.onTaskChanged1 =
        new Microsoft.SharePoint.WorkflowActions.OnTaskChanged();
      this.createTaskWithContentType1 =
  new Microsoft.SharePoint.WorkflowActions.CreateTaskWithContentType();
      this.onWorkflowActivated1 =
        new Microsoft.SharePoint.WorkflowActions.OnWorkflowActivated();
      //
      // onTaskChanged1
      //
```

(continued)

Listing 4-16 *(continued)*

```
        this.onTaskChanged1.AfterProperties = null;
        this.onTaskChanged1.BeforeProperties = null;
        this.onTaskChanged1.Executor = null;
        this.onTaskChanged1.Name = "onTaskChanged1";
        this.onTaskChanged1.TaskId =
               new System.Guid("00000000-0000-0000-0000-000000000000");
        //
        // createTaskWithContentType1
        //
        this.createTaskWithContentType1.ContentTypeId =
   "0x01080100A3440F3CB4E74e5e8B4CF07BAEBAB9B101";
        correlationtoken1.Name = "taskToken";
        correlationtoken1.OwnerActivityName =
   "ConferenceRequestWorkflow";
        this.createTaskWithContentType1.CorrelationToken =
                            correlationtoken1;
        this.createTaskWithContentType1.ListItemId = -1;
        this.createTaskWithContentType1.Name =
   "createTaskWithContentType1";
        this.createTaskWithContentType1.SpecialPermissions = null;
        activitybind1.Name = "ConferenceRequestWorkflow";
        activitybind1.Path = "TaskId";
        activitybind2.Name = "ConferenceRequestWorkflow";
        activitybind2.Path = "TaskProperties";
        this.createTaskWithContentType1.MethodInvoking +=
                        new System.EventHandler(
                this.createTaskWithContentType1_MethodInvoking);
        this.createTaskWithContentType1.SetBinding(Microsoft.SharePoint
 .WorkflowActions.CreateTaskWithContentType.TaskIdProperty, ((System.Workflow
 .ComponentModel.ActivityBind)(activitybind1)));
        this.createTaskWithContentType1.SetBinding(Microsoft.SharePoint
 .WorkflowActions.CreateTaskWithContentType.TaskPropertiesProperty,
 ((System.Workflow.ComponentModel.ActivityBind)(activitybind2)));
        activitybind4.Name = "ConferenceRequestWorkflow";
        activitybind4.Path = "workflowId";
        //
        // onWorkflowActivated1
        //
        correlationtoken2.Name = "workflowToken";
        correlationtoken2.OwnerActivityName =
   "ConferenceRequestWorkflow";
        this.onWorkflowActivated1.CorrelationToken = correlationtoken2;
        this.onWorkflowActivated1.EventName = "OnWorkflowActivated";
        this.onWorkflowActivated1.Name = "onWorkflowActivated1";
        activitybind3.Name = "ConferenceRequestWorkflow";
        activitybind3.Path = "workflowProperties";
        this.onWorkflowActivated1.Invoked += new System.EventHandler<System.Workflow
 .Activities.ExternalDataEventArgs>(this.onWorkflowActivated1_Invoked);
        this.onWorkflowActivated1.SetBinding(Microsoft.SharePoint.WorkflowActions.
 OnWorkflowActivated.WorkflowIdProperty, ((System.Workflow.ComponentModel.ActivityBi
 nd)(activitybind4)));
```

```
        this.onWorkflowActivated1.SetBinding(Microsoft.SharePoint.WorkflowActions.
OnWorkflowActivated.WorkflowPropertiesProperty, ((System.Workflow.ComponentModel
.ActivityBind)(activitybind3)));
        //
        // ConferenceRequestWorkflow
        //
        this.Activities.Add(this.onWorkflowActivated1);
        this.Activities.Add(this.createTaskWithContentType1);
        this.Activities.Add(this.onTaskChanged1);
        this.Name = "ConferenceRequestWorkflow";
        this.CanModifyActivities = false;

      }

      #endregion

      private Microsoft.SharePoint.WorkflowActions.OnTaskChanged
                     onTaskChanged1;
      private Microsoft.SharePoint.WorkflowActions.CreateTaskWithContentType
                     createTaskWithContentType1;
      private Microsoft.SharePoint.WorkflowActions.OnWorkflowActivated
                     onWorkflowActivated1;
    }
  }
```

Your workflow project should include the following files:

- ConferenceRequestWorkflow.cs
- ConferenceRequestWorkflow.designer.cs
- ConferenceRequestInfo.cs
- ConferenceRequestWorkflowAssociationForm.cs
- ConferenceRequestWorkflowInitiationForm.cs
- feature.xml
- ConferenceRequestWorkflow.xml

Press F5 to build and run the project. Visual Studio automatically performs the following tasks for you:

1. It builds the workflow code into a strong-named assembly.
2. It deploys the assembly to the global assembly cache.
3. It copies the feature file and the element manifest file that it references to a feature-specific folder under the FEATURES folder on the file system of the front-end web server. This element manifest file contains the definition of the workflow template.
4. It uses the STSADM.exe command-line utility to install the feature with SharePoint.
5. It uses the STSADM.exe command-line utility to activate the feature within the site whose URL you specified when you were creating the project.

6. It creates a workflow association with the same name, task list, and history list that you specified when you were creating the project on the SharePoint list that you specified when you were creating the project. Keep in mind that this task list contains our ConferenceRequestContentType and ManagerContentType content types.
7. It navigates to the page that displays the SharePoint list on which the workflow association was created.

Next, go ahead and initiate the workflow on a list item in this list. SharePoint will first redirect you to the ConferenceRequestWorkflowInitiationForm.aspx page. Enter the values of the first and last names and the starting and ending dates and click OK to initiate the workflow. The CreateTaskWithContentType activity should create a task with the content type of ManagerContentType in the task list. Navigate to the task list to confirm this. Select the Edit Item menu option from the ECB menu of this task. This should take you to the edit task form shown in Figure 4-14.

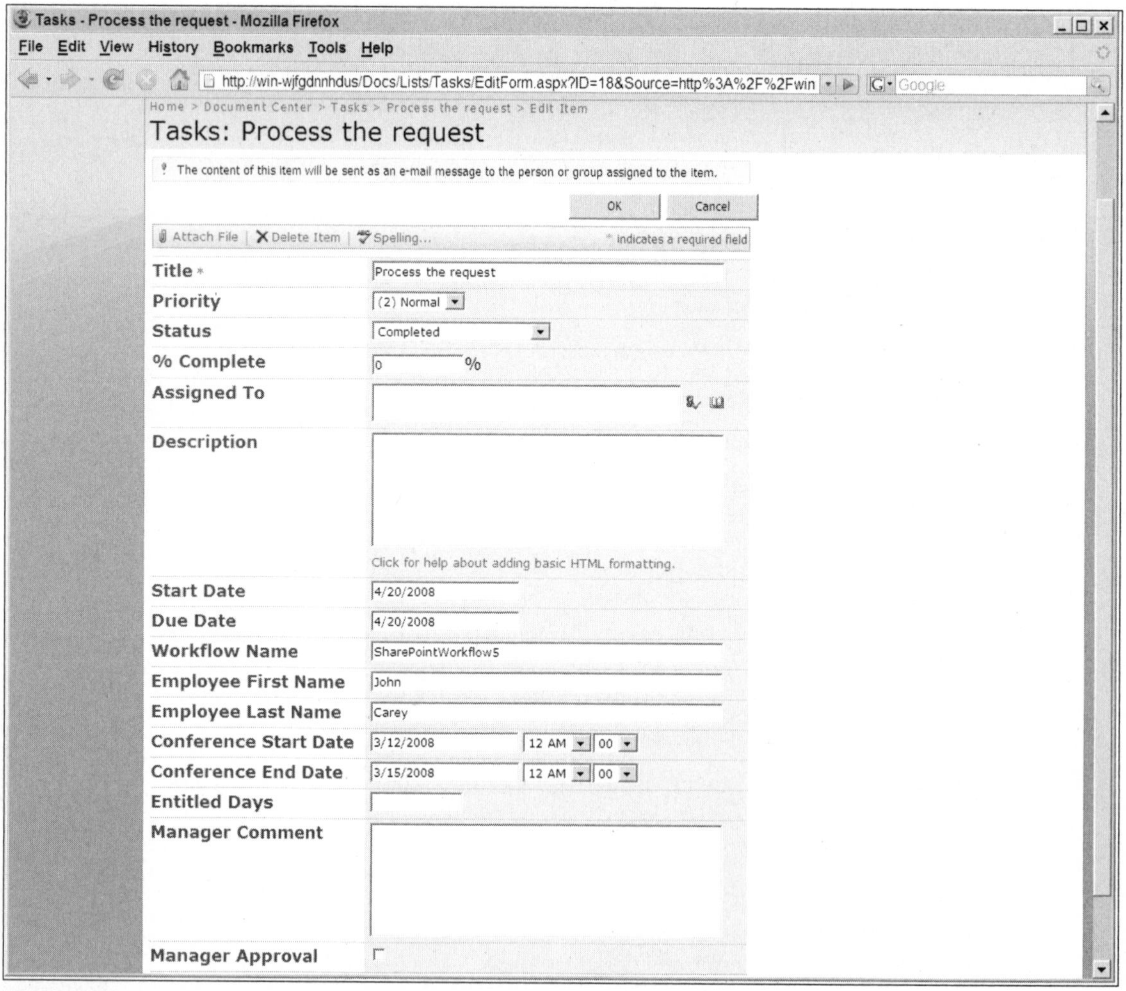

Figure 4-14

This edit task form presents the manager with the following information:

- Employee first name
- Employee last name
- Starting date
- Ending date
- Days to which the employee is entitled. At this point, the value of this field has not been set. The next section will use an UpdateTask activity to retrieve and set the value of this field.
- A checkbox that the manager can check to approve the request
- A text box in which the manager can optionally add a comment

Recall that all the preceding data comes from the fields referenced by the ManagerContentType site content type. In other words, the edit task form shown in Figure 4-14 is tailored toward the ManagerContentType type tasks.

Updating SharePoint Tasks

The UpdateTask activity, shown in Listing 4-17, enables a workflow to invoke the UpdateTask method of the external data exchange task service to update the specified SharePoint task.

Listing 4-17: The UpdateTask activity

```
public sealed class UpdateTask : CallExternalMethodActivity
{
  public static DependencyProperty TaskIdProperty;
  public static DependencyProperty TaskPropertiesProperty;

  public UpdateTask()
  {
    this.InterfaceType = typeof(ITaskService);
    this.MethodName = "UpdateTask";
  }

  protected override void OnMethodInvoking(EventArgs e)
  {
    base.ParameterBindings["taskId"].Value = this.TaskId;
    base.ParameterBindings["properties"].Value = this.TaskProperties;
  }

  public override Type InterfaceType
  {
    get { return typeof(ITaskService); }
  }

  public override string MethodName
```

(continued)

Listing 4-17 *(continued)*

```
    {
      get { return "UpdateTask"; }
    }

    public Guid TaskId { get; set; }
    public SPWorkflowTaskProperties TaskProperties { get; set; }
  }
```

The UpdateTask activity exposes the following properties, which must be set before the activity can be used:

- **TaskId:** Gets or sets a GUID that uniquely identifies the SharePoint task to update. Because this property is defined as a bindable property, it can be bound to a property of the containing workflow or another activity in the workflow to have it automatically pick up its value through activity binding.
- **TaskProperties:** Gets or sets an SPWorkflowTaskProperties object that specifies the names and new values of the SharePoint task properties to update. Because this property is defined as a bindable property, it can be bound to a property of the containing workflow or another activity in the workflow to have it automatically pick up its value through activity binding.
- **CorrelationToken:** Gets or sets a CorrelationToken object. The UpdateTask activity inherits this property from CallExternalMethodActivity.

Next, we'll add an UpdateTask activity to our ConferenceRequestWorkflow workflow, as shown in Figure 4-15.

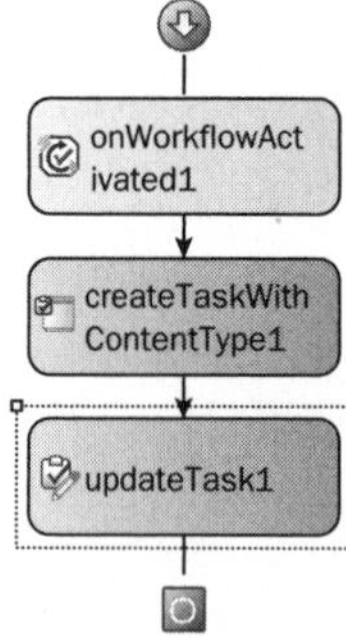

Figure 4-15

The main goal of this activity is to connect to the appropriate data storage to retrieve the number of days to which the employee is entitled and update the task with this information. Recall that the ConferenceRequestContentType content type references a column named Days, which contains the number of days to which employees are entitled. To keep our discussion focused, we'll hard-code this number to 15.

Select the UpdateTask activity, if it hasn't already been selected, to view its properties in the Properties pane, as shown in Figure 4-16. Follow the same procedure discussed earlier:

- Use the same correlation token name that you used for the CreateTaskWithContentType activity. If you don't use the same correlation token, the UpdateTask activity will not update the same task the CreateTaskWithContentType activity created. As discussed in the previous chapter, using the same correlation token name instructs Visual Studio to assign the same CorrelationToken object that was assigned to the CorrelationToken property of the CreateTaskWithContentType activity to the CorrelationToken property of the UpdateTask activity.
- Bind the same TaskId workflow field that you bound to the TaskId property of the CreateTaskWithContentType activity to the TaskId property of the UpdateTask activity.
- Create a new workflow field named TaskProperties2 and bind it to the TaskProperties property of the UpdateTask activity.
- Right-click the UpdateTask activity on the designer surface and select the Generate Handlers menu option to create an empty event handler for the MethodInvoking event of the UpdateTask activity and implement the body of this event handler as follows:

```
private void updateTask1_MethodInvoking(object sender, EventArgs e)
{
  this.TaskProperties2.ExtendedProperties["Days"] = 15;
}
```

This event handler hard-codes the value of the Days field of the task to 15. However, you can use whatever data access code is deemed necessary to retrieve this value from the appropriate data store. For example, you can use a web service proxy to retrieve this value from a web service; ADO.NET, to retrieve this value from an SQL server database; or the SharePoint object model, to retrieve this value from a SharePoint list where the employee information is maintained.

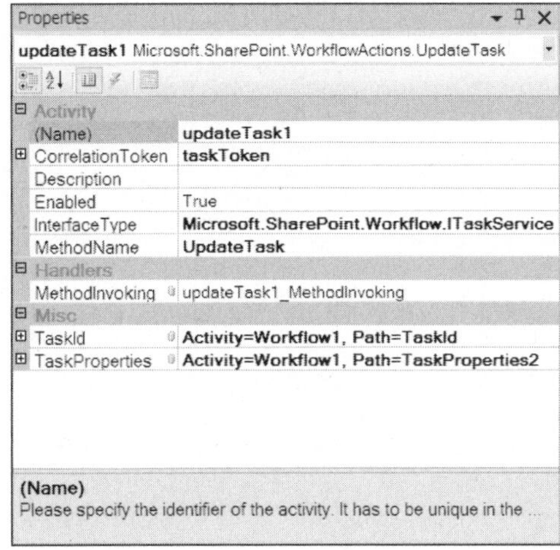

Figure 4-16

Press F5 to compile and run the program. Initiate an instance of our ConferenceRequestWorkflow workflow from a list item on the SharePoint list with which the workflow is associated. You should be redirected to the ConferenceRequestWorkflowInitiationForm.aspx page, where you can enter first and last names and starting and ending dates. Next, navigate to the task list page. You should see the task that the CreateTaskWithContentType activity has created. Select the Edit Item menu option to navigate to the edit task shown in Figure 4-17. As you can see, the UpdateTask activity has set the value of the Entitled Days field of the task to 15.

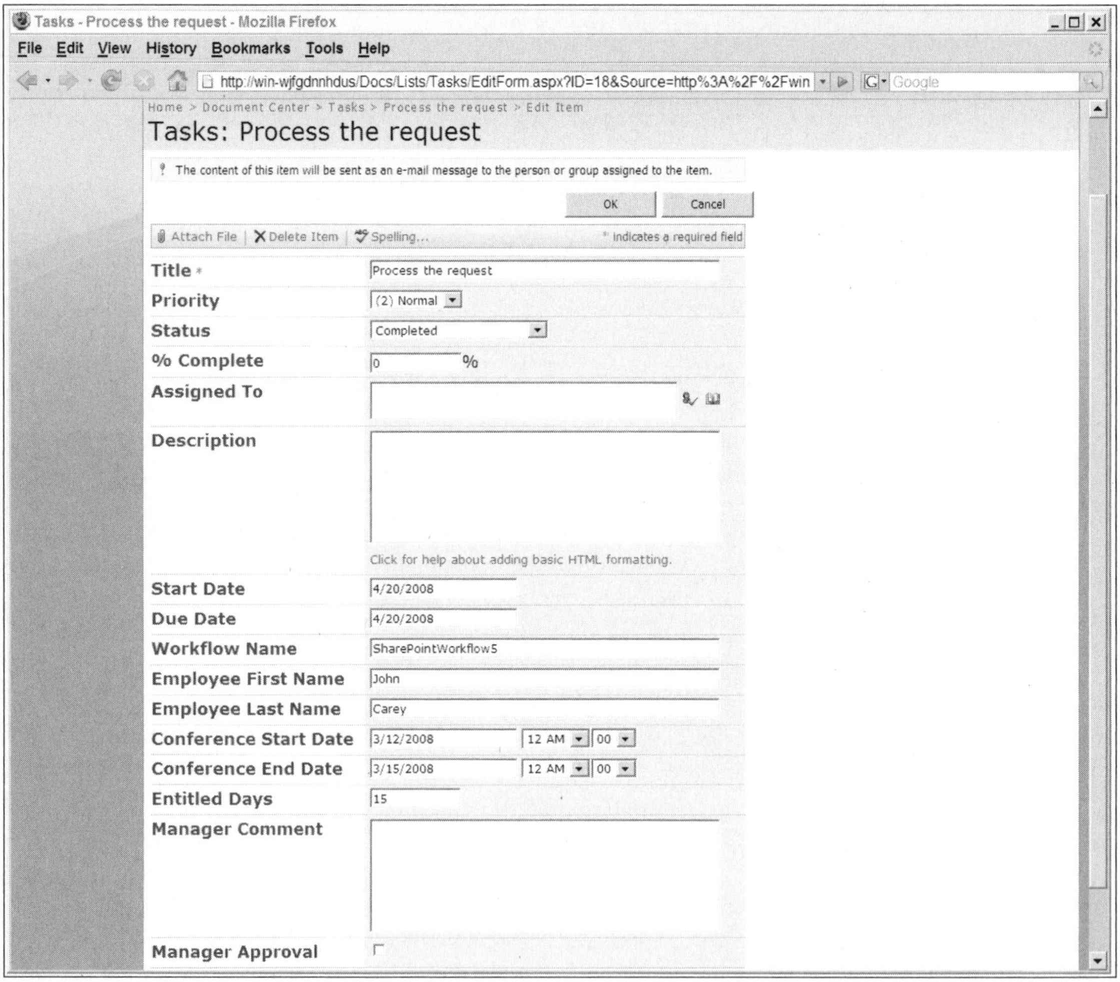

Figure 4-17

Deleting SharePoint Tasks

The DeleteTask activity enables a workflow to invoke the DeleteTask method of the external data exchange task service to delete the specified SharePoint task. This activity inherits from CallExternalMethodActivity and exposes a property named TaskId that must be set to the GUID that uniquely identifies the SharePoint task to delete. Because the TaskId property is bindable, it can be bound to a property of the containing workflow or another activity in the workflow to have it automatically pick up its value through activity binding, as shown in Listing 4-18.

Listing 4-18: The DeleteTask activity

```
public sealed class DeleteTask : CallExternalMethodActivity
{
  public static DependencyProperty TaskIdProperty;

  public DeleteTask()
  {
    this.InterfaceType = typeof(ITaskService);
    this.MethodName = "DeleteTask";
  }

  protected override void OnMethodInvoking(EventArgs e)
  {
    base.ParameterBindings["taskId"].Value = this.TaskId;
  }

  public override Type InterfaceType
  {
    get { return typeof(ITaskService); }
  }

  public override string MethodName
  {
    get { return "DeleteTask";  }
  }

  public Guid TaskId { get; set; }
}
```

Next, we'll improve upon our ConferenceRequestWorkflow workflow by adding a CodeActivity, an IfElseActivity, and a DeleteTask activity. The CodeActivity activity determines whether the number of days the employee has requested exceeds the number of days to which the employee is entitled. If so, it sets a workflow field named CancelRequest to true. The IfElseActivity activity then determines whether this field has been set to true. If so, it executes the DeleteTask activity to delete the task that the CreateTaskWithContentType activity created.

Drag a CodeActivity activity from the toolbox and drop it onto the surface designer below the UpdateTask activity, as shown in Figure 4-18.

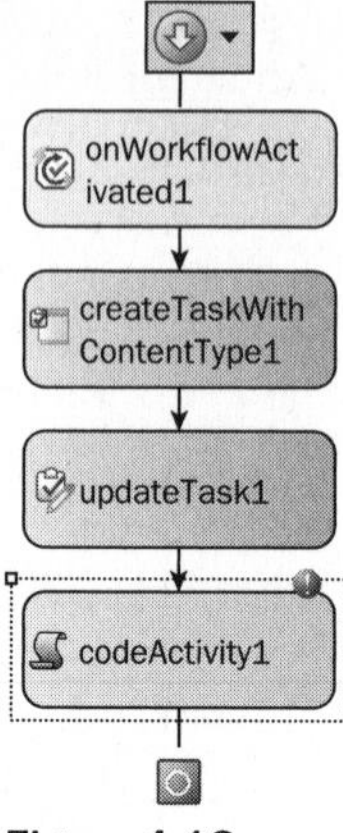

Figure 4-18

Select the CodeActivity activity, if it hasn't already been selected, to view its properties in the Properties pane, as shown in Figure 4-19.

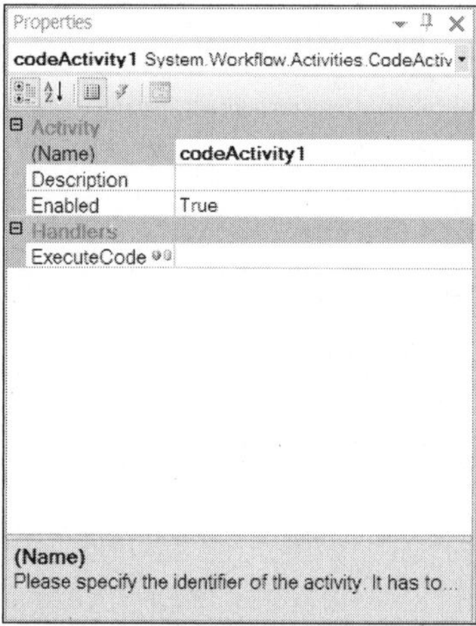

Figure 4-19

The CodeActivity activity exposes an event named ExecuteCode. The execution logic of this activity fires this event to enable you to run custom code. To do so, you need to register an event handler for this event. Right-click the CodeActivity activity on the surface designer and select the Generate Handlers menu option to generate an empty event handler and then add the following code to the body of this event handler:

```
private bool CancelRequest;
private void codeActivity1_ExecuteCode(object sender, EventArgs e)
{
  TimeSpan requestedDays = this.EndingDate - this.StartingDate;
  if (requestedDays > TimeSpan.FromDays(15))
    this.CancelRequest = true;
}
```

The event handler first subtracts the starting date from the ending date to arrive at the requested days. Then it sets the CancelRequest workflow field to true if the number of requested days exceeds the number of days to which the employee is entitled.

Now drag an IfElseActivity activity from the toolbox and drop it onto the designer surface below the CodeActivity activity, as illustrated in Figure 4-20.

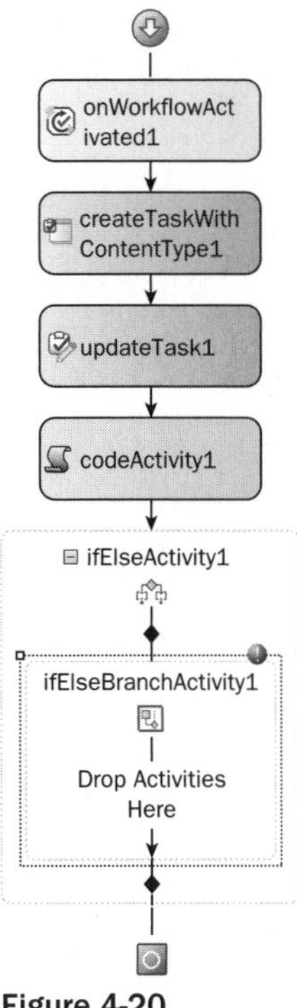

Figure 4-20

Select the IfElseBranchActivity child activity of this IfElseActivity activity to view its properties in the Properties pane, as shown in Figure 4-21.

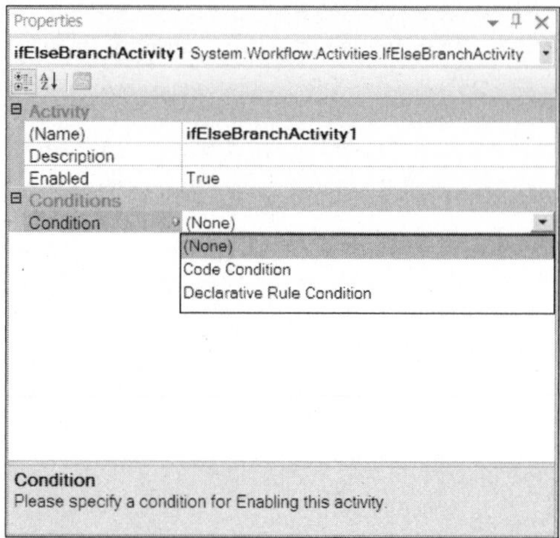

Figure 4-21

As the name suggests, the IfElseBranchActivity activity represents a conditional branch in the IfElseActivity activity. In our case, the IfElseActivity activity contains a single condition branch, which is why this activity only contains a single IfElseActivity activity. As a matter of fact, when you drag and drop an IfElseActivity activity, it originally contains two IfElseBranchActivity child activities. I've deleted one of these child activities.

As Figure 4-21 shows, the IfElseBranchActivity activity exposes a property named Condition that represents the condition under which this activity will execute. In our case, we want this activity to execute only if the value of the CancelRequest workflow field is set to true. Next, we'll specify this condition. Select the Declarative Rule Condition menu option from the menu shown in Figure 4-21 to arrive at what is shown in Figure 4-22.

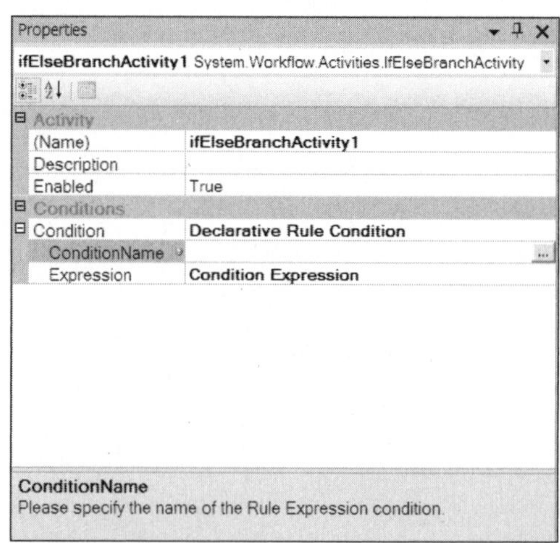

Figure 4-22

Next, click the button shown in the Condition text box to launch the dialog shown in Figure 4-23.

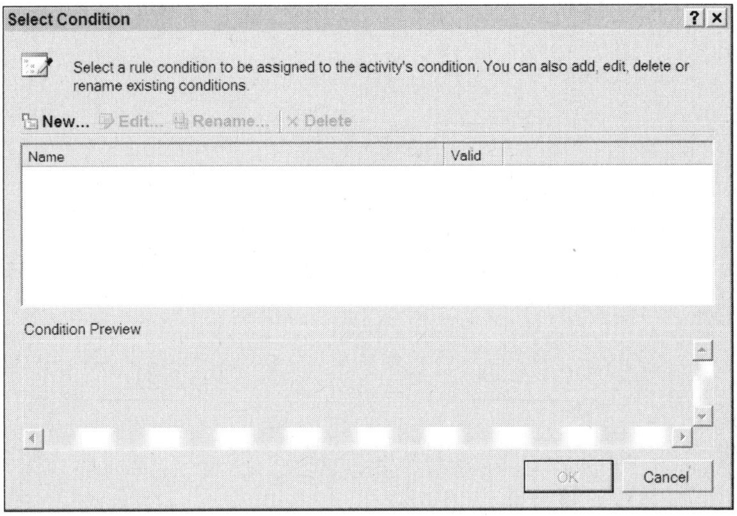

Figure 4-23

Click the New button to launch the dialog shown in Figure 4-24.

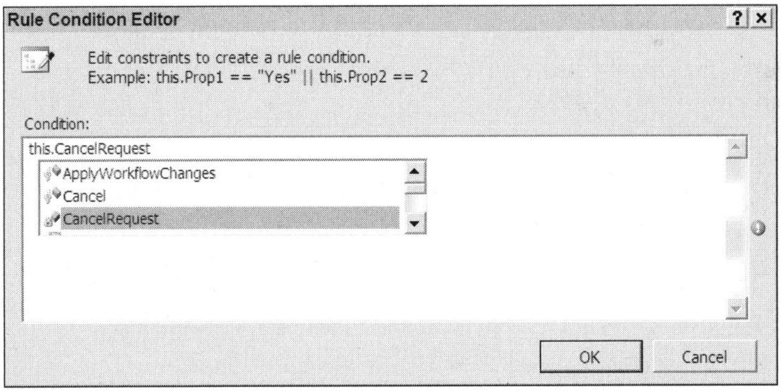

Figure 4-24

Type the keyword **this** followed by a period to view all the public workflow members. As shown in the figure, this text box provides IntelliSense support. Enter the following statement into this text box:

```
this.CancelRequest
```

The IfElseBranchActivity activity will execute only if the preceding condition returns true.

Next, go ahead and drag a DeleteTask activity from the toolbox and drop it onto the designer surface as the child activity of the IfElseBranchActivity activity, as shown in Figure 4-25.

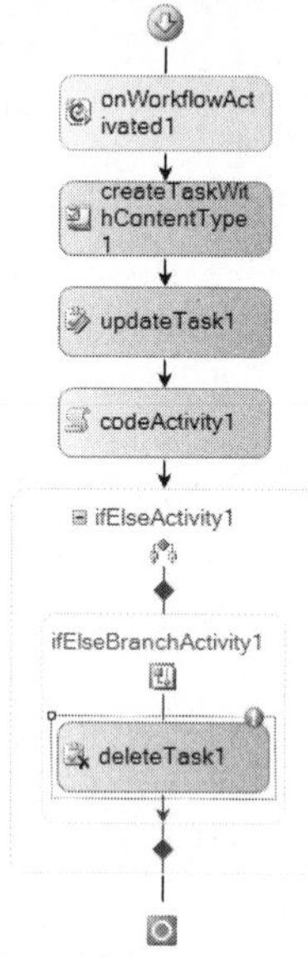

Figure 4-25

Select the DeleteTask activity, if it hasn't already been selected, to view its properties in the Properties pane, as shown in Figure 4-26.

Properties

deleteTask1 Microsoft.SharePoint.WorkflowActions.DeleteTask

Activity	
(Name)	**deleteTask1**
CorrelationToken	
Description	
Enabled	True
InterfaceType	**Microsoft.SharePoint.Workflow.ITaskService**
MethodName	**DeleteTask**
Handlers	
MethodInvoking	
Misc	
TaskId	**00000000-0000-0000-0000-000000000000**

(Name)
Please specify the identifier of the activity. It has to be unique in the wo...

Figure 4-26

Then take the following steps:

- Enter taskToken as the correlation token name to instruct Visual Studio to assign the same CorrelationToken object that was assigned to the CorrelationToken property of the CreateTaskWithContentType activity to the CorrelationToken property of the DeleteTask activity. This causes the DeleteTask activity to delete the same task that the CreateTaskWithContentType activity created.
- Bind the TaskId workflow field to the TaskId property of the DeleteTask activity. Because the same TaskId workflow field is bound to the TaskId property of both the CreateTaskWithContentType and DeleteTask activities, the DeleteTask activity will delete the same task that the CreateTaskWithContentType activity created.

Press F5 to build and run the workflow project, and to navigate to the SharePoint list with which our ConferenceRequestWorkflow is associated. Initiate an instance of this workflow and enter starting and ending dates that add up to more days than entitled days (15 days). Next, navigate to the task list. Notice that this list does not contain a new task. That's because the DeleteTask activity deleted the task that the CreateTaskWithContentType activity created.

Completing SharePoint Tasks

The CompleteTask activity enables a workflow to invoke the CompleteTask method of the external data exchange task service to complete the specified SharePoint task. This activity exposes a property named TaskId that must be set to the GUID that uniquely identifies the SharePoint task to complete. This activity also exposes a string property named TaskOutcome that contains the task outcome. Because these two properties are defined as bindable properties, they can be bound to the properties of the containing workflow or other activities in the workflow so they can automatically pick up their values through activity binding, as shown in Listing 4-19.

Listing 4-19: The CompleteTask activity

```
public sealed class CompleteTask : CallExternalMethodActivity
{
  public static DependencyProperty TaskIdProperty;
  public static DependencyProperty TaskOutcomeProperty;

  public CompleteTask()
  {
    this.InterfaceType = typeof(ITaskService);
    this.MethodName = "CompleteTask";
  }

  protected override void OnMethodInvoking(EventArgs e)
  {
    base.ParameterBindings["taskId"].Value = this.TaskId;
    base.ParameterBindings["taskOutcome"].Value = this.TaskOutcome;
  }

  public override Type InterfaceType
```

(continued)

Listing 4-19 *(continued)*

```
    {
      get { return typeof(ITaskService); }
    }

    public override string MethodName
    {
      get { return "CompleteTask"; }
    }

    public Guid TaskId { get; set; }
    public string TaskOutcome { get; set; }
  }
```

You'll see an example of this activity later in this chapter.

Sending E-mails

This activity invokes the SendEmail method of the SharePoint service to send an e-mail about the workflow instance with the specified instance ID. This activity exposes the workflowId, includeStatus, headers, and body parameters of this method as activity-level bindable properties named WorkflowId, IncludeStatus, Headers, and Body. Note that this activity also features properties named BCC, CC, From, Subject, and To, which are not directly mapped to any parameters on the SendEmail method. This activity's implementation of the OnMethodInvoking method adds the values of these properties to the headers collection parameter of the SendEmail method, as shown in Listing 4-20.

Listing 4-20: The SendEmail activity

```
public sealed class SendEmail : CallExternalMethodActivity
{
  public static DependencyProperty BCCProperty;
  public static DependencyProperty BodyProperty;
  public static DependencyProperty CCProperty;
  public static DependencyProperty FromProperty;
  public static DependencyProperty HeadersProperty;
  public static DependencyProperty IncludeStatusProperty;
  public static DependencyProperty SubjectProperty;
  public static DependencyProperty ToProperty;
  public static DependencyProperty WorkflowIdProperty;

  public SendEmail()
  {
    this.InterfaceType = typeof(ISharePointService);
    this.MethodName = "SendEmail";
  }

  protected override void OnMethodInvoking(EventArgs e)
```

```
{
  StringDictionary headers = this.Headers;
  if (headers == null)
    headers = new StringDictionary();

  if (!string.IsNullOrEmpty(this.To))
    headers["to"] = this.To;

  if (!string.IsNullOrEmpty(this.From))
    headers["from"] = this.From;

  if (!string.IsNullOrEmpty(this.CC))
    headers["cc"] = this.CC;

  if (!string.IsNullOrEmpty(this.BCC))
    headers["bcc"] = this.BCC;

  if (!string.IsNullOrEmpty(this.Subject))
    headers["subject"] = this.Subject;

  base.ParameterBindings["workflowId"].Value = this.WorkflowId;
  base.ParameterBindings["includeStatus"].Value = this.IncludeStatus;
  base.ParameterBindings["headers"].Value = headers;
  base.ParameterBindings["body"].Value = this.Body;
}

public override Type InterfaceType
{
  get { return typeof(ISharePointService); }
}

public override string MethodName
{
  get { return "SendEmail"; }
}

public string BCC { get; set; }
public string Body { get; set; }
public string CC { get; set; }
public string From { get; set; }
public StringDictionary Headers { get; set; }
public bool IncludeStatus { get; set; }
public string Subject { get; set; }
public string To { get; set; }

public Guid WorkflowId
{
  get
  {
    Guid workflowInstanceId =
                (Guid)base.GetValue(WorkflowIdProperty);
    if (Guid.Empty == workflowInstanceId)
```

(continued)

Listing 4-20 *(continued)*

```
            workflowInstanceId = WorkflowEnvironment.WorkflowInstanceId;
          return workflowInstanceId;
        }
        set { base.SetValue(WorkflowIdProperty, value); }
      }
    }
```

As shown in the previous section, our ConferenceRequestWorkflow workflow deletes the task if the number of requested days exceeds the number of days to which the employee is entitled. In this section, we'll enable the workflow to send an e-mail to employees notifying them of the problem.

Drag a SendEmail activity from the toolbox and drop it onto the designer surface below the DeleteTask activity as the child activity of the IfElseBranchActivity activity, as shown in Figure 4-27.

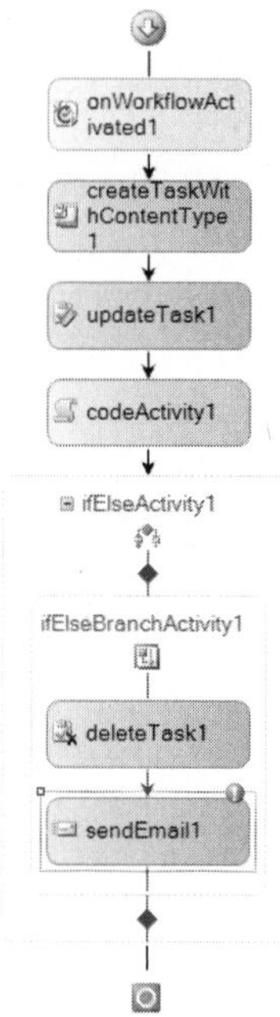

Figure 4-27

Select the SendEmail activity to view its properties in the Properties pane, as shown in Figure 4-28.

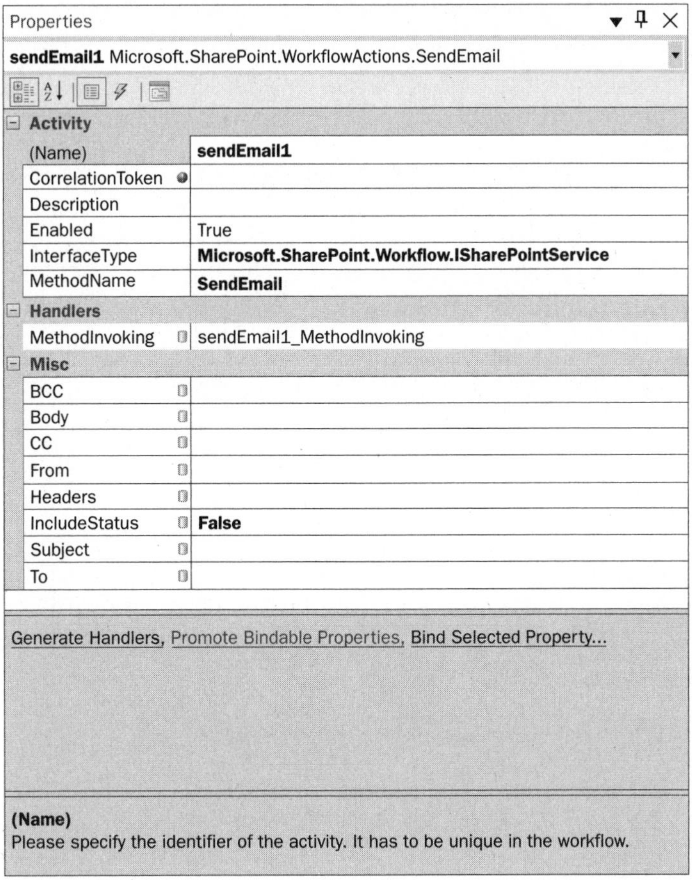

Properties

sendEmail1 Microsoft.SharePoint.WorkflowActions.SendEmail

Activity	
(Name)	**sendEmail1**
CorrelationToken	
Description	
Enabled	True
InterfaceType	**Microsoft.SharePoint.Workflow.ISharePointService**
MethodName	**SendEmail**
Handlers	
MethodInvoking	sendEmail1_MethodInvoking
Misc	
BCC	
Body	
CC	
From	
Headers	
IncludeStatus	**False**
Subject	
To	

Generate Handlers, Promote Bindable Properties, Bind Selected Property...

(Name)
Please specify the identifier of the activity. It has to be unique in the workflow.

Figure 4-28

Assign the same correlation token name that you assigned to the OnWorkflowActivated activity to the SendEmail activity to instruct Visual Studio to assign the same CorrelationToken object that was assigned to the CorrelationToken property of the OnWorkflowActivated activity to the CorrelationToken property of the SendEmail activity. By default, this correlation token is named workflowToken.

Next, create workflow fields named Body, From, Subject, and To and respectively bind them to the Body, From, Subject, and To properties of the SendEmail activity. Then, right-click this activity in the designer surface and select the Generate Handlers menu option to create an empty event handler for the MethodInvoking event of this activity and add the code shown in the following code fragment to this event handler:

```
private void sendEmail1_MethodInvoking(object sender, EventArgs e)
{
  this.From = "EnterFromEmailAddress";
  this.To = "EnterToEmailAddress";
  this.Subject = "Your request was denied!";
  this.Body = "Your requested days exceeds the number of days you're entitled to!";
}
```

Press F5 to run the workflow project and to navigate to the SharePoint list with which the workflow is associated. Next, initiate an instance of the ConferenceRequestWorkflow workflow on a list item in this list and request more than 15 days. If you check your mail, you should see a message.

EnableWorkflowModification

This activity invokes the EnableWorkflowModification method of the SharePoint workflow modification service to enable the workflow modification with the specified ID and context data. This activity exposes the modificationId and contextData parameters of this method as activity-level bindable properties named ModificationId and ContextData, as shown in Listing 4-21.

Listing 4-21: The EnableWorkflowModification activity

```
public sealed class EnableWorkflowModification : CallExternalMethodActivity
{
  public static DependencyProperty ContextDataProperty;
  public static DependencyProperty ModificationIdProperty;

  public EnableWorkflowModification()
  {
    this.InterfaceType = typeof(IWorkflowModificationService);
    this.MethodName = "EnableWorkflowModification";
  }

  protected override void OnMethodInvoking(EventArgs e)
  {
    base.ParameterBindings["modificationId"].Value =
                                   this.ModificationId;
    base.ParameterBindings["contextData"].Value = this.ContextData;
  }

  public override Type InterfaceType
  {
    get { return typeof(IWorkflowModificationService); }
  }

  public override string MethodName
  {
    get { return "EnableWorkflowModification"; }
  }

  public string ContextData { get; set; }
  public Guid ModificationId { get; set; }
}
```

You'll see an example of this activity later in the book.

Implementing Custom CallExternalMethodActivity-Based Activities

If you compare the CallExternalMethodActivity-based activities that ship with SharePoint, you'll realize that they do not cover every method in the SharePoint-specific local service interfaces. More specifically, the methods of the IListItemService are left out:

```
[ExternalDataExchange,
CorrelationParameter("itemId"),
CorrelationParameter("listId"),
CorrelationParameter("id")]
public interface IListItemService
{
  . . .
  [CorrelationInitializer]
  void CheckInListItem(Guid id, Guid listId, int itemId, string comment);

  [CorrelationInitializer]
  void CheckOutListItem(Guid id, Guid listId, int itemId);

  [CorrelationInitializer]
  void CopyListItem(Guid id, Guid listId, int itemId, Guid toList, bool overwrite);

  [CorrelationInitializer]
  int CreateDocument(Guid id, Guid listId, int itemId,
                     Hashtable itemProperties, byte[] fileContents);

  [CorrelationInitializer]
  int CreateListItem(Guid id, Guid listId, int itemId, Hashtable itemProperties);

  [CorrelationInitializer]
  void DeleteListItem(Guid id, Guid listId, int itemId);

  [CorrelationInitializer]
  void InitializeForEvent(Guid id, Guid listId, int itemId);

  [CorrelationInitializer]
  void UndoCheckOutListItem(Guid id, Guid listId, int itemId);

  [CorrelationInitializer]
  void UpdateDocument(Guid id, Guid listId, int itemId,
                      Hashtable itemProperties, bool overwriteFromTemplate,
                      byte[] fileContents);

  [CorrelationInitializer]
  void UpdateListItem(Guid id, Guid listId, int itemId, Hashtable itemProperties);
}
```

You can follow the same recipe that SharePoint uses to implement the CallExternalMethodActivity-based activities discussed in the previous sections to implement custom activities to expose the methods of the IListItemService local service. First, let's formally formulate this recipe:

1. Implement a class that inherits the CallExternalMethodActivity activity. Use the name of the method as the name of this class. For example, choose the name "UpdateDocument" for the class if this class invokes the UpdateDocument method of the SharePoint list item service:

```
public sealed MethodName   : CallExternalMethodActivity
{
  . . .
}
```

2. Implement a default constructor to set the values of the InterfaceType and MethodName properties of the CallExternalMethodActivity activity:

```
public MethodName()
{
  this.InterfaceType = typeof(IListItemService);
  this.MethodName = "EnterMethodNameHere";
}
```

3. Override the InterfaceType property of the CallExternalMethodActivity activity to return the typeof(IListItemService). You must make this property read-only by not implementing its setter method because the value of this property cannot be set:

```
public override Type InterfaceType
{
  get { return typeof(IListItemService); }
}
```

4. Override the MethodName property of the CallExternalMethodActivity activity to return a string that contains the method name, which is the same as the class name. You must make this property read-only by not implementing its setter method:

```
public override string MethodName
{
  get { return "EnterMethodNameHere"; }
}
```

5. Expose the parameters of the method as activity-level bindable properties
6. Expose the return value of the method as an activity-level bindable property. This step applies only if the method returns a value.
7. Override the OnMethodInvoking method of the CallExternalMethodActivity activity to assign the values of these activity-level properties to their respective parameters.
8. Override the OnMethodInvoked method of the CallExternalMethodActivity activity to assign the return value of the method to its respective activity-level property. This step applies only if the method has a return value.

We'll use this eight-step recipe in the following sections to develop custom CallExternalMethodActivity-based activities that enable workflows to invoke those methods of the SharePoint list item service that are not supported by the standard CallExternalMethodActivity-based activities.

Creating SharePoint List Items

The following code presents the implementation of a custom CallExternalMethodActivity-based activity named CreateListItem that enables workflows to invoke the CreateListItem method of the SharePoint list item service:

```
using System.Workflow.ComponentModel;
using System.Workflow.Runtime;
using System.Workflow.Activities;
using Microsoft.SharePoint.Workflow;
using System;
using System.Collections;

namespace Chapter9
{
 public class CreateListItem: CallExternalMethodActivity
 {
    public CreateListItem()
    {
      this.InterfaceType = typeof(IListItemService);
      this.MethodName = "CreateListItem";
    }

    public override Type InterfaceType
    {
      get { return typeof(IListItemService); }
    }

    public override string MethodName
    {
      get { return "CreateListItem"; }
    }

    public static readonly DependencyProperty IdProperty =
           DependencyProperty.Register("Id", typeof(Guid), typeof(CreateListItem));
    public Guid Id
    {
      get { return (Guid)base.GetValue(IdProperty); }
      set { base.SetValue(IdProperty, value); }
    }

    public static readonly DependencyProperty ListIdProperty =
            DependencyProperty.Register("ListId", typeof(Guid),
                                        typeof(CreateListItem));
    public Guid ListId
```

(continued)

(continued)

```
        {
          get { return (Guid)base.GetValue(ListIdProperty); }
          set { base.SetValue(ListIdProperty, value); }
        }

        public static readonly DependencyProperty ItemIdProperty =
                DependencyProperty.Register("ItemId", typeof(int),
                                            typeof(CreateListItem));
        public int ItemId
        {
          get { return (int)base.GetValue(ItemIdProperty); }
          set { base.SetValue(ItemIdProperty, value); }
        }

        public static readonly DependencyProperty ItemPropertiesProperty =
              DependencyProperty.Register("ItemProperties", typeof(Hashtable),
                                          typeof(CreateListItem));
        public Hashtable ItemProperties
        {
          get { return (Hashtable)base.GetValue(ItemPropertiesProperty); }
          set { base.SetValue(ItemPropertiesProperty, value); }
        }

        protected override void OnMethodInvoking(EventArgs e)
        {
          base.ParameterBindings["id"].Value = this.Id;
          base.ParameterBindings["listId"].Value = this.ListId;
          base.ParameterBindings["itemId"].Value = this.ItemId;
          base.ParameterBindings["itemProperties"].Value = this.ItemProperties;
        }

        protected override void OnMethodInvoked(EventArgs e)
        {
          this.ItemId = (int)base.ParameterBindings["(ReturnValue)"].Value;
        }
      }
    }
```

Following our eight-step recipe, the CreateListItem activity takes the following steps:

1. It inherits from the CallExternalMethodActivity activity.
2. It implements a default constructor to set the value of the InterfaceType and MethodName properties of the CallExternalMethodActivity activity to typeof(IListItemService) and "CreateListItem", respectively:

```
public CreateListItem()
{
  this.InterfaceType = typeof(IListItemService);
  this.MethodName = "CreateListItem";
}
```

3. It overrides the InterfaceType property to return typeof(IListItemService):

```
public override Type InterfaceType
{
  get { return typeof(IListItemService); }
}
```

4. It overrides the MethodName property to return "CreateListItem":

```
public override string MethodName
{
  get { return "CreateListItem"; }
}
```

5. It exposes the id, listId, itemId, and itemProperties parameters of the CreateListItem method as Id, ListId, ItemId, and ItemProperties activity-level bindable properties:

```
public static readonly DependencyProperty IdProperty =
       DependencyProperty.Register("Id", typeof(Guid), typeof(CreateListItem));
public Guid Id
{
  get { return (Guid)base.GetValue(IdProperty); }
  set { base.SetValue(IdProperty, value); }
}

public static readonly DependencyProperty ListIdProperty =
        DependencyProperty.Register("ListId", typeof(Guid),
                                    typeof(CreateListItem));
public Guid ListId
{
  get { return (Guid)base.GetValue(ListIdProperty); }
  set { base.SetValue(ListIdProperty, value); }
}

public static readonly DependencyProperty ItemIdProperty =
        DependencyProperty.Register("ItemId", typeof(int),
                                    typeof(CreateListItem));
public int ItemId
{
  get { return (int)base.GetValue(ItemIdProperty); }
  set { base.SetValue(ItemIdProperty, value); }
}

public static readonly DependencyProperty ItemPropertiesProperty =
       DependencyProperty.Register("ItemProperties", typeof(Hashtable),
                                   typeof(CreateListItem));
public Hashtable ItemProperties
{
  get { return (Hashtable)base.GetValue(ItemPropertiesProperty); }
  set { base.SetValue(ItemPropertiesProperty, value); }
}
```

6. It exposes the return value of the CreateListItem method through the activity-level bindable ItemId property.

7. It overrides the OnMethodInvoking method of the CallExternalMethodActivity activity to assign the values of the Id, ListId, ItemId, and ItemProperties activity-level properties to the id, listId, itemId, and itemProperties parameters of the CreateListItem method. Recall that the CallExternalMethodActivity activity invokes the OnMethodInvoking method before it invokes the CreateListItem method on the SharePoint list item service:

```
protected override void OnMethodInvoking(EventArgs e)
{
  base.ParameterBindings["id"].Value = this.Id;
  base.ParameterBindings["listId"].Value = this.ListId;
  base.ParameterBindings["itemId"].Value = this.ItemId;
  base.ParameterBindings["itemProperties"].Value = this.ItemProperties;
}
```

8. It overrides the OnMethodInvoked method of the CallExternalMethodActivity activity to assign the return value of the CreateListItem method to the ItemId activity-level bindable property. Recall that the CallExternalMethodActivity activity invokes the OnMethodInvoked method after it invokes the CreateListItem method on the SharePoint list item service:

```
protected override void OnMethodInvoked(EventArgs e)
{
  this.ItemId = (int)base.ParameterBindings["(ReturnValue)"].Value;
}
```

The following code presents a workflow that uses our custom CreateListItem activity:

```
using System;
using System.ComponentModel;
using System.ComponentModel.Design;
using System.Collections;
using System.Drawing;
using System.Linq;
using System.Workflow.ComponentModel.Compiler;
using System.Workflow.ComponentModel.Serialization;
using System.Workflow.ComponentModel;
using System.Workflow.ComponentModel.Design;
using System.Workflow.Runtime;
using System.Workflow.Activities;
using System.Workflow.Activities.Rules;
using Microsoft.SharePoint;
using Microsoft.SharePoint.Workflow;
using Microsoft.SharePoint.WorkflowActions;
using Microsoft.Office.Workflow.Utility;

namespace Chapter9
{
  public sealed class Workflow2 : SequentialWorkflowActivity
  {
    private LogToHistoryListActivity logToHistoryListActivity2;
    private OnWorkflowActivated onWorkflowActivated1;
```

```
private LogToHistoryListActivity logToHistoryListActivity1;
private CreateListItem createListItem1;
private SequenceActivity sequenceActivity2;
public int ItemId = default(System.Int32);
public Guid ListId = default(System.Guid);

public Workflow2()
{
  InitializeComponent();
}

private void InitializeComponent()
{
  this.CanModifyActivities = true;
  System.Workflow.Runtime.CorrelationToken correlationtoken1 =
                           new System.Workflow.Runtime.CorrelationToken();
  System.Workflow.ComponentModel.ActivityBind activitybind1 =
                          new System.Workflow.ComponentModel.ActivityBind();
  System.Workflow.ComponentModel.ActivityBind activitybind2 =
                          new System.Workflow.ComponentModel.ActivityBind();
  System.Workflow.Runtime.CorrelationToken correlationtoken2 =
                             new System.Workflow.Runtime.CorrelationToken();
  System.Workflow.ComponentModel.ActivityBind activitybind3 =
                         new System.Workflow.ComponentModel.ActivityBind();
  this.logToHistoryListActivity2 =
         new Microsoft.SharePoint.WorkflowActions.LogToHistoryListActivity();
  this.createListItem1 = new Chapter9.CreateListItem();
  this.logToHistoryListActivity1 =
          new Microsoft.SharePoint.WorkflowActions.LogToHistoryListActivity();
  this.onWorkflowActivated1 =
               new Microsoft.SharePoint.WorkflowActions.OnWorkflowActivated();
  //
  // logToHistoryListActivity2
  //
  this.logToHistoryListActivity2.Duration =
                       System.TimeSpan.Parse("-10675199.02:48:05.4775808");
  this.logToHistoryListActivity2.EventId =
     Microsoft.SharePoint.Workflow.SPWorkflowHistoryEventType.WorkflowComment;
  this.logToHistoryListActivity2.HistoryDescription = "Completed";
  this.logToHistoryListActivity2.HistoryOutcome = "Completed";
  this.logToHistoryListActivity2.Name = "logToHistoryListActivity2";
  this.logToHistoryListActivity2.OtherData = "";
  this.logToHistoryListActivity2.UserId = -1;
  //
  // createListItem1
  //
  correlationtoken1.Name = "taskToken";
  correlationtoken1.OwnerActivityName = "Workflow2";
  this.createListItem1.CorrelationToken = correlationtoken1;
  this.createListItem1.InterfaceType =
                   typeof(Microsoft.SharePoint.Workflow.IListItemService);
  activitybind1.Name = "Workflow2";
  activitybind1.Path = "ItemId";
```

(continued)

(continued)

```
            this.createListItem1.ItemProperties = null;
            activitybind2.Name = "Workflow2";
            activitybind2.Path = "ListId";
            this.createListItem1.MethodName = "CreateListItem";
            this.createListItem1.Name = "createListItem1";
            this.createListItem1.MethodInvoking +=
                         new System.EventHandler(this.createListItem1_MethodInvoking);
            this.createListItem1.SetBinding(Chapter9.CreateListItem.ItemIdProperty,
                     ((System.Workflow.ComponentModel.ActivityBind)(activitybind1)));
            this.createListItem1.SetBinding(Chapter9.CreateListItem.ListIdProperty,
                      ((System.Workflow.ComponentModel.ActivityBind)(activitybind2)));
            //
            // logToHistoryListActivity1
            //
            this.logToHistoryListActivity1.Duration =
                                   System.TimeSpan.Parse("-10675199.02:48:05.4775808");
            this.logToHistoryListActivity1.EventId =
               Microsoft.SharePoint.Workflow.SPWorkflowHistoryEventType.WorkflowComment;
            this.logToHistoryListActivity1.HistoryDescription = "Started";
            this.logToHistoryListActivity1.HistoryOutcome = "Started";
            this.logToHistoryListActivity1.Name = "logToHistoryListActivity1";
            this.logToHistoryListActivity1.OtherData = "";
            this.logToHistoryListActivity1.UserId = -1;
            //
            // onWorkflowActivated1
            //
            correlationtoken2.Name = "worflowToken";
            correlationtoken2.OwnerActivityName = "Workflow2";
            this.onWorkflowActivated1.CorrelationToken = correlationtoken2;
            this.onWorkflowActivated1.EventName = "OnWorkflowActivated";
            this.onWorkflowActivated1.Name = "onWorkflowActivated1";
            activitybind3.Name = "Workflow2";
            activitybind3.Path = "workflowProperties";
            this.onWorkflowActivated1.SetBinding(
                                    OnWorkflowActivated.WorkflowPropertiesProperty,
                      ((System.Workflow.ComponentModel.ActivityBind)(activitybind3)));
            //
            // Workflow2
            //
            this.Activities.Add(this.onWorkflowActivated1);
            this.Activities.Add(this.logToHistoryListActivity1);
            this.Activities.Add(this.createListItem1);
            this.Activities.Add(this.logToHistoryListActivity2);
            this.Name = "Workflow2";
            this.CanModifyActivities = false;
        }

        public Guid workflowId = default(System.Guid);
        public SPWorkflowActivationProperties workflowProperties =
                                              new SPWorkflowActivationProperties();

        private void createListItem1_MethodInvoking(object sender, EventArgs e)
```

```
        {
          Hashtable ht = new Hashtable();
          ht["Title"] = "New Title wow";
          createListItem1.SetValue(CreateListItem.ItemPropertiesProperty, ht);
          SPSite siteCollection = new SPSite("http://win-wjfgdnnhdus/Docs");
          SPWeb web = siteCollection.OpenWeb();
          SPList list = web.Lists["Tasks"];
          createListItem1.SetValue(CreateListItem.IdProperty, Guid.NewGuid());
          createListItem1.SetValue(CreateListItem.ListIdProperty, list.ID);
          createListItem1.SetValue(CreateListItem.ItemIdProperty, 1);
        }
      }
    }
```

This workflow registers an event handler named createListItem1_MethodInvoking for the MethodInvoking event of our CreateListItem activity. Our activity inherits this event from the CallExternalMethodActivity activity. This event handler performs the following tasks. First, it instantiates a Hashtable and populates it with the value for the Title field of the list item the activity is about to create. Next, it assigns this Hashtable to the ItemProperties property of our CreateListItem activity. Recall that the OnMethodInvoking method of our activity assigns this Hashtable to the itemProperties of the underlying CreateListItem method. Next, it retrieves the GUID of the SharePoint list on which the workflow wants to create the new list item and assigns this GUID to the ListId property of our custom CreateListItem activity.

If you execute this workflow, it will add a new list item to the specified SharePoint list.

Deleting SharePoint List Items

The following code presents the implementation of a custom CallExternalMethodActivity-based activity named DeleteListItem that invokes the DeleteListItem method on the SharePoint list item service to delete the list item with the specified ID from the SharePoint list with the specified GUID:

```
using System.Workflow.ComponentModel;
using System.Workflow.Runtime;
using System.Workflow.Activities;
using Microsoft.SharePoint.Workflow;
using System;
using System.Collections;

/*
 *   int CreateListItem(Guid id, Guid listId, int itemId, Hashtable
itemProperties);
 */

namespace Chapter9
{
  public class DeleteListItem : CallExternalMethodActivity
  {
    public DeleteListItem()
```

(continued)

(continued)

```
        {
          this.InterfaceType = typeof(IListItemService);
          this.MethodName = "DeleteListItem";
        }

        public override Type InterfaceType
        {
          get { return typeof(IListItemService); }
        }

        public override string MethodName
        {
          get { return "DeleteListItem"; }
        }

        public static readonly DependencyProperty IdProperty =
               DependencyProperty.Register("Id", typeof(Guid), typeof(DeleteListItem));
        public Guid Id
        {
          get { return (Guid)base.GetValue(IdProperty); }
          set { base.SetValue(IdProperty, value); }
        }

        public static readonly DependencyProperty ListIdProperty =
                DependencyProperty.Register("ListId", typeof(Guid),
    typeof(DeleteListItem));
        public Guid ListId
        {
          get { return (Guid)base.GetValue(ListIdProperty); }
          set { base.SetValue(ListIdProperty, value); }
        }

        public static readonly DependencyProperty ItemIdProperty =
                DependencyProperty.Register("ItemId", typeof(int),
    typeof(DeleteListItem));
        public int ItemId
        {
          get { return (int)base.GetValue(ItemIdProperty); }
          set { base.SetValue(ItemIdProperty, value); }
        }

        protected override void OnMethodInvoking(EventArgs e)
        {
          base.ParameterBindings["id"].Value = this.Id;
          base.ParameterBindings["listId"].Value = this.ListId;
          base.ParameterBindings["itemId"].Value = this.ItemId;
        }
      }
    }
```

We've followed the same eight-step recipe to implement the DeleteListItem activity. Here is a workflow that uses this activity:

```
using System;
using System.ComponentModel;
using System.ComponentModel.Design;
using System.Collections;
using System.Drawing;
using System.Linq;
using System.Workflow.ComponentModel.Compiler;
using System.Workflow.ComponentModel.Serialization;
using System.Workflow.ComponentModel;
using System.Workflow.ComponentModel.Design;
using System.Workflow.Runtime;
using System.Workflow.Activities;
using System.Workflow.Activities.Rules;
using Microsoft.SharePoint;
using Microsoft.SharePoint.Workflow;
using Microsoft.SharePoint.WorkflowActions;
using Microsoft.Office.Workflow.Utility;

namespace Chapter9
{
  public sealed class Workflow2 : SequentialWorkflowActivity
  {
    private LogToHistoryListActivity logToHistoryListActivity2;
    private OnWorkflowActivated onWorkflowActivated1;
    private LogToHistoryListActivity logToHistoryListActivity1;
    private SequenceActivity sequenceActivity2;
    public int ItemId = default(System.Int32);
    private DeleteListItem deleteListItem1;
    public Guid ListId = default(System.Guid);

    public Workflow2()
    {
      InitializeComponent();
    }

    private void InitializeComponent()
    {
      this.CanModifyActivities = true;
      System.Workflow.Runtime.CorrelationToken correlationtoken1 =
               new System.Workflow.Runtime.CorrelationToken();
      System.Workflow.Runtime.CorrelationToken correlationtoken2 =
               new System.Workflow.Runtime.CorrelationToken();
      System.Workflow.ComponentModel.ActivityBind activitybind1 =
               new System.Workflow.ComponentModel.ActivityBind();
      this.logToHistoryListActivity2 =
        new Microsoft.SharePoint.WorkflowActions.LogToHistoryListActivity();
      this.deleteListItem1 = new Chapter9.DeleteListItem();
      this.logToHistoryListActivity1 =
        new Microsoft.SharePoint.WorkflowActions.LogToHistoryListActivity();
```

(continued)

(continued)

```
        this.onWorkflowActivated1 =
           new Microsoft.SharePoint.WorkflowActions.OnWorkflowActivated();
        //
        // logToHistoryListActivity2
        //
        this.logToHistoryListActivity2.Duration =
                    System.TimeSpan.Parse("-10675199.02:48:05.4775808");
        this.logToHistoryListActivity2.EventId = Microsoft.SharePoint.Workflow
.SPWorkflowHistoryEventType.WorkflowComment;
        this.logToHistoryListActivity2.HistoryDescription = "Completed";
        this.logToHistoryListActivity2.HistoryOutcome = "Completed";
        this.logToHistoryListActivity2.Name = "logToHistoryListActivity2";
        this.logToHistoryListActivity2.OtherData = "";
        this.logToHistoryListActivity2.UserId = -1;
        //
        // deleteListItem1
        //
        correlationtoken1.Name = "taskToken";
        correlationtoken1.OwnerActivityName = "Workflow2";
        this.deleteListItem1.CorrelationToken = correlationtoken1;
        this.deleteListItem1.Id = new System.Guid("00000000-0000-0000-0000-
000000000000");
        this.deleteListItem1.InterfaceType =
                    typeof(Microsoft.SharePoint.Workflow.IListItemService);
        this.deleteListItem1.ItemId = 0;
        this.deleteListItem1.ListId =
                    new System.Guid("00000000-0000-0000-0000-000000000000");
        this.deleteListItem1.MethodName = "DeleteListItem";
        this.deleteListItem1.Name = "deleteListItem1";
        this.deleteListItem1.MethodInvoking +=
                    new System.EventHandler(this.deleteListItem1_MethodInvoking);
        //
        // logToHistoryListActivity1
        //
        this.logToHistoryListActivity1.Duration =
                    System.TimeSpan.Parse("-10675199.02:48:05.4775808");
        this.logToHistoryListActivity1.EventId = Microsoft.SharePoint.Workflow
.SPWorkflowHistoryEventType.WorkflowComment;
        this.logToHistoryListActivity1.HistoryDescription = "Started";
        this.logToHistoryListActivity1.HistoryOutcome = "Started";
        this.logToHistoryListActivity1.Name = "logToHistoryListActivity1";
        this.logToHistoryListActivity1.OtherData = "";
        this.logToHistoryListActivity1.UserId = -1;
        //
        // onWorkflowActivated1
        //
        correlationtoken2.Name = "workflowToken";
        correlationtoken2.OwnerActivityName = "Workflow2";
        this.onWorkflowActivated1.CorrelationToken = correlationtoken2;
        this.onWorkflowActivated1.EventName = "OnWorkflowActivated";
        this.onWorkflowActivated1.Name = "onWorkflowActivated1";
        activitybind1.Name = "Workflow2";
        activitybind1.Path = "workflowProperties";
```

```
        this.onWorkflowActivated1.SetBinding(Microsoft.SharePoint.WorkflowActions
.OnWorkflowActivated.WorkflowPropertiesProperty, ((System.Workflow.ComponentModel
.ActivityBind)(activitybind1)));
        //
        // Workflow2
        //
        this.Activities.Add(this.onWorkflowActivated1);
        this.Activities.Add(this.logToHistoryListActivity1);
        this.Activities.Add(this.deleteListItem1);
        this.Activities.Add(this.logToHistoryListActivity2);
        this.Name = "Workflow2";
        this.CanModifyActivities = false;

      }

      public Guid workflowId = default(System.Guid);
      public SPWorkflowActivationProperties workflowProperties =
                                        new SPWorkflowActivationProperties();

      private void deleteListItem1_MethodInvoking(object sender, EventArgs e)
      {
        SPSite siteCollection = new SPSite("http://win-wjfgdnnhdus/Docs");
        SPWeb web = siteCollection.OpenWeb();
        SPList list = web.Lists["Tasks"];
        deleteListItem1.SetValue(DeleteListItem.IdProperty, Guid.NewGuid());
        deleteListItem1.SetValue(DeleteListItem.ListIdProperty, list.ID);
        deleteListItem1.SetValue(DeleteListItem.ItemIdProperty, 2);
      }
    }
  }
```

This workflow registers an event handler named deleteListItem1_MethodInvoking for the MethodInvoking event of our DeleteListItem activity, setting the values of the Id, ListId, and ItemId properties of our activity.

Summary

This chapter provided in-depth coverage of those SharePoint activities that inherit from CallExternalMethodActivity, and demonstrated how you implement your own custom CallExternalMethodActivity-based activities to invoke specific methods of standard SharePoint external data exchanges services. The next chapter moves on to those SharePoint activities that inherit from HandleExternalEventActivity.

5

HandleExternalEventActivity-Based SharePoint Activities

This chapter provides in-depth coverage of those SharePoint activities that inherit from HandleExternalEventActivity. You will also learn how to use these activities to implement your own custom SharePoint workflows.

Handling OnTaskChanged Event

The OnTaskChanged activity inherits from HandleExternalEventActivity and is specifically configured and designed to suspend its execution to wait for the SharePoint task service to raise its OnTaskChanged event before the activity resumes its execution. The SharePoint task service fires this event when the SharePoint task with the specified task ID is updated. The following code presents the internal implementation of the OnTaskChanged activity:

```
public sealed class OnTaskChanged : HandleExternalEventActivity
{
  public static DependencyProperty AfterPropertiesProperty;
  public static DependencyProperty BeforePropertiesProperty;
  public static DependencyProperty ExecutorProperty;
  public static DependencyProperty TaskIdProperty;

  public OnTaskChanged()
  {
    this.InterfaceType = typeof(ITaskService);
    this.EventName = "OnTaskChanged";
  }

  protected override void OnInvoked(EventArgs e)
```

(continued)

(continued)

```
    {
      SPTaskServiceEventArgs args = (SPTaskServiceEventArgs)e;
      this.TaskId = args.taskId;
      this.Executor = args.executor;
      this.BeforeProperties = args.beforeProperties;
      this.AfterProperties = args.afterProperties;
    }

    public override string EventName
    {
      get { return "OnTaskChanged"; }
    }

    public string Executor { get; set; }

    public override Type InterfaceType
    {
      get { return typeof(ITaskService); }
    }

    public SPWorkflowTaskProperties AfterProperties { get; set; }
    public SPWorkflowTaskProperties BeforeProperties { get; set; }
    public Guid TaskId { get; set; }
  }
```

This activity overrides the InterfaceType and EventName properties to respectively return the Type object that represents the ITaskServer interface and the string containing the name of the OnTaskChanged event. Note that this activity implements these two properties as read-only because this activity is specifically configured to handle the OnTaskChanged event of the ITaskService service. As such, the value of these two properties cannot be changed. In addition, the constructor of this activity explicitly sets these two properties to the same values to instruct Visual Studio to display these values in the Properties pane.

This activity exposes the taskId, executor, afterProperties, and beforeProperties public fields of the respective SPTaskServiceEventArgs event data object as activity-level bindable properties named TaskId, Executor, AfterProperties, and BeforeProperties.

The previous chapter implemented a custom workflow named ConferenceRequestWorkflow. Recall that the CreateTaskWithContentType activity of this workflow creates a task with the content type of ManagerContentType. The main problem with this workflow is that it completes its execution before the manager of the employee gets the chance to update this task to accept or deny the employee's request. In this chapter, we'll add an OnTaskChanged activity to this workflow to enable it to suspend its execution and wait for the manager to update this task before it resumes execution.

Recall that ConferenceRequestWorkflow includes a CodeActivity that sets a workflow Boolean field named CancelRequest to true or false based on whether the requested days exceed the number of days to which the employee is entitled. Also recall that ConferenceRequestWorkflow includes an IfElseActivity activity right after the CodeActivity activity. This IfElseActivity contains a single

IfElseBranchActivity activity, which executes only if the CancelRequest field is set to true. This IfElseBranchActivity activity contains two child activities: DeleteTask and SendEmail.

The question is, where we should add the OnTaskChanged activity? Obviously, we cannot add it to the existing IfElseBranchActivity activity because we want the OnTaskChanged activity to execute when the CancelRequest field is false — that is, when the requested days do not exceed the number of days to which the employee is entitled. As such, first we need to add a new IfElseBranchActivity activity, which executes when the CancelRequest field is false.

Right-click the IfElseActivity activity on the designer surface and select the Add Branch menu option as shown in Figure 5-1.

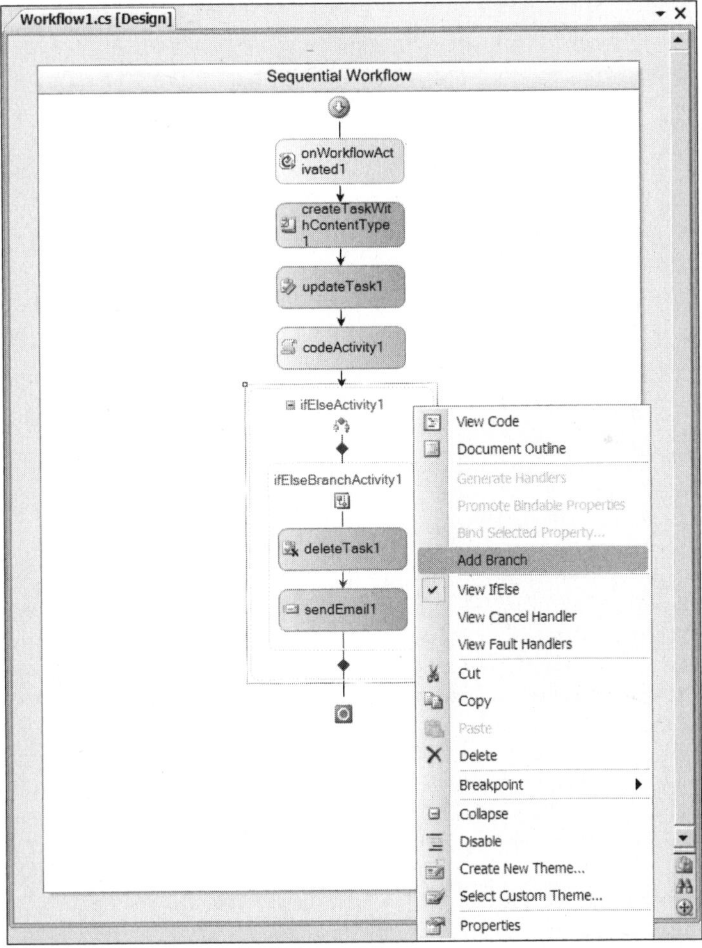

Figure 5-1

This adds a new IfElseBranchActivity activity to the IfElseActivity activity, as shown in Figure 5-2.

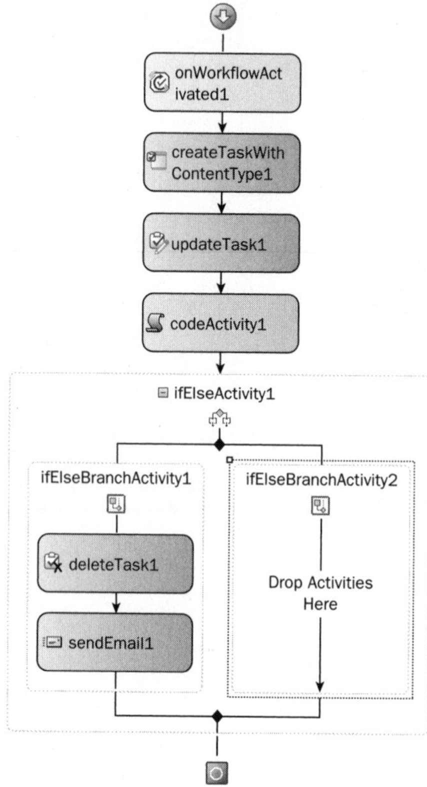

Figure 5-2

We could go ahead and add the OnTaskChanged activity directly to this new IfElseBranchActivity activity, but instead we'll take a different approach, for a reason that will be clear by the end of this section. First, drag a ListenActivity activity from the toolbox and drop it onto the designer surface as the child activity of the new IfElseBranchActivity activity (see Figure 5-3).

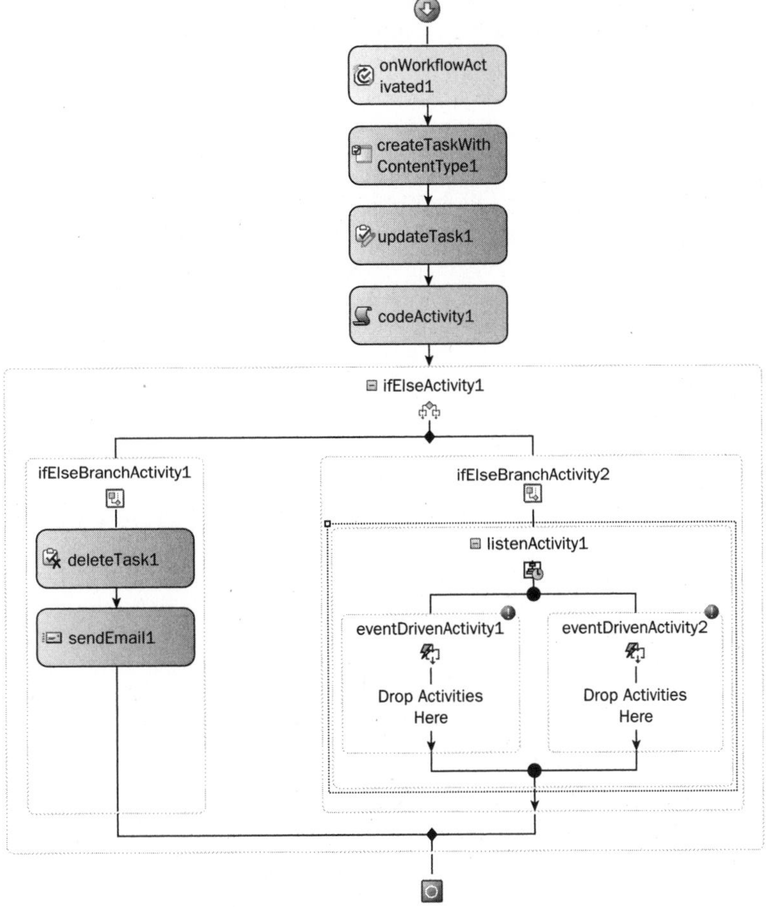

Figure 5-3

The ListenActivity activity contains two or more EventDrivenActivity activities. Every EventDrivenActivity activity requires its first child activity to be an activity that implements the IEventActivity interface. Listing 5-1 presents the definition of this interface.

Listing 5-1: The IEventActivity activity

```
public interface IEventActivity
{
  void Subscribe(ActivityExecutionContext parentContext,
               IActivityEventListener<QueueEventArgs> parentEventHandler);
  void Unsubscribe(ActivityExecutionContext parentContext,
                 IActivityEventListener<QueueEventArgs> parentEventHandler);
  IComparable QueueName { get; }
}
```

The DelayActivity, HandleExternalEventActivity, ReceiveActivity, and WebServiceInputActivity activities are the only standard WF activities that implement the IEventActivity activities. This means that only one of these four activities can be the first child activity of an EventDrivenActivity activity. The rest of the child activities of an EventDrivenActivity activity could be any type of activity.

As Listing 5-1 shows, every IEventActivity activity (that is, DelayActivity, HandleExternalEventActivity, ReceiveActivity, and WebServiceInputActivity) exposes a method named Subscribe, which takes an ActivityExecutionContext object and an IActivityEventListener<QueueEventArgs> object as its arguments. As discussed in the first chapter, the ActivityExecutionContext object represents the current execution context. Listing 5-2 presents the definition of the IActivityEventListener generic interface.

Listing 5-2: The IActivityEventListener generic interface

```
public interface IActivityEventListener<T> where T: EventArgs
{
  void OnEvent(object sender, T e);
}
```

This interface exposes a single method named OnEvent. As the name suggests, this method is invoked when an event is raised. You'll see shortly what event we're talking about here. The ListenActivity activity is one of the many WF activities that implement this interface.

As mentioned, the Subscribe method of an IEventActivity takes an IActivityEventListener<QueueEventArgs> object, which is the ListenActivity activity in our case, as its second argument. This method internally registers the OnEvent method of this object, which is the ListenActivity activity in this case, for the QueueItemAvailable event of a workflow queue whose name is specified in the QueueName property of the IEventActivity activity. Recall from Listing 5-1 that the IEventActivity interface exposes a property named QueueName. As discussed in the first chapter, a workflow queue raises this event when an external entity deposits data into the queue, at which point the OnEvent method that was subscribed for this event is invoked.

To summarize, each EventDrivenActivity child activity of the ListenActivity activity uses the Subscribe method of its IEventActivity child activity (which is always the first child activity) to subscribe to the OnEvent method of the ListenActivity activity for the QueueItemAvailable event of the workflow queue that the IEventActivity child activity creates internally.

When an external entity deposits data into this internal workflow queue, the QueueItemAvailable event is raised and consequently the OnEvent method of the ListenActivity activity is invoked. This method performs the following tasks. First, it invokes the Unsubscribe methods of the IEventActivity child activities (recall from Listing 5-1 that the IEventActivity interface exposes a method named Unsubscribe) of all its child EventDrivenActivity activities. These Unsubscribe methods unsubscribe the OnEvent method of the ListenActivity activity from the QueueItemAvailable events of the workflow queues that these IEventActivity child activities create internally. This means that from this point on, the ListenActivity activity will not respond to the QueueItemAvailable events of any of the IEventActivity child activities of any of its EventDrivenActivity child activities.

Next, the ListenActivity activity registers an event handler for the Closed event of the EventDrivenActivity activity whose first IEventActivity child activity's workflow queue fired its QueueItemAvailable event. Finally, the ListenActivity activity schedules this EventDrivenActivity activity for execution.

Only the first EventDrivenActivity activity whose first IEventActivity child activity's workflow queue fires its QueueItemAvailable event is ever scheduled for execution. The rest of the EventDrivenActivity child activities of the ListenActivity activity are never scheduled for execution. They basically remain in the Initialized state.

As Listing 5-3 shows, the ListenActivity activity by default contains two EventDrivenActivity child activities to address a common scenario. To help you understand this common scenario, imagine a ListenActivity activity with only one EventDrivenActivity child activity. As just discussed, the ListenActivity activity will schedule this EventDrivenActivity child activity for execution only when the workflow queue of the first IEventActivity child activity of this EventDrivenActivity activity fires its QueueItemAvailable event. This workflow queue, like any other workflow queue, fires its QueueItemAvailable event only when an external entity deposits data in the workflow queue. Therefore, if the external entity never deposits the data into this workflow queue, then the ListenActivity activity will never schedule this EventDrivenActivity activity for execution. This means that the ListenActivity activity, and consequently the workflow that contains this activity, can never complete its execution.

That is why the ListenActivity activity by default comes with two EventDrivenActivity activities. The second EventDrivenActivity activity should contain a DelayActivity as the first child activity. Recall that the DelayActivity activity is one of the four activities that implement the IEventActivity interface. The DelayActivity activity, like any other IEventActivity activity, creates an internal workflow queue whose name is provided by its QueueName property. The external entity in this case is a timer service that deposits an empty object into the workflow queue when it times out. This in turn causes the workflow queue of the DelayActivity activity to fire its QueueItemAvailable event and consequently to invoke the OnEvent method of the ListenActivity activity. This means that the ListenActivity activity will schedule the EventDrivenActivity activity that contains the DelayActivity activity for execution. As you can see, the second EventDrivenActivity activity enables you to introduce a timeout mechanism into the ListenActivity activity.

Now that you understand the ListenActivity activity, let's get back to the implementation of our ConferenceRequestWorkflow workflow. First, drag an OnTaskChanged activity and drop it onto the designer surface as the first child activity of one of the EventDrivenActivity child activities of the ListenActivity activity, as illustrated in Figure 5-4.

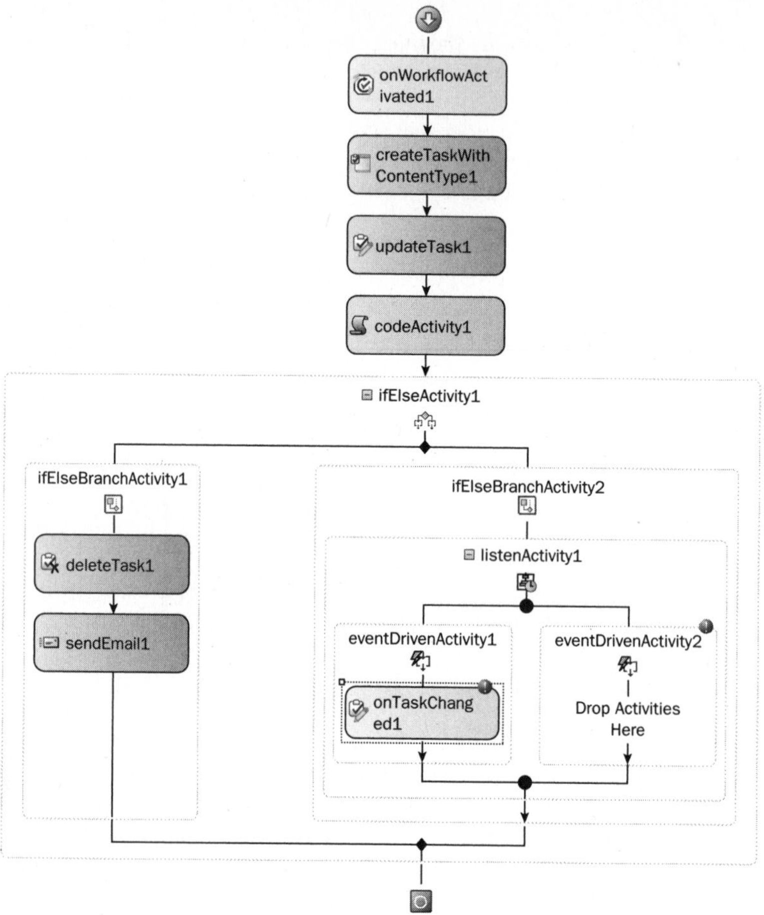

Figure 5-4

The OnTaskChanged activity is an IEventActivity activity because it inherits from the HandleExternalEventActivity activity, which implements the IEventActivity interface. As such, the OnTaskChanged activity can be the first child activity of an EventDrivenActivity activity. Select this OnTaskChanged activity, if it hasn't already been selected, to view its properties in the Properties pane, as Figure 5-5 demonstrates.

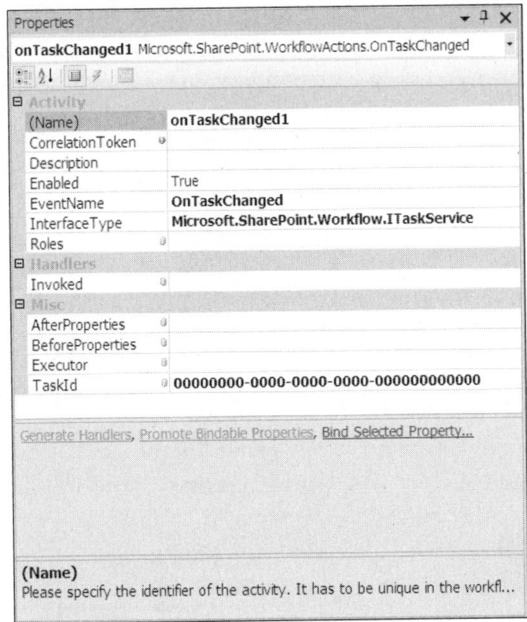

Figure 5-5

Next, take the following steps:

1. Use the same correlation token name that you used for the CreateTaskWithContentType activity to instruct Visual Studio to assign the same CorrelationToken object that was assigned to the CorrelationToken property of the CreateTaskWithContentType activity to the CorrelationToken property of the OnTaskChanged activity. This causes the OnTaskChanged activity to respond only to the OnTaskChanged event that the ITaskService external data exchange service raises when the task that the CreateTaskWithContentType activity created is updated. In other words, the OnTaskChanged activity will not respond to the OnTaskChanged events that this service raises when other tasks are updated.
2. Create three workflow fields named AfterProperties, BeforeProperties, and Executor and respectively bind them to the AfterProperties, BeforeProperties, and Executor properties of the OnTaskChanged activity.
3. Bind the existing TaskId workflow field to the TaskId property of the OnTaskChanged activity, because we want this activity to respond when the task that the CreateTaskWithContentType activity created is updated.

To help you understand the role of the Executor property of the OnTaskChanged activity, let's add a LogToHistoryListActivity activity below the OnTaskChanged activity, as shown in Figure 5-6.

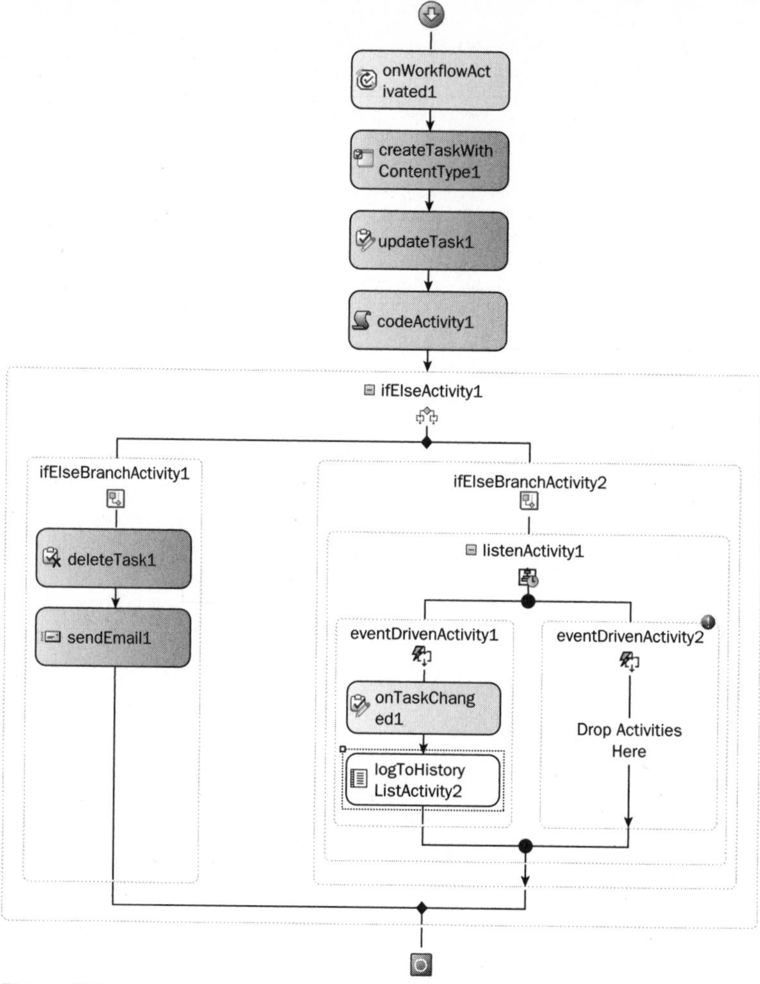

Figure 5-6

Select the LogToHistoryListActivity activity to view its properties in the Properties pane, as Figure 5-7 illustrates.

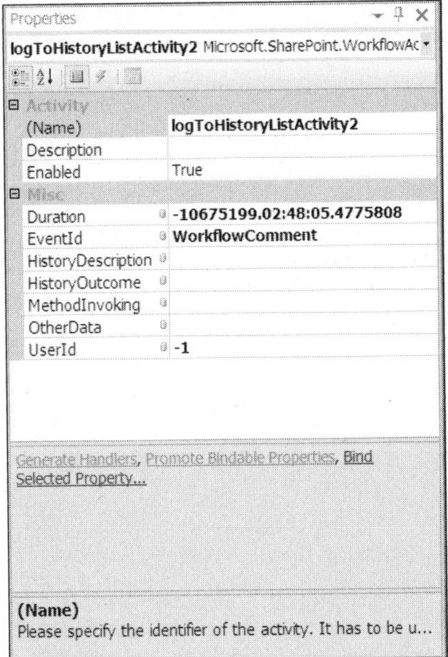

Figure 5-7

Create three workflow fields named HistoryDescription, HistoryOutcome, and UserId, and respectively bind them to the HistoryDescription, HistoryOutcome, and UserId properties of the LogToHistoryListActivity activity. As discussed in the previous chapters, the UserId property of the LogToHistoryListActivity activity is an integer that specifies the user ID of the current user or identity. In other words, this activity expects you to specify the user ID of the current user. This activity then logs the specified history event under this user ID.

The OnTaskChanged activity, conversely, does not expect you to specify the current user. Instead, it returns the user name of the current user to you. This is because the execution of the OnTaskChanged activity is triggered by the user or identity that updates the respective task. Therefore, the OnTaskChanged activity executes under the identity that updates the respective task. The Executor property of this activity returns the user name of this identity. Keep in mind that a SharePoint task can be updated through different mechanisms, such as the SharePoint user interface, a SharePoint web service, the SharePoint object model, and so on.

In our case, we want the LogToHistoryListActivity activity to log the specified history event under the same user that updates the respective task and consequently executes the OnTaskChanged activity. Obviously, we cannot directly bind the Executor property of the OnTaskChanged activity to the UserId property of the LogToHistoryListActivity activity because the Executor and UserId properties are of the System.String and System.Int32 types, respectively. Therefore, we need to determine the user ID of the executor of the OnTaskChanged activity. To do that, right-click the LogToHistoryListActivity activity on the designer surface and select the Generate Handlers menu option. This creates an empty event handler for the MethodInvoking event of the LogToHistoryListActivity activity. Add the code shown here:

```
private void logToHistoryListActivity2_MethodInvoking(object sender, EventArgs e)
{
  this.HistoryDescription = "Information";
  this.HistoryOutcome = "Task " + this.TaskId.ToString() + " was updated!";

  SPPrincipalInfo info =
      SPUtility.ResolvePrincipal(workflowProperties.Web, this.Executor,
                                 SPPrincipalType.All, SPPrincipalSource.All,
                                 null, false);
  this.UserId = (info == null ? -1 : info.PrincipalId);
}
```

This event handler first accesses a reference to the SPPrincipalInfo object containing the complete information about the current principal. The PrincipalId property of this object returns the user ID of the executor. Note the difference between the PrincipalId property and the ID property of the OriginatorUser property of the SPWorkflowActivationProperties object, which was discussed in Chapter 2. The former returns the user ID of the executor of the OnTaskChanged activity — that is, the user ID of the user who updated the task — whereas the latter returns the user ID of the user who initiated the current workflow instance. Therefore, when you need to use a LogToHistoryListActivity activity in your own workflows, you need to decide whether you want to log the history event under the user ID of the user who originated the workflow instance or the user ID of the user who updates the task. *As a best practice, if you're adding a LogToHistoryListActivity activity to report that a task has been updated, deleted, or created, you should log the history event under the user ID of the user who updated, deleted, or created the task.*

Drag a CompleteTask activity from the toolbox and drop it onto the designer surface below the LogToHistoryListActivity activity, as illustrated in Figure 5-8. *Again, as a best practice, always use the CompleteTask activity after the OnTaskChanged activity to mark the task as complete if you don't expect or want more changes to the task.*

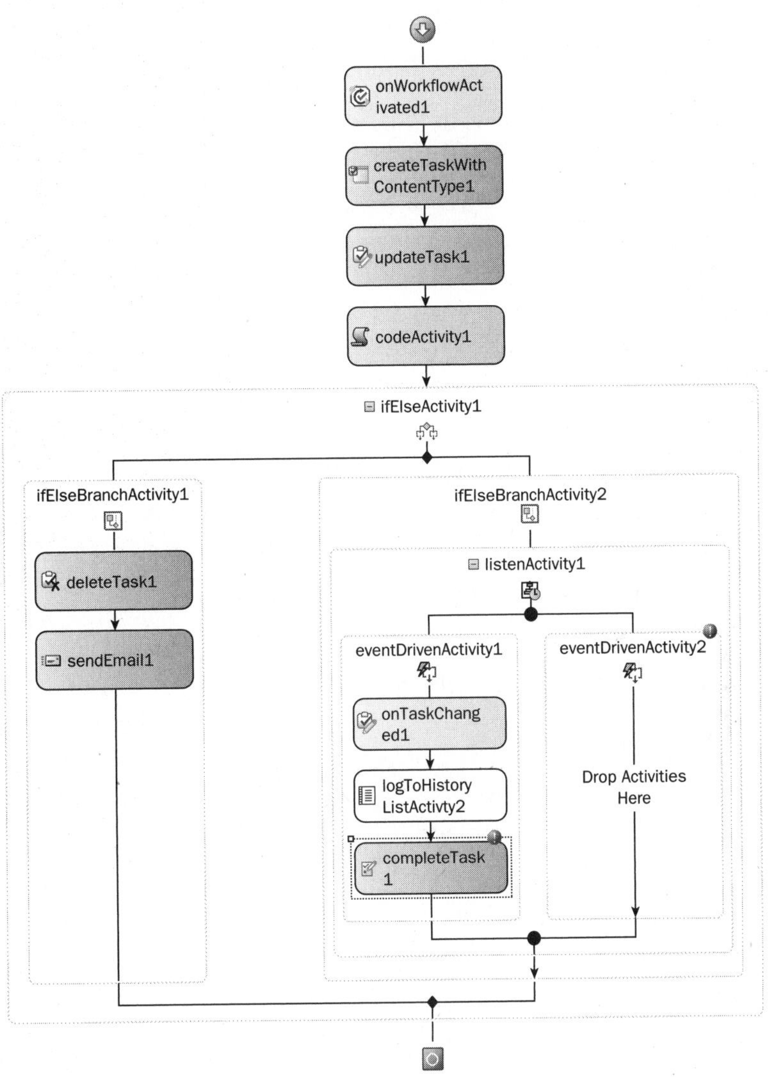

Figure 5-8

Figure 5-9 presents the properties of the CompleteTask activity.

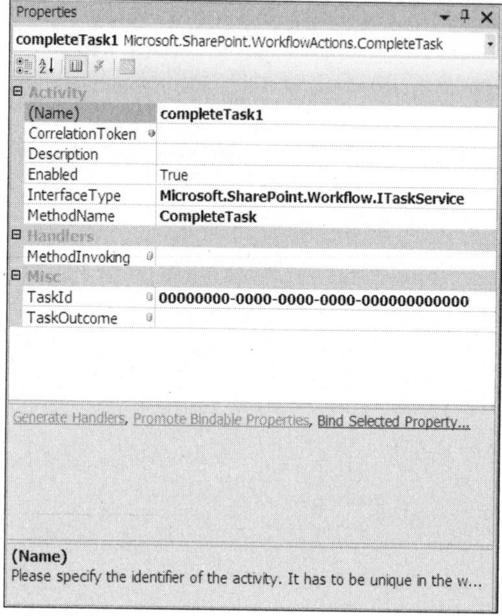

Figure 5-9

Bind the TaskId workflow field to the TaskId property of the CompleteTask activity to instruct this activity to mark the same task that the CreateTaskWithContentType activity created as complete.

So far, we've covered the child activities of one of the EventDrivenActivity child activities of the ListenActivity activity. Next, we'll look at the child activities of the other EventDrivenActivity activity. Drag a DelayActivity activity from the toolbox and drop it onto the designer surface as the first child activity of this EventDrivenActivity activity, as shown in Figure 5-10.

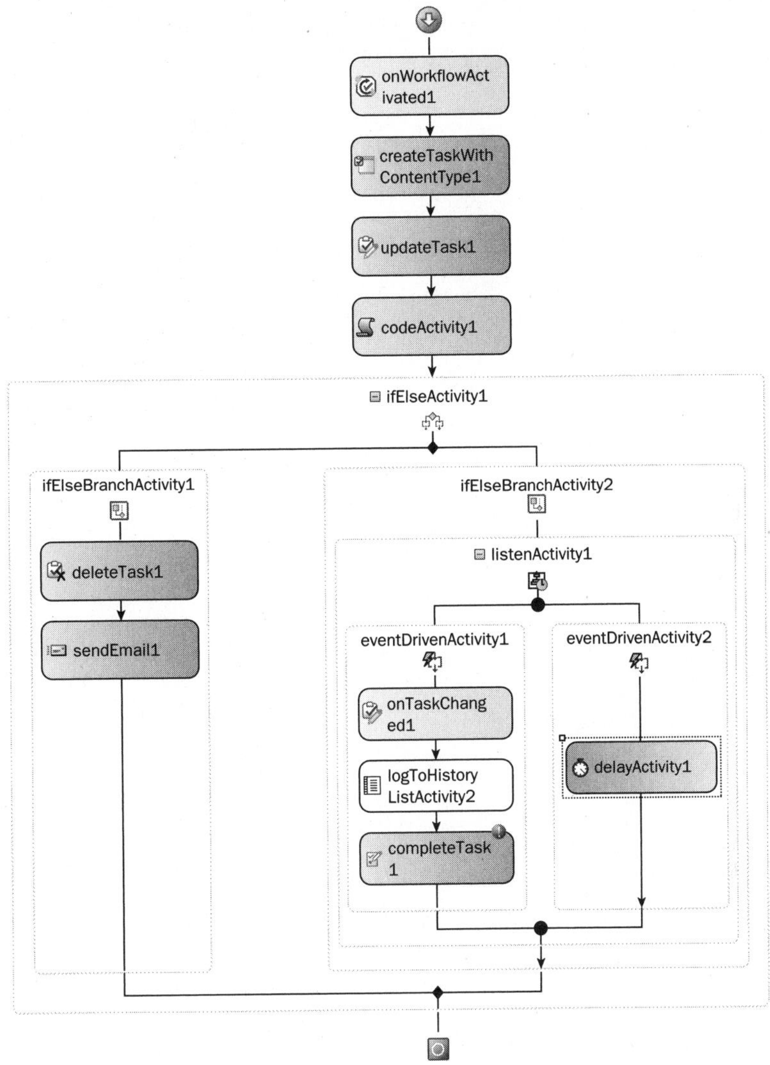

Figure 5-10

Figure 5-11 presents the properties of the DelayActivity activity.

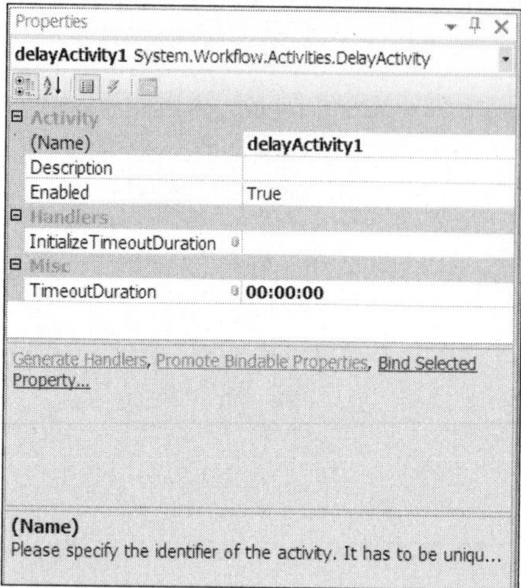

Figure 5-11

This activity exposes a TimeSpan property named TimeoutDuration. Set this property to specify when the DelayActivity activity should time out. When this activity times out, the ListenActivity activity schedules the EventDrivenActivity activity that contains this activity for execution.

Drag a DeleteActivity and a SendEmail activity from the toolbox and drop them onto the designer surface below the DelayActivity activity, as shown in Figure 5-12. Set the properties of these activities as described in Chapter 4.

When the DelayActivity times out — that is, when the specified task is not updated within the time frame specified in the TimeoutDuration property of the DelayActivity activity — the DeleteTask activity executes and deletes the task. The SendEmail activity is then executed to send an e-mail message to the employee indicating that the manager did not process the request within the specified time frame and consequently the request was canceled.

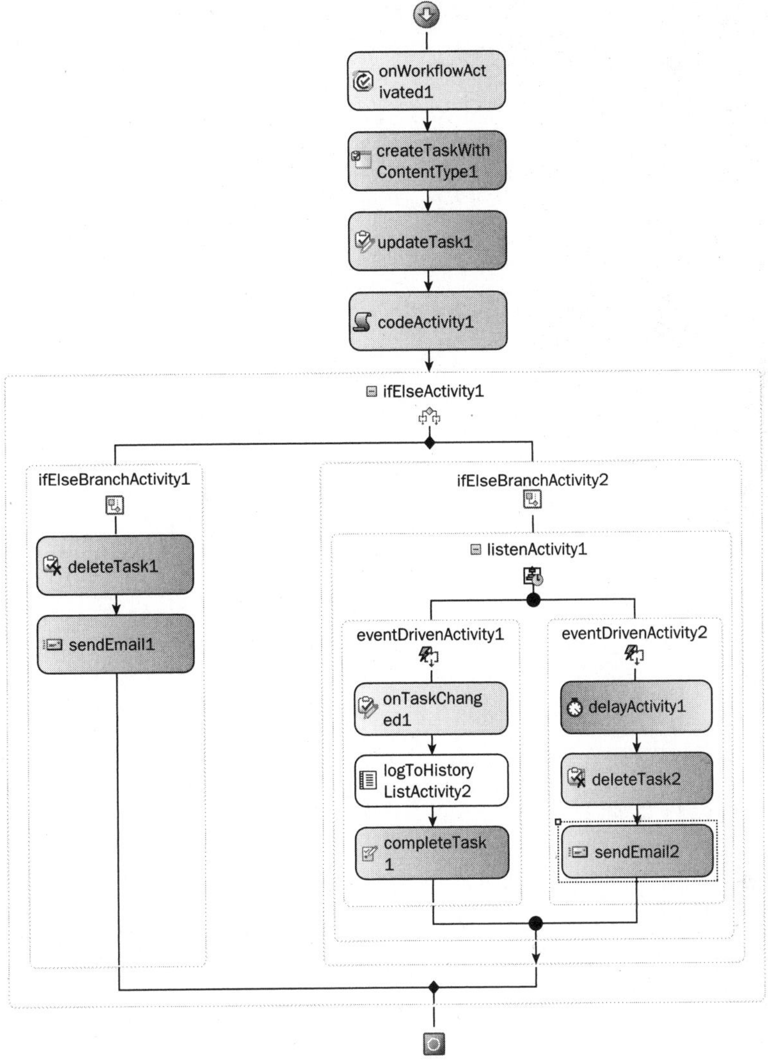

Figure 5-12

Handling OnTaskCreated Event

The OnTaskCreated activity inherits from HandleExternalEventActivity and is specifically configured and designed to suspend its execution to wait for the SharePoint task service to raise its OnTaskCreated event before the activity resumes its execution. The SharePoint task service fires this event when a

SharePoint task is created. The following code presents the internal implementation of the OnTaskCreated activity:

```
public sealed class OnTaskCreated : HandleExternalEventActivity
{
  public static DependencyProperty AfterPropertiesProperty;
  public static DependencyProperty ExecutorProperty;
  public static DependencyProperty TaskIdProperty;

  public OnTaskCreated()
  {
    this.InterfaceType = typeof(ITaskService);
    this.EventName = "OnTaskCreated";
  }

  protected override void OnInvoked(EventArgs e)
  {
    SPTaskServiceEventArgs args = (SPTaskServiceEventArgs)e;
    this.TaskId = args.taskId;
    this.Executor = args.executor;
    this.AfterProperties = args.afterProperties;
  }

  public override string EventName
  {
    get { return "OnTaskCreated"; }
  }

  public string Executor { get; set; }

  public override Type InterfaceType
  {
    get { return typeof(ITaskService); }
  }

  public SPWorkflowTaskProperties AfterProperties { get; set; }
  public Guid TaskId { get; set; }
}
```

This activity exposes three properties named TaskId, Executor, and AfterProperties, which are of the Guid, string, and SPWorkflowTaskProperties types, respectively. As the preceding code shows, the OnTaskCreated activity overrides the OnInvoked method of HandleExternalEventActivity, where it assigns the taskId, executor, and afterProperties public fields of the SPTaskServiceEventArgs object to its respective properties. Recall that HandleExternalEventActivity invokes the OnInvoked method after the task service fires its OnTaskCreated event and after it retrieves the SPTaskServiceEventArgs object deposited into the respective workflow queue.

The AfterProperties property of the OnTaskCreated activity basically provides the containing workflow and its activities with the names and values of the properties of the newly created SharePoint task. The Executor property returns the user name under which the communication from the task service to the current workflow instance flows.

Next, add an OnTaskCreated activity below the CreateTaskWithContentType activity to have our ConferenceRequestWorkflow workflow suspend its execution until the task is actually created, as shown in Figure 5-13.

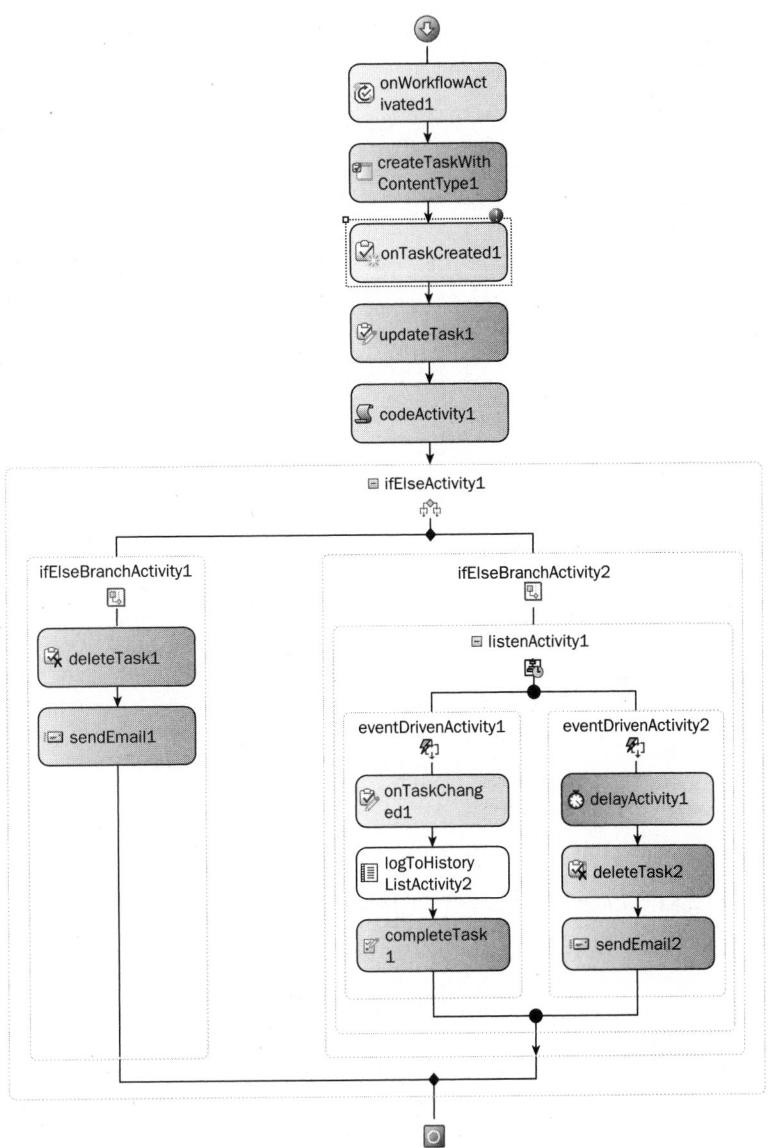

Figure 5-13

Figure 5-14 presents the properties of the OnTaskCreated activity.

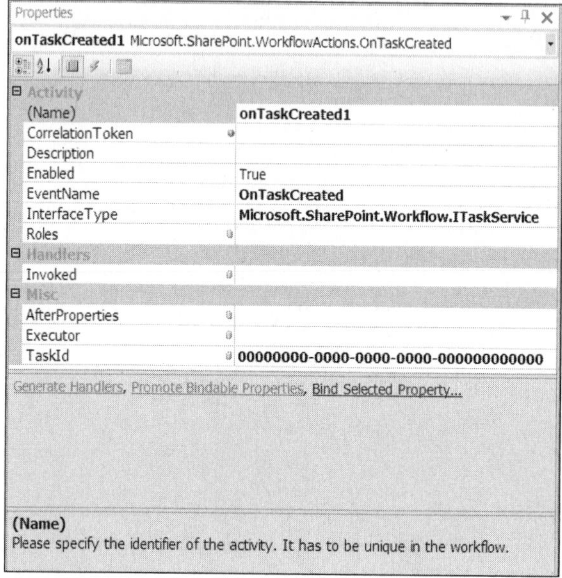

Figure 5-14

The same discussion about the Executor property of the OnTaskChanged activity and its role applies to the Executor property of the OnTaskCreated activity. In other words, the Executor property returns the user name of the user or identity that created the task. *Therefore, if you decide to use a LogToHistoryListActivity activity after an OnTaskCreated activity to report the creation of the task, you should log the history event under the user who created the task, as opposed to the user who initiated the current workflow instance.*

Handling OnTaskDeleted Event

The OnTaskDeleted activity inherits from HandleExternalEventActivity and is specifically configured and designed to respond to the OnTaskDeleted event of the ITaskService service. The SharePoint task service fires this event when a SharePoint task is deleted. The following code presents the internal implementation of the OnTaskDeleted activity:

```
public sealed class OnTaskDeleted : HandleExternalEventActivity
{
  public static DependencyProperty AfterPropertiesProperty;
  public static DependencyProperty ExecutorProperty;
```

```
    public static DependencyProperty TaskIdProperty;

    public OnTaskDeleted()
    {
      this.InterfaceType = typeof(ITaskService);
      this.EventName = "OnTaskDeleted";
    }

    protected override void OnInvoked(EventArgs e)
    {
      SPTaskServiceEventArgs args = (SPTaskServiceEventArgs)e;
      this.TaskId = args.taskId;
      this.Executor = args.executor;
      this.AfterProperties = args.afterProperties;
    }

    public override string EventName
    {
      get { return "OnTaskDeleted"; }
    }

    public string Executor
    {
      get { return (string)base.GetValue(ExecutorProperty); }
      set { base.SetValue(ExecutorProperty, value); }
    }

    public override Type InterfaceType
    {
      get { return typeof(ITaskService); }
    }

    public SPWorkflowTaskProperties AfterProperties { get; set; }
    public Guid TaskId { get; set; }
  }
```

This activity exposes the taskId, executor, and afterProperties public fields of the SPTaskServiceEventArgs object as activity-level properties named TaskId, Executor, and AfterProperties, respectively.

Next, we'll add two OnTaskDeleted activities below the two DeleteTask activities of our ConferenceRequestWorkflow workflow, as Figure 5-15 shows.

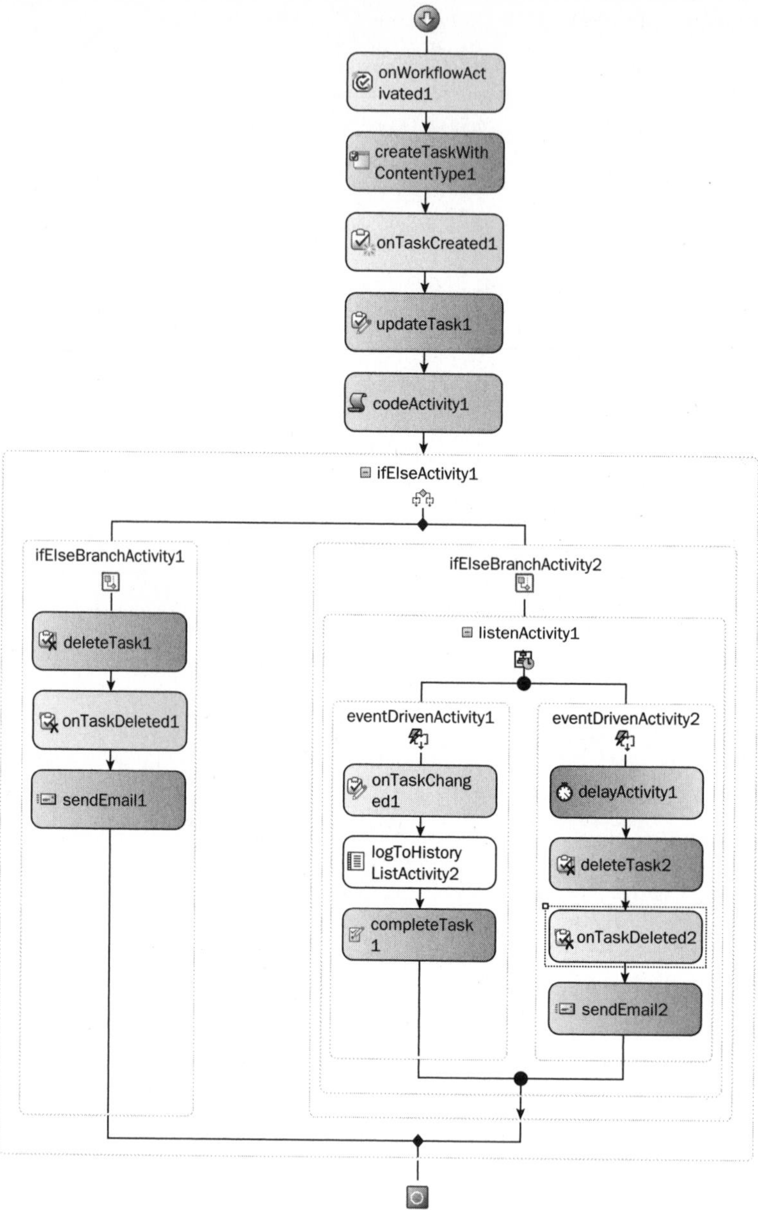
onWorkflowActivated1
createTaskWithContentType1
onTaskCreated1
updateTask1
codeActivity1
ifElseActivity1
ifElseBranchActivity1
deleteTask1
onTaskDeleted1
sendEmail1
ifElseBranchActivity2
listenActivity1
eventDrivenActivity1
onTaskChanged1
logToHistoryListActivity2
completeTask1
eventDrivenActivity2
delayActivity1
deleteTask2
onTaskDeleted2
sendEmail2

Figure 5-15

Figure 5-16 shows the properties of the OnTaskDeleted activity.

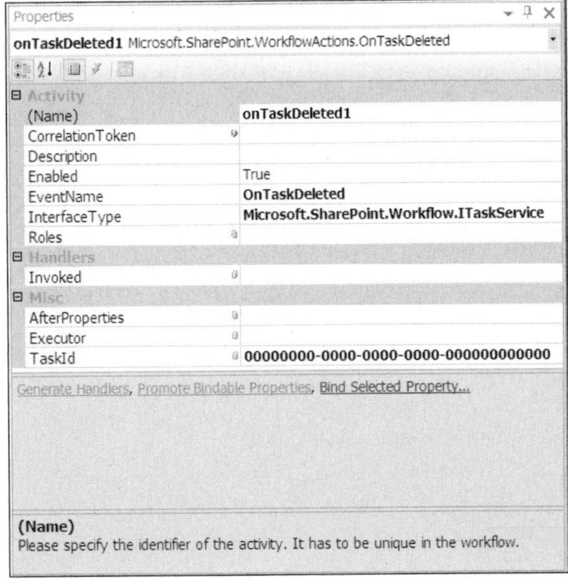

Figure 5-16

You should know by now how to bind workflow fields to the properties of this OnTaskDeleted activity.

Handling OnWorkflowItemChanged Event

The OnWorkflowItemChanged activity responds to the OnWorkflowItemChanged event of the ISharePointService external data exchange service. This service raises this event when the SharePoint list item or document on which the current workflow instance is running is updated. This SharePoint list item or document can be updated through the SharePoint user interface, the SharePoint object model, workflow activities, or SharePoint web services.

The following code presents the internal implementation of the OnWorkflowItemChanged activity:

```
public sealed class OnWorkflowItemChanged : HandleExternalEventActivity
{
  public static DependencyProperty AfterPropertiesProperty;
  public static DependencyProperty BeforePropertiesProperty;
  public static DependencyProperty WorkflowIdProperty;

  public OnWorkflowItemChanged()
  {
    this.InterfaceType = typeof(ISharePointService);
    this.EventName = "OnWorkflowItemChanged";
  }

  protected override void OnInvoked(EventArgs e)
  {
    SPItemEventArgs args = (SPItemEventArgs)e;
    this.WorkflowId = args.workflowId;
    this.BeforeProperties = args.beforeProperties;
    this.AfterProperties = args.afterProperties;
  }

  public override string EventName
  {
    get { return "OnWorkflowItemChanged"; }
  }

  public override Type InterfaceType
  {
    get { return typeof(ISharePointService); }
  }

  public Hashtable AfterProperties { get; set; }
  public Hashtable BeforeProperties { get; set; }
  public Guid WorkflowId
  {
    get
    {
      Guid workflowInstanceId = (Guid)base.GetValue(WorkflowIdProperty);
      if (Guid.Empty == workflowInstanceId)
        workflowInstanceId = WorkflowEnvironment.WorkflowInstanceId;
      return workflowInstanceId;
    }
    set { base.SetValue(WorkflowIdProperty, value); }
  }
}
```

As shown here, the OnWorkflowItemChanged activity exposes the workflowId, beforeProperties, and afterProperties public fields of the respective SPItemEventArgs object as activity-level properties named WorkflowId, BeforeProperties, and AfterProperties. Note that this activity overrides the InterfaceType and EventName properties to return the Type object that represents the ISharePointService interface and "OnWorkflowItemChanged." Also note that these properties are implemented as read-only properties. This is because this activity is specifically designed to listen for the OnWorkflowItemChanged event of the ISharePointService service. The getter of the WorkflowId property returns the value of the WorkflowInstanceId static property of the WorkflowEnvironment class if its value has not been explicitly set.

Next, we'll use an OnWorkflowChanged activity to improve our ConferenceRequestWorkflow workflow. Here's what we want to achieve:

- We want to enable the manager to send an event to all instances of our ConferenceRequestWorkflow workflow. Keep in mind that each employee initiates a separate instance of this workflow. This means that numerous instances of this workflow could be running simultaneously.
- We want to enable the manager to send this event at any time. Therefore, our ConferenceRequestWorkflow workflow must use a flow control construct that enables it to catch this event at any time during its execution logic.
- We want to enable the manager to send this event multiple times over an extended period of time, and the manager may use different event parameters each time. Therefore, our ConferenceRequestWorkflow workflow must use a flow construct that enables it to catch this event each time it is raised.

Therefore, our goal is to come up with a flow control construct that enables our ConferenceRequestWorkflow workflow to catch an event at any time during its execution logic. This event can be raised multiple times over an extended period of time, each time with a different set of event parameters. Next, we'll take a look at two flow control constructs that you're already familiar with to see whether either of these can do the job.

The first flow control construct option is the ParallelActivity activity. Recall that this flow control construct executes two or more execution branches simultaneously. Our ConferenceRequestWorkflow workflow could then have a big ParallelActivity with two branches. One of these branches will contain an OnWorkflowItemChanged activity. The other branch will contain the rest of the activities of our ConferenceRequestWorkflow workflow — that is, everything shown in Figure 5-15 will be in this branch. Figure 5-17 shows the new version of our ConferenceRequestWorkflow workflow.

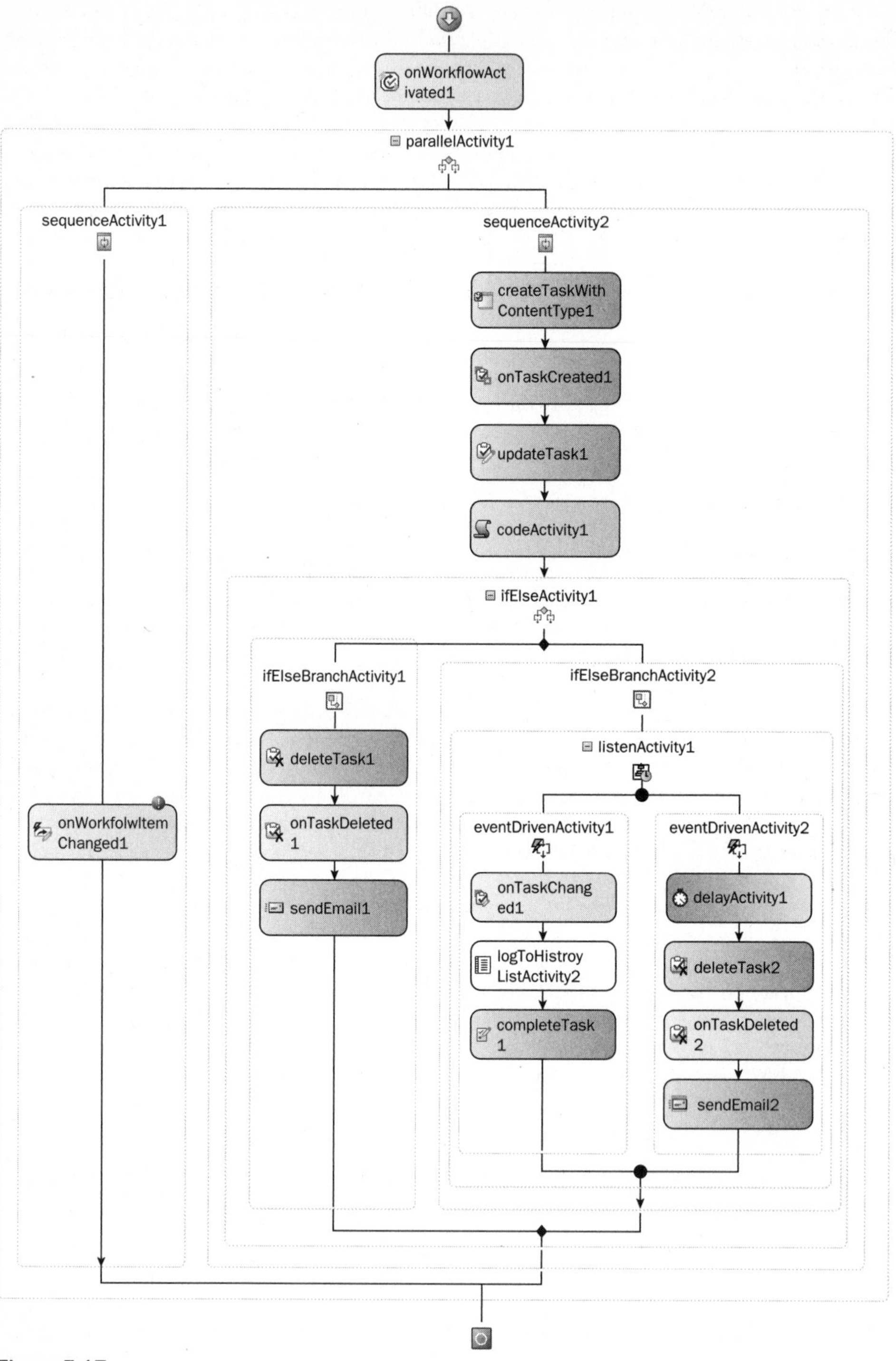
onWorkflowAct
ivated1
parallelActivity1
sequenceActivity1
sequenceActivity2
createTaskWith
ContentType1
onTaskCreated1
updateTask1
codeActivity1
ifElseActivity1
ifElseBranchActivity1
ifElseBranchActivity2
deleteTask1
onTaskDeleted
1
sendEmail1
listenActivity1
onWorkfolwItem
Changed1
eventDrivenActivity1
eventDrivenActivity2
onTaskChang
ed1
logToHistroy
ListActivity2
completeTask
1
delayActivity1
deleteTask2
onTaskDeleted
2
sendEmail2

Figure 5-17

Thanks to the ParallelActivity flow control construct, the OnWorkflowItemChanged activity in the left execution branch responds to the event that the manager sends to the ConferenceRequestWorkflow instance (through updating the list item on which the workflow instance is running) regardless of where the workflow instance is along its execution logic in the right execution branch.

There are two problems with using the ParallelActivity flow control construct in this scenario. One, each execution branch can execute only once. This means that the OnWorkflowItemChanged activity in the left execution branch can only catch one of the events that the manager sends to the workflow instance. Two, the ParallelActivity flow control construct does not return until all execution branches complete. This is a problem in our case because we want the flow control construct to return when the main branch completes its execution, even if the manager does not send any events; sending events is optional. The ParallelActivity activity makes sending events mandatory.

Clearly, the ParallelActivity flow control construct is not the most appropriate construct in this case, so we'll take a look at the ListenActivity flow control construct. Recall that this activity also contains multiple execution branches. Figure 5-18 presents a version of our ConferenceRequestWorkflow workflow that uses a ListenActivity flow control construct.

The trouble with using the ListenActivity flow control construct in this scenario is that when one branch begins its execution, the other branch is never executed. This means that the OnWorkflowItemChanged activity in the left execution branch in Figure 5-18 will never be executed if the right branch executes first. Therefore, the ListenActivity activity is not the right flow control construct in this case either.

What we're looking for is a flow control construct that consists of two branches whereby one branch contains the OnWorkflowItemChanged activity and the other branch contains the rest of the ConferenceRequestWorkflow workflow. We want the branch that contains the rest of the workflow to keep executing while the branch that contains the OnWorkflowItemChanged activity keeps responding to the events that the manager sends to the workflow through updating the list item on which the workflow instance is running. Enter the EventHandlingScopeActivity flow control construct.

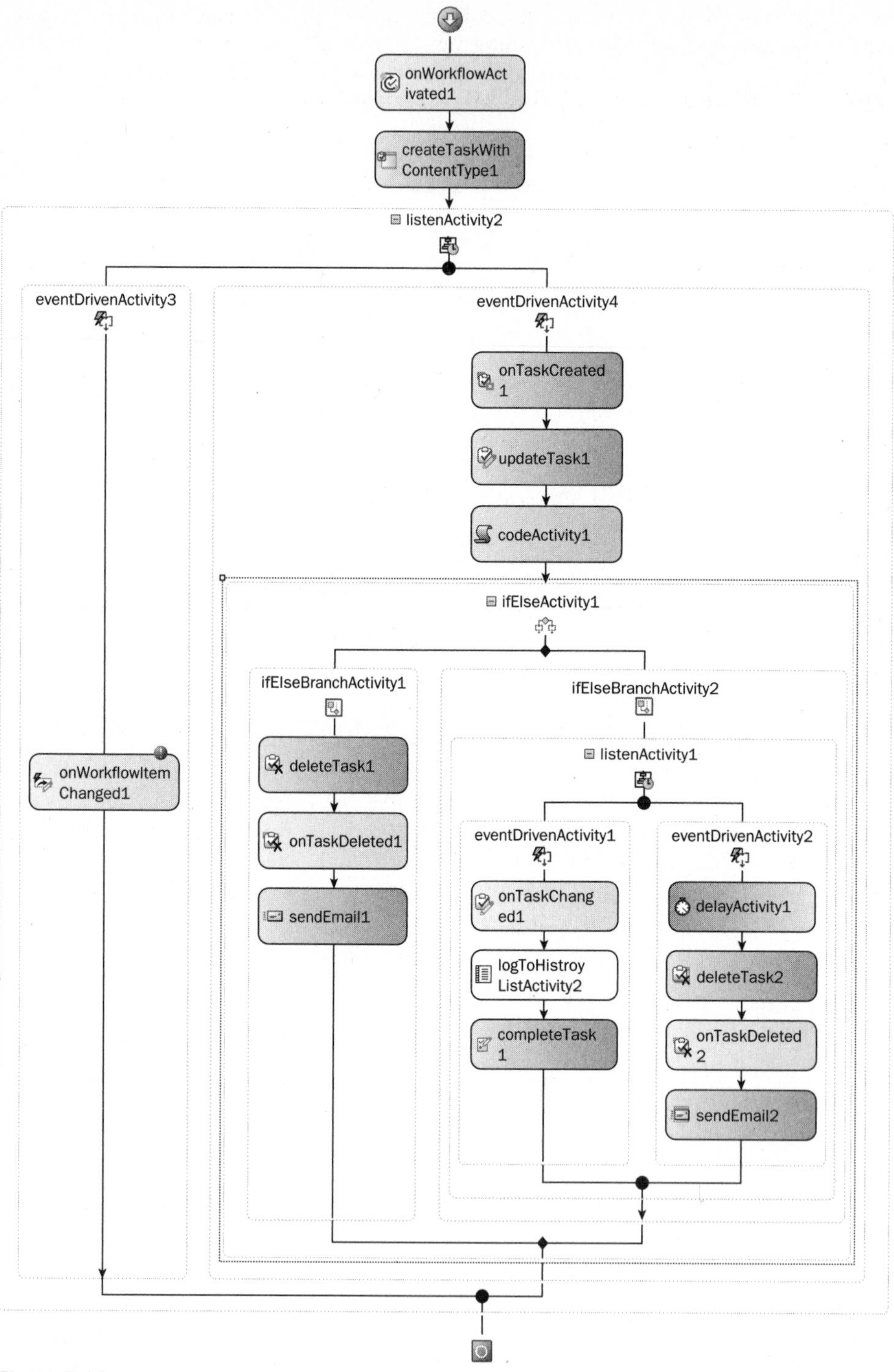

onWorkflowActivated1
createTaskWithContentType1
listenActivity2
eventDrivenActivity3
eventDrivenActivity4
onTaskCreated1
updateTask1
codeActivity1
ifElseActivity1
ifElseBranchActivity1
ifElseBranchActivity2
onWorkflowItemChanged1
deleteTask1
listenActivity1
onTaskDeleted1
eventDrivenActivity1
eventDrivenActivity2
sendEmail1
onTaskChanged1
delayActivity1
logToHistroyListActivity2
deleteTask2
completeTask1
onTaskDeleted2
sendEmail2

Figure 5-18

The best way to understand how the EventHandlingScopeActivity flow control construct works is to take a look at its internal implementation, shown in Listing 5-3.

Listing 5-3: The EventHandlingScopeActivity activity

```
[ActivityValidator(typeof(EventHandlingScopeValidator))]
public sealed class EventHandlingScopeActivity : CompositeActivity,
                  IActivityEventListener<ActivityExecutionStatusChangedEventArgs>
{
  protected override ActivityExecutionStatus Execute(
               ActivityExecutionContext activityExecutionContext)
  {
    Activity bodyActivity = this.BodyActivity;
    if (bodyActivity == null)
      return ActivityExecutionStatus.Closed;

    EventHandlersActivity eventHandlersActivity =
                          this.EventHandlersActivity;
    if (eventHandlersActivity != null)
    {
      eventHandlersActivity.RegisterForStatusChange(
                                Activity.ClosedEvent, this);
      activityExecutionContext.ExecuteActivity(eventHandlersActivity);
    }
    bodyActivity.RegisterForStatusChange(Activity.ClosedEvent, this);
    activityExecutionContext.ExecuteActivity(bodyActivity);
    return base.ExecutionStatus;
  }

  void IActivityEventListener<ActivityExecutionStatusChangedEventArgs>.OnEvent
        (object sender, ActivityExecutionStatusChangedEventArgs args)
  {
    ActivityExecutionContext activityExecutionContext =
                             sender as ActivityExecutionContext;

    args.Activity.UnregisterForStatusChange(
                             Activity.ClosedEvent, this);
    if (args.Activity is EventHandlersActivity)
    {
      if (this.BodyActivity.ExecutionStatus ==
                             ActivityExecutionStatus.Closed)
        activityExecutionContext.CloseActivity();
    }
    else
    {
      EventHandlersActivity eventHandlersActivity =
                        this.EventHandlersActivity;
```

(continued)

Listing 5-3 *(continued)*

```
        if ((eventHandlersActivity == null) ||
            (eventHandlersActivity.ExecutionStatus ==
                                ActivityExecutionStatus.Closed))
          activityExecutionContext.CloseActivity();
        else
          eventHandlersActivity.UnsubscribeAndClose();
      }
    }

    internal Activity BodyActivity
    {
      get
      {
        Activity bodyActivity = null;
        foreach (Activity activity in base.EnabledActivities)
        {
          if (!(activity is EventHandlersActivity))
            bodyActivity = activity;
        }
        return bodyActivity;
      }
    }

    internal EventHandlersActivity EventHandlersActivity
    {
      get
      {
        EventHandlersActivity eventHandlersActivity = null;
        foreach (Activity activity in base.EnabledActivities)
        {
          if (activity is EventHandlersActivity)
            eventHandlersActivity = activity as EventHandlersActivity;
        }
        return eventHandlersActivity;
      }
    }
  }
```

The EventHandlingScopeActivity activity inherits from the CompositeActivity activity and implements the IActivityEventListener<ActivityExecutionStatusChangedEventArgs> interface. Recall from Listing 5-2 that the IActivityEventListener<T> generic interface exposes a single method named OnEvent:

```
void OnEvent(object sender, T args);
```

The generic T type in our case is ActivityExecutionStatusChangedEventArgs, which is the event data class for an activity Closed event. An activity raises its Closed event when it transitions to the Closed state.

As Listing 5-3 shows, EventHandlingScopeActivity exposes two properties: BodyActivity and EventHandlersActivity. As the name suggests, the BodyActivity activity contains the activities that make up the main body, or the main branch, of the EventHandlingScopeActivity. The EventHandlersActivity activity, conversely, contains one or more EventDrivenActivity activities, which run in parallel to the main branch. In other words, the EventHandlingScopeActivity activity consists of one main branch whose root activity is the BodyActivity activity and zero or more parallel branches where the root activity of each branch is an EventDrivenActivity child activity of the EventHandlersActivity activity.

As shown in Listing 5-3, the EventHandlingScopeActivity activity is annotated with the following metadata attribute:

```
[ActivityValidator(typeof(EventHandlingScopeValidator))]
```

This metadata attribute registers the EventHandlingScopeValidator as the validator for the EventHandlingScopeActivity activity. WF calls this validator to validate the EventHandlingScopeActivity activity. This validator ensures that the EventHandlingScopeActivity activity contains only two child activities — that is, the BodyActivity and the EventHandlersActivity.

Next, I'll walk you through the implementation of the Execute method of the EventHandlingScopeActivity activity. This method returns ActivityExecutionStatus.Closed to inform the workflow run time that it has completed its execution if the EventHandlingScopeActivity activity does not contain a body activity:

```
Activity bodyActivity = this.BodyActivity;
if (bodyActivity == null)
  return ActivityExecutionStatus.Closed;
```

The EventHandlersActivity activity branch of the EventHandlingScopeActivity activity never executes if the EventHandlingScopeActivity activity does not have a main branch.

Next, the Execute method checks whether the EventHandlingScopeActivity activity contains the EventHandlersActivity branch. If so, it first registers the OnEvent method of the

EventHandlingScopeActivity activity as the event handler for the Closed event of the EventHandlersActivity activity and then schedules the EventHandlersActivity activity for execution:

```
EventHandlersActivity eventHandlersActivity = this.EventHandlersActivity;
if (eventHandlersActivity != null)
{
  eventHandlersActivity.RegisterForStatusChange(Activity.ClosedEvent, this);
  activityExecutionContext.ExecuteActivity(eventHandlersActivity);
}
```

As shown here, you could have an EventHandlingScopeActivity activity that does not contain the EventHandlersActivity branch.

Next, the Execute method registers the OnEvent method of the EventHandlingScopeActivity activity as event handler for the Closed event of the body activity:

```
bodyActivity.RegisterForStatusChange(Activity.ClosedEvent, this);
```

Then, it schedules the body activity for execution:

```
activityExecutionContext.ExecuteActivity(bodyActivity);
```

The EventHandlingScopeActivity activity schedules both its child activities — that is, the body activity and the EventHandlersActivity activity — for execution simultaneously. At this point, the EventHandlingScopeActivity activity suspends its execution and waits for the EventHandlersActivity activity or the body activity to fire its Closed event and consequently to invoke the OnEvent method of the EventHandlingScopeActivity activity.

As mentioned previously, the EventHandlersActivity activity contains one or more EventDrivenActivity activities running in parallel. Each EventDrivenActivity activity can contain one or more child activities, where the first child activity must be an activity that implements the IEventActivity interface, as discussed earlier. The OnWorkflowItemChanged activity is an IEventActivity activity because it inherits from the HandleExternalEventActivity activity, which implements the IEventActivity interface.

Next, we'll use an EventHandlingScopeActivity activity to enable our ConferenceRequestWorkflow workflow to respond to the events that the manager sends to the workflow instance.
The EventHandlersActivity branch of this EventHandlingScopeActivity will contain a single EventDrivenActivity activity whose first child activity is an OnWorkflowItemChanged activity.
The body activity or main branch of this EventHandlingScopeActivity activity will contain the rest of the ConferenceRequestWorkflow workflow, which we developed in the previous sections.

Follow these steps to convert the latest version of the ConferenceRequestWorkflow workflow shown in Figure 5-15 to the version that uses the EventHandlingScopeActivity activity. First, drag an EventHandlingScopeActivity activity from the toolbox and drop it onto the designer surface below the OnWorkflowActivated activity, as illustrated in Figure 5-19. Recall that the first activity of every SharePoint workflow must be an OnWorkflowActivated activity.

Because the EventHandlingScopeActivity activity can only contain a single activity as its body activity, you need to drag a composite activity such as a SequenceActivity activity from the toolbox and drop it onto the designer surface as the body activity, as Figure 5-20 demonstrates. Because we're using a composite activity as the body activity, we can include other activities inside this composite activity.

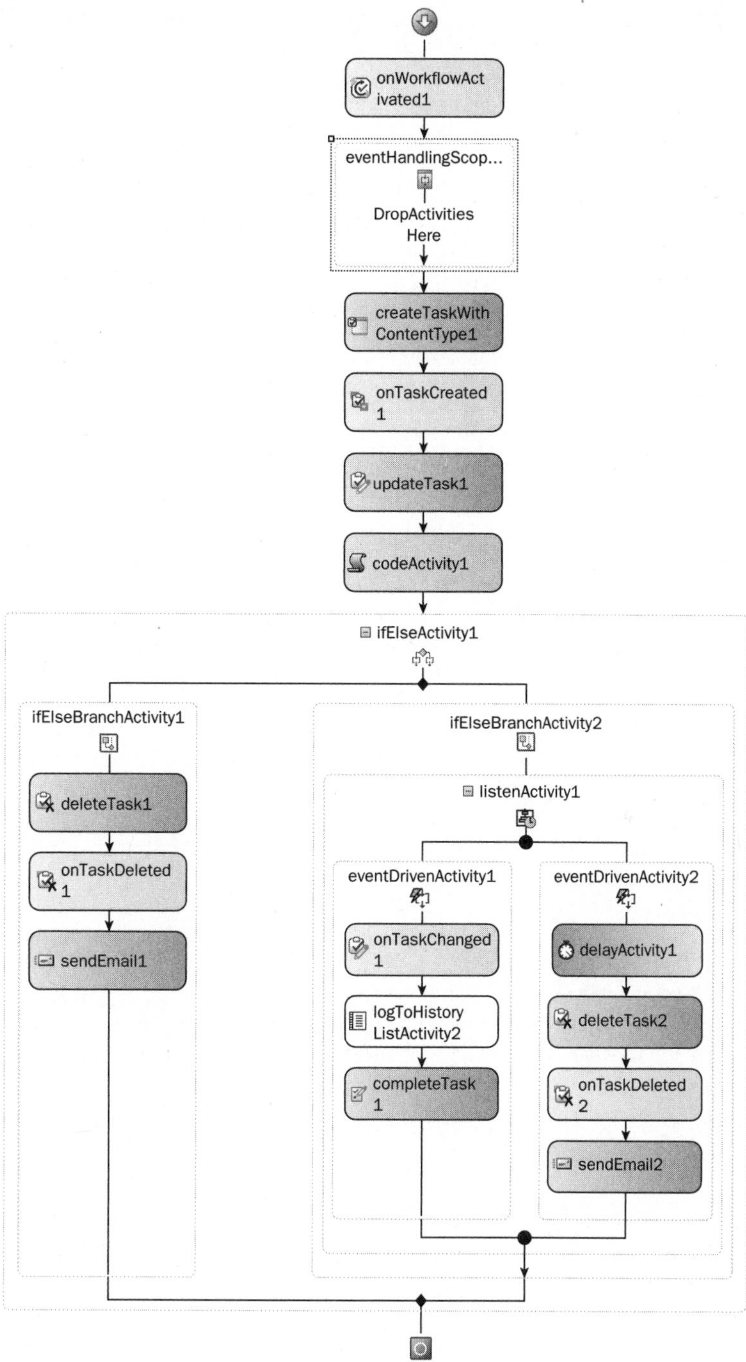
onWorkflowAct
ivated1
eventHandlingScop...
DropActivities
Here
createTaskWith
ContentType1
onTaskCreated
1
updateTask1
codeActivity1
ifElseActivity1
ifElseBranchActivity1
deleteTask1
onTaskDeleted
1
sendEmail1
ifElseBranchActivity2
listenActivity1
eventDrivenActivity1
onTaskChanged
1
logToHistory
ListActivity2
completeTask
1
eventDrivenActivity2
delayActivity1
deleteTask2
onTaskDeleted
2
sendEmail2

Figure 5-19

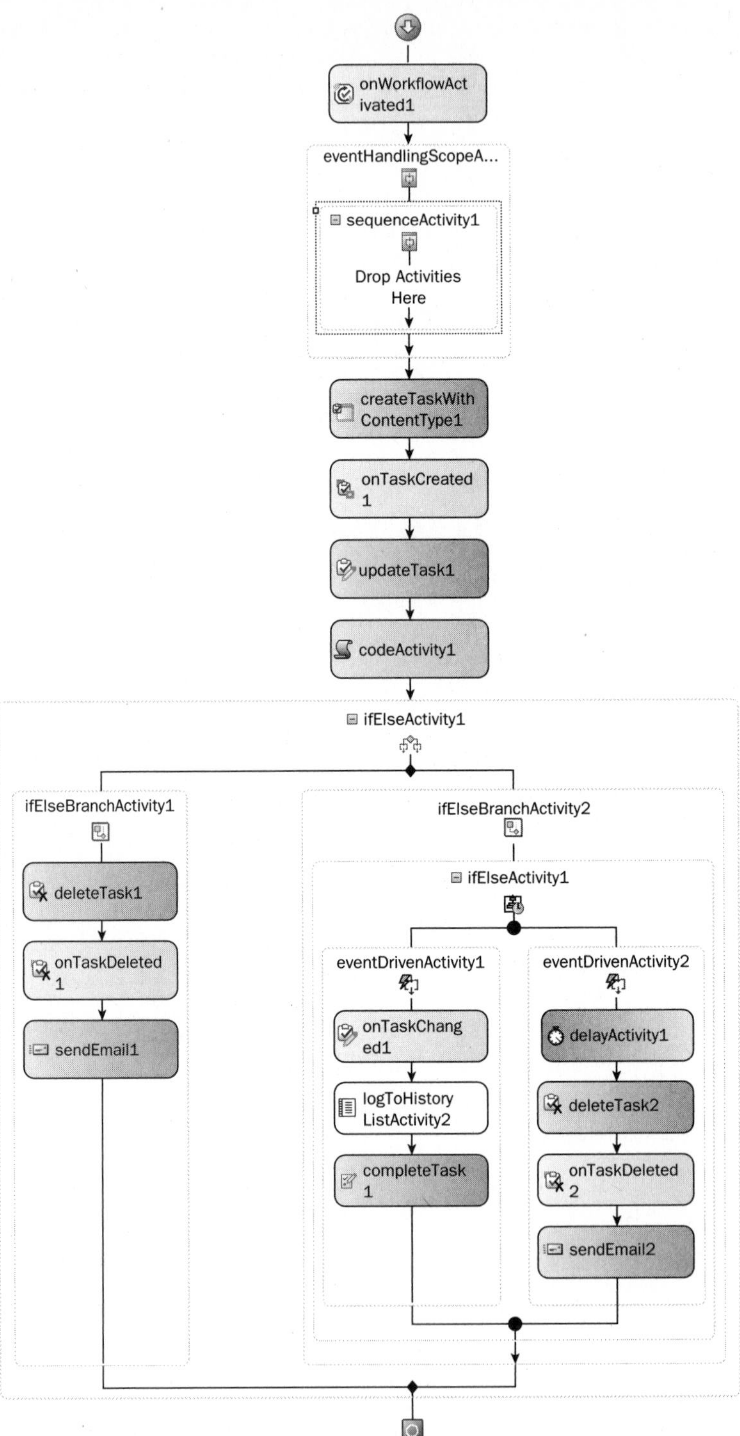

onWorkflowAct
ivated1
eventHandlingScopeA...
sequenceActivity1
Drop Activities
Here
createTaskWith
ContentType1
onTaskCreated
1
updateTask1
codeActivity1
ifElseActivity1
ifElseBranchActivity1
deleteTask1
onTaskDeleted
1
sendEmail1
ifElseBranchActivity2
ifElseActivity1
eventDrivenActivity1
onTaskChang
ed1
logToHistory
ListActivity2
completeTask
1
eventDrivenActivity2
delayActivity1
deleteTask2
onTaskDeleted
2
sendEmail2

Figure 5-20

Next, drag all the activities below the EventHandlingScopeActivity activity in Figure 5-20 and drop them inside the SequenceActivity activity, as Figure 5-21 illustrates. This means that these activities will be executed when the body activity (which is the SequenceActivity in this case) is executed.

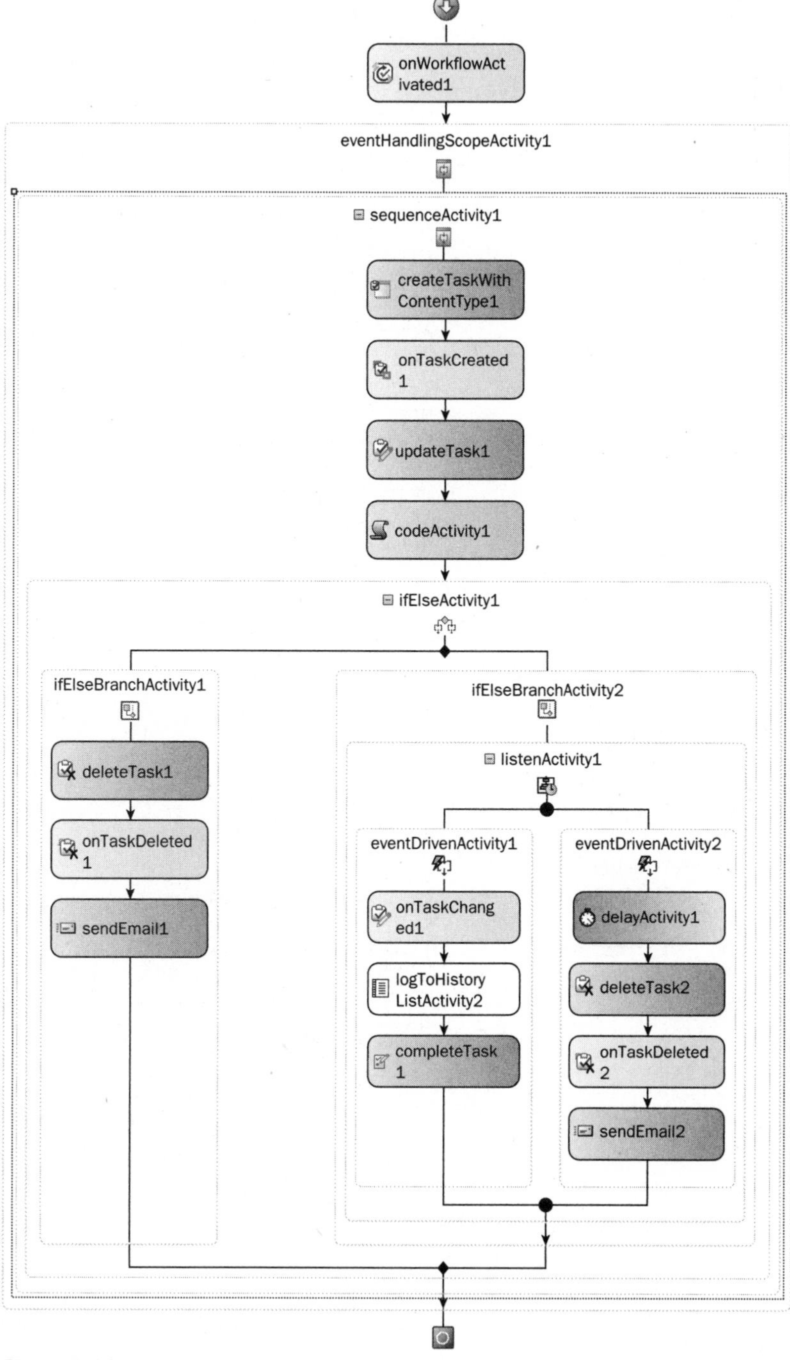

Figure 5-21

Now select the View Event Handlers menu option from the menu shown in Figure 5-22 to switch to the view that displays the EventHandlersActivity activity. Recall that the EventHandlingScopeActivity activity contains up to two child activities — that is, the body activity and the EventHandlersActivity activity.

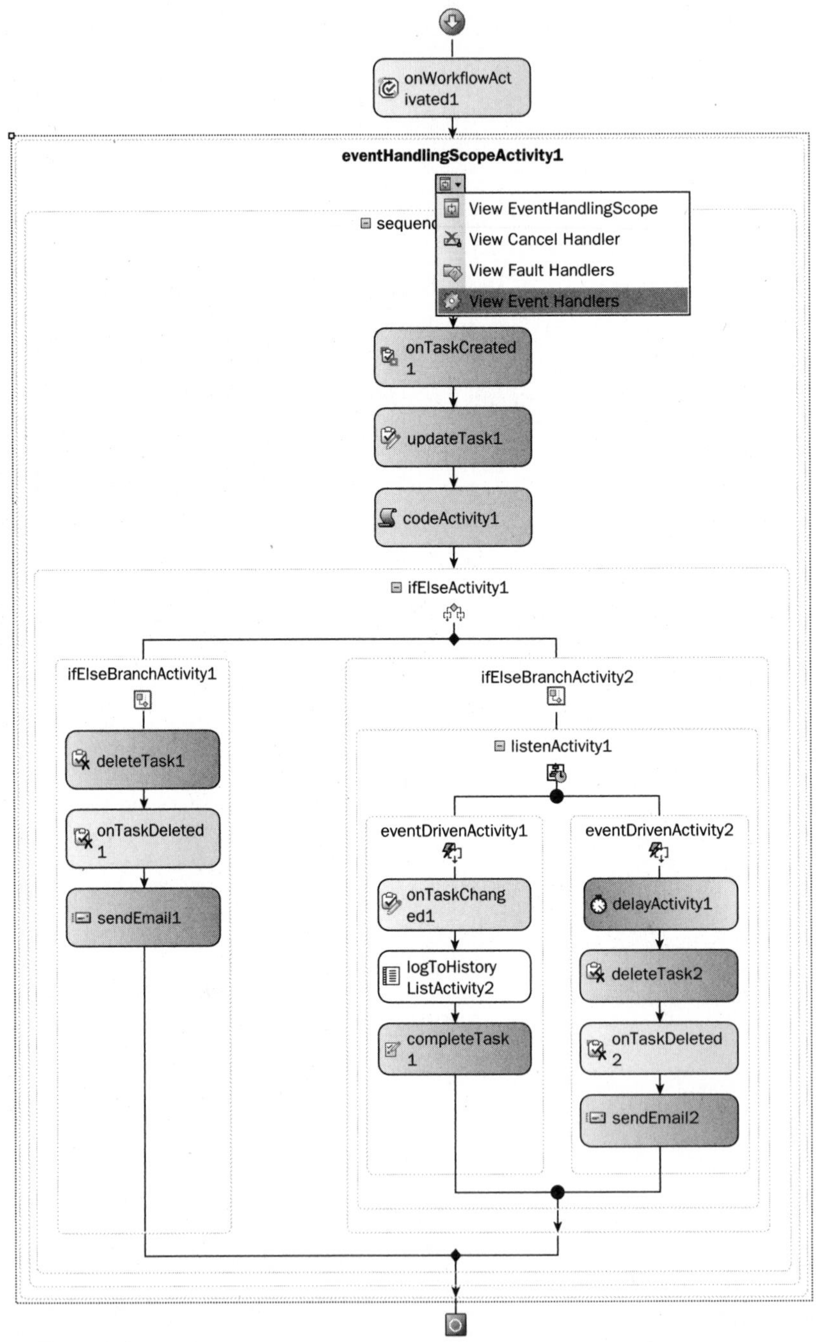

Figure 5-22

Figure 5-23 demonstrates the EventHandlersActivity activity of the EventHandlingScopeActivity activity. Note that the view shown in Figure 5-23 consists of two main parts. The top part, Drop EventDrivenActivity H, is where we will add the child EventDrivenActivity activities of the EventHandlersActivity activity. Recall that the EventHandlersActivity activity can contain zero or more EventDrivenActivity activities.

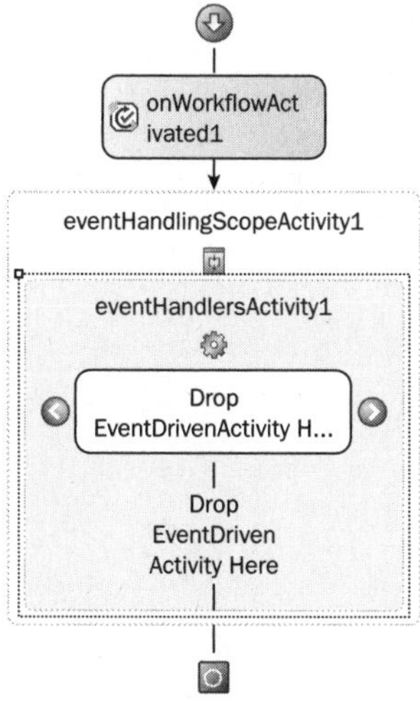

Figure 5-23

Drag an EventDrivenActivity activity from the toolbox and drop it inside the top part of the view, as shown in Figure 5-24.

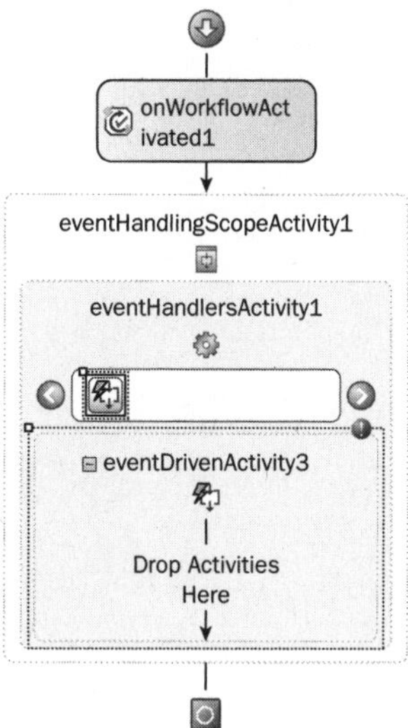

Figure 5-24

Now drag an OnWorkflowItemChanged activity from the toolbox and drop it inside the bottom part of the view, as Figure 5-25 demonstrates. This will automatically add this activity as the first child activity of the EventDrivenActivity activity.

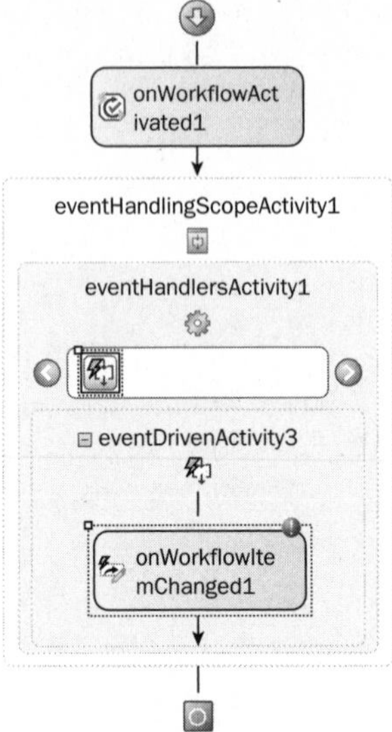

Figure 5-25

Figure 5-26 displays the properties of the OnWorkflowItemChanged activity in the Properties pane.

Properties

onWorkflowItemChanged1 Microsoft.SharePoint.WorkflowActions.OnWorkflowI

Activity	
(Name)	**onWorkflowItemChanged1**
CorrelationToken	
Description	
Enabled	True
EventName	**OnWorkflowItemChanged**
InterfaceType	**Microsoft.SharePoint.Workflow.ISharePointService**
Roles	
Handlers	
Invoked	
Misc	
AfterProperties	
BeforeProperties	

Generate Handlers, Promote Bindable Properties, Bind Selected Property...

(Name)
Please specify the identifier of the activity. It has to be unique in the workflow.

Figure 5-26

You need to use the same correlation token name that you used for the OnWorkflowActivated activity for the OnWorkflowItemChanged activity. Recall that this correlation token name is "workflowToken." Next, create two workflow fields named AfterProperties2 and BeforeProperties2 and bind them to the AfterProperties and BeforeProperties properties of the OnWorkflowItemChanged activity. When the OnWorkflowItemChanged activity finally completes its execution, the rest of the activities in the workflow can access the value of the AfterProperties property of the OnWorkflowItemChanged activity. This property references a Hashtable that contains the new values of the updated fields of the list item on which the workflow instance is running.

This means that the manager can update the specified fields of this list item and the workflow instance can access these field values through the AfterProperties property of the OnWorkflowItemChanged activity. In other words, you can think of this Hashtable as a way for the manager to send information to the running workflow to modify its execution logic.

To keep our discussion focused, we will simply log the content of this Hashtable into the workflow history list. Drag a LogToHistoryListActivity activity from the toolbox and drop it below the OnWorkflowItemChanged activity, as illustrated in Figure 5-27.

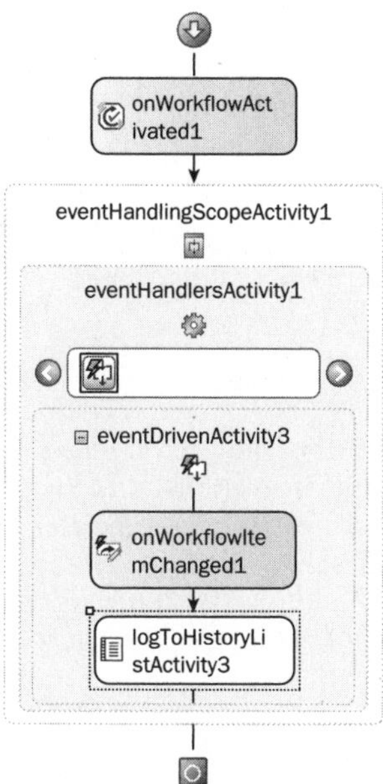

Figure 5-27

Next, bind the HistoryDescription, HistoryOutcome, and UserId workflow fields to the HistoryDescription, HistoryOutcome, and UserId properties of this LogToHistoryListActivity activity. Then, right-click the OnWorkflowItemChanged activity and select the Generate Handlers menu option to add an empty event handler for the Invoked event of this activity and implement the body of this event handler, as shown here:

```
private void onWorkflowItemChanged1_Invoked(object sender, ExternalDataEventArgs e)
{
  SPItemEventArgs args = e as SPItemEventArgs;
  Hashtable afterProperties = args.afterProperties;
  this.HistoryDescription = "New field values";
  this.HistoryOutcome = string.Empty;
  foreach (object key in afterProperties.Keys)
  {
    this.HistoryOutcome += key + ":";
    this.HistoryOutcome += afterProperties[key].ToString();
    this.HistoryOutcome += "#";
  }
}
```

This event handler first accesses the SPItemEventArgs object that contains the event data associated with the OnWorkflowItemChanged event of the underlying ISharePointService external data exchange service. This service instantiates and populates this SPItemEventArgs object when the manager updates the list item on which the current workflow instance is running.

As discussed in the previous chapter, this SPItemEventArgs object exposes a public field named afterProperties, which contains the names and values of the fields of the list item after the manager updates the list item. Our event handler simply iterates through these field names and values and adds them to the HistoryOutcome workflow field. Note that these field name/value pairs are separated by a pound (#) character so we can tell them apart in the entry that the LogToHistoryListActivity activity adds to the workflow history list.

You have two options when it comes to accessing the afterProperties public field of this SPItemEventArgs object. One option is what we have been doing in the previous sections — that is, creating a workflow field named AfterProperties2 and binding it to the afterProperties field. Another option is what we just did — that is, add an event handler for the Invoked event of the OnWorkflowItemChanged activity and directly access the afterProperties field through the SPItemEventArgs object passed into this event handler. The great thing about the former approach is that it enables activity binding whereby you can bind the appropriate properties of other workflow activities to the AfterProperties2 bindable property so they can automatically pick up the value of this property through activity binding.

Press F5 to run the workflow project and to navigate to the page that displays the list with which our ConferenceRequestWorkflow workflow is associated. Next, initiate an instance of our workflow on a list item in this list. Now if you navigate to the page that displays the task list, you should see the task that the CreateTaskWithContentType activity has created. At this point, the workflow instance is idle, waiting for the manager to the update the task before it can continue with its execution.

Return to the page that displays the list with which the workflow is associated and update the list item on which you initiated the workflow instance. If you navigate to the WrkStat.aspx page shown in Figure 5-28, you should see that the workflow history now contains a new entry. This is the entry that the LogToHistoryListActivity child activity of the EventDrivenActivity child activity of the EventHandlersActivity child activity of the EventHandlingScopeActivity activity adds to the workflow history list.

Note that this entry displays the names and values of the fields of the list item after the manager has updated the list item. Our workflow does not use these field values in its execution logic. It simply logs them into the history list. However, you can improve your workflow to have it use these values. Keep in mind that you can add any desired columns to the list item on which you initiate a workflow instance to enable the manager to pass any desired data to the running workflow by updating these columns with this data. In other words, the manager dumps the required data in the specified fields of the list item on which the current workflow instance is running and the workflow instance picks them up through the afterProperties field.

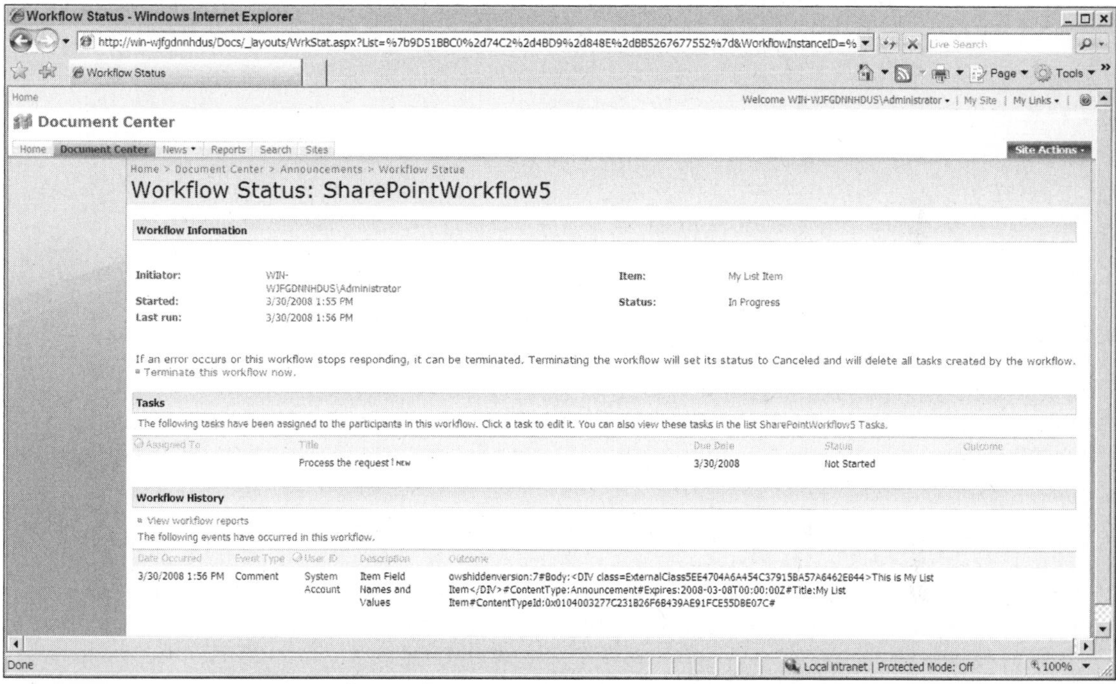

Figure 5-28

In the previous chapters we covered four different ways to pass data to a workflow: association forms, initiation forms, task edit forms, and modification forms. Now we're adding a fifth approach — that is, through updating the list item on which the workflow instance is running. This is a powerful technique that you can use in your own workflows.

If you repeat the same process — that is, if you update the list item on which the current workflow instance is running and navigate to the WrkStat.aspx page again — you should see a second entry in the history list, as shown in Figure 5-29. Thanks to the EventHandlingScopeActivity flow control construct, the same OnWorkflowItemChanged activity can respond to all the events that the manager sends to the workflow instance through updating this list item.

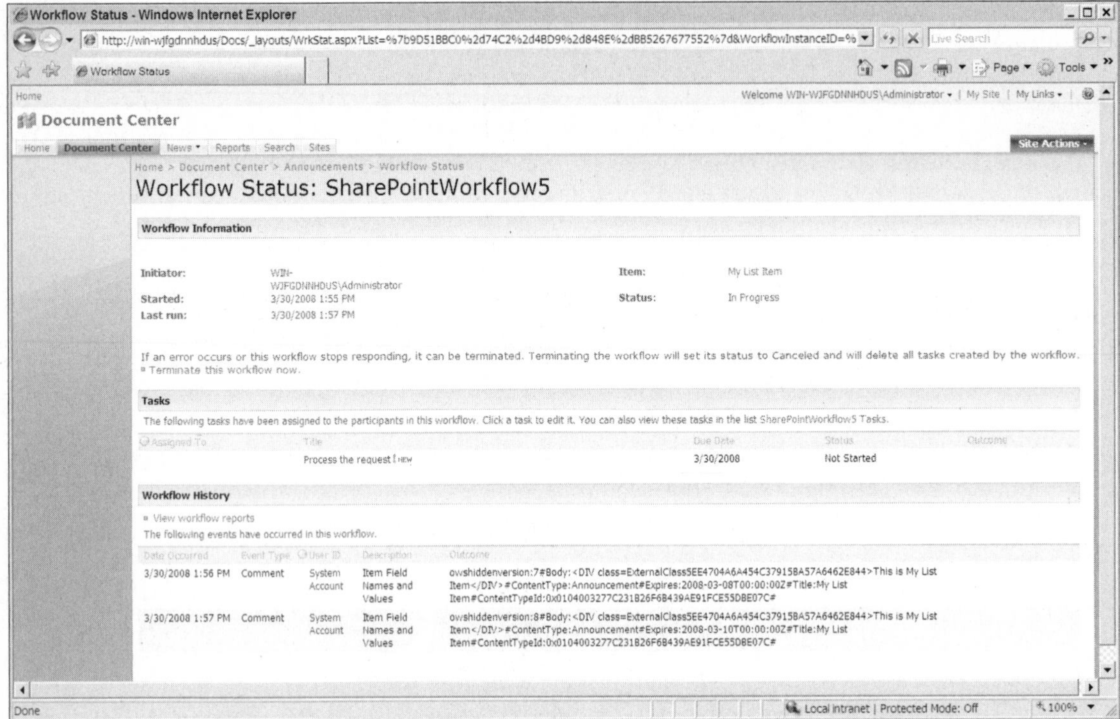

Figure 5-29

Navigate to the page that displays the task list and update the task. Note that the workflow completes its execution. As you can see, thanks to the EventHandlingScopeActivity flow control construct, the workflow completes its execution as soon as its main branch completes its execution.

Handling OnWorkflowItemDeleted Event

The OnWorkflowItemDeleted activity responds to the OnWorkflowItemDeleted event of the ISharePointService external data exchange service. This service raises this event when the SharePoint list item or document on which the current workflow instance is running is deleted. This SharePoint list item or document can be deleted through the SharePoint user interface, the SharePoint object model, workflow activities, or SharePoint web services.

The following code presents the internal implementation of the OnWorkflowItemDeleted activity:

```
public sealed class OnWorkflowItemDeleted : HandleExternalEventActivity
{
  public static DependencyProperty AfterPropertiesProperty;
  public static DependencyProperty BeforePropertiesProperty;
```

```
    public static DependencyProperty WorkflowIdProperty;

    public OnWorkflowItemDeleted()
    {
      this.InterfaceType = typeof(ISharePointService);
      this.EventName = "OnWorkflowItemDeleted";
    }

    protected override void OnInvoked(EventArgs e)
    {
      SPItemEventArgs args = (SPItemEventArgs)e;
      this.WorkflowId = args.workflowId;
      this.BeforeProperties = args.beforeProperties;
      this.AfterProperties = args.afterProperties;
    }

    public override string EventName
    {
      get { return "OnWorkflowItemDeleted"; }
    }

    public override Type InterfaceType
    {
      get { return typeof(ISharePointService); }
    }

    public Hashtable AfterProperties { get; set; }
    public Hashtable BeforeProperties { get; set; }
    public Guid WorkflowId
    {
      get
      {
        Guid workflowInstanceId = (Guid)base.GetValue(WorkflowIdProperty);
        if (Guid.Empty == workflowInstanceId)
          workflowInstanceId = WorkflowEnvironment.WorkflowInstanceId;
        return workflowInstanceId;
      }
      set { base.SetValue(WorkflowIdProperty, value); }
    }
  }
```

Next, we'll modify our ConferenceRequestWorkflow workflow to use the OnWorkflowItemDeleted activity. Drag another EventDrivenActivity activity from the toolbox and drop it inside the EventHandlersActivity activity, as shown in Figure 5-30.

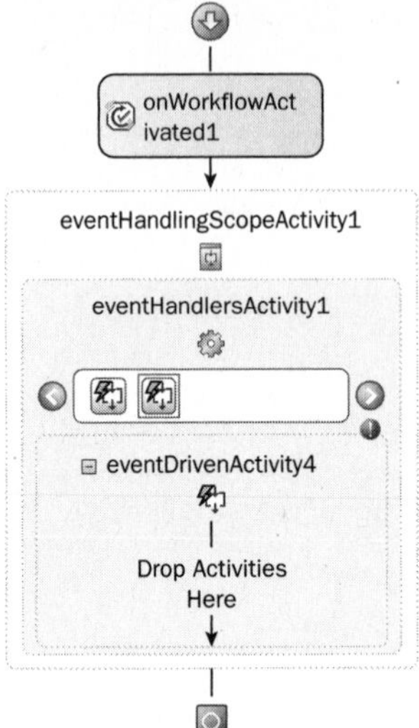

Figure 5-30

Drag an OnWorkflowItemDeleted activity from the toolbox and drop it inside this EventDrivenActivity activity as its first child activity, as Figure 5-31 demonstrates. The EventHandlersActivity activity now contains two branches that execute in parallel. The first branch contains the OnWorkflowItemChanged activity that responds when the manager updates the list item on which the current workflow instance is running. The second branch contains the OnWorkflowItemDeleted activity that responds when the manager deletes this list item.

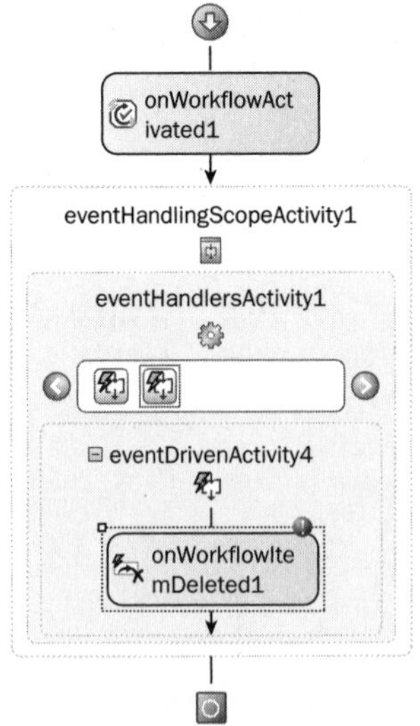

Figure 5-31

Figure 5-32 presents the properties of the OnWorkflowItemDeleted activity in the Properties pane.

Properties

onWorkflowItemDeleted1 Microsoft.SharePoint.WorkflowActions.OnWorkflowIt

Activity	
(Name)	**onWorkflowItemDeleted1**
CorrelationToken	
Description	
Enabled	True
EventName	**OnWorkflowItemDeleted**
InterfaceType	**Microsoft.SharePoint.Workflow.ISharePointService**
Roles	
Handlers	
Invoked	
Misc	
AfterProperties	
BeforeProperties	

Generate Handlers, Promote Bindable Properties, Bind Selected Property...

(Name)
Please specify the identifier of the activity. It has to be unique in the workflow.

Figure 5-32

You must use the same correlation token name that you used for the OnWorkflowActivated activity (that is, “workflowToken”) for the OnWorkflowItemDeletedActivity activity. Next, drag another LogToHistoryListActivity activity and drop it below the OnWorkflowItemDeleted activity, as shown in Figure 5-33.

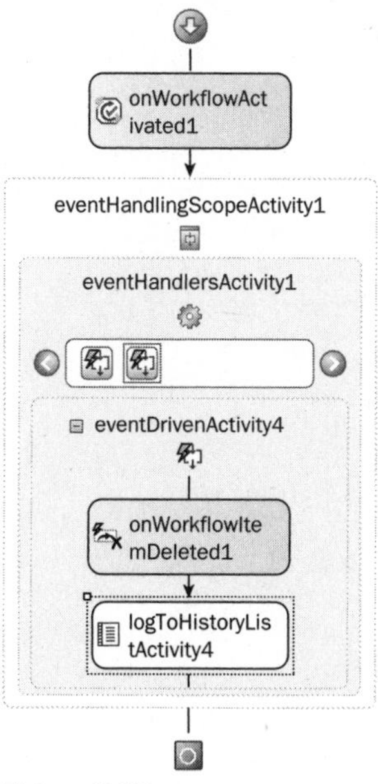

Figure 5-33

Right-click this LogToHistoryListActivity activity and select Generate Handlers to generate an event handler for the MethodInvoking event of this activity and implement the body of this event handler like so:

```
private void logToHistoryListActivity4_MethodInvoking(object sender, EventArgs e)
{
  this.HistoryDescription = "Information";
  this.HistoryOutcome = "The list item was deleted!";
  SPPrincipalInfo info =
      SPUtility.ResolvePrincipal(workflowProperties.Web, this.Executor,
                                 SPPrincipalType.All, SPPrincipalSource.All,
                                 null, false);
  this.UserId = (info == null ? -1 : info.PrincipalId);
}
```

This event handler uses the same logic discussed earlier to determine the user ID of the manager who deleted the task, because we want to log this information under this user ID as opposed to the user ID of the identity who initiated the current workflow instance. Recall that it is the employee who initiates a ConferenceRequestWorkflow workflow instance. You can access the user ID of the initiator or originator through SPWorkflowActivationProperties.OriginatorUser.ID.

Handling OnWorkflowModified Event

The OnWorkflowModified activity responds to the OnWorkflowModified event of the IWorkflowModificationService external data exchange service. This service raises this event when a workflow is modified. I discuss workflow modification in Chapter 7. Listing 5-4 presents the internal implementation of the OnWorkflowModified activity.

Listing 5-4: The OnWorkflowModified activity

```
public sealed class OnWorkflowModified : HandleExternalEventActivity
{
  public static DependencyProperty ContextDataProperty;
  public static DependencyProperty ModificationIdProperty;
  public static DependencyProperty UserProperty;

  public OnWorkflowModified()
  {
    this.InterfaceType = typeof(IWorkflowModificationService);
    this.EventName = "OnWorkflowModified";
  }

  protected override void OnInvoked(EventArgs e)
  {
    SPModificationEventArgs args = (SPModificationEventArgs)e;
    this.ModificationId = args.modificationId;
    this.User = args.user;
    this.ContextData = args.data;
  }

  public override string EventName
```

```
    {
      get { return "OnWorkflowModified"; }
    }

    public override Type InterfaceType
    {
      get { return typeof(IWorkflowModificationService); }
    }

    public string ContextData { get; set; }
    public Guid ModificationId { get; set; }
    public string User { get; set; }
  }
```

The OnWorkflowModified activity exposes the modificationId, user, and data public fields of the respective SPModificationEventArgs object as activity-level bindable properties named ModificationId, User, and ContextData. When the IWorkflowModificationService external data exchange service fires the OnWorkflowModified event, it instantiates and populates this SPModificationEventArgs object with the modification ID, which is the GUID that uniquely identifies the workflow modification, the user name of the user who modified the workflow, and the context data for the workflow modification. Later, in Chapter 7, you'll see an example in which the OnWorkflowModified activity is used.

Summary

This chapter provided in-depth coverage of those SharePoint activities that inherit from HandleExternalEventActivity. You also learned how to use these activities to implement custom SharePoint workflows. We used these activities to enhance the ConferenceRequestWorkflow workflow that we developed in the previous chapter. The following chapters dive into more advanced topics in SharePoint workflow programming.

6

Workflow Security and Management, and Fault Handling

This chapter covers the following three SharePoint workflow programming topics:

- SPWorkflowManager
- Workflow Security
- Fault Handling

SPWorkflowManager

SPWorkflowManager enables you to centrally manage workflow instances across a site collection. Note that SPWorkflowManager has no user interface equivalent. The SharePoint user interface enables users to manage only individual workflow instances running on SharePoint list items. The following code presents the public API of SPWorkflowManager:

```
public class SPWorkflowManager : IDisposable
{
  public static void CancelWorkflow(SPWorkflow workflow);
  public int CountWorkflowAssociations(SPWorkflowTemplate template, SPSite
site);
  public Dictionary<Guid, int> CountWorkflows(SPContentType ct);
  public Dictionary<Guid, int> CountWorkflows(SPList list);
  public int CountWorkflows(SPWorkflowAssociation association);
  public int CountWorkflows(SPWorkflowTemplate template, SPSite site);
  public void Dispose();
  public SPWorkflowCollection GetItemActiveWorkflows(SPListItem item);
  public SPWorkflowTaskCollection GetItemTasks(SPListItem item);
```

(continued)

(continued)

```
    public SPWorkflowTaskCollection GetItemTasks(SPListItem item,
                                                 SPWorkflowFilter filter);
    public SPWorkflowCollection GetItemWorkflows(SPListItem item);
    public SPWorkflowCollection GetItemWorkflows(SPListItem item,
                                                 SPWorkflowFilter filter);
    public SPWorkflowTaskCollection GetWorkflowTasks(SPListItem item,
                                                     SPWorkflow workflow);
    public SPWorkflowTaskCollection GetWorkflowTasks(SPListItem item,
                                                     Guid workflowInstanceId);
    public SPWorkflowTaskCollection GetWorkflowTasks(SPListItem item,
                                   SPWorkflow workflow, SPWorkflowFilter filter);
    public SPWorkflowTaskCollection GetWorkflowTasks(SPListItem item,
                                  Guid workflowInstanceId, SPWorkflowFilter filter);
    public SPWorkflowTemplateCollection GetWorkflowTemplatesByCategory(SPWeb web,
                                                              string strReqCategs);
    public void ModifyWorkflow(SPWorkflow workflow,
                          SPWorkflowModification modification, string contextData);
    public void RemoveWorkflowFromListItem(SPWorkflow workflow);
    public SPWorkflow StartWorkflow(SPListItem item,
                            SPWorkflowAssociation association, string eventData);
    public SPWorkflow StartWorkflow(SPListItem item,
              SPWorkflowAssociation association, string eventData, bool isAutoStart);

    public bool ShuttingDown { get; }
  }
```

SPWorkflowManager exposes a single read-only property of type Boolean named ShuttingDown that specifies whether the workflow manager is shutting down.

Here are the descriptions of the public methods of SPWorkflowManager:

- **CancelWorkflow:** This static method takes an SPWorkflow object as its argument and cancels the workflow instance that the object represents.
- **CountWorkflowAssociations:** This method takes an SPWorkflowTemplate and SPSite objects as its arguments and returns the number of workflow associations created from the workflow template represented by the SPWorkflowTemplate object within the site collection represented by the SPSite object.
- **CountWorkflows:** This method has four overloads, two of which are covered here. The first overload takes an SPWorkflowAssociation object and returns the number of running workflow instances created from the workflow association represented by the SPWorkflowAssociation object. The second overload takes an SPWorkflowTemplate and an SPSite object and returns the number of running workflow instances created from the workflow template represented by the SPWorkflowTemplate object within the SharePoint site collection represented by the SPSite object. Note that both overloads return the number of workflow instances with the SPWorkflowState.Running state. You can see this clearly from the SQL command used in the internal implementation of these two overloads as shown in the boldfaced portions of the following code:

```
public int CountWorkflows(SPWorkflowAssociation workflowAssociation)
{
  SPSqlCommand sqlCommand = new SPSqlCommand();
  sqlCommand.SetStoredProcedure("proc_CountWorkflows");
  sqlCommand.Parameters.AddWithValue("@InternalState", SPWorkflowState.Running);
  sqlCommand.Parameters.AddWithValue("@AssociationId", workflowAssociation.Id);
  sqlCommand.Parameters.AddWithValue("@SiteId", DBNull.Value);
  sqlCommand.Parameters.AddWithValue("@BaseId", DBNull.Value);
  using (SqlDataReader dataReader =
           association.ParentSite.SqlSession.ExecuteReader((SqlCommand)sqlCommand))
  {
    if (!dataReader.Read())
      return 0;

    return reader.GetInt32(0);
  }
}

public int CountWorkflows(SPWorkflowTemplate workflowTemplate,
                           SPSite siteCollection)
{
  SPSqlCommand sqlCommand = new SPSqlCommand();
  sqlCommand.SetStoredProcedure("proc_CountWorkflows");
  sqlCommand.Parameters.AddWithValue("@InternalState", SPWorkflowState.Running);
  sqlCommand.Parameters.AddWithValue("@AssociationId", DBNull.Value);
  sqlCommand.Parameters.AddWithValue("@SiteId", siteCollection.ID);
  sqlCommand.Parameters.AddWithValue("@BaseId", workflowTemplate.Id);
  using (SqlDataReader dataReader =
                siteCollection.SqlSession.ExecuteReader((SqlCommand)sqlCommand))
  {
    if (!dataReader.Read())
      return 0;

    return reader.GetInt32(0);
  }
}
```

- **Dispose:** As a best practice, you should instantiate the SPWorkflowManager within the context of a using statement to ensure that its Dispose method is automatically invoked when the SPWorkflowManager instance goes out of scope.
- **GetItemActiveWorkflows:** This method takes an SPListItem object and returns an SPWorkflowCollection collection that contains SPWorkflow objects representing workflow instances currently running on the SharePoint list item or document represented by the SPListItem object. The following code shows the internal implementation of this method:

```
public SPWorkflowCollection GetItemActiveWorkflows(SPListItem listItem)
{
  return new SPWorkflowCollection(listItem, SPWorkflowState.Running,
                                  SPWorkflowState.None);
}
```

Note that this method internally instantiates an SPWorkflowCollection, passing in SPWorkflowState.Running and SPWorkflowState.None as the second and third arguments. The second and third arguments of the SPWorkflowCollection constructor are known as *inclusive filter states* and *exclusive filter states,* respectively. As the names of these arguments imply, they respectively specify the workflow states that should be included in and excluded from the collection. In this case, we want to include workflow instances with SPWorkflowState. Running. This shows an example of how to use SPWorkflowCollection.

- **GetItemTasks:** This method comes with two overloads. The first overload takes an SPListItem object and returns an SPWorkflowTaskCollection collection that contains the SPWorkflowTask objects representing workflow tasks for the SharePoint list item or document represented by the SPListItem object. The second overload takes an SPListItem and an SPWorkflowFilter object and returns an SPWorkflowTaskCollection collection containing the SPWorkflowTask objects that represent workflow tasks for the SharePoint list item or document represented by the SPListItem object that meet the filter criteria specified by the SPWorkflowFilter object. Recall that you can use SPWorkflowFilter to filter workflow tasks based on to whom the task is assigned and the state of the associated workflow instance.
- **GetItemWorkflows:** This method comes with two overloads. The first overload takes an SPListItem object and returns an SPWorkflowCollection collection that contains the SPWorkflow objects that represent workflow instances that have ever run on the SharePoint list item or document represented by the SPListItem object. The second overload takes an SPListItem object and an SPWorkflowFilter object and returns an SPWorkflowCollection collection that contains the SPWorkflow objects that represent all workflow instances that have ever run on the SharePoint list item or document represented by the SPListItem object and that meet the filter criteria specified by the SPWorkflowFilter object.
- **GetWorkflowTasks:** This method comes with four overloads. The first overload takes an SPListItem object and a GUID and returns an SPWorkflowTaskCollection collection that contains the SPWorkflowTask objects that represent workflow tasks for the workflow instance with the instance ID specified by the GUID running on the SharePoint list item or document represented by the SPListItem object. The second overload takes an SPListItem object and an SPWorkflow object and returns an SPWorkflowTaskCollection collection that contains the SPWorkflowTask objects that represent workflow tasks for the workflow instance represented by the SPWorkflow object running on the SharePoint list item or document represented by the SPListItem object. The third overload takes an SPListItem object, a GUID, and an SPWorkflowFilter and returns an SPWorkflowTaskCollection collection that contains the SPWorkflowTask objects representing workflow tasks for the workflow instance with the instance ID specified by the GUID running on the SharePoint list item or document represented by the SPListItem object and that meets the filter criteria specified in the SPWorkflowFilter object. The fourth overload takes an SPListItem object, an SPWorkflow object, and an SPWorkflowFilter object and returns an SPWorkflowTaskCollection collection that contains the SPWorkflowTask objects that represent workflow tasks for the workflow instance represented by the SPWorkflow object running on the SharePoint list item or document represented by the SPListItem object and that meets the filter criteria specified in the SPWorkflowFilter object.
- **GetWorkflowTemplatesByCategory:** This method takes an SPWeb object and a string as its arguments and returns an SPWorkflowTemplateCollection collection that contains SPWorkflowTemplate objects that represent workflow templates belonging to the category specified in the string argument within the SharePoint site represented by the SPWeb object.

- **ModifyWorkflow:** This method modifies the specified workflow instance. It takes three arguments. The first argument is an SPWorkflow object that represents the workflow instance to modify. The second argument is an SPWorkflowModification object that represents the workflow modification. The third argument is a string that contains the context data for the workflow modification.
- **RemoveWorkflowFromListItem:** This method takes an SPWorkflow object as its argument and removes the workflow instance represented by the SPWorkflow object from the SharePoint list item or document on which it was created.
- **StartWorkflow:** This method comes with two overloads. The first overload takes an SPListItem object, an SPWorkflowAssociation object, a string, and a Boolean as its arguments and creates a workflow instance on the SharePoint list item or document represented by the SPListItem object from the workflow association represented by the SPWorkflowAssociation object. The method starts the workflow instance if the Boolean parameter is true. The method returns an SPWorkflow object that represents the workflow instance. The second overload takes an SPListItem object, an SPWorkflowAssociation object, and a string as its arguments and creates a workflow instance on the SharePoint list item or document represented by the SPListItem object from the workflow association represented by the SPWorkflowAssociation object. This overload automatically starts the workflow instance.

The SPSite class exposes a public property of type SPWorkflowManager named WorkflowManager that you can use in your managed code.

Workflow Security

External data exchange services send messages to a workflow instance through the HandleExternalEventActivity activities that the workflow instance contains. As such, the HandleExternalEventActivity activities that a workflow instance contains are the gateways through which the external world sends messages to the workflow instance. Therefore, you can control access to a workflow instance by controlling which messages are allowed to pass through these gateways. HandleExternalEventActivity encapsulates the logic that determines whether a message from a specified identity is allowed to pass through. This logic uses a bindable property of the HandleExternalEventActivity activity named Roles, which is of the WorkflowRoleCollection type. Listing 6-1 presents the definition of the Roles bindable property.

Listing 6-1: Definition of the the Roles bindable property of HandleExternalEventActivity

```
public static readonly DependencyProperty RolesProperty =
              DependencyProperty.Register("Roles", typeof(WorkflowRoleCollection),
                                          typeof(HandleExternalEventActivity));
public WorkflowRoleCollection Roles
{
  get { return (base.GetValue(RolesProperty) as WorkflowRoleCollection); }
  set { base.SetValue(RolesProperty, value); }
}
```

Listing 6-2 presents the internal implementation of the WorkflowRoleCollection class.

Listing 6-2: Internal implementation of the WorkflowRoleCollection class

```
public sealed class WorkflowRoleCollection : List<WorkflowRole>
{
  public bool IncludesIdentity(string identity)
  {
    if (identity != null)
    {
      foreach (WorkflowRole workflowRole in base)
      {
        if ((workflowRole != null) && workflowRole.IncludesIdentity(identity))
          return true;
      }
    }
    return false;
  }
}
```

As you can see, WorkflowRoleCollection is a collection of WorkflowRole objects. Listing 6-3 contains the definition of the WorkflowRole class.

Listing 6-3: The WorkflowRole class

```
public abstract class WorkflowRole
{
  public abstract IList<string> GetIdentities();
  public abstract bool IncludesIdentity(string identity);

  public abstract string Name { get; set; }
}
```

As the name suggests, a WorkflowRole object represents a workflow role. WF supports role-based security. WorkflowRole is an abstract class that exposes a single read-write string property called Name, which contains the workflow role that the WorkflowRole object represents. WorkflowRole also features an abstract method named GetIdentities that takes no argument and returns an IList collection of string values. Subclasses of WorkflowRole must implement this method to return an IList collection of identities (or user names), which are in the role specified in the Name property. WorkflowRole also features another abstract method named IncludesIdentity that takes a string value and returns a Boolean value. Subclasses of WorkflowRole must implement this method to return a Boolean that indicates whether the specified identity is in the role specified in the Name property.

As shown in Listing 6-2, WorkflowRoleCollection exposes a method named IncludesIdentity that takes an identity as its argument and returns a Boolean. The Execute method of a HandleExternalEventHandler activity invokes the IncludesIdentity method on its Roles collection property (keep in mind that this property is of the WorkflowRoleCollection type), passing in the current user identity, to determine whether the current user is authorized to send messages to the current workflow instance through this HandleExternalEventHandler activity.

The IncludesIdentity method of WorkflowRoleCollection keeps iterating through the WorkflowRole objects in the WorkflowRoleCollection, invoking the IncludesIdentity method of each enumerated

WorkflowRole object until it reaches a WorkflowRole object whose IncludesIdentity method returns true, at which point the method returns true. This signals the HandleExternalEventActivity activity, which invoked the IncludesIdentity method of WorkflowRoleCollection (keep in mind that this HandleExternalEventActivity activity owns this WorkflowRoleCollection), that the specified identity is authorized to send messages to the current workflow instance through the HandleExternalEventActivity activity. If the IncludesIdentity method of none of the WorkflowRole objects in the WorkflowRoleCollection returns true, then the IncludesIdentity method of WorkflowRoleCollection returns false to signal to the HandleExternalEventActivity activity that the specified identity is not authorized to send messages to the current workflow instance through the HandleExternalEventActivity activity.

SharePoint ships with an implementation of the WorkflowRole abstract base class named SPWorkflowRoleProvider. Because the SPWorkflowRoleProvider is an internal class, you cannot directly instantiate an instance of it. SharePoint comes with a public static class named SPWorkflowWorkflowRoleCreator that you can use to create an instance of this internal class, as shown in Listing 6-4.

Listing 6-4: The SPWorkflowWorkflowRoleCreator class

```
public static class SPWorkflowWorkflowRoleCreator
{
  public static WorkflowRole GetWorkflowRoleForGroups(SPWeb site, string Name)
  {
    return new SPWorkflowRoleProvider(site, Name,
                                      SPWorkflowRoleProviderType.Group);
  }

  public static WorkflowRole GetWorkflowRoleForPermission(SPList list,
                                                     SPBasePermissions basePermissions)
  {
    return new SPWorkflowRoleProvider(list, basePermissions,
                                      SPWorkflowRoleProviderType.BasePermission);
  }

  public static WorkflowRole GetWorkflowRoleForPermission(SPListItem listItem,
                                                     SPBasePermissions basePermissions)
  {
    return new SPWorkflowRoleProvider(listItem, basePermissions,
                                      SPWorkflowRoleProviderType.BasePermission);
  }

  public static WorkflowRole GetWorkflowRoleForPermission(SPWeb site,
                                                     SPBasePermissions basePermissions)
  {
    return new SPWorkflowRoleProvider(site, basePermissions,
                                      SPWorkflowRoleProviderType.BasePermission);
  }
}
```

As you can see, the SPWorkflowWorkflowRoleCreator static class includes four static methods:

- **GetWorkflowRoleForGroups:** Use this method to create a WorkflowRole object and then add this WorkflowRole object to the Roles collection of a HandleExternalEventActivity activity in a workflow to instruct this HandleExternalEventActivity activity to allow messages from those identities that are members of the specified SharePoint group in the specified site collection to pass through. This method takes a string that contains the group name as its second argument. It also takes an SPWeb object whose SiteGroups collection contains the SPGroup whose name is specified in the second argument.
- **GetWorkflowRoleForPermission (First Overload):** Use this overload of the GetWorkflowRoleForPermission method to create a WorkflowRole object and add this WorkflowRole object to the Roles collection of a HandleExternalEventActivity activity in a workflow to instruct this HandleExternalEventActivity activity to allow messages from those identities that have the specified base permissions on the specified SharePoint list to pass through. The first argument of this overload references the SPList object that represents the SharePoint list. The second argument of this overload is an SPBasePermissions enumeration value that represents the base permissions.
- **GetWorkflowRoleForPermission (Second Overload):** Use this overload of the GetWorkflowRoleForPermission method to create a WorkflowRole object and add this WorkflowRole object to the Roles collection of a HandleExternalEventActivity activity in a workflow to instruct this HandleExternalEventActivity activity to allow messages from those identities that have the specified base permissions on the specified SharePoint list item to pass through. The first argument of this overload references the SPListItem object that represents the SharePoint list item. The second argument of this overload is an SPBasePermissions enumeration value that represents the base permissions.
- **GetWorkflowRoleForPermission (Third Overload):** Use this overload of the GetWorkflowRoleForPermission method to create a WorkflowRole object and add this WorkflowRole object to the Roles collection of a HandleExternalEventActivity activity in a workflow to instruct this HandleExternalEventActivity activity to allow messages from those identities that have the specified base permissions on the specified SharePoint site to pass through. The first argument of this overload references the SPWeb object that represents the SharePoint site. The second argument of this overload is an SPBasePermissions enumeration value.

The SPBasePermissions enumeration type specifies the available SharePoint built-in permissions. The possible values of this enumeration type are as follows:

- **AddListItems:** This enumeration value specifies the permission to add items to lists and to add web discussion comments. The list here includes both regular SharePoint lists and SharePoint document libraries.
- **ApplyStyleSheets:** This enumeration value specifies the permission to apply style sheets (.css file) to the web site.
- **ApplyThemeAndBorder:** As the name suggests, this enumeration value specifies the permission to apply themes and borders to the entire web site.

- **ApproveItems:** This enumeration value specifies the permission to approve minor versions of list items. The list here includes both regular SharePoint lists and SharePoint document libraries. As such, the list item could be a regular SharePoint list item or a document.
- **AddAndCustomizePages:** As the name suggests, this enumeration value specifies the permission to add and customize (change and delete) pages (HTML and Web Part) through a SharePoint-compatible editor. It also specifies the permission to edit the web site using a SharePoint-compatible editor.
- **AddDelPrivateWebParts:** This enumeration value specifies the permission to add or delete private (personal) Web Parts on a Web Part Page.
- **EditListItems:** This enumeration value specifies the permission to edit list items and web discussion comments in documents, and customize Web Part Pages in document libraries. The list item could be a regular list item or a document.
- **EditMyUserInfo:** This enumeration value specifies that the user has the permission to edit his or her user information.
- **EmptyMask:** This enumeration value specifies that the user has no permissions on the web site.
- **ViewListItems:** This enumeration value specifies the permission to view list items and web discussion comments. The list item could be a regular list item or a document.
- **ViewPages:** This enumeration value specifies the permission to view pages in a web site.
- **ViewUsageData:** This enumeration value specifies the permission to view web site usage reports.
- **ViewVersions:** This enumeration value specifies the permission to view past versions of a list item. The list item could be a regular list item or a document.
- **EnumeratePermissions:** This enumeration value specifies the permission to enumerate permissions on the web site, list, folder, document, or list item.
- **FullMask:** This enumeration value specifies that the user has all permissions on the web site.
- **ManageAlerts:** This enumeration value specifies the permission to manage alerts for all users of the web site.
- **ManagePersonalViews:** This enumeration value specifies the permission to manage personal views, including creating, updating, and deleting personal views of lists.
- **ManageSubwebs:** This enumeration value specifies the permission to manage subsites, including creating subsites.
- **BrowseDirectories:** This enumeration value specifies the permission to browse directories in a web site using Microsoft Office SharePoint Designer 2007 and WebDAV interfaces.
- **BrowseUserInfo:** This enumeration value specifies the permission to browse information about users of the web site.
- **CancelCheckout:** This enumeration value specifies the permission to cancel a checkout by another user.
- **CreateAlerts:** This enumeration value specifies the permission to create e-mail alerts.
- **CreateGroups:** This enumeration value specifies the permission to create a group that can be used anywhere within the site collection.

- **CreateSSCSite:** This enumeration value specifies the permission to use Self-Service Site Creation (SSC) to create a web site.
- **DeleteListItems:** This enumeration value specifies the permission to delete list items from a list and web discussion comments in documents. The list could be a regular SharePoint list or a document library. As such, the list item could be a regular list item or a document.
- **DeleteVersions:** This enumeration value specifies the permission to delete past versions of a list item. The list item could be a regular list item or a document.
- **ManageWeb:** This enumeration value specifies the permission to perform all administrative tasks for the web site as well as manage content, and activate, deactivate, or edit properties of web-site-scoped Features through the object model or the user interface.
- **Open:** This enumeration value specifies the permission to open a web site, list, or folder.
- **OpenItems:** This enumeration value specifies the permission to view the source of documents with server-side file handlers.
- **UpdatePersonalWebParts:** This enumeration value specifies the permission to update Web Parts.
- **UseClientIntegration:** This enumeration value specifies the permission to use features that launch client applications.
- **UseRemoteAPIs:** This enumeration value specifies the permission to use remote APIs such as SOAP, WebDAV, or Microsoft Office SharePoint Designer 2007 to access the web site.
- **ViewFormPages:** This enumeration value specifies the permission to view forms, views, and application pages, and enumerate lists.
- **ManageLists:** This enumeration value specifies the permission to manage lists, including creating and adding lists, adding or removing columns in a list, and adding or removing public views of a list.
- **ManagePermissions:** This enumeration value specifies the permission to manage permissions, including creating and updating permission levels on the web site and assigning permissions to users and groups.

Note that the WorkflowRole objects that the GetWorkflowRoleForPermission overloads return represent base permissions on a specified securable object. The WorkflowRole object that the following overload returns represents base permissions on the specified SPList object. This SPList object is the securable object in this case.

```
public static WorkflowRole GetWorkflowRoleForPermission(SPList list,
                                               SPBasePermissions basePermissions)
```

The WorkflowRole object that the following overload returns, conversely, represents base permissions on a specified SPListItem object. This SPListItem object is the securable object in this case.

```
public static WorkflowRole GetWorkflowRoleForPermission(SPListItem listItem,
                                               SPBasePermissions basePermissions)
```

The WorkflowRole object that the last overload returns represents base permissions on a specified SPWeb object. This means that this SPWeb object is the securable object in this case.

```
public static WorkflowRole GetWorkflowRoleForPermission(SPWeb site,
                                                SPBasePermissions basePermissions)
{
  return new SPWorkflowRoleProvider(site, basePermissions,
                                      SPWorkflowRoleProviderType.BasePermission);
}
```

As shown here, SharePoint ships with three types of securable objects: SPWeb, SPList, and SPListItem. These three classes implement a SharePoint standard interface named ISecurableObject, as defined in Listing 6-5.

Listing 6-5: The ISecurableObject interface

```
public interface ISecurableObject
{
  void BreakRoleInheritance(bool CopyRoleAssignments);
  void CheckPermissions(SPBasePermissions permissionMask);
  bool DoesUserHavePermissions(SPBasePermissions permissionMask);
  void ResetRoleInheritance();

  SPRoleDefinitionBindingCollection AllRolesForCurrentUser { get; }
  SPBasePermissions EffectiveBasePermissions { get; }
  ISecurableObject FirstUniqueAncestor { get; }
  bool HasUniqueRoleAssignments { get; }
  SPReusableAcl ReusableAcl { get; }
  SPRoleAssignmentCollection RoleAssignments { get; }
}
```

A SharePoint site, list, or list item is called a securable object because it has what is known as an *access control list (ACL)*. An ACL is a data structure that contains access control entries (ACEs). Each ACE specifies base permissions for a specific user or group. In other words, a securable object carries with it an ACL that knows which users or groups have which base permissions on the securable object.
A securable object, by default, inherits its parent's ACL. For example, when you create a new SharePoint list, by default it inherits its parent site's ACL. As Listing 6-5 shows, a securable object supports a method named BreakRoleInheritance that enables you to break this role inheritance and create a new ACL for the securable object.

A securable object exposes two methods named CheckPermissions and DoesUserHavePermissions that you can use to check whether the current user has the specified base permissions on the securable object. These methods basically check whether the ACL on the securable object contains an entry (ACE) for the current user for the specified base permissions. The only difference between CheckPermissions and DoesUserHavePermissions is that the former raises an exception if the ACL does not contain an entry for the current user for the specified base permissions, whereas the latter only returns false.

When the Execute method of a HandleExternalEventActivity activity invokes the IncludesIdentity method on its Roles collection property, passing in the current user identity, the IncludesIdentity method iterates through the WorkflowRole objects in the Roles collection and invokes each WorkflowRole object's IncludesIdentity method, passing in the current user identity. Recall that each WorkflowRole object represents specified base permissions on a specified securable object such as a site, list, or list item. The IncludesIdentity method of a WorkflowRole object internally uses the ISecurableObject API of this securable object (shown in Listing 6-5) to check whether the ACL of this securable object contains an entry (ACE) for the current user identity for the specified base permissions. SharePoint workflow security secures access to a workflow instance based on the ACLs on securable objects.

So far I've only covered three static methods of the SPWorkflowWorkflowRoleCreator class shown in Listing 6-4, which are the overloads of the same GetWorkflowRoleForPermissions method. As discussed, these three overloads instantiate and return WorkflowRole objects that represent base permissions on a specified SharePoint site, list, or list item. Next, I'll discuss the fourth static method of the SPWorkflowWorkflowRoleCreator class.

Specifying permissions on individual users can cause the ACLs on securable objects to grow exponentially in large SharePoint farms with many users. To tackle this problem, you should create groups and assign permissions to groups, as opposed to users. The ACLs contain entries for specified groups for specified base permissions, as opposed to specified users for specified base permissions. Note that a SharePoint group is not a role. You can think of a SharePoint group as a bigger user. You can clearly see this in the fact that the SPUser, whose instances represent users, and SPGroup, whose instances represent groups, both inherit from the SPPrincipal base class. In other words, a group, just like a user, is a principal, and not a role.

As shown in Listing 6-4, the SPWorkflowWorkflowRoleCreator class includes a static method named GetWorkflowRoleForGroups that takes a group name that returns a WorkflowRole representing base permissions for the group:

```
public static WorkflowRole GetWorkflowRoleForGroups(SPWeb web, string Name)
```

As discussed earlier, the Execute method of a HandleExternalEventActivity activity invokes the IncludesIdentity method on the WorkflowRoleCollection object that its Roles property references, passing in the current user identity. This method, in turn, invokes the IncludesIdentity methods of the WorkflowRole objects in the collection, passing in the current user identity. The IncludesIdentity method of a WorkflowRole object internally uses the ISecurableObject interface shown in Listing 6-5 to check whether the ACL of the securable object contains an entry for the current user identity for the specified base permissions. The question is: Who is the current user in SharePoint? Whose identity does a HandleExternalEventActivity activity pass into the IncludesIdentity method of the WorkflowRoleCollection object?

The current user in SharePoint is the user who created the reference to the SPSite object that represents the current site collection. The constructor of the SPSite class internally uses the security principal that is creating the reference to create a SharePoint security context. This security principal is the Windows or Forms authentication principal if the code is running in the context of a SharePoint site. This security principal is the Windows principal if the code is running in a console application running on the web server.

Because we're running SharePoint workflows in the context of a SharePoint site, the security principal is the Windows principal if SharePoint is configured to use Windows Integrated Authentication, and is the Forms authentication principal if SharePoint is configured to use Forms authentication.

Next, we'll implement a workflow that demonstrates workflow security in action. As Figure 6-1 shows, our workflow consists of the following activities:

- An OnWorkflowActivated activity, which is always the first activity in every workflow, as discussed earlier
- A CreateTask activity, which creates a SharePoint task
- A LogToHistoryListActivity, which logs a history event to the workflow history list, signaling that a new SharePoint task has been created
- An OnTaskChanged activity, which suspends its execution and consequently suspends the execution of the workflow and waits for the SharePoint task service to fire the OnTaskChanged event. The SharePoint task service fires this event when the associated SharePoint task is updated.
- A LogToHistoryListActivity, which logs a history event to the workflow history list, signaling that the SharePoint task has been updated

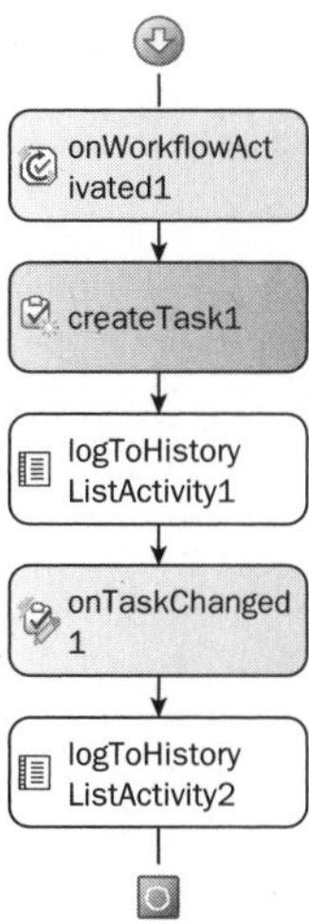

Figure 6-1

Listing 6-6 presents the implementation of this workflow.

Listing 6-6: Workflow demonstrating workflow security features

```
using System;
using System.ComponentModel;
using System.ComponentModel.Design;
using System.Collections;
using System.Drawing;
using System.Linq;
using System.Workflow.ComponentModel.Compiler;
using System.Workflow.ComponentModel.Serialization;
using System.Workflow.ComponentModel;
using System.Workflow.ComponentModel.Design;
using System.Workflow.Runtime;
using System.Workflow.Activities;
using System.Workflow.Activities.Rules;
using Microsoft.SharePoint.Workflow;
using Microsoft.SharePoint;
using Microsoft.SharePoint.WorkflowActions;

namespace Chapter6
{
  public sealed partial class Workflow1 : SequentialWorkflowActivity
  {
    public Workflow1()
    {
      InitializeComponent();
      using(SPSite siteCollection = new SPSite("http://localhost/Docs"))
      {
        using(SPWeb site = siteCollection.OpenWeb())
        {
          WorkflowRole workflowRole =
           SPWorkflowWorkflowRoleCreator.GetWorkflowRoleForGroups(site, "MyGroup");
          Roles.Add(workflowRole);
        }
      }
    }

    private void InitializeComponent()
    {
      this.CanModifyActivities = true;
      ActivityBind activitybind1 = new ActivityBind();
      ActivityBind activitybind2 = new ActivityBind();
      ActivityBind activitybind3 = new ActivityBind();
      ActivityBind activitybind8 = new ActivityBind();
      ActivityBind activitybind4 = new ActivityBind();
      ActivityBind activitybind5 = new ActivityBind();
      CorrelationToken correlationtoken1 = new CorrelationToken();
      ActivityBind activitybind6 = new ActivityBind();
      ActivityBind activitybind7 = new ActivityBind();
      ActivityBind activitybind9 = new ActivityBind();
      ActivityBind activitybind10 = new ActivityBind();
      ActivityBind activitybind11 = new ActivityBind();
```

```
ActivityBind activitybind12 = new ActivityBind();
ActivityBind activitybind13 = new ActivityBind();
CorrelationToken correlationtoken2 = new CorrelationToken();
ActivityBind activitybind14 = new ActivityBind();
this.logToHistoryListActivity2 = new LogToHistoryListActivity();
this.onTaskChanged1 = new OnTaskChanged();
this.logToHistoryListActivity1 = new LogToHistoryListActivity();
this.createTask1 = new CreateTask();
this.onWorkflowActivated1 = new OnWorkflowActivated();

//
// logToHistoryListActivity2
//
this.logToHistoryListActivity2.Duration =
                        System.TimeSpan.Parse("-10675199.02:48:05.4775808");
this.logToHistoryListActivity2.EventId =
                                SPWorkflowHistoryEventType.WorkflowComment;
activitybind1.Name = "Workflow1";
activitybind1.Path = "HistoryDescription";
activitybind2.Name = "Workflow1";
activitybind2.Path = "HistoryOutcome";
this.logToHistoryListActivity2.Name = "logToHistoryListActivity2";
this.logToHistoryListActivity2.OtherData = "";
activitybind3.Name = "Workflow1";
activitybind3.Path = "WorkflowProperties.OriginatorUser.ID";
this.logToHistoryListActivity2.MethodInvoking +=
      new System.EventHandler(this.logToHistoryListActivity2_MethodInvoking);
this.logToHistoryListActivity2.SetBinding(
                         LogToHistoryListActivity.HistoryDescriptionProperty,
                         ((ActivityBind)(activitybind1)));
this.logToHistoryListActivity2.SetBinding(
                         LogToHistoryListActivity.HistoryOutcomeProperty,
                         ((ActivityBind)(activitybind2)));
this.logToHistoryListActivity2.SetBinding(
                         LogToHistoryListActivity.UserIdProperty,
                         ((ActivityBind)(activitybind3)));
activitybind8.Name = "Workflow1";
activitybind8.Path = "Roles";
//
// onTaskChanged1
//
activitybind4.Name = "Workflow1";
activitybind4.Path = "AfterProperties";
activitybind5.Name = "Workflow1";
activitybind5.Path = "BeforeProperties";
correlationtoken1.Name = "taskToken";
correlationtoken1.OwnerActivityName = "Workflow1";
this.onTaskChanged1.CorrelationToken = correlationtoken1;
activitybind6.Name = "Workflow1";
activitybind6.Path = "Executor";
this.onTaskChanged1.Name = "onTaskChanged1";
activitybind7.Name = "Workflow1";
activitybind7.Path = "TaskId";
```

(continued)

Listing 6-6 *(continued)*

```
this.onTaskChanged1.SetBinding(OnTaskChanged.AfterPropertiesProperty,
                              ((ActivityBind)(activitybind4)));
this.onTaskChanged1.SetBinding(OnTaskChanged.BeforePropertiesProperty,
                              ((ActivityBind)(activitybind5)));
this.onTaskChanged1.SetBinding(OnTaskChanged.ExecutorProperty,
                              ((ActivityBind)(activitybind6)));
this.onTaskChanged1.SetBinding(OnTaskChanged.TaskIdProperty,
                              ((ActivityBind)(activitybind7)));
this.onTaskChanged1.SetBinding(HandleExternalEventActivity.RolesProperty,
                              ((ActivityBind)(activitybind8)));
//
// logToHistoryListActivity1
//
this.logToHistoryListActivity1.Duration =
                                     System.TimeSpan.Parse("78.00:00:00");
this.logToHistoryListActivity1.EventId =
                                  SPWorkflowHistoryEventType.WorkflowComment;
activitybind9.Name = "Workflow1";
activitybind9.Path = "HistoryDescription";
activitybind10.Name = "Workflow1";
activitybind10.Path = "HistoryOutcome";
this.logToHistoryListActivity1.Name = "logToHistoryListActivity1";
this.logToHistoryListActivity1.OtherData = "";
activitybind11.Name = "Workflow1";
activitybind11.Path = "WorkflowProperties.OriginatorUser.ID";
this.logToHistoryListActivity1.MethodInvoking +=
     new System.EventHandler(this.logToHistoryListActivity1_MethodInvoking);
this.logToHistoryListActivity1.SetBinding(
                         LogToHistoryListActivity.HistoryDescriptionProperty,
                         ((ActivityBind)(activitybind9)));
this.logToHistoryListActivity1.SetBinding(
                         LogToHistoryListActivity.HistoryOutcomeProperty,
                         ((ActivityBind)(activitybind10)));
this.logToHistoryListActivity1.SetBinding(
                         LogToHistoryListActivity.UserIdProperty,
                         ((ActivityBind)(activitybind11)));
//
// createTask1
//
this.createTask1.CorrelationToken = correlationtoken1;
this.createTask1.ListItemId = -1;
this.createTask1.Name = "createTask1";
this.createTask1.SpecialPermissions = null;
activitybind12.Name = "Workflow1";
activitybind12.Path = "TaskId";
activitybind13.Name = "Workflow1";
activitybind13.Path = "TaskProperties";
this.createTask1.MethodInvoking +=
              new System.EventHandler(this.createTask1_MethodInvoking);
this.createTask1.SetBinding(CreateTask.TaskIdProperty,
                           ((ActivityBind)(activitybind12)));
this.createTask1.SetBinding(CreateTask.TaskPropertiesProperty,
                           ((ActivityBind)(activitybind13)));
```

```
    //
    // onWorkflowActivated1
    //
    correlationtoken2.Name = "workflowToken";
    correlationtoken2.OwnerActivityName = "Workflow1";
    this.onWorkflowActivated1.CorrelationToken = correlationtoken2;
    this.onWorkflowActivated1.EventName = "OnWorkflowActivated";
    this.onWorkflowActivated1.Name = "onWorkflowActivated1";
    activitybind14.Name = "Workflow1";
    activitybind14.Path = "WorkflowProperties";
    this.onWorkflowActivated1.SetBinding(
                              OnWorkflowActivated.WorkflowPropertiesProperty,
                              ((ActivityBind)(activitybind14)));
    //
    // Workflow1
    //
    this.Activities.Add(this.onWorkflowActivated1);
    this.Activities.Add(this.createTask1);
    this.Activities.Add(this.logToHistoryListActivity1);
    this.Activities.Add(this.onTaskChanged1);
    this.Activities.Add(this.logToHistoryListActivity2);
    this.Name = "Workflow1";
    this.CanModifyActivities = false;

  }

  private LogToHistoryListActivity logToHistoryListActivity2;
  private OnTaskChanged onTaskChanged1;
  private CreateTask createTask1;
  private LogToHistoryListActivity logToHistoryListActivity1;
  private OnWorkflowActivated onWorkflowActivated1;

  public SPWorkflowActivationProperties WorkflowProperties =
                                        new SPWorkflowActivationProperties();
  public TimeSpan Duration = default(TimeSpan);
  public Int32 ListItemId = default(Int32);
  public Guid TaskId = default(Guid);
  public SPWorkflowTaskProperties TaskProperties =
                                             new SPWorkflowTaskProperties();
  public String HistoryDescription = default(String);
  public String HistoryOutcome = default(String);

  private void logToHistoryListActivity1_MethodInvoking(object sender,
                                                         EventArgs e)
  {
    this.HistoryDescription = "Information";
    this.HistoryOutcome = "Task " + this.TaskId.ToString() + " is created!";
  }

  public SPWorkflowTaskProperties AfterProperties =
                                             new SPWorkflowTaskProperties();
  public SPWorkflowTaskProperties BeforeProperties =
                                             new SPWorkflowTaskProperties();
```

(continued)

Listing 6-6 *(continued)*

```
        public String Executor = default(String);

        private void logToHistoryListActivity2_MethodInvoking(object sender,
                                                              EventArgs e)
        {
          this.HistoryDescription = "Information";
          this.HistoryOutcome = "Task " + this.TaskId.ToString() + " is changed!";
        }

        private void createTask1_MethodInvoking(object sender, EventArgs e)
        {
          this.TaskId = Guid.NewGuid();
          this.TaskProperties.Title = "Do something";
          this.TaskProperties.PercentComplete = 0;
          this.TaskProperties.DueDate = DateTime.Now.AddMinutes(2);
          this.TaskProperties.StartDate = DateTime.Now;
        }

        public WorkflowRoleCollection Roles = new WorkflowRoleCollection();
      }
    }
```

The constructor of this workflow takes the following steps. First, it creates an SPSite object to represent the site collection with the specified URL:

```
SPSite siteCollection = new SPSite("http://localhost/Docs");
```

As discussed earlier, the constructor of the SPSite class internally uses the principal that instantiates the SPSite object as the current user. Because our workflow runs in the context of a SharePoint site, this principal is the Windows principal if you've configured SharePoint to use Windows authentication. Therefore, the Execute method of the OnTaskChanged activity in our workflow will pass this principal's identity into the IncludesIdentity method of the WorkflowRoleCollection object that its Roles property references when it invokes this method. Keep in mind that the OnTaskChanged activity inherits the HandleExternalEventActivity activity.

The constructor of our workflow then invokes the OpenWeb method on the SPSite object that represents the site collection with the specified URL to return a reference to the SPWeb object that represents the associated site:

```
SPWeb site = siteCollection.OpenWeb();
```

The constructor of our workflow then invokes the GetWorkflowRoleForGroups static method of the SPWorkflowWorkflowRoleCreator class, passing in the SPWeb object and a string that contains a SharePoint group name, to create a WorkflowRole object that represents the base permissions of this group:

```
WorkflowRole workflowRole =
  SPWorkflowWorkflowRoleCreator.GetWorkflowRoleForGroups(site, "MyGroup");
```

The constructor finally adds this WorkflowRole object to the Roles collection field of the workflow:

```
Roles.Add(workflowRole);
```

As shown in Listing 6-6, the Roles collection field of the workflow is bound to the Roles collection property of the OnTaskChanged activity:

```
public WorkflowRoleCollection Roles = new WorkflowRoleCollection();

private void InitializeComponent()
{
  . . .
  ActivityBind activitybind11 = new ActivityBind();
  . . .
  activitybind11.Name = "Workflow1";
  activitybind11.Path = "Roles";
  . . .
  this.onTaskChanged1.SetBinding(HandleExternalEventActivity.RolesProperty,
                                 activitybind11);
  . . .
}
```

This example assumes that the site collection contains a SharePoint group named MyGroup. Go ahead and use the SharePoint user interface to add this group to the site collection, and add your login name to this group as shown in Figure 6-2.

Figure 6-2

Now run the SharePoint workflow. As Figure 6-3 shows, the workflow history list contains an entry indicating that the SharePoint task was created. It also shows this SharePoint task.

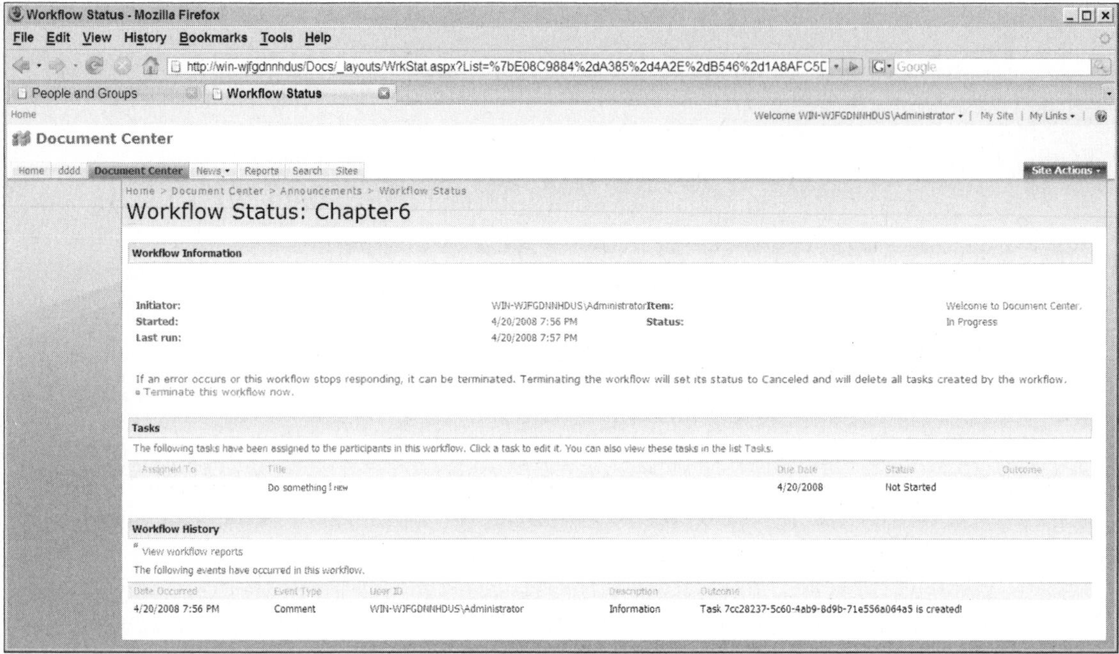

Figure 6-3

Update the task shown in Figure 6-3. When you update the task, the SharePoint task service fires its OnTaskChanged event and sends a message to the OnTaskChanged activity of the current workflow instance under your login name. The OnTaskChanged activity, which inherits from HandleExternalEventActivity, passes your login name into the IncludesIdentity method of the WorkflowRoleCollection object that its Roles property references. This method in turn passes your login name to the IncludesIdentity method of the WorkflowRole object that the constructor of our workflow created and added to the Roles collection.

Because this WorkflowRole object represents the base permissions for the MyGroup SharePoint group and because you're part of this group, the IncludesIdentity method will return true. In other words, the OnTaskChanged activity allows the message that the SharePoint task service sends to the current workflow instance to go through. This means that the OnTaskChanged activity, and consequently the current workflow instance, resumes and completes its execution (as shown in Figure 6-4), which now shows that the workflow history list contains a new entry signaling the completion of the workflow's execution.

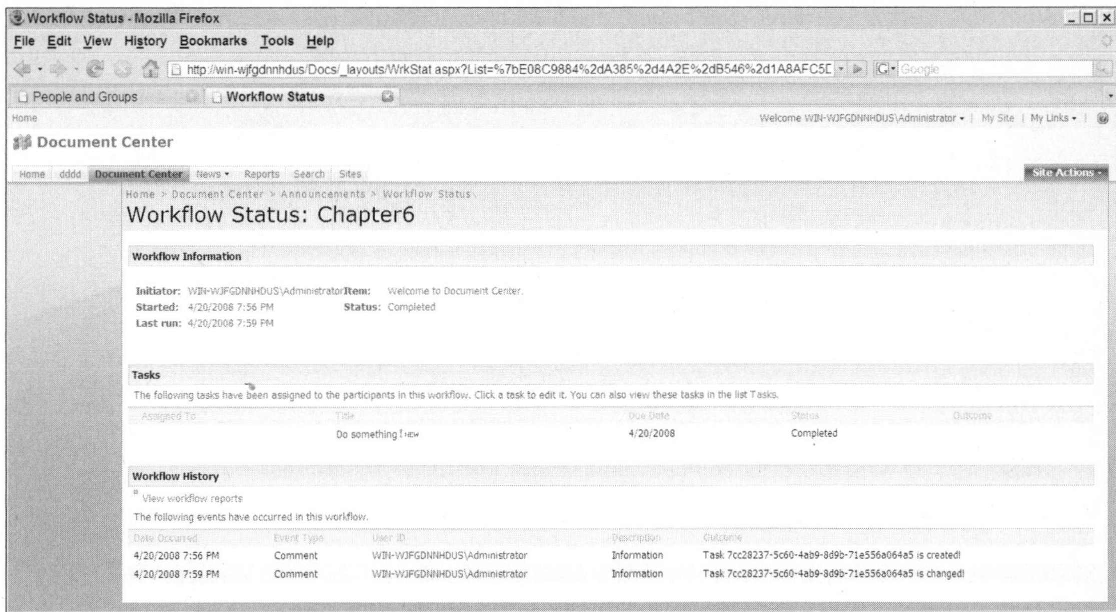

Figure 6-4

Next, remove your login name from the MyGroup SharePoint group shown in Figure 6-2 and then execute the workflow. You should see the same thing shown in Figure 6-5. This means that the CreateTask activity creates the SharePoint task as it did before, because this activity does not use the SharePoint workflow security feature. It does not use it because there is no need to use it. Security becomes an issue when an external entity sends a message to a workflow instance. Now update the SharePoint task as you did before. As Figure 6-5 shows, now the workflow history list contains an error entry. That's because when you update the task, the SharePoint task service raises its OnTaskChanged event and sends a message to the OnTaskChanged activity under your login name. This activity in turns invokes the IncludesIdentity method on its Roles property, passing in your login name, which in turn invokes the IncludesIdentity method on the WorkflowRole object that our workflow created, passing in your login name. Because this WorkflowRole object represents the base permissions for the MyGroup SharePoint group, and because you're not part of this group anymore, this method, and consequently the OnTaskChanged activity, throws an exception.

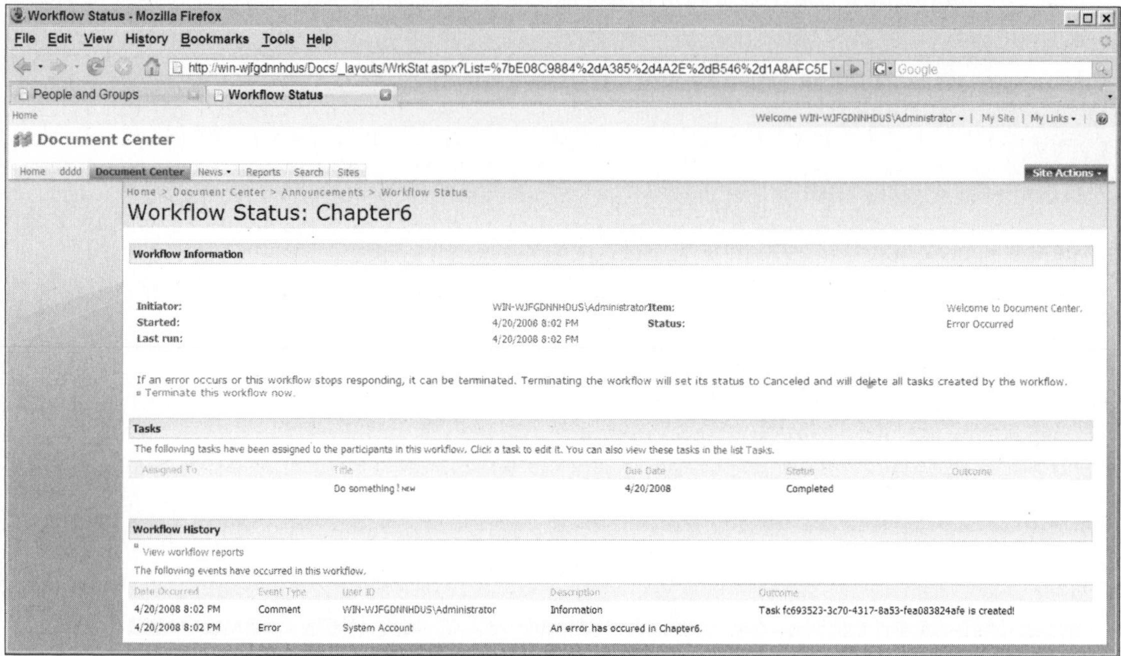

Figure 6-5

The error message shown in Figure 6-5 isn't that helpful, is it? As a developer you need more information to debug a problem like this one. This is where WF fault handling comes in handy.

Fault Handling

When a child activity of a composite activity faults, and WF propagates the fault to the composite activity, the composite activity immediately transitions from the Executing to the Faulting state and its HandleFault method is scheduled with the WF scheduler for execution. When the WF scheduler finally invokes the HandleFault method of the composite activity, this method checks whether any of the child activities of the composite activity are in any state other than Initialized or Closed. If so, it schedules the Cancel method of these child activities for execution. When the Cancel methods of all active child activities are finally invoked and when all active child activities finally transition to the Closed state, the composite activity informs the workflow run time that it is now ready to transition from the Faulting state to the Closed state.

The WF run time first checks whether the composite activity contains an instance of an activity named FaultHandlersActivity. If so, the WF run time schedules the Execute method of this activity for execution. The composite activity is not allowed to transition to the Closed state until the FaultHandlersActivity activity completes its execution and transitions to the Closed state. The FaultHandlersActivity activity can contain zero or more instances of an activity named FaultHandlerActivity. Because the FaultHandlerActivity activity is a composite activity, you can add other activities from the Visual Studio toolbox into this activity as its child activities. You must configure each FaultHandlerActivity activity to handle a fault of a specific type. As such, the FaultHandlerActivity activities of a FaultHandlersActivity activity are more like the C# catch blocks. As each C# catch block contains the code that handles a specific type of exception, each FaultHandlerActivity activity contains child activities that work together to handle a specific type of exception.

Next, we'll add a FaultHandlersActivity activity to our workflow example from the previous section and add a FaultHandlerActivity activity to this FaultHandlersActivity activity and configure this FaultHandlerActivity activity to handle the security exception that is raised when the MyGroup SharePoint group does not contain your login name and you try to update the SharePoint task.

In design view, click the top arrow on the workflow to access the pop-up menu shown in Figure 6-6.

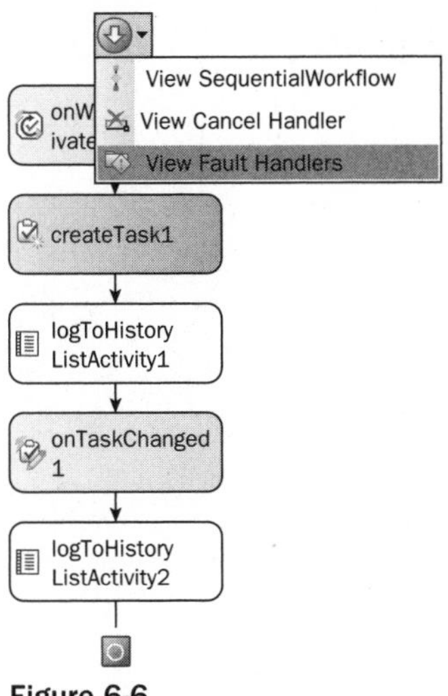

Figure 6-6

Select the View Fault Handlers option. Visual Studio will automatically add the following code to our workflow:

```
private FaultHandlersActivity faultHandlersActivity1;

private void InitializeComponent()
{
  . . .
  this.faultHandlersActivity1 = new FaultHandlersActivity();
  this.faultHandlersActivity1.Name = "faultHandlersActivity1";
  this.Activities.Add(this.faultHandlersActivity1);
  . . .
}
```

Note that this code instantiates a FaultHandlerActivity activity and adds it to the Activities collection property of our workflow. Even though this activity, like any other activity, is added to the Activities collection property of the workflow, the workflow itself does not schedule this activity for execution. In that sense, this activity is fundamentally different from other child activities of the workflow, or any composite activity for that matter. Only the WF run time is allowed to schedule the FaultHandlersActivity activity of a composite activity such as a workflow for execution. Keep in mind that every composite activity can only contain a single instance of the FaultHandlersActivity activity.

After you select the View Fault Handlers option, you should see the fault handler's view of our workflow, as shown in Figure 6-7.

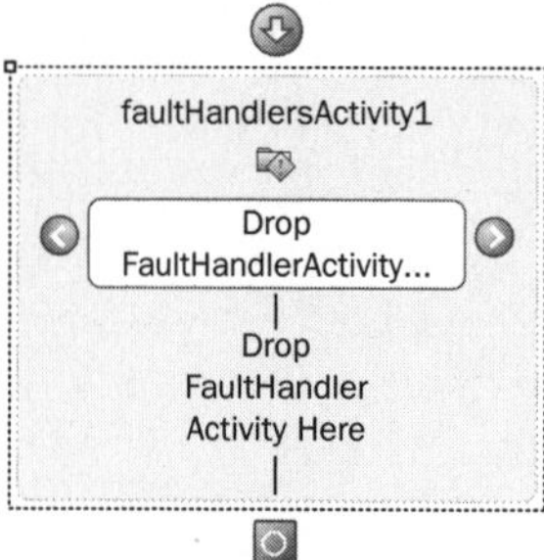

Figure 6-7

This view consists of two parts. The top part, which is the box enclosed within the arrows, is where you need to drop one or more FaultHandlerActivity activities. The bottom part, which is below the box, is where you need to drop the child activities of each FaultHandlerActivity activity.

Next, drag a FaultHandlerActivity activity from the Visual Studio toolbox and drop it into the box enclosed within the arrows, as shown in Figure 6-8.

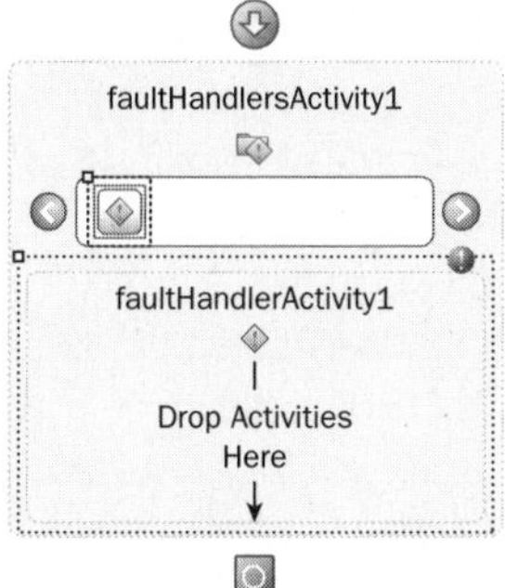

Figure 6-8

Visual Studio automatically generates and adds the following code to our workflow:

```
private FaultHandlerActivity faultHandlerActivity1;

private void InitializeComponent()
{
  . . .
  this.faultHandlersActivity1 = new FaultHandlersActivity();
  this.faultHandlerActivity1.Name = "faultHandlerActivity1";

  this.faultHandlersActivity1.Activities.Add(this.faultHandlerActivity1);
  . . .
}
```

This code instantiates a FaultHandlerActivity activity and adds it to the Activities collection property of the FaultHandlersActivity composite activity.

The top-right corner of the area labeled "Drop Activities Here" shows an exclamation mark (!) because we haven't specified what type of fault or exception this FaultHandlerActivity must handle. You can do this in the Properties pane, which shows the properties of the FaultHandlerActivity activity (see Figure 6-9). Click the FaultType property to make the ellipsis button shown in this figure visible.

Figure 6-9

Click this ellipsis button to launch the dialog shown in Figure 6-10.

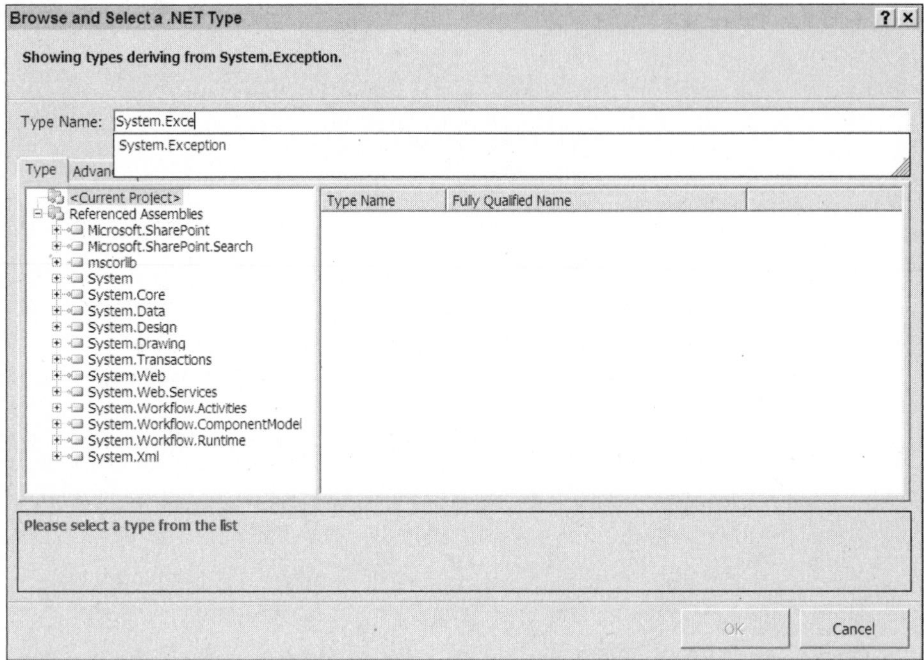

Figure 6-10

This dialog enables you to select or enter an exception type and assign the type to the FaultType property. Select the System.Exception type and click OK. Visual Studio will generate and add the following line of code to our workflow:

```
private void InitializeComponent()
{
  . . .
  this.faultHandlerActivity1.FaultType = typeof(Exception);
  . . .
}
```

This line of code basically assigns the Type object that represents the System.Exception type to the FaultType property of the FaultHandlerActivity activity. This means that this activity handles faults or exceptions of the System.Exception type.

Next, drag a LogToHistoryListActivity activity from the Visual Studio toolbox and drop it into the area that says "Drop Activities Here" (see Figure 6-11).

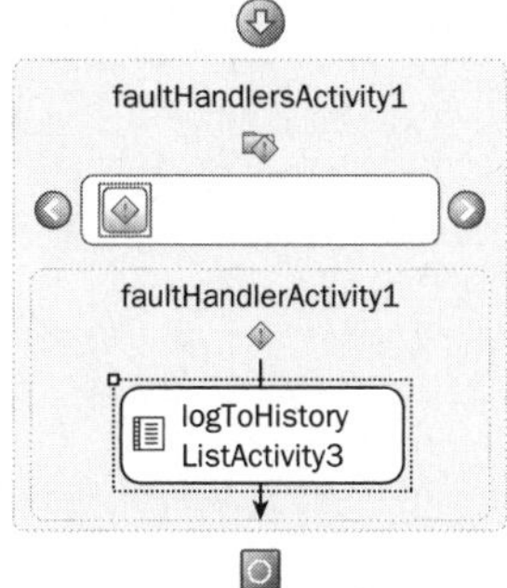

Figure 6-11

Visual Studio will automatically generate and add the following code to our workflow:

```
private LogToHistoryListActivity logToHistoryListActivity3;

private void InitializeComponent()
{
  this.logToHistoryListActivity3 = new LogToHistoryListActivity();
  this.logToHistoryListActivity3.Name = "logToHistoryListActivity3";

  this.faultHandlerActivity1.Activities.Add(this.logToHistoryListActivity3);

      this.logToHistoryListActivity3.MethodInvoking +=
                  new EventHandler(this.logToHistoryListActivity3_MethodInvoking);
}
```

This code instantiates a LogToHistoryListActivity activity and adds it to the Activities collection property of the FaultHandlerActivity activity as its child activity.

Next, bind the properties of this LogToHistoryListActivity activity to the workflow local fields. Then right-click the LogToHistoryListActivity activity and select Generate Handlers to add an event handler for the MethodInvoking event of this activity. Implement the body of this event handler as shown here:

```
private void logToHistoryListActivity3_MethodInvoking(object sender,
                                                       EventArgs e)
{
  LogToHistoryListActivity activity1 = sender as LogToHistoryListActivity;
  FaultHandlerActivity activity2 = activity1.Parent as FaultHandlerActivity;
  Exception fault = activity2.Fault;
  this.HistoryDescription = fault.Message;
  this.HistoryOutcome = fault.StackTrace;
}
```

This event handler first casts its first argument to the LogToHistoryListActivity type:

```
LogToHistoryListActivity activity1 = sender as LogToHistoryListActivity;
```

Next, it accesses the parent activity of the LogToHistoryListActivity activity, which is the FaultHandlerActivity activity:

```
        FaultHandlerActivity activity2 = activity1.Parent as FaultHandlerActivity;
```

Then, it accesses the exception object through the Fault property of the FaultHandlerActivity activity:

```
        Exception fault = activity2.Fault;
```

It then assigns the value of the Message property of the exception object to the HistoryDescription field of the workflow. Keep in mind that this field is bound to the HistoryDescription property of the LogToHistoryListActivity activity. Therefore, the value that we assign to the HistoryDescription field is automatically assigned to the HistoryDescription property of the LogToHistoryListActivity activity through activity binding:

```
        this.HistoryDescription = fault.Message;
```

Finally, it assigns the stack trace of the exception to the HistoryOutcome field of the workflow. Again, keep in mind that this field is bound to the HistoryFault property of the LogToHistoryListActivity activity:

```
        this.HistoryOutcome = fault.StackTrace;
```

The result is that this LogToHistoryListActivity activity logs the error message and the stack trace to the workflow history list.

Listing 6-7 presents the complete code for our workflow.

Listing 6-7: A workflow demonstrating workflow security features with fault handling

```
using System;
using System.ComponentModel;
using System.ComponentModel.Design;
using System.Collections;
using System.Drawing;
using System.Linq;
using System.Workflow.ComponentModel.Compiler;
using System.Workflow.ComponentModel.Serialization;
using System.Workflow.ComponentModel;
using System.Workflow.ComponentModel.Design;
using System.Workflow.Runtime;
using System.Workflow.Activities;
using System.Workflow.Activities.Rules;
using Microsoft.SharePoint.Workflow;
using Microsoft.SharePoint;
using Microsoft.SharePoint.WorkflowActions;

namespace Chapter6
```

```
{
  public sealed partial class Workflow1 : SequentialWorkflowActivity
  {
    public Workflow1()
    {
      InitializeComponent();
      using(SPSite siteCollection = new SPSite("http://localhost/Docs"))
      {
        using(SPWeb site = siteCollection.OpenWeb())
        {
          WorkflowRole workflowRole =
           SPWorkflowWorkflowRoleCreator.GetWorkflowRoleForGroups(site, "MyGroup");
          Roles.Add(workflowRole);
        }
      }
    }

    private void InitializeComponent()
    {
      this.CanModifyActivities = true;
      ActivityBind activitybind1 = new ActivityBind();
      ActivityBind activitybind2 = new ActivityBind();
      ActivityBind activitybind3 = new ActivityBind();
      ActivityBind activitybind4 = new ActivityBind();
      ActivityBind activitybind5 = new ActivityBind();
      ActivityBind activitybind6 = new ActivityBind();
      ActivityBind activitybind11 = new ActivityBind();
      ActivityBind activitybind7 = new ActivityBind();
      ActivityBind activitybind8 = new ActivityBind();
      CorrelationToken correlationtoken1 = new CorrelationToken();
      ActivityBind activitybind9 = new ActivityBind();
      ActivityBind activitybind10 = new ActivityBind();
      ActivityBind activitybind12 = new ActivityBind();
      ActivityBind activitybind13 = new ActivityBind();
      ActivityBind activitybind14 = new ActivityBind();
      ActivityBind activitybind15 = new ActivityBind();
      ActivityBind activitybind16 = new ActivityBind();
      CorrelationToken correlationtoken2 = new CorrelationToken();
      ActivityBind activitybind17 = new ActivityBind();
      this.logToHistoryListActivity3 = new LogToHistoryListActivity();
      this.faultHandlerActivity1 = new FaultHandlerActivity();
      this.cancellationHandlerActivity1 = new CancellationHandlerActivity();
      this.faultHandlersActivity1 = new FaultHandlersActivity();
      this.logToHistoryListActivity2 = new LogToHistoryListActivity();
      this.onTaskChanged1 = new OnTaskChanged();
      this.logToHistoryListActivity1 = new LogToHistoryListActivity();
      this.createTask1 = new CreateTask();
      this.onWorkflowActivated1 = new OnWorkflowActivated();
      //
      // logToHistoryListActivity3
      //
```

(continued)

Listing 6-7 *(continued)*

```
this.logToHistoryListActivity3.Duration =
                              TimeSpan.Parse("-10675199.02:48:05.4775808");
this.logToHistoryListActivity3.EventId =
                               SPWorkflowHistoryEventType.WorkflowComment;
activitybind1.Name = "Workflow1";
activitybind1.Path = "HistoryDescription";
activitybind2.Name = "Workflow1";
activitybind2.Path = "HistoryOutcome";
this.logToHistoryListActivity3.Name = "logToHistoryListActivity3";
this.logToHistoryListActivity3.OtherData = "";
activitybind3.Name = "Workflow1";
activitybind3.Path = "WorkflowProperties.OriginatorUser.ID";
this.logToHistoryListActivity3.MethodInvoking +=
            new EventHandler(this.logToHistoryListActivity3_MethodInvoking);
this.logToHistoryListActivity3.SetBinding(
        LogToHistoryListActivity.HistoryDescriptionProperty, activitybind1);
this.logToHistoryListActivity3.SetBinding(
             LogToHistoryListActivity.HistoryOutcomeProperty, activitybind2);
this.logToHistoryListActivity3.SetBinding(
                    LogToHistoryListActivity.UserIdProperty, activitybind3);
//
// faultHandlerActivity1
//
this.faultHandlerActivity1.Activities.Add(this.logToHistoryListActivity3);
this.faultHandlerActivity1.FaultType = typeof(Exception);
this.faultHandlerActivity1.Name = "faultHandlerActivity1";
//
// cancellationHandlerActivity1
//
this.cancellationHandlerActivity1.Name = "cancellationHandlerActivity1";
//
// faultHandlersActivity1
//
this.faultHandlersActivity1.Activities.Add(this.faultHandlerActivity1);
this.faultHandlersActivity1.Name = "faultHandlersActivity1";
//
// logToHistoryListActivity2
//
this.logToHistoryListActivity2.Duration =
                              TimeSpan.Parse("-10675199.02:48:05.4775808");
this.logToHistoryListActivity2.EventId =
                               SPWorkflowHistoryEventType.WorkflowComment;
activitybind4.Name = "Workflow1";
activitybind4.Path = "HistoryDescription";
activitybind5.Name = "Workflow1";
activitybind5.Path = "HistoryOutcome";
this.logToHistoryListActivity2.Name = "logToHistoryListActivity2";
this.logToHistoryListActivity2.OtherData = "";
activitybind6.Name = "Workflow1";
activitybind6.Path = "WorkflowProperties.OriginatorUser.ID";
this.logToHistoryListActivity2.MethodInvoking +=
            new EventHandler(this.logToHistoryListActivity2_MethodInvoking);
```

```
this.logToHistoryListActivity2.SetBinding(
         LogToHistoryListActivity.HistoryDescriptionProperty, activitybind4);
this.logToHistoryListActivity2.SetBinding(
             LogToHistoryListActivity.HistoryOutcomeProperty, activitybind5);
this.logToHistoryListActivity2.SetBinding(
                     LogToHistoryListActivity.UserIdProperty, activitybind6);
activitybind11.Name = "Workflow1";
activitybind11.Path = "Roles";
//
// onTaskChanged1
//
activitybind7.Name = "Workflow1";
activitybind7.Path = "AfterProperties";
activitybind8.Name = "Workflow1";
activitybind8.Path = "BeforeProperties";
correlationtoken1.Name = "taskToken";
correlationtoken1.OwnerActivityName = "Workflow1";
this.onTaskChanged1.CorrelationToken = correlationtoken1;
activitybind9.Name = "Workflow1";
activitybind9.Path = "Executor";
this.onTaskChanged1.Name = "onTaskChanged1";
activitybind10.Name = "Workflow1";
activitybind10.Path = "TaskId";
this.onTaskChanged1.SetBinding(OnTaskChanged.AfterPropertiesProperty,
                               activitybind7);
this.onTaskChanged1.SetBinding(OnTaskChanged.BeforePropertiesProperty,
                               activitybind8);
this.onTaskChanged1.SetBinding(OnTaskChanged.ExecutorProperty,
                               activitybind9);
this.onTaskChanged1.SetBinding(OnTaskChanged.TaskIdProperty, activitybind10);
this.onTaskChanged1.SetBinding(HandleExternalEventActivity.RolesProperty,
                               activitybind11);
//
// logToHistoryListActivity1
//
this.logToHistoryListActivity1.Duration = TimeSpan.Parse("78.00:00:00");
this.logToHistoryListActivity1.EventId =
                                  SPWorkflowHistoryEventType.WorkflowComment;
activitybind12.Name = "Workflow1";
activitybind12.Path = "HistoryDescription";
activitybind13.Name = "Workflow1";
activitybind13.Path = "HistoryOutcome";
this.logToHistoryListActivity1.Name = "logToHistoryListActivity1";
this.logToHistoryListActivity1.OtherData = "";
activitybind14.Name = "Workflow1";
activitybind14.Path = "WorkflowProperties.OriginatorUser.ID";
this.logToHistoryListActivity1.MethodInvoking +=
             new EventHandler(this.logToHistoryListActivity1_MethodInvoking);
this.logToHistoryListActivity1.SetBinding(
        LogToHistoryListActivity.HistoryDescriptionProperty, activitybind12);
this.logToHistoryListActivity1.SetBinding(
            LogToHistoryListActivity.HistoryOutcomeProperty, activitybind13);
this.logToHistoryListActivity1.SetBinding(
                    LogToHistoryListActivity.UserIdProperty, activitybind14);
```

(continued)

Listing 6-7 *(continued)*

```
    //
    // createTask1
    //
    this.createTask1.CorrelationToken = correlationtoken1;
    this.createTask1.ListItemId = -1;
    this.createTask1.Name = "createTask1";
    this.createTask1.SpecialPermissions = null;
    activitybind15.Name = "Workflow1";
    activitybind15.Path = "TaskId";
    activitybind16.Name = "Workflow1";
    activitybind16.Path = "TaskProperties";
    this.createTask1.MethodInvoking +=
                          new EventHandler(this.createTask1_MethodInvoking);
    this.createTask1.SetBinding(CreateTask.TaskIdProperty, activitybind15);
    this.createTask1.SetBinding(CreateTask.TaskPropertiesProperty,
                           activitybind16);
    //
    // onWorkflowActivated1
    //
    correlationtoken2.Name = "workflowToken";
    correlationtoken2.OwnerActivityName = "Workflow1";
    this.onWorkflowActivated1.CorrelationToken = correlationtoken2;
    this.onWorkflowActivated1.EventName = "OnWorkflowActivated";
    this.onWorkflowActivated1.Name = "onWorkflowActivated1";
    activitybind17.Name = "Workflow1";
    activitybind17.Path = "WorkflowProperties";
    this.onWorkflowActivated1.Invoked +=
      new EventHandler<ExternalDataEventArgs>(this.onWorkflowActivated1_Invoked);
    this.onWorkflowActivated1.SetBinding(
            OnWorkflowActivated.WorkflowPropertiesProperty, activitybind17);
    //
    // Workflow1
    //
    this.Activities.Add(this.onWorkflowActivated1);
    this.Activities.Add(this.createTask1);
    this.Activities.Add(this.logToHistoryListActivity1);
    this.Activities.Add(this.onTaskChanged1);
    this.Activities.Add(this.logToHistoryListActivity2);
    this.Activities.Add(this.faultHandlersActivity1);
    this.Activities.Add(this.cancellationHandlerActivity1);

    this.Name = "Workflow1";
    this.CanModifyActivities = false;
  }

  private CancellationHandlerActivity cancellationHandlerActivity1;
  private LogToHistoryListActivity logToHistoryListActivity3;
  private FaultHandlerActivity faultHandlerActivity1;
  private FaultHandlersActivity faultHandlersActivity1;
  private LogToHistoryListActivity logToHistoryListActivity2;
  private OnTaskChanged onTaskChanged1;
  private CreateTask createTask1;
```

```
private LogToHistoryListActivity logToHistoryListActivity1;
private OnWorkflowActivated onWorkflowActivated1;

public SPWorkflowActivationProperties WorkflowProperties =
                                    new SPWorkflowActivationProperties();

private void onWorkflowActivated1_Invoked(object sender,
                                         ExternalDataEventArgs e)
{
}

public TimeSpan Duration = default(TimeSpan);
public Int32 ListItemId = default(Int32);
public Guid TaskId = default(Guid);
public SPWorkflowTaskProperties TaskProperties =
                                          new SPWorkflowTaskProperties();
public String HistoryDescription = default(String);
public String HistoryOutcome = default(String);

private void logToHistoryListActivity1_MethodInvoking(object sender,
                                                     EventArgs e)
{
  this.HistoryDescription = "Information";
  this.HistoryOutcome = "Task " + this.TaskId.ToString() + " is created!";
}

public SPWorkflowTaskProperties AfterProperties =
                                          new SPWorkflowTaskProperties();
public SPWorkflowTaskProperties BeforeProperties =
                                          new SPWorkflowTaskProperties();
public String Executor = default(String);

private void logToHistoryListActivity2_MethodInvoking(object sender,
                                                     EventArgs e)
{
  this.HistoryDescription = "Information";
  this.HistoryOutcome = "Task " + this.TaskId.ToString() + " is changed!";
}

private void createTask1_MethodInvoking(object sender, EventArgs e)
{
  this.TaskId = Guid.NewGuid();
  this.TaskProperties.Title = "Do something";
  this.TaskProperties.PercentComplete = 0;
  this.TaskProperties.DueDate = DateTime.Now.AddMinutes(2);
  this.TaskProperties.StartDate = DateTime.Now;
}

public WorkflowRoleCollection Roles = new WorkflowRoleCollection();

private void logToHistoryListActivity3_MethodInvoking(object sender,
                                                     EventArgs e)
```

(continued)

Listing 6-7 *(continued)*

```
        {
          LogToHistoryListActivity activity1 = sender as LogToHistoryListActivity;
          FaultHandlerActivity activity2 = activity1.Parent as FaultHandlerActivity;
          Exception fault = activity2.Fault;
          this.HistoryDescription = fault.Message;
          this.HistoryOutcome = fault.StackTrace;
        }
      }
    }
```

If you run this workflow, you'll get the same result shown in Figure 6-3, whereby the CreateTask activity creates a SharePoint task and the OnTaskChanged activity, and consequently the workflow suspends its execution and waits for the SharePoint task services to raise the OnTaskChanged event.

Now go ahead and update the task as you did before. This time around you should get the result shown in Figure 6-12. Thanks to the FaultHandlerActivity activity that we configured to handle the exception, the workflow history list now contains an entry that displays the error message and the stack trace. As the error message clearly states, the current user is not authorized to send massages to the workflow instance through the OnTaskChanged activity.

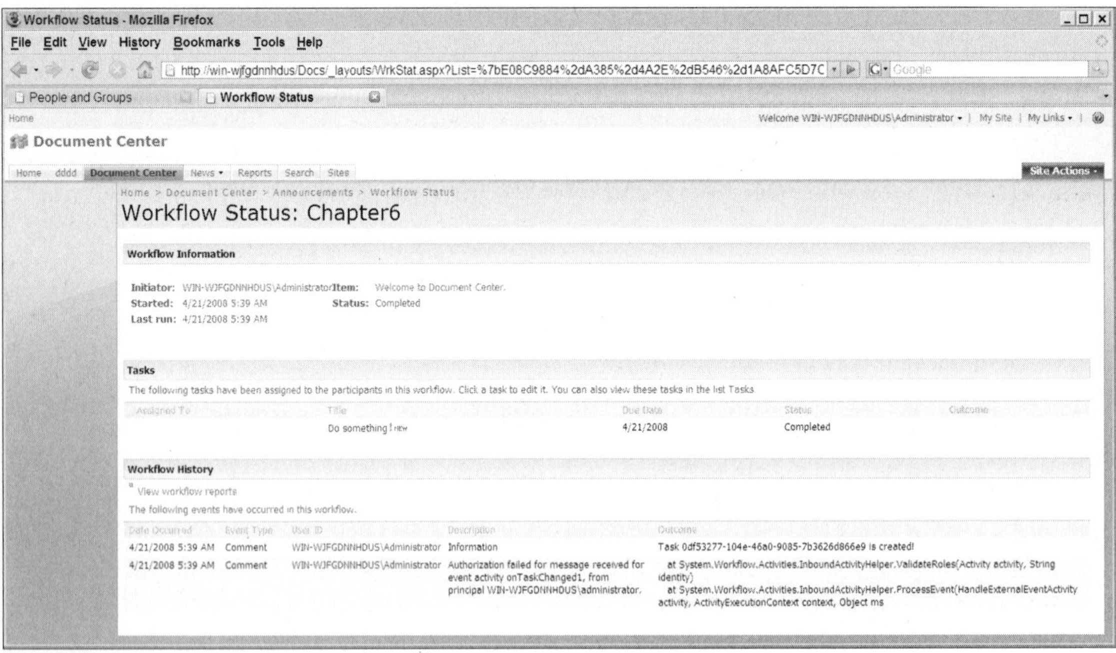

Figure 6-12

Summary

This chapter provided comprehensive coverage of workflow security and management, and fault handling. The next chapter deals with workflow modification and workflow task editing.

7

Workflow Modification and Task Editing

This chapter covers the following two SharePoint workflow programming topics:

- Workflow modification
- Workflow task editing

Implementing a Workflow Modification Input Form

You can modify a running workflow instance. These modifications affect only the workflow instance to which they're applied; they will not affect other workflow instances or the workflow itself. A workflow normally models and represents a business process. For example, the ConferenceRequestWorkflow workflow developed in the previous chapters models the business process through which an employee makes a conference request. A running workflow instance represents and models a running business process. Business rules governing a real-world business process could change after the business process begins. For example, employees may decide to change their information after they make a conference request but before their manager approves or denies the request. As such, you want to be able to modify the running workflow instance that represents a business process whose rules change. Enter workflow modifications.

You must take two main steps to add support for a workflow modification. First, you need to make changes in the workflow itself. Second, you need to implement and deploy a workflow modification form to SharePoint.

Making Changes to the Workflow Itself

This section covers the changes that you need to make to a workflow such as our ConferenceRequestWorkflow workflow to add support for workflow modification. First, you need to add an EventHandlingScopeActivity activity to the appropriate place in your workflow.

In the case of the ConferenceRequestWorkflow workflow, we'll add the EventHandlingScopeActivity activity as the child activity of the IfElseBranchActivity2 activity, as shown in Figure 7-1.

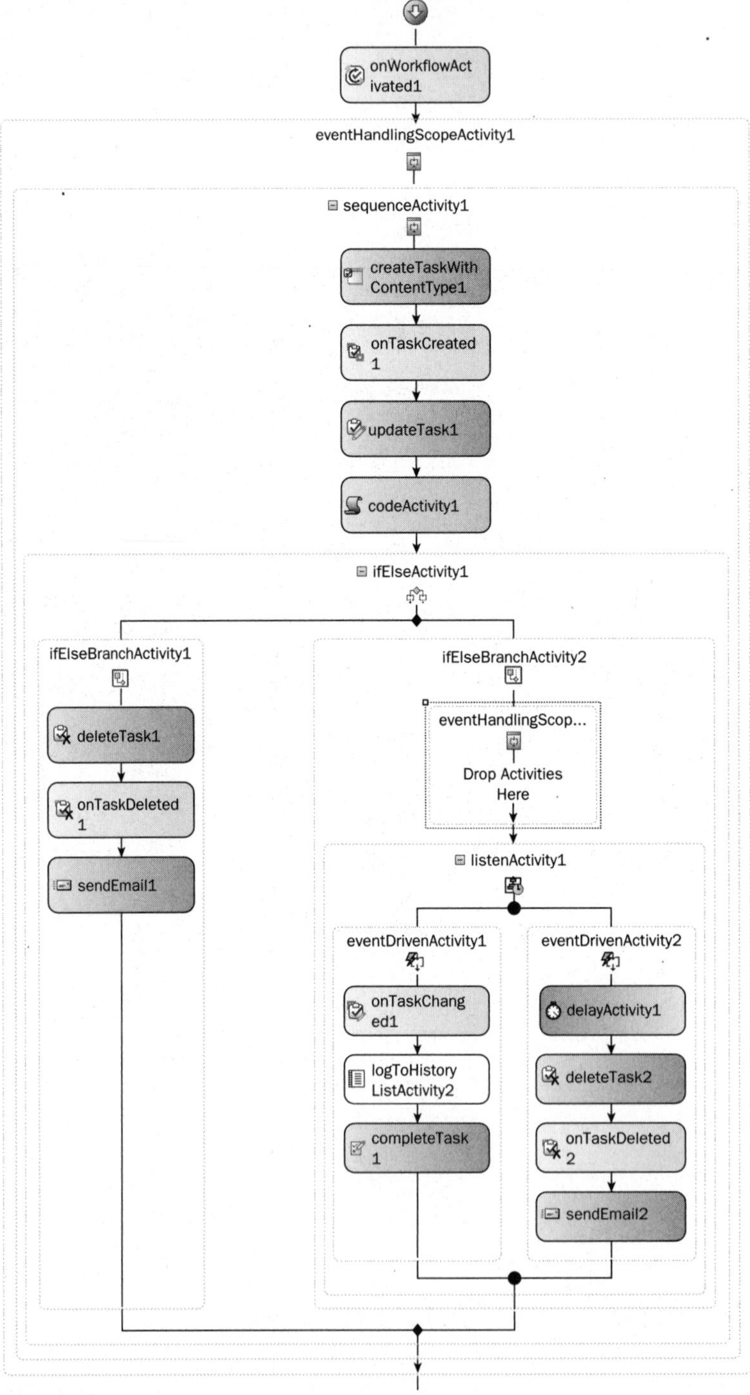

Figure 7-1

Next, you need to add a composite activity such as a SequenceActivity activity as the child activity of the EventHandlingScopeActivity activity (see Figure 7-2). The SequenceActivity activity is merely the main, or body, activity of the EventHandlingScopeActivity activity.

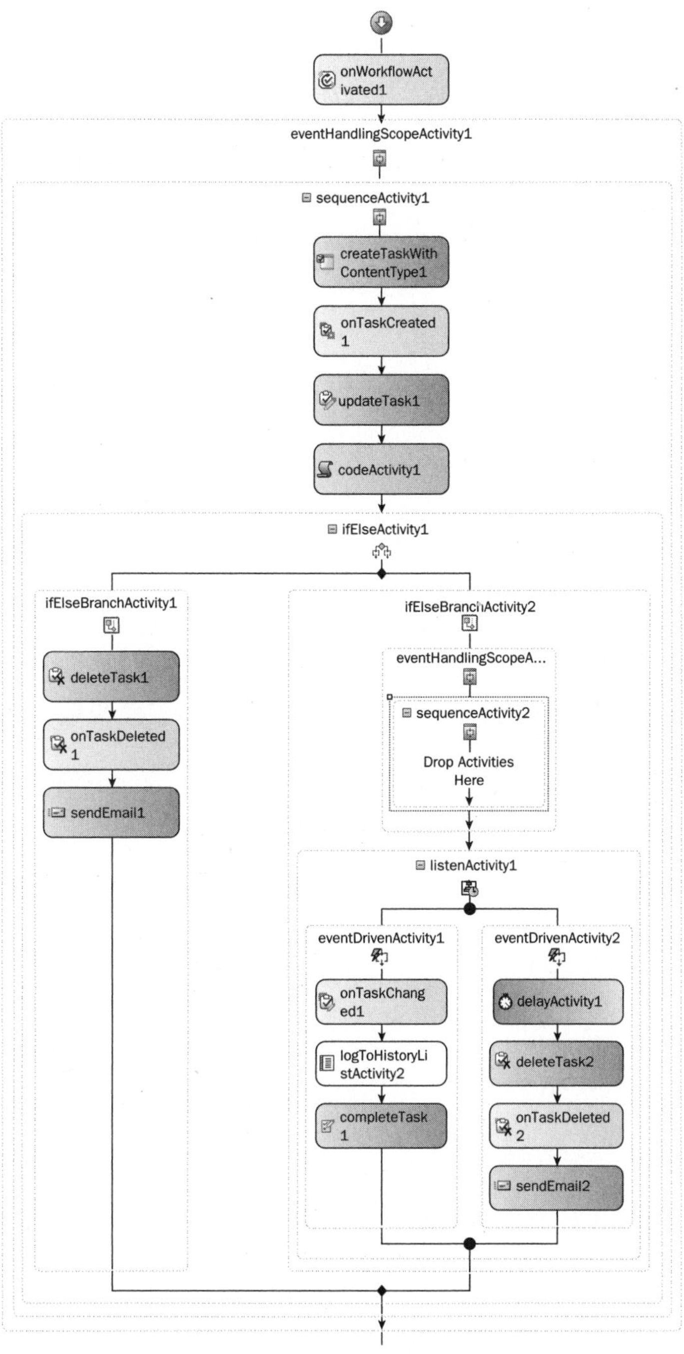

Figure 7-2

Now you need to add an EnableWorkflowModification activity as the first child activity to the main, or body, activity of the EventHandlingScopeActivity activity, which is the SequenceActivity activity in this case (see Figure 7-3).

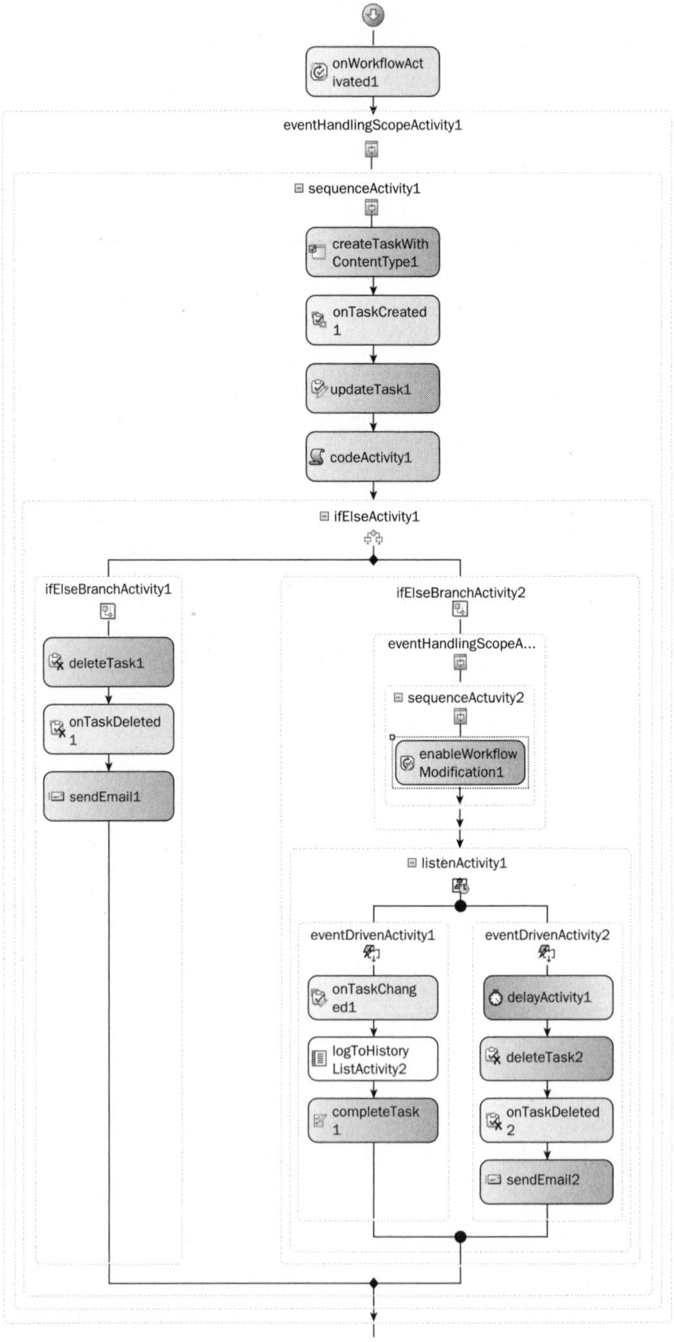

Figure 7-3

Figure 7-4 presents the properties of the EnableWorkflowModification activity in the Properties pane.

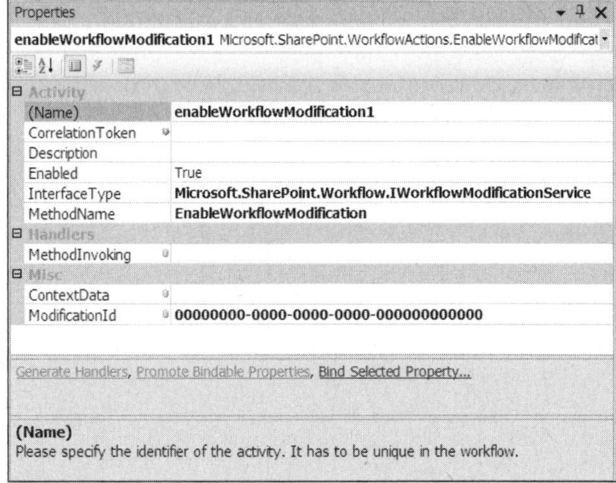

Figure 7-4

Set the correlation token name to an arbitrary name other than the correlation token names used for other activities in the workflow. Here it is set to "modificationToken." You also need to set the OwnerActivityName property to the workflow name, which is ConferenceRequestWorkflow in our case. Create a workflow field named ContextData and bind it to the ContextData property of the EnableWorkflowModification activity. Use the guidgen.exe to generate a GUID and assign it to the ModificationId property of the EnableWorkflowModification activity.

Right-click the EnableWorkflowModification activity and select Generate Handlers to generate an empty event handler for the MethodInvoking event of this activity and implement the body of this event handler like so:

```
private void enableWorkflowModification1_MethodInvoking(object sender, EventArgs e)
{
  ConferenceRequestInfo info = new ConferenceRequestInfo();
  info.EmployeeFirstName = this.EmployeeFirstName;
  info.EmployeeLastName = this.EmployeeLastName;
  info.StartingDate = this.StartingDate;
  info.EndingDate = this.EndingDate;

  using (StringWriter sw = new StringWriter())
  {
    XmlSerializer serializer = new XmlSerializer(typeof(ConferenceRequestInfo));
    serializer.Serialize(sw, info);
    this.ContextData = sw.ToString();
  }
}
```

This event handler first instantiates and populates a ConferenceRequestInfo object with the request information. Then, it uses an XmlSerializer to serialize this object into its string representation and stores this string in the ContextData workflow field. Because this workflow field is bound to the ContextData property of the EnableWorkflowModification activity, the value of this workflow field is automatically assigned to the ContextData property through activity binding. As thoroughly discussed in Chapter 4, under the hood the EnableWorkflowModification activity passes the value of this property as a parameter into the EnableWorkflowModification method of the IWorkflowModificationService service when it invokes this method.

Next, move the entire ListenActivity activity shown in Figure 7-5 inside the main part, or body, of the EventHandlingScopeActivity activity below the EnableWorkflowModification activity. The important point here is that the EnableWorkflowModification activity should be the first child activity of the body of the EventHandlerScopeActivity activity. This ensures that the IWorkflowModificationService service enables the workflow modification before the rest of the body of the EventHandlingScopeActivity activity is executed. Keep in mind that when the execution of the body of the EventHandlerScopeActivity activity is completed, SharePoint automatically disables the workflow modification.

The idea is to enable the workflow modification when the body of the EventHandlingScopeActivity activity starts its execution, and to disable the workflow modification when the body of the EventHandlingScopeActivity activity completes its execution. Enabling the workflow modification prompts SharePoint to display a link in the workflow status page. Users click this link to navigate to the workflow modification form, where they can modify the workflow instance. Disabling the workflow modification, conversely, prompts SharePoint to hide this link.

The net effect in the case of our ConferenceRequestWorkflow workflow is that the workflow modification is enabled and the link to the workflow modification form is displayed before the OnTaskChanged activity starts its execution and waits for the manager to update the task; it is disabled, and the link to the workflow modification form is not displayed, after the OnTaskChanged activity completes its execution — that is, after the manager updates the task. This enables an employee to keep modifying the request information until the manager updates the task. After that the employee is not allowed to modify this information.

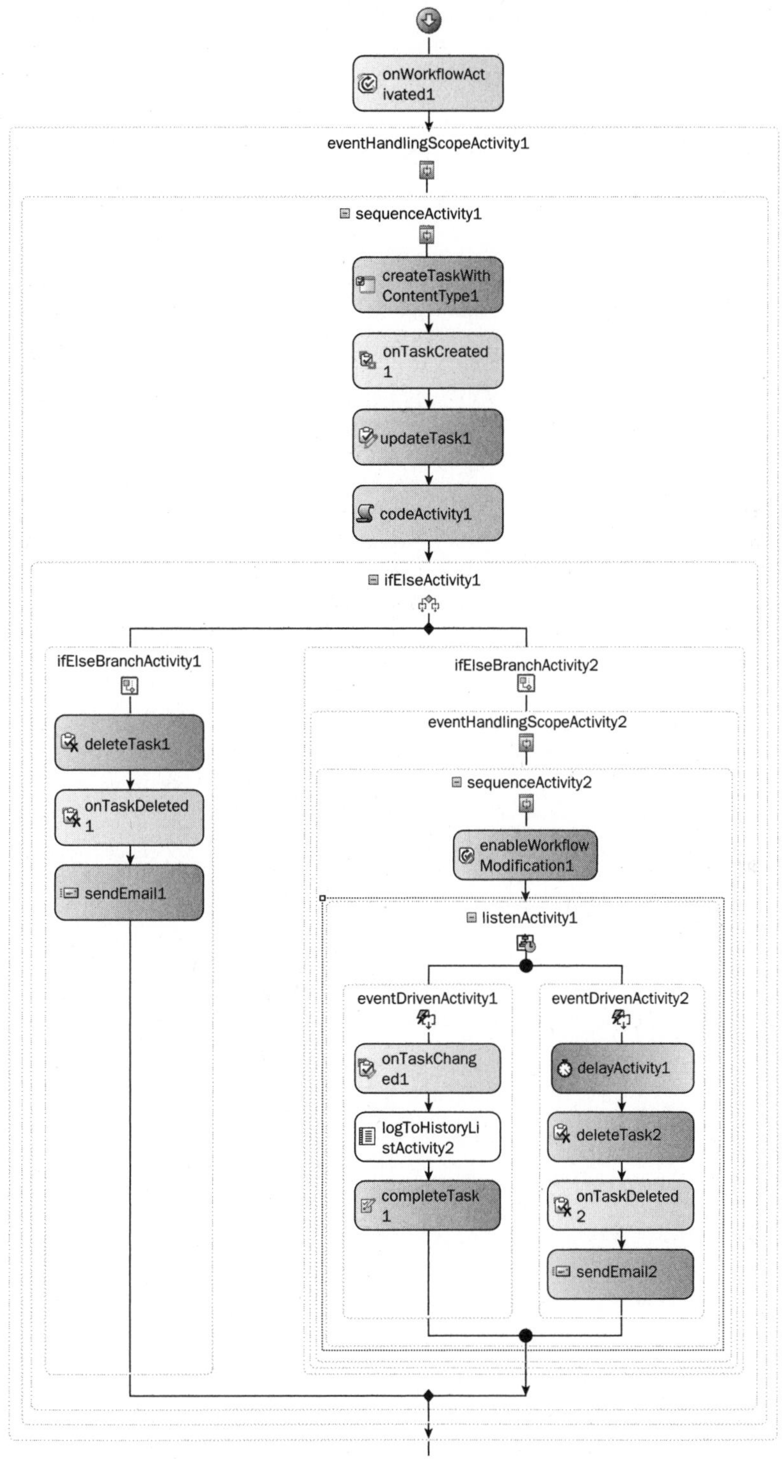
onWorkflowActivated1
eventHandlingScopeActivity1
sequenceActivity1
createTaskWithContentType1
onTaskCreated1
updateTask1
codeActivity1
ifElseActivity1
ifElseBranchActivity1
deleteTask1
onTaskDeleted1
sendEmail1
ifElseBranchActivity2
eventHandlingScopeActivity2
sequenceActivity2
enableWorkflowModification1
listenActivity1
eventDrivenActivity1
onTaskChanged1
logToHistoryListActivity2
completeTask1
eventDrivenActivity2
delayActivity1
deleteTask2
onTaskDeleted2
sendEmail2

Figure 7-5

Select the View Event Handlers option from the menu shown in Figure 7-6 to switch to the Event Handlers view of the EventHandlingScopeActivity activity.

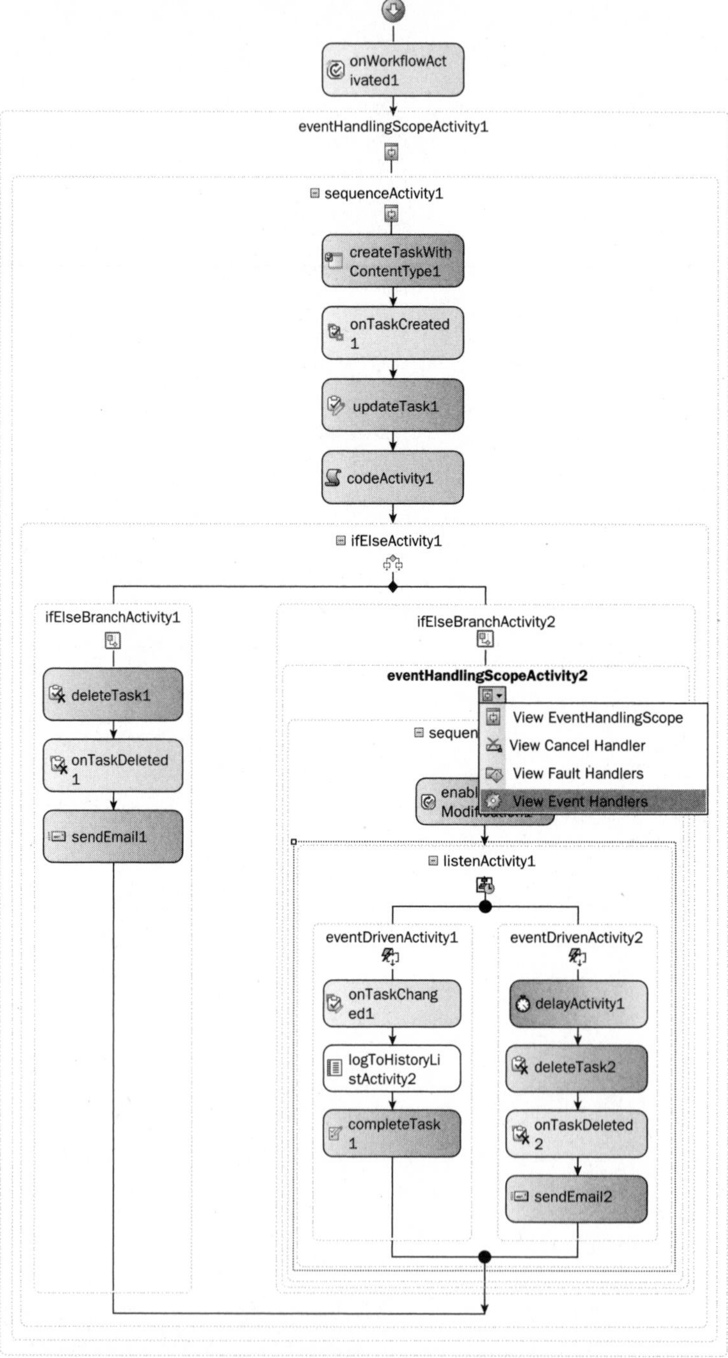

Figure 7-6

Figure 7-7 illustrates the Event Handlers view of the EventHandlingScopeActivity activity. This view basically presents the EventHandlersActivity activity of the EventHandlingScopeActivity activity. Recall that the EventHandlingScopeActivity activity contains two child activities: the main, or body, activity, which is the SequenceActivity in our case, and the EventHandlersActivity activity.

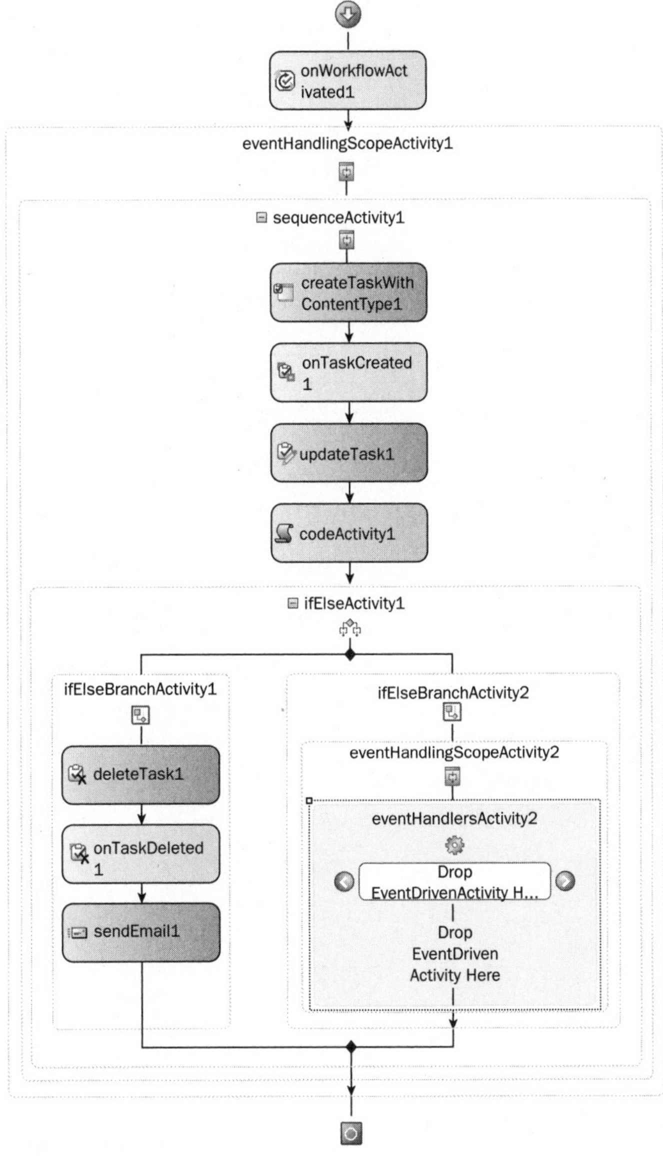

Figure 7-7

Recall that the EventHandlersActivity activity can contain zero or more EventDrivenActivity activities. Next, drag an EventDrivenActivity activity from the toolbox and drop it inside the EventHandlersActivity activity as its child activity, as Figure 7-8 illustrates.

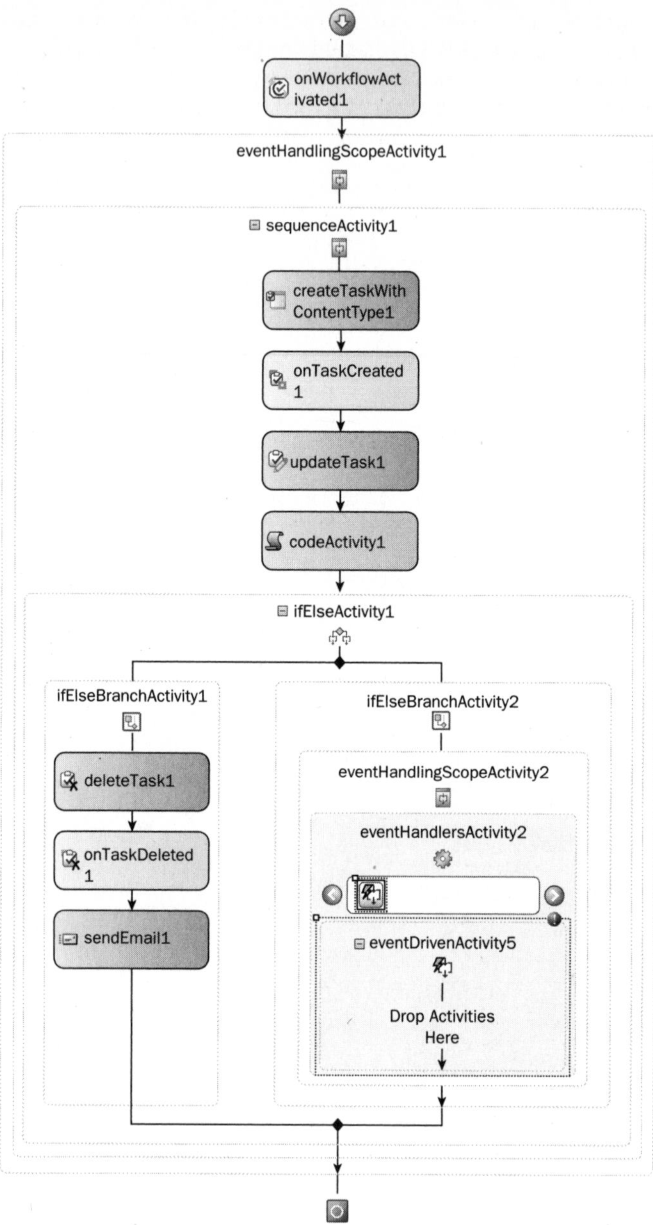

Figure 7-8

Now drag an OnWorkflowModified activity from the toolbox and drop it inside the EventDrivenActivity activity as its first child, as shown in Figure 7-9. Recall that the EventDrivenActivity activity and its child activities execute in parallel with the main, or body, activity of the EventHandlingScopeActivity activity; and that the body in this case contains the OnTaskChanged activity, which is waiting for the manager to update the task. Therefore, the net effect is that while the OnTaskChanged activity is waiting, the OnWorkflowModified activity keeps responding to the OnWorkflowModified events that the IWorkflowModificationService service raises. This service raises an OnWorkflowModified event every time the employee uses the workflow modification form and modifies the request information. The moment the manager updates the task (that is, the moment the OnTaskChanged activity receives the OnTaskChanged event from the ITaskService service), the execution of the body ofthe EventHandlingScopeActivity activity completes. When the execution of the body completes, the EventHandlingScopeActivity activity cancels any further execution of the OnWorkflowModified activity.

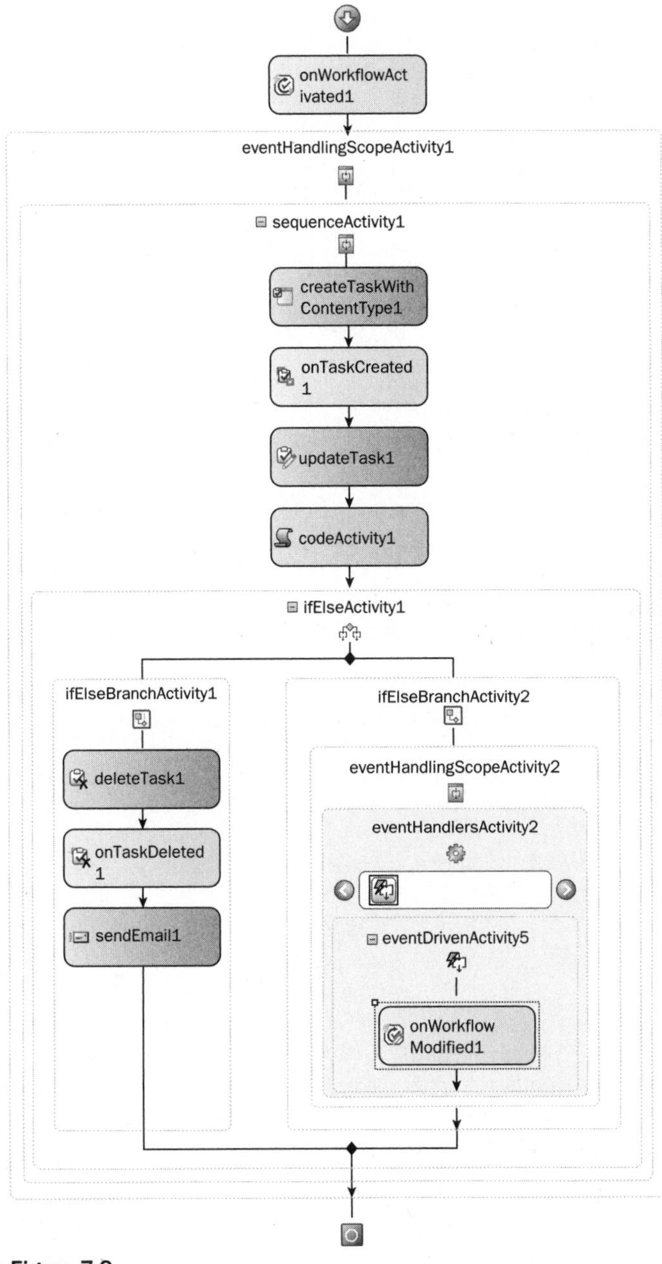

Figure 7-9

Figure 7-10 presents the properties of the OnWorkflowModified activity.

Properties

onWorkflowModified1 Microsoft.SharePoint.WorkflowActions.OnWorkflowModified

Activity	
(Name)	onWorkflowModified1
CorrelationToken	
Description	
Enabled	True
EventName	OnWorkflowModified
InterfaceType	Microsoft.SharePoint.Workflow.IWorkflowModificationService
Roles	
Handlers	
Invoked	
Misc	
ContextData	
ModificationId	00000000-0000-0000-0000-000000000000
User	

Generate Handlers, Promote Bindable Properties, Bind Selected Property...

(Name)
Please specify the identifier of the activity. It has to be unique in the workflow.

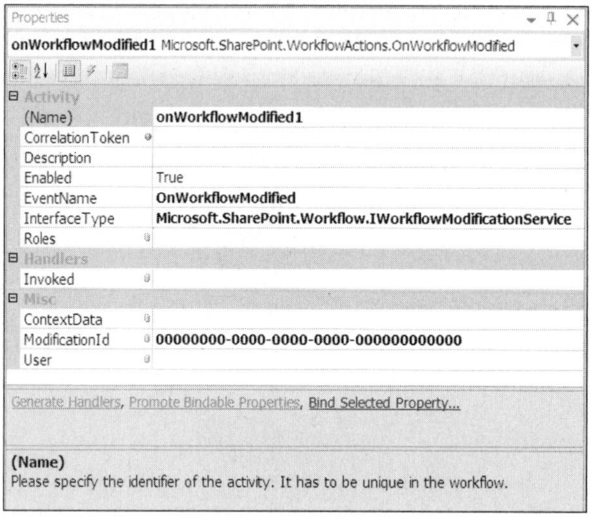

Figure 7-10

Set the same correlation token name ("workflowToken") that was used for the OnWorkflowActivated activity for the OnWorkflowModified activity, to instruct Visual Studio to assign the same CorrelationToken object that was assigned to the CorrelationToken property of the OnWorkflowActivated activity to the CorrelationToken property of the OnWorkflowModified activity. Bind the same ContextData workflow field that you bound to the ContextData property of the EnableWorkflowModification activity to the ContextData property of the OnWorkflowModified activity. Assign the same GUID that you assigned to the ModificationId property of the EnableWorkflowModification activity to the ModificationId property of the OnWorkflowModified activity. Bind the existing Executor workflow field to the User property of the OnWorkflowModified activity. The same argument regarding the user ID of the executor versus the user ID of the user who started the workflow instance applies here.

Next, right-click the OnWorkflowModified activity and select Generate Handlers to add an empty event handler for the Invoked event of this activity and implement the body of this event handler like so:

```
private void onWorkflowModified1_Invoked(object sender, ExternalDataEventArgs e)
{
  ConferenceRequestInfo info = null;

  using (StringReader sr = new StringReader(this.ContextData))
  {
    XmlSerializer serializer = new XmlSerializer(typeof(ConferenceRequestInfo));
    info = (ConferenceRequestInfo)serializer.Deserialize(sr);
  }

  this.EmployeeFirstName = info.EmployeeFirstName;
  this.EmployeeLastName = info.EmployeeLastName;
  this.StartingDate = info.StartingDate;
  this.EndingDate = info.EndingDate;
}
```

As you can see, this event handler first uses an XmlSerializer to deserialize a ConferenceRequestInfo object from the value of the ContextData property and then assigns the values of the properties of this object to the respective workflow fields. Because the OnWorkflowModified activity automatically invokes this event handler when the current workflow instance is modified, these workflow fields are always updated with the latest modifications made to the current workflow instance.

Next, drag a LogToHistoryListActivity activity from the toolbox and drop it inside the EventDrivenActivity activity below the OnWorkflowModified activity, as shown in Figure 7-11.

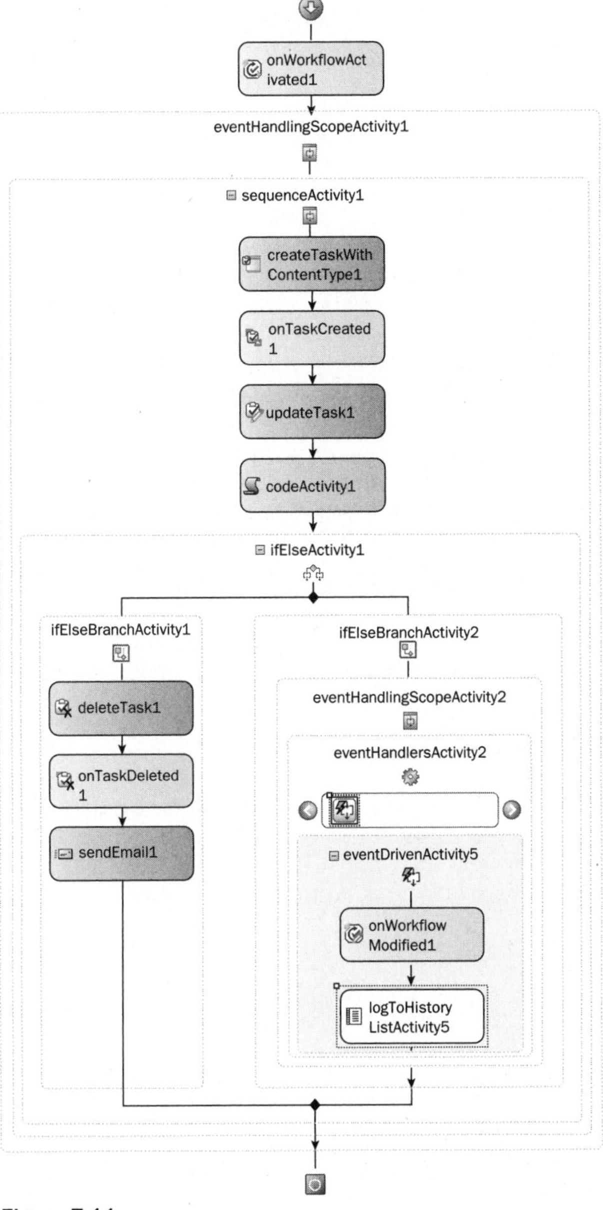

Figure 7-11

Bind the HistoryDescription, HistoryOutcome, and UserId workflow fields to the HistoryDescription, HistoryOutCome, and UserId properties of this LogToHistoryListActivity activity. Then right-click this activity and select Generate Handlers to generate an event handler for the MethodInvoking event of this activity and implement this event handler as follows:

```
private void logToHistoryListActivity5_MethodInvoking(object sender, EventArgs e)
{
  this.HistoryDescription = "Information";
  this.HistoryOutcome = "The workflow " + this.Name + " is updated!";
  SPPrincipalInfo info =
      SPUtility.ResolvePrincipal(workflowProperties.Web, this.Executor,
                                 SPPrincipalType.All, SPPrincipalSource.All,
                                 null, false);
  this.UserId = (info == null ? -1 : info.PrincipalId);
}
```

Note that this event handler logs this history event under the user ID of the actual executor of this event handler — that is, the user who modified the current workflow instance.

The event handler for the Invoked event of the OnWorkflowModified activity sets the values of the EmployeeFirstName, EmployeeLastName, StartingDate, and EndingDate workflow fields to the values of the input fields in the modification form. Next, we need to propagate these changes to the respective task fields. To do so, drag an UpdateTask activity from the toolbox and drop it onto the designer surface below the LogToHistoryListActivity activity just discussed, as shown in Figure 7-12. Then do the following:

- Set the correlation token name for this UpdateTask activity to the same name that was used for the correlation token of the CreateTaskWithContentType activity. This instructs UpdateTask to update the task that CreateTaskWithContentType created.
- Bind the existing TaskId workflow field to the TaskId property of this UpdateTask activity. Recall that the TaskId workflow field specifies the task ID of the task that CreateTaskWithContentType created. We bind this field to the TaskId property of UpdateTask because we want UpdateTask to update the task that CreateTaskWithContentType created.
- Create a new workflow field named TaskProperties3 and bind it to the TaskProperties property of this UpdateTask activity.

Next, right-click the UpdateTask activity and select Generate Handlers to add an event handler for the MethodInvoking event of this activity and implement this event handler as follows:

```
private void updateTask2_MethodInvoking(object sender, EventArgs e)
{
  this.TaskProperties3.ExtendedProperties["EmployeeFirstName"] =
                                                     this.EmployeeFirstName;
  this.TaskProperties3.ExtendedProperties["EmployeeLastName"] =
                                                      this.EmployeeLastName;
  this.TaskProperties3.ExtendedProperties["StartDate"] = this.StartingDate;
  this.TaskProperties3.ExtendedProperties["EndDate"] = this.EndingDate;
}
```

This event handler populates the TaskProperties workflow field, which is bound to the TaskProperties property of the UpdateTask activity, with the values of the EmployeeFirstName, EmployeeLastName,

StartingDate, and EndingDate workflow fields. Keep in mind that the OnWorkflowModified activity sets the values of these four workflow fields to the values of the input fields in the modification form. This means that this UpdateTask activity ends up updating the EmployeeFirstName, EmployeeLastName, StartDate, and EndDate fields of the task with the values of the respective input fields of the modification form.

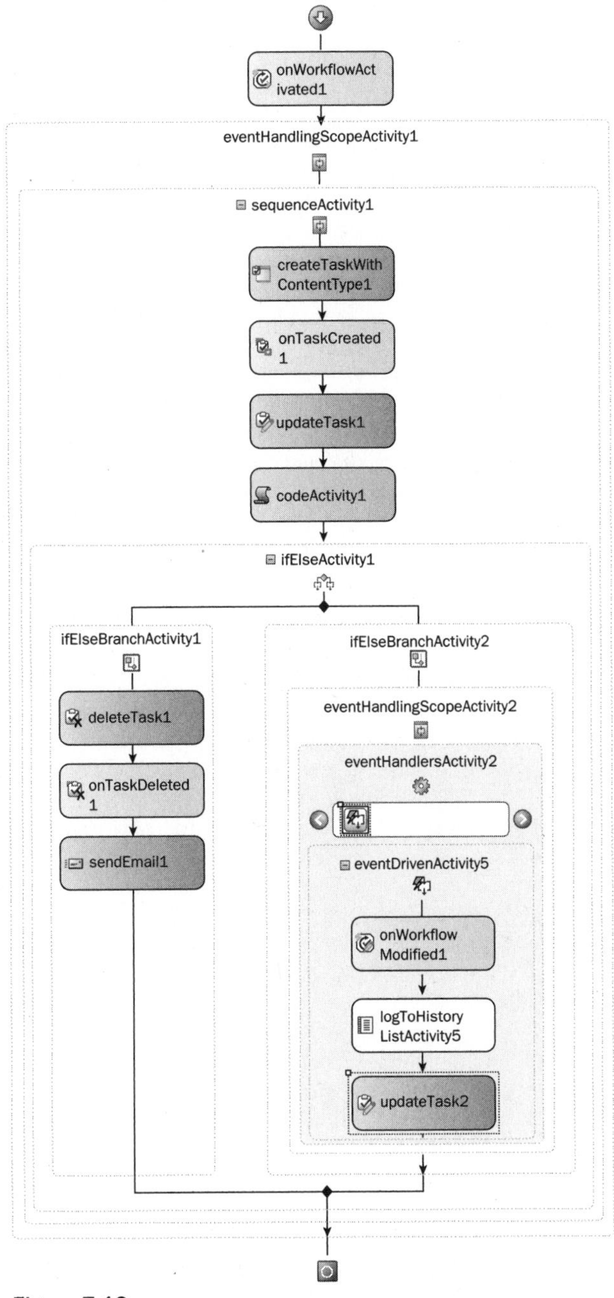

Figure 7-12

Implementing and Deploying the Workflow Modification Form

As discussed earlier, the workflow that supports workflow modification contains an EventHandlingScopeActivity activity with the following characteristics:

- The first child activity of its main, or body, activity is an EnableWorkflowModification activity. Therefore, the workflow modification with the specified modification ID is enabled as soon as the EventHandlingScopeActivity activity comes into scope. This in turn prompts SharePoint to display the link to the respective workflow modification form.
- Its main, or body, activity contains a HandleExternalEventActivity-based activity that follows the EnableWorkflowModification activity. This HandleExternalEventActivity-based activity suspends its execution and waits for an external data exchange service to fire a specified event. In our case, this HandleExternalEventActivity-based activity is an OnTaskChanged activity, which suspends its execution and waits for the ITaskService external data exchange service to fire the OnTaskChanged event.
- The first child activity of one of the EventDrivenActivity child activities of the EventHandlersActivity activity of the EventHandlingScopeActivity activity is an OnWorkflowModified activity.

As long as the HandleExternalEventActivity-derived activity is waiting for the external data exchange service to fire the event, the following is true:

- The workflow modification that the EnableWorkflowModification activity has enabled remains enabled.
- The OnWorkflowModified activity keeps responding to the OnWorkflowModified events that the IWorkflowModificationService external data exchange service raises. That is, the current workflow instance continues to be modified.

As mentioned, when the EnableWorkflowModification activity enables the workflow modification with the specified modification ID, SharePoint needs to render a link in the workflow status page for the current workflow instance. Users click this link to navigate to the workflow modification form to modify the current workflow instance. Rendering a link requires two important pieces of information: the target URL and the link title or text.

SharePoint retrieves these two pieces of information from the workflow template definition as follows: It first retrieves the value of the ModificationUrl attribute on the <Workflow> element from the workflow template definition. This attribute specifies the URL of the workflow modification form. SharePoint renders this URL as the link's target URL.

Next, SharePoint searches the child elements of the <MetaData> child element of this <Workflow> element for a child element whose name contains the specified modification ID and retrieves the text specified within the opening and closing tags of this child element. SharePoint renders this text as the link title.

Note that the <MetaData> element contains child elements whereby the name of each child element consists of three parts separated by the underscore (_) character. The first part is the keyword Modification. The second part is a modification ID, which is the GUID that uniquely identifies the respective workflow modifications. This is the same GUID that was assigned to the ModificationId properties of the EnableWorkflowModification and OnWorkflowModified activities discussed earlier. The third part is the keyword Name. Each of these child elements of the <MetaData> element specifies the name of a specific workflow modification. If your workflow supports multiple modifications, then the <MetaData> element will contain one child element for each workflow modification. Keep in mind that each workflow modification has its own modification ID.

Every workflow supports only a single workflow modification form because the URL of this modification form is provided by the ModificationUrl attribute on the <Workflow> element that defines the workflow template. However, this does not mean that every workflow must support a single workflow modification. A workflow can support multiple modifications as long as each modification has a unique modification ID. When SharePoint renders the target URL of a modification link on a workflow status page, it renders the modification ID as a query string parameter on this URL. This means that the same workflow status page can contain multiple modification links whose target URLs contain different values for the modification query string parameter. When a user clicks a modification link on a workflow status page to navigate to the modification form, the form can retrieve the value of this query string parameter and present the user with the appropriate view of the form or redirect the user to a different page.

Next, we implement a modification form for our ConferenceRequestWorkflow workflow and deploy it to SharePoint. Let's start with the workflow template definition:

```
<?xml version="1.0" encoding="utf-8" ?>
<Elements xmlns="http://schemas.microsoft.com/sharepoint/">
  <Workflow
     Name="SharePointWorkflow5"
     Description="My SharePoint Workflow"
     Id="a28a3693-7b19-4089-834d-10a6b72d5d9a"
     CodeBesideClass="SharePointWorkflow5.Workflow1"
     TaskListContentTypeId="0x01080100A3440F3CB4E74e5e8B4CF07BAEBAB9B1"
     CodeBesideAssembly="SharePointWorkflow5, Version=1.0.0.0, Culture=neutral,
                         PublicKeyToken=1c4a9ebab9f0532c"
     AssociationUrl=
        "_layouts/ConferenceRequest/ConferenceRequestWorkflowAssociationForm.aspx"
    InstantiationUrl=
        "_layouts/ConferenceRequest/ConferenceRequestWorkflowInitiationForm.aspx"
   ModificationUrl=
        "_layouts/ConferenceRequest/ConferenceRequestWorkflowModificationForm
.aspx">
<MetaData>
  <Modification_212a6a61-6ccb-4543-ba13-7d9bc6888cfc_Name>
Modify the current ConferenceRequestWorkflow instance
  </Modification_212a6a61-6ccb-4543-ba13-7d9bc6888cfc_Name>
  <StatusPageUrl>_layouts/WrkStat.aspx</StatusPageUrl>
 </MetaData>
</Workflow>
</Elements>
```

As the top boldfaced portion of this listing shows, the ModificationUrl attribute on the <Workflow> element that defines this workflow template is set to the web application-relative URL of the ConferenceRequestWorkflowModificationForm.aspx modification form. The ConferenceRequestWorkflowModificationForm.aspx modification form is a SharePoint application page, which like any other SharePoint application page is deployed to an application-specific folder (in our case the ConferenceRequest folder) under the following folder on the file system of the front-end web server:

```
Local_Drive:\Program Files\Common Files\microsoft shared\Web Server Extensions\12\
TEMPLATE\LAYOUTS
```

Because this folder is mapped to a virtual directory named _layouts in the current SharePoint web application, the ModificationUrl attribute uses the web application-relative path of this virtual directory.

As the bottom boldfaced portion of the preceding listing shows, the <MetaData> element contains an element named Modification_212a6a61-6ccb-4543-ba13-7d9bc6888cfc_Name, which contains the name of the workflow modification. SharePoint renders this name as the modification link title on the workflow status page for the current workflow instance. Note that the name of the element that contains the modification name includes the modification's ID. This has to be the same modification ID that was assigned to the ModificationId properties of the EnableWorkflowModification and OnWorkflowModified activities. This is how SharePoint knows which name maps to which workflow modification.

Next, we'll implement the ConferenceRequestWorkflowModificationForm.aspx page shown here:

```
<%@ Page Language="C#"
MasterPageFile="~/_layouts/application.master" EnableSessionState="true"
ValidateRequest="False"
Inherits="SharePointWorkflow5.ConferenceRequestWorkflowModificationForm" %>

<%@ Assembly Name="SharePointWorkflow5, Version=1.0.0.0, Culture=neutral, PublicKey
Token=1c4a9ebab9f0532c" %>

<%@ Register TagPrefix="SharePoint" Namespace="Microsoft.SharePoint.WebControls"
Assembly="Microsoft.SharePoint, Version=12.0.0.0, Culture=neutral, PublicKeyToken=7
1e9bce111e9429c" %>

<%@ Register TagPrefix="Utilities" Namespace="Microsoft.SharePoint.Utilities"
Assembly="Microsoft.SharePoint, Version=12.0.0.0, Culture=neutral, PublicKeyToken=7
1e9bce111e9429c" %>

<%@ Register TagPrefix="wssuc" TagName="InputFormSection" Src="/_controltemplates/
InputFormSection.ascx" %>

<%@ Register TagPrefix="wssuc" TagName="InputFormControl" Src="/_controltemplates/
InputFormControl.ascx" %>

<%@ Register TagPrefix="wssuc" TagName="ButtonSection" Src="/_controltemplates/
ButtonSection.ascx" %>

<asp:Content ID="Main" ContentPlaceHolderID="PlaceHolderMain" runat="server">
  <SharePoint:FormDigest ID="FormDigest1" runat="server" />
  <asp:Table CellSpacing="0" CellPadding="0" BorderWidth="0">
```

```
<wssuc:InputFormSection Title="First name"
Description="Specify first name for this workflow modification."
runat="server">
  <template_inputformcontrols>
    <wssuc:InputFormControl runat="server" LabelText="First Name:">
      <Template_Control>
        <SharePoint:InputFormTextBox ID="FirstNameTbx" Title="FirstName"
        width="300" runat="server"/>
      </Template_Control>
    </wssuc:InputFormControl>
  </template_inputformcontrols>
</wssuc:InputFormSection>

<wssuc:InputFormSection Title="Last name"
Description="Specify the last name for this workflow modification."
runat="server">
  <template_inputformcontrols>
    <wssuc:InputFormControl runat="server" LabelText="Last Name:">
      <Template_Control>
        <SharePoint:InputFormTextBox ID="LastNameTbx" Title="LastName"
        width="300" runat="server"/>
      </Template_Control>
    </wssuc:InputFormControl>
  </template_inputformcontrols>
</wssuc:InputFormSection>

<wssuc:InputFormSection Title="Starting date"
Description="Specify the starting date for this workflow modification."
runat="server">
  <template_inputformcontrols>
    <wssuc:InputFormControl runat="server" LabelText="Starting Day:">
      <Template_Control>
        <SharePoint:InputFormTextBox ID="StartingDateTbx"
        Title="StartingDate" width="300" runat="server"/>
      </Template_Control>
    </wssuc:InputFormControl>
  </template_inputformcontrols>
</wssuc:InputFormSection>

<wssuc:InputFormSection Title="Ending date"
Description="Specify the ending date for this workflow modification."
runat="server">
  <template_inputformcontrols>
    <wssuc:InputFormControl runat="server" LabelText="Ending Day:">
      <Template_Control>
        <SharePoint:InputFormTextBox ID="EndingDateTbx"
        Title="EndingDate" width="300" runat="server"/>
      </Template_Control>
    </wssuc:InputFormControl>
  </template_inputformcontrols>
</wssuc:InputFormSection>

<wssuc:ButtonSection runat="server" ShowStandardCancelButton="false">
  <template_buttons>
```

(continued)

(continued)

```
          <asp:PlaceHolder runat="server">
            <asp:Button runat="server" OnClick="OKCallback" Text="OK" />
            <asp:Button runat="server" OnClick="CancelCallback" Text="Cancel" />
          </asp:PlaceHolder>
        </template_buttons>
      </wssuc:ButtonSection>
    </asp:Table>
    </asp:Content>

  <asp:Content ID="Content1" ContentPlaceHolderID="PlaceHolderPageTitle"
  runat="server">
    <%= PlaceHolderPageTitleContent %>
  </asp:Content>

  <asp:Content ID="Content2" ContentPlaceHolderID="PlaceHolderPageTitleInTitleArea"
  runat="server">
    <%= PlaceHolderPageTitleInTitleAreaContent %>
  </asp:Content>
```

Note the following about this modification form:

- Like any other application page, it uses the application.master master file so it can have the same look and feel as other SharePoint pages:

```
MasterPageFile="~/_layouts/application.master"
```

- It uses a code-behind class named ConferenceRequestWorkflowModificationForm, which contains the logic that defines the behavior of this modification form:

```
Inherits="SharePointWorkflow5.ConferenceRequestWorkflowModificationForm"
```

- The code-behind class is compiled into a strong-named assembly and deployed to the global assembly cache:

```
<%@ Assembly Name="SharePointWorkflow5, Version=1.0.0.0, Culture=neutral, PublicKey
Token=1c4a9ebab9f0532c" %>
```

- As a best practice, you should add the code-behind file that contains the code-behind class to the workflow project to compile it into the workflow assembly. This way, the workflow assembly contains everything needed to use the workflow in SharePoint.

The following code presents the implementation of the ConferenceRequestWorkflowModificationForm code-behind class:

```
using System;
using System.IO;
using System.Text;
using System.Web;
using System.Web.UI;
using System.Web.UI.WebControls;
using System.Web.UI.HtmlControls;
```

```
using System.Xml;
using System.Xml.Serialization;
using Microsoft.SharePoint;
using Microsoft.SharePoint.Utilities;
using Microsoft.SharePoint.WebControls;
using Microsoft.SharePoint.Workflow;

namespace SharePointWorkflow5
{
  public class ConferenceRequestWorkflowModificationForm : LayoutsPageBase
  {
    protected string PlaceHolderPageTitleContent;
    protected string PlaceHolderPageTitleInTitleAreaContent;

    protected SPList targetList;
    SPListItem targetListItem;
    protected SPWorkflow workflowInstance;
    protected SPWorkflowModification workflowModification;

    protected InputFormTextBox FirstNameTbx;
    protected InputFormTextBox LastNameTbx;
    protected InputFormTextBox StartingDateTbx;
    protected InputFormTextBox EndingDateTbx;

    protected override void OnLoad(EventArgs e)
    {
      targetList = Web.Lists[new Guid(Request.Params["List"])];
      targetListItem =
                   targetList.GetItemById(int.Parse(Request.Params["ID"]));

      Guid workflowInstanceID = new Guid(Request.Params["WorkflowInstanceID"]);
      workflowInstance = targetListItem.Workflows[workflowInstanceID];
      Guid workflowModificationID = new Guid(Request.Params["ModificationID"]);
      workflowModification =
                          workflowInstance.Modifications[workflowModificationID];
      PlaceHolderPageTitleContent =
                "Modify the current ConferenceRequestWorkflow workflow instance";
      PlaceHolderPageTitleInTitleAreaContent =
                "Modify the ConferenceRequestWorkflow workflow" +
                " instance initiated on the list item " +
                  (string)targetListItem["Title"];

      if (!this.Page.IsPostBack)
      {
        ConferenceRequestInfo info = null;

        using (StringReader sr =
                         new StringReader(workflowModification.ContextData))
        {
          XmlSerializer serializer =
                              new XmlSerializer(typeof(ConferenceRequestInfo));
          info = (ConferenceRequestInfo)serializer.Deserialize(sr);
        }
```

(continued)

(continued)

```
          this.FirstNameTbx.Text = info.EmployeeFirstName;
          this.LastNameTbx.Text = info.EmployeeLastName;
          this.StartingDateTbx.Text = info.StartingDate.ToString();
          this.EndingDateTbx.Text = info.EndingDate.ToString();
        }
      }

      public void CancelCallback(object sender, EventArgs e)
      {
        SPUtility.Redirect(targetList.DefaultViewUrl, SPRedirectFlags.Default,
                           HttpContext.Current);
      }

      public void OKCallback(object sender, EventArgs e)
      {
        try
        {
          ConferenceRequestInfo info = new ConferenceRequestInfo();
          info.EmployeeFirstName = this.FirstNameTbx.Text;
          info.EmployeeLastName = this.LastNameTbx.Text;
          info.StartingDate = DateTime.Parse(this.StartingDateTbx.Text);
          info.EndingDate = DateTime.Parse(this.EndingDateTbx.Text);
          string contextData;

          using (StringWriter sw = new StringWriter())
          {
            XmlSerializer serializer =
                                new XmlSerializer(typeof(ConferenceRequestInfo));
            serializer.Serialize(sw, info);
            contextData = sw.ToString();
          }

          Web.Site.WorkflowManager.ModifyWorkflow(workflowInstance,
                                                  workflowModification,
                                                  contextData);
        }

        catch (SPException exception)
        {
           SPUtility.Redirect("Error.aspx", SPRedirectFlags.RelativeToLayoutsPage,
                              HttpContext.Current,
    "ErrorText=" + SPHttpUtility.UrlKeyValueEncode(exception.Message));
        }

        SPUtility.Redirect(targetList.DefaultViewUrl, SPRedirectFlags.Default,
                           HttpContext.Current);
      }
    }
  }
```

The ConferenceRequestWorkflowModificationForm code-behind class, like the code-behind class of any other application page, inherits from the LayoutsPageBase class. Note that this code-behind class overrides the OnLoad method as follows: First, it retrieves the value of a query string parameter named List. This value is basically the GUID of the SharePoint list on which the current workflow association was created. Next, it creates the actual Guid and uses it as an index into the Lists collection property of the SPWeb object that represents the current site to return a reference to the SPList object representing the SharePoint list:

```
targetList = Web.Lists[new Guid(Request.Params["List"])];
```

Next, OnLoad retrieves the value of a query string parameter named ID. This value is the string representation of the list item ID on which the current workflow was initiated. It then coverts this string representation into the actual ID and invokes the GetItemById method on the SPList object, passing in the ID, to return a reference to the SPListItem object that represents the list item:

```
targetListItem = targetList.GetItemById(int.Parse(Request.Params["ID"]));
```

Next, OnLoad retrieves the value of a query string parameter named WorkflowInstanceID. This value is the string representation of the workflow instance ID. OnLoad then creates the actual Guid and uses it as an index into the Workflows collection property of the SPListItem object to return a reference to the SPWorkflow object that represents the current workflow instance:

```
Guid workflowInstanceID = new Guid(Request.Params["WorkflowInstanceID"]);
workflowInstance = targetListItem.Workflows[workflowInstanceID];
```

OnLoad retrieves the value of a query string parameter named ModificationID. This value is the string representation of the modification ID of the current workflow modification. OnLoad then creates the actual Guid and uses it as an index into the Modifications collection property to return a reference to the SPWorkflowModification object that represents the current modification:

```
Guid workflowModificationID = new Guid(Request.Params["ModificationID"]);
workflowModification = workflowInstance.Modifications[workflowModificationID];
```

As shown later, the event handler for the OK button uses these SPWorkflow and SPWorkflowModification objects. That is why we've made these two variables private fields of the ConferenceRequestWorkflowModificationForm class.

Note that OnLoad takes these steps to populate the input fields of the modification form when the user accesses this form for the first time. It first accesses the value of the ContextData property of the SPWorkflowModification object that represents the current workflow modification. This is the same value that was assigned to the ContextData property of the EnableWorkflowModification activity. Recall that we took these steps within the event handler for the MethodInvoking event of this activity to set the value of this property. First, we created a ConferenceRequestInfo object and assigned the EmployeeFirstName, EmployeeLastName, StartingDate, and EndingDate workflow fields to the respective properties of this object. Then we used an XmlSerializer to serialize this object into a string. Finally, we assigned this string to the ContextData workflow field. Because this workflow field is bound to the ContextData property of the EnableWorkflowModification activity, this string is automatically assigned to this property via activity binding. The ContextData property of the SPWorkflowModification object that represents the current modification basically returns the value of the ContextData property of the EnableWorkflowModification activity.

OnLoad then deserializes a ConferenceRequestInfo object from the value of the ContextData property of the SPWorkflowModification object:

```
using (StringReader sr = new StringReader(workflowModification.ContextData))
{
  XmlSerializer serializer = new XmlSerializer(typeof(ConferenceRequestInfo));
  info = (ConferenceRequestInfo)serializer.Deserialize(sr);
}
```

Finally, OnLoad assigns the property values of this ConferenceRequestInfo object to the respective text boxes on the workflow modification form:

```
this.FirstNameTbx.Text = info.EmployeeFirstName;
this.LastNameTbx.Text = info.EmployeeLastName;
this.StartingDateTbx.Text = info.StartingDate.ToString();
this.EndingDateTbx.Text = info.EndingDate.ToString();
```

After the user makes the required changes and presses OK, the event handler for the OK event is invoked. Let's walk through the implementation of this event handler. This event handler first instantiates a ConferenceRequestInfo object and populates it with the values the user has entered into the respective text boxes on the modification form:

```
ConferenceRequestInfo info = new ConferenceRequestInfo();
info.EmployeeFirstName = this.FirstNameTbx.Text;
info.EmployeeLastName = this.LastNameTbx.Text;
info.StartingDate = DateTime.Parse(this.StartingDateTbx.Text);
info.EndingDate = DateTime.Parse(this.EndingDateTbx.Text);
```

Next, the event handler uses an XmlSerializer to serialize this ConferenceRequestInfo object into its string representation:

```
string contextData;

using (StringWriter sw = new StringWriter())
{
  XmlSerializer serializer =
                          new XmlSerializer(typeof(ConferenceRequestInfo));
  serializer.Serialize(sw, info);
  contextData = sw.ToString();
}
```

Finally, the event handler accesses a reference to the SPWorkflowManager object that the WorkflowManager property of the current site collection references, and invokes the ModifyWorkflow method on this object, passing in the SPWorkflowInstance object that represents the current workflow instance, the SPWorkflowModification object that represents the current workflow modification, and the preceding string representation. Keep in mind that this string representation contains the values of the text boxes on the workflow modification form:

```
Web.Site.WorkflowManager.ModifyWorkflow(workflowInstance,
                                        workflowModification,
                                        contextData);
```

Under the hood, the ModifyWorkflow method causes the IWorkflowModificationService external data exchange service to fire its OnWorkflowModified event, which in turn causes the OnWorkflowModified activity to resume its execution. This service passes an SPModificationEventArgs object to the activity. This object exposes a public field named data that contains the string representation just discussed (the one containing the values of the input fields on the modification form). When the OnWorkflowModified activity fires its Invoked event and consequently invokes the event handler registered for this event, it passes in the same SPModificationEventArgs object it has received from the IWorkflowModificationService service. Recall from the previous sections that this event handler accesses the value of the data public field of this object. The event handler then uses an XmlSerializer to deserialize a ConferenceRequestInfo object from the value of the data public field. Finally, this event handler assigns the values of this object's properties to the respective workflow fields. The net effect is that the values of the input fields on the modification form are automatically assigned to the respective workflow fields. In other words, the user uses the modification form to modify the values of these workflow fields.

Now run the workflow project to navigate to the page that displays the SharePoint list with which our ConferenceRequestWorkflow workflow is associated. Initiate an instance of this workflow. Then navigate to the WrkStat.aspx page for this workflow instance. You should see a modification link titled "Modify the current ConferenceRequestWorkflow instance," as shown in Figure 7-13.

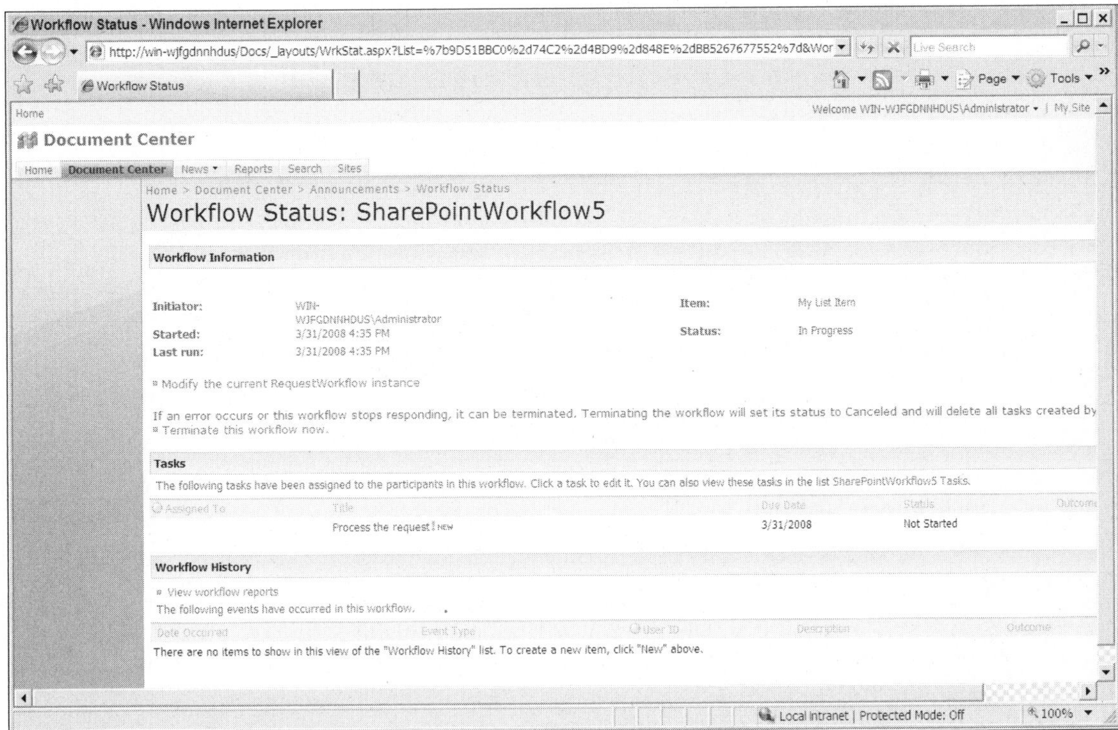

Figure 7-13

Clicking this link will take you to the ConferenceRequestWorkflowModificationForm.aspx application page shown in Figure 7-14.

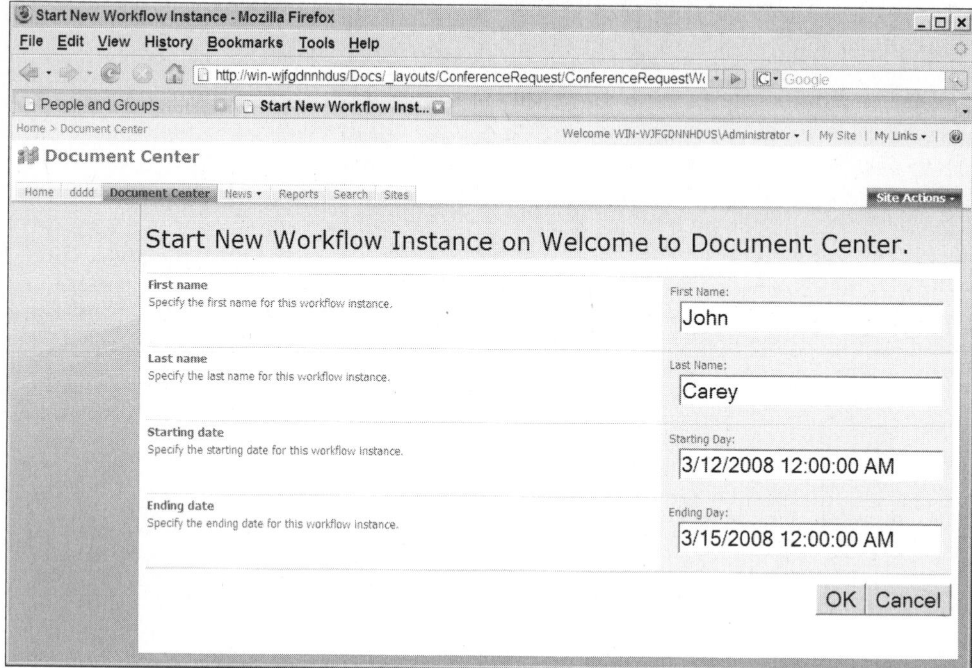

Figure 7-14

Note that the address bar of the modification form page contains the following URL:

```
http://win-wjfgdnnhdus/Docs/_layouts/ConferenceRequest/
ConferenceRequestWorkflowModificationForm.aspx?ID=11&List={9D51BBC0-74C2-
4BD9-848E-BB5267677552}&WorkflowInstanceID={D2DACFF1-0BB5-460D-8E04-84EEB2AC4871}&
Source=%2FDocs%2F%5Flayouts%2FWrkStat%2Easpx%3FList%3D%257b9D51BBC0%252d74C2%252d4BD9
%252d848E%252dBB5267677552%257d%26WorkflowInstanceID%3D%257bD2DACFF1%252d0BB5%252d4
60D%252d8E04%252d84EEB2AC4871%257d&ModificationID=212a6a61-6ccb-4543-ba13-7d9bc6888cfc
```

This URL contains the following query string parameters:

- **ID:** This has the value of 11, which is the ID of the list item on which the current workflow instance was initiated.
- **List:** This has the value of {9D51BBC0-74C2-4BD9-848E-BB5267677552}, which is the GUID of the SharePoint list with which the current workflow association is associated.
- **WorkflowInstanceID:** This has the value of {D2DACFF1-0BB5-460D-8E04-84EEB2AC4871}, which is the workflow instance ID of the current workflow instance.
- **ModificationID:** This has the value of 212a6a61-6ccb-4543-ba13-7d9bc6888cfc, which is the modification ID of the current workflow modification.

Now modify the request information shown in the modification form and click OK. The current workflow instance completes its execution. Why? The OnTaskChanged activity was waiting for the task to change, which is exactly what our modification did. As soon as you press the OK button in the workflow modification form and update the task, the ITaskService external data exchange service fires the OnTaskChanged event, which is the event that OnTaskChanged activity handles. As a result, the OnTaskChanged activity, and consequently the current workflow instance, resumed and completed its execution.

To fix this problem, drag a WhileActivity activity from the toolbox and drop it onto the designer surface below the EnableWorkflowModification activity, as shown in Figure 7-15.

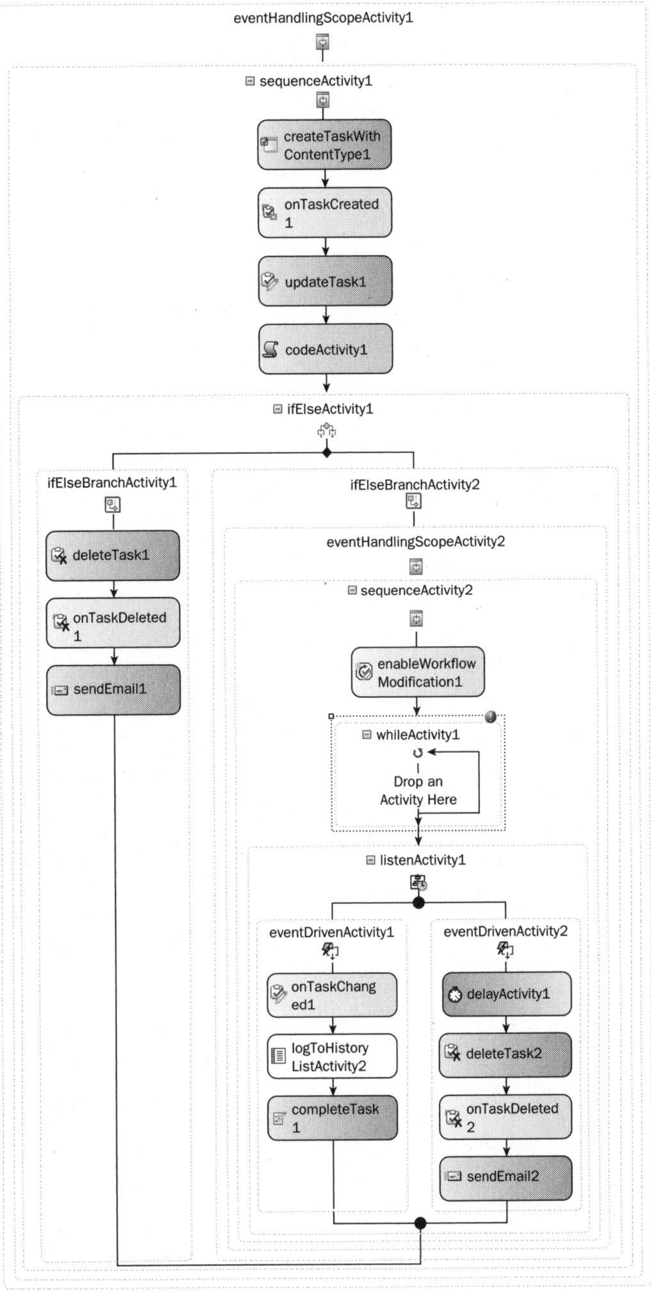

Figure 7-15

Now declare a new workflow field named IsTaskCompleted for our workflow:

```
public bool IsTaskCompleted;
```

Figure 7-16 presents the properties of the WhileActivity activity in the Properties pane. Note that this activity has a property named Condition, which must be set. Follow the same steps taken for IfElseActivity to set this property. Use the following conditional expression:

```
!this.IsTaskCompleted
```

This means that this WhileActivity activity will keep executing its child activity as long as the preceding conditional expression evaluates to true.

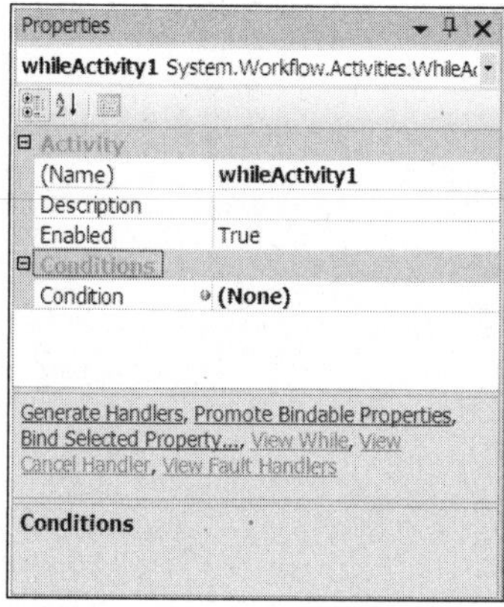

Figure 7-16

Drag the ListenActivity activity, which is located beneath this WhileActivity activity, and drop it inside this WhileActivity activity as its child activity, as shown in Figure 7-17. You should also remove the CompleteTask activity.

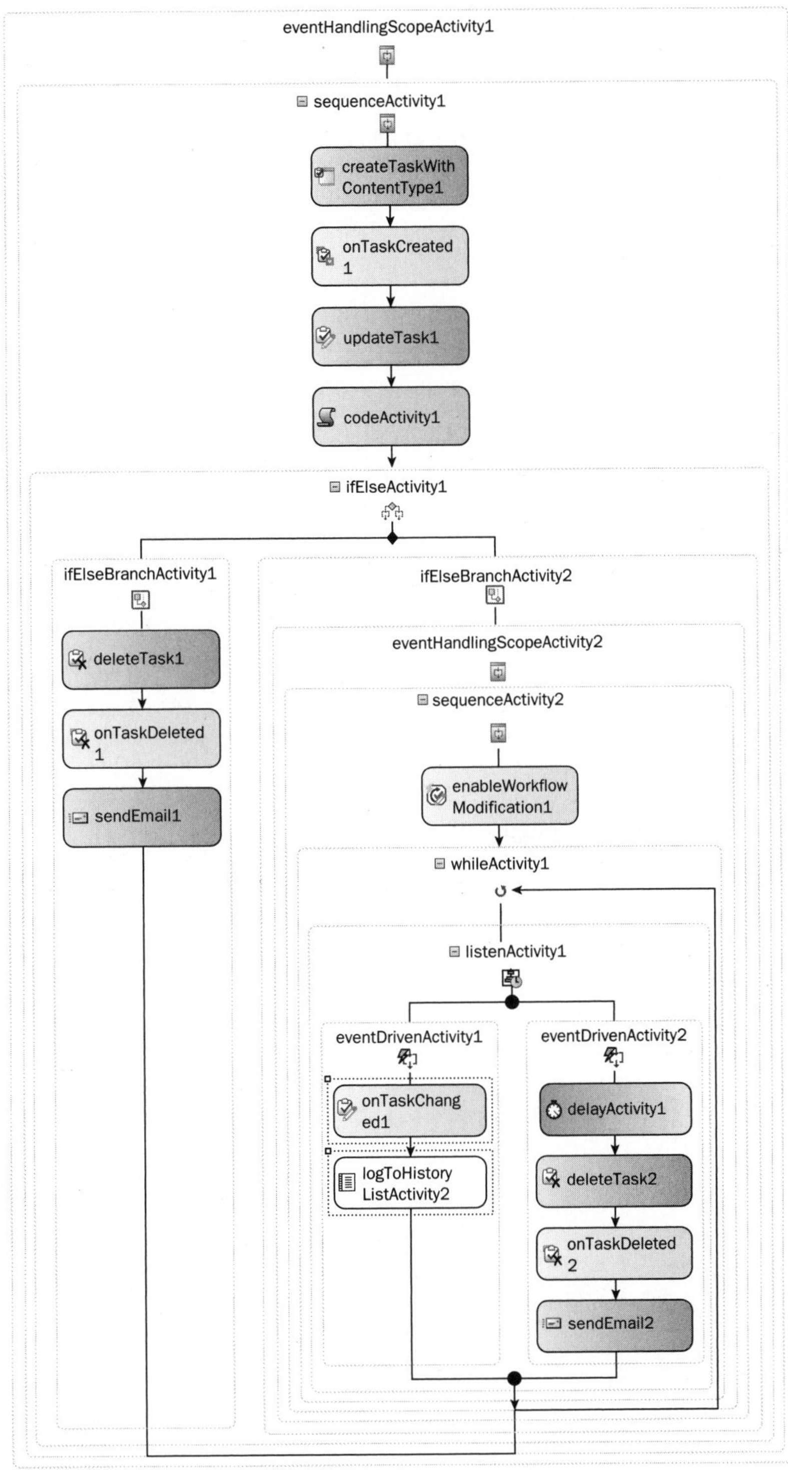
eventHandlingScopeActivity1
sequenceActivity1
createTaskWith ContentType1
onTaskCreated 1
updateTask1
codeActivity1
ifElseActivity1
ifElseBranchActivity1
deleteTask1
onTaskDeleted 1
sendEmail1
ifElseBranchActivity2
eventHandlingScopeActivity2
sequenceActivity2
enableWorkflow Modification1
whileActivity1
listenActivity1
eventDrivenActivity1
onTaskChang ed1
logToHistory ListActivity2
eventDrivenActivity2
delayActivity1
deleteTask2
onTaskDeleted 2
sendEmail2

Figure 7-17

Next, right-click the OnTaskChanged activity inside this ListenActivity activity and select Generate Handlers to add an empty event handler for the Invoked event of the OnTaskChanged activity and implement the body of this event handler like so:

```
private void onTaskChanged1_Invoked(object sender, ExternalDataEventArgs e)
{
  string taskStatus = AfterProperties.ExtendedProperties["TaskStatus"].ToString();

  if (taskStatus.Equals("Completed"))
    this.IsTaskCompleted = true;
}
```

This event handler accesses the value of the TaskStatus field of the task to determine whether the field has been set to "Completed." If so, it sets the IsTaskCompleted workflow field to true. As long as this workflow field is false, the !this.IsTaskCompleted conditional expression evaluates to true, and consequently the WhileActivity activity continues to execute. This means that as long as this workflow field is false, the OnTaskChanged activity will keep on responding to updates made to the task. Therefore, updates that do not set the TaskStatus field to Completed will not cause the current workflow instance to complete. This means that updating the task through the modification form will not cause the current workflow instance to complete because the modification form does not set the value of the TaskStatus field to Completed. This also means that the manager can now continue to update the task (e.g., continue to update a comment) as long as the manager does not change the status of the task to Completed.

What we've just discussed is a general pattern that applies to all cases for which a workflow is only interested in updates made to certain fields of a task. In these cases, you should take the following steps:

1. Declare a public Boolean workflow field with the initial value of false.
2. Place the OnTaskChanged activity inside a WhileActivity activity.
3. Set the conditional expression of the WhileActivity activity so that this activity keeps executing as long as the Boolean workflow field from Step 1 is false.
4. Add an event handler for the Invoked event of the OnTaskChanged activity. This event handler should check the values of the desired fields of the task to determine whether to set the Boolean workflow field from Step 1 to true to signal the WhileActivity activity to complete its execution.

Implementing a Workflow Edit Task Input Form

As our ConferenceRequestWorkflow workflow shows, a SharePoint workflow uses a CreateTask or CreateTaskWithContentType activity to create a SharePoint task, and then uses an OnTaskChanged activity to suspend its execution and wait for an external entity, which could be a person or another program, to update the task before it resumes its execution where it left off.

This section shows you how to develop a custom edit task form to replace the SharePoint standard edit task form (EditForm.aspx). We'll develop an application page named ManagerContentTypeEditTaskForm.aspx that does just that.

Listing 7-1 presents the implementation of this page.

Listing 7-1: The ManagerContentTypeEditTaskForm.aspx page

```
<%@ Page Language="C#"
MasterPageFile="~/_layouts/application.master" EnableSessionState="true"
ValidateRequest="False"
Inherits="SharePointWorkflow5.ManagerContentTypeEditTaskForm" %>

<%@ Assembly Name="SharePointWorkflow5, Version=1.0.0.0, Culture=neutral, PublicKey
Token=1c4a9ebab9f0532c" %>

<%@ Register TagPrefix="SharePoint" Namespace="Microsoft.SharePoint.WebControls"
Assembly="Microsoft.SharePoint, Version=12.0.0.0, Culture=neutral, PublicKeyToken=
71e9bce111e9429c" %>

<%@ Register TagPrefix="Utilities" Namespace="Microsoft.SharePoint.Utilities"
Assembly="Microsoft.SharePoint, Version=12.0.0.0, Culture=neutral, PublicKeyToken=
71e9bce111e9429c" %>

<%@ Register TagPrefix="wssuc" TagName="InputFormSection" Src="/_controltemplates/
InputFormSection.ascx" %>

<%@ Register TagPrefix="wssuc" TagName="InputFormControl" Src="/_controltemplates/
InputFormControl.ascx" %>

<%@ Register TagPrefix="wssuc" TagName="ButtonSection" Src="/_controltemplates/
ButtonSection.ascx" %>

<asp:Content ID="Main" ContentPlaceHolderID="PlaceHolderMain" runat="server">
  <SharePoint:FormDigest ID="FormDigest1" runat="server" />
  <asp:Table CellSpacing="0" CellPadding="0" BorderWidth="0">
    <wssuc:InputFormSection Title="First name"
    Description="Employee first name"
    runat="server">
      <template_inputformcontrols>
        <wssuc:InputFormControl runat="server">
          <Template_Control>
            <asp:Label ID="FirstNameLbl" font-bold="true" width="300"
            runat="server"/>
          </Template_Control>
        </wssuc:InputFormControl>
      </template_inputformcontrols>
    </wssuc:InputFormSection>

    <wssuc:InputFormSection Title="Last name"
    Description="Employee last name"
    runat="server">
      <template_inputformcontrols>
```

(continued)

Listing 7-1 *(continued)*

```
      <wssuc:InputFormControl runat="server">
        <Template_Control>
          <asp:Label ID="LastNameLbl" font-bold="true" width="300"
          runat="server"/>
        </Template_Control>
      </wssuc:InputFormControl>
    </template_inputformcontrols>
  </wssuc:InputFormSection>

  <wssuc:InputFormSection Title="Starting date"
  Description="Starting date"
  runat="server">
    <template_inputformcontrols>
      <wssuc:InputFormControl runat="server">
        <Template_Control>
          <asp:Label ID="StartingDateLbl" font-bold="true" width="300"
          runat="server"/>
        </Template_Control>
      </wssuc:InputFormControl>
    </template_inputformcontrols>
  </wssuc:InputFormSection>

  <wssuc:InputFormSection Title="Ending date"
  Description="Ending date."
  runat="server">
    <template_inputformcontrols>
      <wssuc:InputFormControl runat="server">
        <Template_Control>
          <asp:Label ID="EndingDateLbl" font-bold="true" width="300"
          runat="server"/>
        </Template_Control>
      </wssuc:InputFormControl>
    </template_inputformcontrols>
  </wssuc:InputFormSection>

  <wssuc:InputFormSection Title="Days"
  Description="Days the employee is entitled to."
  runat="server">
    <template_inputformcontrols>
      <wssuc:InputFormControl runat="server">
        <Template_Control>
          <asp:Label ID="DaysLbl" font-bold="true" width="300"
          runat="server"/>
        </Template_Control>
      </wssuc:InputFormControl>
    </template_inputformcontrols>
  </wssuc:InputFormSection>

  <wssuc:InputFormSection Title="Manager Comment"
  Description="Enter an optional comment" runat="server">
    <template_inputformcontrols>
```

```
          <wssuc:InputFormControl runat="server">
            <Template_Control>
              <SharePoint:InputFormTextBox Title="Manager Comment"
              ID="ManagerCommentTbx" runat="server" TextMode="MultiLine"
              Columns="50" Rows="6"/>
            </Template_Control>
          </wssuc:InputFormControl>
        </template_inputformcontrols>
      </wssuc:InputFormSection>

      <wssuc:ButtonSection runat="server" ShowStandardCancelButton="false">
        <template_buttons>
          <asp:PlaceHolder runat="server">
            <asp:Button runat="server" OnClick="ApproveCallback"
            Text="Approve Request" />
            <asp:Button runat="server" OnClick="DenyCallback"
            Text="Deny Request" />
            <asp:Button runat="server" OnClick="CancelCallback" Text="Cancel" />
          </asp:PlaceHolder>
        </template_buttons>
      </wssuc:ButtonSection>
    </asp:Table>
  </asp:Content>

  <asp:Content ID="Content1" ContentPlaceHolderID="PlaceHolderPageTitle"
  runat="server">
    <%= PlaceHolderPageTitleContent %>
  </asp:Content>

  <asp:Content ID="Content2" ContentPlaceHolderID="PlaceHolderPageTitleInTitleArea"
  runat="server">
    <%= PlaceHolderPageTitleInTitleAreaContent %>
  </asp:Content>
```

Because we're taking over the rendering of the entire edit task form, we have to take the required steps to render the form chrome to ensure that our custom form has the same look and feel as the rest of the pages in our site. This is easy to accomplish because our custom edit task form is an application page and, just like any other application page, uses the application.master master page. This master page renders the chrome for us. As such, the @Page directive in Listing 7-1 contains the following attribute:

```
MasterPageFile="~/_layouts/application.master"
```

Our edit task form, like any other content page, consists of several <asp:Content> tags, each providing content for a specific content placeholder in the application.master page. Specifically, our custom edit task form provides contents for the PlaceHolderMain, PlaceHolderPageTitle, and PlaceHolderPageTitleInTitleArea content placeholders.

The content that our edit task form provides for the PlaceHolderMain content placeholder consists of five labels that display the employee's first and last names, starting and ending dates, and the number of days to which the employee is entitled; a text box where the manager can enter a comment; and three buttons that enable the manager to approve or deny the request or cancel the form for now.

You must deploy the ManagerContentTypeEditTaskForm.aspx page to the LAYOUTS subfolder of the following folder on the file system of the front-end web server:

```
Local_Drive:\ProgramFiles\CommonFiles\microsoftshared\WebServerExtensions\12\TEMPLATE\LAYOUTS
```

As a best practice, you should create a folder under the LAYOUTS folder and deploy your page there, as opposed to deploying your page directly to the LAYOUTS folder itself, to avoid possible name conflicts with other pages deployed to the same folder. In our case, create a folder named ConferenceRequest under the LAYOUTS folder and deploy the ManagerContentTypeEditTaskForm.aspx page to that folder.

Note that the @Page directive in Listing 7-1 contains an Inherits attribute that specifies a code-behind class named ManagerContentTypeEditTaskForm:

```
Inherits="SharePointWorkflow5.ManagerContentTypeEditTaskForm"
```

This code-behind class is where the behavior of our edit task form is implemented. Also note that this code-behind class is compiled into a strong-named assembly and deployed to the global assembly cache. **As a best practice, you should add this code-behind class to your workflow project so it is compiled into the same assembly as your workflow.**

```
<%@ Assembly Name="SharePointWorkflow5, Version=1.0.0.0, Culture=neutral, PublicKey
Token=1c4a9ebab9f0532c" %>
```

Listing 7-2 presents the implementation of the ManagerContentTypeEditTaskForm code-behind class.

Listing 7-2: The ManagerContentTypeEditTaskForm code-behind class

```
using System;
using System.IO;
using System.Text;
using System.Web;
using System.Web.UI;
using System.Web.UI.WebControls;
using System.Web.UI.HtmlControls;
using System.Xml;
using System.Xml.Serialization;
using Microsoft.SharePoint;
using Microsoft.SharePoint.Utilities;
using Microsoft.SharePoint.WebControls;
using Microsoft.SharePoint.Workflow;
using System.Collections;

namespace SharePointWorkflow5
{
  public class ManagerContentTypeEditTaskForm : LayoutsPageBase
  {
    protected string PlaceHolderPageTitleContent;
    protected string PlaceHolderPageTitleInTitleAreaContent;

    protected SPList targetTasksList;
    SPListItem targetTask;
```

```
    protected SPWorkflow workflowInstance;
    protected SPWorkflowModification workflowModification;

    protected Label FirstNameLbl;
    protected Label LastNameLbl;
    protected Label StartingDateLbl;
    protected Label EndingDateLbl;
    protected Label DaysLbl;
    protected InputFormTextBox ManagerCommentTbx;

    protected override void OnLoad(EventArgs e)
    {
      targetTasksList = Web.Lists[new Guid(Request.Params["List"])];
      targetTask =
               targetTasksList.GetItemById(int.Parse(Request.Params["ID"]));

      PlaceHolderPageTitleContent = "Process Request";
      PlaceHolderPageTitleInTitleAreaContent = "Process Request";

      if (!this.Page.IsPostBack)
      {
        this.FirstNameLbl.Text = (string)targetTask["EmployeeFirstName"];
        this.LastNameLbl.Text = (string)targetTask["EmployeeLastName"];
        this.StartingDateLbl.Text = targetTask["StartDate"].ToString();
        this.EndingDateLbl.Text = targetTask["EndDate"].ToString();
        this.DaysLbl.Text = targetTask["Days"].ToString();
      }
    }

    public void CancelCallback(object sender, EventArgs e)
    {
      SPUtility.Redirect(targetTasksList.DefaultViewUrl, SPRedirectFlags.Default,
                         HttpContext.Current);
    }

    public void ApproveCallback(object sender, EventArgs e)
    {
      try
      {
        Hashtable taskProperties = new Hashtable();
        taskProperties["TaskStatus"] = "Completed";
        taskProperties["ManagerApproval"] = true;
        taskProperties["ManagerComment"] = this.ManagerCommentTbx.Text;
        SPWorkflowTask.AlterTask(targetTask, taskProperties, true);
      }

      catch (Exception exception)
      {
        SPUtility.Redirect("Error.aspx", SPRedirectFlags.RelativeToLayoutsPage,
                           HttpContext.Current,
  "ErrorText=" + SPHttpUtility.UrlKeyValueEncode(exception.Message));
      }

      SPUtility.Redirect(targetTasksList.DefaultViewUrl, SPRedirectFlags.Default,
                         HttpContext.Current);
```

(continued)

Listing 7-2 *(continued)*

```
      }

      public void DenyCallback(object sender, EventArgs e)
      {
        try
        {
          Hashtable taskProperties = new Hashtable();
          taskProperties["TaskStatus"] = "Completed";
          taskProperties["ManagerApproval"] = false;
          taskProperties["ManagerComment"] = this.ManagerCommentTbx.Text;
          SPWorkflowTask.AlterTask(targetTask, taskProperties, true);
        }

        catch (Exception exception)
        {
          SPUtility.Redirect("Error.aspx", SPRedirectFlags.RelativeToLayoutsPage,
                             HttpContext.Current,
   "ErrorText=" + SPHttpUtility.UrlKeyValueEncode(exception.Message));
        }

        SPUtility.Redirect(targetTasksList.DefaultViewUrl, SPRedirectFlags.Default,
                           HttpContext.Current);
      }
    }
  }
```

ManagerContentTypeEditTaskForm, like any other application page code-behind class, inherits from the LayoutsPageBase base class. This base class is fully aware of the SharePoint context within which the form is executing, such as the current site or site collection, and contains public properties such as Web and Site that expose the current SharePoint context. An application page code-behind class inherits these properties and can use them to access the current SharePoint context.

As shown in Listing 7-2, ManagerContentTypeEditTaskForm overrides the OnLoad method where it performs these tasks. First, it retrieves the value of a query string parameter named List. This value is the string representation of the GUID of the SharePoint tasks list. Next, it creates the actual Guid object that represent this GUID and uses it as an index into the Lists collection property of the SPWeb object representing the current site to return a reference to an SPList object that represents the tasks list:

```
targetTasksList = Web.Lists[new Guid(Request.Params["List"])];
```

ManagerContentTypeEditTaskForm inherits the Web property from LayoutsPageBase. This property references the SPWeb object that represents the current site. This is an example of the SharePoint contextual information referred to earlier.

Next, OnLoad accesses the value of a query string parameter named ID, which is the string representation of the current task's ID. OnLoad then converts this string into an integer and passes it into the GetItemById method of the SPList object that represents the current task list to return a reference to the SPListItem object that represents the current task:

```
targetTask = targetTasksList.GetItemById(int.Parse(Request.Params["ID"]));
```

If the page is being loaded for the first time, OnLoad accesses the values of the EmployeeFirstName, EmployeeLastName, StartDate, EndDate, and Days fields of the current task and renders them in their respective labels:

```
this.FirstNameLbl.Text = (string)targetTask["EmployeeFirstName"];
this.LastNameLbl.Text = (string)targetTask["EmployeeLastName"];
this.StartingDateLbl.Text = targetTask["StartDate"].ToString();
this.EndingDateLbl.Text = targetTask["EndDate"].ToString();
this.DaysLbl.Text = targetTask["Days"].ToString();
```

As Listing 6-1 (in the preceding chapter) shows, our custom edit task form registers methods named ApproveCallback and DenyCallback as event handlers for the Click events of the Approve and Deny buttons, respectively. As shown in Listing 7-2, both event handlers use a similar logic, which begins with instantiating a Hashtable:

```
Hashtable taskProperties = new Hashtable();
```

Then it sets the TaskStatus field of the current task to "Completed" to mark the task as completed:

```
taskProperties["TaskStatus"] = "Completed";
```

Next, it sets the ManagerApproval field of the current task to true if the Approve button is clicked. Otherwise, it sets it false:

```
taskProperties["ManagerApproval"] = true;
```

It then sets the ManagerComment field to the comment that the manager has entered the comment text box:

```
taskProperties["ManagerComment"] = this.ManagerCommentTbx.Text;
```

Finally, it invokes a static method named AlterTask to a class named SPWorkflowTask, passing in the SPListItem object that represents the current task and the Hashtable that contains the field values:

```
SPWorkflowTask.AlterTask(targetTask, taskProperties, true);
```

This method updates the current task in the content database.

So far we've implemented the ManagerContentTypeEditTaskForm.aspx page and its code-behind class. Next, we need to update the element manifest file that defines the ManagerContentType site content type to add a reference to the ManagerContentTypeEditTaskForm.aspx page. Recall that we've defined this site content type in an element manifest file named ConferenceRequestContentTypes.xml, which we deployed to the following feature-specific folder on the file system of the front-end web server:

```
Local_Drive:\Program Files\Common Files\microsoft shared\Web Server Extensions\
12\TEMPLATE\FEATURES\ConferenceRequest
```

Listing 7-3 presents an excerpt from this element manifest file.

Listing 7-3: The ManagerContentType site content type

```
<?xml version="1.0" encoding="utf-8" ?>
<Elements xmlns="http://schemas.microsoft.com/sharepoint/">
  . . .
  <ContentType
    ID="0x01080100A3440F3CB4E74e5e8B4CF07BAEBAB9B101"
    Name="ManagerContentType"
    Description="Provision a new ManagerContentType"
    Version="0"
    Group="Conference Request Content Types" >
    <FieldRefs>
      <FieldRef ID="{D90A2BE9-0230-4d0e-8C33-192CF9F54A27}" Name="ManagerComment"
      DisplayName="Manager Comment" />
      <FieldRef ID="{29BBEEC4-BE8E-4efb-9646-F4A132222B45}" Name="ManagerApproval"
      DisplayName="Manager Approval" />
    </FieldRefs>

    <XmlDocuments>
      <XmlDocument
      NamespaceURI=
    "http://schemas.microsoft.com/sharepoint/v3/contenttype/
    forms/url">
          <FormUrls
        xmlns="http://schemas.microsoft.com/sharepoint/v3/contenttype/forms/url">
            <Edit>
    _layouts/ConferenceRequest/ManagerContentTypeEditTaskForm.aspx
            </Edit>
        </FormUrls>
      </XmlDocument>
    </XmlDocuments>

  </ContentType>
  . . .
</Elements>
```

As shown in the boldfaced portion of this XML fragment, we've added an element named <XmlDocuments> as the child element of the <ContentType> element that defines the ManagerContentType site content type. This child element is the main extensibility point of a site content type. To extend a site content type, you simply add one or more <XmlDocument> child elements to the <XmlDocuments> element. You can include any valid XML document between the opening and closing tags of each <XmlDocument> child element. You can then access these XML documents through the SharePoint object model to perform whatever tasks deemed necessary.

SharePoint uses the same extensibility point of a site content type to enable you to add support for custom list item forms, including displaying list item forms, editing list item forms, and adding new list item forms for a site content type. All you need to do is the following:

1. Add an <XmlDocument> child element to the <XmlDocuments> element.
2. Add a <FormUrls> child element to the <XmlDocument> element from Step 1.
3. Add one or more of the following child elements to the <FormUrls> element from Step 2:
    - An <Edit> child element: You must specify the URL to your custom edit list item form within the opening and closing tags of this child element.
    - A <Display> child element: You must specify the URL to your custom view list item form within the opening and closing tags of this child element.
    - A <New> child element: You must specify the URL to your custom new list item form within the opening and closing tags of this child element.

In our case, we're only interested in adding support for a custom edit list item or task form. As such, the <FormUrls> element only contains the <Edit> child element to provide a reference to the ManagerContentTypeEditTaskForm.aspx application page.

Note that when you update a site content type, the update does not affect the list content types that were provisioned from the site content type. You have to either explicitly push the changes down to these list content types or remove these list content types from their lists and add the site content type back in these lists. This is because when you add a site content type to a list, SharePoint adds a local copy of the site content type definition to the list. This local copy is known as a *list content type*. As such, changes made to a site content type do not affect the list content types provisioned from it.

After propagating the changes made to our ManagerContentType site content type to the list content type provisioned from it, press F5 to run the workflow project and to navigate to the page that displays the SharePoint list with which our workflow is associated. Because we've added the file that contains the ManagerContentTypeEditTaskForm code-behind class to the workflow project, this code-behind class is compiled into the same assembly as the workflow and deployed to the global assembly cache.

Next, initiate an instance of the ConferenceRequestWorkflow workflow on a list item in this list. This should add a new task to the tasks list. Navigate to the page that displays the tasks list and select the Edit Item. SharePoint should direct you to the ManagerContentTypeEditTaskForm.aspx application page (see Figure 7-18).

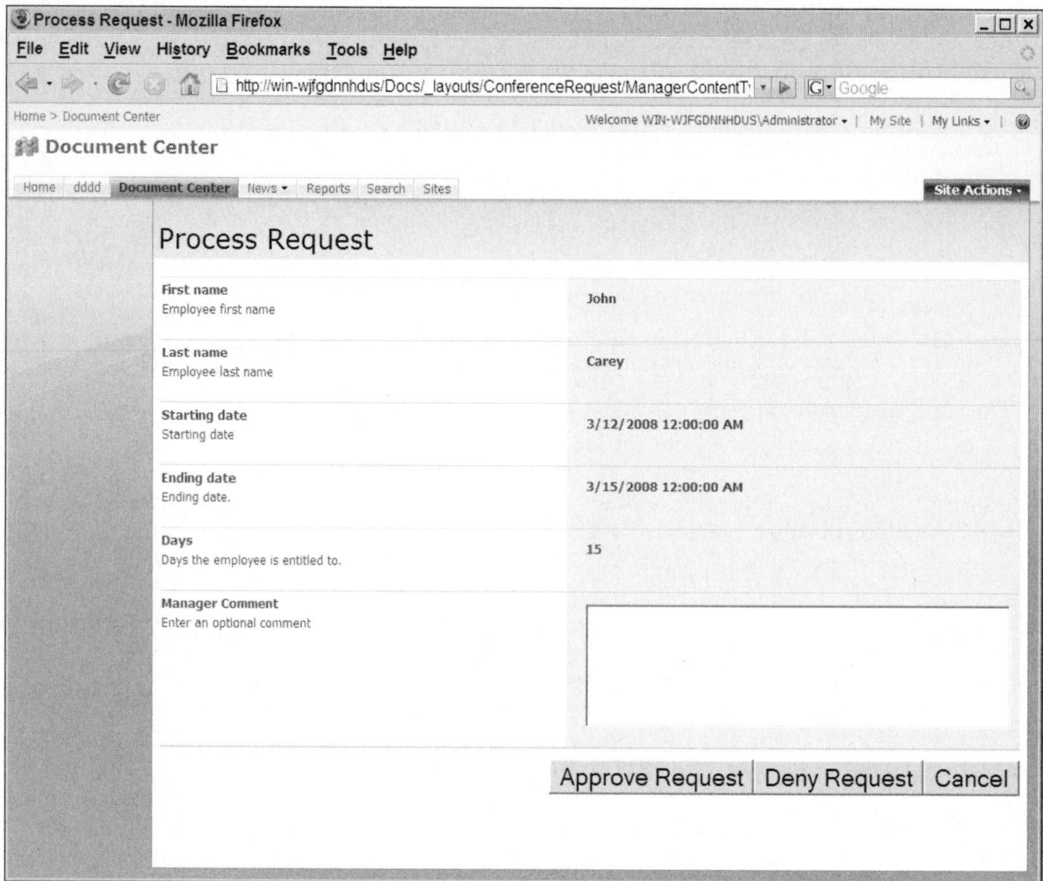

Figure 7-18

Listing 7-4 presents the complete code for the ConferenceRequestWorkflow.cs file of the ConferenceRequestWorkflow workflow that we've been implementing here and in earlier chapters.

Listing 7-4: The ConferenceRequestWorkflow.cs file

```
using System;
using System.ComponentModel;
using System.ComponentModel.Design;
using System.Collections;
using System.Drawing;
using System.Linq;
using System.Workflow.ComponentModel.Compiler;
using System.Workflow.ComponentModel.Serialization;
using System.Workflow.ComponentModel;
using System.Workflow.ComponentModel.Design;
using System.Workflow.Runtime;
using System.Workflow.Activities;
using System.Workflow.Activities.Rules;
```

```
using Microsoft.SharePoint;
using Microsoft.SharePoint.Workflow;
using Microsoft.SharePoint.WorkflowActions;
using Microsoft.Office.Workflow.Utility;
using System.Xml;
using System.Xml.Serialization;
using System.IO;
using Microsoft.SharePoint.Utilities;

namespace SharePointWorkflow5
{
  public sealed partial class Workflow1 : SequentialWorkflowActivity
  {
    public Workflow1()
    {
      InitializeComponent();
    }

    public Guid workflowId = default(System.Guid);
    public SPWorkflowActivationProperties workflowProperties =
                                          new SPWorkflowActivationProperties();
    public Guid TaskId = default(System.Guid);
    public SPWorkflowTaskProperties TaskProperties = new Microsoft.SharePoint.
Workflow.SPWorkflowTaskProperties();

    private void createTaskWithContentType1_MethodInvoking(object sender,
                                                           EventArgs e)
    {
      this.TaskId = Guid.NewGuid();
      this.TaskProperties.Title = "Process the request";
      this.TaskProperties.PercentComplete = 0;
      this.TaskProperties.DueDate = DateTime.Now.AddMinutes(2);
      this.TaskProperties.StartDate = DateTime.Now;
      this.TaskProperties.ExtendedProperties["EmployeeFirstName"] =
                                                      this.EmployeeFirstName;
      this.TaskProperties.ExtendedProperties["EmployeeLastName"] =
                                                      this.EmployeeLastName;
      this.TaskProperties.ExtendedProperties["ConferenceStartDate"] =
                                                      this.StartingDate;
      this.TaskProperties.ExtendedProperties["ConferenceEndDate"] =
                                                      this.EndingDate;


    }

    public string EmployeeFirstName = default(string);
    public string EmployeeLastName = default(string);
    public DateTime StartingDate = default(DateTime);
    public DateTime EndingDate = default(DateTime);

    private void onWorkflowActivated1_Invoked(object sender,
                                              ExternalDataEventArgs e)
    {
      ConferenceRequestInfo info = null;
```

(continued)

Listing 7-4 *(continued)*

```
        using (StringReader sr = new StringReader(workflowProperties.InitiationData))
        {
          XmlSerializer serializer =
                        new XmlSerializer(typeof(ConferenceRequestInfo));
          info = (ConferenceRequestInfo)serializer.Deserialize(sr);
        }

        this.EmployeeFirstName = info.EmployeeFirstName;
        this.EmployeeLastName = info.EmployeeLastName;
        this.StartingDate = info.StartingDate;
        this.EndingDate = info.EndingDate;
      }

      public SPWorkflowTaskProperties TaskProperties2 =
                new Microsoft.SharePoint.Workflow.SPWorkflowTaskProperties();

      private void updateTask1_MethodInvoking(object sender, EventArgs e)
      {
        this.TaskProperties2.ExtendedProperties["EntitledDays"] = 15;
      }

      private bool CancelRequest;
      private void codeActivity1_ExecuteCode(object sender, EventArgs e)
      {
        TimeSpan requestedDays = this.EndingDate - this.StartingDate;
        if (requestedDays > TimeSpan.FromDays(15))
          this.CancelRequest = true;
      }

      public String Body = default(System.String);
      public String From = default(System.String);
      public String To = default(System.String);
      public String Subject = default(System.String);

      private void sendEmail1_MethodInvoking(object sender, EventArgs e)
      {
        this.From = "EnterEmailAddress";
        this.To = "EnterEmailAddress";
        this.Subject = "Your request denied!";
        this.Body =
    "Your requested days exceeds the number of days you're entitled to!";
      }

      public String HistoryDescription = default(System.String);
      public String HistoryOutcome = default(System.String);

      private void logToHistoryListActivity1_MethodInvoking(object sender,
                                                            EventArgs e)
      {
        LogToHistoryListActivity hist = sender as LogToHistoryListActivity;
```

```
      FaultHandlerActivity fha = hist.Parent as FaultHandlerActivity;
      Exception fault = fha.Fault;
      this.HistoryDescription = fault.Message;
      this.HistoryOutcome = fault.StackTrace;
    }

    public SPWorkflowTaskProperties AfterProperties =
            new Microsoft.SharePoint.Workflow.SPWorkflowTaskProperties();
    public SPWorkflowTaskProperties BeforeProperties =
            new Microsoft.SharePoint.Workflow.SPWorkflowTaskProperties();
    public String Executor = default(System.String);
    public String TaskOutcome = default(System.String);
    public Int32 UserId = default(System.Int32);

    private void logToHistoryListActivity2_MethodInvoking(object sender,
                                                          EventArgs e)
    {
      this.HistoryDescription = "Information";
      this.HistoryOutcome = "Task " + this.TaskId.ToString() + " was updated!";
      SPPrincipalInfo info =
          SPUtility.ResolvePrincipal(workflowProperties.Web, this.Executor,
                                     SPPrincipalType.All, SPPrincipalSource.All,
                                     null, false);
      this.UserId = (info == null ? -1 : info.PrincipalId);
    }

    private void sendEmail2_MethodInvoking(object sender, EventArgs e)
    {
      this.From = "EnterEmailAddress";
      this.To = "EnterEmailAddress";
      this.Subject = "Your request canceled!";
      this.Body =
  "Your manager did not process your request within the specified timeframe!";
    }

    public SPWorkflowTaskProperties AfterProperties1 =
                   new Microsoft.SharePoint.Workflow.SPWorkflowTaskProperties();
    public String Executor1 = default(System.String);
    public SPWorkflowTaskProperties AfterProperties2 =
                   new Microsoft.SharePoint.Workflow.SPWorkflowTaskProperties();
    public String Executor2 = default(System.String);
    public SPWorkflowTaskProperties AfterProperties3 =
                   new Microsoft.SharePoint.Workflow.SPWorkflowTaskProperties();
    public String Executor3 = default(System.String);

    private void logToHistoryListActivity3_MethodInvoking(object sender,
                                                          EventArgs e)
    {
      SPPrincipalInfo info =
          SPUtility.ResolvePrincipal(workflowProperties.Web, this.Executor,
                                     SPPrincipalType.All, SPPrincipalSource.All,
                                     null, false);
      this.UserId = (info == null ? -1 : info.PrincipalId);
    }
```

(continued)

Listing 7-4 *(continued)*

```
private void onWorkflowItemChanged1_Invoked(object sender,
                                            ExternalDataEventArgs e)
{
  SPItemEventArgs args = e as SPItemEventArgs;
  Hashtable afterProperties = args.afterProperties;
  this.HistoryDescription = "Item Field Names and Values";
  this.HistoryOutcome = string.Empty;
  foreach (object key in afterProperties.Keys)
  {
    this.HistoryOutcome += key + ":";
    this.HistoryOutcome += afterProperties[key].ToString();
    this.HistoryOutcome += "#";
  }
}

private void onWorkflowItemDeleted1_Invoked(object sender,
                                            ExternalDataEventArgs e)
{

}

private void logToHistoryListActivity4_MethodInvoking(object sender,
                                                      EventArgs e)
{
  this.HistoryDescription = "Information";
  this.HistoryOutcome = "The list item was deleted!";
  SPPrincipalInfo info =
      SPUtility.ResolvePrincipal(workflowProperties.Web, this.Executor,
                           SPPrincipalType.All, SPPrincipalSource.All,
                           null, false);
        this.UserId = (info == null ? -1 : info.PrincipalId);
}

public String ContextData = default(System.String);
public bool IsTaskCompleted;

private void onWorkflowModified1_Invoked(object sender,
                                         ExternalDataEventArgs e)
{
  ConferenceRequestInfo info = null;

  using (StringReader sr = new StringReader(this.ContextData))
  {
    XmlSerializer serializer =
              new XmlSerializer(typeof(ConferenceRequestInfo));
    info = (ConferenceRequestInfo)serializer.Deserialize(sr);
  }

  this.EmployeeFirstName = info.EmployeeFirstName;
  this.EmployeeLastName = info.EmployeeLastName;
  this.StartingDate = info.StartingDate;
```

```
    this.EndingDate = info.EndingDate;
  }

  private void enableWorkflowModification1_MethodInvoking(object sender,
                                                         EventArgs e)
  {
    ConferenceRequestInfo info = new ConferenceRequestInfo();
    info.EmployeeFirstName = this.EmployeeFirstName;
    info.EmployeeLastName = this.EmployeeLastName;
    info.StartingDate = this.StartingDate;
    info.EndingDate = this.EndingDate;

    using (StringWriter sw = new StringWriter())
    {
      XmlSerializer serializer =
                new XmlSerializer(typeof(ConferenceRequestInfo));
      serializer.Serialize(sw, info);
      this.ContextData = sw.ToString();
    }
  }

  private void logToHistoryListActivity5_MethodInvoking(object sender,
                                                        EventArgs e)
  {
    this.HistoryDescription = "Information";
    this.HistoryOutcome = "The workflow " + this.Name + " is updated!";
    SPPrincipalInfo info =
        SPUtility.ResolvePrincipal(workflowProperties.Web, this.Executor,
                               SPPrincipalType.All, SPPrincipalSource.All,
                               null, false);
    this.UserId = (info == null ? -1 : info.PrincipalId);
  }

  private void onTaskChanged1_Invoked(object sender, ExternalDataEventArgs e)
  {
    Guid taskStatusGuid = new Guid("c15b34c3-ce7d-490a-b133-3f4de8801b76");
    string taskStatus =
           AfterProperties.ExtendedProperties[taskStatusGuid].ToString();
    if (taskStatus.Equals("Completed"))
      this.IsTaskCompleted = true;
  }

  public SPWorkflowTaskProperties TaskProperties3 =
          new Microsoft.SharePoint.Workflow.SPWorkflowTaskProperties();

  private void updateTask2_MethodInvoking(object sender, EventArgs e)
  {
    this.TaskProperties3.ExtendedProperties["EmployeeFirstName"] =
                                           this.EmployeeFirstName;
    this.TaskProperties3.ExtendedProperties["EmployeeLastName"] =
                                           this.EmployeeLastName;
    this.TaskProperties3.ExtendedProperties["ConferenceStartDate"] =
                                           this.StartingDate;
```

(continued)

Listing 7-4 *(continued)*

```
        this.TaskProperties3.ExtendedProperties["ConferenceEndDate"] =
                                                    this.EndingDate;
      }

    }
  }
```

Listings 7-5 presents the complete code for the ConferenceRequestWorkflow.designer.cs file of the ConferenceRequestWorkflow workflow that we've been implementing in earlier chapters.

Listing 7-5: The ConferenceRequestWorkflow.designer.cs file

```
using System;
using System.ComponentModel;
using System.ComponentModel.Design;
using System.Collections;
using System.Drawing;
using System.Reflection;
using System.Workflow.ComponentModel.Compiler;
using System.Workflow.ComponentModel.Serialization;
using System.Workflow.ComponentModel;
using System.Workflow.ComponentModel.Design;
using System.Workflow.Runtime;
using System.Workflow.Activities;
using System.Workflow.Activities.Rules;

namespace SharePointWorkflow5
{
  public sealed partial class Workflow1
  {
    #region Designer generated code

    /// <summary>
    /// Required method for Designer support - do not modify
    /// the contents of this method with the code editor.
    /// </summary>
    [System.Diagnostics.DebuggerNonUserCode]
    private void InitializeComponent()
    {
      this.CanModifyActivities = true;
      System.Workflow.ComponentModel.ActivityBind activitybind1 =
                          new System.Workflow.ComponentModel.ActivityBind();
      System.Workflow.Runtime.CorrelationToken correlationtoken1 =
                          new System.Workflow.Runtime.CorrelationToken();
      System.Workflow.ComponentModel.ActivityBind activitybind2 =
                          new System.Workflow.ComponentModel.ActivityBind();
      System.Workflow.ComponentModel.ActivityBind activitybind3 =
                          new System.Workflow.ComponentModel.ActivityBind();
      System.Workflow.ComponentModel.ActivityBind activitybind4 =
                          new System.Workflow.ComponentModel.ActivityBind();
      System.Workflow.Runtime.CorrelationToken correlationtoken2 =
                          new System.Workflow.Runtime.CorrelationToken();
```

```
System.Workflow.ComponentModel.ActivityBind activitybind5 =
                     new System.Workflow.ComponentModel.ActivityBind();
System.Workflow.ComponentModel.ActivityBind activitybind6 =
                     new System.Workflow.ComponentModel.ActivityBind();
System.Workflow.Runtime.CorrelationToken correlationtoken3 =
                     new System.Workflow.Runtime.CorrelationToken();
System.Workflow.ComponentModel.ActivityBind activitybind7 =
                     new System.Workflow.ComponentModel.ActivityBind();
System.Workflow.ComponentModel.ActivityBind activitybind8 =
                     new System.Workflow.ComponentModel.ActivityBind();
System.Workflow.ComponentModel.ActivityBind activitybind9 =
                     new System.Workflow.ComponentModel.ActivityBind();
System.Workflow.ComponentModel.ActivityBind activitybind10 =
                     new System.Workflow.ComponentModel.ActivityBind();
System.Workflow.ComponentModel.ActivityBind activitybind11 =
                     new System.Workflow.ComponentModel.ActivityBind();
System.Workflow.ComponentModel.ActivityBind activitybind12 =
                     new System.Workflow.ComponentModel.ActivityBind();
System.Workflow.Runtime.CorrelationToken correlationtoken4 =
                     new System.Workflow.Runtime.CorrelationToken();
System.Workflow.ComponentModel.ActivityBind activitybind13 =
                     new System.Workflow.ComponentModel.ActivityBind();
System.Workflow.ComponentModel.ActivityBind activitybind14 =
                     new System.Workflow.ComponentModel.ActivityBind();
System.Workflow.ComponentModel.ActivityBind activitybind15 =
                     new System.Workflow.ComponentModel.ActivityBind();
System.Workflow.ComponentModel.ActivityBind activitybind16 =
                     new System.Workflow.ComponentModel.ActivityBind();
System.Workflow.ComponentModel.ActivityBind activitybind17 =
                     new System.Workflow.ComponentModel.ActivityBind();
System.Workflow.ComponentModel.ActivityBind activitybind18 =
                     new System.Workflow.ComponentModel.ActivityBind();
System.Workflow.ComponentModel.ActivityBind activitybind19 =
                     new System.Workflow.ComponentModel.ActivityBind();
System.Workflow.ComponentModel.ActivityBind activitybind20 =
                     new System.Workflow.ComponentModel.ActivityBind();
System.Workflow.Runtime.CorrelationToken correlationtoken5 =
                     new System.Workflow.Runtime.CorrelationToken();
System.Workflow.Activities.Rules.RuleConditionReference
ruleconditionreference1 =
             new System.Workflow.Activities.Rules.RuleConditionReference();
System.Workflow.ComponentModel.ActivityBind activitybind21 =
             new System.Workflow.ComponentModel.ActivityBind();
System.Workflow.ComponentModel.ActivityBind activitybind22 =
             new System.Workflow.ComponentModel.ActivityBind();
System.Workflow.ComponentModel.ActivityBind activitybind23 =
             new System.Workflow.ComponentModel.ActivityBind();
System.Workflow.ComponentModel.ActivityBind activitybind24 =
             new System.Workflow.ComponentModel.ActivityBind();
System.Workflow.Runtime.CorrelationToken correlationtoken6 =
             new System.Workflow.Runtime.CorrelationToken();
System.Workflow.ComponentModel.ActivityBind activitybind25 =
             new System.Workflow.ComponentModel.ActivityBind();
System.Workflow.ComponentModel.ActivityBind activitybind26 =
             new System.Workflow.ComponentModel.ActivityBind();
```

(continued)

Listing 7-5 *(continued)*

```
System.Workflow.ComponentModel.ActivityBind activitybind27 =
            new System.Workflow.ComponentModel.ActivityBind();
System.Workflow.Runtime.CorrelationToken correlationtoken7 =
            new System.Workflow.Runtime.CorrelationToken();
System.Workflow.ComponentModel.ActivityBind activitybind28 =
            new System.Workflow.ComponentModel.ActivityBind();
System.Workflow.ComponentModel.ActivityBind activitybind29 =
            new System.Workflow.ComponentModel.ActivityBind();
System.Workflow.Runtime.CorrelationToken correlationtoken8 =
            new System.Workflow.Runtime.CorrelationToken();
System.Workflow.ComponentModel.ActivityBind activitybind30 =
            new System.Workflow.ComponentModel.ActivityBind();
System.Workflow.ComponentModel.ActivityBind activitybind31 =
            new System.Workflow.ComponentModel.ActivityBind();
System.Workflow.ComponentModel.ActivityBind activitybind32 =
            new System.Workflow.ComponentModel.ActivityBind();
System.Workflow.ComponentModel.ActivityBind activitybind33 =
            new System.Workflow.ComponentModel.ActivityBind();
System.Workflow.Activities.Rules.RuleConditionReference
ruleconditionreference2 =
   new System.Workflow.Activities.Rules.RuleConditionReference();
System.Workflow.Runtime.CorrelationToken correlationtoken9 =
   new System.Workflow.Runtime.CorrelationToken();
System.Workflow.ComponentModel.ActivityBind activitybind34 =
             new System.Workflow.ComponentModel.ActivityBind();
System.Workflow.ComponentModel.ActivityBind activitybind35 =
             new System.Workflow.ComponentModel.ActivityBind();
System.Workflow.ComponentModel.ActivityBind activitybind36 =
             new System.Workflow.ComponentModel.ActivityBind();
System.Workflow.Runtime.CorrelationToken correlationtoken10 =
             new System.Workflow.Runtime.CorrelationToken();
System.Workflow.ComponentModel.ActivityBind activitybind37 =
             new System.Workflow.ComponentModel.ActivityBind();
System.Workflow.ComponentModel.ActivityBind activitybind38 =
             new System.Workflow.ComponentModel.ActivityBind();
System.Workflow.Runtime.CorrelationToken correlationtoken11 =
             new System.Workflow.Runtime.CorrelationToken();
System.Workflow.ComponentModel.ActivityBind activitybind39 =
             new System.Workflow.ComponentModel.ActivityBind();
System.Workflow.ComponentModel.ActivityBind activitybind40 =
             new System.Workflow.ComponentModel.ActivityBind();
System.Workflow.ComponentModel.ActivityBind activitybind42 =
             new System.Workflow.ComponentModel.ActivityBind();
System.Workflow.Runtime.CorrelationToken correlationtoken12 =
             new System.Workflow.Runtime.CorrelationToken();
System.Workflow.ComponentModel.ActivityBind activitybind41 =
             new System.Workflow.ComponentModel.ActivityBind();
this.sendEmail2 = new Microsoft.SharePoint.WorkflowActions.SendEmail();
this.onTaskDeleted2 =
           new Microsoft.SharePoint.WorkflowActions.OnTaskDeleted();
this.deleteTask2 = new Microsoft.SharePoint.WorkflowActions.DeleteTask();
this.delayActivity1 = new System.Workflow.Activities.DelayActivity();
```

```
this.logToHistoryListActivity2 =
     new Microsoft.SharePoint.WorkflowActions.LogToHistoryListActivity();
this.onTaskChanged1 =
              new Microsoft.SharePoint.WorkflowActions.OnTaskChanged();
this.eventDrivenActivity2 =
              new System.Workflow.Activities.EventDrivenActivity();
this.eventDrivenActivity1 =
              new System.Workflow.Activities.EventDrivenActivity();
this.updateTask2 = new Microsoft.SharePoint.WorkflowActions.UpdateTask();
this.logToHistoryListActivity5 =
        new Microsoft.SharePoint.WorkflowActions.LogToHistoryListActivity();
this.onWorkflowModified1 =
        new Microsoft.SharePoint.WorkflowActions.OnWorkflowModified();
this.listenActivity1 = new System.Workflow.Activities.ListenActivity();
this.eventDrivenActivity5 =
        new System.Workflow.Activities.EventDrivenActivity();
this.whileActivity1 = new System.Workflow.Activities.WhileActivity();
this.enableWorkflowModification1 =
     new Microsoft.SharePoint.WorkflowActions.EnableWorkflowModification();
this.logToHistoryListActivity1 =
     new Microsoft.SharePoint.WorkflowActions.LogToHistoryListActivity();
this.eventHandlersActivity2 =
     new System.Workflow.Activities.EventHandlersActivity();
this.sequenceActivity2 = new System.Workflow.Activities.SequenceActivity();
this.faultHandlerActivity1 =
     new System.Workflow.ComponentModel.FaultHandlerActivity();
this.eventHandlingScopeActivity2 =
     new System.Workflow.Activities.EventHandlingScopeActivity();
this.faultHandlersActivity1 =
     new System.Workflow.ComponentModel.FaultHandlersActivity();
this.sendEmail1 = new Microsoft.SharePoint.WorkflowActions.SendEmail();
this.onTaskDeleted1 =
     new Microsoft.SharePoint.WorkflowActions.OnTaskDeleted();
this.deleteTask1 = new Microsoft.SharePoint.WorkflowActions.DeleteTask();
this.logToHistoryListActivity4 =
     new Microsoft.SharePoint.WorkflowActions.LogToHistoryListActivity();
this.onWorkflowItemDeleted1 =
     new Microsoft.SharePoint.WorkflowActions.OnWorkflowItemDeleted();
this.logToHistoryListActivity3 =
     new Microsoft.SharePoint.WorkflowActions.LogToHistoryListActivity();
this.onWorkflowItemChanged1 =
     new Microsoft.SharePoint.WorkflowActions.OnWorkflowItemChanged();
this.ifElseBranchActivity2 =
     new System.Workflow.Activities.IfElseBranchActivity();
this.ifElseBranchActivity1 =
     new System.Workflow.Activities.IfElseBranchActivity();
this.eventDrivenActivity4 =
     new System.Workflow.Activities.EventDrivenActivity();
this.eventDrivenActivity3 =
     new System.Workflow.Activities.EventDrivenActivity();
this.ifElseActivity1 = new System.Workflow.Activities.IfElseActivity();
this.codeActivity1 = new System.Workflow.Activities.CodeActivity();
this.updateTask1 = new Microsoft.SharePoint.WorkflowActions.UpdateTask();
```

(continued)

Listing 7-5 *(continued)*

```
this.onTaskCreated1 =
            new Microsoft.SharePoint.WorkflowActions.OnTaskCreated();
this.createTaskWithContentType1 =
        new Microsoft.SharePoint.WorkflowActions.CreateTaskWithContentType();
this.eventHandlersActivity1 =
        new System.Workflow.Activities.EventHandlersActivity();
this.sequenceActivity1 = new System.Workflow.Activities.SequenceActivity();
this.eventHandlingScopeActivity1 =
        new System.Workflow.Activities.EventHandlingScopeActivity();
this.onWorkflowActivated1 =
        new Microsoft.SharePoint.WorkflowActions.OnWorkflowActivated();
//
// sendEmail2
//
this.sendEmail2.BCC = null;
activitybind1.Name = "Workflow1";
activitybind1.Path = "Body";
this.sendEmail2.CC = null;
correlationtoken1.Name = "workflowToken";
correlationtoken1.OwnerActivityName = "Workflow1";
this.sendEmail2.CorrelationToken = correlationtoken1;
activitybind2.Name = "Workflow1";
activitybind2.Path = "From";
this.sendEmail2.Headers = null;
this.sendEmail2.IncludeStatus = false;
this.sendEmail2.Name = "sendEmail2";
activitybind3.Name = "Workflow1";
activitybind3.Path = "Subject";
activitybind4.Name = "Workflow1";
activitybind4.Path = "To";
this.sendEmail2.MethodInvoking +=
        new System.EventHandler(this.sendEmail2_MethodInvoking);
this.sendEmail2.SetBinding(
          Microsoft.SharePoint.WorkflowActions.SendEmail.FromProperty,
          ((System.Workflow.ComponentModel.ActivityBind)(activitybind2)));
this.sendEmail2.SetBinding(
          Microsoft.SharePoint.WorkflowActions.SendEmail.BodyProperty,
          ((System.Workflow.ComponentModel.ActivityBind)(activitybind1)));
this.sendEmail2.SetBinding(
          Microsoft.SharePoint.WorkflowActions.SendEmail.ToProperty,
          ((System.Workflow.ComponentModel.ActivityBind)(activitybind4)));
this.sendEmail2.SetBinding(
          Microsoft.SharePoint.WorkflowActions.SendEmail.SubjectProperty,
          ((System.Workflow.ComponentModel.ActivityBind)(activitybind3)));
//
// onTaskDeleted2
//
correlationtoken2.Name = "taskToken";
correlationtoken2.OwnerActivityName = "Workflow1";
this.onTaskDeleted2.CorrelationToken = correlationtoken2;
activitybind5.Name = "Workflow1";
activitybind5.Path = "Executor3";
```

```
      this.onTaskDeleted2.Name = "onTaskDeleted2";
      activitybind6.Name = "Workflow1";
      activitybind6.Path = "TaskId";
      this.onTaskDeleted2.SetBinding(Microsoft.SharePoint.WorkflowActions
.OnTaskDeleted.TaskIdProperty, ((System.Workflow.ComponentModel.ActivityBind)
(activitybind6)));
      this.onTaskDeleted2.SetBinding(Microsoft.SharePoint.WorkflowActions
.OnTaskDeleted.ExecutorProperty, ((System.Workflow.ComponentModel.ActivityBind)
(activitybind5)));
      //
      // deleteTask2
      //
      correlationtoken3.Name = "taskToken";
      correlationtoken3.OwnerActivityName = "Workflow1";
      this.deleteTask2.CorrelationToken = correlationtoken3;
      this.deleteTask2.Name = "deleteTask2";
      activitybind7.Name = "Workflow1";
      activitybind7.Path = "TaskId";
      this.deleteTask2.SetBinding(Microsoft.SharePoint.WorkflowActions.DeleteTask
.TaskIdProperty, ((System.Workflow.ComponentModel.ActivityBind)(activitybind7)));
      //
      // delayActivity1
      //
      this.delayActivity1.Name = "delayActivity1";
      this.delayActivity1.TimeoutDuration = System.TimeSpan.Parse("00:10:00");
      //
      // logToHistoryListActivity2
      //
      this.logToHistoryListActivity2.Duration =
                System.TimeSpan.Parse("-10675199.02:48:05.4775808");
      this.logToHistoryListActivity2.EventId =
        Microsoft.SharePoint.Workflow.SPWorkflowHistoryEventType.WorkflowComment;
      activitybind8.Name = "Workflow1";
      activitybind8.Path = "HistoryDescription";
      activitybind9.Name = "Workflow1";
      activitybind9.Path = "HistoryOutcome";
      this.logToHistoryListActivity2.Name = "logToHistoryListActivity2";
      this.logToHistoryListActivity2.OtherData = "";
      activitybind10.Name = "Workflow1";
      activitybind10.Path = "UserId";
      this.logToHistoryListActivity2.MethodInvoking +=
        new System.EventHandler(this.logToHistoryListActivity2_MethodInvoking);
      this.logToHistoryListActivity2.SetBinding(Microsoft.SharePoint
.WorkflowActions.LogToHistoryListActivity.HistoryDescriptionProperty,
((System.Workflow.ComponentModel.ActivityBind)(activitybind8)));
      this.logToHistoryListActivity2.SetBinding(Microsoft.SharePoint
.WorkflowActions.LogToHistoryListActivity.HistoryOutcomeProperty,
((System.Workflow.ComponentModel.ActivityBind)(activitybind9)));
```

(continued)

Listing 7-5 *(continued)*

```
        this.logToHistoryListActivity2.SetBinding(Microsoft.SharePoint
.WorkflowActions.LogToHistoryListActivity.UserIdProperty, ((System.Workflow
.ComponentModel.ActivityBind)(activitybind10)));
        //
        // onTaskChanged1
        //
        activitybind11.Name = "Workflow1";
        activitybind11.Path = "AfterProperties";
        activitybind12.Name = "Workflow1";
        activitybind12.Path = "BeforeProperties";
        correlationtoken4.Name = "taskToken";
        correlationtoken4.OwnerActivityName = "Workflow1";
        this.onTaskChanged1.CorrelationToken = correlationtoken4;
        activitybind13.Name = "Workflow1";
        activitybind13.Path = "Executor";
        this.onTaskChanged1.Name = "onTaskChanged1";
        activitybind14.Name = "Workflow1";
        activitybind14.Path = "TaskId";
        this.onTaskChanged1.Invoked +=
          new System.EventHandler<System.Workflow.Activities.ExternalDataEventArgs>(
                                                   this.onTaskChanged1_Invoked);
        this.onTaskChanged1.SetBinding(
         Microsoft.SharePoint.WorkflowActions.OnTaskChanged.BeforePropertiesProperty,
         ((System.Workflow.ComponentModel.ActivityBind)(activitybind12)));
        this.onTaskChanged1.SetBinding(
                Microsoft.SharePoint.WorkflowActions.OnTaskChanged.TaskIdProperty,
                ((System.Workflow.ComponentModel.ActivityBind)(activitybind14)));
        this.onTaskChanged1.SetBinding(
                Microsoft.SharePoint.WorkflowActions.OnTaskChanged.ExecutorProperty,
               ((System.Workflow.ComponentModel.ActivityBind)(activitybind13)));
        this.onTaskChanged1.SetBinding(
          Microsoft.SharePoint.WorkflowActions.OnTaskChanged.AfterPropertiesProperty,
         ((System.Workflow.ComponentModel.ActivityBind)(activitybind11)));
        //
        // eventDrivenActivity2
        //
        this.eventDrivenActivity2.Activities.Add(this.delayActivity1);
        this.eventDrivenActivity2.Activities.Add(this.deleteTask2);
        this.eventDrivenActivity2.Activities.Add(this.onTaskDeleted2);
        this.eventDrivenActivity2.Activities.Add(this.sendEmail2);
        this.eventDrivenActivity2.Name = "eventDrivenActivity2";
        //
        // eventDrivenActivity1
        //
        this.eventDrivenActivity1.Activities.Add(this.onTaskChanged1);
        this.eventDrivenActivity1.Activities.Add(this.logToHistoryListActivity2);
        this.eventDrivenActivity1.Name = "eventDrivenActivity1";
        //
        // updateTask2
        //
        this.updateTask2.CorrelationToken = correlationtoken4;
        this.updateTask2.Name = "updateTask2";
```

```
        activitybind15.Name = "Workflow1";
        activitybind15.Path = "TaskId";
        activitybind16.Name = "Workflow1";
        activitybind16.Path = "TaskProperties3";
        this.updateTask2.MethodInvoking +=
                    new System.EventHandler(this.updateTask2_MethodInvoking);
        this.updateTask2.SetBinding(
              Microsoft.SharePoint.WorkflowActions.UpdateTask.TaskIdProperty,
             ((System.Workflow.ComponentModel.ActivityBind)(activitybind15)));
        this.updateTask2.SetBinding(
              Microsoft.SharePoint.WorkflowActions.UpdateTask.TaskPropertiesProperty,
              ((System.Workflow.ComponentModel.ActivityBind)(activitybind16)));
        //
        // logToHistoryListActivity5
        //
        this.logToHistoryListActivity5.Duration =
                              System.TimeSpan.Parse("-10675199.02:48:05.4775808");
        this.logToHistoryListActivity5.EventId =
            Microsoft.SharePoint.Workflow.SPWorkflowHistoryEventType.WorkflowComment;
        activitybind17.Name = "Workflow1";
        activitybind17.Path = "HistoryDescription";
        activitybind18.Name = "Workflow1";
        activitybind18.Path = "HistoryOutcome";
        this.logToHistoryListActivity5.Name = "logToHistoryListActivity5";
        this.logToHistoryListActivity5.OtherData = "";
        activitybind19.Name = "Workflow1";
        activitybind19.Path = "UserId";
        this.logToHistoryListActivity5.MethodInvoking +=
          new System.EventHandler(this.logToHistoryListActivity5_MethodInvoking);
        this.logToHistoryListActivity5.SetBinding(Microsoft.SharePoint
.WorkflowActions.LogToHistoryListActivity.HistoryDescriptionProperty,
((System.Workflow.ComponentModel.ActivityBind)(activitybind17)));
        this.logToHistoryListActivity5.SetBinding(Microsoft.SharePoint
.WorkflowActions.LogToHistoryListActivity.HistoryOutcomeProperty,
((System.Workflow.ComponentModel.ActivityBind)(activitybind18)));
        this.logToHistoryListActivity5.SetBinding(Microsoft.SharePoint
.WorkflowActions.LogToHistoryListActivity.UserIdProperty, ((System.Workflow
.ComponentModel.ActivityBind)(activitybind19)));
        //
        // onWorkflowModified1
        //
        activitybind20.Name = "Workflow1";
        activitybind20.Path = "ContextData";
        correlationtoken5.Name = "modificationToken";
        correlationtoken5.OwnerActivityName = "Workflow1";
        this.onWorkflowModified1.CorrelationToken = correlationtoken5;
        this.onWorkflowModified1.ModificationId =
                         new System.Guid("212a6a61-6ccb-4543-ba13-7d9bc6888cfc");
        this.onWorkflowModified1.Name = "onWorkflowModified1";
        this.onWorkflowModified1.Invoked += new System.EventHandler<System.Workflow.
Activities.ExternalDataEventArgs>(this.onWorkflowModified1_Invoked);
```

(continued)

Listing 7-5 *(continued)*

```
        this.onWorkflowModified1.SetBinding(Microsoft.SharePoint.WorkflowActions
.OnWorkflowModified.ContextDataProperty, ((System.Workflow.ComponentModel
.ActivityBind)(activitybind20)));
        //
        // listenActivity1
        //
        this.listenActivity1.Activities.Add(this.eventDrivenActivity1);
        this.listenActivity1.Activities.Add(this.eventDrivenActivity2);
        this.listenActivity1.Name = "listenActivity1";
        //
        // eventDrivenActivity5
        //
        this.eventDrivenActivity5.Activities.Add(this.onWorkflowModified1);
        this.eventDrivenActivity5.Activities.Add(this.logToHistoryListActivity5);
        this.eventDrivenActivity5.Activities.Add(this.updateTask2);
        this.eventDrivenActivity5.Name = "eventDrivenActivity5";
        //
        // whileActivity1
        //
        this.whileActivity1.Activities.Add(this.listenActivity1);
        ruleconditionreference1.ConditionName = "Condition2";
        this.whileActivity1.Condition = ruleconditionreference1;
        this.whileActivity1.Name = "whileActivity1";
        //
        // enableWorkflowModification1
        //
        activitybind21.Name = "Workflow1";
        activitybind21.Path = "ContextData";
        this.enableWorkflowModification1.CorrelationToken = correlationtoken5;
        this.enableWorkflowModification1.ModificationId =
                    new System.Guid("212a6a61-6ccb-4543-ba13-7d9bc6888cfc");
        this.enableWorkflowModification1.Name = "enableWorkflowModification1";
        this.enableWorkflowModification1.MethodInvoking +=
            new System.EventHandler(this.enableWorkflowModification1_MethodInvoking);
        this.enableWorkflowModification1.SetBinding(Microsoft.SharePoint
.WorkflowActions.EnableWorkflowModification.ContextDataProperty, ((System.Workflow
.ComponentModel.ActivityBind)(activitybind21)));
        //
        // logToHistoryListActivity1
        //
        this.logToHistoryListActivity1.Duration =
                          System.TimeSpan.Parse("-10675199.02:48:05.4775808");
        this.logToHistoryListActivity1.EventId =
           Microsoft.SharePoint.Workflow.SPWorkflowHistoryEventType.WorkflowComment;
        activitybind22.Name = "Workflow1";
        activitybind22.Path = "HistoryDescription";
        activitybind23.Name = "Workflow1";
        activitybind23.Path = "HistoryOutcome";
        this.logToHistoryListActivity1.Name = "logToHistoryListActivity1";
        this.logToHistoryListActivity1.OtherData = "";
```

```
            this.logToHistoryListActivity1.UserId = -1;
            this.logToHistoryListActivity1.MethodInvoking +=
               new System.EventHandler(this.logToHistoryListActivity1_MethodInvoking);
            this.logToHistoryListActivity1.SetBinding(Microsoft.SharePoint
.WorkflowActions.LogToHistoryListActivity.HistoryDescriptionProperty,
((System.Workflow.ComponentModel.ActivityBind)(activitybind22)));
            this.logToHistoryListActivity1.SetBinding(Microsoft.SharePoint
.WorkflowActions.LogToHistoryListActivity.HistoryOutcomeProperty,
((System.Workflow.ComponentModel.ActivityBind)(activitybind23)));
            //
            // eventHandlersActivity2
            //
            this.eventHandlersActivity2.Activities.Add(this.eventDrivenActivity5);
            this.eventHandlersActivity2.Name = "eventHandlersActivity2";
            //
            // sequenceActivity2
            //
            this.sequenceActivity2.Activities.Add(this.enableWorkflowModification1);
            this.sequenceActivity2.Activities.Add(this.whileActivity1);
            this.sequenceActivity2.Name = "sequenceActivity2";
            //
            // faultHandlerActivity1
            //
            this.faultHandlerActivity1.Activities.Add(this.logToHistoryListActivity1);
            this.faultHandlerActivity1.FaultType = typeof(System.Exception);
            this.faultHandlerActivity1.Name = "faultHandlerActivity1";
            //
            // eventHandlingScopeActivity2
            //
            this.eventHandlingScopeActivity2.Activities.Add(this.sequenceActivity2);
            this.eventHandlingScopeActivity2.Activities.Add(this.eventHandlersActivity2);
            this.eventHandlingScopeActivity2.Name = "eventHandlingScopeActivity2";
            //
            // faultHandlersActivity1
            //
            this.faultHandlersActivity1.Activities.Add(this.faultHandlerActivity1);
            this.faultHandlersActivity1.Name = "faultHandlersActivity1";
            //
            // sendEmail1
            //
            this.sendEmail1.BCC = null;
            activitybind24.Name = "Workflow1";
            activitybind24.Path = "Body";
            this.sendEmail1.CC = null;
            correlationtoken6.Name = "workflowToken";
            correlationtoken6.OwnerActivityName = "Workflow1";
            this.sendEmail1.CorrelationToken = correlationtoken6;
            activitybind25.Name = "Workflow1";
            activitybind25.Path = "From";
            this.sendEmail1.Headers = null;
            this.sendEmail1.IncludeStatus = false;
            this.sendEmail1.Name = "sendEmail1";
```

(continued)

Listing 7-5 *(continued)*

```
activitybind26.Name = "Workflow1";
activitybind26.Path = "Subject";
activitybind27.Name = "Workflow1";
activitybind27.Path = "To";
this.sendEmail1.MethodInvoking +=
            new System.EventHandler(this.sendEmail1_MethodInvoking);
this.sendEmail1.SetBinding(
       Microsoft.SharePoint.WorkflowActions.SendEmail.FromProperty,
       ((System.Workflow.ComponentModel.ActivityBind)(activitybind25)));
this.sendEmail1.SetBinding(
       Microsoft.SharePoint.WorkflowActions.SendEmail.BodyProperty,
      ((System.Workflow.ComponentModel.ActivityBind)(activitybind24)));
this.sendEmail1.SetBinding(
     Microsoft.SharePoint.WorkflowActions.SendEmail.ToProperty,
     ((System.Workflow.ComponentModel.ActivityBind)(activitybind27)));
this.sendEmail1.SetBinding(
       Microsoft.SharePoint.WorkflowActions.SendEmail.SubjectProperty,
      ((System.Workflow.ComponentModel.ActivityBind)(activitybind26)));
//
// onTaskDeleted1
//
correlationtoken7.Name = "taskToken";
correlationtoken7.OwnerActivityName = "Workflow1";
this.onTaskDeleted1.CorrelationToken = correlationtoken7;
activitybind28.Name = "Workflow1";
activitybind28.Path = "Executor2";
this.onTaskDeleted1.Name = "onTaskDeleted1";
activitybind29.Name = "Workflow1";
activitybind29.Path = "TaskId";
this.onTaskDeleted1.SetBinding(
     Microsoft.SharePoint.WorkflowActions.OnTaskDeleted.TaskIdProperty,
    ((System.Workflow.ComponentModel.ActivityBind)(activitybind29)));
this.onTaskDeleted1.SetBinding(
     Microsoft.SharePoint.WorkflowActions.OnTaskDeleted.ExecutorProperty,
    ((System.Workflow.ComponentModel.ActivityBind)(activitybind28)));
//
// deleteTask1
//
correlationtoken8.Name = "taskToken";
correlationtoken8.OwnerActivityName = "Workflow1";
this.deleteTask1.CorrelationToken = correlationtoken8;
this.deleteTask1.Name = "deleteTask1";
activitybind30.Name = "Workflow1";
activitybind30.Path = "TaskId";
this.deleteTask1.SetBinding(
       Microsoft.SharePoint.WorkflowActions.DeleteTask.TaskIdProperty,
      ((System.Workflow.ComponentModel.ActivityBind)(activitybind30)));
//
// logToHistoryListActivity4
//
this.logToHistoryListActivity4.Duration =
              System.TimeSpan.Parse("-10675199.02:48:05.4775808");
```

```
        this.logToHistoryListActivity4.EventId =
            Microsoft.SharePoint.Workflow.SPWorkflowHistoryEventType.WorkflowComment;
        this.logToHistoryListActivity4.HistoryDescription = "";
        this.logToHistoryListActivity4.HistoryOutcome = "";
        this.logToHistoryListActivity4.Name = "logToHistoryListActivity4";
        this.logToHistoryListActivity4.OtherData = "";
        this.logToHistoryListActivity4.UserId = -1;
        this.logToHistoryListActivity4.MethodInvoking +=
            new System.EventHandler(this.logToHistoryListActivity4_MethodInvoking);
        //
        // onWorkflowItemDeleted1
        //
        this.onWorkflowItemDeleted1.CorrelationToken = correlationtoken6;
        this.onWorkflowItemDeleted1.Name = "onWorkflowItemDeleted1";
        this.onWorkflowItemDeleted1.Invoked += new System.EventHandler
<System.Workflow.Activities.ExternalDataEventArgs>(this.onWorkflowItemDeleted1_
Invoked);
        //
        // logToHistoryListActivity3
        //
        this.logToHistoryListActivity3.Duration =
                System.TimeSpan.Parse("-10675199.02:48:05.4775808");
        this.logToHistoryListActivity3.EventId =
           Microsoft.SharePoint.Workflow.SPWorkflowHistoryEventType.WorkflowComment;
        activitybind31.Name = "Workflow1";
        activitybind31.Path = "HistoryDescription";
        activitybind32.Name = "Workflow1";
        activitybind32.Path = "HistoryOutcome";
        this.logToHistoryListActivity3.Name = "logToHistoryListActivity3";
        this.logToHistoryListActivity3.OtherData = "";
        activitybind33.Name = "Workflow1";
        activitybind33.Path = "UserId";
        this.logToHistoryListActivity3.MethodInvoking +=
          new System.EventHandler(this.logToHistoryListActivity3_MethodInvoking);
        this.logToHistoryListActivity3.SetBinding(
Microsoft.SharePoint.WorkflowActions.LogToHistoryListActivity.
HistoryDescriptionProperty, ((System.Workflow.ComponentModel.ActivityBind)(activity
bind31)));
        this.logToHistoryListActivity3.SetBinding(Microsoft.SharePoint
.WorkflowActions.LogToHistoryListActivity.HistoryOutcomeProperty,
((System.Workflow.ComponentModel.ActivityBind)(activitybind32)));
        this.logToHistoryListActivity3.SetBinding(Microsoft.SharePoint
.WorkflowActions.LogToHistoryListActivity.UserIdProperty, ((System.Workflow
.ComponentModel.ActivityBind)(activitybind33)));
        //
        // onWorkflowItemChanged1
        //
        this.onWorkflowItemChanged1.AfterProperties = null;
        this.onWorkflowItemChanged1.BeforeProperties = null;
        this.onWorkflowItemChanged1.CorrelationToken = correlationtoken6;
        this.onWorkflowItemChanged1.Name = "onWorkflowItemChanged1";
```

(continued)

Listing 7-5 *(continued)*

```
        this.onWorkflowItemChanged1.Invoked += new System.EventHandler
<System.Workflow.Activities.ExternalDataEventArgs>(this.onWorkflowItemChanged1_
Invoked);
        //
        // ifElseBranchActivity2
        //
        this.ifElseBranchActivity2.Activities.Add(this.eventHandlingScopeActivity2);
        this.ifElseBranchActivity2.Name = "ifElseBranchActivity2";
        //
        // ifElseBranchActivity1
        //
        this.ifElseBranchActivity1.Activities.Add(this.deleteTask1);
        this.ifElseBranchActivity1.Activities.Add(this.onTaskDeleted1);
        this.ifElseBranchActivity1.Activities.Add(this.sendEmail1);
        this.ifElseBranchActivity1.Activities.Add(this.faultHandlersActivity1);
        ruleconditionreference2.ConditionName = "Condition1";
        this.ifElseBranchActivity1.Condition = ruleconditionreference2;
        this.ifElseBranchActivity1.Name = "ifElseBranchActivity1";
        //
        // eventDrivenActivity4
        //
        this.eventDrivenActivity4.Activities.Add(this.onWorkflowItemDeleted1);
        this.eventDrivenActivity4.Activities.Add(this.logToHistoryListActivity4);
        this.eventDrivenActivity4.Name = "eventDrivenActivity4";
        //
        // eventDrivenActivity3
        //
        this.eventDrivenActivity3.Activities.Add(this.onWorkflowItemChanged1);
        this.eventDrivenActivity3.Activities.Add(this.logToHistoryListActivity3);
        this.eventDrivenActivity3.Name = "eventDrivenActivity3";
        //
        // ifElseActivity1
        //
        this.ifElseActivity1.Activities.Add(this.ifElseBranchActivity1);
        this.ifElseActivity1.Activities.Add(this.ifElseBranchActivity2);
        this.ifElseActivity1.Name = "ifElseActivity1";
        //
        // codeActivity1
        //
        this.codeActivity1.Name = "codeActivity1";
        this.codeActivity1.ExecuteCode +=
                new System.EventHandler(this.codeActivity1_ExecuteCode);
        //
        // updateTask1
        //
        correlationtoken9.Name = "taskToken";
        correlationtoken9.OwnerActivityName = "Workflow1";
        this.updateTask1.CorrelationToken = correlationtoken9;
        this.updateTask1.Name = "updateTask1";
        activitybind34.Name = "Workflow1";
        activitybind34.Path = "TaskId";
        activitybind35.Name = "Workflow1";
        activitybind35.Path = "TaskProperties2";
```

```
      this.updateTask1.MethodInvoking +=
              new System.EventHandler(this.updateTask1_MethodInvoking);
      this.updateTask1.SetBinding(
         Microsoft.SharePoint.WorkflowActions.UpdateTask.TaskPropertiesProperty,
        ((System.Workflow.ComponentModel.ActivityBind)(activitybind35)));
      this.updateTask1.SetBinding(
         Microsoft.SharePoint.WorkflowActions.UpdateTask.TaskIdProperty,
        ((System.Workflow.ComponentModel.ActivityBind)(activitybind34)));
      //
      // onTaskCreated1
      //
      activitybind36.Name = "Workflow1";
      activitybind36.Path = "AfterProperties1";
      correlationtoken10.Name = "taskToken";
      correlationtoken10.OwnerActivityName = "Workflow1";
      this.onTaskCreated1.CorrelationToken = correlationtoken10;
      activitybind37.Name = "Workflow1";
      activitybind37.Path = "Executor1";
      this.onTaskCreated1.Name = "onTaskCreated1";
      activitybind38.Name = "Workflow1";
      activitybind38.Path = "TaskId";
      this.onTaskCreated1.SetBinding(
           Microsoft.SharePoint.WorkflowActions.OnTaskCreated.TaskIdProperty,
          ((System.Workflow.ComponentModel.ActivityBind)(activitybind38)));
      this.onTaskCreated1.SetBinding(
             Microsoft.SharePoint.WorkflowActions.OnTaskCreated.ExecutorProperty,
            ((System.Workflow.ComponentModel.ActivityBind)(activitybind37)));
      this.onTaskCreated1.SetBinding(
        Microsoft.SharePoint.WorkflowActions.OnTaskCreated.AfterPropertiesProperty,
        ((System.Workflow.ComponentModel.ActivityBind)(activitybind36)));
      //
      // createTaskWithContentType1
      //
      this.createTaskWithContentType1.ContentTypeId =
 "0x01080100A3440F3CB4E74e5e8B4CF07BAEBAB9B101";
      correlationtoken11.Name = "taskToken";
      correlationtoken11.OwnerActivityName = "Workflow1";
      this.createTaskWithContentType1.CorrelationToken = correlationtoken11;
      this.createTaskWithContentType1.ListItemId = -1;
      this.createTaskWithContentType1.Name = "createTaskWithContentType1";
      this.createTaskWithContentType1.SpecialPermissions = null;
      activitybind39.Name = "Workflow1";
      activitybind39.Path = "TaskId";
      activitybind40.Name = "Workflow1";
      activitybind40.Path = "TaskProperties";
      this.createTaskWithContentType1.MethodInvoking +=
        new System.EventHandler(this.createTaskWithContentType1_MethodInvoking);
      this.createTaskWithContentType1.SetBinding(Microsoft.SharePoint
.WorkflowActions.CreateTaskWithContentType.TaskPropertiesProperty,
((System.Workflow.ComponentModel.ActivityBind)(activitybind40)));
```

(continued)

Listing 7-5 *(continued)*

```
        this.createTaskWithContentType1.SetBinding(Microsoft.SharePoint
.WorkflowActions.CreateTaskWithContentType.TaskIdProperty, ((System.Workflow
.ComponentModel.ActivityBind)(activitybind39)));
        //
        // eventHandlersActivity1
        //
        this.eventHandlersActivity1.Activities.Add(this.eventDrivenActivity3);
        this.eventHandlersActivity1.Activities.Add(this.eventDrivenActivity4);
        this.eventHandlersActivity1.Name = "eventHandlersActivity1";
        //
        // sequenceActivity1
        //
        this.sequenceActivity1.Activities.Add(this.createTaskWithContentType1);
        this.sequenceActivity1.Activities.Add(this.onTaskCreated1);
        this.sequenceActivity1.Activities.Add(this.updateTask1);
        this.sequenceActivity1.Activities.Add(this.codeActivity1);
        this.sequenceActivity1.Activities.Add(this.ifElseActivity1);
        this.sequenceActivity1.Name = "sequenceActivity1";
        //
        // eventHandlingScopeActivity1
        //
        this.eventHandlingScopeActivity1.Activities.Add(this.sequenceActivity1);
        this.eventHandlingScopeActivity1.Activities.Add(this.eventHandlersActivity1);
        this.eventHandlingScopeActivity1.Name = "eventHandlingScopeActivity1";
        activitybind42.Name = "Workflow1";
        activitybind42.Path = "workflowId";
        //
        // onWorkflowActivated1
        //
        correlationtoken12.Name = "workflowToken";
        correlationtoken12.OwnerActivityName = "Workflow1";
        this.onWorkflowActivated1.CorrelationToken = correlationtoken12;
        this.onWorkflowActivated1.EventName = "OnWorkflowActivated";
        this.onWorkflowActivated1.Name = "onWorkflowActivated1";
        activitybind41.Name = "Workflow1";
        activitybind41.Path = "workflowProperties";
        this.onWorkflowActivated1.Invoked += new System.EventHandler<System.Workflow
.Activities.ExternalDataEventArgs>(this.onWorkflowActivated1_Invoked);
        this.onWorkflowActivated1.SetBinding(Microsoft.SharePoint.WorkflowActions
.OnWorkflowActivated.WorkflowIdProperty, ((System.Workflow.ComponentModel.ActivityB
ind)(activitybind42)));
        this.onWorkflowActivated1.SetBinding(Microsoft.SharePoint.WorkflowActions
.OnWorkflowActivated.WorkflowPropertiesProperty, ((System.Workflow.ComponentModel
.ActivityBind)(activitybind41)));
        //
        // Workflow1
        //
        this.Activities.Add(this.onWorkflowActivated1);
        this.Activities.Add(this.eventHandlingScopeActivity1);
        this.Name = "Workflow1";
        this.CanModifyActivities = false;
```

```
}

#endregion

private Microsoft.SharePoint.WorkflowActions.UpdateTask updateTask2;
private Microsoft.SharePoint.WorkflowActions.OnTaskChanged onTaskChanged1;
private WhileActivity whileActivity1;
private Microsoft.SharePoint.WorkflowActions.LogToHistoryListActivity
                                    logToHistoryListActivity2;
private SequenceActivity sequenceActivity2;
private Microsoft.SharePoint.WorkflowActions.EnableWorkflowModification
                                    enableWorkflowModification1;
private Microsoft.SharePoint.WorkflowActions.OnWorkflowModified
                                    onWorkflowModified1;
private EventDrivenActivity eventDrivenActivity5;
private Microsoft.SharePoint.WorkflowActions.LogToHistoryListActivity
                                    logToHistoryListActivity5;
private EventHandlersActivity eventHandlersActivity2;
private EventHandlingScopeActivity eventHandlingScopeActivity2;
private Microsoft.SharePoint.WorkflowActions.LogToHistoryListActivity
                                    logToHistoryListActivity4;
private Microsoft.SharePoint.WorkflowActions.OnWorkflowItemDeleted
                                    onWorkflowItemDeleted1;
private EventDrivenActivity eventDrivenActivity4;
private EventHandlingScopeActivity eventHandlingScopeActivity1;
private Microsoft.SharePoint.WorkflowActions.SendEmail sendEmail2;
private Microsoft.SharePoint.WorkflowActions.OnTaskDeleted onTaskDeleted2;
private Microsoft.SharePoint.WorkflowActions.DeleteTask deleteTask2;
private DelayActivity delayActivity1;
private Microsoft.SharePoint.WorkflowActions.LogToHistoryListActivity
                                    logToHistoryListActivity1;
private EventDrivenActivity eventDrivenActivity2;
private EventDrivenActivity eventDrivenActivity1;
private FaultHandlerActivity faultHandlerActivity1;
private ListenActivity listenActivity1;
private FaultHandlersActivity faultHandlersActivity1;
private Microsoft.SharePoint.WorkflowActions.SendEmail sendEmail1;
private Microsoft.SharePoint.WorkflowActions.OnTaskDeleted onTaskDeleted1;
private Microsoft.SharePoint.WorkflowActions.DeleteTask deleteTask1;
private IfElseBranchActivity ifElseBranchActivity2;
private IfElseBranchActivity ifElseBranchActivity1;
private IfElseActivity ifElseActivity1;
private CodeActivity codeActivity1;
private Microsoft.SharePoint.WorkflowActions.UpdateTask updateTask1;
private Microsoft.SharePoint.WorkflowActions.OnTaskCreated onTaskCreated1;
private Microsoft.SharePoint.WorkflowActions.CreateTaskWithContentType
                                    createTaskWithContentType1;
private SequenceActivity sequenceActivity1;
private EventDrivenActivity eventDrivenActivity3;
private EventHandlersActivity eventHandlersActivity1;
private Microsoft.SharePoint.WorkflowActions.OnWorkflowItemChanged
                                    onWorkflowItemChanged1;
```

(continued)

Listing 7-5 *(continued)*

```
        private Microsoft.SharePoint.WorkflowActions.LogToHistoryListActivity
                                               logToHistoryListActivity3;
        private Microsoft.SharePoint.WorkflowActions.OnWorkflowActivated
                                               onWorkflowActivated1;
    }
}
```

Summary

This chapter provided in-depth coverage of both workflow modification and workflow task editing. So far, you've learned throughout this book how to implement custom activities. The next chapter demonstrates how you can deploy these custom activities to Microsoft Office SharePoint Designer 2007 and how to take advantage of SharePoint Designer 2007 features.

8

Developing Custom Office SharePoint Designer 2007 Actions and Conditions

Office SharePoint Designer 2007 enables workflow designers to develop workflows in purely graphical fashion without any code. Office SharePoint Designer 2007 comes with a set of prebuilt actions and conditions that workflow developers can use out of the box. Oftentimes, modeling real-life business processes requires running custom code on the server that is not supported by any of the prebuilt actions and conditions shipped with Microsoft Office SharePoint Designer 2007.

This chapter shows you how to implement custom actions and conditions to encapsulate custom code, which can run on the server when these actions and conditions are executed, and how to import these custom actions and conditions to Office SharePoint Designer 2007 to enable workflow developers to use them in purely graphical fashion without any code.

Recipe for Implementing a Custom Action

Follow these steps to implement a custom Office SharePoint Designer 2007 action to enable workflow developers to run your custom code on the server without writing any code:

1. Implement a custom Windows Workflow Foundation activity that encapsulates your custom code. We will expose this WF activity as an Office SharePoint Designer 2007 action.
2. Compile the WF activity from Step 1 into a strong-named assembly.
3. Install the strong-named assembly from Step 2 in the global assembly cache (GAC).

4. Register the WF activity from Step 1 as an authorized type to authorize the activity and consequently your custom code to run on the server.
5. Implement an .actions XML file to describe the WF activity from Step 1 to Office SharePoint Designer 2007 as an action.
6. Deploy the .actions XML file from Step 5 to the file system of each front-end web server in the SharePoint farm.
7. Test your custom action in Office SharePoint Designer 2007.

In this chapter, we'll follow these steps to implement a custom action that enables workflow developers to run simple custom code, which simply echoes the user inputs.

Implementing a Custom SharePoint Activity

Following our recipe, the first order of business is to implement a custom WF activity named CustomActivity that encapsulates our custom code, as shown in Listing 8-1.

Listing 8-1: The CustomActivity custom WF activity

```
using System;
using System.Workflow.ComponentModel;
using Microsoft.SharePoint;

namespace Chapter8
{
 public class CustomActivity: Activity
 {
    public static readonly DependencyProperty StringPropertyProperty =
        DependencyProperty.Register("StringProperty", typeof(string),
                                    typeof(CustomActivity));
    public string StringProperty
    {
      get { return (string)base.GetValue(StringPropertyProperty); }
      set { base.SetValue(StringPropertyProperty, value); }
    }

    public static readonly DependencyProperty DateTimePropertyProperty =
        DependencyProperty.Register("DateTimeProperty", typeof(DateTime),
                                    typeof(CustomActivity));
    public DateTime DateTimeProperty
    {
      get { return (DateTime)base.GetValue(DateTimePropertyProperty); }
      set { base.SetValue(DateTimePropertyProperty, value); }
    }

    public static readonly DependencyProperty StringOutputPropertyProperty =
        DependencyProperty.Register("StringOutputProperty", typeof(string),
                                    typeof(CustomActivity));
    public string StringOutputProperty
```

```
        {
          get { return (string)base.GetValue(StringOutputPropertyProperty); }
          set { base.SetValue(StringOutputPropertyProperty, value); }
        }

        protected override ActivityExecutionStatus Execute(
                                      ActivityExecutionContext executionContext)
        {
          this.StringOutputProperty = "You entered " + this.StringProperty + ", " +
                                      this.DateTimeProperty.ToString();
          return ActivityExecutionStatus.Closed;
        }
    }
}
```

CustomActivity exposes an input string property named StringProperty, an input DateTime property named DateTimeProperty, and an output string property named StringOutputProperty. Notice that CustomActivity follows this pattern to implement each of the three properties:

1. Defines a field of the DependencyProperty type. By convention, the name of the field is the name of the property suffixed with the word "Property."
2. Defines a public read-write property whose getter and setter, respectively, delegate to the GetValue and SetValue methods. Note that the field from Step 1 is passed into these methods as an argument.

This pattern enables workflow developers to do the following:

- Bind the properties of other activities in the workflow or the fields of the workflow itself to the StringProperty and DateTimeProperty properties of CustomActivity. In other words, this enables workflow developers to set the values of these two properties through activity binding. An activity binding automatically assigns the value of the target property to the source property. The source property in this case is the StringProperty or DateTimeProperty property, and the target property is the property of another activity in the workflow or the property of the workflow itself. Activity binding is a very powerful technique that enables workflow developers to chain together several activities whereby the input properties of one activity in the chain are bound to the output properties of a previous activity in the chain. You must follow the previous two-step pattern to implement the properties of your custom activities to enable activity binding.
- Bind the StringOutputProperty property of CustomActivity to an input property of another activity or a property of the workflow itself. In other words, the outcome of the execution of CustomActivity is automatically assigned to an input property of another activity through activity binding as just discussed.

Compiling a Custom SharePoint Activity to a Strong-Named Assembly

You must compile your custom WF activity into a strong-named assembly. The most convenient way to do this is to configure Visual Studio to do it for you!

Installing Assembly in GAC

You must install the strong-named assembly that contains your custom WF activity in the global assembly cache (GAC) to make it available to SharePoint. You have two options for installing an assembly in the GAC. You can launch Windows Explorer, navigate to the assembly folder, and drag and drop your assembly there. Another option is to use the gacutil.exe command-line utility.

Registering a Custom SharePoint Activity As an Authorized Type

Next, you need to register your custom WF activity as an authorized type to authorize it to run on the server. To do so, navigate to the root folder of your web application, which should have a path such as following:

```
Local_Drive:\inetpub\wwwroot\wss\VirtualDirectories\3000
```

Open the web.config file and search for the following section:

```
<System.Workflow.ComponentModel.WorkflowCompiler>
  <authorizedTypes>
    <authorizedType
    Assembly="System.Workflow.Activities, Version=3.0.0.0, Culture=neutral,
              PublicKeyToken=31bf3856ad364e35"
    Namespace="System.Workflow.*" TypeName="*" Authorized="True" />

    <authorizedType
    Assembly="System.Workflow.ComponentModel, Version=3.0.0.0, Culture=neutral,
              PublicKeyToken=31bf3856ad364e35"
    Namespace="System.Workflow.*" TypeName="*" Authorized="True" />

    . . .
  </authorizedTypes>
</System.Workflow.ComponentModel.WorkflowCompiler>
```

As shown here, this section has already registered several standard types as authorized. You need to add a new <authorizedType> child element to the <system.Workflow.ComponentModel.WorkflowCompiler> element to authorize your custom WF activity to run on the server. The <authorizedType> element features the following attributes that you need to set:

- **Assembly:** Set this attribute to the strong name of the assembly that contains your custom WF activity. The strong name of an assembly consists of four parts: assembly name, version, culture, and public key token.

- **Namespace:** Set this attribute to the complete namespace containment hierarchy of your custom WF activity. You can optionally use (*) asterisk to include all subnamespaces of a namespace.
- **TypeName:** Set this attribute to the class name of your custom WF activity. You can optionally use (*) asterisk to authorize all types in the namespace specified in the Namespace attribute to run on the server.
- **Authorized:** Set this attribute to true to authorize your custom WF activity to run on the server. If you have used asterisk in the TypeName attribute, this will authorize all types in the namespace specified in the Namespace attribute to run on the server.

Implementing an .Actions XML File

Now you need to implement an XML file with the .actions extension to describe your custom WF activity to Office SharePoint Designer 2007. Listing 8-2 presents the content of the CustomActivity.actions XML file that describes our CustomActivity WF activity to Office SharePoint Designer 2007. Don't forget to replace the value of the PublicKeyToken in Listing 8-2 with the actual public key token of your assembly.

Listing 8-2: The CustomActivity.actions file

```
<?xml version="1.0" encoding="utf-8" ?>
<WorkflowInfo Language="en-us">
  <Actions Sequential="then" Parallel="and">
    <Action Name="Execute custom code" AppliesTo="all" Category="My Custom Actions"
   ClassName="Chapter8.CustomActivity"
   Assembly="Chapter8, Version=1.0.0.0, Culture=neutral,
             PublicKeyToken=636dfad85c01d3c8">
      <RuleDesigner
      Sentence="Execute custom code with %1 and %2 on the server (Output: %3) ">
        <FieldBind Field="StringProperty" DesignerType="ParameterNames"
        Text="this StringProperty value" Id="1"/>
        <FieldBind Field="DateTimeProperty" DesignerType="ParameterNames"
        Text="this DateTimeProperty value" Id="2"/>
        <FieldBind Field="StringOutputProperty" DesignerType="ParameterNames"
        Text="StringOutputProperty" Id="3"/>
      </RuleDesigner>
      <Parameters>
        <Parameter Name="StringProperty" Type="System.String, mscorlib"
        Direction="In" />
        <Parameter Name="DateTimeProperty" Type="System.DateTime, mscorlib"
        Direction="In" />
        <Parameter Name="StringOutputProperty" Type="System.String, mscorlib"
        Direction="Out" />
      </Parameters>
    </Action>
  </Actions>
</WorkflowInfo>
```

Deploying the .Actions XML File

Next, deploy the .actions XML file that describes your custom WF activity to the following folder on the file system of each front-end web server:

```
%Program Files%\Common Files\Microsoft Shared\web server extensions\12\
TEMPLATE\1033\Workflow\
```

Using Visual Studio

You can perform all the steps discussed in the previous sections in Visual Studio as follows. Launch Visual Studio and select File ⇨ New Project to launch the New Project dialog, shown in Figure 8-1. Select the Workflow option under the Visual C# section of the Project Types pane and then select the Workflow Activity Library option from the Templates pane, as shown in Figure 8-1.

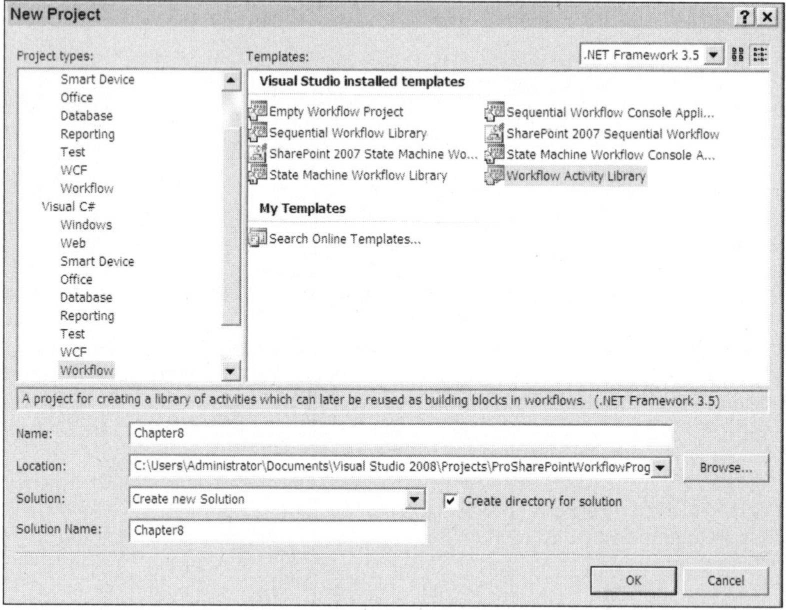

Figure 8-1

Name the project Chapter8. This will create a Workflow Activity Library project, which includes two files named Activity1.cs and Activity1.designer.cs. Delete Activity1.designer.cs and rename Activity1.cs to CustomActivity.cs. Replace the contents of CustomActivity.cs with Listing 8-1. Next, add a reference to the Microsoft.SharePoint.dll assembly, which is located in the following folder:

```
%Program Files%\Common Files\Microsoft Shared\web server extensions\12\ISAPI
```

Next, we'll configure Visual Studio to generate a strong-named assembly every time we build the project. To do so, right-click the project in the Solution Explorer and select Properties from the pop-up menu as shown in Figure 8-2.

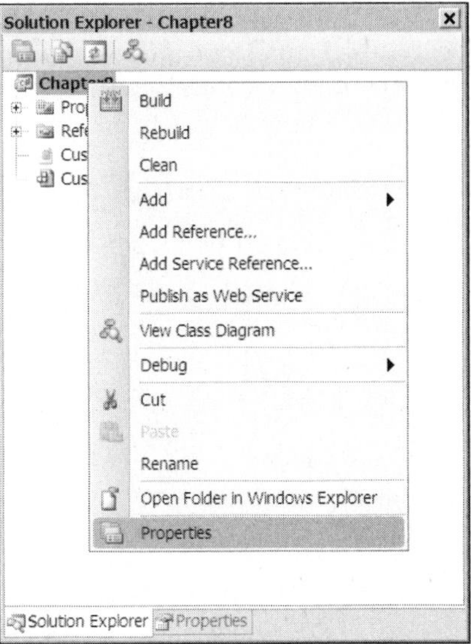

Figure 8-2

This will launch the Properties window shown in Figure 8-3. Switch to the Signing tab, check the "Sign the assembly" toggle, and select the "<New . . .>" option from the drop-down list box to launch the Create Strong Name Key dialog shown in Figure 8-4.

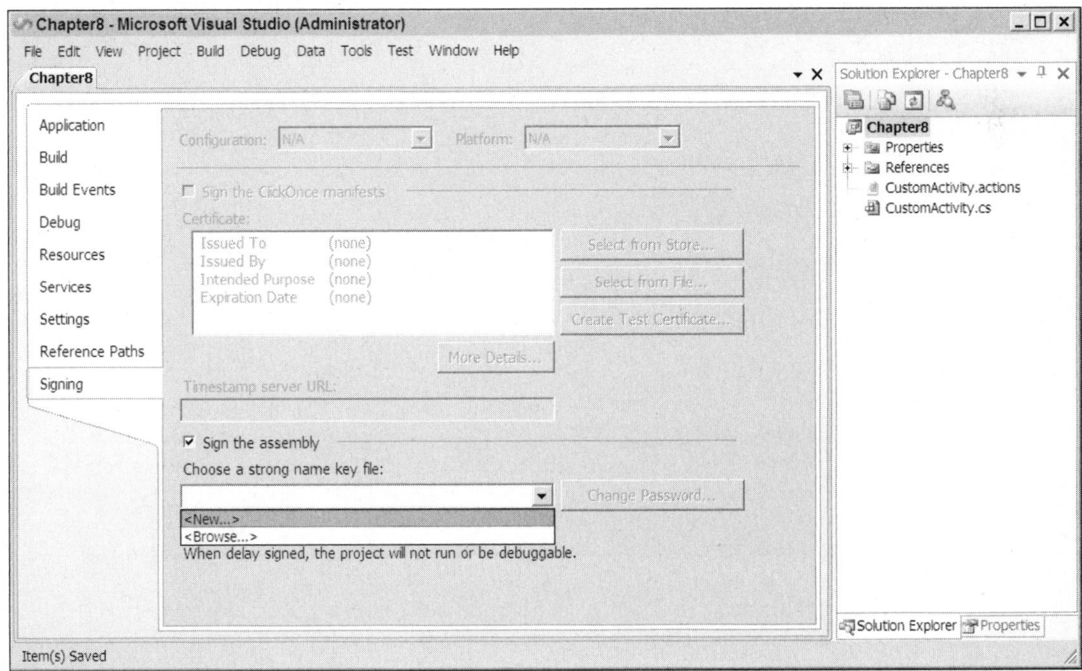

Figure 8-3

Enter a name for the key file, uncheck the "Protect my key file with a password" toggle, and click OK. This will create a key file with the specified name and add it to the root folder of the project. This key file contains that key that Visual Studio uses to sign the assembly.

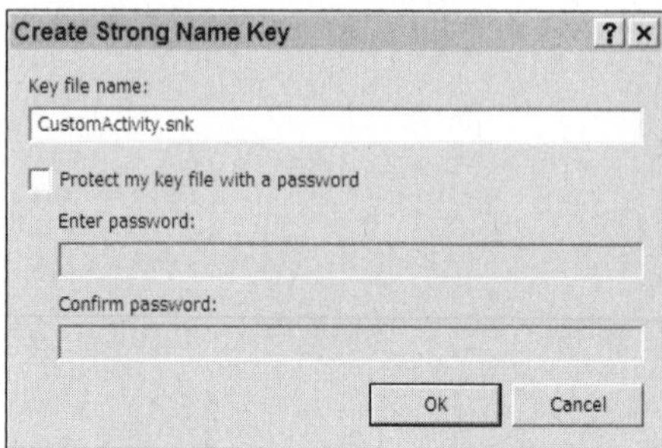

Figure 8-4

Save your changes. Next, we'll configure Visual Studio to install the strong-named assembly in the global assembly cache every time we build the project. To do so, go back to the Properties page shown in Figure 8-3 and switch to the Build Events tab and enter the following command line into the "Post-build event command line" text box, as shown in Figure 8-5:

```
"Local_Drive:\Program Files\Microsoft Visual Studio 8\SDK\v2.0\Bin\gacutil.exe" /
if "$(TargetPath)"
```

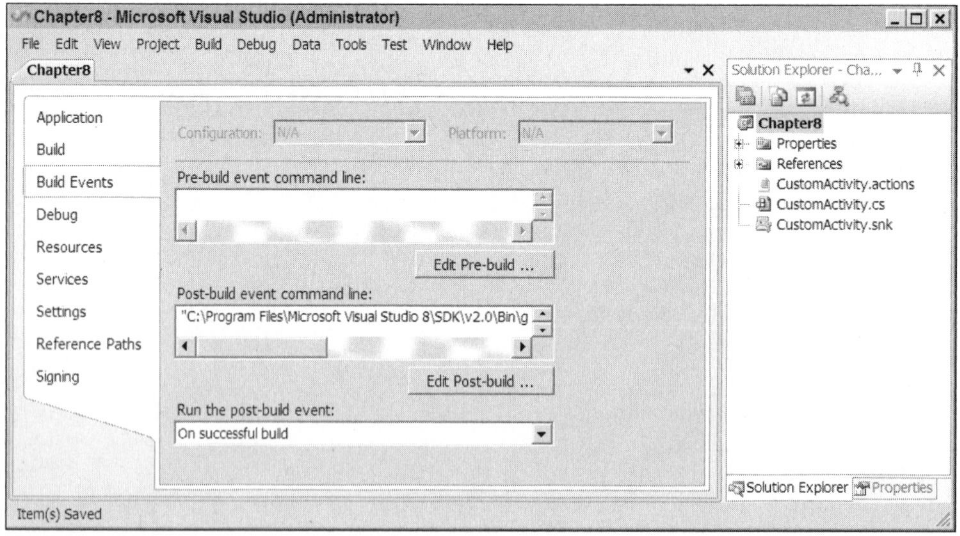

Figure 8-5

Thanks to this post-build event command line, Visual Studio will install the assembly to the global assembly cache every time you build the project.

Next, add a new XML file named CustomActivity.actions to the project and add Listing 8-2 to this file. Then add the following command lines below the previous command line in the "Post-build event command line" text box shown in Figure 8-5 to have Visual Studio automatically copy the CustomActivity.actions file to the Workflow folder on the file system of the front-end web server every time you build the project:

```
"C:\Program Files\Microsoft Visual Studio 8\SDK\v2.0\Bin\gacutil.exe" /if
"$(TargetPath)"
cd $(ProjectDir)
xcopy /y CustomActivity.actions "c:\Program Files\Common Files\microsoft shared\
Web Server Extensions\12\TEMPLATE\1033\Workflow"
```

As Listing 8-2 shows, the <Action> element that describes our CustomActivity WF activity to SharePoint features an attribute named Assembly, which is set to the strong name of the assembly that contains our WF activity. This strong name consists of the assembly name, version, culture, and public key token. There are different ways to get the public key token of an assembly. One approach is to do it from within Visual Studio as follows. Select the External Tools menu option from the Tools menu in Visual Studio to launch the External Tools dialog shown in Figure 8-6.

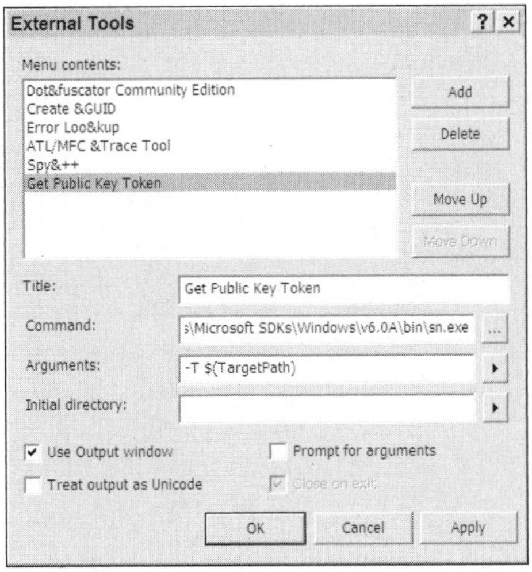

Figure 8-6

This dialog enables you to add an external tool to Visual Studio. Enter **Get Public Key Token** into the Title text box; enter the full path to the sn.exe command-line utility tool into the Command text box; and enter **-T $(TargetPath)** into the Arguments text box. Check the "Use Output window" toggle to have Visual Studio print the public key token in the output window. To find out the full path to the sn.exe command-line utility, launch the Visual Studio command prompt and type **where sn.exe** at the prompt. The $(TargetPath) provides the full path to the strong-named assembly. If you click the OK button shown in Figure 8-6, it will add a new menu option to the Tools menu of Visual Studio, as shown in Figure 8-7.

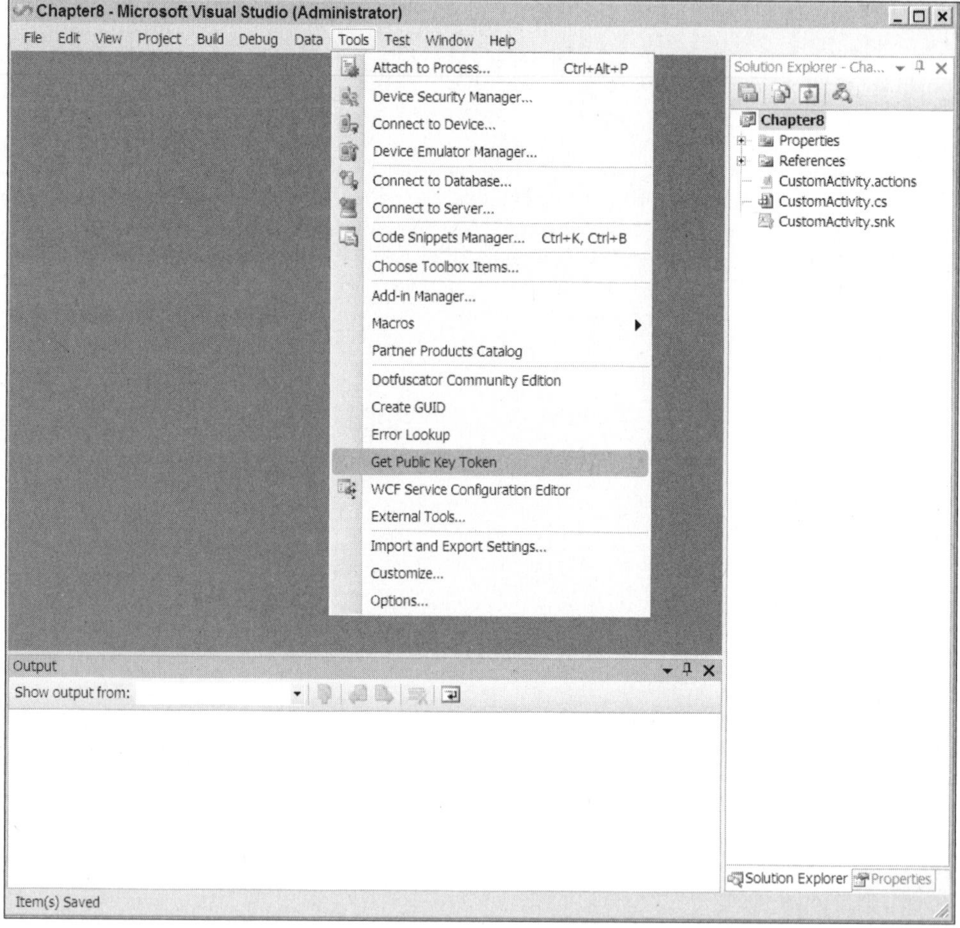

Figure 8-7

If you select the Get Public Key Token menu option, the public key token of the assembly is printed into the output window, as shown in Figure 8-8.

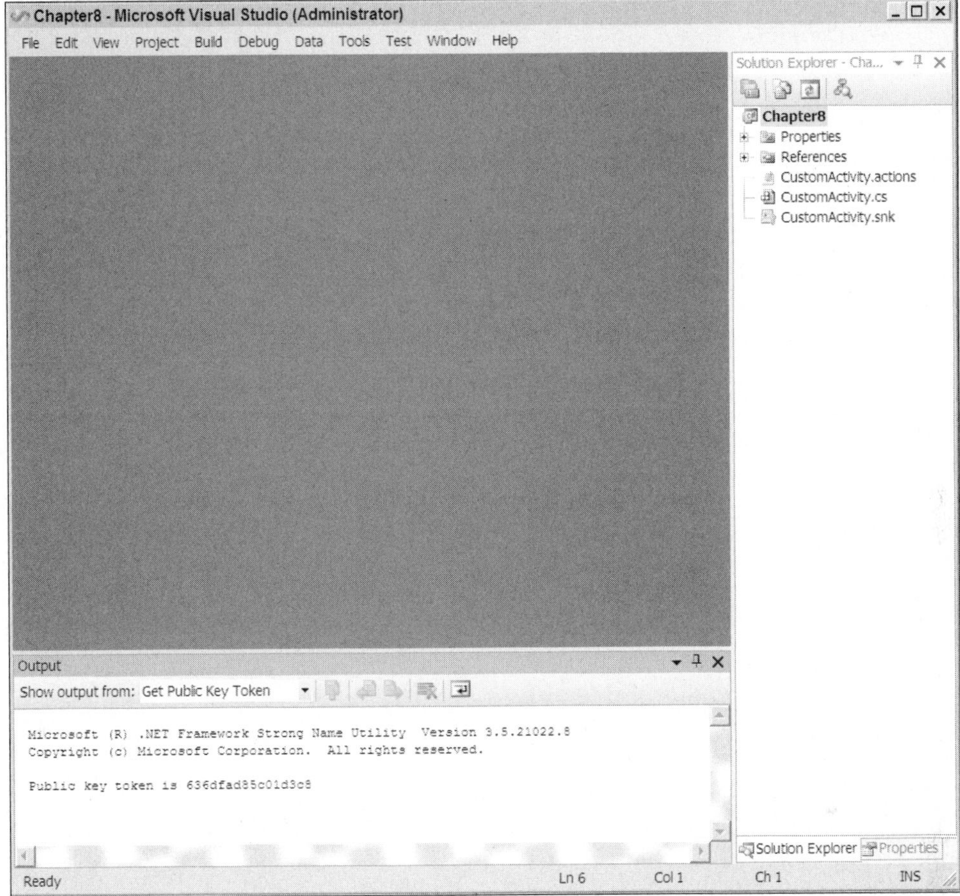

Figure 8-8

Don't forget to add the following entry to the web.config file of the web application:

```
<System.Workflow.ComponentModel.WorkflowCompiler>
  <authorizedTypes>
    . . .
    <authorizedType
    Assembly="Chapter8, Version=1.0.0.0, Culture=neutral,
              PublicKeyToken=636dfad85c01d3c8"
    Namespace="Chapter8" TypeName="*" Authorized="True" />
  </authorizedTypes>
</System.Workflow.ComponentModel.WorkflowCompiler>
```

Testing Your Custom Action in Office SharePoint Designer 2007

Launch Office SharePoint Designer 2007. Select File ⇨ New ⇨ Workflows to launch the Workflow Designer wizard shown in Figure 8-9. In this section, we'll use the Workflow Designer to design a workflow that uses our custom action.

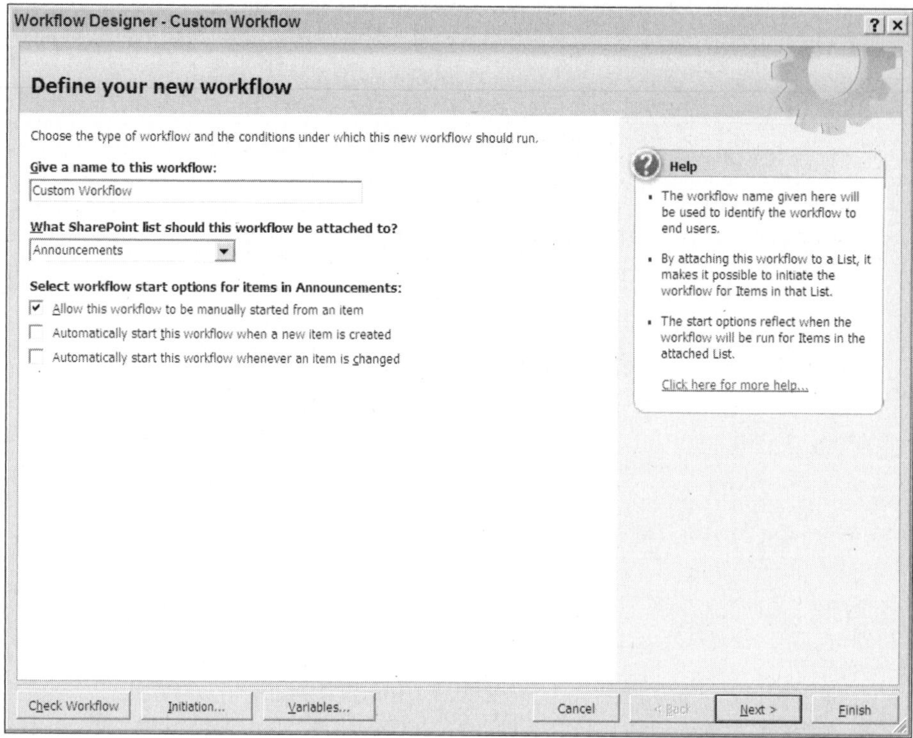

Figure 8-9

Enter a unique name for the workflow and select a SharePoint list from the drop-down list box. Office SharePoint Designer 2007 will automatically associate the workflow with the selected SharePoint list when you are done designing the workflow. Notice the following main differences between designing a workflow in Office SharePoint Designer 2007 and Visual Studio:

- When designing a workflow in Office SharePoint Designer 2007, you must specify the SharePoint list with which the workflow will be associated. The workflow association is part of the very design of the workflow itself. This is very different from designing a workflow in Visual Studio, where the workflow association is not established during the design of the workflow.
- A workflow designed in Office SharePoint Designer 2007 can be associated with one and only one SharePoint list. Once the association between a workflow and the SharePoint list is established during the workflow design, it can never be removed. After you design and save a workflow in Office SharePoint Designer 2007, you can always reopen the workflow to edit it.

However, such edits do not apply to the workflow association. In other words, Office SharePoint Designer 2007 allows you to edit every aspect of a workflow except its association. This is very different from workflows designed in Visual Studio, where you can always remove a workflow association and establish a new one. Besides, the same workflow designed in Visual Studio can be associated with multiple SharePoint lists.

- A workflow designed in Office SharePoint Designer 2007 cannot be associated with a SharePoint list content type or a site content type. It can only be associated with a SharePoint list. A workflow designed in Visual Studio, conversely, can be associated with SharePoint lists, list content types, and site content types.

Now back to the Workflow Designer wizard shown in Figure 8-9. First, toggle on/off the desired initiation or activation options for the workflow. You have three activation options. The first option enables users to initiate a workflow instance from the workflow association manually from the SharePoint user interface. The second option instructs SharePoint to initiate a workflow instance from the workflow association automatically every time a new list item is added to the SharePoint list with which the workflow is associated. The third option instructs SharePoint to initiate a workflow instance from the workflow association automatically every time a list item in the SharePoint list associated with the workflow is updated.

Click the Next button to navigate to the next step of the Workflow Designer wizard, shown in Figure 8-10.

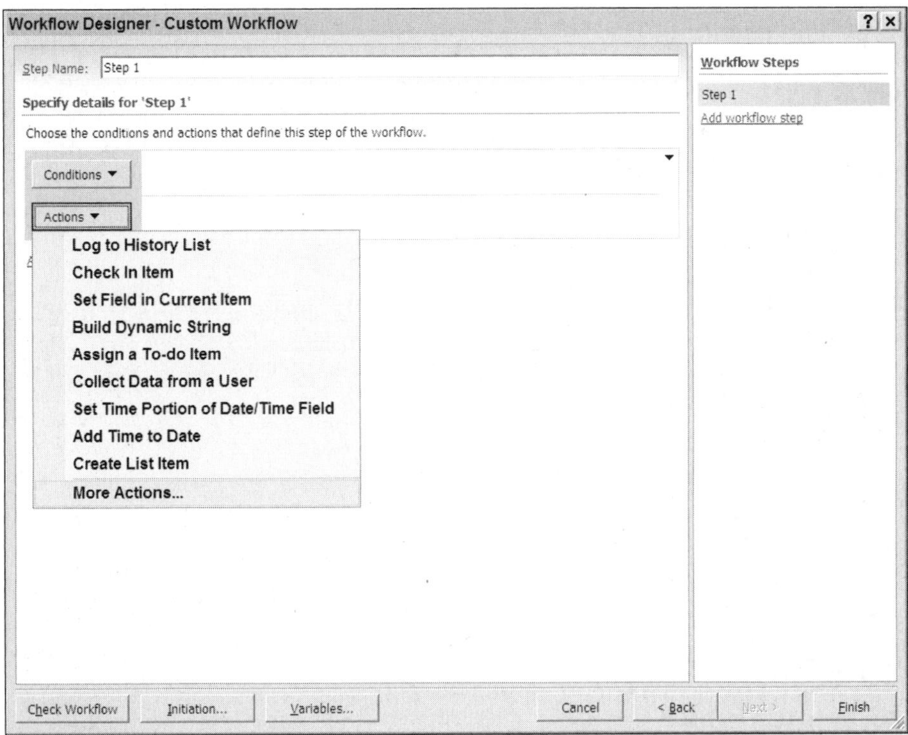

Figure 8-10

Click the Actions menu shown and select the More Actions option to launch the Workflow Actions dialog box shown in Figure 8-11.

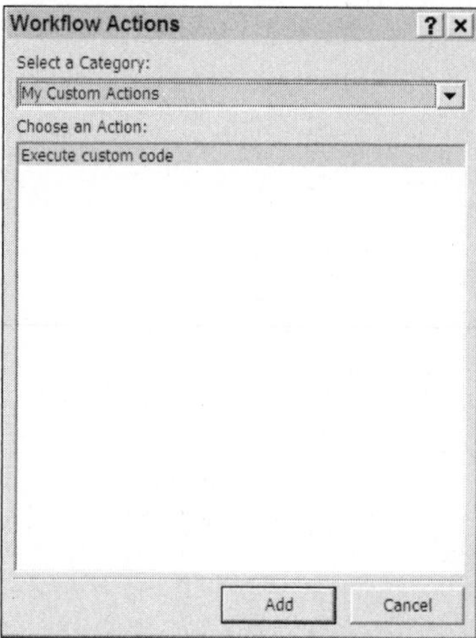

Figure 8-11

Select My Custom Actions from the Select a Category menu to view all actions in the My Custom Actions category. Recall from Listing 8-2 that we set the Category attribute on the <Action> element that describes our CustomActivity activity to My Custom Actions to instruct the Workflow Actions dialog shown in Figure 8-8 to display the name of our custom action under the My Custom Actions category:

```
<Actions Sequential="then" Parallel="and">
  <Action Name="Execute custom code" . . . Category="My Custom Actions">
    . . .
  </Action>
</Actions>
```

Select Execute Custom Code from the Workflow Actions dialog shown in Figure 8-11. Recall from Listing 8-2 that we set the Name attribute on the <Action> element that describes our CustomActivity activity to "Execute custom code" to instruct the Workflow Actions dialog shown in Figure 8-11 to use "Execute custom code" as the name of our custom action:

```
<Actions Sequential="then" Parallel="and">
  <Action Name="Execute custom code" . . . Category="My Custom Actions">
    . . .
  </Action>
</Actions>
```

Next, click the Add button on the Workflow Actions dialog shown in Figure 8-11 to return to the Workflow Designer wizard step shown in Figure 8-12.

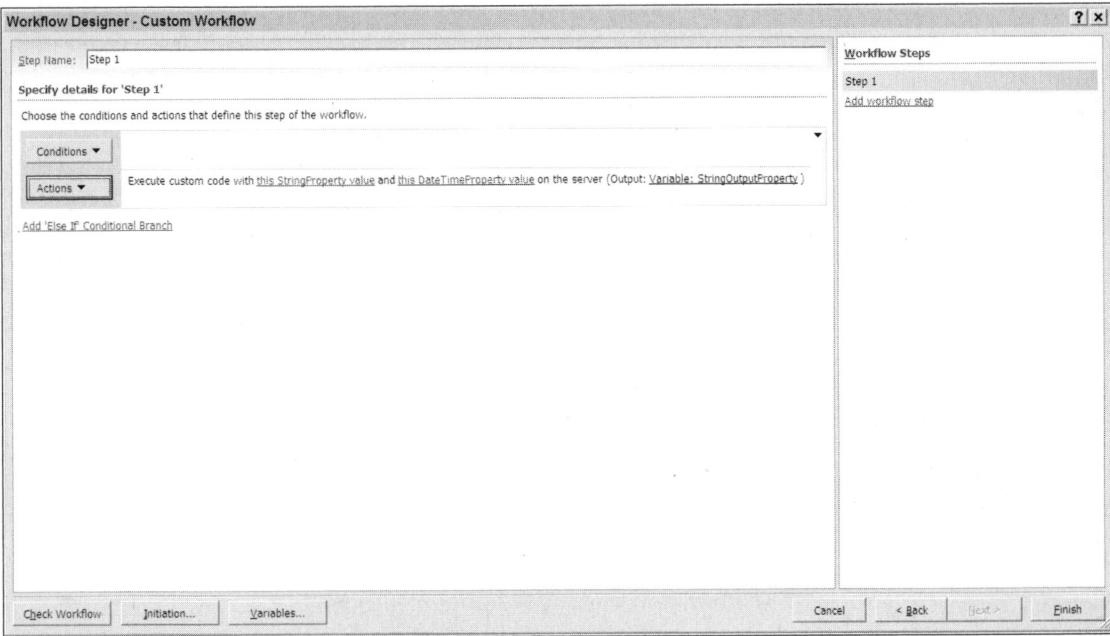

Figure 8-12

Note that this Workflow Designer wizard step now contains the following rule designer sentence:

```
Execute custom code with this StringProperty value and this DateTimeProperty value
on the server (Output: StringOutputProperty)
```

The Workflow Designer wizard uses the instructions that our .actions XML file provides to build the preceding rule designer sentence. Recall from Listing 8-2 that we set the Sentence attribute on the <Action> element that describes our CustomActivity activity to the value shown in boldface in the following excerpt:

```
<Action . . .>
  <RuleDesigner
  Sentence="Execute custom code with %1 and %2 on the server (Output: %3)">
    . . .
  </RuleDesigner>
  . . .
</Action>
```

The Workflow Designer wizard replaces the %1, %2, and %3 placeholder variables in this rule designer sentence with the values of the Text attributes on the <FieldBind> child elements whose Id attributes are set to 1, 2, and 3, respectively, as shown in the following excerpt from Listing 8-2:

```
<Action Name="Execute custom code" . . .>
  <RuleDesigner
  Sentence="Execute custom code with %1 and %2 on the server (Output: %3)">
    <FieldBind Field="StringProperty" DesignerType="ParameterNames"
    Text="this StringProperty value" Id="1"/>
    <FieldBind Field="DateTimeProperty" DesignerType="ParameterNames"
    Text="this DateTimeProperty value" Id="2"/>
    <FieldBind Field="StringOutputProperty" DesignerType="ParameterNames"
    Text="StringOutputProperty" Id="3"/>
  </RuleDesigner>
  . . .
</Action>
```

As shown here, you can use the Sentence attribute on the <RuleDesigner> element, and the Text and Id attributes on the <FieldBind> elements, to tell the Workflow Designer wizard what rule sentence to display to users.

Now return to the Workflow Designer wizard step shown in Figure 8-12 and click the Initiation button to launch the Workflow Initiation Parameters dialog box shown in Figure 8-13.

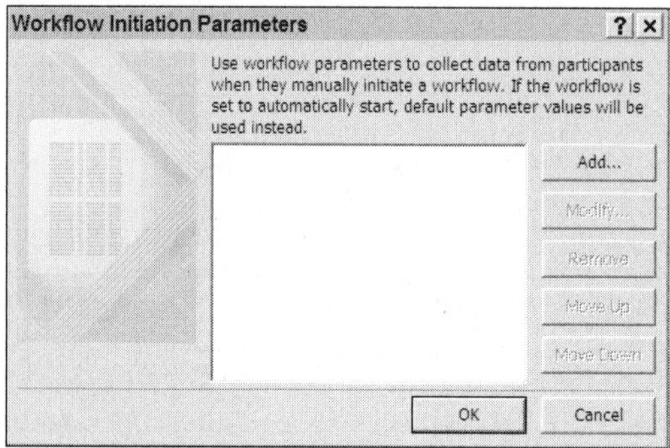

Figure 8-13

This dialog box enables us to design a workflow initiation form for our workflow. Because our CustomActivity WF activity exposes two input properties named StringProperty and DateTimeProperty, we need to add two input controls to our workflow initiation form to collect the user inputs for these two properties.

Click the Add button on the Workflow Initiation Parameters wizard shown in Figure 8-5 to launch the Add Field dialog box shown in Figure 8-14.

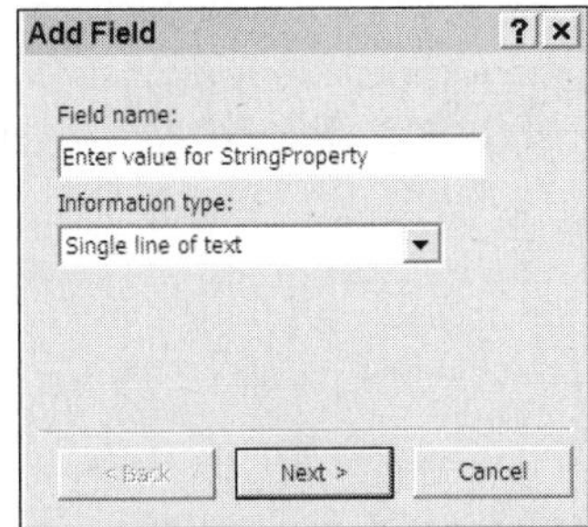

Figure 8-14

Enter "**Enter value for StringProperty**" in the Field Name text box and select the "Single line of text" menu option from the Information Type drop-down list box. Click Next to navigate to the next step of the Workflow Initiation Parameters wizard, shown in Figure 8-15.

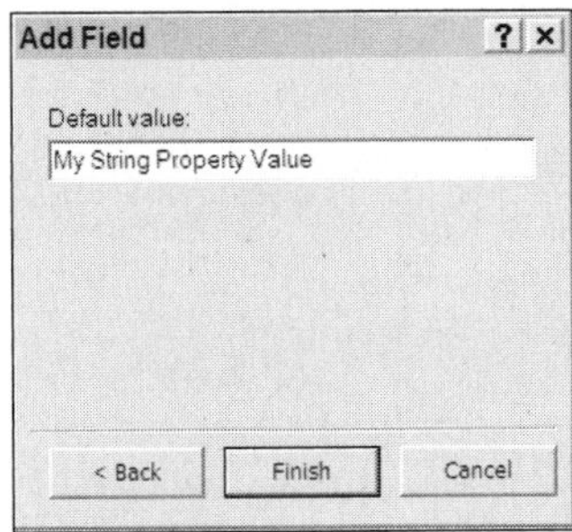

Figure 8-15

This step provides you with the appropriate interface to specify a default value. In this case this interface is a text box because we selected the "Single line of text" option from the Information Type drop-down list box in the previous step. Enter a default value of "My String Property Value" in the Default Value text box and click the Finish button. This instructs Office SharePoint Designer 2007 to render a label titled "Enter value for StringProperty" and a text box. Office SharePoint Designer 2007 automatically displays the default value of "My String Property Value" inside the text box. Finally, click the Finish button. This instructs Office SharePoint Designer 2007 to add a label titled "Enter value for StringProperty" and a textbox control to our workflow initiation form.

Now go back to the Workflow Initiation Parameters dialog box shown in Figure 8-13 and click the Add button to launch the Add Field wizard once again. Enter "**Enter value for DateTimeProperty**" in the Field Name text box and select the Date and Time menu option from the Information Type drop-down list box as shown in Figure 8-16.

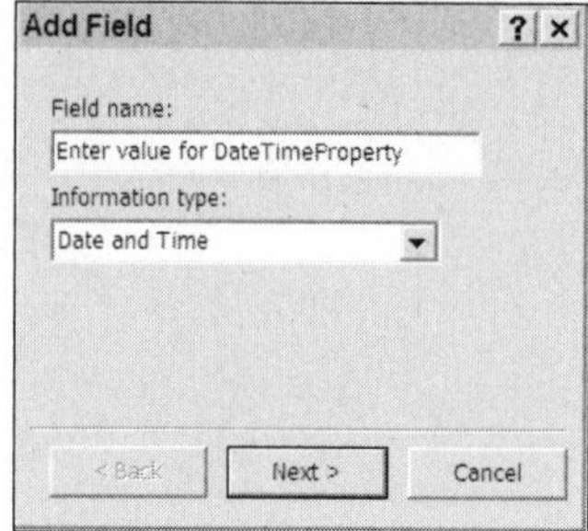

Figure 8-16

Click Next to launch the Add Field dialog shown in Figure 8-17 to specify a default date time value. As you can see, the option that you select from the Information Type drop-down list box determines what type of dialog box is used to specify the default value.

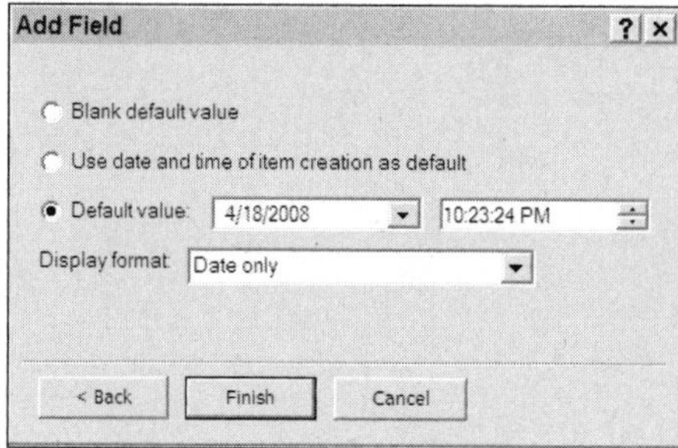

Figure 8-17

Next, click the Finish button. This instructs Office SharePoint Designer 2007 to add a label titled "Enter value for DateTimeProperty" and an appropriate date/time input control to the workflow initiation form.

So far, we've created our workflow initiation form. As you'll see later, when a user initiates a workflow instance from the workflow association, SharePoint automatically presents the user with the workflow initiation form to collect the user inputs. If the workflow is configured to be initiated automatically every time a list item is added to the SharePoint list and/or every time a list item in the SharePoint list is updated, SharePoint will not display the workflow initiation form. In such cases, the default values for the workflow initiation form's input controls are used.

When the user enters the desired values in the workflow initiation form's input controls and clicks the Start button on the form to initiate a workflow instance from the workflow association, SharePoint automatically passes the user's input values to the workflow instance. These values are then exposed to the constituent activities of a workflow through workflow local variables. Next, I'll show you how to bind these workflow local variables to the StringProperty and DateTimeProperty properties of our custom action.

Now go back to the Workflow Designer and click the "this StringProperty value" link. This should display the drop-down list box shown in Figure 8-18.

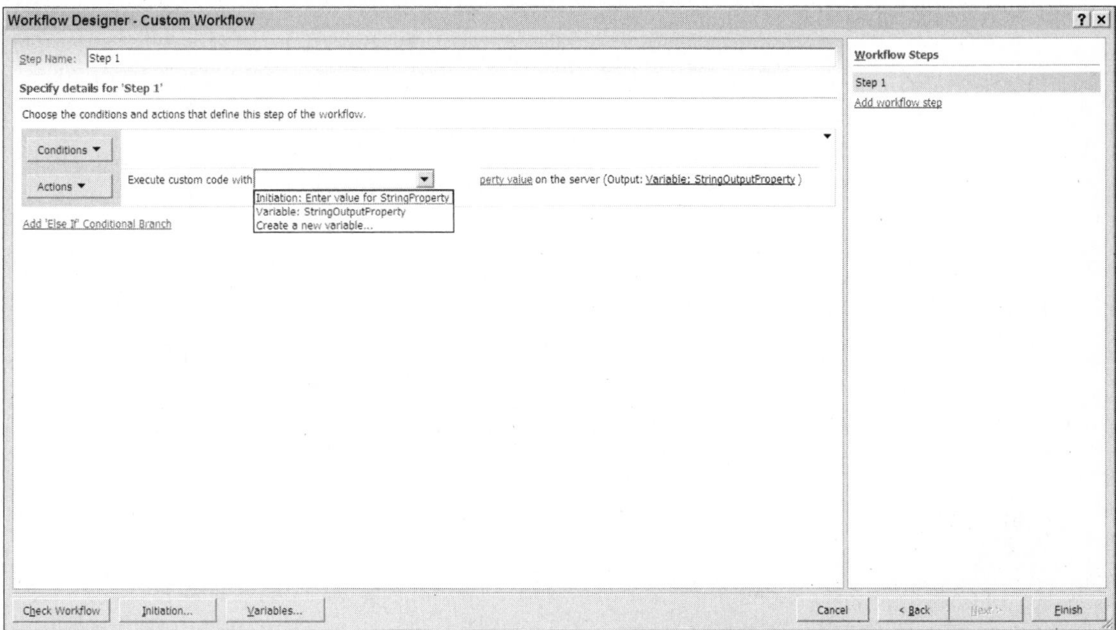

Figure 8-18

Notice that this drop-down list box displays the "Enter value for StringProperty" field that we added to the workflow initiation form. Select this option to bind the value that the user enters into the respective input control to the StringProperty property of our CustomActivity WF activity. Such binding is possible because our CustomActivity WF activity defines its StringProperty property as a bindable property, as shown in the following excerpt from Listing 8-1:

```
public static readonly DependencyProperty StringPropertyProperty =
    DependencyProperty.Register("StringProperty", typeof(string),
                                typeof(CustomActivity));
public string StringProperty
{
  get { return (string)base.GetValue(StringPropertyProperty); }
  set { base.SetValue(StringPropertyProperty, value); }
}
```

Next, click the "this DateTimeProperty value" link on the Workflow Designer to display the drop-down list box shown in Figure 8-19.

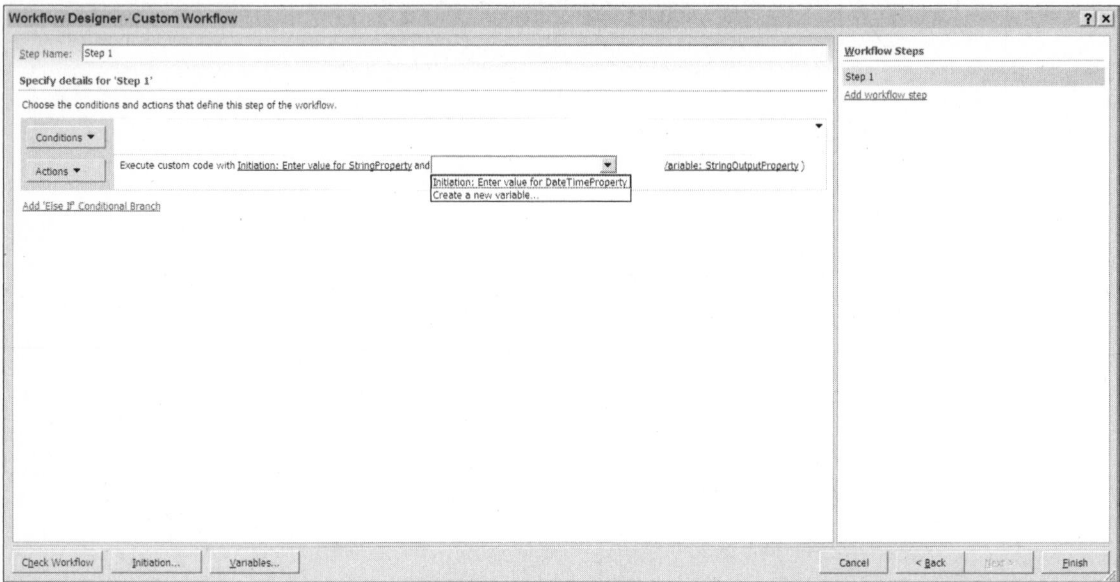

Figure 8-19

Note that this drop-down list box displays the "Enter value for DateTimeProperty" field that we added to our workflow initiation form. Select this option to bind the value that the user enters into the respective input control to the DateTimeProperty property of our CustomActivity WF activity. Once again, such binding is possible because our CustomActivity WF activity defines its DateTimeProperty property as a bindable property, as shown in the following excerpt from Listing 8-1:

```
public static readonly DependencyProperty DateTimePropertyProperty =
    DependencyProperty.Register("DateTimeProperty", typeof(DateTime),
                                typeof(CustomActivity));
public DateTime DateTimeProperty
{
  get { return (DateTime)base.GetValue(DateTimePropertyProperty); }
  set { base.SetValue(DateTimePropertyProperty, value); }
}
```

Thanks to the bindable properties of our CustomActivity WF activity, a workflow designer can pass the values that a user enters into the workflow initiation form to the appropriate properties of this activity through activity binding in purely declarative and graphical fashion without any code. You must always define the appropriate properties of your custom activity as bindable to enable workflow developers to specify their values in this manner. Otherwise, your custom activity could not be used in a code-free workflow editor such as Office SharePoint Designer 2007.

So far, you've learned how to set the input properties of our CustomActivity WF activity in graphical fashion through activity binding. What about the StringOutputProperty output property of our CustomActivity WF activity? Recall that this output property echoes the values of its input properties. Can workflow developers access the value of this property in purely declarative and graphical fashion without any code? The answer is a definite yes.

Go back to the Workflow Designer shown in Figure 8-19 and click the Variables button to launch the Workflow Local Variables dialog box shown in Figure 8-20.

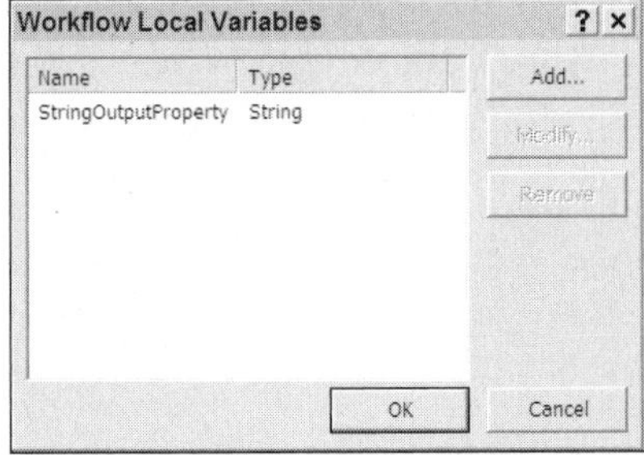

Figure 8-20

Click the Add button on the Workflow Local Variables dialog to launch the Edit Variable dialog box shown in Figure 8-21. This dialog box enables you to add a local variable to your workflow.

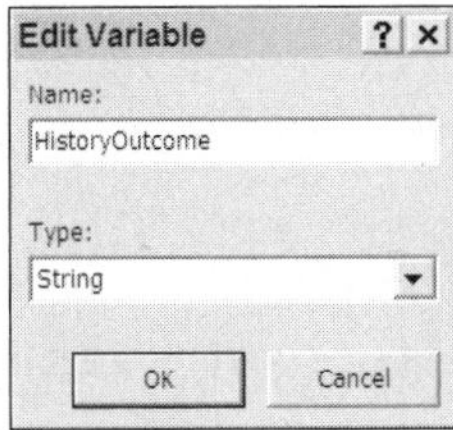

Figure 8-21

Enter **HistoryOutcome** into the Name text box as the name of the local variable and select String from the Type drop-down list box to specify that the local variable is of the System.String .NET type (refer to Figure 8-21).

Back in the Workflow Designer, click the Actions button and select the Build Dynamic String action, as shown in Figure 8-22.

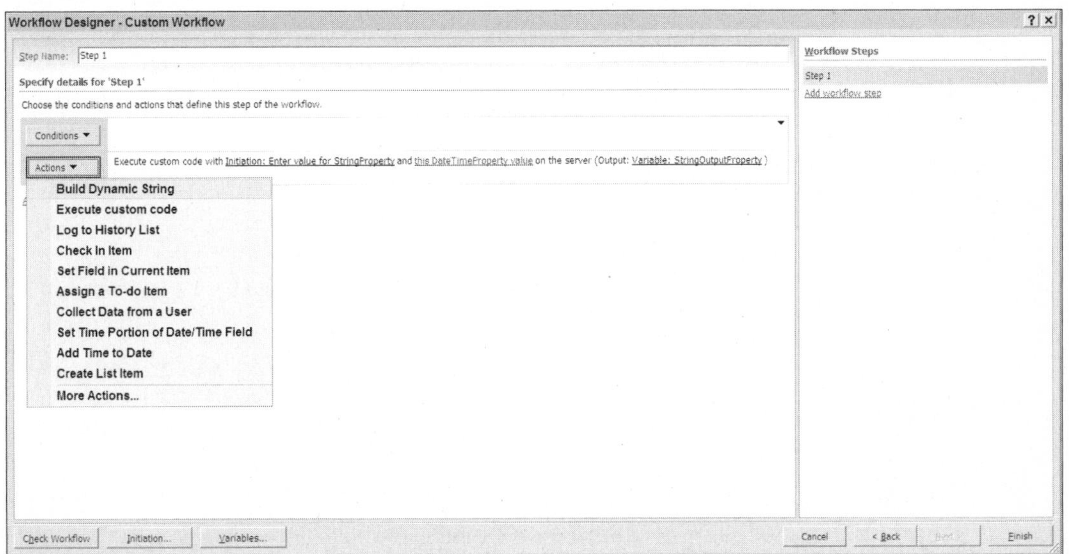

Figure 8-22

If the menu does not display the Build Dynamic String option, click the More Actions option to access the Build Dynamic String action. This will add the Build Dynamic String action to our workflow, as shown in Figure 8-23.

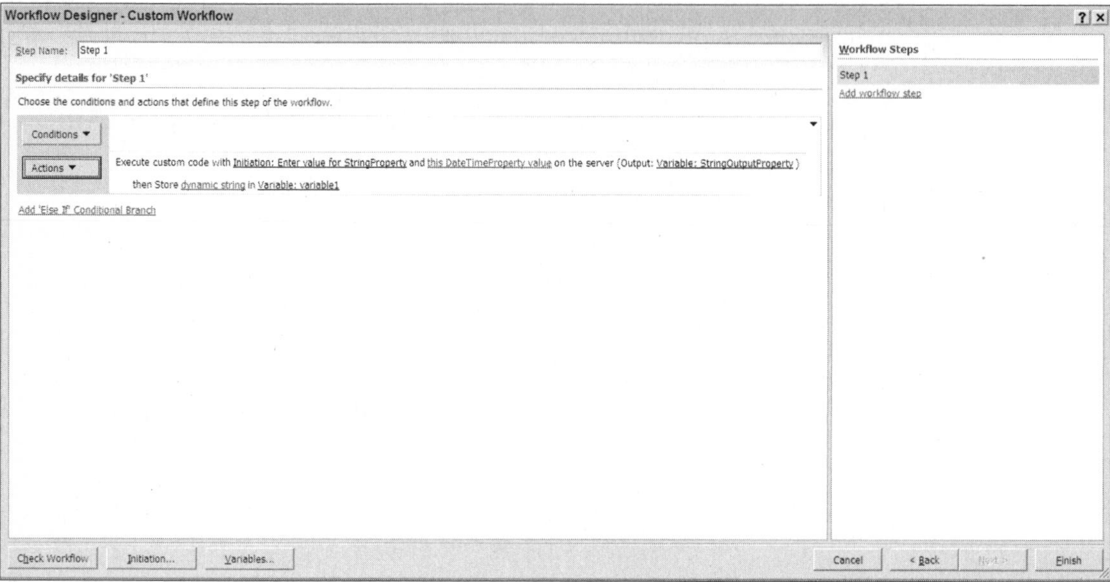

Figure 8-23

The Build Dynamic String action enables us to build a string and assign it to a workflow local variable. Note that the Build Dynamic String action takes two input parameters and assigns the value of the first parameter to the second parameter. Click the Dynamic String link to display the String Builder dialog box shown in Figure 8-24. Enter the text "**The outcome of CustomActivity:**"

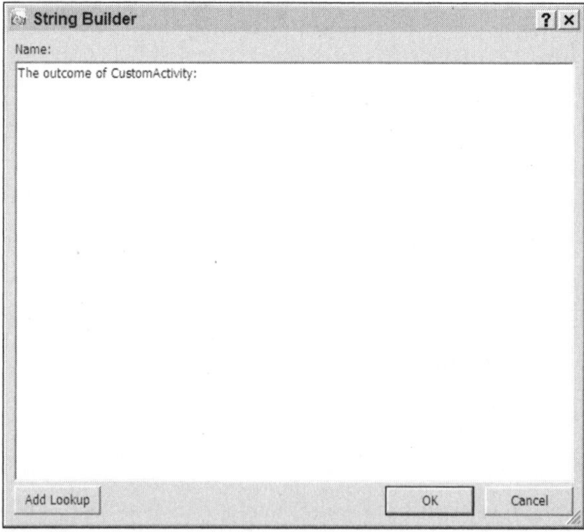

Figure 8-24

Click the Add Lookup button to launch the Define Workflow Lookup dialog box shown in Figure 8-25. Select Workflow Data from the Source drop-down list box and StringOutputProperty from the Field drop-down list box.

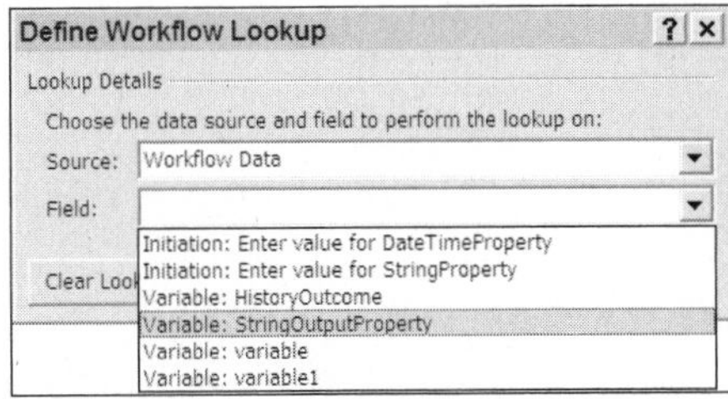

Figure 8-25

This will add the data binding expression shown in Figure 8-26. Click OK to accept the changes. Because the properties of the Build Dynamic String activity are bindable, the workflow designer can bind the output of our custom activity to the input of the Build Dynamic String activity, enabling data transfer from our activity to the Build Dynamic String activity through the activity binding process.

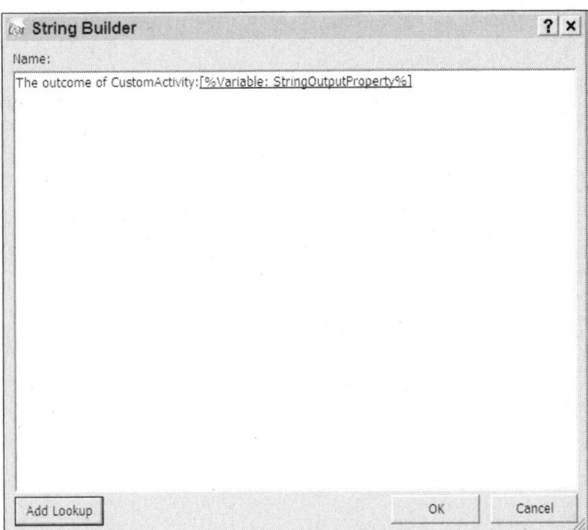

Figure 8-26

Back in the Workflow Designer, click the second link on the rule sentence of the Build Dynamic String action and select the HistoryOutcome option from the drop-down list box, as shown in Figure 8-27.

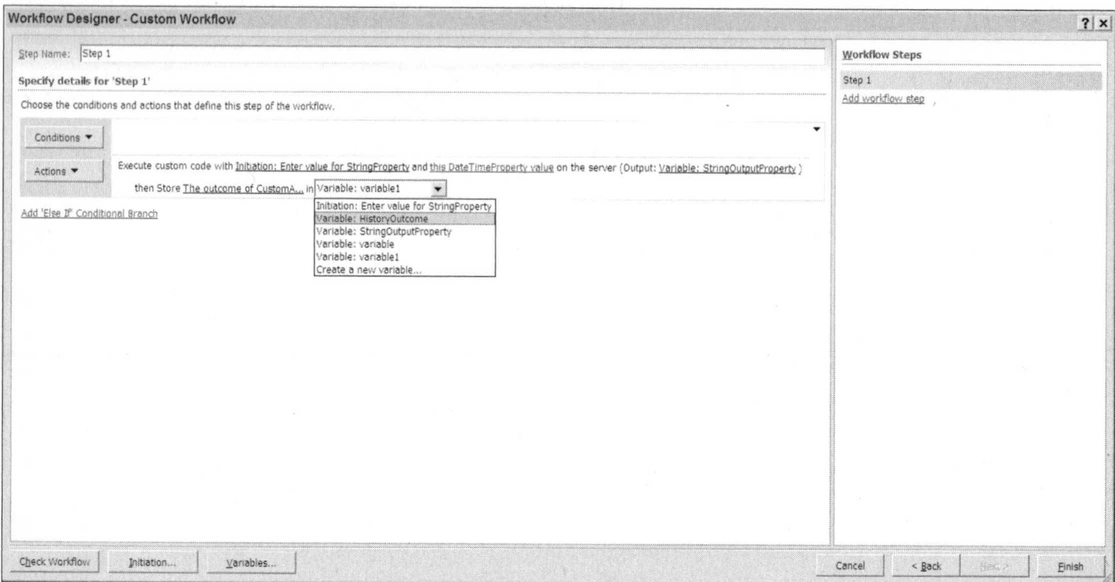

Figure 8-27

From the Workflow Designer wizard step shown in Figure 8-27, click the Actions menu and select the Log To History List menu item, as shown in Figure 8-28. If this menu item is not shown, select the More Actions option to launch the Workflow Actions dialog shown in Figure 8-11 to select the Log To History List action.

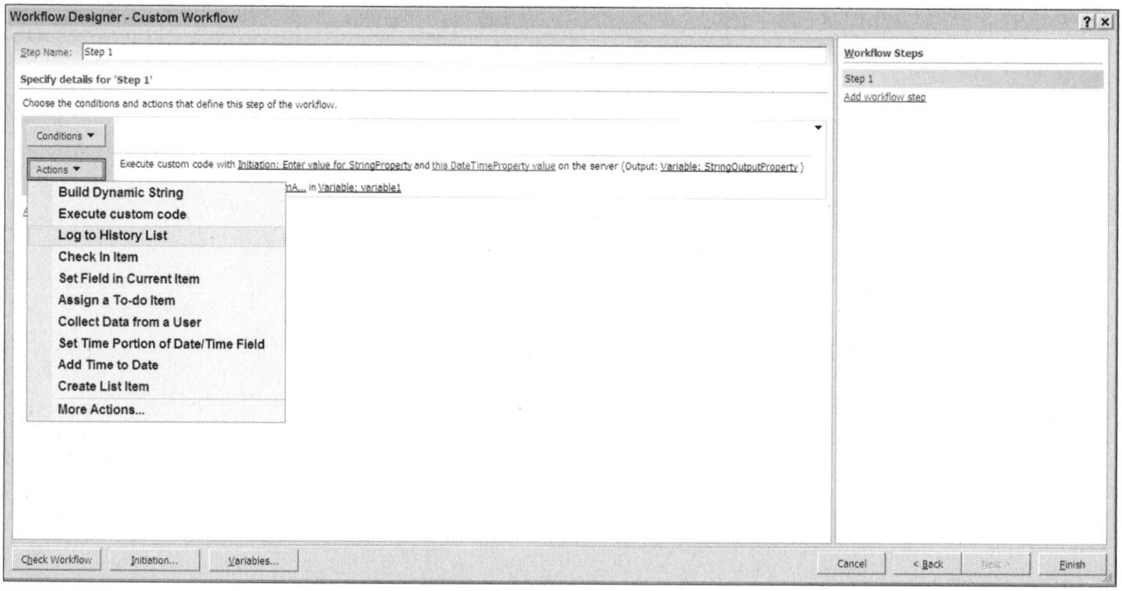

Workflow Designer - Custom Workflow

Step Name: Step 1

Specify details for 'Step 1'

Choose the conditions and actions that define this step of the workflow.

Conditions

Actions

Execute custom code with Initiation: Enter value for StringProperty and this DateTimeProperty value on the server (Output: Variable: StringOutputProperty)

Build Dynamic String
Execute custom code
Log to History List
Check In Item
Set Field in Current Item
Assign a To-do Item
Collect Data from a User
Set Time Portion of Date/Time Field
Add Time to Date
Create List Item
More Actions...

Workflow Steps

Step 1

Add workflow step

Check Workflow | Initiation... | Variables... | Cancel | < Back | Next > | Finish

Figure 8-28

This will append the Log to History List action to our workflow, as shown in Figure 8-29.

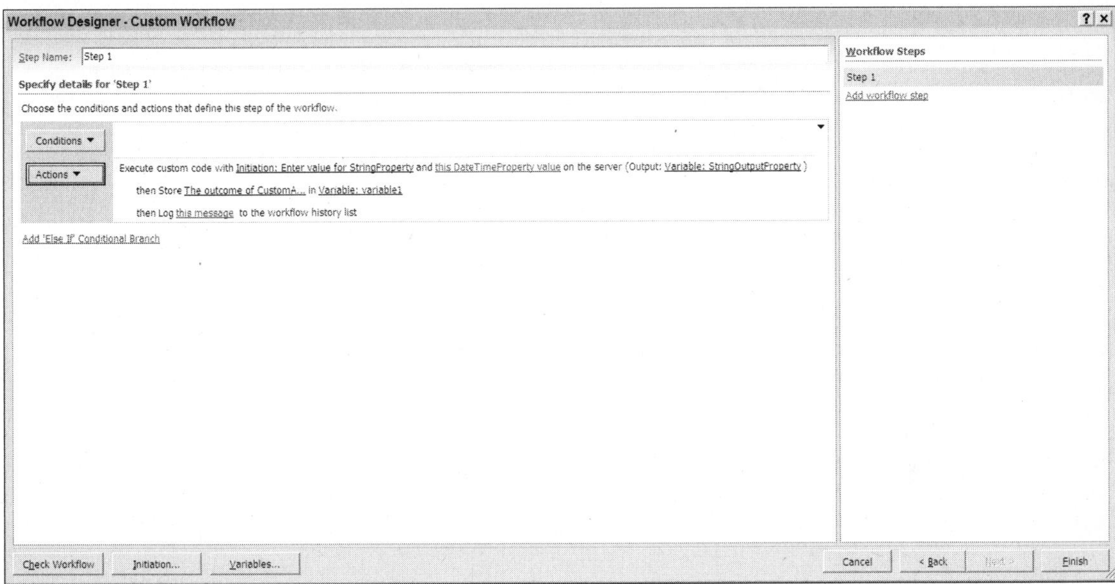

Figure 8-29

Click the This Message link to see the interface shown in Figure 8-30.

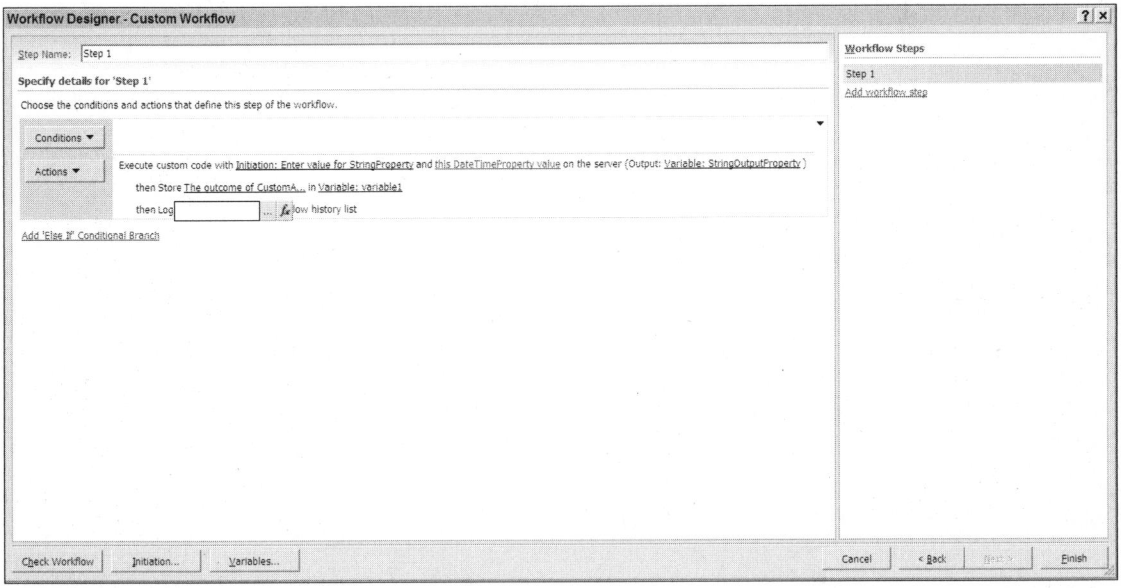

Figure 8-30

Click the Data Binding button (the button next to the ellipse button) on this interface to launch the Define Workflow Lookup dialog box shown in Figure 8-31. Select the Workflow Data option from the top drop-down list box and the HistoryOutcome option from the bottom drop-down list box.

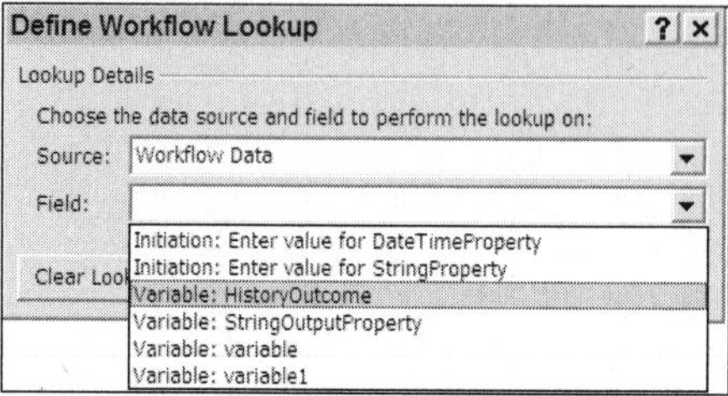

Figure 8-31

Workflow Designer should now look like Figure 8-32.

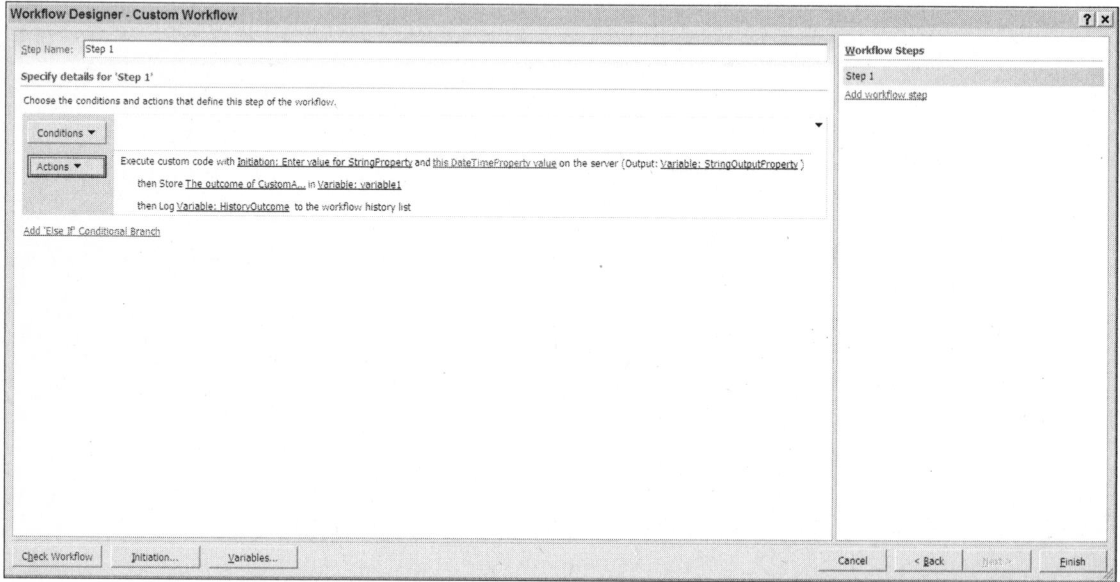

Figure 8-32

Click the Finish button on Workflow Designer to save the workflow. Office SharePoint Designer 2007 stores all workflows for a SharePoint Web application in a folder named Workflows in the content database. Figure 8-33 shows this folder.

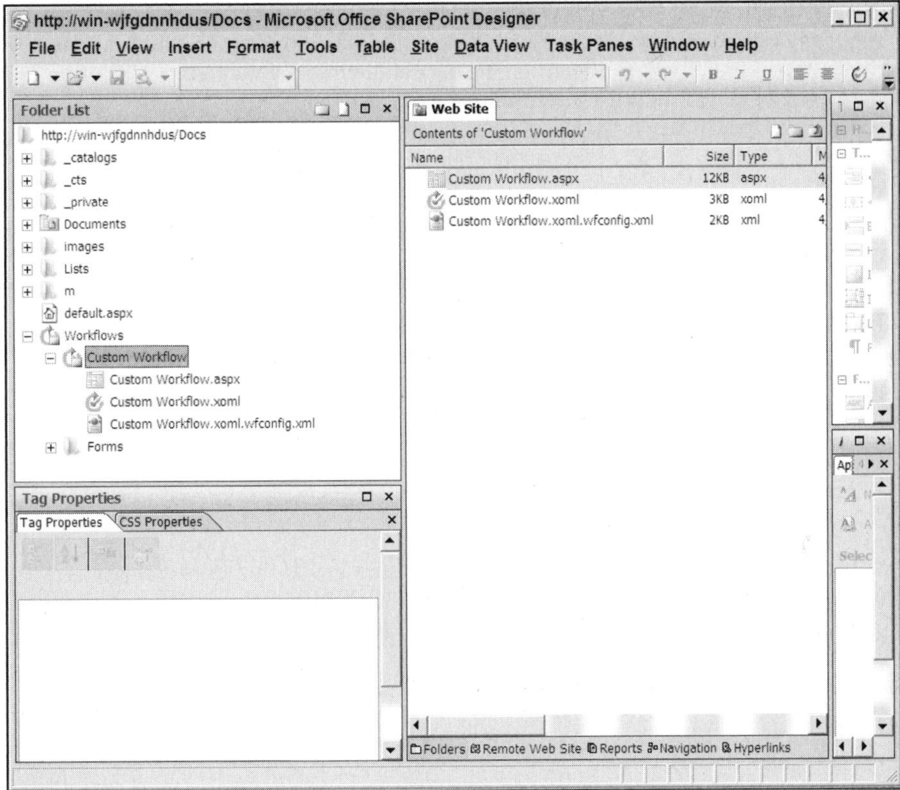

Figure 8-33

Note that each workflow is stored in a separate folder under the Workflows folder. Each workflow's folder contains the workflow initiation form (if any), the XOML file that contains the definition of the workflow, and the workflow configuration file.

Recipe for Implementing a Custom Condition

Every condition represents a .NET method or function that takes zero or more parameters and returns a Boolean. A workflow uses conditions to introduce different execution branches. As a workflow is executing, when it reaches one or more conditions, it invokes their associated .NET methods, passing in the required parameter values. Which execution branch the workflow executes next depends on whether these .NET methods return true or false. Follow these steps to implement a custom condition and add it to Office SharePoint Designer 2007:

1. Implement a .NET class.
2. Add one public method to this class for each condition. Each method must take the required parameters, consume these parameter values, and return a Boolean. You should make these methods static. Each method must take at least three parameters of the

Microsoft.SharePoint.WorkflowActions.WorkflowContext, System.String, and System.Int32 types, in that order. When the method associated with a condition is invoked, these three required parameter values are automatically passed into the method. The method can then use these parameter values in its execution logic to determine whether to return false or true. The System.String and System.Int32 parameters, respectively, contain the GUID of the current SharePoint list and the ID of the current SharePoint list item. Each method can optionally take extra parameters if the execution logic of the method requires inputs from the workflow.

3. Compile the .NET class into a strong-named assembly.
4. Deploy the assembly to the global assembly cache (GAC).
5. Implement an .actions file to describe your custom conditions to Office SharePoint Designer 2007.
6. Deploy the .actions file to the following folder on the file system of the front-end web server as discussed earlier:

```
%Program Files%\Common Files\Microsoft Shared\web server
extensions\12\TEMPLATE\1033\Workflow\
```

Recall that when a condition method is invoked, it receives a WorkflowContext object as its first argument. The method can then use the methods and properties of this object in its execution logic. The WorkflowContext class exposes a method named GetListItem as follows:

```
public SPListItem GetListItem(SPList list, int listItem);
```

This method takes an SPList object and an integer that specifies the ID of a list item in the SharePoint list represented by the SPList object and returns an SPListItem object that represents the list item. The WorkflowContext class also exposes the following two properties:

```
public SPSite Site { get; }
public SPWeb Web { get; }
```

As you may have guessed already, the Site property returns the SPSite object that represents the current site collection, and the Web property returns the SPWeb object that represents the current site.

Next, we'll use this recipe to implement a custom condition named "Title field contains keywords2." The .NET method associated with this custom condition provides a simplified version of the internal implementation of the SharePoint "Title field contains keywords" condition. My goal is to help you understand the following:

- How to implement a custom condition
- How to deploy it to Office SharePoint Designer 2007
- The roles of the required Microsoft.SharePoint.WorkflowActions.WorkflowContext, System.String, and System.Int32 parameters of a condition method

The following code listing presents the implementation of our custom condition method:

```
using System;
using Microsoft.SharePoint.WorkflowActions;
using Microsoft.SharePoint;

namespace Chapter8
{
 public class Helper
 {
    public static bool WordsInTitle(WorkflowContext context, string listId,
                                    int listItem, string words)
    {
      SPWeb web = context.Web;
      Guid listGuid = new Guid(listId);
      SPList list = web.Lists[listGuid];
      SPListItem item = context.GetListItem(list, listItem);
      string str = item["Title"].ToString();
      return ((str != null) && str.Contains(words));
    }
 }
}
```

As you can see, our WordsInTitle custom condition method, just like any other custom condition method, is a public static method that takes the three Microsoft.SharePoint.WorkflowActions.WorkflowContext, System.String, and System.Int32 parameters. Our custom condition method also takes a fourth parameter of the System.String type that contains the keywords for which our method will search the Title field of the current SharePoint list item. This method first uses the Web property of the WorkflowContext object passed into it as its first argument to access the SPWeb object that represents the current site:

```
SPWeb web = context.Web;
```

Next, it creates a Guid from the string passed into it as its second argument. Recall that this string contains the GUID of the current SharePoint list:

```
      Guid listGuid = new Guid(listId);
```

Then, it uses this Guid as an index into the Lists collection property of the SPWeb object that represents the current site to return a reference to the SPList object that represents the current SharePoint list:

```
      SPList list = web.Lists[listGuid];
```

Next, it invokes the GetListItem method on the WorkflowContext object passed into it as its first argument, passing in the SPList object and the string containing the ID of the current list item, to return a reference to the SPListItem object that represents the current list item. Recall that the string containing the ID of the current list item is passed into the WordsInTitle method as its third argument:

```
      SPListItem item = context.GetListItem(list, listItem);
```

Then, WordsInTitle uses the "Title" string as an index into this SPListItem object to return the value of the Title field:

```
      string str = item["Title"].ToString();
```

Finally, it uses the Contains method to determine whether the Title field value contains the specified keywords. Recall that the keywords are passed into the WordsInTitle method as its fourth argument:

```
return ((str != null) && str.Contains(words));
```

As the implementation of this sample custom condition method shows, your custom condition method can use the methods and properties of the WorkflowContext object passed into it as its first argument, the GUID of the current list passed into it as its second argument, and the ID of the current list item passed into it as its third argument in the logic that determines whether the method should return true or false.

The following .actions file describes our custom condition to Office SharePoint Designer 2007:

```
<?xml version="1.0" encoding="utf-8"?>
<WorkflowInfo Language="en-us">
  <Conditions And="and" Or="or" Not="not" When="If" Else="Else if">
    <Condition Name="Title field contains keywords2"
      FunctionName="WordsInTitle"
      ClassName="Chapter8.Helper"
      Assembly="Chapter8, Version=1.0.0.0, Culture=neutral, PublicKeyToken=636dfad8
5c01d3c8"
      AppliesTo="all"
      UsesCurrentItem="true">
      <RuleDesigner Sentence="Title field contains %1">
        <FieldBind Id="1" Field="_1_" Text="keywords" DesignerType="Text" />
      </RuleDesigner>
      <Parameters>
        <Parameter Name="_1_" Type="System.String, mscorlib" Direction="In" />
      </Parameters>
    </Condition>
  </Conditions>
</WorkflowInfo>
```

Note that this .actions file sets the AppliesTo attribute on the <Condition> element to All to instruct Office SharePoint Designer 2007 to make the condition available to workflow developers regardless of whether the workflow they're designing is associated with a standard SharePoint list or a document library. Also note that the UsesCurrentItem attribute on the <Condition> element is set to true because our condition method does use the current list item in its execution logic. The next chapter provides in-depth coverage of the XML markup language that you need to use to implement the .actions file describing your custom conditions to Office SharePoint Designer 2007.

Next, let's use our custom action in a workflow, as shown in Figure 8-34. Here, we've used the Conditions button to select our custom condition from the list of available conditions. Note that this workflow contains two execution branches. The first branch executes only if the method associated with our custom condition returns true. The second branch executes only if this method returns false. Both branches contain a LogToHistoryListActivity activity to log the appropriate information into the workflow history list.

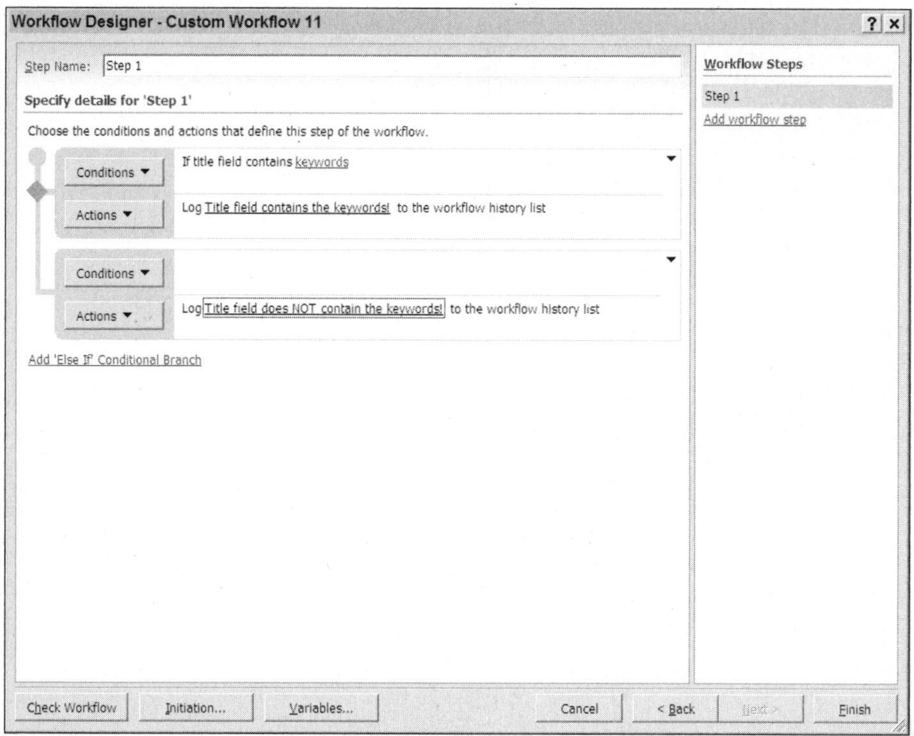

Figure 8-34

Use the steps discussed earlier in this chapter to create a workflow initiation form that contains a text box titled "Enter keywords."

Click the "keywords" link in the rule designer sentence associated with our custom condition. Because we've set the DesignerType attribute on the <FieldBind> element that represents the parameter of the method associated with our custom condition to Text, clicking this link pops up the interface shown in Figure 8-35. The next chapter provides detailed coverage of the DesignerType attribute and its values.

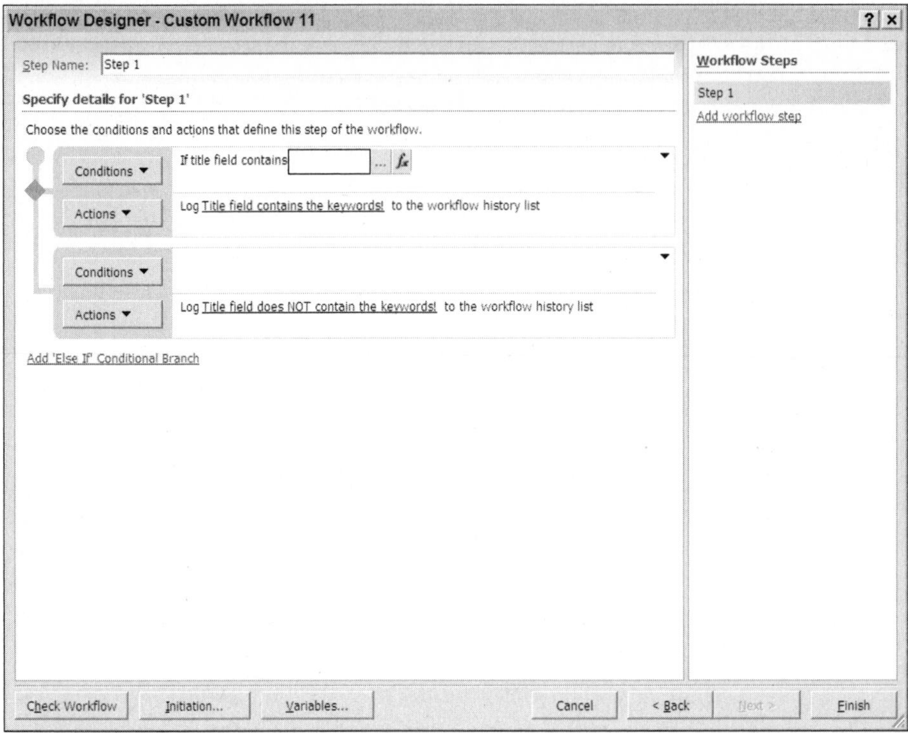

Figure 8-35

Click the data binding button (the button next to the ellipsis button) and follow the steps discussed earlier in this chapter to bind the keywords parameter of the method associated with our custom condition to the "Enter keywords" workflow local variable. The Workflow Designer should now look like Figure 8-36.

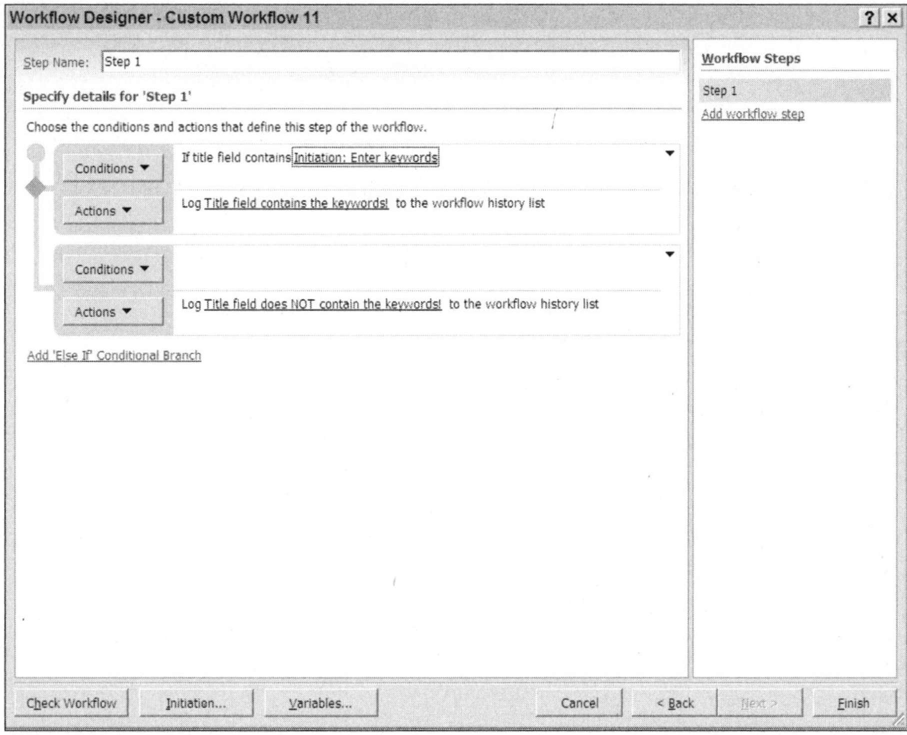

Figure 8-36

Finally, click the Finish button (see Figure 8-36) to create and store the workflow. If you run the workflow on an item in its associated list, you'll be redirected to the workflow initiation form shown in Figure 8-37. Enter "**Document**" and click Start to start the workflow.

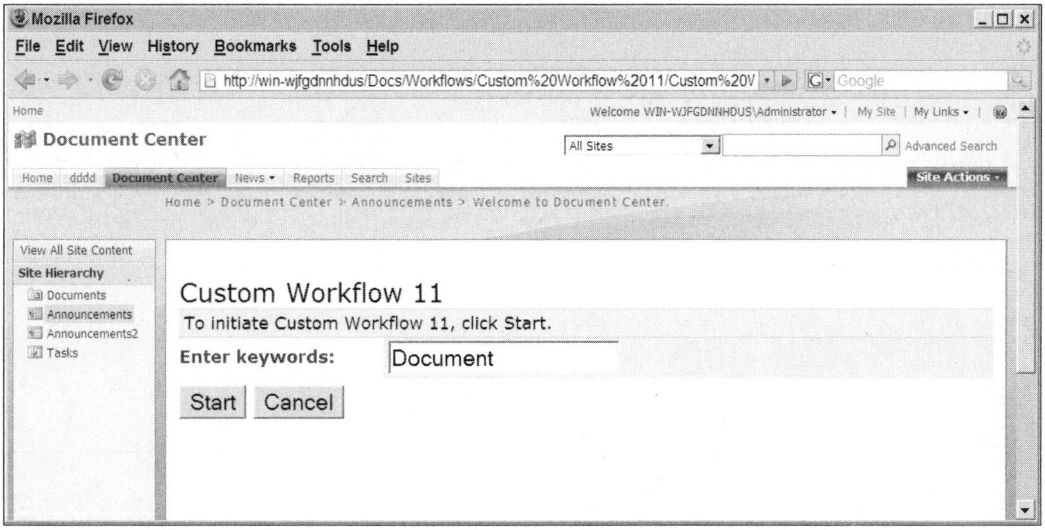

Figure 8-37

As Figure 8-38 shows, the workflow history list contains the message "Title field contains the keywords!," which indicates that the first branch of the workflow was executed. Rerun the workflow and this time enter text that the Title of the current list item does not contain. You should see the message "Title field does NOT contain the keywords!" in the workflow history list.

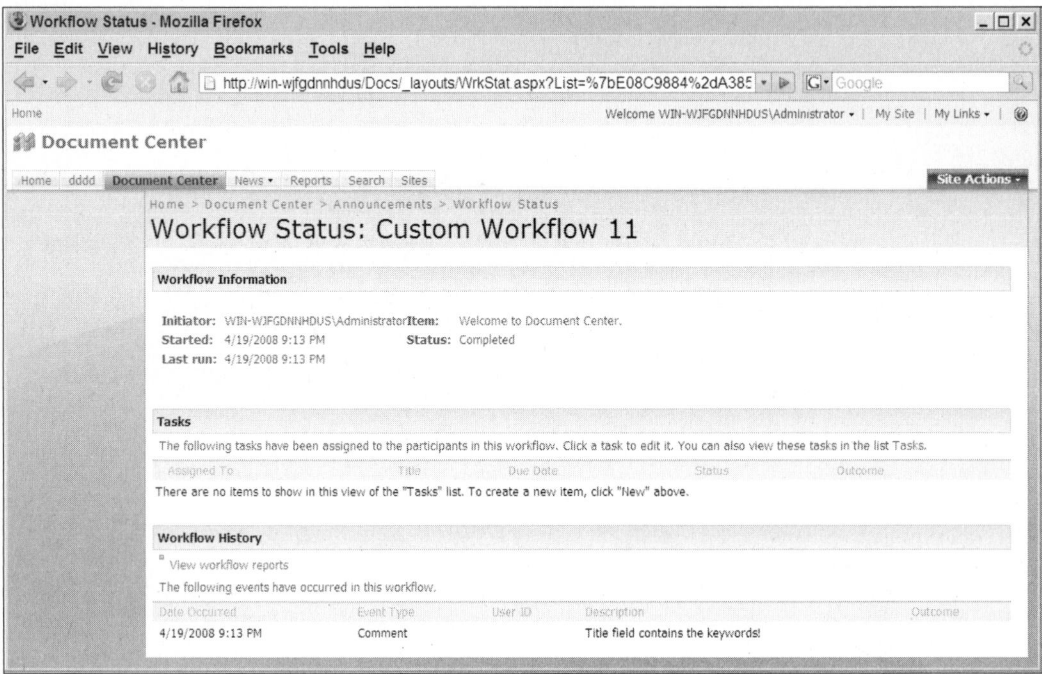

Figure 8-38

Summary

This chapter presented detailed, step-by-step recipes for implementing and deploying custom activities and custom conditions to Office SharePoint Designer 2007. The chapter used these recipes to implement and deploy a custom activity and custom condition. As shown in this chapter, you must implement an .actions file to describe your custom activity and custom condition to the Office SharePoint Designer 2007. The next chapter provides in-depth coverage of the workflow actions and conditions XML markup language. You'll need to use this markup language to implement an .actions file.

9

Workflow Actions and Conditions XML Markup Language

The previous chapter walked you through the implementation, deployment, and testing of an Office SharePoint Designer 2007 custom action and custom condition. As you saw, you must implement an .actions XML file to describe your custom WF activity and custom condition to Office SharePoint Designer 2007. You must use the workflow actions and conditions XML markup language to implement this XML file. In this chapter, we will dive into the details of this markup language.

An .actions XML document, like any other XML document, features a single XML element known as a *document element*. The document element in this case is an element named <WorkflowInfo>. This document element features a single optional attribute named Language. Set the value of this attribute to a language/culture pair:

```
<WorkflowInfo Language="en-us">
  . . .
</WorkflowInfo>
```

The <WorkflowInfo> document element features two child elements named <Actions> and <Conditions>. I discuss the <Conditions> element later in this chapter. The <Actions> element has two required attributes as follows:

- **Sequential:** Office SharePoint Designer 2007 displays this text in the rule designer sentence when users arrange two or more actions in sequential order. The default is "then."
- **Parallel:** Office SharePoint Designer 2007 displays this text in the rule sentence when users arrange two or more actions in parallel. The default is "and."

In the case of our example:

```
<WorkflowInfo Language="en-us">
  <Actions Sequential="then" Parallel="and">
    . . .
  </Actions>
</WorkflowInfo>
```

The <Actions> element supports two child elements named <Action> and <Default>. Use an <Action> element to describe your custom WF activity to Office SharePoint Designer 2007. The following sections cover the attributes and child elements of the <Action> element.

Attributes of the Action Element

This section discusses the attributes of the <Action> element.

Name

Set this required attribute to the friendly name of your custom WF activity. Office SharePoint Designer 2007 displays this friendly name to workflow designers:

```
<WorkflowInfo Language="en-us">
  <Actions Sequential="then" Parallel="and">
    <Action Name="Execute custom code" . . .>
      . . .
    </Action>
  </Actions>
</WorkflowInfo>
```

ClassName

Set this required attribute to the fully qualified name of your custom WF activity. The fully qualified name of a type includes its complete namespace containment hierarchy in addition to the name of the type:

```
<WorkflowInfo Language="en-us">
  <Actions Sequential="then" Parallel="and">
    <Action Name="Execute custom code" ClassName="Chapter9.CustomActivity">
      . . .
    </Action>
  </Actions>
</WorkflowInfo>
```

Assembly

Set this required attribute to the strong name of the assembly that contains your custom WF activity. The strong name of an assembly consists of four parts: assembly name, version, culture, and public key token:

```
<WorkflowInfo Language="en-us">
  <Actions Sequential="then" Parallel="and">
    <Action Name="Execute custom code" ClassName="Chapter9.CustomActivity"
    Assembly="Chapter9. Version=1.0.0.0, Culture=neutral,
              PublicKeyToken=37bb2ef3e98409ac">
      . . .
    </Action>
  </Actions>
</WorkflowInfo>
```

Category

Set this optional attribute to the name of the category under which you would like Office SharePoint Designer 2007 to display the friendly name of your custom WF activity to users:

```
<WorkflowInfo Language="en-us">
  <Actions Sequential="then" Parallel="and">
    <Action Name="Execute custom code" ClassName="Chapter9.CustomActivity"
    Assembly="Chapter9 Version=1.0.0.0, Culture=neutral,
              PublicKeyToken=37bb2ef3e98409ac"
    Category="My Custom Actions">
      . . .
    </Action>
  </Actions>
</WorkflowInfo>
```

CreatesTask

This attribute specifies whether the WF activity that the <Action> element describes creates SharePoint tasks. SharePoint ships with three activities named CollectDataTask, TodoItemTask, and GroupAssignedTask, which set this attribute to true because they create SharePoint tasks as part of their execution logic.

The following XML fragment shows an excerpt from a wss.actions file that describes the CollectDataTask activity to Office SharePoint Designer 2007. As the boldfaced portions of this XML fragment illustrate, the CreatesTask attribute is set to true to signal to Office SharePoint Designer 2007 that this activity creates a SharePoint task as part of its execution logic. Note that this activity exposes a bindable integer output property named TaskId, which contains the task ID of the SharePoint task that this activity creates:

```
<Action Name="Collect Data from a User"
ClassName="Microsoft.SharePoint.WorkflowActions.CollectDataTask"
Assembly="Microsoft.SharePoint.WorkflowActions, Version=12.0.0.0, Culture=neutral,
          PublicKeyToken=71e9bce111e9429c"
AppliesTo="all" CreatesTask="true" Category="Task Actions">
  <RuleDesigner Sentence="Collect %1 from %2 (Output to %3)">
    <FieldBind Field="Title, ContentTypeId" DesignerType="Survey"
    Text="data" Id="1"/>
    <FieldBind Field="AssignedTo" DesignerType="SinglePerson"
    Text="this user" Id="2"/>
    <FieldBind Field="TaskId" DesignerType="ParameterNames" Text="collect" Id="3"/>
  </RuleDesigner>
  <Parameters>
    <Parameter Name="__Context"
    Type="Microsoft.SharePoint.WorkflowActions.WorkflowContext,
          Microsoft.SharePoint.WorkflowActions" Direction="In" />
    <Parameter Name="ContentTypeId" Type="System.String, mscorlib"
    Direction="In" />
    <Parameter Name="AssignedTo" Type="System.String, mscorlib" Direction="In" />
    <Parameter Name="Title" Type="System.String, mscorlib" Direction="In" />
    <Parameter Name="TaskId" Type="System.Int32, mscorlib" Direction="Out" />
  </Parameters>
</Action>
```

The wss.actions file is where SharePoint describes SharePoint standard activities to SharePoint Designer 2007. This file is located in the following folder in the file system of each front-end web server:

```
Local_Drive:\Program Files\Common Files\microsoft shared\Web Server
Extensions\12\TEMPLATE\1033\Workflow
```

The following excerpt from the wss.actions file describes the TodoItemTask activity to Office SharePoint Designer 2007. As shown in the boldfaced portions of this excerpt, the CreatesTask attribute is set to true because this activity creates a SharePoint task, which is assigned to the people specified in the AssignedTo input property of the activity:

```
<Action Name="Assign a To-do Item"
ClassName="Microsoft.SharePoint.WorkflowActions.TodoItemTask"
Assembly="Microsoft.SharePoint.WorkflowActions, Version=12.0.0.0, Culture=neutral,
          PublicKeyToken=71e9bce111e9429c"
AppliesTo="all" CreatesTask="true" Category="Task Actions">
  <RuleDesigner Sentence="Assign %1 to %2">
    <FieldBind Field="Title, ContentTypeId" DesignerType="Survey"
    Text="a to-do item" Id="1"/>
    <FieldBind Field="AssignedTo" DesignerType="Person" Text="these users" Id="2"/>
  </RuleDesigner>
  <Parameters>
    <Parameter Name="__Context"
```

```
    Type="Microsoft.SharePoint.WorkflowActions.WorkflowContext,
          Microsoft.SharePoint.WorkflowActions" Direction="In" />
    <Parameter Name="ContentTypeId" Type="System.String, mscorlib"
    Direction="In" />
    <Parameter Name="AssignedTo" Type="System.Collections.ArrayList, mscorlib"
    Direction="In" />
    <Parameter Name="Title" Type="System.String, mscorlib" Direction="In" />
  </Parameters>
</Action>
```

The following excerpt from wss.actions describes the GroupAssignedTask activity to Office SharePoint Designer 2007. The CreateTasks attribute is set to true because this activity creates a SharePoint task and assigns it to the people specified in its AssignedTo property, as shown in the boldfaced portions of the this excerpt:

```
<Action Name="Assign a Form to a Group"
ClassName="Microsoft.SharePoint.WorkflowActions.GroupAssignedTask"
Assembly="Microsoft.SharePoint.WorkflowActions, Version=12.0.0.0, Culture=neutral,
          PublicKeyToken=71e9bce111e9429c"
AppliesTo="all" CreatesTask="true" Category="Task Actions">
  <RuleDesigner Sentence="Assign %1 to %2">
    <FieldBind Field="Title,ContentTypeId" DesignerType="Survey"
    Text="a custom form" Id="1"/>
    <FieldBind Field="AssignedTo" DesignerType="Person" Text="these users" Id="2"/>
  </RuleDesigner>
  <Parameters>
    <Parameter Name="__Context"
     Type="Microsoft.SharePoint.WorkflowActions.WorkflowContext,
          Microsoft.SharePoint.WorkflowActions" Direction="In" />
    <Parameter Name="ContentTypeId" Type="System.String, mscorlib"
    Direction="In" />
    <Parameter Name="AssignedTo" Type="System.Collections.ArrayList, mscorlib"
    Direction="In" />
    <Parameter Name="Title" Type="System.String, mscorlib" Direction="In" />
  </Parameters>
</Action>
```

CreatesInList

This optional attribute specifies whether the WF activity that the <Action> element describes creates a list item in a SharePoint list. SharePoint ships with two WF activities named CreateItemActivity and CopyItemActivity that create list items in a specified SharePoint list. The following XML fragment is an excerpt from the wss.actions file, which describes CreateItemActivity to Office SharePoint Designer 2007:

```
<Action Name="Create List Item"
ClassName="Microsoft.SharePoint.WorkflowActions.CreateItemActivity"
Assembly="Microsoft.SharePoint.WorkflowActions, Version=12.0.0.0, Culture=neutral,
          PublicKeyToken=71e9bce111e9429c"
AppliesTo="all" CreatesInList="ListId" Category="List Actions">
  <RuleDesigner Sentence="Create item in %1 (Output to %2)">
    <FieldBind Field="ListId, ItemProperties, Overwrite" Text="this list" Id="1"
```

(continued)

(continued)

```
      DesignerType="CreateListItem" />
      <FieldBind Field="NewItemId" DesignerType="ParameterNames"
      Text="create" Id="2"/>
    </RuleDesigner>
    <Parameters>
      <Parameter Name="__Context"
      Type="Microsoft.SharePoint.WorkflowActions.WorkflowContext" Direction="In" />
      <Parameter Name="ListId" Type="System.String, mscorlib" Direction="In" />
      <Parameter Name="ItemProperties" Type="System.Collections.Hashtable, mscorlib"
      Direction="In" />
      <Parameter Name="Overwrite" Type="System.Boolean, mscorlib" Direction="In"
      InitialValue="false" />
      <Parameter Name="NewItemId" Type="System.Int32, mscorlib" Direction="Out" />
    </Parameters>
  </Action>
```

As the boldfaced portions of this XML fragment show, the CreatesInList attribute is set to "ListId," which is the name of the property of the CreateItemActivity activity that contains the GUID of the SharePoint list in which the activity creates the list item.

The following XML fragment shows an excerpt from the wss.actions file that describes CopyItemActivity to Office SharePoint Designer 2007, where the CreatesInList attribute is set to "ToListId," which is the name of the property of the CopyItemActivity activity that contains the GUID of the SharePoint list to which the activity copies the specified list item:

```
  <Action Name="Copy List Item" AppliesTo="all" Category="List Actions"
  ClassName="Microsoft.SharePoint.WorkflowActions.CopyItemActivity"
  Assembly="Microsoft.SharePoint.WorkflowActions, Version=12.0.0.0, Culture=neutral,
            PublicKeyToken=71e9bce111e9429c"
  CreatesInList="ToListId">
    <RuleDesigner Sentence="Copy item in %1 to %2">
      <FieldBind Field="ListId, ListItem" Text="this list" Id="1"
      DesignerType="ChooseListItem" />
      <FieldBind Field="ToListId" Text="this list" Id="2" DesignerType="ListNames" />
    </RuleDesigner>
    <Parameters>
      <Parameter Name="__Context"
      Type="Microsoft.SharePoint.WorkflowActions.WorkflowContext" Direction="In" />
      <Parameter Name="ListId" Type="System.String, mscorlib" Direction="In" />
      <Parameter Name="ListItem" Type="System.Int32, mscorlib" Direction="In" />
      <Parameter Name="ToListId" Type="System.String, mscorlib" Direction="In" />
      <Parameter Name="Overwrite" Type="System.Boolean, mscorlib" Direction="In"
      InitialValue="false" />
    </Parameters>
  </Action>
```

AppliesTo

The following list describes the possible values of this required attribute:

- **List:** This value specifies that the WF activity that the <Action> element describes can only be used in workflows associated with a standard SharePoint list.

- **Doclib**: This value specifies that the WF activity that the <Action> element describes can only be used in workflows associated with a SharePoint document library.
- **All:** This value specifies that the WF activity that the <Action> element describes can be used in both workflows associated with a SharePoint list and a document library.

The following XML fragment shows an example in which this attribute is set to All:

```
<WorkflowInfo Language="en-us">
  <Actions Sequential="then" Parallel="and">
    <Action Name="Execute custom code" ClassName="Chapter9.CustomActivity"
    Assembly="Chapter9 Version=1.0.0.0, Culture=neutral,
              PublicKeyToken=37bb2ef3e98409ac"
    Category="My Custom Actions" AppliesTo="All">
      . . .
    </Action>
  </Actions>
</WorkflowInfo>
```

ListModeration

This Boolean attribute specifies whether the WF activity that the <Action> element describes applies to a SharePoint list and has content approval enabled. SharePoint ships with an activity named SetModerationStatusActivity. The <Action> element that describes this activity sets ListModeration to true. Note that this activity exposes an input property named ModerationStatus, with possible values of Approved, Rejected, and Pending, as shown in the following XML excerpt:

```
<Action Name="Set Content Approval Status" AppliesTo="list"
ClassName="Microsoft.SharePoint.WorkflowActions.SetModerationStatusActivity"
Assembly="Microsoft.SharePoint.WorkflowActions, Version=12.0.0.0, Culture=neutral,
          PublicKeyToken=71e9bce111e9429c"
ListModeration="true" Category="Core Actions" UsesCurrentItem="true">
  <RuleDesigner Sentence="Set content approval status to %1 with %2">
    <FieldBind Field="ModerationStatus" DesignerType="Dropdown" Id="1"
    Text="this status">
      <Option Name="Approved" Value="Approved"/>
      <Option Name="Rejected" Value="Denied"/>
      <Option Name="Pending" Value="Pending"/>
    </FieldBind>
    <FieldBind Field="Comments" Text="comments" Id="2" DesignerType="TextArea" />
  </RuleDesigner>
  <Parameters>
    <Parameter Name="ModerationStatus" Type="System.String, mscorlib"
    Direction="In" />
    <Parameter Name="Comments" Type="System.String, mscorlib"
    Direction="Optional" />
    <Parameter Name="__Context"
    Type="Microsoft.SharePoint.WorkflowActions.WorkflowContext,
          Microsoft.SharePoint.WorkflowActions" />
    <Parameter Name="__ListId" Type="System.String, mscorlib" Direction="In" />
    <Parameter Name="__ListItem" Type="System.Int32, mscorlib" Direction="In" />
  </Parameters>
</Action>
```

UsesCurrentItem

This attribute specifies whether the WF activity that the <Action> element describes uses or modifies the current list item as part of its execution logic. SharePoint comes with an activity named SetFieldActivity, which is described in the following excerpt from the wss.actions file. As shown in the boldfaced portions of this excerpt, the UsesCurrentItem attribute is set to true because this activity sets the specified field in the current list item to the specified value. Note that this activity exposes two input properties named FieldName and Value, which respectively specify the name and value of the field whose value is being set. This activity exposes an input integer property named __ListItem that specifies the ID of the current list item:

```
<Action Name="Set Field in Current Item"
ClassName="Microsoft.SharePoint.WorkflowActions.SetFieldActivity"
Assembly="Microsoft.SharePoint.WorkflowActions, Version=12.0.0.0, Culture=neutral,
          PublicKeyToken=71e9bce111e9429c"
AppliesTo="list" UsesCurrentItem="true" Category="Core Actions">
  <RuleDesigner Sentence="Set %1 to %2">
    <FieldBind Field="FieldName" Text="field" Id="1"
    DesignerType="writablefieldNames" />
    <FieldBind Field="Value" Text="value" Id="2" TypeFrom="FieldName"/>
  </RuleDesigner>
  <Parameters>
    <Parameter Name="FieldName" Type="System.String, mscorlib" Direction="In" />
    <Parameter Name="Value" Type="System.Object, mscorlib" Direction="In" />
    <Parameter Name="__Context"
    Type="Microsoft.SharePoint.WorkflowActions.WorkflowContext,
          Microsoft.SharePoint.WorkflowActions" Direction="In"/>
    <Parameter Name="__ListId" Type="System.String, mscorlib" Direction="In" />
    <Parameter Name="__ListItem" Type="System.Int32, mscorlib" Direction="In" />
  </Parameters>
</Action>
```

So far, we've discussed the attributes of the <Action> element. The <Action> element supports two child elements named <RuleDesigner> and <Parameters>, which are discussed in the following sections.

RuleDesigner Child Element of Action Element

Use the <RuleDesigner> element to provide Office SharePoint Designer 2007 with the information that it needs to render a rule designer sentence for your custom WF activity. This element supports a single required attribute named Sentence that must contain the text for the rule designer sentence. This text must contain a placeholder variable for each input and output properties of your custom WF activity. A placeholder variable consists of two parts: The first part is a percent (%) character and the second part is a non-negative integer. This non-negative integer must be equal to the value of the Id attribute on a <FieldBind> child element of the <RuleDesigner> element. Here is an example:

```
<WorkflowInfo Language="en-us">
  <Actions Sequential="then" Parallel="and">
    <Action Name="Execute custom code" ClassName="Chapter9.CustomActivity"
    Assembly="Chapter9 Version=1.0.0.0, Culture=neutral,
              PublicKeyToken=37bb2ef3e98409ac"
    Category="My Custom Actions" AppliesTo="All">
      <RuleDesigner Sentence="Execute custom code with %1 and %2 (Output: %3)">
        . . .
      </RuleDesigner>
      . . .
    </Action>
  </Actions>
</WorkflowInfo>
```

The <RuleDesigner> element can contain zero or more <FieldBind> child elements. Each <FieldBind> child element has the following characteristics:

- It binds a property of your custom WF activity to a placeholder variable in the rule designer sentence. You must specify the name of the property in the Field attribute of the <FieldBind> child element whose Id attribute is set to the same non-negative integer number specified in the placeholder variable.
- It specifies the type of control that Office SharePoint Designer 2007 presents to users when they click the placeholder variable to specify a value for it or bind another variable to it.

The <FieldBind> element supports the attributes discussed in the following sections.

DesignerType Attribute of the FieldBind Element

Set this optional attribute to tell Office SharePoint Designer 2007 what type of control to present to users when they click the associated placeholder variable in the rule designer sentence. If you do not specify a value for this attribute, by default Office SharePoint Designer 2007 presents users with a text box followed by an ellipsis button and a lookup button for binding. The following sections describe the possible values of the DesignerType attribute.

Boolean

Set the DesignerType attribute to Boolean to have Office SharePoint Designer 2007 display a drop-down list box populated with two values, true and false, when users click the placeholder variable in the rule designer sentence that represents a Boolean property of your custom WF activity. Here is an example:

```
<RuleDesigner Sentence="Execute custom code with %1">
  <FieldBind Name="BooleanProperty" DesignerType="Boolean" Id="1"
  Text="this value" />
</RuleDesigner>
<Parameters>
  <Parameter Name="BooleanProperty" Type="System.Boolean, mscorlib"
  Direction="In" />
</Parameters>
```

ChooseDoclibItem

This value for the DesignerType attribute instructs Office SharePoint Designer 2007 to display the document library item selector control when users click the placeholder variable in the rule designer sentence. Obviously, this only makes sense if the execution logic of the activity that the <Action> element represents requires the workflow developer to select a list item from a specified list.

SharePoint ships with three standard activities, CheckOutItemActivity, CheckInItemActivity, and UndoCheckoutItemActivity, which a workflow can use to respectively check out, check in, and undo checkout of a specified list item. Before discussing the <Action> elements, which describe these activities, we'll take a look at the CheckInItemActivity activity to see the list item selector control in action.

Figure 9-1 presents the rule sentence for the CheckInItemActivity activity.

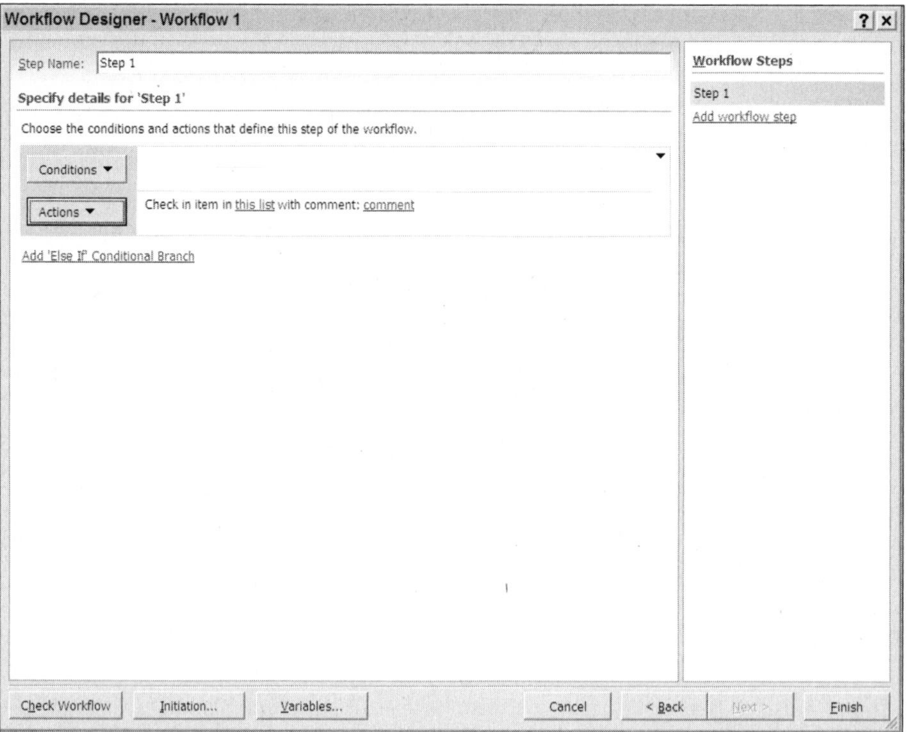

Figure 9-1

When the user clicks the This List link shown in this rule designer sentence, Office SharePoint Designer 2007 launches the list item selector control shown in Figure 9-2.

Figure 9-2

The list item selector control contains a drop-down list box that displays the list of available SharePoint lists to choose from. After the workflow developer makes the required selections and clicks OK, the list item selector control automatically assigns the GUID of the selected SharePoint list to the ListId property of the CheckInItemActivity. This property is of the System.String type.

After the user selects a SharePoint list from here, the list item selector control displays the rest of its user interface, enabling the user to select and locate the desired list item in the selected SharePoint list, as shown in Figure 9-3.

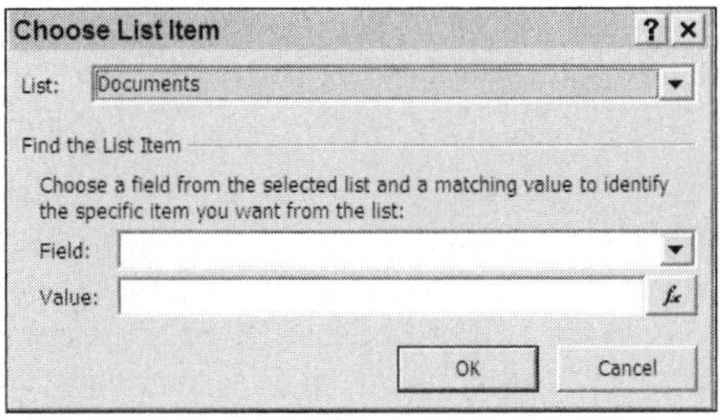

Figure 9-3

The bottom part of the list item selector control contains a drop-down list box that displays all the fields of the selected SharePoint list. The workflow developer selects a field from this drop-down list box, specifies a value for this field in the text box below this drop-down list box, and clicks OK to have the list item selector control select the list item with the specified field value from the selected SharePoint list. The list item selector control assigns the ID of the selected list item to the ListItem property of the CheckInItemActivity activity. The main function of the list item selector control is to enable the workflow developer to set the values of the ListId and ListItem properties of the CheckInItemActivity activity in purely graphical fashion without any code.

The following excerpt from wss.actions presents the <Action> elements that describe the CheckOutItemActivity, CheckInItemActivity, and UndoCheckoutItemActivity activities to Office SharePoint Designer 2007:

```
<Action Name="Check Out Item"
ClassName="Microsoft.SharePoint.WorkflowActions.CheckOutItemActivity"
Assembly="Microsoft.SharePoint.WorkflowActions, Version=12.0.0.0, Culture=neutral,
          PublicKeyToken=71e9bce111e9429c"
AppliesTo="all" Category="List Actions">
  <RuleDesigner Sentence="Check out item in %1">
    <FieldBind Field="ListId, ListItem" Text="this list" Id="1"
```

(continued)

(continued)

```
      DesignerType="ChooseDoclibItem" />
    </RuleDesigner>
    <Parameters>
      <Parameter Name="__Context"
      Type="Microsoft.SharePoint.WorkflowActions.WorkflowContext" Direction="In" />
      <Parameter Name="ListId" Type="System.String, mscorlib" Direction="In" />
      <Parameter Name="ListItem" Type="System.Int32, mscorlib" Direction="In" />
    </Parameters>
  </Action>

  <Action Name="Check In Item"
  ClassName="Microsoft.SharePoint.WorkflowActions.CheckInItemActivity"
  Assembly="Microsoft.SharePoint.WorkflowActions, Version=12.0.0.0, Culture=neutral,
          PublicKeyToken=71e9bce111e9429c"
  AppliesTo="all" Category="List Actions">
    <RuleDesigner Sentence="Check in item in %1 with comment: %2">
      <FieldBind Field="ListId,ListItem" Text="this list" Id="1"
      DesignerType="ChooseDoclibItem" />
      <FieldBind Field="Comment" Text="comment" Id="2"
      DesignerType="TextArea"></FieldBind>
    </RuleDesigner>
    <Parameters>
      <Parameter Name="__Context"
      Type="Microsoft.SharePoint.WorkflowActions.WorkflowContext" Direction="In" />
      <Parameter Name="ListId" Type="System.String, mscorlib" Direction="In" />
      <Parameter Name="ListItem" Type="System.Int32, mscorlib" Direction="In" />
      <Parameter Name="Comment" Type="System.String, mscorlib" Direction="In" />
    </Parameters>
  </Action>

  <Action Name="Discard Check Out Item"
  ClassName="Microsoft.SharePoint.WorkflowActions.UndoCheckOutItemActivity"
  Assembly="Microsoft.SharePoint.WorkflowActions, Version=12.0.0.0, Culture=neutral,
          PublicKeyToken=71e9bce111e9429c"
  AppliesTo="all" Category="List Actions">
    <RuleDesigner Sentence="Discard check out of item in %1">
      <FieldBind Field="ListId,ListItem" Text="this list" Id="1"
      DesignerType="ChooseDoclibItem" />
    </RuleDesigner>
    <Parameters>
      <Parameter Name="__Context"
      Type="Microsoft.SharePoint.WorkflowActions.WorkflowContext" Direction="In" />
      <Parameter Name="ListId" Type="System.String, mscorlib" Direction="In" />
      <Parameter Name="ListItem" Type="System.Int32, mscorlib" Direction="In" />
    </Parameters>
  </Action>
```

As shown in the boldfaced portions, all three activities expose two properties named ListId and ListItem. The ListItem property is where the list item selector control stores the ID of the list item to check out, check in, or undo checkout. The ListId property is where the list item selector control stores the GUID of the SharePoint list to which this list item belongs. Note that the DesignerType attribute on the <FieldBind> elements that bind the ListId and ListItem properties of these activities to the %1 placeholder variable in the rule sentence is set to ChooseDoclibItem. This instructs Office SharePoint

Designer 2007 to present workflow developers with the list item selector control when they click this placeholder variable. Workflow developers click this variable to select a list item from a SharePoint list to check out, check in, or undo checkout.

ChooseListItem

This value for the DesignerType attribute instructs Office SharePoint Designer 2007 to display the list item selector control when the user clicks a specified placeholder variable in the rule sentence. Both the ChooseDoclibItem and the ChooseListItem values launch the same list item selector control discussed earlier.

SharePoint ships with two standard activities named CopyItemActivity and DeleteItemActivity, which enable a workflow to copy a specified list item from a specified SharePoint list to another SharePoint list and to delete a specified list item, respectively. As the following excerpt from wss.actions shows, the DesignerType attribute in both cases is set to ChooseListItem:

```
<Action Name="Copy List Item"
  ClassName="Microsoft.SharePoint.WorkflowActions.CopyItemActivity"
  Assembly="Microsoft.SharePoint.WorkflowActions, Version=12.0.0.0,
            Culture=neutral, PublicKeyToken=71e9bce111e9429c"
  CreatesInList="ToListId" AppliesTo="all" Category="List Actions">
  <RuleDesigner Sentence="Copy item in %1 to %2">
    <FieldBind Field="ListId, ListItem" Text="this list" Id="1"
    DesignerType="ChooseListItem" />
    <FieldBind Field="ToListId" Text="this list" Id="2" DesignerType="ListNames" />
  </RuleDesigner>
  <Parameters>
    <Parameter Name="__Context"
    Type="Microsoft.SharePoint.WorkflowActions.WorkflowContext" Direction="In" />
    <Parameter Name="ListId" Type="System.String, mscorlib" Direction="In" />
    <Parameter Name="ListItem" Type="System.Int32, mscorlib" Direction="In" />
    <Parameter Name="ToListId" Type="System.String, mscorlib" Direction="In" />
    <Parameter Name="Overwrite" Type="System.Boolean, mscorlib" Direction="In"
    InitialValue="false" />
  </Parameters>
</Action>

<Action Name="Delete Item"
ClassName="Microsoft.SharePoint.WorkflowActions.DeleteItemActivity"
Assembly="Microsoft.SharePoint.WorkflowActions, Version=12.0.0.0, Culture=neutral,
          PublicKeyToken=71e9bce111e9429c"
AppliesTo="all" Category="List Actions">
  <RuleDesigner Sentence="Delete item in %1">
    <FieldBind Field="ListId, ListItem" Text="this list" Id="1"
    DesignerType="ChooseListItem" />
  </RuleDesigner>
  <Parameters>
    <Parameter Name="__Context"
    Type="Microsoft.SharePoint.WorkflowActions.WorkflowContext" Direction="In" />
    <Parameter Name="ListId" Type="System.String, mscorlib" Direction="In" />
    <Parameter Name="ListItem" Type="System.Int32, mscorlib" Direction="In" />
  </Parameters>
</Action>
```

CreateListItem

This value for the DesignerType attribute instructs Office SharePoint Designer 2007 to launch the create list item control when the workflow developer clicks a specified placeholder variable in the rule sentence. SharePoint comes with a standard activity named CreateListItem that enables workflows to create list items. Before describing the details of the <Action> element, which describes this activity, we'll take a look at the create list item control in action.

Figure 9-4 presents the rule sentence for the CreateListItem activity.

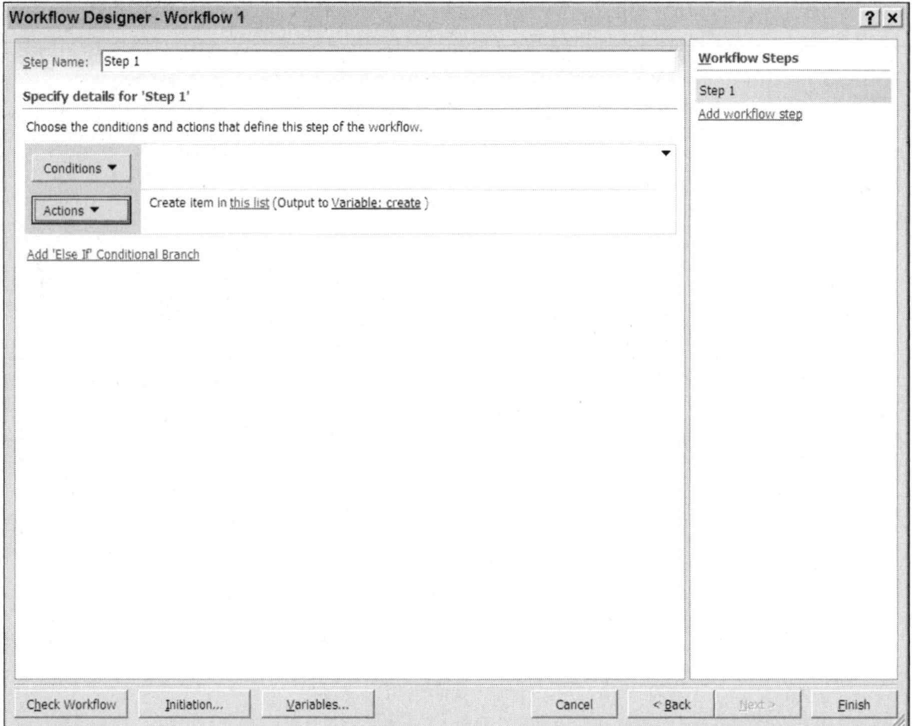

Figure 9-4

When the workflow developer clicks the This List placeholder variable, Office SharePoint Designer 2007 presents the workflow developer with the create list item control shown in Figure 9-5.

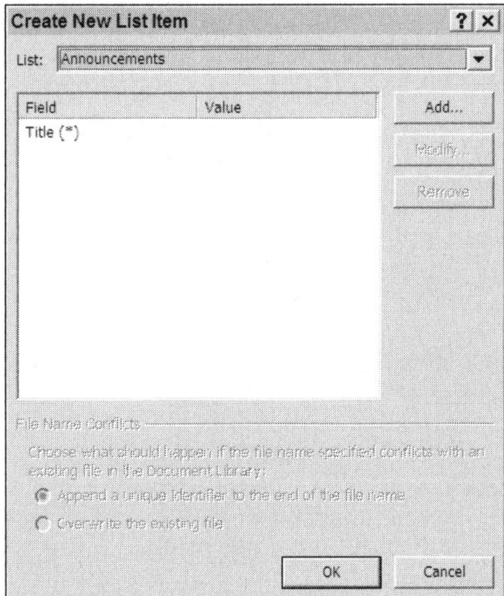

Figure 9-5

This control contains a drop-down list box that displays the list of available SharePoint lists to choose from. When the workflow developer selects a SharePoint list from this drop-down list box, the create list item selector displays some of the fields of the selected SharePoint list. The Add button launches the dialog shown in Figure 9-6, which enables the user to add more of the fields of the selected SharePoint list and to specify the values of these fields. The Modify button enables the user to specify the values of the displayed fields.

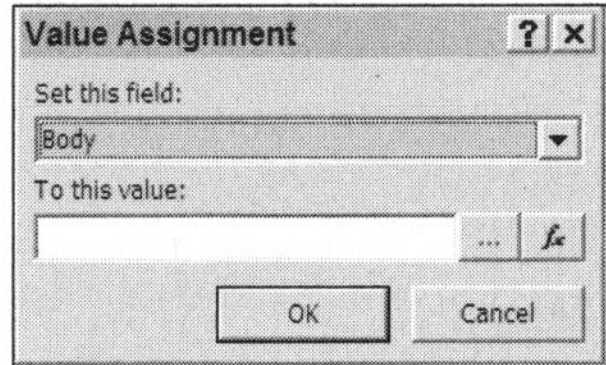

Figure 9-6

When the user finally clicks the OK button in Figure 9-5, the create list item control takes the following steps:

1. It assigns the ID of the selected SharePoint list to the ListId property of the CreateItemActivity activity.
2. It stores the names and values of the fields of the newly created list item in the ItemProperties property of the CreateItemActivity activity. This property is of the Hashtable type.
3. It stores the ID of the newly created list item in the NewItemId output property of the CreateItemActivity activity.

The following excerpt from wss.actions presents the <Action> element that describes the CreateItemActivity activity:

```
<Action Name="Create List Item"
ClassName="Microsoft.SharePoint.WorkflowActions.CreateItemActivity"
Assembly="Microsoft.SharePoint.WorkflowActions, Version=12.0.0.0, Culture=neutral,
          PublicKeyToken=71e9bce111e9429c"
AppliesTo="all" CreatesInList="ListId" Category="List Actions">
  <RuleDesigner Sentence="Create item in %1 (Output to %2)">
    <FieldBind Field="ListId, ItemProperties, Overwrite" Text="this list" Id="1"
    DesignerType="CreateListItem" />
    <FieldBind Field="NewItemId" DesignerType="ParameterNames"
    Text="create" Id="2"/>
  </RuleDesigner>
  <Parameters>
    <Parameter Name="__Context"
    Type="Microsoft.SharePoint.WorkflowActions.WorkflowContext" Direction="In" />
    <Parameter Name="ListId" Type="System.String, mscorlib" Direction="In" />
    <Parameter Name="ItemProperties" Type="System.Collections.Hashtable, mscorlib"
    Direction="In" />
    <Parameter Name="Overwrite" Type="System.Boolean, mscorlib" Direction="In"
    InitialValue="false" />
    <Parameter Name="NewItemId" Type="System.Int32, mscorlib" Direction="Out" />
  </Parameters>
</Action>
```

The preceding XML fragment accomplishes the following:

- It defines a <FieldBind> element.
- It sets the Field attribute on this <FieldBind> element to a comma-separated list of three substrings that contain the names of the properties of the CreateItemActivity activity where the create list item control can store the ID of the selected SharePoint list, the names and values of the fields of the newly created list item, and a Boolean value that specifies whether the newly created list item overrides an existing list item:

```
<FieldBind Field="ListId, ItemProperties, Overwrite" Text="this list" Id="1"
DesignerType="CreateListItem" />
```

- It sets the DesignerType attribute on this <FieldBind> element to CreateListItem:

```
<FieldBind Field="ListId, ItemProperties, Overwrite" Text="this list" Id="1"
DesignerType="CreateListItem" />
```

Date

Set the DesignerType attribute to Date to have Office SharePoint Designer 2007 display the date/time selector control when the workflow developer clicks a placeholder variable in the rule sentence that represents a DataTime property of your custom WF activity.

DropDown

Set the DesignerType attribute to Dropdown to have Office SharePoint Designer 2007 display a drop-down list box populated with predetermined static values when workflow developers click the placeholder variable in the rule sentence that represents a property of your custom WF activity. You must use a separate <Option> child element within the <FieldBind> element to specify each static value.

SharePoint ships with an activity named SetModerationStatusActivity, which is described by the <Action> element shown in the following excerpt from wss.actions:

```
<Action Name="Set Content Approval Status"
ClassName="Microsoft.SharePoint.WorkflowActions.SetModerationStatusActivity"
Assembly="Microsoft.SharePoint.WorkflowActions, Version=12.0.0.0, Culture=neutral,
         PublicKeyToken=71e9bce111e9429c"
AppliesTo="list" ListModeration="true" Category="Core Actions"
UsesCurrentItem="true">
  <RuleDesigner Sentence="Set content approval status to %1 with %2">
    <FieldBind Field="ModerationStatus" DesignerType="Dropdown" Id="1"
    Text="this status">
      <Option Name="Approved" Value="Approved"/>
      <Option Name="Rejected" Value="Denied"/>
      <Option Name="Pending" Value="Pending"/>
    </FieldBind>
    <FieldBind Field="Comments" Text="comments" Id="2" DesignerType="TextArea" />
  </RuleDesigner>
  <Parameters>
    <Parameter Name="ModerationStatus" Type="System.String, mscorlib"
    Direction="In" />
    <Parameter Name="Comments" Type="System.String, mscorlib"
    Direction="Optional" />
    <Parameter Name="__Context"
    Type="Microsoft.SharePoint.WorkflowActions.WorkflowContext,
          Microsoft.SharePoint.WorkflowActions" />
    <Parameter Name="__ListId" Type="System.String, mscorlib" Direction="In" />
    <Parameter Name="__ListItem" Type="System.Int32, mscorlib" Direction="In" />
  </Parameters>
</Action>
```

As the boldfaced portion of this excerpt illustrates, this XML fragment contains a <FieldBind> element that binds the ModerationStatus property of the SetModerationStatusActivity activity to the %1 placeholder variable in the rule sentence. Note that the DesignerType attribute on this <FieldBind> element is set to Dropdown to have Office SharePoint Designer 2007 display a drop-down list box when the workflow developer clicks this placeholder variable. Also note that this <FieldBind> element contains three <Option> child elements specifying the names and values of the items that the drop-down list box displays. When the workflow developer selects an item, the drop-down list assigns the value (not the name) of the item to the ModerationStatus property of the SetModerationStatusActivity activity.

The Dropdown designer type is great for situations where the execution logic of your custom WF activity branches is based on the value of a given property. The following custom WF activity exposes a bindable property named MyProperty, which takes three possible values of Value1, Value2, and Value3. This custom WF activity executes a different IfElseBranchActivity activity depending on the value of the MyProperty property:

```
using System;
using System.Workflow.ComponentModel;
using Microsoft.SharePoint;
using System.Workflow.Activities;

namespace Chapter9
{
  public class CustomActivity : SequenceActivity
  {
    private IfElseBranchActivity ifElseBranchActivity2;
    private IfElseBranchActivity ifElseBranchActivity1;
    private IfElseBranchActivity ifElseBranchActivity3;
    private IfElseActivity ifElseActivity1;
    private Microsoft.SharePoint.WorkflowActions.LogToHistoryListActivity
                               logToHistoryListActivity1;
    public static readonly DependencyProperty MyPropertyProperty =
        DependencyProperty.Register("MyProperty", typeof(string),
                                 typeof(CustomActivity));
    public string HistoryDescription = default(System.String);
    public string HistoryOutcome = default(System.String);
    private Microsoft.SharePoint.WorkflowActions.LogToHistoryListActivity
                                 logToHistoryListActivity3;
    private Microsoft.SharePoint.WorkflowActions.LogToHistoryListActivity
                                  logToHistoryListActivity2;
    public int UserId = default(System.Int32);

    public string MyProperty
    {
      get { return (string)base.GetValue(MyPropertyProperty); }
      set { base.SetValue(MyPropertyProperty, value); }
    }

    private void InitializeComponent()
    {
      this.CanModifyActivities = true;
      System.Workflow.ComponentModel.ActivityBind activitybind1 =
                      new System.Workflow.ComponentModel.ActivityBind();
      System.Workflow.ComponentModel.ActivityBind activitybind2 =
                      new System.Workflow.ComponentModel.ActivityBind();
      System.Workflow.ComponentModel.ActivityBind activitybind3 =
                      new System.Workflow.ComponentModel.ActivityBind();
      System.Workflow.ComponentModel.ActivityBind activitybind4 =
                      new System.Workflow.ComponentModel.ActivityBind();
      System.Workflow.ComponentModel.ActivityBind activitybind5 =
                      new System.Workflow.ComponentModel.ActivityBind();
      System.Workflow.ComponentModel.ActivityBind activitybind6 =
                      new System.Workflow.ComponentModel.ActivityBind();
      System.Workflow.ComponentModel.ActivityBind activitybind7 =
                      new System.Workflow.ComponentModel.ActivityBind();
      System.Workflow.ComponentModel.ActivityBind activitybind8 =
                      new System.Workflow.ComponentModel.ActivityBind();
```

```
        System.Workflow.ComponentModel.ActivityBind activitybind9 =
                        new System.Workflow.ComponentModel.ActivityBind();
        System.Workflow.Activities.Rules.RuleConditionReference
        ruleconditionreference1 =
            new System.Workflow.Activities.Rules.RuleConditionReference();
        System.Workflow.Activities.Rules.RuleConditionReference
        ruleconditionreference2 =
             new System.Workflow.Activities.Rules.RuleConditionReference();
        System.Workflow.Activities.Rules.RuleConditionReference
        ruleconditionreference3 =
                 new System.Workflow.Activities.Rules.RuleConditionReference();
        this.logToHistoryListActivity3 =
           new Microsoft.SharePoint.WorkflowActions.LogToHistoryListActivity();
        this.logToHistoryListActivity2 =
           new Microsoft.SharePoint.WorkflowActions.LogToHistoryListActivity();
        this.logToHistoryListActivity1 =
            new Microsoft.SharePoint.WorkflowActions.LogToHistoryListActivity();
        this.ifElseBranchActivity3 =
            new System.Workflow.Activities.IfElseBranchActivity();
        this.ifElseBranchActivity2 =
            new System.Workflow.Activities.IfElseBranchActivity();
        this.ifElseBranchActivity1 =
            new System.Workflow.Activities.IfElseBranchActivity();
        this.ifElseActivity1 = new System.Workflow.Activities.IfElseActivity();
        //
        // logToHistoryListActivity3
        //
        this.logToHistoryListActivity3.Duration =
                      System.TimeSpan.Parse("-10675199.02:48:05.4775808");
        this.logToHistoryListActivity3.EventId =
           Microsoft.SharePoint.Workflow.SPWorkflowHistoryEventType.WorkflowComment;
        activitybind1.Name = "CustomActivity";
        activitybind1.Path = "HistoryDescription";
        activitybind2.Name = "CustomActivity";
        activitybind2.Path = "HistoryOutcome";
        this.logToHistoryListActivity3.Name = "logToHistoryListActivity3";
        this.logToHistoryListActivity3.OtherData = "";
        activitybind3.Name = "CustomActivity";
        activitybind3.Path = "UserId";
        this.logToHistoryListActivity3.MethodInvoking +=
          new System.EventHandler(this.logToHistoryListActivity1_MethodInvoking);
        this.logToHistoryListActivity3.SetBinding(Microsoft.SharePoint
.WorkflowActions.LogToHistoryListActivity.HistoryDescriptionProperty,
((System.Workflow.ComponentModel.ActivityBind)(activitybind1)));
        this.logToHistoryListActivity3.SetBinding(Microsoft.SharePoint
.WorkflowActions.LogToHistoryListActivity.HistoryOutcomeProperty,
((System.Workflow.ComponentModel.ActivityBind)(activitybind2)));
        this.logToHistoryListActivity3.SetBinding(Microsoft.SharePoint
.WorkflowActions.LogToHistoryListActivity.UserIdProperty,
((System.Workflow.ComponentModel.ActivityBind)(activitybind3)));
        //
        // logToHistoryListActivity2
        //
```

(continued)

(continued)

```
        this.logToHistoryListActivity2.Duration =
                System.TimeSpan.Parse("-10675199.02:48:05.4775808");
        this.logToHistoryListActivity2.EventId =
           Microsoft.SharePoint.Workflow.SPWorkflowHistoryEventType.WorkflowComment;
        activitybind4.Name = "CustomActivity";
        activitybind4.Path = "HistoryDescription";
        activitybind5.Name = "CustomActivity";
        activitybind5.Path = "HistoryOutcome";
        this.logToHistoryListActivity2.Name = "logToHistoryListActivity2";
        this.logToHistoryListActivity2.OtherData = "";
        activitybind6.Name = "CustomActivity";
        activitybind6.Path = "UserId";
        this.logToHistoryListActivity2.MethodInvoking +=
           new System.EventHandler(this.logToHistoryListActivity1_MethodInvoking);
        this.logToHistoryListActivity2.SetBinding(Microsoft.SharePoint
  .WorkflowActions.LogToHistoryListActivity.HistoryDescriptionProperty,
  ((System.Workflow.ComponentModel.ActivityBind)(activitybind4)));
        this.logToHistoryListActivity2.SetBinding(Microsoft.SharePoint
  .WorkflowActions.LogToHistoryListActivity.HistoryOutcomeProperty,
  ((System.Workflow.ComponentModel.ActivityBind)(activitybind5)));
        this.logToHistoryListActivity2.SetBinding(Microsoft.SharePoint
  .WorkflowActions.LogToHistoryListActivity.UserIdProperty,
  ((System.Workflow.ComponentModel.ActivityBind)(activitybind6)));
        //
        // logToHistoryListActivity1
        //
        this.logToHistoryListActivity1.Duration =
                       System.TimeSpan.Parse("-10675199.02:48:05.4775808");
        this.logToHistoryListActivity1.EventId =
            Microsoft.SharePoint.Workflow.SPWorkflowHistoryEventType.WorkflowComment;
        activitybind7.Name = "CustomActivity";
        activitybind7.Path = "HistoryDescription";
        activitybind8.Name = "CustomActivity";
        activitybind8.Path = "HistoryOutcome";
        this.logToHistoryListActivity1.Name = "logToHistoryListActivity1";
        this.logToHistoryListActivity1.OtherData = "";
        activitybind9.Name = "CustomActivity";
        activitybind9.Path = "UserId";
        this.logToHistoryListActivity1.MethodInvoking +=
             new System.EventHandler(this.logToHistoryListActivity1_MethodInvoking);
        this.logToHistoryListActivity1.SetBinding(Microsoft.SharePoint
  .WorkflowActions.LogToHistoryListActivity.HistoryDescriptionProperty,
  ((System.Workflow.ComponentModel.ActivityBind)(activitybind7)));
        this.logToHistoryListActivity1.SetBinding(Microsoft.SharePoint
  .WorkflowActions.LogToHistoryListActivity.HistoryOutcomeProperty,
  ((System.Workflow.ComponentModel.ActivityBind)(activitybind8)));
        this.logToHistoryListActivity1.SetBinding(Microsoft.SharePoint
  .WorkflowActions.LogToHistoryListActivity.UserIdProperty,
  ((System.Workflow.ComponentModel.ActivityBind)(activitybind9)));
        //
        // ifElseBranchActivity3
        //
        this.ifElseBranchActivity3.Activities.Add(this.logToHistoryListActivity3);
```

```
        ruleconditionreference1.ConditionName = "Condition3";
        this.ifElseBranchActivity3.Condition = ruleconditionreference1;
        this.ifElseBranchActivity3.Name = "ifElseBranchActivity3";
        //
        // ifElseBranchActivity2
        //
        this.ifElseBranchActivity2.Activities.Add(this.logToHistoryListActivity2);
        ruleconditionreference2.ConditionName = "Condition2";
        this.ifElseBranchActivity2.Condition = ruleconditionreference2;
        this.ifElseBranchActivity2.Name = "ifElseBranchActivity2";
        //
        // ifElseBranchActivity1
        //
        this.ifElseBranchActivity1.Activities.Add(this.logToHistoryListActivity1);
        ruleconditionreference3.ConditionName = "Condition1";
        this.ifElseBranchActivity1.Condition = ruleconditionreference3;
        this.ifElseBranchActivity1.Name = "ifElseBranchActivity1";
        //
        // ifElseActivity1
        //
        this.ifElseActivity1.Activities.Add(this.ifElseBranchActivity1);
        this.ifElseActivity1.Activities.Add(this.ifElseBranchActivity2);
        this.ifElseActivity1.Activities.Add(this.ifElseBranchActivity3);
        this.ifElseActivity1.Name = "ifElseActivity1";
        //
        // CustomActivity
        //
        this.Activities.Add(this.ifElseActivity1);
        this.Name = "CustomActivity";
        this.CanModifyActivities = false;

      }

      private void logToHistoryListActivity1_MethodInvoking(object sender,
                                                             EventArgs e)
      {
        this.HistoryDescription = "MyProperty";
        this.HistoryOutcome = this.MyProperty;
      }
    }
  }
```

The following XML document presents the content of the .actions files that describes the preceding custom WF activity to Office SharePoint Designer 2007:

```
<?xml version="1.0" encoding="utf-8" ?>
<WorkflowInfo Language="en-us">
  <Actions Sequential="then" Parallel="and">
    <Action Name="Execute custom code" AppliesTo="all" Category="My Custom Actions"
   ClassName="Chapter9.CustomActivity"
   Assembly="Chapter9, Version=1.0.0.0, Culture=neutral,
             PublicKeyToken=252d221e933b41ec">
      <RuleDesigner
```

(continued)

(continued)

```
        Sentence="Execute custom code with %1 on the server">
          <FieldBind Field="MyProperty" DesignerType="DropDown"
          Text="this MyProperty value" Id="1">
            <Option Name="Name1" Value="Value1" />
            <Option Name="Name2" Value="Value2" />
            <Option Name="Name3" Value="Value3" />
          </FieldBind>
        </RuleDesigner>
        <Parameters>
          <Parameter Name="MyProperty" Type="System.String, mscorlib"
          Direction="In" />
        </Parameters>
      </Action>
    </Actions>
  </WorkflowInfo>
```

This XML document defines a <FieldBind> element that binds the MyProperty property of our CustomActivity activity to the %1 placeholder variable in the rule designer sentence. Note that the DesignerType attribute on this <FieldBind> element is set to DropDown to have Office SharePoint Designer 2007 display a drop-down list box populated with the values specified in the <Option> child elements of this <FieldBind> element. As Figure 9-7 shows, when the workflow developer clicks the %1 placeholder variable in the rule designer sentence, the Workflow Designer interface renders a drop-down list box that displays the values of the Name attributes of the <Option> child elements of the <FieldBind> element.

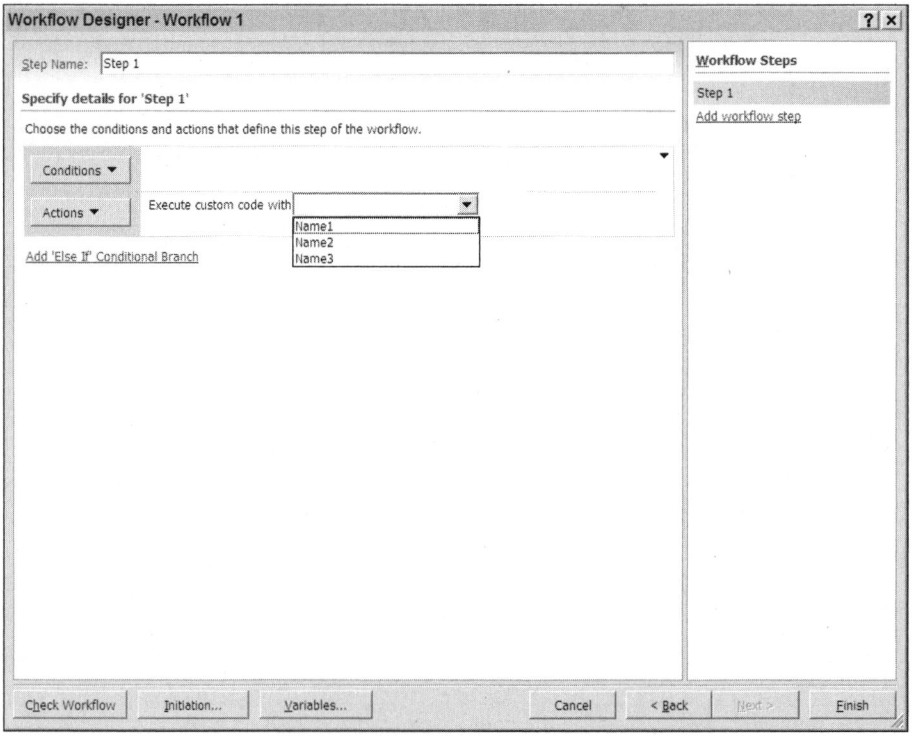

Workflow Designer - Workflow 1

Step Name: Step 1

Specify details for 'Step 1'

Choose the conditions and actions that define this step of the workflow.

Conditions

Actions — Execute custom code with [Name1 / Name2 / Name3]

Add 'Else If' Conditional Branch

Workflow Steps

Step 1

Add workflow step

Check Workflow | Initiation... | Variables... | Cancel | < Back | Next > | Finish

Figure 9-7

Email

Set the DesignerType attribute to Email to have Office SharePoint Designer 2007 display an e-mail advanced control when workflow developers click a placeholder variable in the rule sentence. This control presents workflow developers with standard e-mail fields, including To, From, CC, Subject, and Body.

SharePoint comes with a WF activity named EmailActivity, which enables workflows to send e-mails. Figure 9-8 presents the rule sentence for this activity.

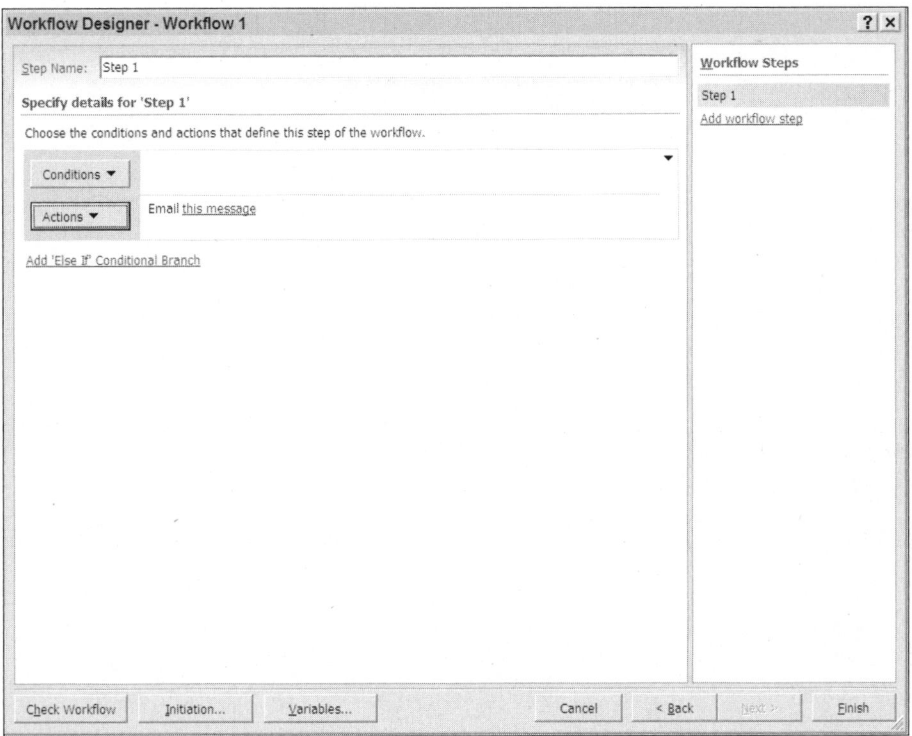

Figure 9-8

When the workflow developer clicks the This Message placeholder variable in this rule sentence, Office SharePoint Designer 2007 launches the e-mail advanced control shown in Figure 9-9.

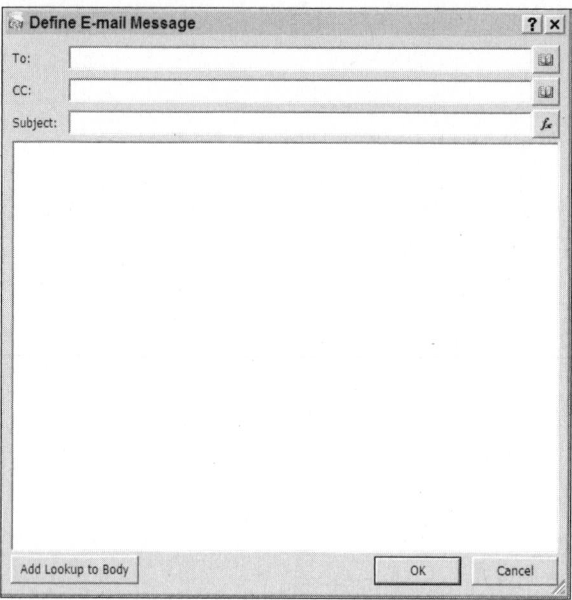

Figure 9-9

This powerful dialog box enables the workflow developer to use a combination of text and property binding to specify values for the TO, CC, SUBJECT, and BODY parameters. When the workflow developer clicks the OK button, the dialog assigns these values to the To, CC, Subject, and Body properties of the EmailActivity activity.

The following excerpt from wss.actions presents the <Action> element that describes the EmailActivity activity to Office SharePoint Designer 2007:

```
<Action Name="Send an Email"
ClassName="Microsoft.SharePoint.WorkflowActions.EmailActivity"
Assembly="Microsoft.SharePoint.WorkflowActions, Version=12.0.0.0, Culture=neutral,
          PublicKeyToken=71e9bce111e9429c"
Category="Core Actions" AppliesTo="all">
  <RuleDesigner Sentence="Email %1">
    <FieldBind Field="To,CC,Subject,Body" Text="this message"
    DesignerType="Email" Id="1"/>
  </RuleDesigner>
  <Parameters>
    <Parameter Name="__Context" Direction="In"
    Type="Microsoft.SharePoint.WorkflowActions.WorkflowContext,
          Microsoft.SharePoint.WorkflowActions" />
    <Parameter Name="Body" Type="System.String, mscorlib" Direction="Optional" />
    <Parameter Name="To" Type="System.Collections.ArrayList, mscorlib"
    Direction="In" />
    <Parameter Name="CC" Type="System.Collections.ArrayList, mscorlib"
    Direction="Optional" />
    <Parameter Name="Subject" Type="System.String, mscorlib" Direction="In" />
  </Parameters>
</Action>
```

As shown in the preceding excerpt, you must take the following steps to take advantage of the e-mail advanced control:

- Add a property of the System.String type to your custom WF activity where the e-mail control can store the value that the workflow developer enters for the body of the e-mail message.
- Add a property of the ArrayList type to your custom WF activity where the e-mail control can store the value that the workflow developer enters for the "to" part of the e-mail.
- Add a property of the ArrayList type to your custom WF activity where the e-mail control can store the value that the workflow developer enters for the "cc" part of the e-mail.
- Add a property of the System.String type to your custom WF activity where the e-mail control can store the value that the workflow developer enters for the subject of the e-mail message.
- Add a <FieldBind> element.
- Set the Field attribute on this <FieldBind> element to a comma-separated list of the names of the preceding four properties:

```
<FieldBind Field="To,CC,Subject,Body" Text="this message"
DesignerType="Email" Id="1"/>
```

- Set the DesignerType attribute on this <FieldBind> element to Email.

The following code listing presents the implementation of a custom activity named CustomActivity2 that exposes four properties named To, CC, Subject, and Body and uses the values of these properties in its execution logic:

```
using System;
using System.Workflow.ComponentModel;
using Microsoft.SharePoint;
using System.Workflow.Activities;
using System.Collections;

namespace Chapter9
{
  public class CustomActivity2 : SequenceActivity
  {
    public string HistoryDescription = default(System.String);
    public string HistoryOutcome = default(System.String);
    private Microsoft.SharePoint.WorkflowActions.LogToHistoryListActivity
                  logToHistoryListActivity1;
    public int UserId = default(System.Int32);
    private Microsoft.SharePoint.WorkflowActions.LogToHistoryListActivity
                  logToHistoryListActivity4;
    private Microsoft.SharePoint.WorkflowActions.LogToHistoryListActivity
                  logToHistoryListActivity3;
    private Microsoft.SharePoint.WorkflowActions.LogToHistoryListActivity
                  logToHistoryListActivity2;

    public static readonly DependencyProperty ToProperty =
        DependencyProperty.Register("To", typeof(ArrayList),
                                    typeof(CustomActivity2));
```

(continued)

(continued)

```
        public ArrayList To
        {
          get { return (ArrayList)base.GetValue(ToProperty); }
          set { base.SetValue(ToProperty, value); }
        }

        public static readonly DependencyProperty CCProperty =
            DependencyProperty.Register("CC", typeof(ArrayList),
                                        typeof(CustomActivity2));
        public ArrayList CC
        {
          get { return (ArrayList)base.GetValue(CCProperty); }
          set { base.SetValue(CCProperty, value); }
        }

        public static readonly DependencyProperty SubjectProperty =
            DependencyProperty.Register("Subject", typeof(string),
                                        typeof(CustomActivity2));
        public string Subject
        {
          get { return (string)base.GetValue(SubjectProperty); }
          set { base.SetValue(SubjectProperty, value); }
        }

        public static readonly DependencyProperty BodyProperty =
            DependencyProperty.Register("Body", typeof(string),
                                        typeof(CustomActivity2));
        public string Body
        {
          get { return (string)base.GetValue(BodyProperty); }
          set { base.SetValue(BodyProperty, value); }
        }

        public CustomActivity2()
        {
          this.InitializeComponent();
        }

        private void InitializeComponent()
        {
          this.CanModifyActivities = true;
          System.Workflow.ComponentModel.ActivityBind activitybind1 =
                              new System.Workflow.ComponentModel.ActivityBind();
          System.Workflow.ComponentModel.ActivityBind activitybind2 =
                              new System.Workflow.ComponentModel.ActivityBind();
          System.Workflow.ComponentModel.ActivityBind activitybind3 =
                              new System.Workflow.ComponentModel.ActivityBind();
          System.Workflow.ComponentModel.ActivityBind activitybind4 =
                              new System.Workflow.ComponentModel.ActivityBind();
          System.Workflow.ComponentModel.ActivityBind activitybind5 =
                              new System.Workflow.ComponentModel.ActivityBind();
          System.Workflow.ComponentModel.ActivityBind activitybind6 =
                              new System.Workflow.ComponentModel.ActivityBind();
```

```
        System.Workflow.ComponentModel.ActivityBind activitybind7 =
                        new System.Workflow.ComponentModel.ActivityBind();
        System.Workflow.ComponentModel.ActivityBind activitybind8 =
                        new System.Workflow.ComponentModel.ActivityBind();
        System.Workflow.ComponentModel.ActivityBind activitybind9 =
                        new System.Workflow.ComponentModel.ActivityBind();
        System.Workflow.ComponentModel.ActivityBind activitybind10 =
                        new System.Workflow.ComponentModel.ActivityBind();
        System.Workflow.ComponentModel.ActivityBind activitybind11 =
                        new System.Workflow.ComponentModel.ActivityBind();
        System.Workflow.ComponentModel.ActivityBind activitybind12 =
                        new System.Workflow.ComponentModel.ActivityBind();
        this.logToHistoryListActivity4 =
              new Microsoft.SharePoint.WorkflowActions.LogToHistoryListActivity();
        this.logToHistoryListActivity3 =
             new Microsoft.SharePoint.WorkflowActions.LogToHistoryListActivity();
        this.logToHistoryListActivity2 =
             new Microsoft.SharePoint.WorkflowActions.LogToHistoryListActivity();
        this.logToHistoryListActivity1 =
             new Microsoft.SharePoint.WorkflowActions.LogToHistoryListActivity();
        //
        // logToHistoryListActivity4
        //
        this.logToHistoryListActivity4.Duration =
              System.TimeSpan.Parse("-10675199.02:48:05.4775808");
        this.logToHistoryListActivity4.EventId =
          Microsoft.SharePoint.Workflow.SPWorkflowHistoryEventType.WorkflowComment;
        activitybind1.Name = "CustomActivity2";
        activitybind1.Path = "HistoryDescription";
        activitybind2.Name = "CustomActivity2";
        activitybind2.Path = "HistoryOutcome";
        this.logToHistoryListActivity4.Name = "logToHistoryListActivity4";
        this.logToHistoryListActivity4.OtherData = "";
        activitybind3.Name = "CustomActivity2";
        activitybind3.Path = "UserId";
        this.logToHistoryListActivity4.MethodInvoking +=
          new System.EventHandler(this.logToHistoryListActivity4_MethodInvoking);
        this.logToHistoryListActivity4.SetBinding(Microsoft.SharePoint
.WorkflowActions.LogToHistoryListActivity.HistoryDescriptionProperty,
((System.Workflow.ComponentModel.ActivityBind)(activitybind1)));
        this.logToHistoryListActivity4.SetBinding(Microsoft.SharePoint
.WorkflowActions.LogToHistoryListActivity.HistoryOutcomeProperty,
((System.Workflow.ComponentModel.ActivityBind)(activitybind2)));
        this.logToHistoryListActivity4.SetBinding(Microsoft.SharePoint
.WorkflowActions.LogToHistoryListActivity.UserIdProperty,
((System.Workflow.ComponentModel.ActivityBind)(activitybind3)));
        //
        // logToHistoryListActivity3
        //
        this.logToHistoryListActivity3.Duration =
                   System.TimeSpan.Parse("-10675199.02:48:05.4775808");
        this.logToHistoryListActivity3.EventId =
          Microsoft.SharePoint.Workflow.SPWorkflowHistoryEventType.WorkflowComment;
```

(continued)

(continued)

```
        activitybind4.Name = "CustomActivity2";
        activitybind4.Path = "HistoryDescription";
        activitybind5.Name = "CustomActivity2";
        activitybind5.Path = "HistoryOutcome";
        this.logToHistoryListActivity3.Name = "logToHistoryListActivity3";
        this.logToHistoryListActivity3.OtherData = "";
        activitybind6.Name = "CustomActivity2";
        activitybind6.Path = "UserId";
        this.logToHistoryListActivity3.MethodInvoking +=
          new System.EventHandler(this.logToHistoryListActivity3_MethodInvoking);
        this.logToHistoryListActivity3.SetBinding(Microsoft.SharePoint
  .WorkflowActions.LogToHistoryListActivity.HistoryDescriptionProperty,
  ((System.Workflow.ComponentModel.ActivityBind)(activitybind4)));
        this.logToHistoryListActivity3.SetBinding(Microsoft.SharePoint
  .WorkflowActions.LogToHistoryListActivity.HistoryOutcomeProperty,
  ((System.Workflow.ComponentModel.ActivityBind)(activitybind5)));
        this.logToHistoryListActivity3.SetBinding(Microsoft.SharePoint
  .WorkflowActions.LogToHistoryListActivity.UserIdProperty,
  ((System.Workflow.ComponentModel.ActivityBind)(activitybind6)));
        //
        // logToHistoryListActivity2
        //
        this.logToHistoryListActivity2.Duration =
              System.TimeSpan.Parse("-10675199.02:48:05.4775808");
        this.logToHistoryListActivity2.EventId =
            Microsoft.SharePoint.Workflow.SPWorkflowHistoryEventType.WorkflowComment;
        activitybind7.Name = "CustomActivity2";
        activitybind7.Path = "HistoryDescription";
        activitybind8.Name = "CustomActivity2";
        activitybind8.Path = "HistoryOutcome";
        this.logToHistoryListActivity2.Name = "logToHistoryListActivity2";
        this.logToHistoryListActivity2.OtherData = "";
        activitybind9.Name = "CustomActivity2";
        activitybind9.Path = "UserId";
        this.logToHistoryListActivity2.MethodInvoking +=
          new System.EventHandler(this.logToHistoryListActivity2_MethodInvoking);
        this.logToHistoryListActivity2.SetBinding(Microsoft.SharePoint
  .WorkflowActions.LogToHistoryListActivity.HistoryDescriptionProperty,
  ((System.Workflow.ComponentModel.ActivityBind)(activitybind7)));
        this.logToHistoryListActivity2.SetBinding(Microsoft.SharePoint
  .WorkflowActions.LogToHistoryListActivity.HistoryOutcomeProperty,
  ((System.Workflow.ComponentModel.ActivityBind)(activitybind8)));
        this.logToHistoryListActivity2.SetBinding(Microsoft.SharePoint
  .WorkflowActions.LogToHistoryListActivity.UserIdProperty,
  ((System.Workflow.ComponentModel.ActivityBind)(activitybind9)));
        //
        // logToHistoryListActivity1
        //
        this.logToHistoryListActivity1.Duration =
                System.TimeSpan.Parse("-10675199.02:48:05.4775808");
        this.logToHistoryListActivity1.EventId =
           Microsoft.SharePoint.Workflow.SPWorkflowHistoryEventType.WorkflowComment;
```

```
        activitybind10.Name = "CustomActivity2";
        activitybind10.Path = "HistoryDescription";
        activitybind11.Name = "CustomActivity2";
        activitybind11.Path = "HistoryOutcome";
        this.logToHistoryListActivity1.Name = "logToHistoryListActivity1";
        this.logToHistoryListActivity1.OtherData = "";
        activitybind12.Name = "CustomActivity2";
        activitybind12.Path = "UserId";
        this.logToHistoryListActivity1.MethodInvoking +=
           new System.EventHandler(this.logToHistoryListActivity1_MethodInvoking);
        this.logToHistoryListActivity1.SetBinding(Microsoft.SharePoint
.WorkflowActions.LogToHistoryListActivity.HistoryDescriptionProperty,
((System.Workflow.ComponentModel.ActivityBind)(activitybind10)));
        this.logToHistoryListActivity1.SetBinding(Microsoft.SharePoint
.WorkflowActions.LogToHistoryListActivity.HistoryOutcomeProperty,
((System.Workflow.ComponentModel.ActivityBind)(activitybind11)));
        this.logToHistoryListActivity1.SetBinding(Microsoft.SharePoint
.WorkflowActions.LogToHistoryListActivity.UserIdProperty,
((System.Workflow.ComponentModel.ActivityBind)(activitybind12)));
        //
        // CustomActivity2
        //
        this.Activities.Add(this.logToHistoryListActivity1);
        this.Activities.Add(this.logToHistoryListActivity2);
        this.Activities.Add(this.logToHistoryListActivity3);
        this.Activities.Add(this.logToHistoryListActivity4);
        this.Name = "CustomActivity2";
        this.CanModifyActivities = false;

      }

      private void logToHistoryListActivity1_MethodInvoking(object sender,
                                                            EventArgs e)
      {
        this.HistoryDescription = "To";
        this.HistoryOutcome = string.Empty;

        for (int i = 0; i < this.To.Count; i++)
        {
          if (i != 0)
            this.HistoryOutcome += ";";
          this.HistoryOutcome += this.To[i];
        }
      }

      private void logToHistoryListActivity2_MethodInvoking(object sender,
                                                            EventArgs e)
      {
        this.HistoryDescription = "CC";
        this.HistoryOutcome = string.Empty;

        for (int i = 0; i < this.CC.Count; i++)
        {
```

(continued)

(continued)

```
          if (i != 0)
            this.HistoryOutcome += ";";
          this.HistoryOutcome += this.CC[i];
        }
      }

      private void logToHistoryListActivity3_MethodInvoking(object sender,
                                                            EventArgs e)
      {
        this.HistoryDescription = "Subject";
        this.HistoryOutcome = this.Subject;
      }

      private void logToHistoryListActivity4_MethodInvoking(object sender,
                                                            EventArgs e)
      {
        this.HistoryDescription = "Body";
        this.HistoryOutcome = this.Body;
      }
    }
  }
```

The following XML document presents the content of the .actions files that describe the preceding custom WF activity to Office SharePoint Designer 2007:

```
<?xml version="1.0" encoding="utf-8" ?>
<WorkflowInfo Language="en-us">
  <Actions Sequential="then" Parallel="and">
    <Action Name="Execute custom code 2" AppliesTo="all"
    Category="My Custom Actions"
    ClassName="Chapter9.CustomActivity2"
    Assembly="Chapter9, Version=1.0.0.0, Culture=neutral,
             PublicKeyToken=252d221e933b41ec">
      <RuleDesigner
      Sentence="Execute custom code with %1 on the server">
        <FieldBind Field="To,CC,Subject,Body" Text="this message"
        DesignerType="Email" Id="1"/>
      </RuleDesigner>
      <Parameters>
        <Parameter Name="Body" Type="System.String, mscorlib"
        Direction="Optional" />
        <Parameter Name="To" Type="System.Collections.ArrayList, mscorlib"
        Direction="In" />
        <Parameter Name="CC" Type="System.Collections.ArrayList, mscorlib"
        Direction="Optional" />
        <Parameter Name="Subject" Type="System.String, mscorlib" Direction="In" />
      </Parameters>
    </Action>
  </Actions>
</WorkflowInfo>
```

Note that the DesignerType attribute on the <FieldBind> element, which binds the To, CC, Subject, and Body properties of the CustomActivity activity to the %1 placeholder variable in the rule designer sentence, is set to Email. Figure 9-10 shows this rule designer sentence in action.

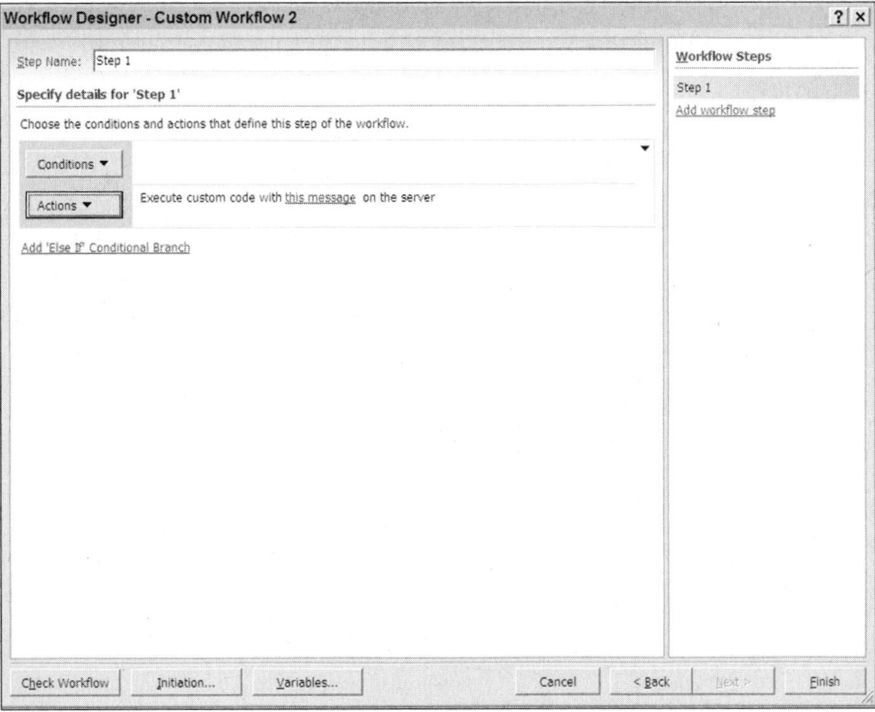

Figure 9-10

Now go ahead and click the This Message link in this rule designer sentence. Workflow Designer launches the Define E-mail Message dialog box shown in Figure 9-11 to enable you to set the values of the To, CC, Subject, and Body properties of the CustomActivity2 activity in purely graphical fashion without any code.

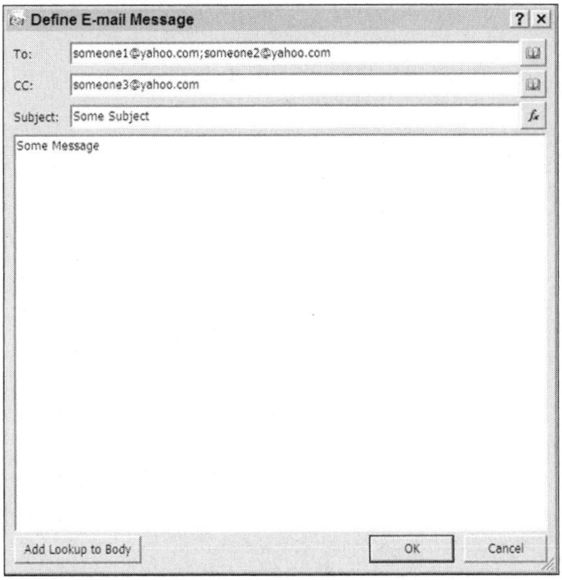

Figure 9-11

Enter values for the To, CC, Subject, and Body text boxes shown in Figure 9-11 and click the OK button. The rule sentence now should look like Figure 9-12.

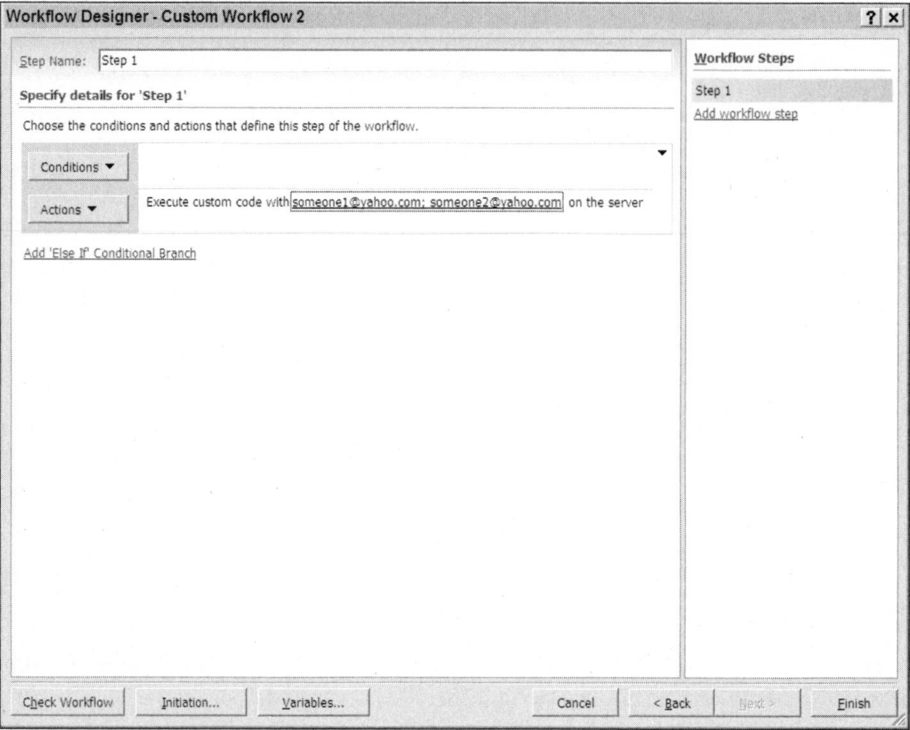

Figure 9-12

Click the Finish button in Figure 9-12 to create and store the workflow. Next, navigate to the page that shows the SharePoint list with which this workflow is associated and initiate an instance of this workflow on a list item in this list. Then navigate to the workflow status page for this workflow instance, as shown in Figure 9-13, which shows the content of the workflow history list after you run the workflow that contains the CustomActivity2 activity.

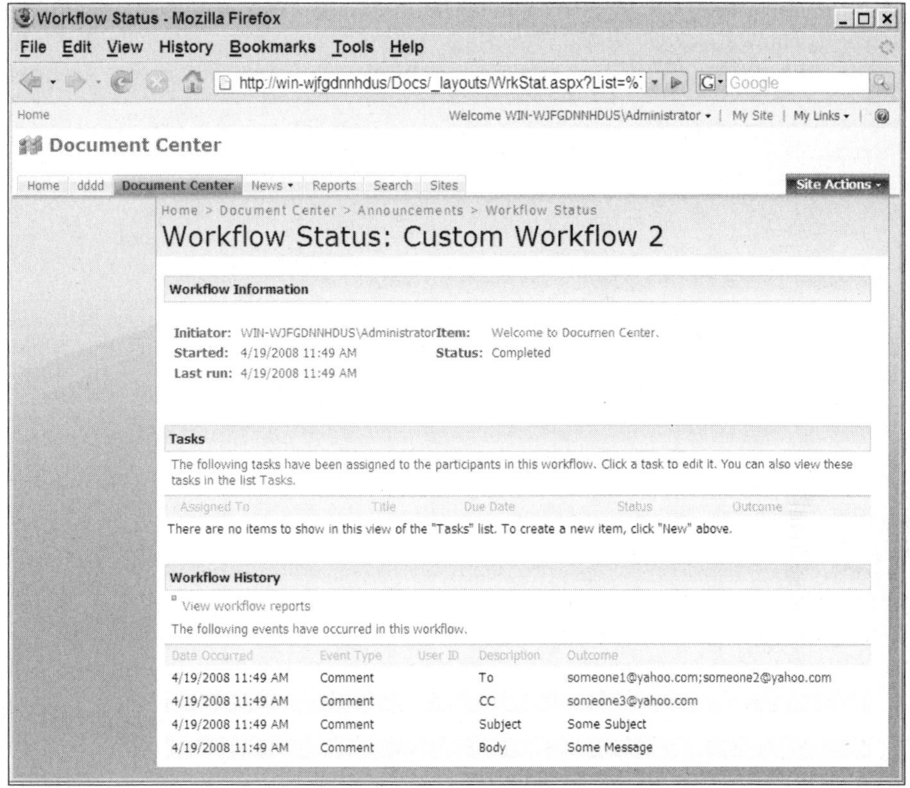

Figure 9-13

FieldNames

Set the DesignerType attribute to FieldNames to have Office SharePoint Designer 2007 display a drop-down list box populated with all field names in the SharePoint list or document library with which the current workflow is associated when workflow developers click the respective placeholder variable in the rule sentence.

SharePoint ships with a WF activity named WaitForActivity, which enables a workflow to wait for the field with the specified name in the current list item to change. This activity exposes a bindable string property named FieldName, which the workflow developer must set to the name of the field whose value change triggers the WaitForActivity activity to resume its execution where it left off. The following XML fragment presents the portion of the wss.actions file defining the <FieldBind> element that binds the FieldName property of the WaitForActivity activity to the %1 placeholder variable in the rule designer sentence:

```
<Action Name="Wait For Field Change in Current Item"
ClassName="Microsoft.SharePoint.WorkflowActions.WaitForActivity"
Assembly="Microsoft.SharePoint.WorkflowActions, Version=12.0.0.0, Culture=neutral,
          PublicKeyToken=71e9bce111e9429c"
AppliesTo="list" UsesCurrentItem="true" Category="Core Actions">
```

(continued)

(continued)

```
    <RuleDesigner Sentence="Wait for %1 %2 %3">
      <FieldBind Field="FieldName" Text="field" Id="1" DesignerType="fieldNames" />
      . . .
    </RuleDesigner>
    <Parameters>
      <Parameter Name="FieldName" Type="System.String, mscorlib" Direction="In" />
      . . .
    </Parameters>
  </Action>
```

When the workflow developer clicks the %1 placeholder variable in the rule designer sentence, the Workflow Designer displays a drop-down list box containing the field names of the SharePoint list or document library with which the current workflow is associated.

Now we'll develop a custom WF activity named CustomActivity3 that exposes a bindable property named FieldName, as shown in the following code:

```
using System;
using System.Workflow.ComponentModel;
using Microsoft.SharePoint;
using System.Workflow.Activities;
using System.Collections;

namespace Chapter9
{
  public class CustomActivity3 : SequenceActivity
  {
    public string HistoryDescription = default(System.String);
    public string HistoryOutcome = default(System.String);
    private Microsoft.SharePoint.WorkflowActions.LogToHistoryListActivity
              logToHistoryListActivity1;
    public int UserId = default(System.Int32);

    public static readonly DependencyProperty FieldNameProperty =
        DependencyProperty.Register("FieldName", typeof(string),
                                    typeof(CustomActivity3));
    public string FieldName
    {
      get { return (string)base.GetValue(FieldNameProperty); }
      set { base.SetValue(FieldNameProperty, value); }
    }

    public CustomActivity3()
    {
      this.InitializeComponent();
    }

    private void InitializeComponent()
    {
      this.CanModifyActivities = true;
      System.Workflow.ComponentModel.ActivityBind activitybind1 =
                          new System.Workflow.ComponentModel.ActivityBind();
      System.Workflow.ComponentModel.ActivityBind activitybind2 =
                          new System.Workflow.ComponentModel.ActivityBind();
```

```
            System.Workflow.ComponentModel.ActivityBind activitybind3 =
                             new System.Workflow.ComponentModel.ActivityBind();
            this.logToHistoryListActivity1 =
               new Microsoft.SharePoint.WorkflowActions.LogToHistoryListActivity();
            //
            // logToHistoryListActivity1
            //
            this.logToHistoryListActivity1.Duration =
                        System.TimeSpan.Parse("-10675199.02:48:05.4775808");
            this.logToHistoryListActivity1.EventId =
               Microsoft.SharePoint.Workflow.SPWorkflowHistoryEventType.WorkflowComment;
            activitybind1.Name = "CustomActivity3";
            activitybind1.Path = "HistoryDescription";
            activitybind2.Name = "CustomActivity3";
            activitybind2.Path = "HistoryOutcome";
            this.logToHistoryListActivity1.Name = "logToHistoryListActivity1";
            this.logToHistoryListActivity1.OtherData = "";
            activitybind3.Name = "CustomActivity3";
            activitybind3.Path = "UserId";
            this.logToHistoryListActivity1.MethodInvoking +=
              new System.EventHandler(this.logToHistoryListActivity1_MethodInvoking);
            this.logToHistoryListActivity1.SetBinding(Microsoft.SharePoint
.WorkflowActions.LogToHistoryListActivity.HistoryDescriptionProperty,
((System.Workflow.ComponentModel.ActivityBind)(activitybind1)));
            this.logToHistoryListActivity1.SetBinding(Microsoft.SharePoint
.WorkflowActions.LogToHistoryListActivity.HistoryOutcomeProperty,
((System.Workflow.ComponentModel.ActivityBind)(activitybind2)));
            this.logToHistoryListActivity1.SetBinding(Microsoft.SharePoint
.WorkflowActions.LogToHistoryListActivity.UserIdProperty,
((System.Workflow.ComponentModel.ActivityBind)(activitybind3)));
            //
            // CustomActivity3
            //
            this.Activities.Add(this.logToHistoryListActivity1);
            this.Name = "CustomActivity3";
            this.CanModifyActivities = false;
        }

        private void logToHistoryListActivity1_MethodInvoking(object sender,
                                                               EventArgs e)
        {
            this.HistoryDescription = "FieldName";
            this.HistoryOutcome = this.FieldName;
        }
    }
}
```

The following XML document presents the content of the .actions file that describes the preceding custom activity to Office SharePoint Designer 2007:

```
<?xml version="1.0" encoding="utf-8" ?>
<WorkflowInfo Language="en-us">
  <Actions Sequential="then" Parallel="and">
    <Action Name="Execute custom code 3" AppliesTo="all"
```

(continued)

(continued)

```
      Category="My Custom Actions"
      ClassName="Chapter9.CustomActivity3"
      Assembly="Chapter9, Version=1.0.0.0, Culture=neutral, PublicKeyToken=252d221e93
3b41ec">
        <RuleDesigner
        Sentence="Execute custom code with %1 on the server">
          <FieldBind Field="FieldName" Text="this field name"
          DesignerType="FieldNames" Id="1"/>
        </RuleDesigner>
        <Parameters>
          <Parameter Name="FieldName" Type="System.String, mscorlib"
          Direction="In" />
        </Parameters>
      </Action>
    </Actions>
</WorkflowInfo>
```

This .actions file contains a <FieldBind> element that binds the FieldName property of our CustomActivity3 activity to the %1 placeholder variable in the rule designer sentence. Note that the DesignerType attribute on this <FieldBind> element is set to FieldNames to instruct SharePoint Designer 2007 to present the workflow developer with a list of the field names of the SharePoint list with which the workflow is associated.

Next, let's take a look at the Workflow Designer where this custom activity is used. Select the Announcements SharePoint list from the Workflow Designer, as shown in Figure 9-14.

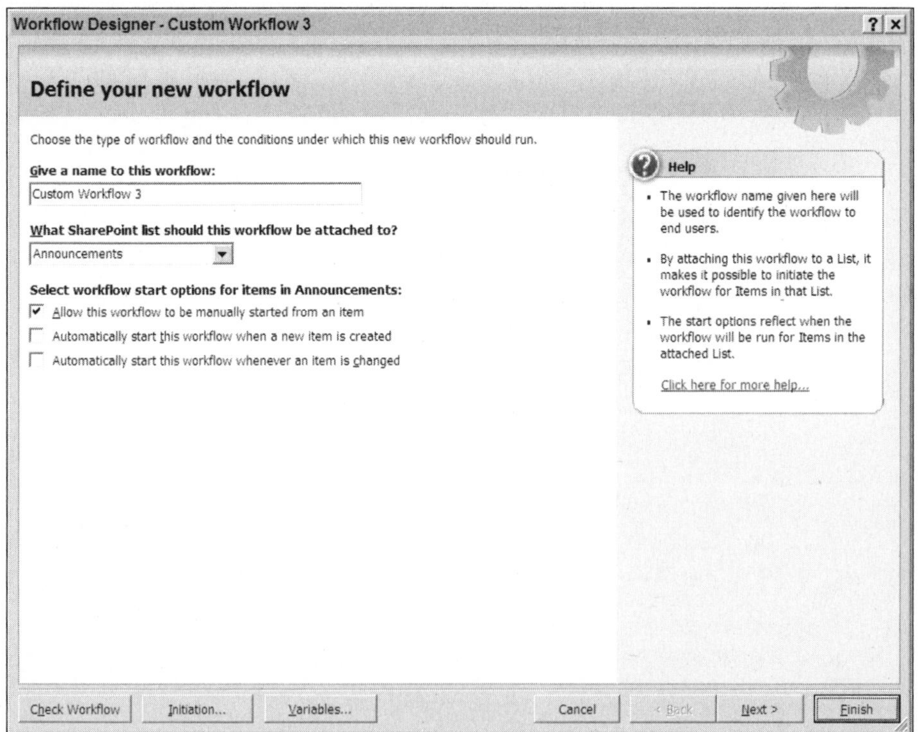

Figure 9-14

Click Next to navigate to the next step, shown in Figure 9-15, which added an instance of our CustomActivity3 activity to the workflow.

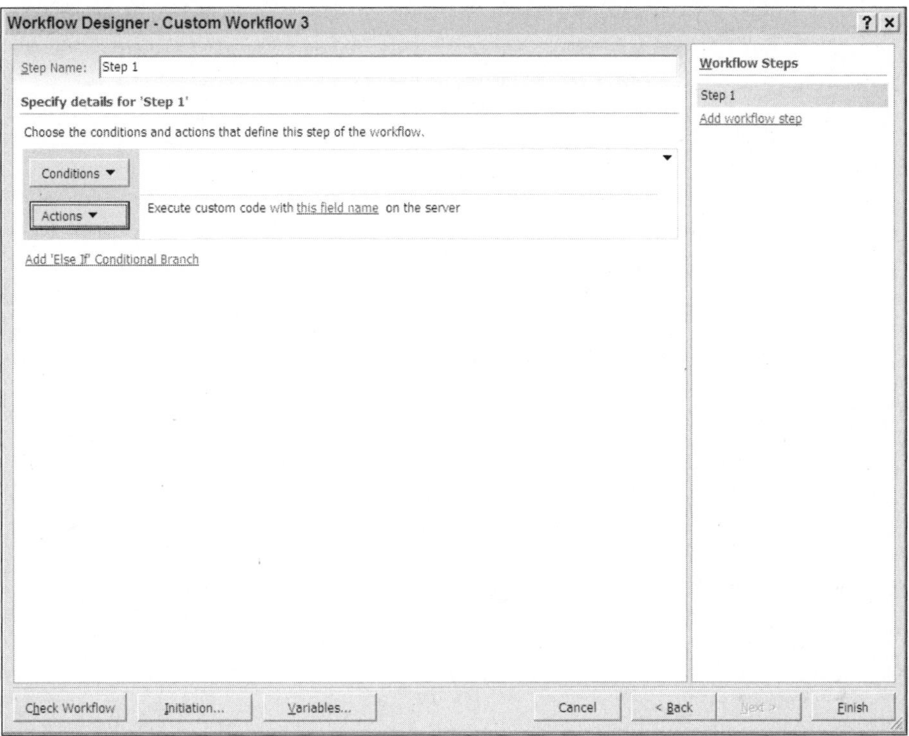

Figure 9-15

As Figure 9-16 shows, when the workflow developer clicks the placeholder variable link in the rule designer, Workflow Designer displays a drop-down list box populated with the field names of the Announcements SharePoint list.

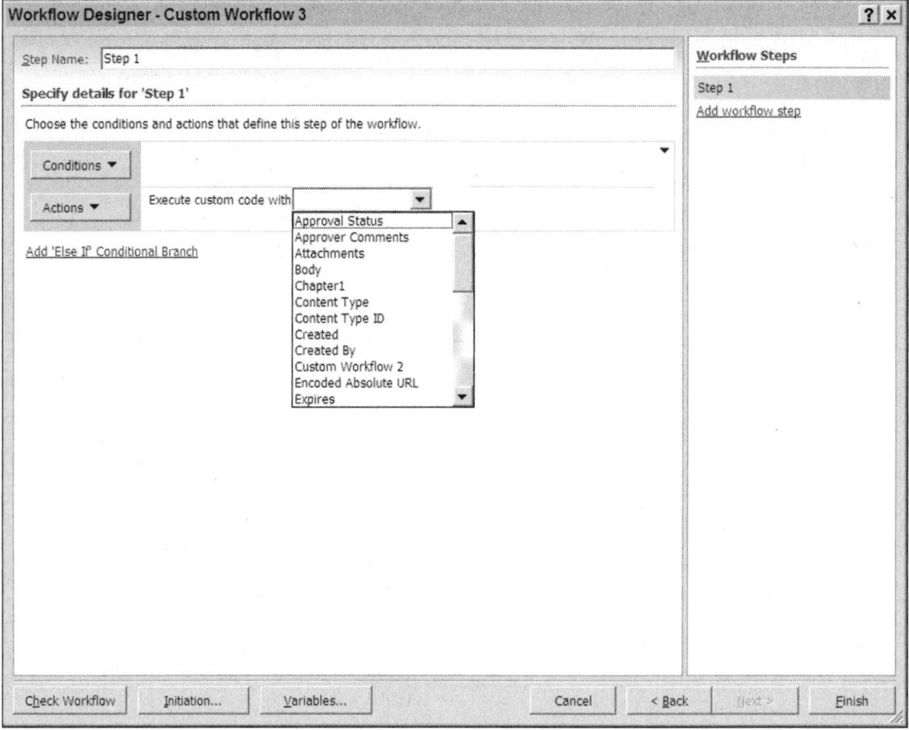

Figure 9-16

Now go back to the previous page and select the Documents SharePoint list. As Figure 9-17 shows, this time around the drop-down list box displays the field names of the Documents list.

Figure 9-18 shows the content of the history workflow list after the workflow containing the CustomActivity3 custom activity executes. In this case, the workflow developer has selected the _ModerationComments field of the Announcements SharePoint list.

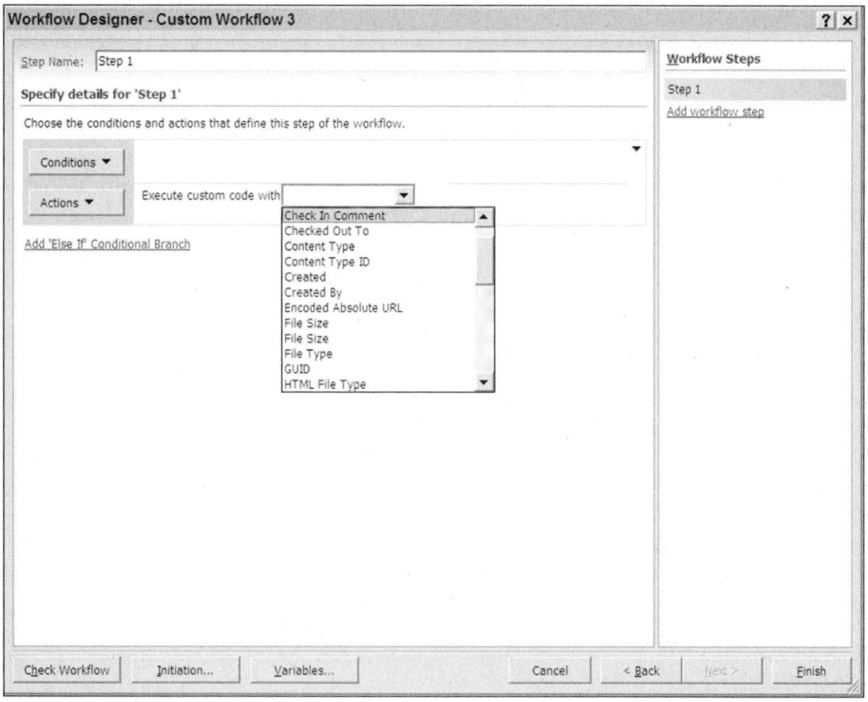

Figure 9-17

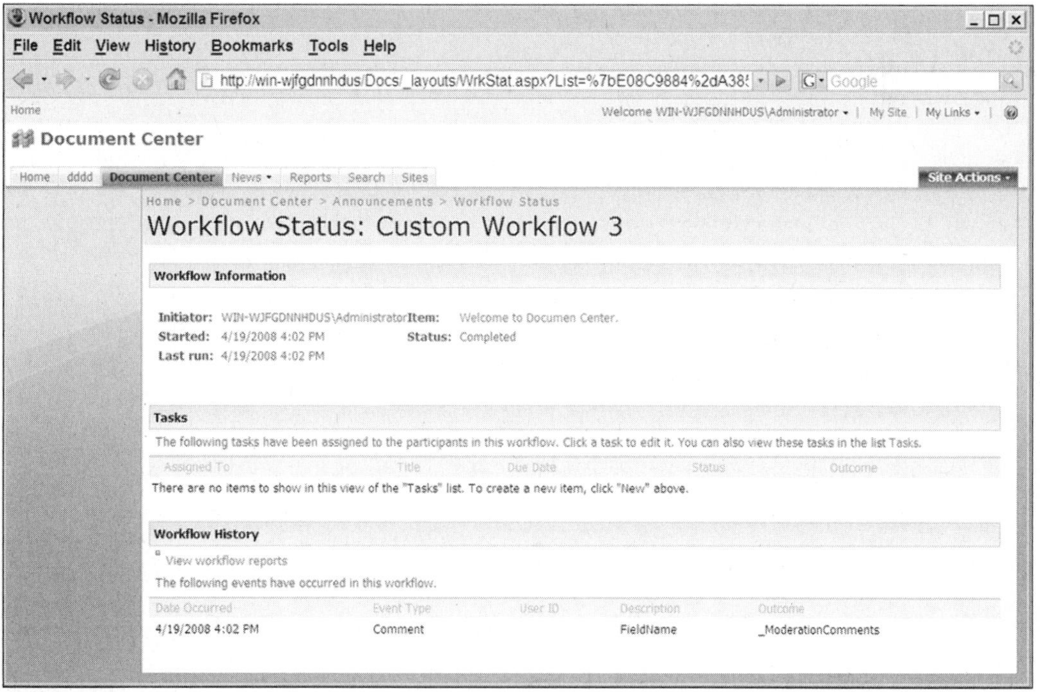

Figure 9-18

Operator

Set the DesignerType attribute to Operator to have Office SharePoint Designer 2007 display a drop-down list box populated with the list of available operators when the workflow developer clicks a placeholder variable in the respective rule designer sentence.

SharePoint ships with a WF activity named WaitForActivity, which enables a workflow to wait for the field with the specified name in the current list item in the current SharePoint list to change.

This activity exposes the following three important bindable properties:

- **Operator:** Gets or sets the string that contains the operator specifying the type of change that can resume and complete the execution of the WaitForActivity activity
- **FieldName:** Gets or sets the name of the field whose change resumes and completes the execution of the WaitForActivity activity. This acts as the left operand of the operator.
- **Value:** Gets or sets the object that acts as the right operand of the operator. This is basically the value with which the value of the field is compared.

The following excerpt from wss.actions describes the WaitForActivity activity to Office SharePoint Designer 2007:

```
<Action Name="Wait For Field Change in Current Item"
ClassName="Microsoft.SharePoint.WorkflowActions.WaitForActivity"
Assembly="Microsoft.SharePoint.WorkflowActions, Version=12.0.0.0, Culture=neutral,
          PublicKeyToken=71e9bce111e9429c"
AppliesTo="list" UsesCurrentItem="true" Category="Core Actions">
  <RuleDesigner Sentence="Wait for %1 %2 %3">
    <FieldBind Field="FieldName" Text="field" Id="1" DesignerType="fieldNames" />
    <FieldBind Field="Operator" Id="2" DesignerType="Operator"
    OperatorTypeFrom="FieldName" Text="this test">
      <Option Name="to equal" Value="Equal"/>
      <Option Name="to not equal" Value="NotEqual"/>
      <Option Name="to be greater than" Value="GreaterThan"
      TypeFilter="System.Double;System.Int32;System.Uint32;System.DateTime"/>
      <Option Name="to be greater than or to equal" Value="GreaterThanOrEqual"
      TypeFilter="System.Double;System.Int32;System.Uint32;System.DateTime"/>
      <Option Name="to be less than" Value="LessThan"
      TypeFilter="System.Double;System.Int32;System.Uint32;System.DateTime"/>
      <Option Name="to be less than or to equal" Value="LessThanOrEqual"
      TypeFilter="System.Double;System.Int32;System.Uint32;System.DateTime"/>
      <Option Name="to be empty" Value="IsEmpty"
      TypeFilter="System.String" UnaryHides="Value"/>
      <Option Name="to be not empty" Value="NotIsEmpty"
      TypeFilter="System.String" UnaryHides="Value"/>
      <Option Name="to begin with" Value="StartsWith"
      TypeFilter="System.String"/>
      <Option Name="to not begin with" Value="NotStartsWith"
      TypeFilter="System.String"/>
      <Option Name="to end with" Value="EndsWith"
      TypeFilter="System.String"/>
```

```
      <Option Name="to not end with" Value="NotEndsWith"
      TypeFilter="System.String"/>
      <Option Name="to contain" Value="Contains" TypeFilter="System.String"/>
      <Option Name="to not contain" Value="NotContains"
      TypeFilter="System.String"/>
      <Option Name="to match regular expression" Value="Matches"
      TypeFilter="System.String"/>
      <Option Name="to equal (ignoring case)" Value="EqualNoCase"
      TypeFilter="System.String"/>
      <Option Name="to contain (ignoring case)" Value="ContainsNoCase"
      TypeFilter="System.String"/>
      <Option Name="to equal (ignoring time)" Value="EqualNoTime"
      TypeFilter="System.DateTime"/>
    </FieldBind>
    <FieldBind Field="Value" Text="value" Id="3" TypeFrom="FieldName"/>
  </RuleDesigner>
  <Parameters>
    <Parameter Name="FieldName" Type="System.String, mscorlib" Direction="In" />
    <Parameter Name="Operator" Type="System.String, mscorlib" Direction="In"
    InitialValue="Equal" />
    <Parameter Name="Value" Type="System.Object, mscorlib" Direction="In" />
    <Parameter Name="__Context" Direction="In"
    Type="Microsoft.SharePoint.WorkflowActions.WorkflowContext,
          Microsoft.SharePoint.WorkflowActions" />
    <Parameter Name="__ListId" Type="System.String, mscorlib, mscorlib"
    Direction="In" />
    <Parameter Name="__ListItem" Type="System.Int32, mscorlib, mscorlib"
    Direction="In" />
  </Parameters>
</Action>
```

Note the following:

- The AppliesTo attribute on the <Action> element is set to "list" to tell Office SharePoint Designer 2007 that this WF activity can be used only in workflows associated with standard SharePoint lists as opposed to SharePoint document libraries.
- The UsesCurrentItem attribute on the <Action> element is set to true to tell Office SharePoint Designer 2007 that this WF activity uses the current list item — that is, the list item on which the current workflow instance is running.
- The <RuleDesigner> element contains a <FieldBind> child element that binds the FieldName property of the WaitForActivity activity to the %1 placeholder variable in the rule sentence. Note that the DesignerType attribute on this <FieldBind> child element is set to FieldNames to have Office SharePoint Designer 2007 present the workflow developer with a drop-down list box populated with the field names of the current SharePoint list. Office SharePoint Designer 2007 automatically assigns the field name that the workflow developer selects from this drop-down list box to the FieldName property of the WaitForActivity activity. Keep in mind that the WaitForActivity activity internally uses the value of the FieldName property as the left operand of the operator specified in the Operator property:

```
<FieldBind Field="FieldName" Text="field" Id="1" DesignerType="fieldNames" />
```

- The <RuleDesigner> element contains a <FieldBind> child element that binds the Value property of the WaitForActivity activity to the %3 placeholder variable in the rule sentence. Note that the TypeFrom attribute on this <FieldBind> child element is set to reference the FieldName property of the WaitForActivity activity to specify that the value specified in the Value property is of the same type as the field whose name is specified in FieldName property. The WaitForActivity activity internally uses the value of the Value property as the right operand of the operator specified in the Operator property:

  ```
  <FieldBind Field="Value" Text="value" Id="3" TypeFrom="FieldName"/>
  ```

- The <RuleDesigner> element contains a <FieldBind> child element that binds the Operator property of the WaitForActivity activity to the %2 placeholder variable in the rule sentence. TheOperatorTypeName attribute on this <FieldBind> element is set to reference the FieldName property of the WaitForActivity activity to specify that the operator specified in the Operator property applies to the same .NET data type as the data type of the field whose name is specified in the FieldName property.

  As the following excerpt shows, each <Option> child element of this <FieldBind> element specifies a specific operator:

  ```
  <FieldBind Field="Operator" Id="2" DesignerType="Operator"
  OperatorTypeFrom="FieldName" Text="this test">
    <Option Name="to equal" Value="Equal"/>
    <Option Name="to not equal" Value="NotEqual"/>
    <Option Name="to be greater than" Value="GreaterThan"
    TypeFilter="System.Double;System.Int32;System.Uint32;System.DateTime"/>
    <Option Name="to be greater than or to equal" Value="GreaterThanOrEqual"
    TypeFilter="System.Double;System.Int32;System.Uint32;System.DateTime"/>
    <Option Name="to be less than" Value="LessThan"
    TypeFilter="System.Double;System.Int32;System.Uint32;System.DateTime"/>
    <Option Name="to be less than or to equal" Value="LessThanOrEqual"
    TypeFilter="System.Double;System.Int32;System.Uint32;System.DateTime"/>
    <Option Name="to be empty" Value="IsEmpty"
    TypeFilter="System.String" UnaryHides="Value"/>
    <Option Name="to be not empty" Value="NotIsEmpty"
    TypeFilter="System.String" UnaryHides="Value"/>
    <Option Name="to begin with" Value="StartsWith"
    TypeFilter="System.String"/>
    <Option Name="to not begin with" Value="NotStartsWith"
    TypeFilter="System.String"/>
    <Option Name="to end with" Value="EndsWith"
    TypeFilter="System.String"/>
    <Option Name="to not end with" Value="NotEndsWith"
    TypeFilter="System.String"/>
    <Option Name="to contain" Value="Contains" TypeFilter="System.String"/>
    <Option Name="to not contain" Value="NotContains"
    TypeFilter="System.String"/>
    <Option Name="to match regular expression" Value="Matches"
    TypeFilter="System.String"/>
    <Option Name="to equal (ignoring case)" Value="EqualNoCase"
    TypeFilter="System.String"/>
    <Option Name="to contain (ignoring case)" Value="ContainsNoCase"
  ```

```
    TypeFilter="System.String"/>
    <Option Name="to equal (ignoring time)" Value="EqualNoTime"
    TypeFilter="System.DateTime"/>
  </FieldBind>
```

- Each <Option> element has an attribute named Name, which is set to the name of the operator, and an attribute named Value, which is set to the value that Office SharePoint Designer 2007 assigns to the Value property of the WaitForActivity activity if the workflow developer selects this operator. In other words, the Name attribute provides a friendly name for the value specified in the Value attribute. The drop-down list box that Office SharePoint Designer 2007 presents to the workflow developer shows the value of the Name attribute. The TypeFilter attribute of some <Option> elements are set. This attribute specifies the .NET data types to which the specified operator is applicable. When Office SharePoint Designer 2007 is populating the drop-down list box, it uses the value of this attribute to display only those operators that are applicable to the data type of the field that the workflow developer has selected as the left operand of the operator.

In addition to the WaitForActivity activity, SharePoint ships with two more activities named AddTimeToDateActivity and SetTimeFieldActivity that make use of operators. The following listing presents the <Action> element that describes the AddTimeToDateActivity activity to Office SharePoint Designer 2007:

```
<Action Name="Add Time to Date"
ClassName="Microsoft.SharePoint.WorkflowActions.AddTimeToDateActivity"
Assembly="Microsoft.SharePoint.WorkflowActions, Version=12.0.0.0, Culture=neutral,
          PublicKeyToken=71e9bce111e9429c"
AppliesTo="all" Category="Core Actions">
  <RuleDesigner Sentence="Add %1 %2 to %3  (Output to %4)">
    <FieldBind Field="AddValue" DesignerType="Integer" Id="1" Text="this many"/>
    <FieldBind Field="Units" Text="units" Id="2" DesignerType="Operator"
    OperatorTypeFrom="DropDownMenu" >
      <Option Name="minutes" Value="minutes"/>
      <Option Name="hours" Value="hours"/>
      <Option Name="days" Value="days"/>
      <Option Name="months" Value="months"/>
      <Option Name="years" Value="years"/>
    </FieldBind>
    <FieldBind Field="DateValue" Text="date" Id="3" DesignerType="Date" />
    <FieldBind Field="DateVariable" Text="date" Id="4"
    DesignerType="parameterNames" />
  </RuleDesigner>
  <Parameters>
    <Parameter Name="__Context" Direction="In"
    Type="Microsoft.SharePoint.WorkflowActions.WorkflowContext,
          Microsoft.SharePoint.WorkflowActions"/>
    <Parameter Name="AddValue" Type="System.Double, mscorlib" Direction="In" />
    <Parameter Name="Units" Type="System.String, mscorlib" Direction="In"
    InitialValue="minutes" />
    <Parameter Name="DateValue" Type="System.DateTime, mscorlib" Direction="In"
    InitialValue="" />
    <Parameter Name="DateVariable" Type="System.DateTime, mscorlib"
    Direction="Out" />
  </Parameters>
</Action>
```

Note that AddTimeToDateActivity exposes four bindable properties: AddValue, which is of the System.Double .NET type; Units, which is of the System.String .NET type; DateValue, which of the System.DateTime .NET type; and DateVariable, which is of the System.DateTime .NET type. The execution logic of AddTimeToDateActivity basically adds the value specified in the AddValue property to the value specified in the DateValue property and assigns the result to the DateVariable output property. AddTimeToDateActivity uses the operator or unit that the workflow developer has selected from the list of available operators or units (minutes, hours, days, months, and years) to determine how to convert the value specified in the AddValue property before it adds it to the value specified in the DateValue property. Notice that the OperatorTypeFrom attribute on the <FieldBind> element that binds the Units property to the %2 placeholder variable in the rule sentence is set to DropDownMenu to specify that the type of data that these operators operate on is specified in the drop-down list box itself. For example, if the workflow developer selects the following operator, we're dealing with minutes as opposed to hours:

```
<Option Name="minutes" Value="minutes"/>
```

Float

If your custom WF activity exposes a property of the float type, you should set the DesignerType attribute on the <FieldBind> element that binds this property to a placeholder variable in the rule sentence to Float in order to have Office SharePoint Designer 2007 display a text box that only allows floating-point values.

Integer

If your custom WF activity exposes a non-negative integer property, you should set the DesignerType attribute on the <FieldBind> element that binds this property to a placeholder variable in the rule sentence to Integer in order to have Office SharePoint Designer 2007 display a text box that only allows non-negative integer values.

ListNames

Set the DesignerType attribute to ListNames to have Office SharePoint Designer 2007 display a drop-down list box populated with all lists in the current site when users click the placeholder variable in the rule sentence that binds to a property of your custom WF activity. The following excerpt shows the <Action> element that describes the CopyItemActivity activity:

```
<Action Name="Copy List Item"
ClassName="Microsoft.SharePoint.WorkflowActions.CopyItemActivity"
Assembly="Microsoft.SharePoint.WorkflowActions, Version=12.0.0.0, Culture=neutral,
          PublicKeyToken=71e9bce111e9429c"
CreatesInList="ToListId" AppliesTo="all" Category="List Actions">
  <RuleDesigner Sentence="Copy item in %1 to %2">
    <FieldBind Field="ListId, ListItem" Text="this list" Id="1"
    DesignerType="ChooseListItem" />
    <FieldBind Field="ToListId" Text="this list" Id="2" DesignerType="ListNames" />
  </RuleDesigner>
  <Parameters>
    <Parameter Name="__Context"
    Type="Microsoft.SharePoint.WorkflowActions.WorkflowContext" Direction="In" />
    <Parameter Name="ListId" Type="System.String, mscorlib" Direction="In" />
```

```
      <Parameter Name="ListItem" Type="System.Int32, mscorlib" Direction="In" />
      <Parameter Name="ToListId" Type="System.String, mscorlib" Direction="In" />
      <Parameter Name="Overwrite" Type="System.Boolean, mscorlib" Direction="In"
      InitialValue="false" />
    </Parameters>
  </Action>
```

The <RuleDesigner> element contains a <FieldBind> child element that binds the ToListId property of the CopyItemActivity activity to the %2 placeholder variable in the rule sentence. Note that the DesignerType attribute on this <FieldBind> element is set to ListNames to have Office SharePoint Designer 2007 display a drop-down list box populated with the names of all lists in the current site. Office SharePoint Designer 2007 automatically assigns the list name that the workflow developer selects from this drop-down list box to the ToListId property. This is the SharePoint list into which the specified list item is copied.

Next, we'll implement a custom activity named CustomActivity4 that exposes a string property named ListId, as shown in the following code listing:

```
using System;
using System.Workflow.ComponentModel;
using Microsoft.SharePoint;
using System.Workflow.Activities;
using System.Collections;

namespace Chapter9
{
  public class CustomActivity4 : SequenceActivity
  {
    public string HistoryDescription = default(System.String);
    public string HistoryOutcome = default(System.String);
    private Microsoft.SharePoint.WorkflowActions.LogToHistoryListActivity
                  logToHistoryListActivity1;
    public int UserId = default(System.Int32);

    public static readonly DependencyProperty ListIdProperty =
        DependencyProperty.Register("ListId", typeof(string),
                                       typeof(CustomActivity4));
    public string ListId
    {
      get { return (string)base.GetValue(ListIdProperty); }
      set { base.SetValue(ListIdProperty, value); }
    }

    public CustomActivity4()
    {
      this.InitializeComponent();
    }

    private void InitializeComponent()
    {
      this.CanModifyActivities = true;
```

(continued)

(continued)

```
        System.Workflow.ComponentModel.ActivityBind activitybind1 =
                       new System.Workflow.ComponentModel.ActivityBind();
        System.Workflow.ComponentModel.ActivityBind activitybind2 =
                       new System.Workflow.ComponentModel.ActivityBind();
        System.Workflow.ComponentModel.ActivityBind activitybind3 =
                       new System.Workflow.ComponentModel.ActivityBind();
        this.logToHistoryListActivity1 =
                new Microsoft.SharePoint.WorkflowActions.LogToHistoryListActivity();
        //
        // logToHistoryListActivity1
        //
        this.logToHistoryListActivity1.Duration =
                     System.TimeSpan.Parse("-10675199.02:48:05.4775808");
        this.logToHistoryListActivity1.EventId =
           Microsoft.SharePoint.Workflow.SPWorkflowHistoryEventType.WorkflowComment;
        activitybind1.Name = "CustomActivity4";
        activitybind1.Path = "HistoryDescription";
        activitybind2.Name = "CustomActivity4";
        activitybind2.Path = "HistoryOutcome";
        this.logToHistoryListActivity1.Name = "logToHistoryListActivity1";
        this.logToHistoryListActivity1.OtherData = "";
        activitybind3.Name = "CustomActivity4";
        activitybind3.Path = "UserId";
        this.logToHistoryListActivity1.MethodInvoking +=
           new System.EventHandler(this.logToHistoryListActivity1_MethodInvoking);
        this.logToHistoryListActivity1.SetBinding(Microsoft.SharePoint
.WorkflowActions.LogToHistoryListActivity.HistoryDescriptionProperty,
((System.Workflow.ComponentModel.ActivityBind)(activitybind1)));
        this.logToHistoryListActivity1.SetBinding(Microsoft.SharePoint
.WorkflowActions.LogToHistoryListActivity.HistoryOutcomeProperty,
((System.Workflow.ComponentModel.ActivityBind)(activitybind2)));
        this.logToHistoryListActivity1.SetBinding(Microsoft.SharePoint
.WorkflowActions.LogToHistoryListActivity.UserIdProperty,
((System.Workflow.ComponentModel.ActivityBind)(activitybind3)));
        //
        // CustomActivity4
        //
        this.Activities.Add(this.logToHistoryListActivity1);
        this.Name = "CustomActivity4";
        this.CanModifyActivities = false;
      }

      private void logToHistoryListActivity1_MethodInvoking(object sender,
                                                             EventArgs e)
      {
        this.HistoryDescription = "ListId";
        this.HistoryOutcome = this.ListId;
      }
    }
}
```

The following XML document presents the content of the .actions file that describes the preceding custom activity to Office SharePoint Designer 2007:

```
<?xml version="1.0" encoding="utf-8" ?>
<WorkflowInfo Language="en-us">
  <Actions Sequential="then" Parallel="and">
     <Action Name="Execute custom code 4" AppliesTo="all"
     Category="My Custom Actions"
     ClassName="Chapter9.CustomActivity4"
    Assembly="Chapter9, Version=1.0.0.0, Culture=neutral, PublicKeyToken=252d221e93
3b41ec">
      <RuleDesigner
      Sentence="Execute custom code with %1 on the server">
        <FieldBind Field="ListId" Text="this list name"
        DesignerType="ListNames" Id="1"/>
      </RuleDesigner>
      <Parameters>
        <Parameter Name="ListId" Type="System.String, mscorlib" Direction="In" />
      </Parameters>
    </Action>
  </Actions>
</WorkflowInfo>
```

Note that this XML document defines a <FieldBind> element that binds the ListId property of our custom activity to the %1 placeholder variable in the rule designer sentence. As you can see, the DesignerType attribute on this <FieldBind> element is set to ListNames to have Office SharePoint Designer 2007 display the names of all SharePoint lists in the current site so the workflow developer can set the value of the ListId property in graphical fashion without any code, as shown in Figure 9-19.

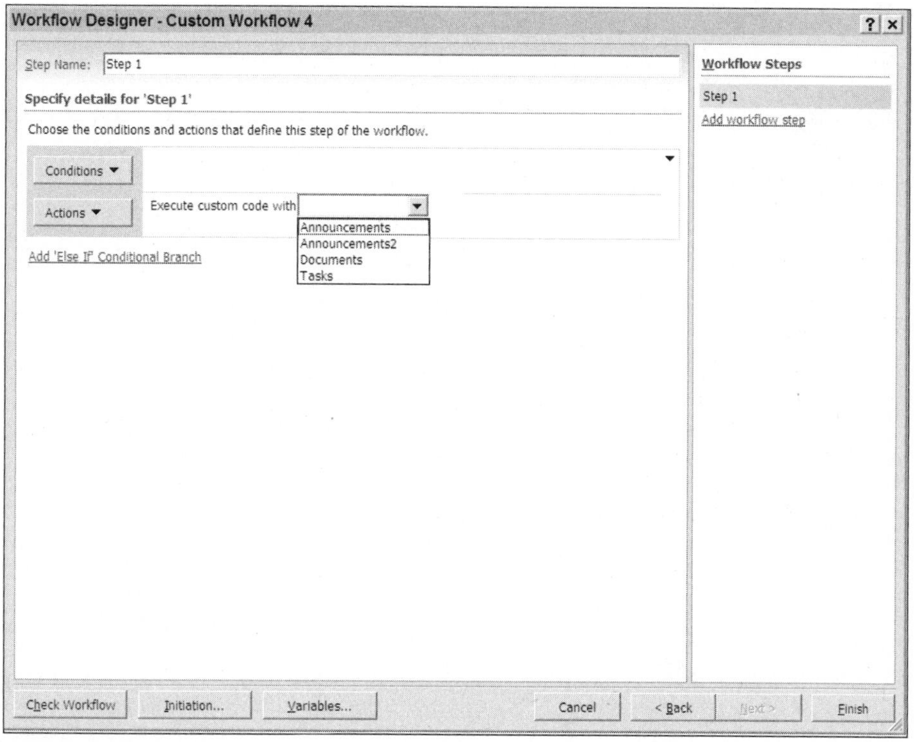

Figure 9-19

Figure 9-20 presents the content of the history workflow list for the workflow that uses our custom activity.

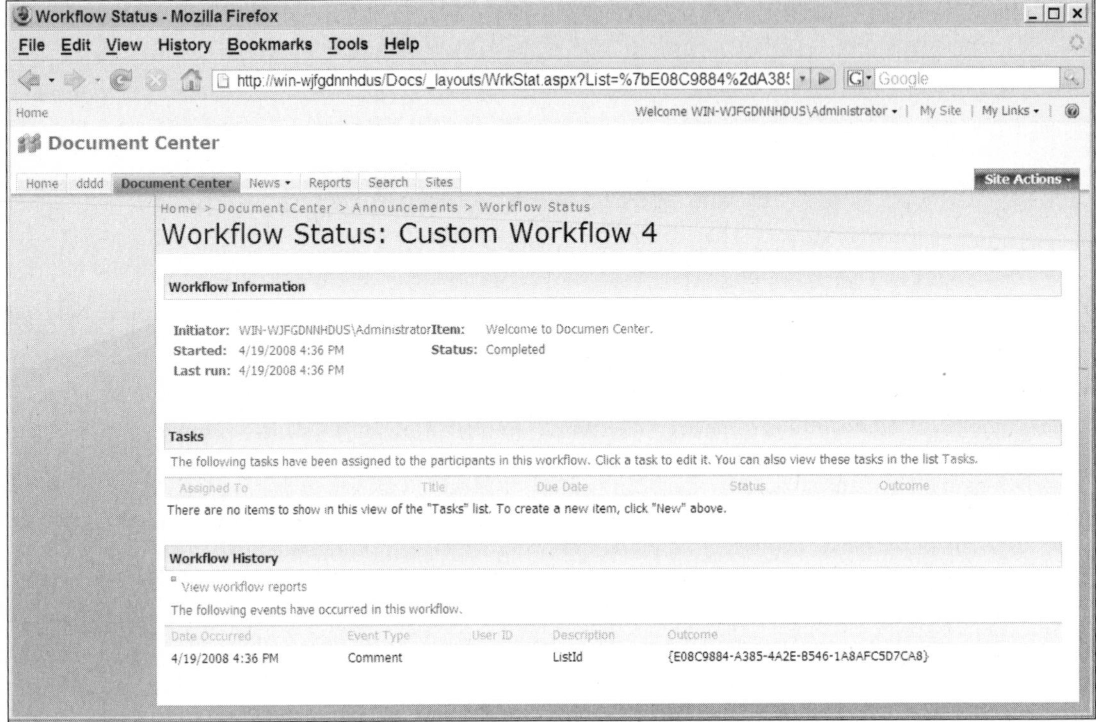

Figure 9-20

Note that the history workflow list contains an entry showing the GUID of the SharePoint list that the workflow developer selected from the list of available SharePoint lists.

ParameterNames

If your custom WF activity contains a property that the workflow designer needs to bind to a local workflow variable, you must set the DesignerType attribute on the <FieldBind> element that binds the property to a placeholder variable in the rule designer sentence to ParameterNames in order to have Office SharePoint Designer 2007 display a drop-down list box populated with all workflow local variables. This enables the workflow developer to set the value of the property in a graphical fashion. A workflow local variable is either a variable that the workflow developer creates on a workflow or the return parameter of the activities that make up the workflow. This enables a workflow developer to chain a number of activities together whereby the output of one activity is bound to the input of another activity.

Person

If your custom activity exposes an input collection property that must be populated with the appropriate user names, you should set the DesignerType attribute on the <FieldBind> element that binds this property to a placeholder variable in the rule sentence to Person in order to have Office SharePoint

Designer 2007 display the Select Users dialog box. This enables the workflow developer to set the value of this collection property in a graphical fashion.

The SharePoint TodoItemTask activity exposes a property named AssignedTo, which is of the System.Collections.ArrayList .NET type. As the following excerpt shows, the DesignerType attribute on the <FieldBind> element associated with this property is set to Person:

```
<Action Name="Assign a To-do Item"
ClassName="Microsoft.SharePoint.WorkflowActions.TodoItemTask"
Assembly="Microsoft.SharePoint.WorkflowActions, Version=12.0.0.0, Culture=neutral,
          PublicKeyToken=71e9bce111e9429c"
AppliesTo="all" CreatesTask="true" Category="Task Actions">
  <RuleDesigner Sentence="Assign %1 to %2">
    <FieldBind Field="Title,ContentTypeId" DesignerType="Survey"
    Text="a to-do item" Id="1"/>
    <FieldBind Field="AssignedTo" DesignerType="Person" Text="these users" Id="2"/>
  </RuleDesigner>
  <Parameters>
    <Parameter Name="__Context" Direction="In"
    Type="Microsoft.SharePoint.WorkflowActions.WorkflowContext,
          Microsoft.SharePoint.WorkflowActions" />
    <Parameter Name="ContentTypeId" Type="System.String, mscorlib"
    Direction="In" />
    <Parameter Name="AssignedTo" Type="System.Collections.ArrayList, mscorlib"
    Direction="In" />
    <Parameter Name="Title" Type="System.String, mscorlib" Direction="In" />
  </Parameters>
</Action>
```

SharePoint comes with another activity named GroupAssignedTask, which also exposes a collection property named AssignedTo. As shown in the following excerpt, the <Action> element that describes this activity also sets the DesignerType attribute to Person:

```
<Action Name="Assign a Form to a Group"
ClassName="Microsoft.SharePoint.WorkflowActions.GroupAssignedTask"
Assembly="Microsoft.SharePoint.WorkflowActions, Version=12.0.0.0, Culture=neutral,
          PublicKeyToken=71e9bce111e9429c"
AppliesTo="all" CreatesTask="true" Category="Task Actions">
  <RuleDesigner Sentence="Assign %1 to %2">
    <FieldBind Field="Title,ContentTypeId" DesignerType="Survey"
    Text="a custom form" Id="1"/>
    <FieldBind Field="AssignedTo" DesignerType="Person" Text="these users" Id="2"/>
  </RuleDesigner>
  <Parameters>
    <Parameter Name="__Context" Direction="In"
    Type="Microsoft.SharePoint.WorkflowActions.WorkflowContext,
          Microsoft.SharePoint.WorkflowActions" />
    <Parameter Name="ContentTypeId" Type="System.String, mscorlib"
    Direction="In" />
    <Parameter Name="AssignedTo" Type="System.Collections.ArrayList, mscorlib"
    Direction="In" />
    <Parameter Name="Title" Type="System.String, mscorlib" Direction="In" />
  </Parameters>
</Action>
```

Next, we'll implement a custom activity named CustomActivity5 that exposes a property named Users, which is of the System.Collection.ArrayList .NET type, as shown in the following code listing:

```
using System;
using System.Workflow.ComponentModel;
using Microsoft.SharePoint;
using System.Workflow.Activities;
using System.Collections;

namespace Chapter9
{
  public class CustomActivity5 : SequenceActivity
  {
    public string HistoryDescription = default(System.String);
    public string HistoryOutcome = default(System.String);
    private Microsoft.SharePoint.WorkflowActions.LogToHistoryListActivity
                     logToHistoryListActivity1;
    public int UserId = default(System.Int32);

    public static readonly DependencyProperty UsersProperty =
        DependencyProperty.Register("Users", typeof(ArrayList),
                                    typeof(CustomActivity5));
    public ArrayList Users
    {
      get { return (ArrayList)base.GetValue(UsersProperty); }
      set { base.SetValue(UsersProperty, value); }
    }

    public CustomActivity5()
    {
      this.InitializeComponent();
    }

    private void InitializeComponent()
    {
      this.CanModifyActivities = true;
      System.Workflow.ComponentModel.ActivityBind activitybind1 =
                    new System.Workflow.ComponentModel.ActivityBind();
      System.Workflow.ComponentModel.ActivityBind activitybind2 =
                    new System.Workflow.ComponentModel.ActivityBind();
      System.Workflow.ComponentModel.ActivityBind activitybind3 =
                    new System.Workflow.ComponentModel.ActivityBind();
      this.logToHistoryListActivity1 =
          new Microsoft.SharePoint.WorkflowActions.LogToHistoryListActivity();
      //
      // logToHistoryListActivity1
      //
      this.logToHistoryListActivity1.Duration =
                  System.TimeSpan.Parse("-10675199.02:48:05.4775808");
      this.logToHistoryListActivity1.EventId =
         Microsoft.SharePoint.Workflow.SPWorkflowHistoryEventType.WorkflowComment;
      activitybind1.Name = "CustomActivity5";
      activitybind1.Path = "HistoryDescription";
```

```
        activitybind2.Name = "CustomActivity5";
        activitybind2.Path = "HistoryOutcome";
        this.logToHistoryListActivity1.Name = "logToHistoryListActivity1";
        this.logToHistoryListActivity1.OtherData = "";
        activitybind3.Name = "CustomActivity5";
        activitybind3.Path = "UserId";
        this.logToHistoryListActivity1.MethodInvoking +=
           new System.EventHandler(this.logToHistoryListActivity1_MethodInvoking);
        this.logToHistoryListActivity1.SetBinding(Microsoft.SharePoint
  .WorkflowActions.LogToHistoryListActivity.HistoryDescriptionProperty,
  ((System.Workflow.ComponentModel.ActivityBind)(activitybind1)));
        this.logToHistoryListActivity1.SetBinding(Microsoft.SharePoint
  .WorkflowActions.LogToHistoryListActivity.HistoryOutcomeProperty,
  ((System.Workflow.ComponentModel.ActivityBind)(activitybind2)));
        this.logToHistoryListActivity1.SetBinding(Microsoft.SharePoint
  .WorkflowActions.LogToHistoryListActivity.UserIdProperty,
  ((System.Workflow.ComponentModel.ActivityBind)(activitybind3)));
        //
        // CustomActivity5
        //
        this.Activities.Add(this.logToHistoryListActivity1);
        this.Name = "CustomActivity5";
        this.CanModifyActivities = false;
      }

      private void logToHistoryListActivity1_MethodInvoking(object sender,
                                                             EventArgs e)
      {
        this.HistoryDescription = "Users";
        this.HistoryOutcome = string.Empty;
        for (int i = 0; i < this.Users.Count; i++)
        {
          if (i != 0)
            this.HistoryOutcome += ";";
          this.HistoryOutcome += this.Users[i];
        }
      }
    }
  }
```

The following XML document presents the .actions file that describes the preceding custom activity:

```
<?xml version="1.0" encoding="utf-8" ?>
<WorkflowInfo Language="en-us">
  <Actions Sequential="then" Parallel="and">
    <Action Name="Execute custom code 5" AppliesTo="all"
    Category="My Custom Actions"
   ClassName="Chapter9.CustomActivity5"
    Assembly="Chapter9, Version=1.0.0.0, Culture=neutral,
             PublicKeyToken=252d221e933b41ec">
      <RuleDesigner
      Sentence="Execute custom code with %1 on the server">
```

(continued)

(continued)

```
          <FieldBind Field="Users" Text="these users" DesignerType="Person" Id="1"/>
        </RuleDesigner>
        <Parameters>
          <Parameter Name="Users" Type="System.Collection.ArrayList, mscorlib"
          Direction="In" />
        </Parameters>
      </Action>
    </Actions>
  </WorkflowInfo>
```

Note that the .actions file defines a <FieldBind> element that represents the Users property of our custom activity. As you can see, the DesignerType attribute on this element is set to Person.

Figure 9-21 shows the Workflow Designer that displays the rule designer sentence for our custom action.

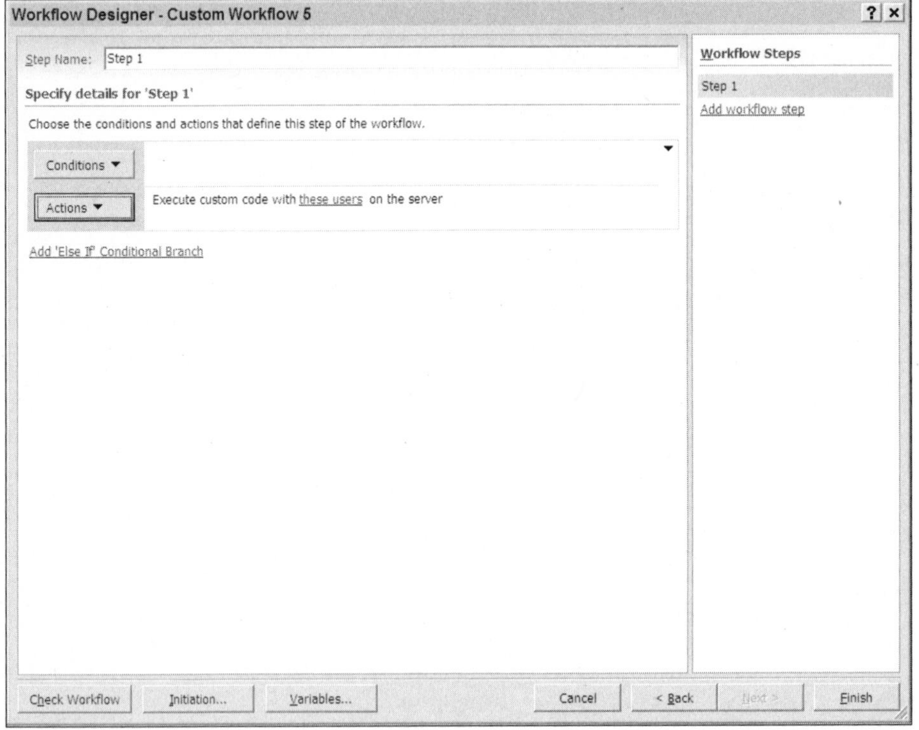

Figure 9-21

When the workflow developer clicks the These Users link in this rule sentence, Workflow Designer launches the Select Users dialog box shown in Figure 9-22. This dialog box enables the workflow developer to select and add users. Under the hood, the Select Users dialog box packs the selected users in a System.Collection.ArrayList object and assigns this object to the Users property of our custom activity.

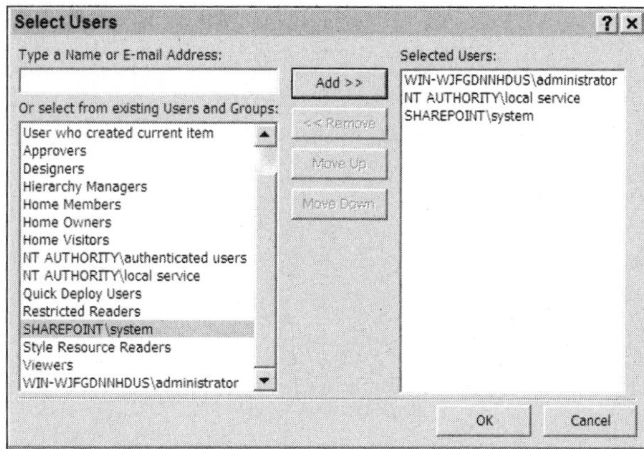

Figure 9-22

As Figure 9-23 shows, our custom activity adds an entry to the workflow history list, which contains the users that the workflow designer selected.

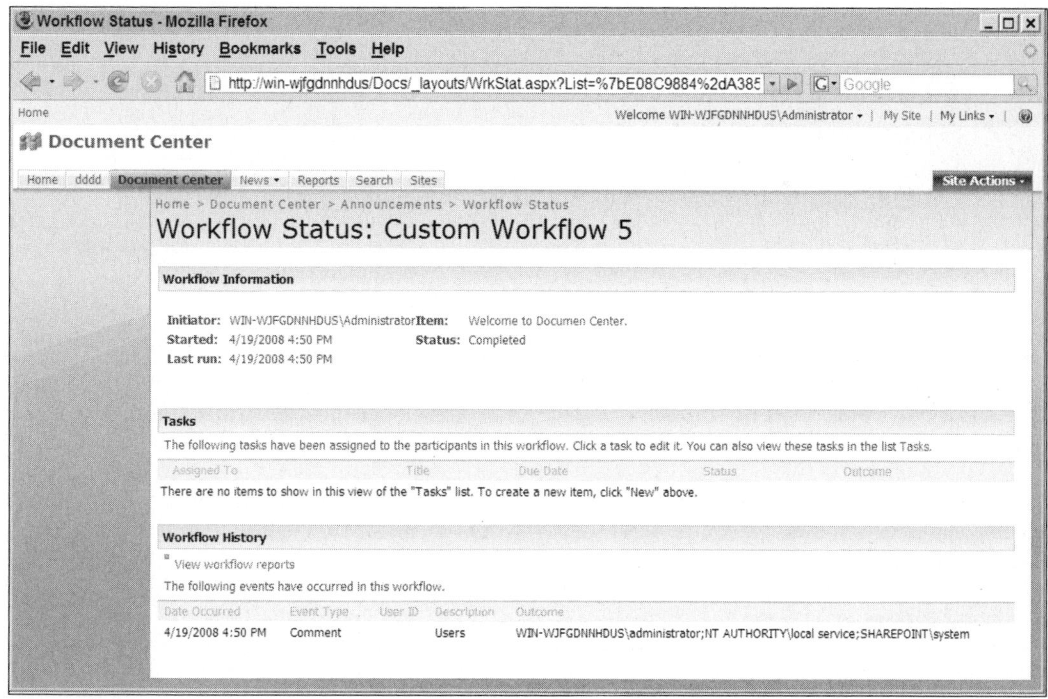

Figure 9-23

SinglePerson

The previous section discussed the scenario in which your custom activity exposes a collection property that the workflow developer must populate with the appropriate user names. This section discusses the scenario in which your custom activity exposes a non-collection property that the workflow developer must set to the appropriate user name.

The SharePoint CollectDataTask activity is an example of such an activity. This activity exposes a non-collection string property named AssignedTo, which the workflow developer must set to the user from whom this activity must collect data. The following <Action> element describes this activity:

```
<Action Name="Collect Data from a User"
ClassName="Microsoft.SharePoint.WorkflowActions.CollectDataTask"
Assembly="Microsoft.SharePoint.WorkflowActions, Version=12.0.0.0, Culture=neutral,
          PublicKeyToken=71e9bce111e9429c"
AppliesTo="all" CreatesTask="true" Category="Task Actions">
  <RuleDesigner Sentence="Collect %1 from %2  (Output to %3)">
    <FieldBind Field="Title,ContentTypeId" DesignerType="Survey"
    Text="data" Id="1"/>
    <FieldBind Field="AssignedTo" DesignerType="SinglePerson"
    Text="this user" Id="2"/>
    <FieldBind Field="TaskId" DesignerType="ParameterNames" Text="collect" Id="3"/>
  </RuleDesigner>
  <Parameters>
    <Parameter Name="__Context" Direction="In"
    Type="Microsoft.SharePoint.WorkflowActions.WorkflowContext,
          Microsoft.SharePoint.WorkflowActions" />
    <Parameter Name="ContentTypeId" Type="System.String, mscorlib"
    Direction="In" />
    <Parameter Name="AssignedTo" Type="System.String, mscorlib" Direction="In" />
    <Parameter Name="Title" Type="System.String, mscorlib" Direction="In" />
    <Parameter Name="TaskId" Type="System.Int32, mscorlib" Direction="Out" />
  </Parameters>
</Action>
```

The <FieldBind> element that binds the AssignedTo property to the %2 placeholder variable in the rule sentence has its DesignerType attribute set to SinglePerson in order to have Office SharePoint Designer 2007 display the appropriate dialog box for the workflow developer to set the value of this property in a graphical manner.

The following code listing presents the implementation of a custom activity named CustomActivity6 that exposes a string property named User that the workflow developer must set to the appropriate user name:

```
using System;
using System.Workflow.ComponentModel;
using Microsoft.SharePoint;
using System.Workflow.Activities;
using System.Collections;

namespace Chapter9
```

```
{
  public class CustomActivity6 : SequenceActivity
  {
    public string HistoryDescription = default(System.String);
    public string HistoryOutcome = default(System.String);
    private Microsoft.SharePoint.WorkflowActions.LogToHistoryListActivity
                      logToHistoryListActivity1;
    public int UserId = default(System.Int32);

    public static readonly DependencyProperty UserProperty =
        DependencyProperty.Register("User", typeof(string),
                                    typeof(CustomActivity6));
    public string User
    {
      get { return (string)base.GetValue(UserProperty); }
      set { base.SetValue(UserProperty, value); }
    }

    public CustomActivity6()
    {
      this.InitializeComponent();
    }

    private void InitializeComponent()
    {
      this.CanModifyActivities = true;
      System.Workflow.ComponentModel.ActivityBind activitybind1 =
                     new System.Workflow.ComponentModel.ActivityBind();
      System.Workflow.ComponentModel.ActivityBind activitybind2 =
                     new System.Workflow.ComponentModel.ActivityBind();
      System.Workflow.ComponentModel.ActivityBind activitybind3 =
                     new System.Workflow.ComponentModel.ActivityBind();
      this.logToHistoryListActivity1 =
           new Microsoft.SharePoint.WorkflowActions.LogToHistoryListActivity();
      //
      // logToHistoryListActivity1
      //
      this.logToHistoryListActivity1.Duration =
                         System.TimeSpan.Parse("-10675199.02:48:05.4775808");
      this.logToHistoryListActivity1.EventId =
         Microsoft.SharePoint.Workflow.SPWorkflowHistoryEventType.WorkflowComment;
      activitybind1.Name = "CustomActivity6";
      activitybind1.Path = "HistoryDescription";
      activitybind2.Name = "CustomActivity6";
      activitybind2.Path = "HistoryOutcome";
      this.logToHistoryListActivity1.Name = "logToHistoryListActivity1";
      this.logToHistoryListActivity1.OtherData = "";
      activitybind3.Name = "CustomActivity6";
      activitybind3.Path = "UserId";
      this.logToHistoryListActivity1.MethodInvoking +=
        new System.EventHandler(this.logToHistoryListActivity1_MethodInvoking);
      this.logToHistoryListActivity1.SetBinding(Microsoft.SharePoint
.WorkflowActions.LogToHistoryListActivity.HistoryDescriptionProperty,
((System.Workflow.ComponentModel.ActivityBind)(activitybind1)));
```

(continued)

(continued)

```
        this.logToHistoryListActivity1.SetBinding(Microsoft.SharePoint
.WorkflowActions.LogToHistoryListActivity.HistoryOutcomeProperty,
((System.Workflow.ComponentModel.ActivityBind)(activitybind2)));
        this.logToHistoryListActivity1.SetBinding(Microsoft.SharePoint
.WorkflowActions.LogToHistoryListActivity.UserIdProperty,
((System.Workflow.ComponentModel.ActivityBind)(activitybind3)));
        //
        // CustomActivity6
        //
        this.Activities.Add(this.logToHistoryListActivity1);
        this.Name = "CustomActivity6";
        this.CanModifyActivities = false;
      }

      private void logToHistoryListActivity1_MethodInvoking(object sender,
                                                            EventArgs e)
      {
        this.HistoryDescription = "User";
        this.HistoryOutcome = this.User;
      }
    }
}
```

The following XML document contains the content of the .actions file that describes this custom activity:

```
<?xml version="1.0" encoding="utf-8" ?>
<WorkflowInfo Language="en-us">
  <Actions Sequential="then" Parallel="and">
    <Action Name="Execute custom code 6" AppliesTo="all"
    Category="My Custom Actions"
    ClassName="Chapter9.CustomActivity6"
    Assembly="Chapter9, Version=1.0.0.0, Culture=neutral, PublicKeyToken=252d221e93
3b41ec">
      <RuleDesigner
      Sentence="Execute custom code with %1 on the server">
        <FieldBind Field="User" Text="this user" DesignerType="SinglePerson"
        Id="1"/>
      </RuleDesigner>
      <Parameters>
        <Parameter Name="User" Type="System.String, mscorlib" Direction="In" />
      </Parameters>
    </Action>
  </Actions>
</WorkflowInfo>
```

Figure 9-24 shows the rule designer sentence associated with this custom activity.

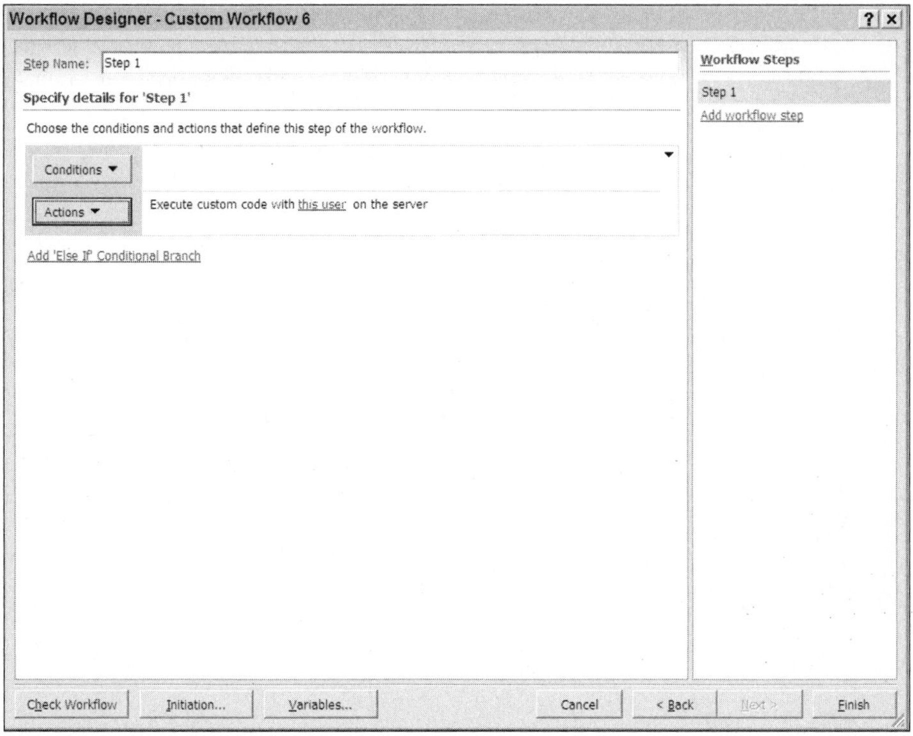

Figure 9-24

When the workflow developer clicks the This User link in this rule sentence, Office SharePoint Designer 2007 launches the Select Users dialog shown in Figure 9-25. Note that this dialog does not allow the workflow developer to add more than one user.

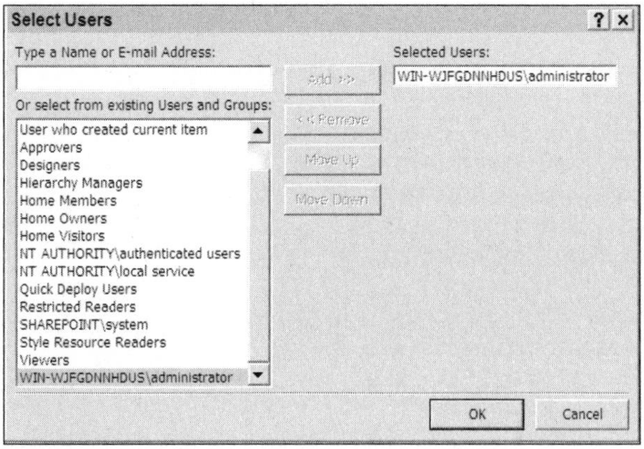

Figure 9-25

When the workflow designer clicks the OK button on the Select Users dialog box, the selected user is automatically assigned to the User property of our custom activity. As Figure 9-26 shows, when the workflow that contains our custom activity executes, our custom action adds an entity to the workflow history list that contains the selected user.

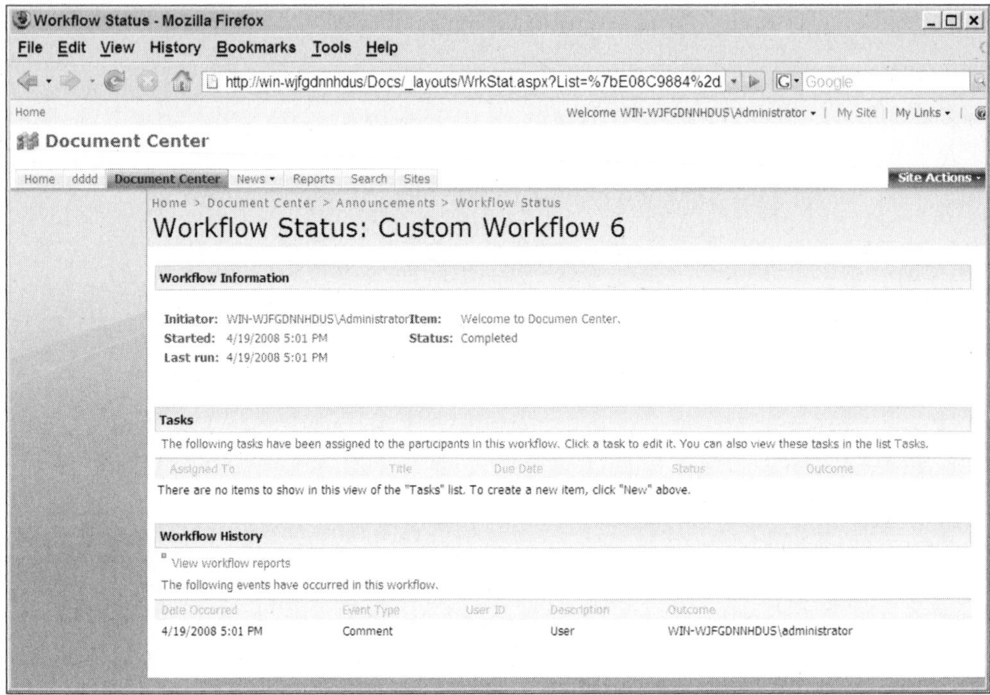

Figure 9-26

StringBuilder

If the DesignerType attribute on a <FieldBind> element is set to StringBuilder, when the workflow designer clicks the associated placeholder variable in the rule sentence, Office SharePoint Designer 2007 launches the String Builder dialog box. To help you understand the role of this dialog box and the StringBuilder attribute value, let's implement a custom WF activity named CustomActivity7 that makes use of them. Listing 9-1 presents the implementation of this custom activity.

Listing 9-1: The CustomActivity activity

```
using System;
using System.Workflow.ComponentModel;
using Microsoft.SharePoint;
using System.Workflow.Activities;
using System.Collections;
using Microsoft.SharePoint.WorkflowActions;

namespace Chapter9
```

```
{
  public class CustomActivity7 : SequenceActivity
  {
    public string HistoryDescription = default(System.String);
    public string HistoryOutcome = default(System.String);
    private Microsoft.SharePoint.WorkflowActions.LogToHistoryListActivity
              logToHistoryListActivity1;
    public int UserId = default(System.Int32);

    public static readonly DependencyProperty StringPropertyProperty =
        DependencyProperty.Register("StringProperty", typeof(string),
                                    typeof(CustomActivity7));
    public string StringProperty
    {
      get { return (string)base.GetValue(StringPropertyProperty); }
      set { base.SetValue(StringPropertyProperty, value); }
    }

    public CustomActivity7()
    {
      this.InitializeComponent();
    }

    private void InitializeComponent()
    {
      this.CanModifyActivities = true;
      System.Workflow.ComponentModel.ActivityBind activitybind1 =
                    new System.Workflow.ComponentModel.ActivityBind();
      System.Workflow.ComponentModel.ActivityBind activitybind2 =
                    new System.Workflow.ComponentModel.ActivityBind();
      System.Workflow.ComponentModel.ActivityBind activitybind3 =
                    new System.Workflow.ComponentModel.ActivityBind();
      this.logToHistoryListActivity1 =
              new Microsoft.SharePoint.WorkflowActions.LogToHistoryListActivity();
      //
      // logToHistoryListActivity1
      //
      this.logToHistoryListActivity1.Duration =
                       System.TimeSpan.Parse("-10675199.02:48:05.4775808");
      this.logToHistoryListActivity1.EventId =
         Microsoft.SharePoint.Workflow.SPWorkflowHistoryEventType.WorkflowComment;
      activitybind1.Name = "CustomActivity7";
      activitybind1.Path = "HistoryDescription";
      activitybind2.Name = "CustomActivity7";
      activitybind2.Path = "HistoryOutcome";
      this.logToHistoryListActivity1.Name = "logToHistoryListActivity1";
      this.logToHistoryListActivity1.OtherData = "";
      activitybind3.Name = "CustomActivity7";
      activitybind3.Path = "UserId";
      this.logToHistoryListActivity1.MethodInvoking +=
        new System.EventHandler(this.logToHistoryListActivity1_MethodInvoking);
```

(continued)

Listing 9-1 *(continued)*

```
      this.logToHistoryListActivity1.SetBinding(Microsoft.SharePoint
.WorkflowActions.LogToHistoryListActivity.HistoryDescriptionProperty,
((System.Workflow.ComponentModel.ActivityBind)(activitybind1)));
      this.logToHistoryListActivity1.SetBinding(Microsoft.SharePoint
.WorkflowActions.LogToHistoryListActivity.HistoryOutcomeProperty,
((System.Workflow.ComponentModel.ActivityBind)(activitybind2)));
      this.logToHistoryListActivity1.SetBinding(Microsoft.SharePoint
.WorkflowActions.LogToHistoryListActivity.UserIdProperty,
((System.Workflow.ComponentModel.ActivityBind)(activitybind3)));
      //
      // CustomActivity7
      //
      this.Activities.Add(this.logToHistoryListActivity1);
      this.Name = "CustomActivity7";
      this.CanModifyActivities = false;
    }

    protected override ActivityExecutionStatus Execute(
                                  ActivityExecutionContext context)
    {
      if (this.StringProperty != null)
      {
        Activity parent = context.Activity;
        while (parent.Parent != null)
        {
          parent = parent.Parent;
        }
        this.HistoryOutcome =
            Helper.ProcessStringField(this.StringProperty, parent, null);
      }

      return base.Execute(context);
    }

    private void logToHistoryListActivity1_MethodInvoking(object sender,
                                                    EventArgs e)
    {
      this.HistoryDescription = "StringProperty";
    }
  }
}
```

Note that this activity exposes a bindable string property named StringProperty. The following XML document contains the content of the .actions file that describes this custom activity to Office SharePoint Designer 2007:

```
<?xml version="1.0" encoding="utf-8" ?>
<WorkflowInfo Language="en-us">
  <Actions Sequential="then" Parallel="and">
     <Action Name="Execute custom code 7" AppliesTo="all"
```

```
      Category="My Custom Actions"
      ClassName="Chapter9.CustomActivity7"
      Assembly="Chapter9, Version=1.0.0.0, Culture=neutral, PublicKeyToken=252d221e9
33b41ec">
        <RuleDesigner
        Sentence="Execute custom code with %1 on the server">
          <FieldBind Field="StringProperty" Text="this value for StringProperty"
          DesignerType="StringBuilder" Id="1"/>
        </RuleDesigner>
        <Parameters>
          <Parameter Name="StringProperty"
          Type="System.String, mscorlib" Direction="In" />
        </Parameters>
      </Action>
    </Actions>
  </WorkflowInfo>
```

The <FieldBind> element that represents the StringProperty property of our custom activity has its DesignerType attribute set to StringBuilder to instruct Office SharePoint Designer 2007 to launch the String Builder dialog when the workflow designer clicks the associated placeholder variable in the rule designer sentence.

Now we'll create a workflow that uses our custom activity. Figure 9-27 shows a workflow that contains an instance of our custom activity.

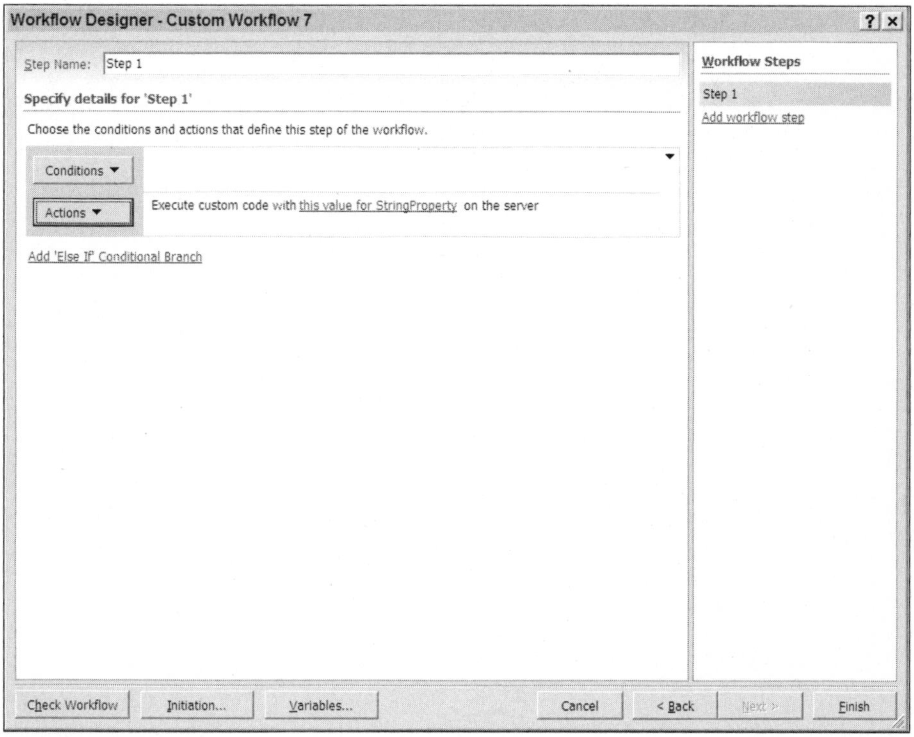

Figure 9-27

Add two workflow local variables named DateVariable, of the Date and Time type, and NumberVariable, of the Number type, following the same steps discussed in the previous chapter. Next, click the "this value for StringProperty" link in the rule designer sentence. Because we have set the DesignerType attribute to StringBuilder, Office SharePoint Designer 2007 automatically launches the String Builder dialog box shown in Figure 9-28.

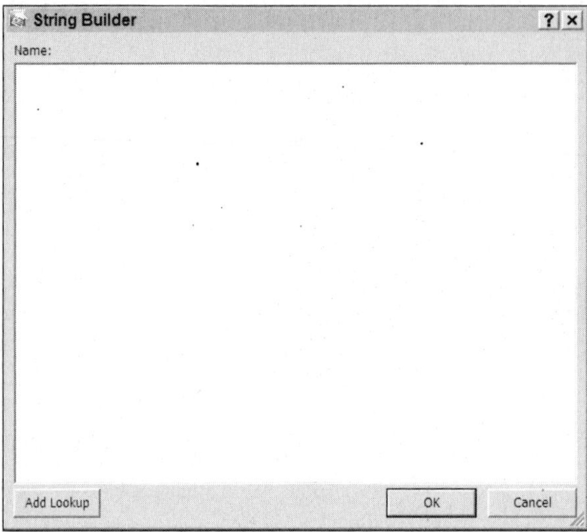

Figure 9-28

Add the text "**Date Variable is :**" to the String Builder editor area. Then click the Add Lookup button to launch the Define Workflow Lookup dialog shown in Figure 9-29.

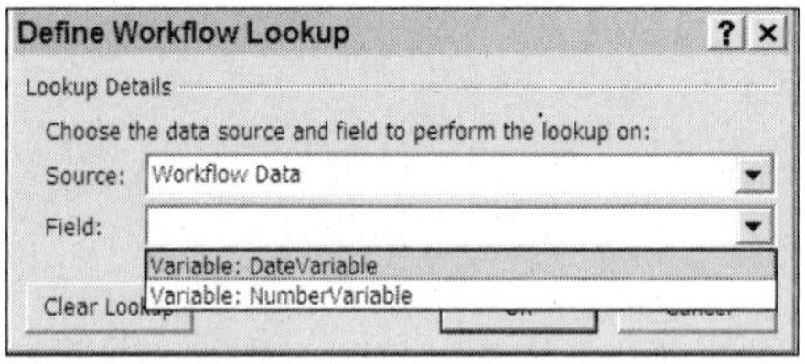

Define Workflow Lookup
Lookup Details
Choose the data source and field to perform the lookup on:
Source: Workflow Data
Field:
Variable: DateVariable
Variable: NumberVariable
Clear Lookup

Figure 9-29

Select the Workflow Data menu option from the Source drop-down list box and the DateVariable option from the Field drop-down list box and click the OK button. This will add the text shown in Figure 9-30.

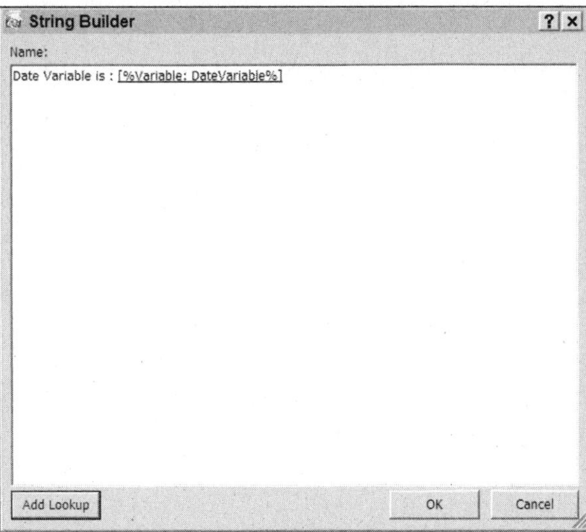

Figure 9-30

Note that the text uses what is known as a *data binding expression* to bind the DateVariable workflow local variable. Repeat the same procedure to add a second data binding expression, as shown in Figure 9-31.

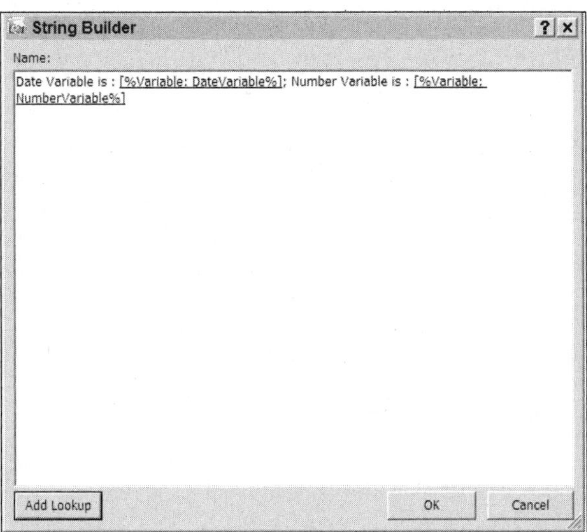

Figure 9-31

When you click OK (refer to Figure 9-31), the String Builder dialog box automatically assigns the string shown here "as is" to the StringProperty property of our custom activity. It is important to understand that the String Builder dialog box does not do anything with the data binding expressions. It is the responsibility of our custom activity to evaluate these data binding expressions at run time. As Listing 9-1 shows, the Execute method of our custom activity passes the value of the StringProperty, which includes the data binding expressions, to a helper method named ProcessStringField on a standard SharePoint helper class named Helper to evaluate these data binding expressions:

```
protected override ActivityExecutionStatus Execute(
                                    ActivityExecutionContext context)
{
  if (this.StringProperty != null)
  {
    Activity parent = context.Activity;
    while (parent.Parent != null)
    {
      parent = parent.Parent;
    }
    this.HistoryOutcome = Helper.ProcessStringField(
                                    this.StringProperty, parent, null);
  }

  return base.Execute(context);
}
```

Our custom activity overrides the Execute method of its base class — that is, the SequenceActivity activity — to include the call into the ProcessStringField method. As you can see, our custom activity's implementation of the Execute method finally invokes the Execute method of its base class. This is important because it is the Execute method of the SequenceActivity activity that triggers the call into the Execute method of the LogToHistoryListActivity activity's Execute method, which in turn logs the specified information to the workflow history list.

To keep our discussions focused, we'll add two Set Workflow Variable actions to our workflow to set the values of the DateVariable and NumberVariable workflow local fields, as shown in Figure 9-32.

Following the same steps discussed in the previous chapter, bind the "workflow variable" placeholder variables of these two Set Workflow Variable actions to the DateVariable and NumberVariable local workflow variables, respectively, as shown in Figure 9-33.

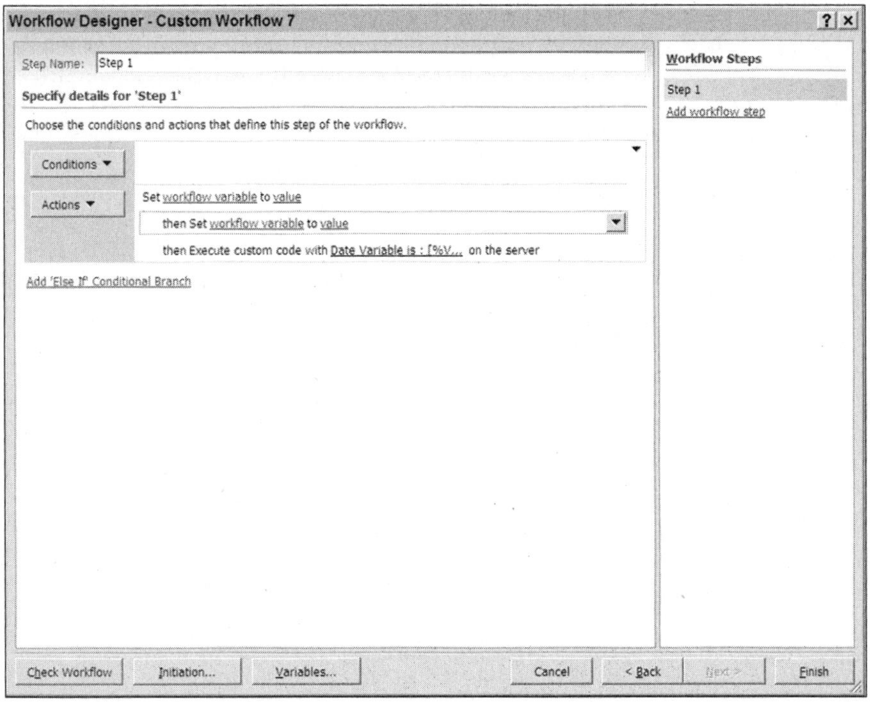

Figure 9-32

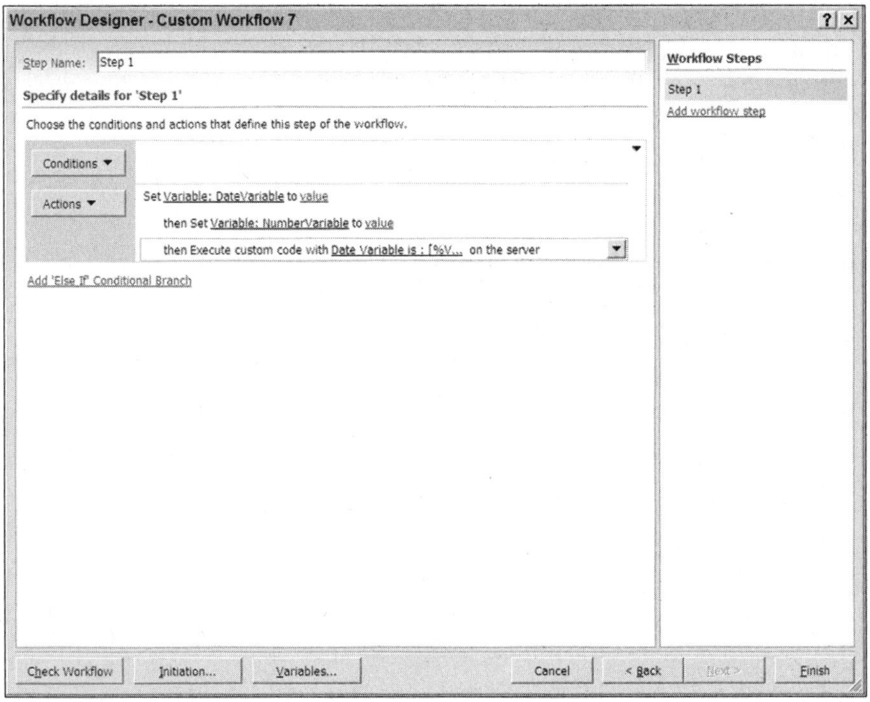

Figure 9-33

Next, click the value placeholder variable of the top Set Workflow Variable action to display the user interface, which consists of a text box and two buttons, as shown in Figure 9-34.

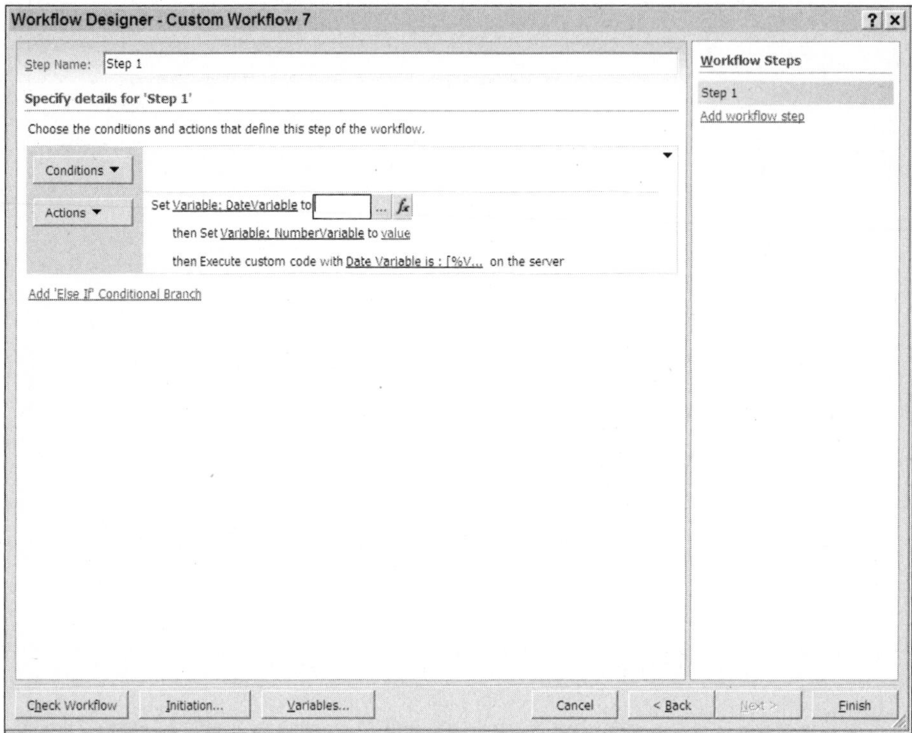

Figure 9-34

Click the first button to launch the Date Value dialog shown in Figure 9-35 and check the Current Date radio button to use the current date as the value of the value placeholder.

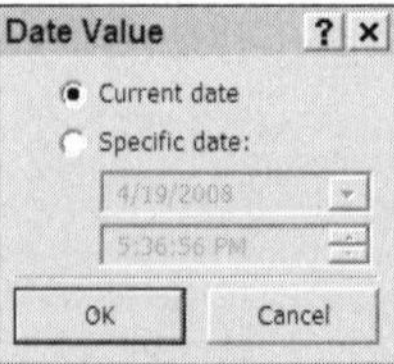

Figure 9-35

Next, click the value placeholder to display the user interface, which consists of a text box and a button. Enter the number 45 as the value of the value placeholder variable, as shown in Figure 9-36.

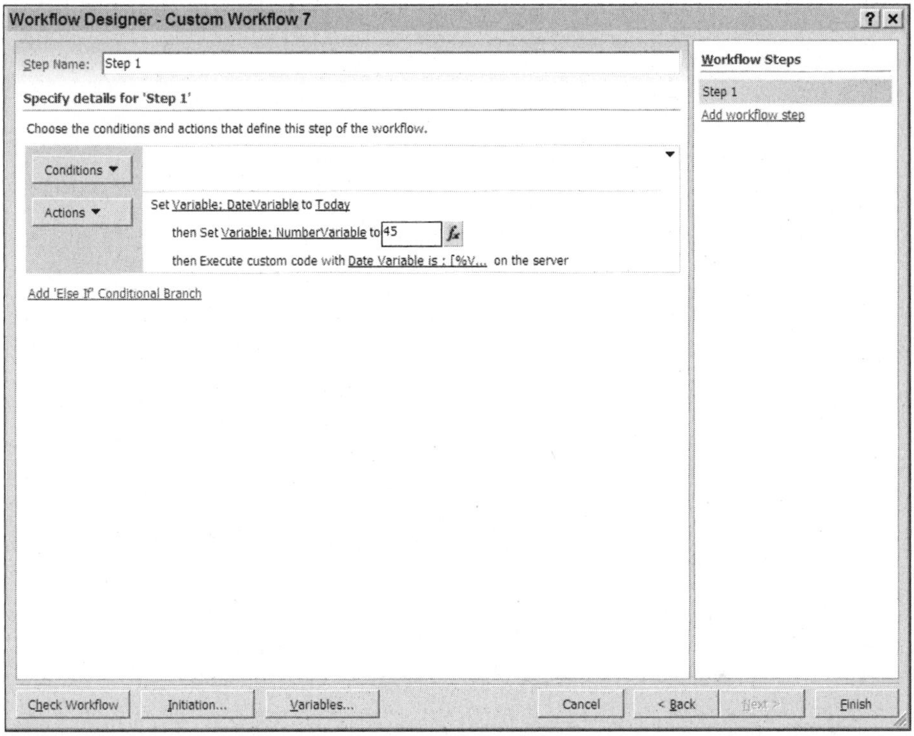

Figure 9-36

Click the Finish button to create and store the workflow. Then navigate to the SharePoint list with which the workflow is associated and initiate an instance of the workflow on a list item in this list. Figure 9-37 presents the outcome of the execution of the workflow that contains our custom activity. As you can see, the entry that our custom activity logs into the workflow history list contains the outcome of the evaluation of the data binding expressions that the workflow developer adds to the String Builder dialog box.

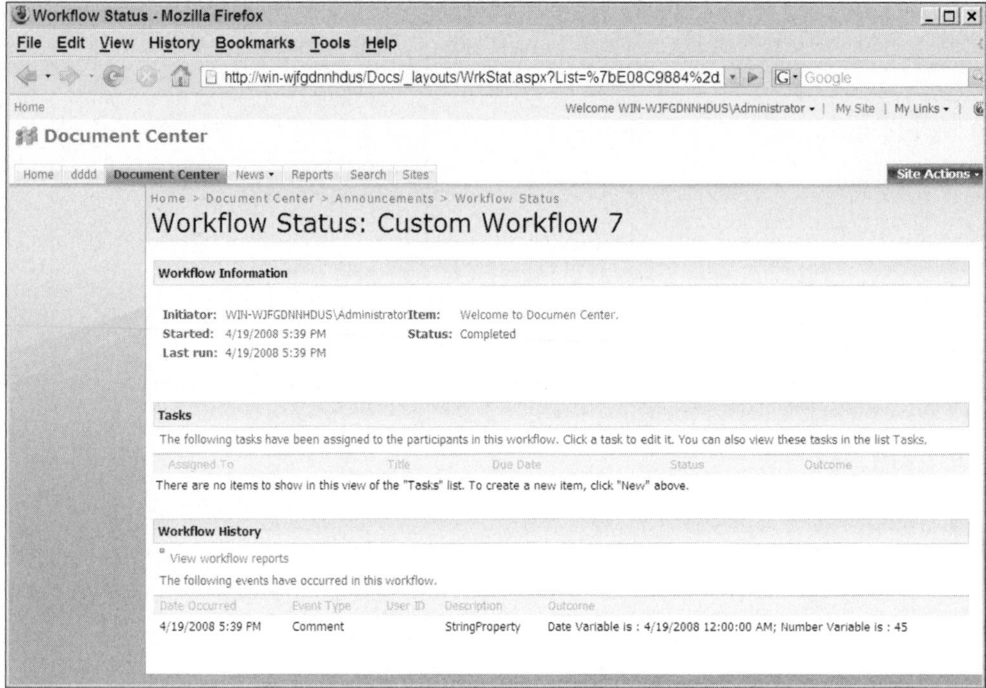

Figure 9-37

SharePoint ships with a standard activity named BuildStringActivity that makes use of the String Builder dialog box. This activity, which exposes two string properties named Variable and StringValue, simply evaluates the string assigned to its StringValue, including all the data binding expressions that the string contains, and assigns the outcome of this evaluation to its Variable property. The following <Action> element describes this activity to Office SharePoint Designer 2007:

```
<Action Name="Build Dynamic String"
ClassName="Microsoft.SharePoint.WorkflowActions.BuildStringActivity"
Assembly="Microsoft.SharePoint.WorkflowActions, Version=12.0.0.0, Culture=neutral,
          PublicKeyToken=71e9bce111e9429c"
AppliesTo="all" Category="Core Actions">
  <RuleDesigner Sentence="Store %1 in %2">
    <FieldBind Field="StringValue" Text="dynamic string" Id="1"
    DesignerType="stringbuilder" />
    <FieldBind Field="Variable" Text="variable" Id="2"
    DesignerType="ParameterNames"/>
  </RuleDesigner>
  <Parameters>
    <Parameter Name="Variable" Type="System.String, mscorlib" Direction="Out" />
    <Parameter Name="StringValue" Type="System.String, mscorlib" Direction="In" />
  </Parameters>
</Action>
```

Note that the DesignerType attribute on the <FieldBind> element that represents the StringValue property is set to StringBuilder as expected. Because the BuildStringActivity activity is marked with the Toolbox(false) metadata attribute, it cannot be added to Visual Studio's toolbox. As our latest custom activity shows, it is very easy to duplicate the functionality of this activity in your own custom activities if you need to.

Text and TextArea

If your custom WF activity exposes a string property and you want to enable workflow developers to specify the value of this property, either statically through hard-coding a fixed value or dynamically through activity binding, set the DesignerType attribute on the <FieldBind> element that represents this property to Text or TextArea. Let's take a look at an example.

The following code listing presents the implementation of a custom activity named CustomActivity8 that exposes a string property named StringProperty:

```
using System;
using System.Workflow.ComponentModel;
using Microsoft.SharePoint;
using System.Workflow.Activities;
using System.Collections;
using Microsoft.SharePoint.WorkflowActions;

namespace Chapter9
{
  public class CustomActivity8 : SequenceActivity
  {
    public string HistoryDescription = default(System.String);
    public string HistoryOutcome = default(System.String);
    private LogToHistoryListActivity logToHistoryListActivity1;
    public int UserId = default(System.Int32);

    public static readonly DependencyProperty StringPropertyProperty =
        DependencyProperty.Register("StringProperty", typeof(string),
                                    typeof(CustomActivity8));
    public string StringProperty
    {
      get { return (string)base.GetValue(StringPropertyProperty); }
      set { base.SetValue(StringPropertyProperty, value); }
    }

    public CustomActivity8()
    {
      this.InitializeComponent();
    }

    private void InitializeComponent()
    {
      this.CanModifyActivities = true;
      System.Workflow.ComponentModel.ActivityBind activitybind1 =
                        new System.Workflow.ComponentModel.ActivityBind();
```

(continued)

(continued)

```
        System.Workflow.ComponentModel.ActivityBind activitybind2 =
                        new System.Workflow.ComponentModel.ActivityBind();
        System.Workflow.ComponentModel.ActivityBind activitybind3 =
                        new System.Workflow.ComponentModel.ActivityBind();
        this.logToHistoryListActivity1 =
                new Microsoft.SharePoint.WorkflowActions.LogToHistoryListActivity();
        //
        // logToHistoryListActivity1
        //
        this.logToHistoryListActivity1.Duration =
                System.TimeSpan.Parse("-10675199.02:48:05.4775808");
        this.logToHistoryListActivity1.EventId =
           Microsoft.SharePoint.Workflow.SPWorkflowHistoryEventType.WorkflowComment;
        activitybind1.Name = "CustomActivity8";
        activitybind1.Path = "HistoryDescription";
        activitybind2.Name = "CustomActivity8";
        activitybind2.Path = "HistoryOutcome";
        this.logToHistoryListActivity1.Name = "logToHistoryListActivity1";
        this.logToHistoryListActivity1.OtherData = "";
        activitybind3.Name = "CustomActivity8";
        activitybind3.Path = "UserId";
        this.logToHistoryListActivity1.MethodInvoking +=
          new System.EventHandler(this.logToHistoryListActivity1_MethodInvoking);
        this.logToHistoryListActivity1.SetBinding(Microsoft.SharePoint
.WorkflowActions.LogToHistoryListActivity.HistoryDescriptionProperty,
((System.Workflow.ComponentModel.ActivityBind)(activitybind1)));
        this.logToHistoryListActivity1.SetBinding(Microsoft.SharePoint
.WorkflowActions.LogToHistoryListActivity.HistoryOutcomeProperty,
((System.Workflow.ComponentModel.ActivityBind)(activitybind2)));
        this.logToHistoryListActivity1.SetBinding(Microsoft.SharePoint
.WorkflowActions.LogToHistoryListActivity.UserIdProperty,
((System.Workflow.ComponentModel.ActivityBind)(activitybind3)));
        //
        // CustomActivity8
        //
        this.Activities.Add(this.logToHistoryListActivity1);
        this.Name = "CustomActivity8";
        this.CanModifyActivities = false;
      }

      private void logToHistoryListActivity1_MethodInvoking(object sender,
                                                            EventArgs e)
      {
        this.HistoryDescription = "StringProperty";
        this.HistoryOutcome = this.StringProperty;
      }
    }
}
```

The following XML document presents the content of the .actions file that describes this custom activity to Office SharePoint Designer 2007:

```
<?xml version="1.0" encoding="utf-8" ?>
<WorkflowInfo Language="en-us">
  <Actions Sequential="then" Parallel="and">
    <Action Name="Execute custom code 8" AppliesTo="all"
    Category="My Custom Actions"
    ClassName="Chapter9.CustomActivity8"
    Assembly="Chapter9, Version=1.0.0.0, Culture=neutral,
             PublicKeyToken=252d221e933b41ec">
      <RuleDesigner
      Sentence="Execute custom code with %1 on the server">
        <FieldBind Field="StringProperty" Text="this StringProperty value"
        DesignerType="Text" Id="1"/>
      </RuleDesigner>
      <Parameters>
        <Parameter Name="StringProperty" Type="System.String, mscorlib"
        Direction="In" />
      </Parameters>
    </Action>
  </Actions>
</WorkflowInfo>
```

As you can see, the DesignerType attribute on the <FieldBind> element that represents the StringProperty property is set to Text. Next, let's design a workflow that uses our custom activity, as shown in Figure 9-38.

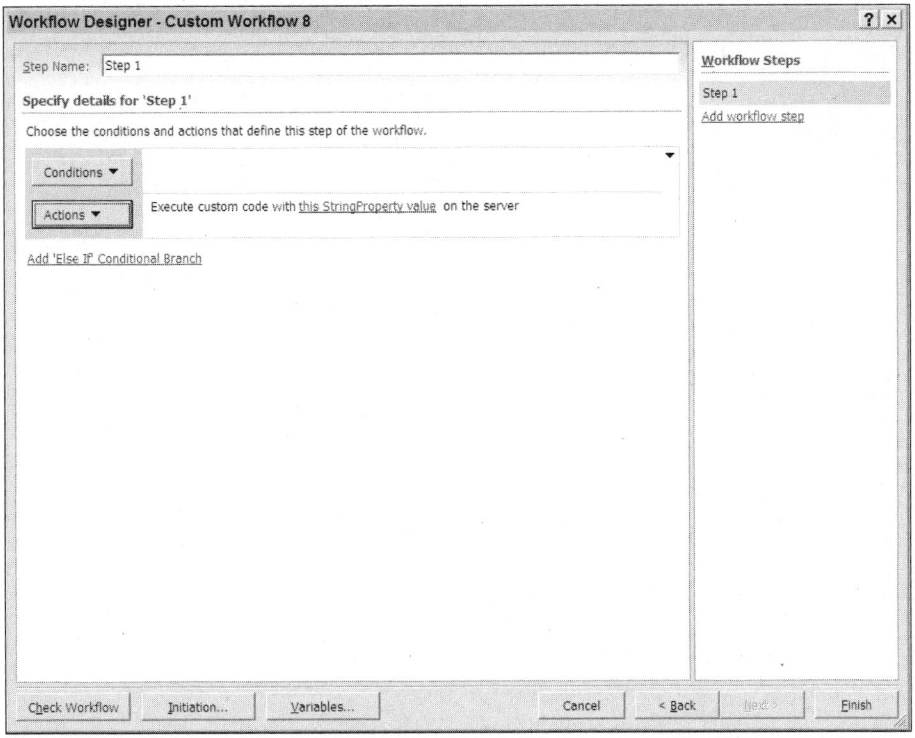

Figure 9-38

If you click the "this StringProperty value" link in the rule designer sentence, you'll get the interface shown in Figure 9-39.

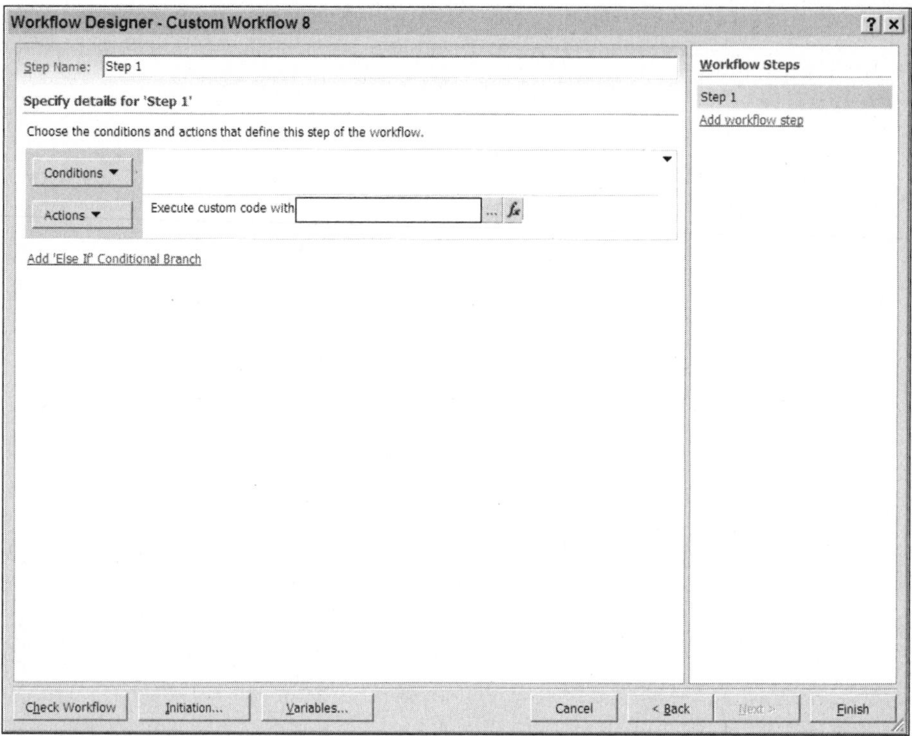

Figure 9-39

This interface consists of three elements: a text box where you can enter a fixed value, a button that takes you to a bigger text box if you need more room to enter the value, and a button that launches the Define Workflow Lookup dialog shown in Figure 9-40, which enables you to set the value through activity binding.

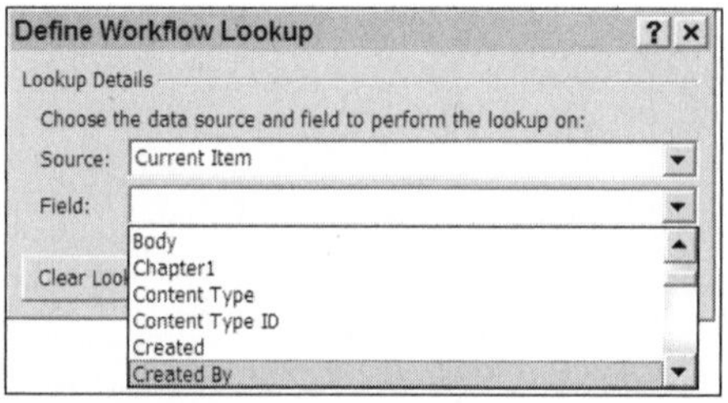

Figure 9-40

Select the Current Item from the Source drop-down list and a field name from the Field drop-down list to bind to this field of the selected item. Workflow Designer should now look like Figure 9-41.

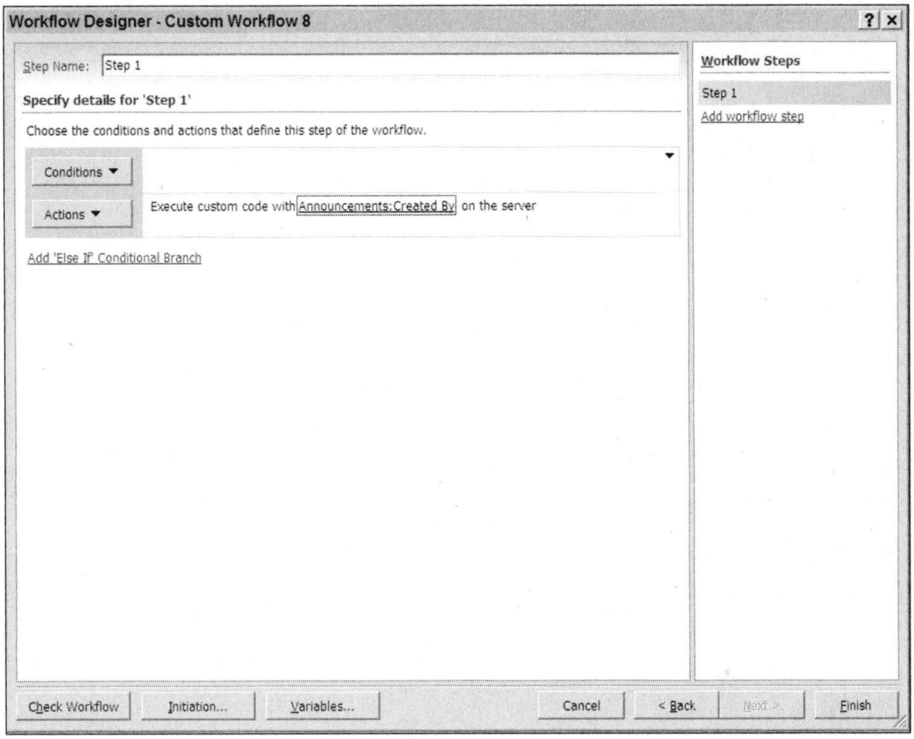

Figure 9-41

Click the Finish button shown in Figure 9-41 to create and store the workflow. Then navigate to the SharePoint list with which the workflow is associated and initiate an instance of the workflow on a list item in this list. Figure 9-42 presents the outcome of the execution of this workflow instance. As you can see, our custom activity has added an entry to the workflow history list. Notice that this log displays the outcome of the evaluation of the data binding expression.

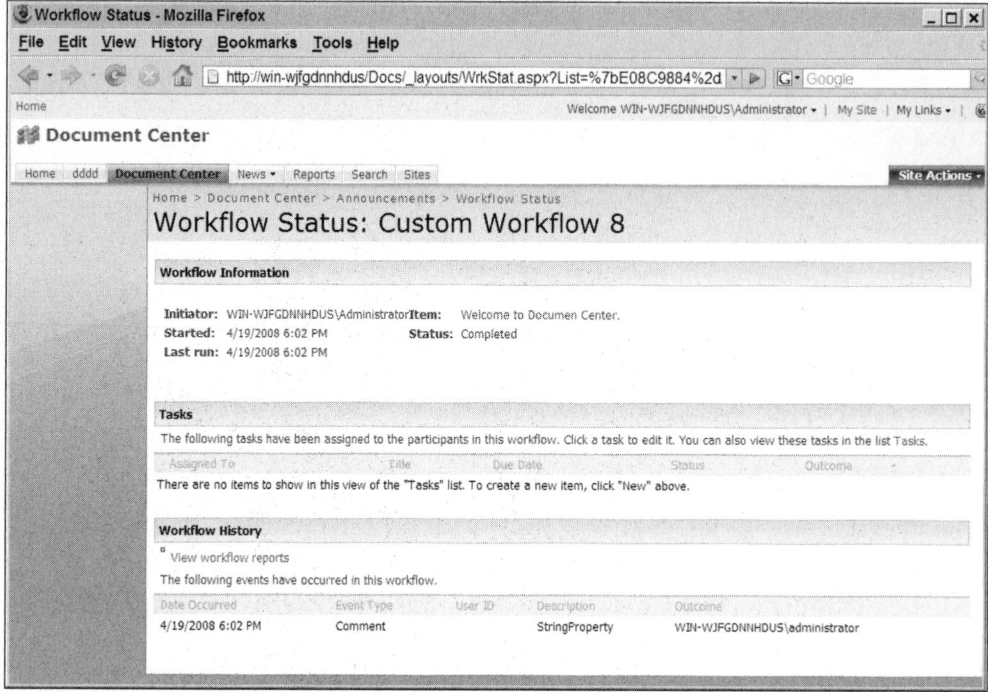

Figure 9-42

UpdateListItem

Take the following steps to enable your custom WF activity to update a list item:

1. Expose a bindable property of the System.String type named ListId. This is where the GUID of the SharePoint list whose item is being updated will be stored.
2. Expose a bindable property of the System.Int32 type named ListItem. This is where the ID of the SharePoint list item being updated will be stored.
3. Expose a bindable property of the System.Collection.Hashtable type named ItemProperties. This is where the names and values of the fields of the SharePoint list item being updated will be stored.
4. Define a <FieldBind> element that binds ListId, ListItem, and ItemProperties properties to a placeholder variable in the rule designer sentence of the action associated with your custom WF activity.
5. Set the DesignerType attribute on this <FieldBind> element to UpdateListItem.

The following code listing presents the implementation of a custom WF activity named CustomActivity9 that follows the preceding recipe:

```
using System;
using System.Workflow.ComponentModel;
using Microsoft.SharePoint;
using System.Workflow.Activities;
using System.Collections;
using Microsoft.SharePoint.WorkflowActions;

namespace Chapter9
{
  public class CustomActivity9 : SequenceActivity
  {
    public string HistoryDescription = default(System.String);
    public string HistoryOutcome = default(System.String);
    private LogToHistoryListActivity logToHistoryListActivity1;
    public int UserId = default(System.Int32);
    private LogToHistoryListActivity logToHistoryListActivity3;
    private LogToHistoryListActivity logToHistoryListActivity2;

    public static readonly DependencyProperty ListIdProperty =
        DependencyProperty.Register("ListId", typeof(string),
                                    typeof(CustomActivity9));
    public string ListId
    {
      get { return (string)base.GetValue(ListIdProperty); }
      set { base.SetValue(ListIdProperty, value); }
    }

    public static readonly DependencyProperty ListItemProperty =
        DependencyProperty.Register("ListItem", typeof(int),
                                    typeof(CustomActivity9));
    public int ListItem
    {
      get { return (int)base.GetValue(ListItemProperty); }
      set { base.SetValue(ListItemProperty, value); }
    }

    public static readonly DependencyProperty ItemPropertiesProperty =
        DependencyProperty.Register("ItemProperties", typeof(Hashtable),
                                    typeof(CustomActivity9));
    public Hashtable ItemProperties
    {
      get { return (Hashtable)base.GetValue(ItemPropertiesProperty); }
      set { base.SetValue(ItemPropertiesProperty, value); }
    }

    public CustomActivity9()
    {
      this.InitializeComponent();
    }

    private void InitializeComponent()
```

(continued)

(continued)

```
        {
          this.CanModifyActivities = true;
          System.Workflow.ComponentModel.ActivityBind activitybind1 =
                              new System.Workflow.ComponentModel.ActivityBind();
          System.Workflow.ComponentModel.ActivityBind activitybind2 =
                              new System.Workflow.ComponentModel.ActivityBind();
          System.Workflow.ComponentModel.ActivityBind activitybind3 =
                              new System.Workflow.ComponentModel.ActivityBind();
          System.Workflow.ComponentModel.ActivityBind activitybind4 =
                              new System.Workflow.ComponentModel.ActivityBind();
          System.Workflow.ComponentModel.ActivityBind activitybind5 =
                              new System.Workflow.ComponentModel.ActivityBind();
          System.Workflow.ComponentModel.ActivityBind activitybind6 =
                              new System.Workflow.ComponentModel.ActivityBind();
          System.Workflow.ComponentModel.ActivityBind activitybind7 =
                              new System.Workflow.ComponentModel.ActivityBind();
          System.Workflow.ComponentModel.ActivityBind activitybind8 =
                              new System.Workflow.ComponentModel.ActivityBind();
          System.Workflow.ComponentModel.ActivityBind activitybind9 =
                              new System.Workflow.ComponentModel.ActivityBind();
          this.logToHistoryListActivity3 =
               new Microsoft.SharePoint.WorkflowActions.LogToHistoryListActivity();
          this.logToHistoryListActivity2 =
              new Microsoft.SharePoint.WorkflowActions.LogToHistoryListActivity();
          this.logToHistoryListActivity1 =
              new Microsoft.SharePoint.WorkflowActions.LogToHistoryListActivity();
          //
          // logToHistoryListActivity3
          //
          this.logToHistoryListActivity3.Duration =
                 System.TimeSpan.Parse("-10675199.02:48:05.4775808");
          this.logToHistoryListActivity3.EventId =
            Microsoft.SharePoint.Workflow.SPWorkflowHistoryEventType.WorkflowComment;
          activitybind1.Name = "CustomActivity9";
          activitybind1.Path = "HistoryDescription";
          activitybind2.Name = "CustomActivity9";
          activitybind2.Path = "HistoryOutcome";
          this.logToHistoryListActivity3.Name = "logToHistoryListActivity3";
          this.logToHistoryListActivity3.OtherData = "";
          activitybind3.Name = "CustomActivity9";
          activitybind3.Path = "UserId";
          this.logToHistoryListActivity3.MethodInvoking +=
            new System.EventHandler(this.logToHistoryListActivity3_MethodInvoking);
          this.logToHistoryListActivity3.SetBinding(Microsoft.SharePoint
    .WorkflowActions.LogToHistoryListActivity.HistoryDescriptionProperty,
    ((System.Workflow.ComponentModel.ActivityBind)(activitybind1)));
          this.logToHistoryListActivity3.SetBinding(Microsoft.SharePoint
    .WorkflowActions.LogToHistoryListActivity.HistoryOutcomeProperty,
    ((System.Workflow.ComponentModel.ActivityBind)(activitybind2)));
          this.logToHistoryListActivity3.SetBinding(Microsoft.SharePoint
    .WorkflowActions.LogToHistoryListActivity.UserIdProperty,
    ((System.Workflow.ComponentModel.ActivityBind)(activitybind3)));
```

```
        //
        // logToHistoryListActivity2
        //
        this.logToHistoryListActivity2.Duration =
                System.TimeSpan.Parse("-10675199.02:48:05.4775808");
        this.logToHistoryListActivity2.EventId =
           Microsoft.SharePoint.Workflow.SPWorkflowHistoryEventType.WorkflowComment;
        activitybind4.Name = "CustomActivity9";
        activitybind4.Path = "HistoryDescription";
        activitybind5.Name = "CustomActivity9";
        activitybind5.Path = "HistoryOutcome";
        this.logToHistoryListActivity2.Name = "logToHistoryListActivity2";
        this.logToHistoryListActivity2.OtherData = "";
        activitybind6.Name = "CustomActivity9";
        activitybind6.Path = "UserId";
        this.logToHistoryListActivity2.MethodInvoking +=
           new System.EventHandler(this.logToHistoryListActivity2_MethodInvoking);
        this.logToHistoryListActivity2.SetBinding(Microsoft.SharePoint
.WorkflowActions.LogToHistoryListActivity.HistoryDescriptionProperty,
((System.Workflow.ComponentModel.ActivityBind)(activitybind4)));
        this.logToHistoryListActivity2.SetBinding(Microsoft.SharePoint
.WorkflowActions.LogToHistoryListActivity.HistoryOutcomeProperty,
((System.Workflow.ComponentModel.ActivityBind)(activitybind5)));
        this.logToHistoryListActivity2.SetBinding(Microsoft.SharePoint
.WorkflowActions.LogToHistoryListActivity.UserIdProperty,
((System.Workflow.ComponentModel.ActivityBind)(activitybind6)));
        //
        // logToHistoryListActivity1
        //
        this.logToHistoryListActivity1.Duration =
                System.TimeSpan.Parse("-10675199.02:48:05.4775808");
        this.logToHistoryListActivity1.EventId =
           Microsoft.SharePoint.Workflow.SPWorkflowHistoryEventType.WorkflowComment;
        activitybind7.Name = "CustomActivity9";
        activitybind7.Path = "HistoryDescription";
        activitybind8.Name = "CustomActivity9";
        activitybind8.Path = "HistoryOutcome";
        this.logToHistoryListActivity1.Name = "logToHistoryListActivity1";
        this.logToHistoryListActivity1.OtherData = "";
        activitybind9.Name = "CustomActivity9";
        activitybind9.Path = "UserId";
        this.logToHistoryListActivity1.MethodInvoking +=
           new System.EventHandler(this.logToHistoryListActivity1_MethodInvoking);
        this.logToHistoryListActivity1.SetBinding(Microsoft.SharePoint
.WorkflowActions.LogToHistoryListActivity.HistoryDescriptionProperty,
((System.Workflow.ComponentModel.ActivityBind)(activitybind7)));
        this.logToHistoryListActivity1.SetBinding(Microsoft.SharePoint
.WorkflowActions.LogToHistoryListActivity.HistoryOutcomeProperty,
((System.Workflow.ComponentModel.ActivityBind)(activitybind8)));
        this.logToHistoryListActivity1.SetBinding(Microsoft.SharePoint
.WorkflowActions.LogToHistoryListActivity.UserIdProperty,
((System.Workflow.ComponentModel.ActivityBind)(activitybind9)));
```

(continued)

(continued)

```
        //
        // CustomActivity9
        //
        this.Activities.Add(this.logToHistoryListActivity1);
        this.Activities.Add(this.logToHistoryListActivity2);
        this.Activities.Add(this.logToHistoryListActivity3);
        this.Name = "CustomActivity9";
        this.CanModifyActivities = false;
      }

      private void logToHistoryListActivity1_MethodInvoking(object sender,
                                                            EventArgs e)
      {
        this.HistoryDescription = "ListId";
        this.HistoryOutcome = this.ListId;
      }

      private void logToHistoryListActivity2_MethodInvoking(object sender,
                                                            EventArgs e)
      {
        this.HistoryDescription = "ListItem";
        this.HistoryOutcome = this.ListItem.ToString();
      }

      private void logToHistoryListActivity3_MethodInvoking(object sender,
                                                            EventArgs e)
      {
        this.HistoryDescription = "ItemProperties";
        this.HistoryOutcome = string.Empty;

        int i = 0;
        foreach (string key in this.ItemProperties.Keys)
        {
          if (i != 0)
            this.HistoryOutcome += ";";
          this.HistoryOutcome = this.ItemProperties[key].ToString();
          i++;
        }
      }
    }
  }
```

Here is the .actions file that describes the preceding custom activity:

```
<?xml version="1.0" encoding="utf-8" ?>
<WorkflowInfo Language="en-us">
  <Actions Sequential="then" Parallel="and">
    <Action Name="Execute custom code 9" AppliesTo="all"
    Category="My Custom Actions"
    ClassName="Chapter9.CustomActivity9"
    Assembly="Chapter9, Version=1.0.0.0, Culture=neutral,
PublicKeyToken=252d221e933b41ec">
```

```
      <RuleDesigner
      Sentence="Execute custom code with %1 on the server">
        <FieldBind Field="ListId,ListItem,ItemProperties" Text="this list" Id="1"
        DesignerType="UpdateListItem" />
      </RuleDesigner>
      <Parameters>
        <Parameter Name="ListId" Type="System.String, mscorlib" Direction="In" />
        <Parameter Name="ListItem" Type="System.Int32, mscorlib" Direction="In" />
        <Parameter Name="ItemProperties"
        Type="System.Collections.Hashtable, mscorlib"
        Direction="In" />
      </Parameters>
    </Action>
  </Actions>
</WorkflowInfo>
```

Next, let's use this activity in a workflow, as shown in Figure 9-43.

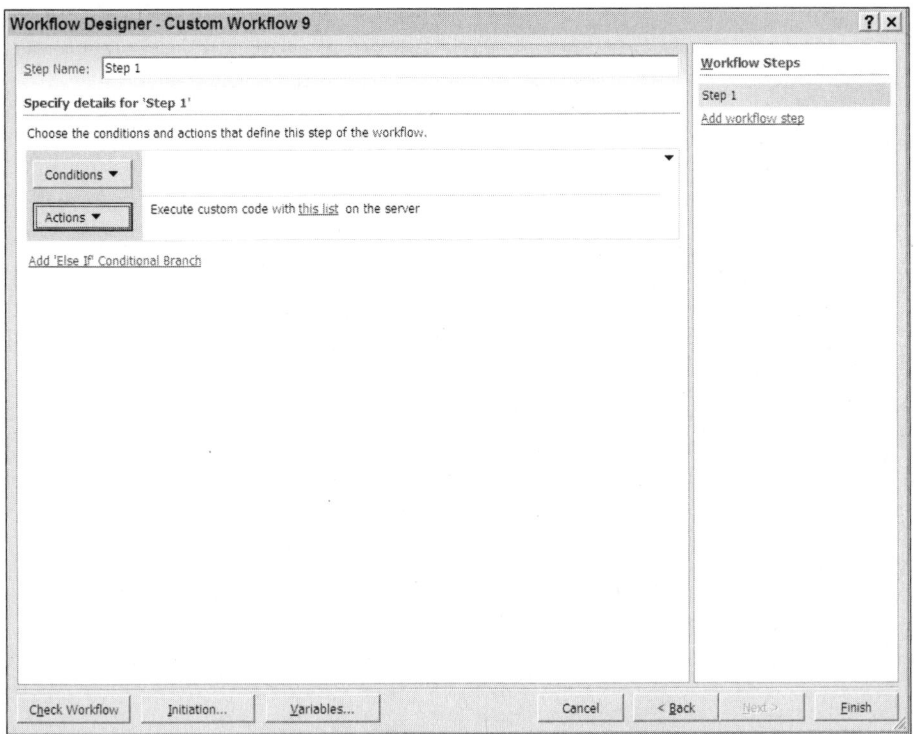

Figure 9-43

Now follow the steps discussed in the previous chapter to create a workflow initiation form with two input fields of the "Single line of text" type, named "Enter value for Body field" and "Enter value for Title field." Click the This List link in the rule designer sentence shown in Figure 9-43. Because we set the DesignerType attribute to UpdateListItem, Workflow Designer automatically launches the Update List

Item dialog box, shown in Figure 9-44, to enable workflow developers to set the values of the ListId, ListItem, and ItemProperties properties of our custom WF activity in a purely graphical fashion.

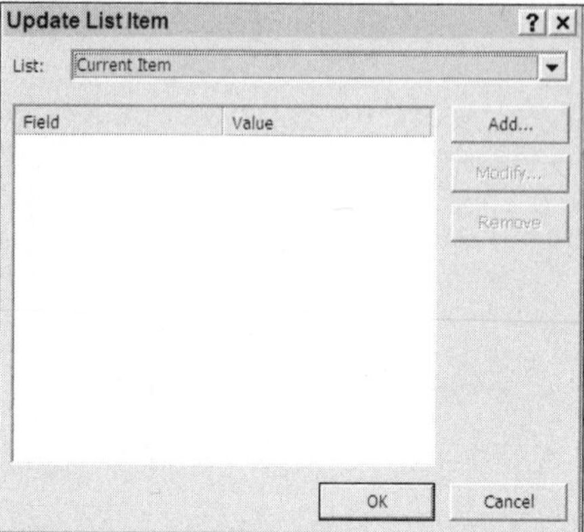

Figure 9-44

Click the Add button on the Update List Item dialog box to launch the Value Assignment dialog box shown in Figure 9-45.

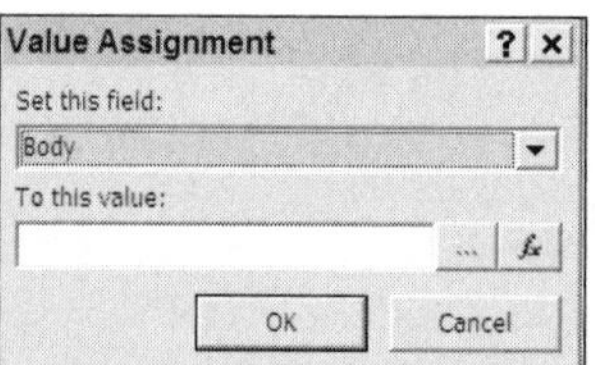

Figure 9-45

Select the Body field from the Set This Field drop-down list box and click the data binding button to launch the Define Workflow Lookup dialog box shown in Figure 9-46.

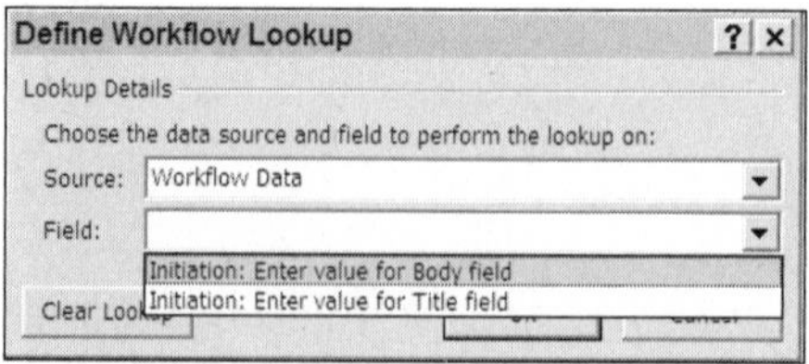

Figure 9-46

Select the Workflow Data option from the Source drop-down list box and the "Enter value for Body field" option from the Field drop-down list box and click OK. This will bind the "Enter value for Body field" input field of the workflow initiation form to the Body field of the current list item. Repeat the same steps to bind the "Enter value for Title field" input field of the workflow initiation form to the Subject field of the current list item. The Update List Item dialog box should now look like Figure 9-47.

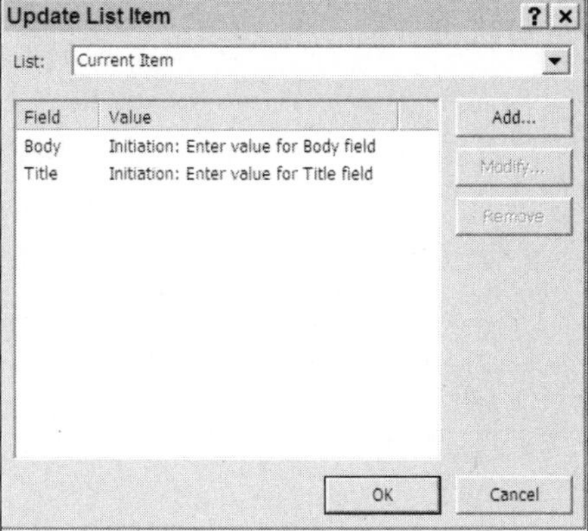

Figure 9-47

Click OK. The Workflow Designer should now look like Figure 9-48.

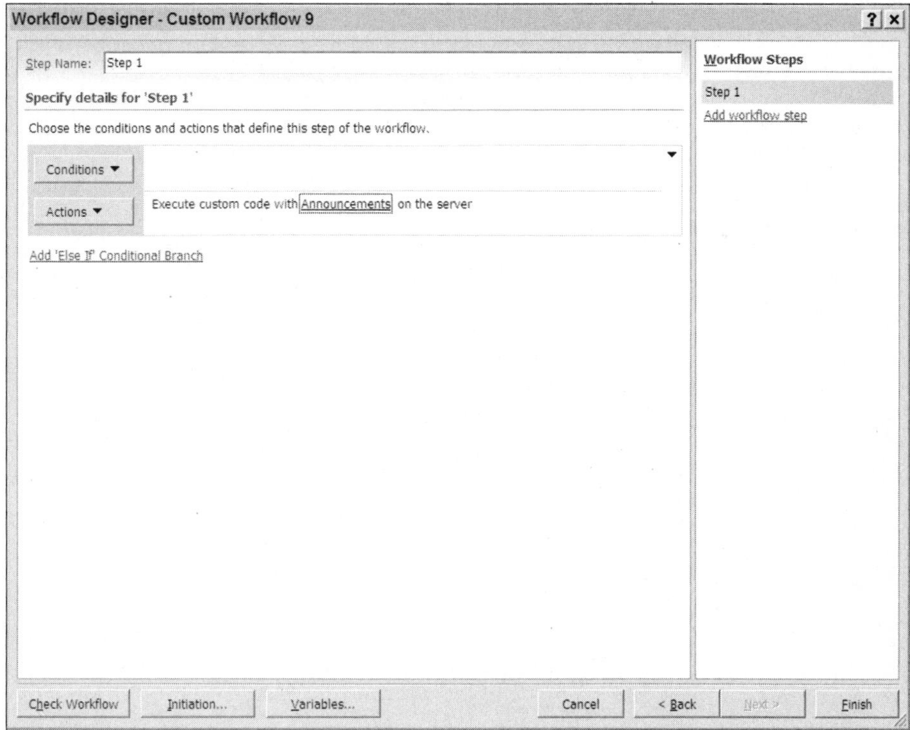

Figure 9-48

Click the Finish button to create and store the workflow. Then navigate to the SharePoint list with which the workflow is associated and initiate an instance of the workflow on a list item in this list. SharePoint should display the initiation form shown in Figure 9-49.

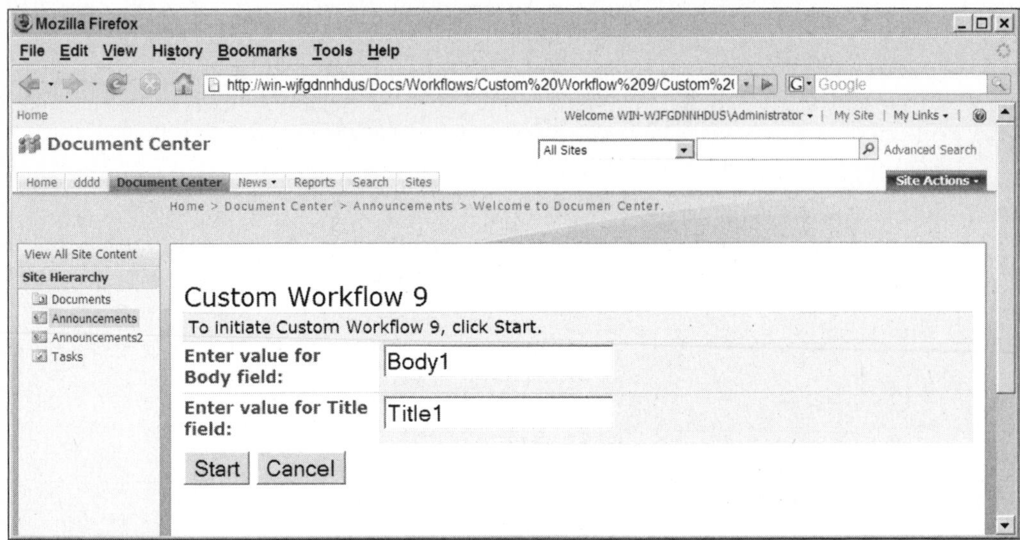

Figure 9-49

Click the Start button shown in Figure 9-49 to start the workflow instance. Figure 9-50 shows the outcome of the execution of this workflow. As you can see, our custom activity has added three entries to the workflow history list, which respectively display the values of the ListId, ListItem, and ItemProperties properties.

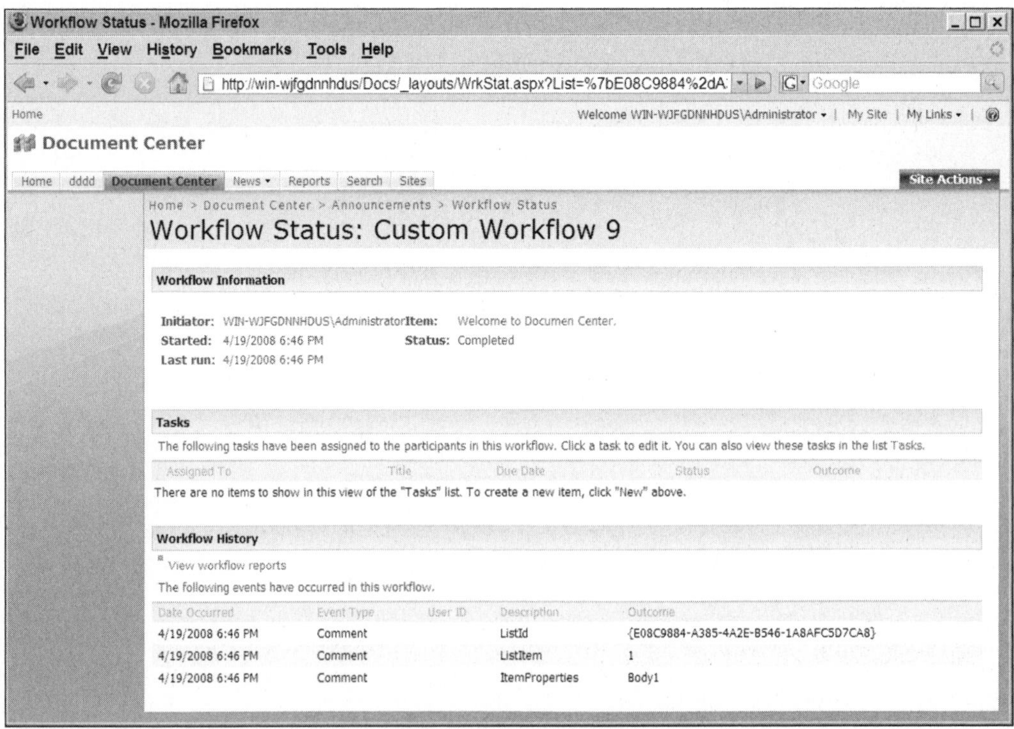

Figure 9-50

The previous discussions showed you how to enable workflow developers to set the ListId, ListItem, and ItemProperties properties of our custom activity through the Update List Item dialog box. SharePoint ships with an activity named UpdateItemActivity that you can use in your own custom activity so your activity does not have to implement the logic that updates a list item. The following excerpt presents the <Action> element that describes the UpdateItemActivity activity:

```
<Action Name="Update List Item"
ClassName="Microsoft.SharePoint.WorkflowActions.UpdateItemActivity"
Assembly="Microsoft.SharePoint.WorkflowActions, Version=12.0.0.0, Culture=neutral,
          PublicKeyToken=71e9bce111e9429c"
AppliesTo="all" Category="List Actions">
  <RuleDesigner Sentence="Update item in %1">
    <FieldBind Field="ListId,ListItem,ItemProperties" Text="this list" Id="1"
    DesignerType="UpdateListItem" />
  </RuleDesigner>
  <Parameters>
    <Parameter Name="__Context"
    Type="Microsoft.SharePoint.WorkflowActions.WorkflowContext" Direction="In" />
    <Parameter Name="ListId" Type="System.String, mscorlib" Direction="In" />
    <Parameter Name="ListItem" Type="System.Int32, mscorlib" Direction="In" />
    <Parameter Name="ItemProperties" Type="System.Collections.Hashtable, mscorlib"
    Direction="In" />
  </Parameters>
</Action>
```

WritablefieldNames

If your custom WF activity has a string property whose value must be set to the name of one of the writable fields of a current item, you must set the DesignerType attribute on the <FieldBind> element that represents this property to WritableFieldNames.

For example, the following code listing presents the code for a custom activity named CustomActivity10 that exposes a string property whose value must be set to the name of a writable field in the current item:

```
using System;
using System.Workflow.ComponentModel;
using Microsoft.SharePoint;
using System.Workflow.Activities;
using System.Collections;
using Microsoft.SharePoint.WorkflowActions;

namespace Chapter9
{
  public class CustomActivity10 : SequenceActivity
  {
    public string HistoryDescription = default(System.String);
    public string HistoryOutcome = default(System.String);
    private LogToHistoryListActivity logToHistoryListActivity1;
```

(continued)

(continued)

```
        public int UserId = default(System.Int32);

        public static readonly DependencyProperty FieldNameProperty =
            DependencyProperty.Register("FieldName", typeof(string),
                                        typeof(CustomActivity10));
        public string FieldName
        {
          get { return (string)base.GetValue(FieldNameProperty); }
          set { base.SetValue(FieldNameProperty, value); }
        }

        public CustomActivity10()
        {
          this.InitializeComponent();
        }

        private void InitializeComponent()
        {
          this.CanModifyActivities = true;
          System.Workflow.ComponentModel.ActivityBind activitybind1 =
                          new System.Workflow.ComponentModel.ActivityBind();
          System.Workflow.ComponentModel.ActivityBind activitybind2 =
                          new System.Workflow.ComponentModel.ActivityBind();
          System.Workflow.ComponentModel.ActivityBind activitybind3 =
                          new System.Workflow.ComponentModel.ActivityBind();
          this.logToHistoryListActivity1 =
              new Microsoft.SharePoint.WorkflowActions.LogToHistoryListActivity();
          //
          // logToHistoryListActivity1
          //
          this.logToHistoryListActivity1.Duration =
                      System.TimeSpan.Parse("-10675199.02:48:05.4775808");
          this.logToHistoryListActivity1.EventId =
            Microsoft.SharePoint.Workflow.SPWorkflowHistoryEventType.WorkflowComment;
          activitybind1.Name = "CustomActivity10";
          activitybind1.Path = "HistoryDescription";
          activitybind2.Name = "CustomActivity10";
          activitybind2.Path = "HistoryOutcome";
          this.logToHistoryListActivity1.Name = "logToHistoryListActivity1";
          this.logToHistoryListActivity1.OtherData = "";
          activitybind3.Name = "CustomActivity10";
          activitybind3.Path = "UserId";
          this.logToHistoryListActivity1.MethodInvoking +=
            new System.EventHandler(this.logToHistoryListActivity1_MethodInvoking);
          this.logToHistoryListActivity1.SetBinding(Microsoft.SharePoint
.WorkflowActions.LogToHistoryListActivity.HistoryDescriptionProperty,
((System.Workflow.ComponentModel.ActivityBind)(activitybind1)));
```

```
      this.logToHistoryListActivity1.SetBinding(Microsoft.SharePoint
.WorkflowActions.LogToHistoryListActivity.HistoryOutcomeProperty,
((System.Workflow.ComponentModel.ActivityBind)(activitybind2)));
      this.logToHistoryListActivity1.SetBinding(Microsoft.SharePoint
.WorkflowActions.LogToHistoryListActivity.UserIdProperty,
((System.Workflow.ComponentModel.ActivityBind)(activitybind3)));
      //
      // CustomActivity10
      //
      this.Activities.Add(this.logToHistoryListActivity1);
      this.Name = "CustomActivity10";
      this.CanModifyActivities = false;
    }

    private void logToHistoryListActivity1_MethodInvoking(object sender,
                                                          EventArgs e)
    {
      this.HistoryDescription = "FieldName";
      this.HistoryOutcome = this.FieldName;
    }
  }
}
```

Here is the .actions file that describes this custom activity:

```
<?xml version="1.0" encoding="utf-8" ?>
<WorkflowInfo Language="en-us">
  <Actions Sequential="then" Parallel="and">
    <Action Name="Execute custom code 10" AppliesTo="all" UsesCurrentItem="true"
    Category="My Custom Actions"
    ClassName="Chapter9.CustomActivity10"
    Assembly="Chapter9, Version=1.0.0.0, Culture=neutral,
             PublicKeyToken=252d221e933b41ec">
      <RuleDesigner
      Sentence="Execute custom code with %1 on the server">
        <FieldBind Field="FieldName" Text="this field name"
        DesignerType="WritableFieldNames" Id="1"/>
      </RuleDesigner>
      <Parameters>
        <Parameter Name="FieldName" Type="System.String, mscorlib"
        Direction="In" />
      </Parameters>
    </Action>
  </Actions>
</WorkflowInfo>
```

As shown in the preceding .actions file, you must set the UsesCurrentItem attribute on the <Action> element to true in addition to setting the DesignerType attribute on the <FieldBind> element to WritableFieldNames because your activity is updating the current item.

Figure 9-51 shows a workflow that uses this custom activity.

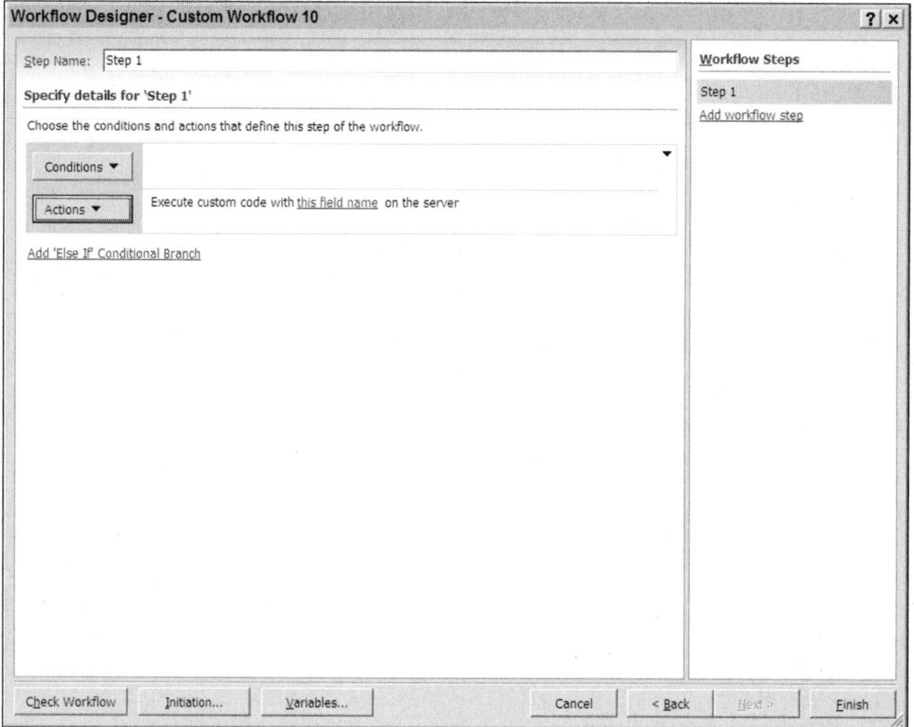

Figure 9-51

If you click the This Field Name link in the rule designer sentence, the drop-down list box shown in Figure 9-52 pops up. Note that this drop-down list box displays only the writable fields of the current item.

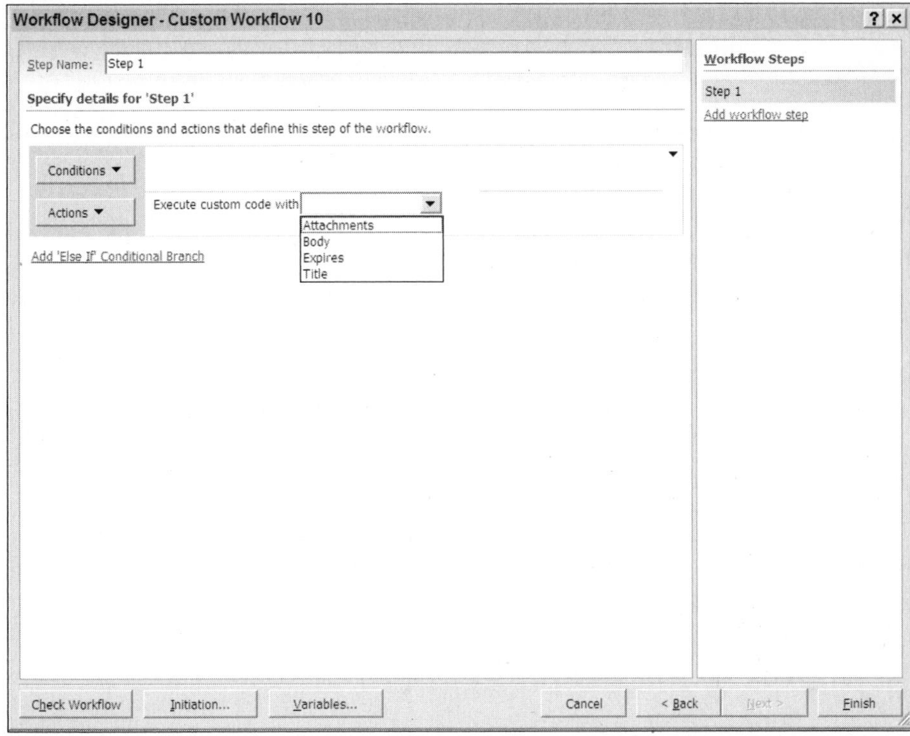

Figure 9-52

SharePoint ships with an activity named SetFieldActivity that makes use of the WritableFieldNames value, as shown in the following excerpt:

```
<Action Name="Set Field in Current Item"
ClassName="Microsoft.SharePoint.WorkflowActions.SetFieldActivity"
Assembly="Microsoft.SharePoint.WorkflowActions, Version=12.0.0.0, Culture=neutral,
          PublicKeyToken=71e9bce111e9429c"
AppliesTo="list" UsesCurrentItem="true" Category="Core Actions">
  <RuleDesigner Sentence="Set %1 to %2">
    <FieldBind Field="FieldName" Text="field" Id="1"
    DesignerType="writablefieldNames" />
    <FieldBind Field="Value" Text="value" Id="2" TypeFrom="FieldName"/>
  </RuleDesigner>
  <Parameters>
    <Parameter Name="FieldName" Type="System.String, mscorlib" Direction="In" />
    <Parameter Name="Value" Type="System.Object, mscorlib" Direction="In" />
    <Parameter Name="__Context" Direction="In"
    Type="Microsoft.SharePoint.WorkflowActions.WorkflowContext,
          Microsoft.SharePoint.WorkflowActions" />
    <Parameter Name="__ListId" Type="System.String, mscorlib" Direction="In" />
    <Parameter Name="__ListItem" Type="System.Int32, mscorlib" Direction="In" />
  </Parameters>
</Action>
```

Field Attribute of FieldBind Element

Set the Field attribute of the <FieldBind> element to the name of the property of your custom WF activity, which the element binds to the specified placeholder variable in the rule sentence. You have seen numerous examples of the Field attribute throughout this chapter.

Id Attribute of FieldBind Element

Set the Id attribute of the <FieldBind> element to the non-negative integer value specified in the respective placeholder variable in the rule sentence. You have also seen numerous examples of the Id attribute throughout this chapter.

OperatorTypeFrom Attribute of FieldBind Element

This attribute is applicable only when you set the DesignerType attribute on the <FieldBind> element to Operator. The value of the OperatorTypeFrom attribute specifies the .NET data type that the operators support. Set the value of this attribute to the name of a property on your custom WF activity to specify that the respective operators only support the .NET data type of this property. Set the value of this attribute to the DropDownMenu to specify that the selected operator itself determines the supported .NET data type. You've seen examples of both these cases in previous sections of this chapter.

Text Attribute of FieldBind Element

Set the Text attribute on the <FieldBind> element to specify the text that Office SharePoint Designer 2007 should display in place of the respective placeholder variable in the rule sentence. You've seen numerous examples of this attribute throughout this chapter.

TypeFrom Attribute of FieldBind Element

As shown throughout this chapter, workflow developers click a placeholder variable in a rule designer sentence to launch the user interface that enables them to specify a value for the variable. This user interface normally presents workflow developers with some kind of input control where they can specify the value. Obviously, the type of value specified in this input control must match the type of value expected by the placeholder variable. For example, if the input control is used to specify a value for a specified field in the current item, the type of the value must match the type of the field. To help Office SharePoint Designer 2007 restrict the values that workflow developers can enter into the input control to the valid types, set the TypeForm attribute on the associated <FieldBind> element of the placeholder variable to the appropriate value. Let's look at a few examples.

The following <Action> element describes the SetFieldActivity activity. The TypeName attribute on the <FieldBind> element that represents the Value property of this activity is set to the FieldName property, which contains the name of the field whose value is being set. This tells Office SharePoint Designer 2007 that the value that workflow developers assign to the Value property must be of the same type as the field whose value is being set.

```
<Action Name="Set Field in Current Item"
ClassName="Microsoft.SharePoint.WorkflowActions.SetFieldActivity"
Assembly="Microsoft.SharePoint.WorkflowActions, Version=12.0.0.0, Culture=neutral,
          PublicKeyToken=71e9bce111e9429c"
AppliesTo="list" UsesCurrentItem="true" Category="Core Actions">
  <RuleDesigner Sentence="Set %1 to %2">
    <FieldBind Field="FieldName" Text="field" Id="1"
    DesignerType="writablefieldNames" />
    <FieldBind Field="Value" Text="value" Id="2" TypeFrom="FieldName"/>
  </RuleDesigner>
  <Parameters>
    <Parameter Name="FieldName" Type="System.String, mscorlib" Direction="In" />
    <Parameter Name="Value" Type="System.Object, mscorlib" Direction="In" />
    <Parameter Name="__Context" Direction="In"
    Type="Microsoft.SharePoint.WorkflowActions.WorkflowContext,
          Microsoft.SharePoint.WorkflowActions" />
    <Parameter Name="__ListId" Type="System.String, mscorlib" Direction="In" />
    <Parameter Name="__ListItem" Type="System.Int32, mscorlib" Direction="In" />
  </Parameters>
</Action>
```

The following <Action> element describes the WaitForActivity activity. The TypeFrom attribute on the <FieldBind> element that represents the Value property of the activity is set to the FieldName property of the activity, which contains the name of the field whose value change triggers resumption of the activity's execution. Again, this enables Office SharePoint Designer 2007 to restrict the values that workflow developers enter to values of the same type as the field.

```
<Action Name="Wait For Field Change in Current Item"
ClassName="Microsoft.SharePoint.WorkflowActions.WaitForActivity"
Assembly="Microsoft.SharePoint.WorkflowActions, Version=12.0.0.0, Culture=neutral,
          PublicKeyToken=71e9bce111e9429c"
AppliesTo="list" UsesCurrentItem="true" Category="Core Actions">
  <RuleDesigner Sentence="Wait for %1 %2 %3">
    <FieldBind Field="FieldName" Text="field" Id="1" DesignerType="fieldNames" />
    <FieldBind Id="2" Field="Operator" DesignerType="Operator"
    OperatorTypeFrom="FieldName" Text="this test">
      <Option Name="to equal" Value="Equal"/>
      <Option Name="to not equal" Value="NotEqual"/>
      <Option Name="to be greater than or to equal" Value="GreaterThanOrEqual"
      TypeFilter="System.Double;System.Int32;System.Uint32;System.DateTime"/>
      . . .
    </FieldBind>
    <FieldBind Field="Value" Text="value" Id="3" TypeFrom="FieldName"/>
  </RuleDesigner>
  <Parameters>
    <Parameter Name="FieldName" Type="System.String, mscorlib" Direction="In" />
    <Parameter Name="Operator" Type="System.String, mscorlib" Direction="In"
    InitialValue="Equal" />
    <Parameter Name="Value" Type="System.Object, mscorlib" Direction="In" />
    . . .
  </Parameters>
</Action>
```

The following <Action> element describes the SetVariableActivity activity. Note that the TypeForm attribute on the <FieldBind> element that represents the Value property of the activity is set to the Variable property of the activity. This tells Office SharePoint Designer 2007 to restrict the entered values to the values of the same type as the Variable property. This is because this activity internally assigns the value of the Value property to the Variable property.

```
<Action Name="Set Workflow Variable"
ClassName="Microsoft.SharePoint.WorkflowActions.SetVariableActivity"
Assembly="Microsoft.SharePoint.WorkflowActions, Version=12.0.0.0, Culture=neutral,
          PublicKeyToken=71e9bce111e9429c"
AppliesTo="all" Category="Core Actions">
  <RuleDesigner Sentence="Set %1 to %2">
    <FieldBind Field="Variable,ValueType" Text="workflow variable" Id="1"
    DesignerType="parameterNames" />
    <FieldBind Field="Value" Text="value" Id="2" TypeFrom="Variable"/>
  </RuleDesigner>
  <Parameters>
    <Parameter Name="Variable" Type="System.Object, mscorlib" Direction="Out" />
    <Parameter Name="Value" Type="System.Object, mscorlib" Direction="In" />
    <Parameter Name="ValueType" Type="System.String, mscorlib" Direction="In" />
  </Parameters>
</Action>
```

Value Attribute of FieldBind Element

Do not use this attribute because it is reserved.

So far we've discussed the attributes of the <FieldBind> element. The <FieldBind> element also supports a child element named <Option>, which is discussed in the following section.

Option Child Element of FieldBind Element

As discussed, a <FieldBind> element binds the WF activity property whose name is specified in the Field attribute to the placeholder variable whose non-negative integer number is the same as the value specified in the Id attribute. When the workflow developer clicks on the respective placeholder variable, Office SharePoint Designer 2007 presents the workflow developer with the appropriate control to specify the value of the property bound to the placeholder variable. One of these controls is a drop-down list box that displays a list of options. In such cases, you must use <Option> elements to tell Office SharePoint Designer 2007 what options to display in the drop-down list box. An <Option> element supports the following attributes:

- **Name:** The drop-down list box displays the value of this attribute to workflow developers.
- **Value:** Office SharePoint Designer 2007 assigns the value of the Value attribute on the <Option> element that the workflow developer selects to the respective property of the WF activity.
- **TypeFilter:** This attribute is applicable only when you set the DesignerType attribute on the parent <FieldBind> element to Operator. Set the value of this attribute to a comma-separated list of substrings, where each substring contains the fully qualified name of a .NET type. Office SharePoint Designer 2007 uses the value of this attribute to determine whether to display the respective options. For example, the following <Action> element describes the MathActivity

activity. This XML document defines a <FieldBind> element whose DesignerType attribute is set to Operator. This element contains a number of <Option> child elements that display the available math operators to workflow designers:

```
<Action Name="Do Calculation"
ClassName="Microsoft.SharePoint.WorkflowActions.MathActivity"
Assembly="Microsoft.SharePoint.WorkflowActions, Version=12.0.0.0, Culture=neutral,
          PublicKeyToken=71e9bce111e9429c"
AppliesTo="all" Category="Core Actions">
  <RuleDesigner Sentence="Calculate %1 %2 %3  (Output to %4)">
    <FieldBind Field="Operand1" Text="value" Id="1" TypeFrom="*ValueType" />
    <FieldBind Id="2" Field="Operator" DesignerType="Operator"
    OperatorTypeFrom="Variable" Text="this operation">
      <Option Name="plus" Value="add"
      TypeFilter="System.Double;System.Int32;System.Uint32;System.String"/>
      <Option Name="minus" Value="sub"
      TypeFilter="System.Double;System.Int32;System.Uint32"/>
      <Option Name="multiply by" Value="times"
      TypeFilter="System.Double;System.Int32;System.Uint32"/>
      <Option Name="divided by" Value="divide"
      TypeFilter="System.Double;System.Int32;System.Uint32"/>
      <Option Name="mod" Value="mod"
      TypeFilter="System.Double;System.Int32;System.Uint32"/>
    </FieldBind>
    <FieldBind Field="Operand2" Text="value" Id="3" TypeFrom="*ValueType" />
    <FieldBind Field="Variable,ValueType" Text="calc" Id="4"
    DesignerType="parameterNames" />
  </RuleDesigner>
  <Parameters>
    <Parameter Name="Variable" Type="System.Object, mscorlib" Direction="Out" />
    <Parameter Name="Operand1" Type="System.Object, mscorlib" Direction="In" />
    <Parameter Name="Operand2" Type="System.Object, mscorlib" Direction="In" />
    <Parameter Name="ValueType" Type="System.String, mscorlib" Direction="In"
    InitialValue="System.Double, mscorlib"/>
    <Parameter Name="Operator" Type="System.String, mscorlib" Direction="In"
    InitialValue="add"/>
  </Parameters>
</Action>
```

The TypeFilter attribute on the <Option> element that represents the Add operation is set to the following value:

```
<Option Name="plus" Value="add"
TypeFilter="System.Double;System.Int32;System.Uint32;System.String"/>
```

The TypeFilter attribute on the <Option> element that represents the Division operation, conversely, is set as follows:

```
<Option Name="divided by" Value="divide"
TypeFilter="System.Double;System.Int32;System.Uint32"/>
```

This is because you can add two strings but you cannot divide one string by another. Setting the TypeFilter attribute in these cases enables Office SharePoint Designer 2007 to hide the Division option from workflow developers when the operands are strings.

- **UnaryHides:** This attribute is applicable only when you set the DesignerType attribute on the parent <FieldBind> element to Operator. If you set the UnaryHides attribute to the value of the Name attribute of another <FieldBind> element, when the user selects this option Office SharePoint Designer 2007 automatically hides the placeholder variable associated with this <FieldBind>.

  The following shows an example. This excerpt contains the <Action> element that describes the WaitForActivity activity:

```
<Action Name="Wait For Field Change in Current Item"
ClassName="Microsoft.SharePoint.WorkflowActions.WaitForActivity"
Assembly="Microsoft.SharePoint.WorkflowActions, Version=12.0.0.0, Culture=neutral,
          PublicKeyToken=71e9bce111e9429c"
AppliesTo="list" UsesCurrentItem="true" Category="Core Actions">
  <RuleDesigner Sentence="Wait for %1 %2 %3">
    <FieldBind Field="FieldName" Text="field" Id="1" DesignerType="fieldNames" />
    <FieldBind Id="2" Field="Operator" DesignerType="Operator"
    OperatorTypeFrom="FieldName" Text="this test">
      . . .
      <Option Name="to be empty" Value="IsEmpty"
      TypeFilter="System.String" UnaryHides="Value"/>
      <Option Name="to be not empty" Value="NotIsEmpty"
      TypeFilter="System.String" UnaryHides="Value"/>
      . . .
    </FieldBind>
    <FieldBind Field="Value" Text="value" Id="3" TypeFrom="FieldName"/>
  </RuleDesigner>
  <Parameters>
    <Parameter Name="FieldName" Type="System.String, mscorlib" Direction="In" />
    <Parameter Name="Operator" Type="System.String, mscorlib" Direction="In"
    InitialValue="Equal" />
    <Parameter Name="Value" Type="System.Object, mscorlib" Direction="In" />
    . . .
  </Parameters>
</Action>
```

  As the boldfaced portions of the preceding XML fragment show, the UnaryHides attributes of two <Option> elements are set to reference the <FieldBind> element with the Name attribute value of Value:

```
<FieldBind Field="Value" Text="value" Id="3" TypeFrom="FieldName"/>
```

  When the user selects one of these two options, Office SharePoint Designer 2007 automatically hides the %3 placeholder variable in the rule sentence. This makes sense because these two operators are unary, so it doesn't make sense to specify a right operand for them.

Parameters Child Element of Action Element

The <Parameters> child element of an <Action> element is where you describe the bindable properties of your custom WF activity to Office SharePoint Designer 2007. This child element features no attributes and contains <Parameter> child elements whereby each <Parameter> child element describes a particular bindable property.

The <Parameter> element supports the following attributes:

- **Type:** Specifies the .NET data type of the bindable property
- **Name:** Specifies the name of the bindable property
- **InitialValue:** Specifies the default initial value of the bindable property. For example, the following <Action> element describes the AddTimeToDateActivity activity. This activity exposes two properties named Units and DateValue. As the boldfaced portions of the following XML document show, the InitialValue attributes on the <Parameter> elements that represent these two properties are set to minutes and empty string, respectively:

```
<Action Name="Add Time to Date"
ClassName="Microsoft.SharePoint.WorkflowActions.AddTimeToDateActivity"
Assembly="Microsoft.SharePoint.WorkflowActions, Version=12.0.0.0, Culture=neutral,
          PublicKeyToken=71e9bce111e9429c"
AppliesTo="all" Category="Core Actions">
  <RuleDesigner Sentence="Add %1 %2 to %3  (Output to %4)">
    <FieldBind Field="AddValue" DesignerType="Integer" Id="1" Text="this many"/>
    <FieldBind Field="Units" Text="units" Id="2" DesignerType="Operator"
    OperatorTypeFrom="DropDownMenu" >
      <Option Name="minutes" Value="minutes"/>
      <Option Name="hours" Value="hours"/>
      <Option Name="days" Value="days"/>
      <Option Name="months" Value="months"/>
      <Option Name="years" Value="years"/>
    </FieldBind>
    <FieldBind Field="DateValue" Text="date" Id="3" DesignerType="Date" />
    <FieldBind Field="DateVariable" Text="date" Id="4"
    DesignerType="parameterNames" />
  </RuleDesigner>
  <Parameters>
    <Parameter Name="__Context" Direction="In"
    Type="Microsoft.SharePoint.WorkflowActions.WorkflowContext,
          Microsoft.SharePoint.WorkflowActions"/>
    <Parameter Name="AddValue" Type="System.Double, mscorlib" Direction="In" />
    <Parameter Name="Units" Type="System.String, mscorlib" Direction="In"
    InitialValue="minutes" />
    <Parameter Name="DateValue" Type="System.DateTime, mscorlib" Direction="In"
    InitialValue="" />
    <Parameter Name="DateVariable" Type="System.DateTime, mscorlib"
    Direction="Out" />
  </Parameters>
</Action>
```

- **Direction:** Specifies the direction of the bindable property — that is, whether it is an input or output. The possible values are In, Out, and Optional.

You have seen numerous examples of the <Parameter> element throughout this chapter.

Conditions

As mentioned earlier in this chapter, every .actions file has a document element named <WorkflowInfo>, which supports two child elements named <Actions> and <Conditions>. The previous sections of this chapter provided in-depth coverage of the <Actions> element and its attributes and child elements. This section discusses the <Conditions> element. The <Conditions> element contains the <Condition> child elements that describe specified conditions to Office SharePoint Designer 2007. The <Condition> element supports the attributes and child elements discussed in the following sections.

Condition Attributes

The <Condition> element exposes the following attributes.

AppliesTo

The possible values for this attribute are as follows:

- **List:** Set this attribute to this value to instruct Office SharePoint Designer 2007 to make this condition available to workflow developers only when the workflow is associated with a SharePoint list.
- **Doclib:** Set this attribute to this value to instruct Office SharePoint Designer 2007 to make this condition available to workflow developers only when the workflow is associated with a SharePoint document library.
- **All:** Set this attribute to this value to instruct Office SharePoint Designer 2007 always to make this condition available to workflow developers.
- **None:** Set this attribute to this value to instruct Office SharePoint Designer 2007 never to make this condition available to workflow developers.

FunctionName

Set this attribute to the name of the .NET method associated with the condition. When the execution logic of a workflow reaches the condition, this method is automatically invoked, passing in the required parameter values. The workflow then uses the return Boolean value of this method to determine which execution path to take next.

ClassName

Set this attribute to the name of the .NET class that contains the .NET method associated with the condition.

Assembly

Set this attribute to the strong name of the assembly that contains the .NET class containing the .NET method associated with the condition.

Type

The possible values of this optional attribute are Custom and Advanced. Set this attribute to Custom if the condition compares a value in the current SharePoint list or document library item with the value specified in the workflow editor. Set this attribute to Advanced if the condition compares any two values.

Child Elements of Condition Element

The <Condition> element supports the same two child elements that the <Action> element supports — that is, the <RuleDesigner> and <Parameters> child elements. The only two differences between the two are as follows. The <Parameters> child element of the <Action> element describes the properties of the respective WF activity, whereas the <Parameters> child element of the <Condition> element describes the parameters of the .NET method associated with the condition. The <RuleDesigner> child element of the <Action> element describes the rule sentence whereby the placeholder variables are bound to the properties of the WF activity, whereas the <RuleDesigner> child element of the <Condition> element describes the rule sentence whereby the placeholder variables are bound to the parameters of the .NET method associated with the condition.

The previous chapter provided an example of a custom condition with an .actions file that used a <Condition> element to describe the custom condition to Office SharePoint Designer 2007.

Summary

This chapter provided in-depth coverage of the workflow actions and conditions XML markup language and used numerous examples to show you how to use this markup language to describe your own custom activities to Office SharePoint Designer 2007.

10

Deploying Workflows and Actions through SharePoint Solution Package

The examples and recipes presented in the previous chapters did not use SharePoint solution packages for deployment. Instead, they used a manual approach to make the steps involved in the deployment of SharePoint workflows explicit, so you can gain a better understanding of the process. For example, this manual approach requires you to directly create the required folders in the file system of the front-end web server and copy the required files into these folders.

This manual approach was taken for educational purposes. You should not use it to deploy your SharePoint workflows to a production machine because of its following downsides:

- ❑ The manual approach requires console access to the front-end web servers in the server farm. System administrators are very reluctant to provide such access to developers.
- ❑ This approach requires you to manually deploy the same deployment files to all front-end web servers in the server farm. This is prone to error and unmanageable in server farms that contain numerous web servers.
- ❑ The manual approach also requires you to manually deploy the same deployment files to all front-end web servers that will be added to the same server farm in the future. This is also prone to error and unmanageable.

Instead, you should use SharePoint solution packages. A SharePoint solution package automatically creates the specified folders and copies the specified files to these folders.

As you'll see in this chapter, implementing a SharePoint solution package requires you to know what files you need to deploy and to which folders on the file system of each front-end web server in the server farm you should deploy them. Thanks to the manual approach taken in the previous chapters, you should now know what these files are and where they should be deployed. You're now in a good position to dive into SharePoint solution packages.

Cabinet and DDF Files

A SharePoint solution package enables you to compress all your deployment files into a single compressed file, which is then deployed as a single unit. This compressed file is a cabinet file with a .wsp extension. You must use the makecab operating system command-line utility to create this cabinet file. You also must feed this command-line utility a file known as a *data description file* (.ddf), which instructs the utility which files to add into the cabinet file, how to lay out these files inside the cabinet file, what name and extension to use for the cabinet file, and in which directory to place this file. Because a SharePoint solution package is a cabinet file with the .wsp extension, the data description file that you feed the makecab command-line utility should instruct this utility to create a cabinet file with the .wsp extension.

The following makecab command-line utility compresses the files specified in the cab.ddf file into a cabinet file based on the structure or layout specified in the cab.ddf. In other words, the specified files are laid out inside the .wsp file as instructed in the cab.ddf file.

```
makecab /f cab.ddf
```

A data description file (.ddf) consists of two parts: header and body. The header tells the makecab utility what name and extension to use for the cabinet file and in which directory to create the cabinet file. The body tells the makecab utility what files to compress into the cabinet file and how to lay out these files in the cabinet file.

Listing 10-1 presents an example of a simple data description file named cab.ddf.

Listing 10-1: A simple data description file

```
;** Header **
.Option Explicit
.Set CabinetNameTemplate=cab.wsp
.set DiskDirectoryTemplate=CDROM
.Set CompressionType=MSZIP
.Set UniqueFiles="ON"
.Set Cabinet=on
.Set DiskDirectory1=cab

;** Body **
MyDir1\MyFile1.txt MyCabDir1\MyTextFiles\MyFile1.txt
MyDir2\MyImage1.jpg MyCabDir1\MyImageFiles\MyImage1.jpg
```

Use the CabinetNameTemplate header to tell makecab what name and extension to use for the cabinet file. SharePoint solution packages should always use the extension .wsp. Use the DiskDirectory1 header to tell makecab in which folder (from the folder in which the makecab runs) to create the cabinet file or the SharePoint solution package. If the folder does not already exist, makecab automatically creates this folder.

As Listing 10-1 shows, the body of a data description file contains a number of lines, with each line consisting of two parts. The first part provides the full folder path (from the folder in which the makecab utility runs) of the file to add to the cabinet file. For example, the first part of the first line of the body of the ddf file shown in Listing 10-1 is as follows:

```
MyDir1\MyFile1.txt
```

This tells the makecab command-line utility to add the MyFile1.txt file, which is in the MyDir1 subfolder of the folder where the utility is running, into the cabinet file.

The second part of a line in the body of a .ddf file provides the full folder path of the location in the cabinet file in which to add the file specified in the first part. For example, the second part of the first line of the body of the .ddf file shown in Listing 10-1 is as follows:

```
MyCabDir1\MyTextFiles\MyFile1.txt
```

This tells the makecab utility to add the MyDir1\MyFile1.txt file as MyFile1.txt to a folder named MyTextFiles in a folder named MyCabDir1 in the cabinet file. If the cabinet file does not already contain the MyCabDir1 folder, then the makecab utility creates this folder. If the MyCabDir1 folder does not already contain the MyTextFiles folder, then the makecab utility creates this folder as well.

As Listing 10-1 shows, you can add any type of file, such as text and image files, into a cabinet file. Note that when the second line of the body of the .ddf file shown in Listing 10-1 runs, makecab retrieves the MyImage1.jpg image file from the MyDir2 subfolder of the folder in which the makecab utility is running and adds it as MyImage1.jpg to a folder named MyImageFiles in the MyCabDir1 folder. In this case, the cabinet file will contain a single folder named MyCabDir1, which contains two subfolders named MyTextFiles and MyImageFiles, which in turn contain the MyFile1.txt and MyImage1.jpg files, respectively.

To see this in action, create a folder named Testing on your local drive. Then create two subfolders named MyDir1 and MyDir2 in the Testing folder. Next, create a text file named MyFile1.txt and add it to the MyDir1 folder. Then, download a .jpg file from your favorite site, name the file MyImage1.jpg, and add it to the MyDir2 folder. Next, create another text file inside the Testing directory, name this text file cab.ddf, and add the content of Listing 10-1 to this text file. Finally, run the makecab utility from the Testing folder as follows:

```
makecab /f cab.ddf
```

This should create a subfolder named cab in the folder from which you ran the makecab utility. If you change directory to this subfolder, you should see a file named cab.wsp in it. This is the cabinet file. Next, download and install your favorite cabinet file viewer and open this cab.wsp file in the viewer. The viewer should show you the content of this cabinet file, which consists of a single folder named MyCabDir2, which contains two subfolders named MyTextFiles and MyImageFiles. If you change folder in the viewer to the MyTextFiles and MyImageFiles folders, you should see the MyImage1.txt and MyFile1.jpg files in these two folders.

As this example clearly shows, the .ddf file tells the makecab utility not only to add the MyFile1.txt and MyImage1.jpg files to the cabinet file, but also to create a specified hierarchy of folders in the cabinet file and to place these files in specific folders in this hierarchy.

Solution Manifest

So far you've learned a great deal about the .ddf file and its role in creating a cabinet file. Creating a cabinet file is only half the story. When a solution package (the cabinet file with .wsp extension) is deployed to SharePoint, SharePoint needs to decompress the files in the solution package and deploy them. This raises the following questions:

- How does SharePoint know what types of files the solution package contains?
- How does SharePoint know in which folders in the folder hierarchy in the cabinet file each file type is located?
- How does SharePoint know where to deploy these files in the file system of each front-end web server in the server farm? As you've seen throughout this book, different types of files are deployed into different folders in the file system of each front-end web server.
- Deploying some types of files requires creating new folders. For example, deployment of a new feature requires creation of a feature-specific subfolder in the Features folder. How does SharePoint know what folders to create and where in the file system of each front-end web server to create them?

As you can see, SharePoint needs to know in which folder in the solution package each deployment file is located, to which folder in the file system of each front-end web server to deploy each deployment file, whether to create a new folder for a deployment file, and what to name the new folder (if any) and in which folder in the file system of each front-end web server to create the new folder (if any).

To address these SharePoint needs, every solution package also contains a special file named solution manifest (manifest.xml). This file, in conjunction with the file cabinet folder hierarchy in which each deployment file resides, provides SharePoint with the complete information it needs to decompress and deploy the deployment files into the right folders in the file system of each front-end web server in the server farm.

Listing 10-2 presents only the portion of the structure of the manifest.xml file that we will use in this chapter to deploy our SharePoint workflow deployment files. Complete coverage of the elements that make up the manifest.xml file is beyond the scope of this book.

Listing 10-2: Portion of the structure of the manifest.xml file

```
<?xml version="1.0" encoding="utf-8" ?>
<Solution xmlns="http://schemas.microsoft.com/sharepoint/" SolutionId="">
  <FeatureManifests>
    <FeatureManifest Location=""/>
    <FeatureManifest Location=""/>
  </FeatureManifests>

  <TemplateFiles>
    <TemplateFile Location=""/>
    <TemplateFile Location=""/>
  </TemplateFiles>

  <Assemblies>
    <Assembly DeploymentTarget="GlobalAssemblyCache | WebApplication" Location=""/>
  </Assemblies>
</Solution>
```

As shown here, a solution manifest is an XML file with a document element named <Solution>, which supports an attribute named SolutionId. You must set this attribute to a Guid that uniquely identifies the solution package. Use the guidgen.exe utility discussed earlier to generate and copy and paste a Guid as the value of this attribute. A solution package, just like a feature, is identified by a Guid.

The elements and attributes that you need in order to implement your solution manifest XML file belong to the following namespace:

```
http://microsoft.schemas.com/sharepoint/
```

The <Solution> document element shown in Listing 10-2 supports the following important child elements:

- <FeatureManifests>: This child element instructs SharePoint which features to copy to which folders in the FEATURES system folder of each front-end web server in the server farm, and to install these features. Note that this child element does not instruct SharePoint to activate these features. You still have to activate them.
- <TemplateFiles>: This child element instructs SharePoint which template files to copy to which folders in the TEMPLATE system folder of each front-end web server in the server farm.
- <Assemblies>: This child element instructs SharePoint which assemblies to install in the global assembly cache and which assemblies to install in the local bin directory of the web application in each front-end web server in the server farm.

In the following two sections, we will implement two SharePoint solution packages to deploy the workflows and activities developed in the previous chapters.

Deploying Workflows

Recall that Chapters 4, 5, and 7 implemented a workflow named ConferenceRequestWorkflow that enables an employee to make a conference request. Those chapters used the manual approach to deploy the deployment files to SharePoint. This section implements a SharePoint solution package to deploy these files. First, let's enumerate these deployment files:

- **ConferenceRequestSiteColumnsAndContentTypesFeature.xml:** This is the feature file shown in Listing 4-9. Recall that this feature references the element manifest file that defines our custom site columns and site content types.
- **ConferenceRequestSiteContentTypes.xml:** This is the element manifest file shown in Listing 4-7, which defines our custom site content types.
- **ConferenceRequestSiteColumns.xml:** This is the element manifest file shown in Listing 4-8, which defines our custom site columns.
- **ConferenceRequestWorkflowAssociationForm.aspx:** This is the association form shown in Listing 4-10.
- **ConferenceRequestWorkflowInitiationForm.aspx:** This file contains the initiation form shown in Listing 4-13.

- **feature.xml:** This file contains the feature that deploys our workflow, as shown in Listing 10-3.
- **workflow.xml:** This file defines our workflow template, as shown in Listing 10-4.
- **ConferenceRequestWorkflowModificationForm.aspx:** This file contains the workflow modification form shown in Chapter 7.
- **ManagerContentTypeEditTaskForm.aspx:** This file contains the edit task form shown in Listing 7-1.
- **SharePointWorkflow5.dll:** This assembly contains the following compiled code:
    - **ConferenceRequestInfo.cs:** This file contains Listing 4-12.
    - **ConferenceRequestWorkflowAssociationForm.cs:** This file contains Listing 4-11.
    - **ConferenceRequestWorkflowInitiationForm.cs:** This file contains Listing 4-14.
    - **ConferenceRequestWorkflowModificationForm.cs:** This file contains the code for the ConferenceRequestWorkflowModificationForm presented in Chapter 7.
    - **ManagerContentTypeEditTaskForm.cs:** This file contains Listing 7-2.
    - **ConferenceRequestWorkflow.cs:** This file contains the code-behind for the ConferenceRequestWorkflow workflow shown in Listing 7-4.
    - **ConferenceRequestWorkflow.designer.cs:** This file contains the designer code for the ConferenceRequestWorkflow workflow shown in Listing 7-5.
    - **WorkflowAssociationTarget.cs:** This file contains the definition of the WorkflowAssociationTarget enumeration shown in Listing 4-12.

Visual Studio Solution Explorer, shown in Figure 10-1, presents these deployment files.

Figure 10-1

Listing 10-3 presents the feature that deploys our workflow.

Listing 10-3: The feature deploying our workflow

```
<?xml version="1.0" encoding="utf-8" ?>
<Feature  Id="160b0278-c4af-47a3-b947-2d1edb1da529"
Title="SharePointWorkflow5 feature"
Description="My SharePoint Workflow Feature"
Version="12.0.0.0"
Scope="Site"
ReceiverAssembly="Microsoft.Office.Workflow.Feature, Version=12.0.0.0,
Culture=neutral, PublicKeyToken=71e9bce111e9429c"
ReceiverClass="Microsoft.Office.Workflow.Feature.WorkflowFeatureReceiver"
xmlns="http://schemas.microsoft.com/sharepoint/">
  <ElementManifests>
    <ElementManifest Location="workflow.xml" />
  </ElementManifests>
  <Properties>
    <Property Key="GloballyAvailable" Value="true" />
    <!-- Value for RegisterForms key indicates the path to the forms relative to
feature file location -->
    <!-- if you don't have forms, use *.xsn -->
    <Property Key="RegisterForms" Value="*.xsn" />
  </Properties>
</Feature>
```

Listing 10-4 presents our workflow template.

Listing 10-4: The workflow.xml file

```
<?xml version="1.0" encoding="utf-8" ?>
<Elements xmlns="http://schemas.microsoft.com/sharepoint/">
  <Workflow
  Name="SharePointWorkflow5"
  Description="My SharePoint Workflow"
  Id="a28a3693-7b19-4089-834d-10a6b72d5d9a"
  CodeBesideClass="SharePointWorkflow5.Workflow1"
  TaskListContentTypeId="0x01080100A3440F3CB4E74e5e8B4CF07BAEBAB9B1"
  CodeBesideAssembly="SharePointWorkflow5, Version=1.0.0.0, Culture=neutral,
                    PublicKeyToken=1c4a9ebab9f0532c"
AssociationUrl="_layouts/ConferenceRequest/
ConferenceRequestWorkflowAssociationForm.aspx"
InstantiationUrl="_layouts/ConferenceRequest/
ConferenceRequestWorkflowInitiationForm.aspx"
ModificationUrl="_layouts/ConferenceRequest/
ConferenceRequestWorkflowModificationForm.aspx">
    <Categories/>
    <MetaData>
      <Modification_212a6a61-6ccb-4543-ba13-7d9bc6888cfc_Name>Modify the current
ConferenceRequestWorkflow instance</Modification_212a6a61-6ccb-4543-ba13-
7d9bc6888cfc_Name>
      <StatusPageUrl>_layouts/WrkStat.aspx</StatusPageUrl>
    </MetaData>
  </Workflow>
</Elements>
```

The first order of business is to implement the data description file (.ddf), as shown in Listing 10-5.

Listing 10-5: The data description file

```
; * My Solution Package*
.Option Explicit
.Set CabinetNameTemplate=MySolutionPackage.wsp
.set DiskDirectoryTemplate=CDROM
.Set CompressionType=MSZIP
.Set UniqueFiles="ON"
.Set Cabinet=on
.Set DiskDirectory1=MySolutionPackage

manifest.xml manifest.xml
feature.xml SharePointWorkflow5\feature.xml
workflow.xml SharePointWorkflow5\workflow.xml
ConferenceRequestSiteColumnsAndContentTypesFeature.xml ConferenceRequest\
feature.xml
ConferenceRequestSiteColumns.xml ConferenceRequest\ConferenceRequestSiteColumns.xml
ConferenceRequestSiteContentTypes.xml ConferenceRequest\
ConferenceRequestSiteContentTypes.xml
ConferenceRequestWorkflowAssociationForm.aspx LAYOUTS\ConferenceRequest\
ConferenceRequestWorkflowAssociationForm.aspx
ConferenceRequestWorkflowInitiationForm.aspx LAYOUTS\ConferenceRequest\
ConferenceRequestWorkflowInitiationForm.aspx
ConferenceRequestWorkflowModificationForm.aspx LAYOUTS\ConferenceRequest\
ConferenceRequestWorkflowModificationForm.aspx
ManagerContentTypeEditTaskForm.aspx LAYOUTS\ConferenceRequest\
ManagerContentTypeEditTaskForm.aspx

bin\Release\SharePointWorkflow5.dll SharePointWorkflow5.dll
```

We use the CabinetNameTemplate header to specify MySolutionPackage.wsp as the name of our SharePoint solution package, and use the DiskDirectory1 header to have the makecab utility add the MySolutionPackage.wsp file into a directory named MySolutionPackage in the root directory of our project.

The first line in the body of the data description file instructs makecab to copy the manifest file from the root directory of our project, which is where we run the makecab utility, to the root of our solution package:

```
manifest.xml manifest.xml
```

The second and third lines tell makecab to create a folder named SharePointWorkflow5 in our solution package and copy the feature.xml and workflow.xml files from the root directory of our project to this folder:

```
feature.xml SharePointWorkflow5\feature.xml
workflow.xml SharePointWorkflow5\workflow.xml
```

The fourth line tells makecab to create a folder named ConferenceRequest in our solution package and copy the ConferenceRequestSiteColumnsAndContentTypesFeature.xml file as feature.xml into this folder:

```
ConferenceRequestSiteColumnsAndContentTypesFeature.xml ConferenceRequest\
feature.xml
```

The fifth and sixth lines tell makecab to copy the ConferenceRequestSiteColumns.xml and ConferenceRequestSiteContentTypes.xml files into the ConferenceRequest folder in our solution package:

```
ConferenceRequestSiteColumns.xml ConferenceRequest\ConferenceRequestSiteColumns.xml
ConferenceRequestSiteContentTypes.xml ConferenceRequest\
ConferenceRequestSiteContentTypes.xml
```

Lines seven through ten tell makecab to first create a folder named LAYOUTS in the root of our solution package and then create a subfolder named ConferenceRequest in this folder; and finally to copy the ConferenceRequestWorkflowAssociationForm.aspx, ConferenceRequestWorkflowInitiationForm.aspx, ConferenceRequestWorkflowModificationForm.aspx, and ManagerContentTypeEditTaskForm.aspx files into this ConferenceRequest subfolder:

```
ConferenceRequestWorkflowAssociationForm.aspx LAYOUTS\ConferenceRequest\
ConferenceRequestWorkflowAssociationForm.aspx
ConferenceRequestWorkflowInitiationForm.aspx LAYOUTS\ConferenceRequest\
ConferenceRequestWorkflowInitiationForm.aspx
ConferenceRequestWorkflowModificationForm.aspx LAYOUTS\ConferenceRequest\
ConferenceRequestWorkflowModificationForm.aspx
ManagerContentTypeEditTaskForm.aspx LAYOUTS\ConferenceRequest\
ManagerContentTypeEditTaskForm.aspx
```

The last line tells makecab to copy the assembly that contains all our code into the root of our solution package:

```
bin\Release\SharePointWorkflow5.dll SharePointWorkflow5.dll
```

The next order of business is to implement the manifest.xml file as shown in Listing 10-6.

Listing 10-6: The manifest.xml file

```
<?xml version="1.0" encoding="utf-8" ?>
<Solution
xmlns="http://schemas.microsoft.com/sharepoint/"
SolutionId="{89755660-9837-483f-B19B-09B19A7AA6FA}">
  <FeatureManifests>
    <FeatureManifest Location="SharePointWorkflow5\feature.xml"/>
    <FeatureManifest Location="ConferenceRequest\feature.xml"/>
  </FeatureManifests>

  <TemplateFiles>
    <TemplateFile Location="LAYOUTS\ConferenceRequest\
ConferenceRequestWorkflowAssociationForm.aspx"/>
```

(continued)

Listing 10-6 *(continued)*

```
    <TemplateFile Location="LAYOUTS\ConferenceRequest\
ConferenceRequestWorkflowInitiationForm.aspx"/>
    <TemplateFile Location="LAYOUTS\ConferenceRequest\
ConferenceRequestWorkflowModificationForm.aspx"/>
    <TemplateFile Location="LAYOUTS\ConferenceRequest\
ManagerContentTypeEditTaskForm.aspx"/>
  </TemplateFiles>

  <Assemblies>
    <Assembly DeploymentTarget="GlobalAssemblyCache" Location="SharePointWorkflow5
.dll" />
  </Assemblies>
</Solution>
```

The first <FeatureManifest> child element of the <FeatureManifests> element tells SharePoint to deploy the feature.xml file from the SharePointWorkflow5 folder of our solution package to the SharePointWorkflow5 folder in the Features folder in the file system of each front-end web server in the server farm. SharePoint automatically creates the SharePointWorkflow5 folder if it hasn't already been created:

```
<FeatureManifest Location="SharePointWorkflow5\feature.xml"/>
```

The second <FeatureManifest> child element of the <FeatureManifests> element tells SharePoint to deploy the feature.xml file from the ConferenceRequest folder of our solution package to the ConferenceRequest folder in the Features folder in the file system of each front-end web server in the server farm. SharePoint automatically creates the ConferenceRequest folder if it hasn't already been created:

```
<FeatureManifest Location="ConferenceRequest\feature.xml"/>
```

The <TemplateFile> child elements of the <TemplateFiles> element tell SharePoint to deploy the ConferenceRequestWorkflowAssociationForm.aspx, ConferenceRequestWorkflowInitiationForm .aspx, ConferenceRequestWorkflowModificationForm.aspx, and ManagerContentTypeEditTaskForm.aspx files from the ConferenceRequest subfolder of the LAYOUTS folder of our solution package to the ConferenceRequest subfolder of the LAYOUTS folder in the file system of each front-end web server in the server farm. SharePoint automatically creates the ConferenceRequest folder if it hasn't already been created:

```
<TemplateFile Location="LAYOUTS\ConferenceRequest\
ConferenceRequestWorkflowAssociationForm.aspx"/>
    <TemplateFile Location="LAYOUTS\ConferenceRequest\
ConferenceRequestWorkflowInitiationForm.aspx"/>
    <TemplateFile Location="LAYOUTS\ConferenceRequest\
ConferenceRequestWorkflowModificationForm.aspx"/>
    <TemplateFile Location="LAYOUTS\ConferenceRequest\
ManagerContentTypeEditTaskForm.aspx"/>
```

The <Assembly> child element of the <Assemblies> element tells SharePoint to install the SharePointWorkflow5.dll from the root of our solution package to the global assembly cache:

```
<Assembly DeploymentTarget="GlobalAssemblyCache" Location="SharePointWorkflow5.dll" />
```

Listing 10-7 presents a batch file that contains all the required command lines.

Listing 10-7: The batch file

```
if Exist MySolutionPackage\MySolutionPackage.wsp Del MySolutionPackage\
MySolutionPackage.wsp
makecab /f MySolutionPackage.ddf

@SET STSADM="c:\program files\common files\microsoft shared\web server
extensions\12\bin\stsadm"

%STSADM% -o deactivatefeature -name ConferenceRequest -url http://win-wjfgdnnhdus
%STSADM% -o deactivatefeature -name SharePointWorkflow5 -url http://win-wjfgdnnhdus

%STSADM% -o retractsolution -name MySolutionPackage.wsp -local
%STSADM% -o execadmsvcjobs
%STSADM% -o deletesolution -name MySolutionPackage.wsp -override
%STSADM% -o execadmsvcjobs

%STSADM% -o addsolution -filename MySolutionPackage\MySolutionPackage.wsp
%STSADM% -o execadmsvcjobs
%STSADM% -o deploysolution -name MySolutionPackage.wsp -allowGacDeployment -local
%STSADM% -o execadmsvcjobs

%STSADM% -o activatefeature -name ConferenceRequest -url http://win-wjfgdnnhdus
%STSADM% -o activatefeature -name SharePointWorkflow5 -url http://win-wjfgdnnhdus
```

Note that this batch file also activates the features that define our site columns, site content types, and workflow template. As discussed earlier, the <FeatureManifest> child elements of the <FeatureManifests> element of the manifest.xml file do not tell SharePoint to activate the respective features. They only tell SharePoint to install them. Our batch file contains direct commands for activating these features.

Deploying Actions

The previous chapter implemented 10 custom activities and manually deployed them as SharePoint Designer actions. This section implements a solution package to deploy these actions. The deployment files are as follows:

- **CustomActivity.actions:** This file contains Listing 10-8.
- **Chapter9.dll:** This assembly contains all the .cs files shown in Figure 10-2. Recall that these .cs files contain the implementation of the custom activities that we developed in the previous chapter.

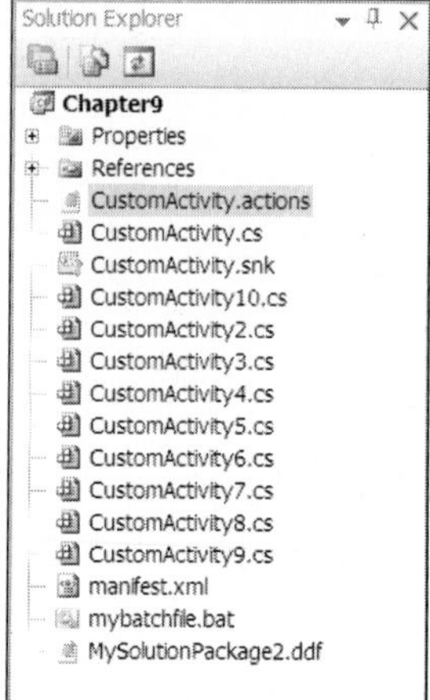

Figure 10-2

Listing 10-8 presents the .actions file that describes our custom activities to the SharePoint Designer.

Listing 10-8: The CustomActivity.actions file

```
<?xml version="1.0" encoding="utf-8" ?>
<WorkflowInfo Language="en-us">
  <Actions Sequential="then" Parallel="and">
    <Action Name="Execute custom code" AppliesTo="all" Category="My Custom Actions"
   ClassName="Chapter9.CustomActivity"
  Assembly="Chapter9, Version=1.0.0.0, Culture=neutral,
             PublicKeyToken=252d221e933b41ec">
      <RuleDesigner
      Sentence="Execute custom code with %1 on the server">
        <FieldBind Field="MyProperty" DesignerType="DropDown"
        Text="this MyProperty value" Id="1">
          <Option Name="Name1" Value="Value1" />
          <Option Name="Name2" Value="Value2" />
          <Option Name="Name3" Value="Value3" />
        </FieldBind>
      </RuleDesigner>
      <Parameters>
        <Parameter Name="MyProperty" Type="System.String, mscorlib"
        Direction="In" />
      </Parameters>
    </Action>

    <Action Name="Execute custom code 2" AppliesTo="all"
    Category="My Custom Actions"
   ClassName="Chapter9.CustomActivity2"
   Assembly="Chapter9, Version=1.0.0.0, Culture=neutral,
            PublicKeyToken=252d221e933b41ec">
      <RuleDesigner
      Sentence="Execute custom code with %1 on the server">
        <FieldBind Field="To,CC,Subject,Body" Text="this message"
        DesignerType="Email" Id="1"/>
      </RuleDesigner>
```

```
  <Parameters>
    <Parameter Name="Body" Type="System.String, mscorlib"
    Direction="Optional" />
    <Parameter Name="To" Type="System.Collections.ArrayList, mscorlib"
    Direction="In" />
    <Parameter Name="CC" Type="System.Collections.ArrayList, mscorlib"
    Direction="Optional" />
    <Parameter Name="Subject" Type="System.String, mscorlib" Direction="In" />
  </Parameters>
</Action>

<Action Name="Execute custom code 3" AppliesTo="all"
Category="My Custom Actions"
ClassName="Chapter9.CustomActivity3"
Assembly="Chapter9, Version=1.0.0.0, Culture=neutral,
          PublicKeyToken=252d221e933b41ec">
  <RuleDesigner
  Sentence="Execute custom code with %1 on the server">
    <FieldBind Field="FieldName" Text="this field name"
    DesignerType="FieldNames" Id="1"/>
  </RuleDesigner>
  <Parameters>
    <Parameter Name="FieldName" Type="System.String, mscorlib"
    Direction="In" />
  </Parameters>
</Action>

<Action Name="Execute custom code 4" AppliesTo="all"
Category="My Custom Actions"
ClassName="Chapter9.CustomActivity4"
Assembly="Chapter9, Version=1.0.0.0, Culture=neutral,
          PublicKeyToken=252d221e933b41ec">
  <RuleDesigner
  Sentence="Execute custom code with %1 on the server">
    <FieldBind Field="ListId" Text="this list name"
    DesignerType="ListNames" Id="1"/>
  </RuleDesigner>
  <Parameters>
    <Parameter Name="ListId" Type="System.String, mscorlib" Direction="In" />
  </Parameters>
</Action>

<Action Name="Execute custom code 5" AppliesTo="all"
Category="My Custom Actions"
ClassName="Chapter9.CustomActivity5"
Assembly="Chapter9, Version=1.0.0.0, Culture=neutral,
          PublicKeyToken=252d221e933b41ec">
  <RuleDesigner
  Sentence="Execute custom code with %1 on the server">
    <FieldBind Field="Users" Text="these users" DesignerType="Person" Id="1"/>
  </RuleDesigner>
  <Parameters>
    <Parameter Name="Users" Type="System.Collection.ArrayList, mscorlib"
    Direction="In" />
```

(continued)

Listing 10-8 *(continued)*

```
    </Parameters>
  </Action>

  <Action Name="Execute custom code 6" AppliesTo="all"
  Category="My Custom Actions"
  ClassName="Chapter9.CustomActivity6"
  Assembly="Chapter9, Version=1.0.0.0, Culture=neutral,
            PublicKeyToken=252d221e933b41ec">
    <RuleDesigner
    Sentence="Execute custom code with %1 on the server">
      <FieldBind Field="User" Text="this user"
      DesignerType="SinglePerson" Id="1"/>
    </RuleDesigner>
    <Parameters>
      <Parameter Name="User" Type="System.String, mscorlib" Direction="In" />
    </Parameters>
  </Action>

  <Action Name="Execute custom code 7" AppliesTo="all"
  Category="My Custom Actions"
  ClassName="Chapter9.CustomActivity7"
  Assembly="Chapter9, Version=1.0.0.0, Culture=neutral,
            PublicKeyToken=252d221e933b41ec">
    <RuleDesigner
    Sentence="Execute custom code with %1 on the server">
      <FieldBind Field="StringProperty" Text="this value for StringProperty"
      DesignerType="StringBuilder" Id="1"/>
    </RuleDesigner>
    <Parameters>
      <Parameter Name="StringProperty" Type="System.String, mscorlib"
      Direction="In" />
    </Parameters>
  </Action>

  <Action Name="Execute custom code 8" AppliesTo="all"
  Category="My Custom Actions"
  ClassName="Chapter9.CustomActivity8"
  Assembly="Chapter9, Version=1.0.0.0, Culture=neutral,
            PublicKeyToken=252d221e933b41ec">
    <RuleDesigner
    Sentence="Execute custom code with %1 on the server">
      <FieldBind Field="StringProperty" Text="this StringProperty value"
      DesignerType="Text" Id="1"/>
    </RuleDesigner>
    <Parameters>
      <Parameter Name="StringProperty" Type="System.String, mscorlib"
      Direction="In" />
    </Parameters>
  </Action>

  <Action Name="Execute custom code 9" AppliesTo="all"
```

```
    Category="My Custom Actions"
    ClassName="Chapter9.CustomActivity9"
    Assembly="Chapter9, Version=1.0.0.0, Culture=neutral,
              PublicKeyToken=252d221e933b41ec">
      <RuleDesigner
      Sentence="Execute custom code with %1 on the server">
        <FieldBind Field="ListId,ListItem,ItemProperties" Text="this list" Id="1"
        DesignerType="UpdateListItem" />

      </RuleDesigner>
      <Parameters>
        <Parameter Name="ListId" Type="System.String, mscorlib" Direction="In" />
        <Parameter Name="ListItem" Type="System.Int32, mscorlib" Direction="In" />
        <Parameter Name="ItemProperties"
        Type="System.Collections.Hashtable, mscorlib" Direction="In" />

      </Parameters>
    </Action>

    <Action Name="Execute custom code 10" AppliesTo="all" UsesCurrentItem="true"
    Category="My Custom Actions"
    ClassName="Chapter9.CustomActivity10"
    Assembly="Chapter9, Version=1.0.0.0, Culture=neutral,
              PublicKeyToken=252d221e933b41ec">
      <RuleDesigner
      Sentence="Execute custom code with %1 on the server">
        <FieldBind Field="FieldName" Text="this field name"
        DesignerType="WritableFieldNames" Id="1"/>
      </RuleDesigner>
      <Parameters>
        <Parameter Name="FieldName" Type="System.String, mscorlib"
        Direction="In" />
      </Parameters>
    </Action>

  </Actions>
</WorkflowInfo>
```

Listing 10-9 presents the data description file.

Listing 10-9: The data description file

```
; * My Solution Package2*
.Option Explicit
.Set CabinetNameTemplate=MySolutionPackage2.wsp
.set DiskDirectoryTemplate=CDROM
.Set CompressionType=MSZIP
.Set UniqueFiles="ON"
.Set Cabinet=on
.Set DiskDirectory1=MySolutionPackage2

manifest.xml manifest.xml
CustomActivity.actions 1033\Workflow\CustomActivity.actions
bin\Release\Chapter9.dll Chapter9.dll
```

The first line of the body of this data description file tells makecab to copy the manifest.xml file from the root directory of the project, which is the directory from which we run makecab, to the root of our solution package:

```
manifest.xml manifest.xml
```

The second line tells makecab to first create a folder named 1033 in the root of our solution package and then create a subfolder named Workflow in this folder, and finally to copy the CustomActivity.actions file from the root directory of the project to this subfolder:

```
CustomActivity.actions 1033\Workflow\CustomActivity.actions
```

The last line tells makecab to copy the Chapter9.dll assembly, which contains all our custom activities, to the root of our solution package:

```
bin\Release\Chapter9.dll Chapter9.dll
```

Listing 10-10 presents the manifest.xml file.

Listing 10-10: The manifest.xml file

```
<?xml version="1.0" encoding="utf-8" ?>
<Solution
xmlns="http://schemas.microsoft.com/sharepoint/"
SolutionId="{DD43C230-761E-4bd3-BB09-51BF53E19DF5}">
  <TemplateFiles>
    <TemplateFile Location="1033\Workflow\CustomActivity.actions"/>
  </TemplateFiles>

  <Assemblies>
    <Assembly DeploymentTarget="GlobalAssemblyCache" Location="Chapter9.dll" />
  </Assemblies>
</Solution>
```

The <TemplateFile> child element of the <TemplateFiles> element tells SharePoint to deploy the CustomActivity .actions file from the Workflow subfolder of the 1033 folder of our solution package to the Workflow folder in the file system of each front-end web server in the server farm:

```
<TemplateFile Location="1033\Workflow\CustomActivity.actions"/>
```

The <Assembly> child element of the <Assemblies> element tells SharePoint to install the Chapter9.dll assembly from the root of our solution package to the global assembly cache:

```
<Assembly DeploymentTarget="GlobalAssemblyCache" Location="Chapter9.dll" />
```

Listing 10-11 presents the batch file that contains the required commands.

Listing 10-11: The batch file

```
if Exist MySolutionPackage2\MySolutionPackage2.wsp Del MySolutionPackage2\
MySolutionPackage2.wsp
makecab /f MySolutionPackage2.ddf

@SET STSADM="c:\program files\common files\microsoft shared\web server
extensions\12\bin\stsadm"

%STSADM% -o retractsolution -name MySolutionPackage2.wsp -local
%STSADM% -o execadmsvcjobs
%STSADM% -o deletesolution -name MySolutionPackage2.wsp -override
%STSADM% -o execadmsvcjobs

%STSADM% -o addsolution -filename MySolutionPackage2\MySolutionPackage2.wsp
%STSADM% -o execadmsvcjobs
%STSADM% -o deploysolution -name MySolutionPackage2.wsp -allowGacDeployment -local
%STSADM% -o execadmsvcjobs
```

Summary

This chapter showed you how to use a SharePoint solution package to deploy your SharePoint workflows and actions solutions. The discussions of the chapter were presented in the context of examples where SharePoint solution packages were used.

Index

A

B

C

D

E

F

G

H

I

J

K

L

M

N

O

Q

R

S

T

U

V

W

X

powered by
books24x7
Programmer to Programmer